D0450345

Dog Owner's Home

VETERINARY

Handbook

This book is not intended as a substitute for the medical advice of veterinarians. Readers should regularly consult a veterinarian in matters relating to their dog's health, and particularly with respect to any symptoms that may require medical attention.

In writing this book, we have described the signs and symptoms that will lead you to a preliminary idea of what is happening with your dog, so you can weigh the severity of the problem. Knowing when to call your veterinarian is very important. Delays can be dangerous.

At the same time, we have sought to provide guidance for the acute or emergency situations that you must handle on your own until you can get your dog to a veterinarian. Life-saving procedures such as artificial respiration and heart massage, and what to do in the event of poisonings, obstetrical problems, and other emergencies are explained step by step.

But a veterinary handbook is not a substitute for professional care. Advice from a book can never be as helpful or as safe as actual medical advice. No text can replace the interview and the hands-on examination that enables a veterinarian to make a speedy and accurate diagnosis.

However, the knowledge provided in this book will enable you to more effectively cooperate and better understand your interactions with your veterinarian. You'll be more alert to the signs of health problems and better able to describe them. You'll know more about basic care for your dog, and you'll be prepared in an emergency.

Dog Owner's Home

VETERINARY

Handbook

4th Edition

Debra M. Eldredge, DVM
Liisa D. Carlson, DVM
Delbert G. Carlson, DVM
James M. Giffin, MD

Edited by Beth Adelman

BICENTENNIAL
1807
WILEY
2007
BICENTENNIAL

Wiley Publishing, Inc.

Howell Book House
Published by Wiley Publishing, Inc., Hoboken, New Jersey

For general information on our other products and services or to obtain technical support please contact our Customer Care Department within the U.S. at (800) 762-2974, outside the U.S. at (317) 572-3993 or fax (317) 572-4002.

Wiley also publishes its books in a variety of electronic formats. Some content that appears in print may not be available in electronic books. For more information about Wiley products, please visit our web site at www.wiley.com.

Library of Congress Cataloging-in-Publication Data:
Dog owner's home veterinary handbook / Debra M. Eldredge . . . [et al.]. — 4th ed.
      p. cm.
   Includes index.
   Rev. ed. of: Dog owner's home veterinary handbook / James M. Giffin and Liisa Carlson, 2000.
   ISBN-13: 978-0-470-06785-7 (cloth)
   ISBN-10: 0-470-06785-3
   1. Dogs—Diseases—Handbooks, manuals, etc. I. Eldredge, Debra. II. Giffin, James M. Dog owner's home veterinary handbook.
   SF991.C25 2007
   636.7'089—dc22
                                        2007016275
Printed in the United States of America

10 9 8 7 6

Fourth Edition

Edited by Beth Adelman
Cover design by Ruth Acosta
Book production by Wiley Publishing, Inc. Composition Services

FINDING IT QUICKLY

A special **Index of Signs and Symptoms** is on the inside of the front cover for fast referral. Consult this if your dog exhibits any unexplained behavior. It will help you locate the problem.

The detailed **Contents** outlines the organs and body systems that are the sites of disease. If you can locate the problem anatomically, look here first.

The **General Index** begins on page 607 and gives you a comprehensive guide to the book's medical information. Where a page number is in bold, it indicates more detailed coverage of the subject.

Cross-references note pertinent supplementary information.

A **Glossary** on page 585 defines medical terms used preferentially to best explain the subject or condition. Many of these words are now being used commonly among veterinarians and their clients. Glossary terms will usually be found in italics in the text. (Italics may also be used for emphasis.)

ACKNOWLEDGMENTS

I would like to thank Roxanne Cerda for thinking of me for this project and my incredible agent, Jessica Faust of Book Ends, for making it work. I can't say enough good things about working with Beth Adelman as my editor—it has been fun! Sandy Young, DVM, has done a great job in her technical review. And Marcella Durand has found us some images we thought might be impossible to find.

My thanks to my family, who have endured weird meals at weird times and dealt with the stress of occasional computer illnesses.

A special thank you to my three personal dogs, who oversaw this project. Ms Dani, my Belgian Tervuren bitch, offered counsel and company while making sure the school bus returned Kate and Tom every day. Hokey, my young male Belgian Tervuren, simply makes me smile—every day and often. Susan, the almost 15-year-old Pembroke Welsh Corgi who came to us as an 8-year-old, has been my shadow, my support, and an exemplification of true love.

—Debra Eldredge, DVM

Tribute to a Dog

The one absolutely unselfish friend that man can have in this selfish world, the one that never deserts him, the one that never proves ungrateful or treacherous, is his dog. A man's dog stands by him in prosperity and in poverty, in health and in sickness. He will sleep on the cold ground, where the wintry winds blow and the snow drives fiercely, if only he may be near his master's side. He will kiss the hand that has no food to offer; he will lick the wounds and sores that come in encounter with the roughness of the world. He guards the sleep of his pauper master as if he were a prince. When all other friends desert, he remains. When riches take wings and reputation falls to pieces, he is as constant in his love as the sun in its journey through the heavens.

—Senator George Vest, 1870

CONTENTS

Chapter 4: THE SKIN AND COAT **101**

Chapter 8: THE MOUTH AND THROAT

INTRODUCTION

The *Dog Owner's Home Veterinary Handbook* has been a familiar title on my bookshelf for more than two decades. It's the book I turn to, time and again, for definitive answers on canine health.

I've owned several editions of this book, always replacing my old one with the latest. But I have been surprised to learn that many dog breeders, and several of my journalist colleagues, have all three editions, going all the way back to 1980, because they just can't bear to part with them. Go to a canine sporting event and ask the exhibitors which health book they turn to most often. Chances are, it will be this one. Type in the title on any Internet search engine and you will see hundreds of web sites that recommend it.

This is an old book with a long legacy, but also a new one with some exciting additions. You'll find the latest information here on vaccine protocols; flea, tick, and heartworm preventives; raw diets; arthritis medications and supplements; treatments for cancer and kidney disease; and treatments for cognitive dysfunction in senior dogs. New drugs and surgical techniques are explained, and the latest information on how to prevent bloat is detailed. Canine influenza, one of the newest diseases of dogs, is covered. You'll also find the latest information on what we know about the canine senses, and possible organic causes of behavior problems such as aggression and compulsive behaviors.

When the third edition was published in 2000, therapies using supplements, nutraceuticals, and holistic modalities such as acupuncture were largely untested. Now, for illnesses where holistic treatments have proven to be beneficial, they are listed under the Treatments section.

Another new development is that scientists have described the canine genome. The result is a wealth of information on breed dispositions for certain genetic conditions, and on genetic testing for certain diseases—all of which is discussed in this edition.

According to a 2006 study by Veterinary Pet Insurance Co., the top ten canine medical conditions for which their policy holders filed claims were:

1. Skin allergies
2. Ear infections
3. Stomach upsets
4. Bladder infections
5. Benign tumors

6. Osteoarthritis
7. Sprains
8. Eye infections
9. Enteritis (diarrhea)
10. Hypothyroidism

You will also find all of those common canine health problems here—covered completely and comprehensively. And, whatever troubles your dog, you will find it described clearly and have a variety of treatment options to discuss with your veterinarian.

As an editor, it's always an honor to work on a book that is already a classic in its field and will continue to be one. I also had the pleasure of working on the third edition with Dr. James Giffin. Because I was involved, I tend to look at that edition very critically. I have spent seven years wishing there were things we had done differently. At last, I have my chance. In this edition, the cross-references are easier to use, the index is expanded, there's an index of charts and tables, and overall, when you come home with your dog from the veterinarian's office full of questions, it's easier to find what you are looking for.

—*Beth Adelman, Editor*

EMERGENCIES

Emergency care is just that—care applied to a potentially serious condition as soon as possible while you are trying to reach your veterinarian. One of the cardinal rules in dealing with any emergency is for you to remain calm. If you panic, you won't be thinking clearly and you will panic your dog. Take a deep breath, quietly reassure your dog, and then do what is necessary. Don't hesitate to ask for help, and remember that your dog is relying on you.

Home Emergency Medical Kit	
Container for equipment	Tweezers
Penlight	Scissors
Blanket	Grooming clippers
Nylon leash	Needle-nose pliers
Muzzle (nylon or leather)	K-Y lubricant or petroleum jelly
Rectal thermometer	Rubbing alcohol
Surgical gloves	Betadine or similar antiseptic scrub
Cotton balls	Hydrogen peroxide
Cotton swabs	Topical antibiotic ointment
Gauze pads (3 inches, 70 mm, square)	Sterile saline eye wash
Gauze roll (3 inches, 70 mm, wide)	List of emergency phone numbers:
Ace bandage (3 inches, 70 mm, wide)	Your veterinarian's office
Surgical adhesive tape (1 inch, 25 mm wide)	24-hour emergency clinic
Syringe (plastic) without a needle	ASPCA Animal Poison Control Center (888) 426-4435
Compressed activated charcoal tables (5 grams each)	

Handling and Restraint

Any dog, no matter how docile he may be, has the potential to bite when he is severely injured, frightened, or in pain. It is important to recognize this and take proper precautions to keep from being bitten.

An injured dog who growls, snarls, or raises his hackles is sending a clear message. Do not approach or attempt to restrain this dog. Call your local animal shelter or animal care and control agency for help.

MUZZLES

All dogs should be muzzled for any handling or treatment that may be frightening or painful. Cloth muzzles are easy to store and can be slipped on easily. Soft muzzles with Velcro closures in the back can be ordered through your veterinarian or a pet supply store. An open cage muzzle is preferred for an injured or sick dog. It allows the dog to breathe easily, and if the dog vomits he will not aspirate the vomitus. Keep the muzzle with your Home Emergency Medical Kit (see page 1).

If you don't have a commercial muzzle, you can make an acceptable substitute using adhesive tape, a piece of cloth, a length of roll gauze, or a leash. Wind the tape around the dog's muzzle. Or make a large loop with the other materials that you can slip over the dog's muzzle. Then tighten this down around the dog's muzzle, bring the two ends under the dog's ears, and tie the ends behind his head. Make sure the muzzle is not so tight that the dog cannot open his mouth slightly to breathe.

There are circumstances in which a dog should not be muzzled. It can be dangerous to muzzle a dog who is vomiting, coughing, having difficulty breathing, or aggressively resisting the muzzle. Never muzzle an unconscious dog.

RESTRAINING FOR EXAMINATION AND TREATMENT

For the cooperative dog, routine procedures such as grooming, bathing, and even medicating seldom require restraint. Gentle handling and a soothing voice will coax most dogs to accept such handling. Approach the task with quiet confidence. Dogs are quick to sense anxiety in their owners and copy it.

For examinations and treatments that may excite or hurt the dog, it is important to restrain the dog *before* attempting the treatment. Once a dog is restrained, he usually settles down and accepts the procedure with little complaint.

A cage muzzle should be used if the dog is vomiting or breathing rapidly.

A cloth muzzle is convenient and can be slipped on easily.

A strip of adhesive tape makes an expedient temporary muzzle.

The headlock is an excellent restraint for a large dog. First muzzle the dog. Then hold the dog securely against your chest with one arm around his neck and the other around his waist. This is the most commonly used restraint for a quick procedure such as giving an injection.

To restrain a small dog, support the abdomen with one arm and grasp the outside front leg. Immobilize the head with the other arm. Hold the dog close to your body.

The headlock is an excellent restraint for a large dog. For treatment, the dog should be muzzled.

This is a good way to restrain and carry a small dog.

An Elizabethan collar, named for the high neck ruff popular during the reign of Queen Elizabeth I of England, is also an excellent way of restraining dogs who are prone to bite. The collar is also used to keep a dog from scratching at his ears, removing sutures, and biting at wounds and skin sores. These collars can be purchased from pet supply stores and some veterinarians (your veterinarian may also be able to lend you one). The size of the collar must be tailored to the dog. For the dog to be able to eat and drink, the outer edge of the collar should not extend more than one to two inches beyond the dog's nose. Most dogs adjust well to an Elizabethan collar. If the dog refuses to eat or drink with the collar on, temporarily remove it.

An Elizabethan collar is an excellent restraint for dogs who tend to snap.

A newer option is the BiteNot collar. This high-necked collar prevents a dog from turning his head to bite. As with an Elizabethan collar, good fit is important. The collar must be just as long as the dog's neck.

Another way to restrain the dog is to lay him on his side by grasping the inside front and back legs and then sliding the dog down your knees to the floor. Hold his legs out straight and keep pressure with your forearms on his chest and pelvis to prevent him from getting up.

A BiteNot collar is a humane restraint frequently used by veterinarians. It may be more comfortable for a dog than the Elizabethan collar.

To lay the dog down on his side, grasp the inside front and back legs and slide him down your knees.

Hold his legs out straight and use your forearms to keep him on the floor.

CARRYING AN INJURED DOG

Incorrectly picking up or carrying a dog can make injuries much worse. Never pick up a dog by his front legs, as this can result in a dislocated elbow or shoulder.

Carry a small dog cuddled in your arms with the injured side away from your body. With a large dog, place one arm around his chest or between his front legs. Place the other arm around his rump—or between his back legs if you suspect a hind-limb injury. Hold the dog close to your chest so you can't drop him if he squirms.

Carry an injured dog with one arm around his chest and the other around his back legs.

TRANSPORTING AN INJURED DOG

A dog in shock should be transported lying down on a flat surface or in a hammock stretcher to facilitate breathing and to prevent a sudden drop in blood pressure.

Suspect a broken back or spinal cord injury in any dog who is unconscious or unable to stand after a fall from a height or after being struck by a car. These dogs require special handling. See *Treating Head Injuries*, page 358, and *Spinal Cord Injuries*, page 375, for more on what to do in these cases.

Artificial Respiration and Heart Massage

Artificial respiration is the emergency procedure used to assist air exchange in an unconscious dog. Heart massage (chest compressions) is used when no heartbeat can be felt or heard. When chest compressions are combined with artificial respiration, it is called cardiopulmonary resuscitation (CPR). Because cessation of breathing is soon followed by heart stoppage and vice versa, CPR is required in most life-threatening situations.

While CPR can be performed by one person, it is easier and more often successful when done by two. One person does the artificial respiration while the other does the chest compressions.

To determine which basic life-support technique will be required in an unconscious dog, see the chart on the next page. The following emergencies may require artificial respiration or CPR:

- Shock
- Poisoning
- Prolonged seizure
- Coma
- Head injury
- Electric shock
- Obstructed airway (choking)
- Sudden cessation of heart activity and breathing

Artificial Respiration or CPR?

Is the dog breathing? Observe the rise and fall of the chest. Feel for air against your cheek.

If **YES,** pull out the tongue and clear the airway. Observe.

If **NO**, feel for a pulse.

Does the dog have a pulse? Feel for the femoral artery located on the inside of the mid-thigh.

If **YES**, start artificial respiration.

If **NO**, start CPR.

ARTIFICIAL RESPIRATION

Lay the dog on a flat surface with his right side down. Open his mouth and pull his tongue forward as far as you can. Clear any secretions with a cloth or handkerchief. Check for a foreign body. If present, remove it if possible. If it is impossible to dislodge, perform the *Heimlich Maneuver*, described on page 316.

For puppies and small dogs under 30 pounds (13.6 kg)

1. Pull the tongue forward so it is even with the canine teeth. Close the dog's mouth.
2. Place your mouth over the dog's nose. Blow gently into the dog's nostrils. The chest will expand.
3. Release your mouth to let the air return. Excess air will escape through the dog's lips, preventing overinflation of the lungs and overdistension of the stomach.
4. If the chest does not rise and fall, blow more forcefully or seal the lips.
5. Continue at a rate of 20 to 30 breaths per minute (one breath every two to three seconds).
6. Continue until the dog breathes on his own, or as long as the heart beats.

For medium and large dogs

1. Proceed as for small dogs, but seal the lips by placing a hand around the dog's muzzle to prevent the escape of air.
2. If the chest does not rise and fall, blow more forcefully.
3. The breathing rate is 20 breaths per minute (one breath every three seconds).

CPR

CRP is a combination of artificial respiration and heart massage. If a dog needs heart massage, he also needs artificial respiration. On the other hand, if the dog resists your attempts to perform CPR, he probably does not need it!

For puppies and small dogs under 30 pounds (13.6 kg)

1. Place the dog on a flat surface, right side down.

2. Place your cupped hands on either side of the rib cage *over the heart*, immediately behind the point of the elbow. (For puppies, use your thumb on one side of the chest and the rest of your fingers on the other.)

3. Compress the chest 1 inch to 1½ inches (2.5 to 4 cm—that should be one-quarter to one-third the width of the chest). Squeeze for a count of 1, then release for a count of 1. Continue at a rate of 100 compressions per minute.

4. With one-person CPR, administer a breath after every five compressions. With two-person CPR, administer a breath after every two to three compressions.

To begin CPR, open the dog's mouth and pull his tongue forword as far as you can. Check for a foreign body.

Feel for the femoral pulse in the mid-thigh to determine if the dog has a heartbeat.

For artificial respiration, blow gently into the dog's nose every two to three seconds.

Chest compressions on a small dog. Note the placement of the hands on either side of the chest. The compression rate is 100 per minute.

Two-person CPR on a large dog. Note the placement of the hands for chest compressions. The compression rate is 80 per minute.

For medium and large dogs

1. Place the dog on a flat surface, right side down. Position yourself behind the dog's back.
2. Place the heel of one hand over the widest portion of the rib cage, *not over the heart*. Place the heel of your other hand on top of the first.
3. Keep both elbows straight and push down firmly on the rib cage. Compress the chest one-quarter to one-third of its width. Compress for a count of 1, then release for a count of 1. Continue at a rate of 80 compressions per minute.
4. With one-person CPR, administer a breath after every five compressions. With two-person CPR, administer a breath after every two to three compressions.

Continue CPR until the dog breathes on his own and has a steady pulse. If vital signs do not return after 10 minutes of CPR, the likelihood of success is remote. Consider stopping CPR.

Note that CPR has the potential to cause complications, including broken ribs and *pneumothorax*. Also, *never* practice artificial respiration or heart massage on a healthy dog; you can seriously injure the dog.

Shock

Shock is caused by insufficient blood flow and oxygen to meet the body's needs. Adequate blood flow requires effective heart pumping, open, intact blood vessels, and sufficient blood volume to maintain flow and pressure. Adequate oxygenation requires an open respiratory tract and enough energy to breathe. Any condition that adversely affects the circulatory or respiratory systems can cause shock.

The cardiovascular system of an animal in shock will try to compensate for inadequate oxygen and blood flow by increasing the heart and respiratory rates, constricting the skin's blood vessels, and maintaining fluid in the circulation by reducing urinary output. This requires additional energy at a time when the vital organs aren't getting enough oxygen to carry out normal activities. After a time, shock becomes self-perpetuating. Untreated, it results in death.

Common causes of shock are hemorrhage, heart failure, anaphylactic (allergic) reactions, dehydration (heat stroke, vomiting, diarrhea), poisoning, and toxic shock associated with *sepsis* and *peritonitis*.

Signs of early shock include panting, rapid heart rate, bounding pulses, and a bright red color to the mucous membranes of the lips, gums, and tongue. Many of these signs will be missed or considered mild—perhaps regarded as signs of a dog who overexerted himself. The later signs are when most owners notice and respond to their dog's condition. Signs of late shock (the ones seen most often) are pale skin and mucous membranes, a drop in body temperature, cold feet and legs, a slow respiratory rate, apathy and depression, unconsciousness, and a weak or absent pulse.

Treatment: First, evaluate. Is the dog breathing? Is there a heartbeat? What is the extent of the injuries? Is the dog in shock?

If so, proceed as follows:

1. If the dog is not breathing, administer artificial respiration (see page 8).

2. If there is no heartbeat or pulse, administer CPR (see page 8).

3. If the dog is unconscious, check to be sure that the airway is open. Clear secretions from the mouth with your fingers and a piece of cloth. Pull the tip of the tongue foreword beyond the front teeth to make it easier for the dog to breathe. Keep the dog's head lower than his body by placing a blanket beneath his hindquarters.

4. Control bleeding as described under *Wounds*, page 42.

5. Wrap the dog in a coat or blanket to provide warmth and protect injured extremities.

6. Transport the dog to a veterinary hospital.

This is the best way to transport a dog in shock. If you don't have a stretcher, use a camp cot, a wooden plank, or even a folded wire crate with a blanket laid on top.

To avoid aggravating the shock:

- Calm the dog and speak soothingly.
- Allow the dog to assume the most comfortable position in which breathing is easiest. An animal will naturally adopt the position of least pain.
- When possible, splint or support any broken bones before moving the dog (see *Broken Bones*, page 15).
- All dogs who are unconscious or found lying down after an accident must be considered to have spinal cord injuries and should be handled accordingly (see *Spinal Cord Injuries*, page 375).
- Transport large dogs on a flat surface or in a hammock stretcher. Carry small dogs in a blanket with the injured parts protected.
- Avoid using a muzzle except for short periods, such as when moving the dog from the scene of the accident into a car, or from a car into the veterinary clinic. Muzzling can interfere with breathing in some situations.

ANAPHYLACTIC SHOCK

Anaphylactic shock is an immediate, serious allergic reaction. It occurs when a dog is exposed to an *allergen* to which he has been sensitized. Sensitivity occurs through prior contact.

The most common drug allergen that causes anaphylactic shock is penicillin. The venom in the stings of bees and wasps can also occasionally produce anaphylactic shock. Some dogs have been known to experience shock after a vaccination, but this is not common.

A dog receiving emergency treatment for anaphylactic shock, in this case following a routine vaccination. The dog responded well, and 30 minutes later was fine.

Anaphylactic shock causes signs and symptoms different from those previously described for shock. Initially there may be local signs at the point of contact, including pain, itching, swelling, and redness of the skin. With acute anaphylaxis, the allergic response becomes generalized, either immediately or over the course of several hours. Signs are agitation, diarrhea, vomiting, difficulty breathing, *stridor* (harsh breathing sounds) from a swollen voice box, weakness, and circulatory collapse. In untreated cases, coma and death follow.

Treatment: Emergency treatment of anaphylactic shock involves administering intravenous or subcutaneous adrenaline, oxygen, antihistamines, IV fluids, and hydrocortisone—drugs not available in the home. This is why it is best to have your veterinarian give vaccines—he or she has the drugs and equipment to treat allergic reactions in time.

A dog who has had an allergic reaction to a drug in the past should not be given that drug again.

Acute Painful Abdomen

An acute painful abdomen is an emergency that may lead to death of the dog unless treatment is started at once. The signs of an acute abdomen are the sudden onset of pain, along with whining and crying, retching and vomiting, extreme restlessness and inability to find a comfortable position, grunting, and labored breathing. The abdomen is extremely painful when pressed.

Characteristically, the dog may assume a prayer position with his chest to the floor and his rump in the air. As the condition worsens, the dog's pulse becomes weak and thready, the mucous membranes become pale, and the dog goes into shock.

If you see any of these signs, call your veterinarian at once! Early surgical intervention is life-saving.

One of the following conditions may be the cause of acute abdomen:

- Bloat
- Urinary stones obstructing the bladder
- Trauma to the abdomen with internal injury
- Rupture of the bladder
- Poisoning
- Rupture of the pregnant uterus
- Peritonitis
- Acute pancreatitis
- Intestinal obstruction
- Twisting of the intestines

Broken Bones

Most fractures are caused by automobile accidents and falls from a height. The bones most commonly broken are the femur, pelvis, skull, jaw, and spine. Fractures are classified as open or closed. In an open fracture (also called a compound fracture), a wound exposes the bone. Often the bone is seen sticking through the skin. These fractures are contaminated by dirt and bacteria and thus are accompanied by a high rate of bone infection.

Signs of bone fracture include pain, swelling, inability to bear weight, and deformity with shortening of the affected leg.

Treatment: Injuries that cause fractures can also cause shock, blood loss, and trauma to internal organs. Controlling shock takes precedence over treating any fractures (see *Shock*, page 11).

A dog in pain is often uncooperative and may bite in self-defense. Take precautions to avoid being bitten. If necessary, muzzle the dog (see *Handling and Restraint*, page 2).

Open wounds over bones should be covered with a sterile dressing, using several gauze pads, if available. If you cannot get gauze pads, cover the wound with a clean cloth or towel and wrap loosely. If there is continued bleeding, carefully apply pressure to the site.

Splinting fractures relieves pain and prevents shock and further tissue damage while the dog is being transported to the veterinary hospital. The decision to splint is based on a number of factors, including the severity and location of the injury, the time it will take to get professional help, the presence of other injuries, and the availability of materials. Note that improper splinting can cause more harm than good. Do not attempt to splint the leg if the dog resists.

Always splint the limb in the position in which you find it. Do not attempt to straighten a crooked leg.

An effective splint is one that crosses the joints above and below the fracture. When the fracture is below the knee or elbow, fold a magazine, a newspaper, or a piece of thick cardboard around the leg. A cardboard roll, such as for paper towels or toilet paper, may work if you slit it open. Extend the splint from the toes to a point well above the knee or elbow. Hold the splint in place by wrapping it with a roll of gauze, a necktie, or tape. Do not wrap tightly.

Fractures above the elbow and knee are difficult to splint. The best way to prevent further damage is to keep the dog as still as possible.

Dogs in shock should be transported lying down, either on a flat surface or in a hammock stretcher, to facilitate breathing and prevent a drop in blood pressure. Head injuries and spinal cord injuries require special handling and transport, as described in chapter 12.

Fractures where the ends of bones are at angles or far apart must be reduced under general anesthesia by a veterinarian, to bring the ends together and realign the bone. This is accomplished by pulling on the leg to overcome the

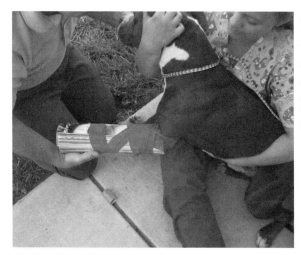

A magazine makes a good temporary splint for leg fractures below the elbow or knee. Hold the magazine in place with tape. An effective splint crosses the joints above and below the fracture site.

muscular forces causing the displacement. Once reduced, the position of the bones must be maintained. In most dogs, with fractures above the knee or elbow the position is held with pins and metal plates, while fractures below the knee or elbow are immobilized with splints and casts. Fractures involving joints usually require open surgery and repair with pins, screws, and wire.

Displaced jaw fractures cause malposition of the teeth. The jaw should be adjusted and the teeth wired together to maintain the correct position until healing is complete.

Depressed skull fractures may require surgery to elevate the depressed fragments.

Burns

Burns are caused by heat, chemicals, electric shocks, or radiation. Hot liquids may scald a dog. Sunburn is an example of a radiation burn. It occurs on the noses of dogs with insufficient pigment and on the skin of white-coated dogs who are clipped short in summer.

The extent of skin damage depends upon the length of exposure.

A first-degree burn causes the skin to become red, slightly swollen, and painful. It usually heals in about five days.

A second-degree burn is deeper and there is blistering. These burns are extremely painful. If there is no infection, healing is usually complete in 21 days.

A third-degree burn involves the full thickness of skin and extends into the subcutaneous fat. These burns appear charred, dry, and leathery. The hair comes out easily when pulled. Deep burns, because they destroy nerve endings, usually are not as painful as second-degree burns.

If more than 50 percent of the dog's body surface is involved with second-degree burns, or if more than 30 percent is involved with third-degree burns, survival is unlikely.

Treatment: All but minor burns require professional attention. Protect the area from further injury by wrapping it with a loose-fitting damp gauze dressing and proceed at once to the veterinary clinic. Extensive burns require intensive care to treat shock, adjust fluid and electrolyte losses, and prevent secondary infection.

If your dog appears to be suffering from electrical shock, use a wooden implement to slide any cords away from him before you touch him. Alternatively, unplug all cords or turn off the circuit breakers so that you won't get a shock too.

Small superficial burns that involve less than 5 percent of the body surface can be treated at home. Apply cool compresses (*not ice packs*) for 20 minutes to relieve pain and lessen the depth of the injury. Clip the coat over the burn and wash the skin gently with a surgical antiseptic such as dilute chlorhexidine solution (see *Wounds*, page 42). Apply a topical antibiotic ointment such as triple antibiotic, and bandage the area. The bandage should be removed daily and the wound medicated and redressed.

When acid, alkali, gasoline, kerosene, or other chemicals have caused the burn, or even come in contact with the skin, immediately flush the area with large amounts of water for 10 minutes. Wear rubber or plastic gloves and bathe the dog with mild soap and water. Blot dry. If there are any signs of burning (such as redness or blistering), call your veterinarian for further instructions.

Cold Exposure

HYPOTHERMIA (LOW BODY TEMPERATURE)

Prolonged exposure to cold will result in a drop in body temperature. Toy breeds, breeds with short coats, puppies, and very old dogs are most susceptible to hypothermia. Because a wet coat loses its insulating properties, hypothermia is a potential complication for all dogs who have been submerged in cold water. Hypothermia also occurs along with shock, after a long course of anesthesia, and in newborn puppies who get chilled because of inadequately heated whelping quarters. Prolonged cold exposure burns up stored energy and results in a low blood sugar.

Signs of hypothermia are violent shivering followed by listlessness, a rectal temperature below 95°F (35°C), weak pulse, lethargy, and coma. Note that hypothermic dogs can withstand prolonged periods of cardiac arrest, because the low body temperature also lowers the metabolic rate. CPR may be successful in such individuals.

To take a dog's rectal temperature using a digital thermometer, lubricate the thermometer and then insert it gently. You can place a hand under the dog's tummy to keep him from sitting down.

Treatment: Wrap the dog in a blanket or coat and carry him into a warm building. If the dog is wet (he fell into icy water), dry him vigorously with towels. Wrap the dog in a warm blanket and take his rectal temperature. If the temperature is above 95°F, continue the warm blankets and encourage the dog to swallow a sugar solution such as honey, or 4 teaspoons (32g) of sugar dissolved in a pint of water.

If the dog's rectal temperature is below 95°F, notify your veterinarian. While awaiting instructions, begin rapid warming by applying warm water bottles wrapped in towels to the dog's armpits and chest, then wrap the dog in a blanket. The temperature of the packs should be about that of a baby bottle (warm to the wrist). Take the rectal temperature every 10 minutes. Change the warming packs until the rectal temperature reaches 100°F (37.8°C). Do not apply heat directly to the dog, as this may cause burns. For the same reason, do not use a hair dryer to warm the dog.

How to warm a chilled puppy is discussed in *Reviving a Weak Puppy*, page 495.

FROSTBITE

Frostbite occurs when a part of the body freezes. It often accompanies hypothermia. Frostbite tends to involve the tail, ear tips, pads of the feet, and scrotum. These parts are the most exposed and least protected by fur. Frostbite of the ears is discussed on page 211.

Frostbitten skin is pale white or blue. As circulation returns, it becomes red and swollen and may begin to peel. Eventually it looks black with a line of demarcation between live and dead tissue. Dead skin and tissue separates from the body in one to three weeks.

Treatment: Apply warm (not hot) water soaks to the frostbitten part for 20 minutes, or until the tissue becomes flushed. Never use snow or ice; tissue damage is made much more severe if thawing is followed by refreezing. Do not rub or massage the affected parts. Handle them carefully. Take your dog to a veterinarian for further evaluation and treatment.

Note that as sensation returns, frostbitten parts can be painful. Prevent the dog from biting at the skin and inflicting further injury using the restraint techniques described in *Handling and Restraint*, page 2. The total extent of damage may not be apparent for a week or more.

Dehydration

Dehydration occurs when a dog loses body fluids faster than he can replace them. Dehydration usually involves the loss of both water and electrolytes. In dogs, the most common causes of dehydration are severe vomiting and diarrhea. Dehydration can also be caused by inadequate fluid intake, often associated with fever and severe illness. A rapid loss of fluids also occurs with heat stroke (see page 42).

A prominent sign of dehydration is loss of skin elasticity. When the skin along the back is pulled up, it should spring back into place. In a dehydrated animal, the skin stays up in a ridge.

Another sign of dehydration is dryness of the mouth. The gums, which should be wet and glistening, become dry and tacky. The saliva is thick and tenacious. In an advanced case, the eyes are sunken and the dog exhibits signs of shock, including collapse.

Treatment: A dog who is visibly dehydrated should receive immediate veterinary attention, including intravenous fluids, to replace fluids and prevent further loss.

Loss of skin elasticity is a sign of dehydration. Note that this dog is getting intravenous fluids, which are extremely important in serious cases.

For mild dehydration, if the dog is not vomiting you can give him an electrolyte solution by bottle or syringe into the cheek pouch (see *How to Give Medications*, page 566). Balanced electrolyte solutions for treating dehydration in children, such as Ringer's lactate with 5 percent dextrose in water or Pedialyte solution, are available at drugstores and are also suitable for dogs. Gatorade is another short-term substitute to help replace fluids. Administer the solution at a rate of 2 to 4 ml per pound (1 to 2 ml per kilo) of body weight per hour, depending on the severity of the dehydration (or as directed by your veterinarian).

Treatment of dehydration in infant puppies is discussed in *Dehydration*, page 493.

Drowning and Suffocation

Any condition that prevents oxygen from getting to the tissues causes suffocation. The most common emergencies in this category are drowning, smothering in an airtight space, being overcome by toxic fumes (smoke, gasoline, propane, refrigerants, solvents, and others), choking from a foreign body in the throat, being poisoned by carbon monoxide, and suffering a penetrating wound of the chest.

Signs of oxygen deprivation (called *hypoxia*) are extreme anxiety, straining to breathe, and gasping for air (often with the head and neck extended), followed by loss of consciousness as the dog succumbs. The tongue and mucous membranes turn blue, a condition called *cyanosis*.

One exception to the blue color of hypoxia is carbon monoxide poisoning. Carbon monoxide turns the blood and mucous membranes bright red. Carbon monoxide poisoning is seen in dogs who are trapped in burning buildings, transported in the trunk of a car, or left in an unventilated enclosure such as a garage with the car engine turned on.

Although most dogs are good swimmers, drowning can occur if a dog swims too far out and becomes fatigued, falls through ice, is caught in a flood, or is unable to climb out of a swimming pool.

The sudden onset of gasping and struggling to breathe in a healthy dog suggests a foreign object lodged in the throat (see *Choking*, page 316).

Treatment: The immediate need is to reestablish breathing with fresh air. If breathing is shallow or absent, begin artificial respiration (see page 8). As soon as possible, transport your dog to the nearest veterinary facility for ventilation support.

Carbon monoxide poisoning is frequently associated with smoke inhalation and burns of the mouth and throat. Carbon monoxide binds with hemoglobin and blocks the delivery of oxygen to the tissues. Even though the dog is breathing deeply, oxygen transport will be compromised for several hours. Breathing a high concentration of oxygen helps to overcome these effects. A veterinarian will be able to provide this therapy using an oxygen mask, a nasal tube, or an oxygen cage.

If the dog has an open wound in the chest (*pneumothorax*) with air sucking in and out, pinch the skin together over the wound to seal the chest. Maintain the seal with a bandage wrapped around the chest and transport the dog to the nearest veterinary facility.

The first step in treating drowning is to remove water from the dog's lungs. Hold the unconscious dog upside down by his middle (hold a small dog by his back legs) and allow as much water as possible to run out his nose and mouth. Then quickly position the dog on his right side with his head lower than his chest (accomplish this by placing a blanket or coat beneath his hindquarters) and begin artificial respiration. Check for a pulse. If there is none, begin CPR (see page 8). Continue until the dog breathes on his own or until no pulse is felt for 10 minutes. Dogs who drown in cold water are often hypothermic and can sometimes be resuscitated even though they have been under water for a considerable time.

Following resuscitation, the dog should be seen and treated by a veterinarian. Inhalation pneumonia is a frequent complication.

Electric Shock

Electric shock (electrocution) can occur when dogs bite electric cords or come into contact with downed wires. A lightning strike is a rare cause of electrocution, but a dog does not have to be struck to be seriously injured or killed. A tall tree with deep roots and spreading branches can act as a conduit for a bolt of lightning, conducting electricity through the ground to any animal in the immediate vicinity. Most lightning strikes are fatal. The singed hair and skin give evidence of the cause of death.

A dog who gets an electric shock may be burned. The electric shock may cause an irregular heartbeat with circulatory collapse, followed by cardiac arrest. Electric current also damages the capillaries of the lungs and leads to the accumulation of fluid in the air sacs, a condition called *pulmonary edema*.

A characteristic sign of electric shock injury is finding the unconscious dog on the floor near an electrical outlet. Electric shocks cause involuntary muscle contractions of the dog's jaw that may prevent him from releasing his hold on a live wire. Dogs who survive electric shock may cough, have difficulty breathing, drool, have an offensive mouth odor, and have burns in the mouth.

Treatment: If your dog is found in contact with an electric cord or appliance, *do not touch the dog.* First shut off the main power and pull the plug. If that's not possible, use a piece of wood to move the source of the electricity off the dog, or to move the dog away from the electricity. If the dog is unconscious and is not breathing, administer artificial respiration (page 8) or CPR, if needed (page 8). Dogs who revive from electric shock should be seen by a veterinarian at once.

The treatment of mouth burns is discussed on page 234.

Prevention: Electric cord shocks can be prevented by placing cords in inaccessible locations, covering cords with plastic sleeves, unplugging cords when not in use, and providing appropriate chewing toys for puppies and dogs.

Heat Stroke

Heat stroke is an emergency and requires immediate treatment. Because dogs do not sweat (except to a minor degree through their foot pads), they do not tolerate high environmental temperatures as well as humans do. Dogs depend upon panting to exchange warm air for cool air. But when air temperature is close to body temperature, cooling by panting is not an efficient process.

Common situations that can set the stage for heat stroke in dogs include:

- Being left in a car in hot weather
- Exercising strenuously in hot, humid weather
- Being a *brachycephalic* breed, especially a Bulldog, Pug, or Pekingese
- Suffering from a heart or lung disease that interferes with efficient breathing
- Being muzzled while put under a hair dryer
- Suffering from a high fever or seizures
- Being confined on concrete or asphalt surfaces
- Being confined without shade and fresh water in hot weather
- Having a history of heat stroke

Heat stroke begins with heavy panting and difficulty breathing. The tongue and mucous membranes appear bright red. The saliva is thick and tenacious, and the dog often vomits. The rectal temperature rises to 104° to 110°F (40° to 43.3°C). The dog becomes progressively unsteady and passes bloody diarrhea. As shock sets in, the lips and mucous membranes turn gray. Collapse, seizures, coma, and death rapidly ensue.

Treatment: Emergency measures to cool the dog must begin at once. Move the dog out of the source of heat, preferably into an air-conditioned building. Take his rectal temperature every 10 minutes. Mild cases may be resolved by moving the dog into a cool environment.

If the rectal temperature is above 104°F, begin rapid cooling by spraying the dog with a garden hose or immersing him in a tub of cool water (not ice water) for up to two minutes. Alternatively, place the wet dog in front of an electric fan. Cool packs applied to the groin area may be helpful, as well as wiping his paws off with cool water. Monitor his rectal temperature and continue the cooling process until the rectal temperature falls below 103°F (39°C). At this point, stop the cooling process and dry the dog. Further cooling may induce hypothermia and shock.

Following an episode of heat stroke, take your dog to a veterinarian as soon as possible. Heat stroke can be associated with laryngeal *edema* (see page 315). This seriously worsens the breathing problem and may require an emergency *tracheostomy*. An injection of cortisone before the onset of respiratory distress may prevent this problem.

Other consequences of hyperthermia include kidney failure, spontaneous bleeding, irregular heartbeat, and seizures. These complications can occur hours or days later.

Prevention:

- Dogs with airway disease and breathing problems should be kept indoors with air conditioning or at least a fan during periods of high heat and humidity.
- Never leave your dog in a car with the windows closed, even if the car is parked in the shade.
- When traveling by car, crate the dog in a well-ventilated dog carrier, or better yet, an open wire cage.
- Restrict exercise in hot weather.
- Always provide shade and plenty of cool water to dogs outdoors, particularly those kenneled on cement or asphalt surfaces.
- Offer cooler surfaces outdoors for dogs to lie on, such as wooden planking, mats, or grass.

Poisoning

A poison is any substance harmful to the body. Dogs, being curious by nature, tend to explore out-of-the-way places such as wood piles, weed thickets, and storage areas. These environs put them into contact with insects, dead animals, toxic plants, and poison baits. It also means the exact cause of poisoning will not be known in many cases.

Intentional, malicious poisoning is a factor to consider whenever a dog is found dead without apparent cause. However, several studies have shown that most cases of sudden death are caused by accidents and natural events. Malicious poisoning does occur, but it is far less common than accidental poisoning.

General recommendations for the treatment of poisoning are discussed in the next section. In the sections that follow, specific poisons are discussed in the order in which they are most frequently seen by veterinarians.

GENERAL TREATMENT OF POISONING

If your dog ingests an unknown substance, it is important to determine whether that substance is a poison. Most products have labels that list their ingredients, but if the label doesn't tell you the composition and toxicity of the product, call the ASPCA Animal Poison Control Center at (888) 426-4435 for specific information. The Poison Control Center has a staff of licensed veterinarians and board-certified toxicologists on call 24 hours a day, every day of the year. You will be charged a consultation fee of $50 per case, which can be charged to most major credit cards. There is no charge for follow-up calls in critical cases. At your request, they will also contact your veterinarian. You can also log onto www.aspca.org and click on "Animal Poison Control Center" for more information, including a list of toxic and nontoxic plants.

Other poison control hotlines include the Angell Animal Poison Control Hotline, operated by Angell Animal Medical Centers and the Massachusetts SPCA (877-226-4355, www.smspca.org) and the Animal Poison Hotline, operated by the North Shore Animal League and PROSAR International Animal Poison Center at (888) 232-8870.

In some cases, you can call the emergency room at your local hospital, which may be able to give you information about how to treat the poison. Specific antidotes are available for some poisons, but they cannot be administered unless the poison is known, or at least suspected by the circumstances. Some product labels have phone numbers you can call for safety information about their products.

When signs of poisoning develop, the most important consideration is to get your dog to the nearest emergency veterinary facility at once. If possible, find the poison and bring the container with you. This provides the emergency personnel with an immediate diagnosis and expedites treatment.

If the dog has ingested the substance recently, residual poison is often present in his stomach. An initial and most important step is to rid the dog's stomach of any remaining poison. The most effective way to empty the stomach is to pass a stomach tube, remove as much of the stomach contents as possible, and then wash the stomach out with large volumes of water. This must be done by your veterinarian.

In many cases it is preferable to induce vomiting at the scene rather than proceed directly to the veterinary hospital. For example, if you see the dog swallow the poisonous substance, it is obviously best to make the dog vomit it right back up. Similarly, if the poison was ingested within two hours but it will take 30 minutes or longer to get to a veterinary facility, it is frequently advisable to induce vomiting at home. However:

DO NOT *induce vomiting*

- If the dog has already vomited
- If the dog is in a stupor, breathing with difficulty, or shows any sign of neurologic involvement

- If the dog is unconscious or convulsing
- If the dog has swallowed an acid, alkali, cleaning solution, household chemical, or petroleum product
- If the dog has swallowed a sharp object that could lodge in the esophagus or perforate the stomach
- If the label on the product says, "Do not induce vomiting."

How to Induce Vomiting and Prevent Poison Absorption

Induce vomiting by giving the dog hydrogen peroxide. A 3 percent solution is most effective. Give 1 teaspoon (5 ml) per 10 pounds (4.5 kg) body weight of the dog. Repeat every 15 to 20 minutes, up to three times, until the dog vomits. Walking the dog after giving each dose may help to stimulate vomiting.

Syrup of ipecac has been recommended in the past, but hydrogen peroxide is a better choice for dogs. Syrup of ipecac (*not* ipecac fluid extract, which is 14 times stronger) is only 50 percent effective and can be dangerous to dogs. *It should not be used to induce vomiting unless specifically advised by your veterinarian.* The dose is .5 to 1 ml per pound (.45 kg) of body weight, with a maximum dose of 15 ml (1 tablespoon). Repeat in 20 minutes (once only) if the dog does not vomit.

Once the poison has been cleared from the dog's stomach, give him activated charcoal to bind any remaining poison and prevent further absorption. The most effective and easily administered home oral charcoal product is compressed activated charcoal, which comes in 5-gram tablets (recommended for the Home Emergency Medical Kit). The dose is one tablet per 10 pounds (4.5 kg) of body weight. Products that come in a liquid or as a powder made into a slurry are extremely difficult to administer at home with a syringe or medicine bottle. The slurry is dense and gooey, and few dogs will swallow it voluntarily. These products are best administered by stomach tube. This is routinely done by your veterinarian after flushing out the stomach.

If activated charcoal is not available, coat the intestines with milk and egg whites using ¼ cup (60 ml) egg whites and ¼ cup milk per 10 pounds (4.5 kg) of body weight. Administer into the dog's cheek pouch using a plastic syringe (see *How to Give Medications*, page 567).

Intensive care in a veterinary hospital improves the survival rate for dogs who have been poisoned. Intravenous fluids support circulation, treat shock, and protect the kidneys. A large urine output assists in eliminating the poison. Corticosteroids may be given for their anti-inflammatory effects. A dog in a coma may benefit from tracheal intubation and artificial ventilation during the acute phase of respiratory depression.

Seizures

Seizures caused by poisons are associated with prolonged periods of *hypoxia* and the potential for brain damage. Continuous or recurrent seizures are controlled with intravenous diazepam (Valium) or barbiturates, which must be administered by a veterinarian.

Note that seizures caused by strychnine and other central nervous system poisons may be mistaken for epilepsy. This could be a problem, because immediate veterinary attention is needed in cases of poisoning, but not for most epileptic seizures. Seizures caused by poisoning usually are continuous or recur within minutes. Between seizures the dog may exhibit tremors, lack of coordination, weakness, abdominal pain, and diarrhea. In contrast, most epileptic seizures are brief, seldom lasting more than two minutes, and are followed by a quiet period in which the dog appears dazed but otherwise normal. If your dog is having a seizure, see the treatment section under *Epilepsy*, page 369.

CONTACT POISONS

If your dog's coat or skin comes in contact with a poisonous substance or toxic chemical, flush the site with large amounts of water for 30 minutes. Wear rubber or plastic gloves and give the dog a complete bath in *lukewarm* water. Even if the substance is not irritating to the skin, it must be removed. Otherwise the dog may lick it off and swallow it.

DRUG POISONS

Unintentional overdose with veterinary medications and accidental ingestion of both human and veterinary pills are the most common causes of poisoning in pets. Veterinary products, in particular, are often flavored to encourage a dog to take them, and will be eagerly consumed if they are discovered.

Many people give over-the-counter medications to their dogs without veterinary approval, to treat a variety of symptoms; they believe that what works for people works for dogs. Unfortunately, this is not correct. Drugs given to dogs in human dosages are often toxic—and some human drugs cannot be given to dogs in any amount.

Common pain relievers such as ibuprofen (Advil) and acetaminophen (Tylenol) are a particular problem. Dogs and cats do not have the necessary enzymes to detoxify and eliminate these drugs. This can lead to the accumulation of dangerous substances in the animal that are left behind when the drugs are metabolized. As few as two Tylenol tablets can produce severe organ damage in a medium-size dog. Symptoms develop quickly and include abdominal pain, salivation, vomiting, and weakness.

Other human drugs that produce a variety of toxic effects and are commonly involved in accidental poisonings include antihistamines, sleeping pills, diet pills, heart pill, blood pressure pills, and vitamins.

Treatment: If you suspect your pet has swallowed any drug, immediately induce vomiting. Call your veterinarian for further instructions. A specific antidote may be available for the drug in question.

Prevention: Accidental poisoning can be prevented by always consulting your veterinarian before administering any medication. Follow instructions exactly for frequency and dosage. Store all drugs in a secure place to prevent inadvertent consumption by pets and children. *Never assume that a human drug is safe for pets!*

RODENT POISONS

Common rat and mouse poisons include anticoagulants and hypercalcemic agents. Both can be deadly if your dog ingests them.

Anticoagulants

Anticoagulant rat and mouse poisons are the most commonly used household poisons. These products account for a large number of accidental poisonings in dogs and cats. Anticoagulants block the synthesis of vitamin K, essential for normal blood clotting. Vitamin K deficiency results in spontaneous bleeding.

Observable signs of poisoning do not occur until several days after exposure. The dog may become weak and pale from blood loss, have nose bleeds, vomit blood, have rectal bleeding, develop *hematomas* and bruises beneath the skin, or have hemorrhages beneath the gums. The dog may be found dead from bleeding into the chest or abdomen.

There are two generations of anticoagulants, both in current use. The first generation are cumulative poisons that require multiple feedings over several days to kill the rodent. These poisons contain the anticoagulants warfarin and hydroxycoumadin.

Second-generation anticoagulants contain bromadiolone and brodifacoum, poisons that are 50 to 200 times more toxic than warfarin and hydroxycoumadin. These products are more dangerous to pets and are capable of killing rodents after a single feeding. It is even possible for a small dog to be poisoned by eating a dead rodent with residual poison in its stomach.

Closely related to the second-generation anticoagulants are the long-acting anticoagulants of the indanedione class (pindone, diphacinone, diphenadione, and chlorphacinone). These products are extremely toxic.

Treatment: Seek immediate veterinary help. If at all possible, bring in the product container so the veterinarian can identify the poison. This is important because treatment depends on whether the poison was a first- or second-generation anticoagulant. With observed or suspected recent ingestion, induce vomiting (see page 25).

Treatment of spontaneous bleeding caused by all anticoagulants involves administering fresh whole blood or frozen plasma in amounts determined by the rate and volume of blood loss. Vitamin K_1 is a specific antidote. It is given by subcutaneous injection and repeated subcutaneously or orally as necessary until clotting time returns to normal. With first-generation anticoagulants, this often occurs within a week. With long-acting anticoagulants, treatment takes up to a month because of the length of time the poison remains in the dog's system.

Hypercalcemic Agents

Hypercalcemic agents are poisons that contain vitamin D (cholecalciferol) as their effective agent. Cholecalciferol poisons work by raising the calcium content in blood serum to toxic levels, eventually producing cardiac arrhythmias and death. They are becoming increasingly popular because rodents do not develop resistance to them and, with the rare exception of a puppy or small dog, dogs who eat poisoned rodents will not develop toxicity. In virtually all cases, the dog must eat the poison itself to become ill.

In dogs, signs of hypercalcemia appear 18 to 36 hours after ingesting the poison. They include thirst and frequent urination, vomiting, generalized weakness, muscle twitching, seizures, and, finally, death. Among survivors, the effects of an elevated serum calcium may persist for weeks.

Treatment: If you suspect your dog has ingested one of these poisons within the past four hours, induce vomiting (see page 25) and notify your veterinarian. Veterinary treatment involves correcting the fluid and electrolyte imbalances and lowering calcium levels using diuretics, prednisone, oral phosphorus binders, and a low-calcium prescription diet. Calcitonin is a specific antidote, but it is difficult to obtain and has only short-term effects.

ANTIFREEZE

Poisoning by antifreeze that contains ethylene glycol is one of the most common small animal toxicities. Antifreeze has a sweet taste that appeals to dogs. Exposure typically occurs when antifreeze drips from the car radiator and is lapped up by the pet. Dogs may also drink from the toilet bowl in vacation homes that have been winterized by pouring antifreeze into the bowl.

Less than 3 ounces (88 ml) is enough to poison a medium-size dog. The poison primarily affects the brain and the kidneys. Signs of toxicity are dose-related, and occur within 30 minutes to 12 hours after ingestion. They include depression, vomiting, an uncoordinated "drunken" gait, and seizures. Coma and death can occur in a matter of hours. Dogs who recover from acute intoxication frequently develop kidney failure one to three days later. Death is common.

Treatment: If you see or suspect that your pet has ingested even a small amount of antifreeze, immediately induce vomiting (see page 25) and take your dog to the veterinarian. If treatment will be delayed, administer activated charcoal (see page 25) to prevent further absorption of ethylene glycol. A specific antidote (4-methylpyrazole) is available to treat poisoning. It is most effective when given shortly after ingestion and early in the course of treatment. Intensive care in an animal hospital may prevent kidney failure.

Prevention: This common cause of pet and child poisoning can be prevented by keeping all antifreeze containers tightly closed and properly stored, preventing spills, and properly disposing of used antifreeze. A new generation of antifreeze products contain propylene glycol rather than ethylene glycol. The U.S. Food and Drug Administration has labeled propylene glycol as "generally recognized as safe," which means it can be added to foods. However, that is in small amounts. Ingesting propylene glycol antifreeze can cause lack of coordination and, possibly, seizures, but is unlikely to be fatal.

POISON BAITS

Animal baits containing strychnine, sodium fluoroacetate, phosphorus, zinc phosphide, and metaldehyde are used in rural areas to control gophers, coyotes, and other predators. They are also used in stables and barns to eliminate rodents. These baits are highly palatable and therefore may be accidentally ingested by a dog. Many are extremely toxic and kill in a matter of minutes. Fortunately, they are being used less frequently because of livestock losses, concerns about persistence in the environment, and the potential to poison pets and children.

Strychnine

Strychnine is used as a rat, gopher, mole, and coyote poison. In concentrations greater than 0.5 percent its use is restricted to certified exterminators. It is available to the public in concentrations of 0.3 percent or less. With better regulation and the use of lower concentrations, strychnine is becoming a less common cause of accidental poisoning.

Signs of strychnine poisoning appear within two hours of ingestion. They include agitation, excitability, and apprehension, followed rather quickly by intensely painful convulsions with rigid extension of all four limbs. Seizures last about 60 seconds, during which time the dog throws his head back, stops breathing, and turns blue. The slightest stimulation, even touching the dog or clapping the hands, can trigger a seizure. This type of seizure response is typical only of strychnine.

Other signs of poisoning include tremors, champing, drooling, uncoordinated muscle spasms, collapse, and paddling of the legs.

Treatment: Induce vomiting (see page 25) immediately after ingestion. But do not induce vomiting if the dog is unresponsive, convulsing, or having difficulty breathing. Cover the dog with a coat or blanket and proceed as quickly as possible to the nearest veterinary clinic. Further treatment involves administering intravenous diazepam (Valium) or barbiturates to control seizures. The dog is placed in a dark, quiet room and disturbed as little as possible.

Sodium Fluoroacetate

Sodium fluoroacetate (compound 1080/1081), a very potent rat and gopher poison, is restricted to licensed pest control operators and is used infrequently in the United States. Dogs and cats have been poisoned by eating a dead rodent that has ingested the poison. The onset is sudden and begins with vomiting, followed by agitation, staggering, convulsions, and collapse.

Treatment: Treatment is similar to that described for strychnine poisoning (on this page).

Metaldehyde

This poison, often combined with arsenic, is found in rat, snail, and slug baits. It is also used as a solid fuel for camp stoves. The dry form looks and tastes like dog food. Signs of toxicity include excitation, drooling and slobbering, uncoordinated gait, muscle tremors, inability to stand, and continuous seizures that eventually lead to death from respiratory paralysis. Signs many appear immediately or up to three hours after ingestion. Dogs who survive the acute poisoning may die from secondary liver failure.

Treatment: Treatment is similar to that described for strychnine poisoning (on this page).

Phosphorus

This extremely toxic chemical is used in rat and roach poisons and is also found in fireworks, matches, and matchboxes. A poisoned dog may have a garlic odor to his breath. The first signs of intoxication are vomiting and diarrhea. This is followed by an interval of normal behavior, then by further vomiting, cramps, pain in the abdomen, convulsions, and coma.

Treatment: Induce vomiting (see page 25) when you suspect the dog has ingested a product or poison that contains phosphorus. Do not coat the bowel with milk or egg whites, as this can actually promote absorption. Take your dog to the nearest veterinary facility. There is no specific antidote.

Zinc Phosphide

This substance is found in rat poisons and is used by pest control professionals as a grain fumigant. Zinc phosphide in the stomach releases gas that has the odor of garlic or rotten fish. Intoxication causes depression, rapid labored breathing, vomiting (often of blood), weakness, convulsions, and death.

Treatment: Treatment is similar to that described for strychnine poisoning (page 33). The lavage must be done at a veterinary clinic. There is no specific antidote. The stomach should be lavaged with 5 percent sodium bicarbonate, which raises the gastric pH and delays the formation of gas.

INSECTICIDES

There are dozens of products sold at hardware, home repair, and agricultural stores to kill ants, termites, wasps, garden pests, and other insects. Most of them contain organophosphates and carbamates as their active ingredients. With the development of pyrethrin insecticides that are equally effective but much less toxic, organophosphates and carbamates are being used less frequently.

Organophosphates and Carbamates

The organophosphates include chlorpyrifos, diazinon, phosmet, fenthion, cythioate, and tetrachlorvinphos. The common carbamates are carbyl and propexur. Most cases of organophosphate or carbamate poisoning occur because the dog ingested a poison bait. Exposure to high concentrations of chemicals in sprays and dusts also occurs.

Signs of toxicity are hyperexcitability, excessive salivation and drooling, frequent urination, diarrhea, muscle twitching, weakness, staggering, collapse, and coma. Death is by respiratory failure.

Treatment: If you suspect that your dog has ingested an insecticide poison, immediately induce vomiting (see page 25) and notify your veterinarian. With any sign of toxicity, the first priority is to get your dog to the veterinarian as quickly as possible.

The specific antidote for organophosphate poisoning (*not* carbamate poisoning) is 2-PAM (protopam chloride). Atropine is given for both organophosphate and carbamate poisoning to control excessive salivation, vomiting, frequent urination and defecation, and to reverse a slow heart rate. Seizures are controlled with diazepam (Valium) or barbiturates.

In the event of skin exposure, give the dog a bath with soapy water and rinse thoroughly to remove residual insecticide.

Chlorinated Hydrocarbons

These compounds, of which the prototype is DDT, are added to sprays and dusts to control plant pests. Their use has been curtailed because of persistent toxicity in the environment. Only lindane and methoxychlor are approved for use around livestock. Chlorinated hydrocarbons are readily inhaled and easily absorbed through the skin. Toxicity can occur from repeated or excessive exposure.

Signs of toxicity appear rapidly. They include hyperexcitability with twitching of the face, followed by muscle tremors that begin at the head and progress back to involve the neck, shoulder, trunk, and rear legs. Seizures and convulsions are followed by respiratory paralysis and death.

Treatment: There is no specific antidote. Treatment includes supporting life functions, removing ingested poison from the stomach, and controlling seizures.

Pyrethrins and Pyrethroids

These compounds are incorporated into many insecticidal shampoos, sprays, dusts, dips, foggers, and sprays. Pyrethrins and the synthetic pyrethroids are much safer to use on and around dogs (and humans) than are other insecticides, and they are being used more widely. Many over-the-counter topical flea-control products have concentrated pyrethrins as their active ingredients. Some dogs may be adversely affected by that level of pyrethrins. Common chemicals in this class include permethrin, allethrin, fenvalerate, resmethrin, and sumethrin.

Signs of toxicity include drooling, depression, muscle tremors, staggering, vomiting, and rapid labored breathing. Toxicity occurs primarily in small dogs. Death is rare. Simultaneous exposure to organophosphates increases the toxicity of pyrethroids.

Treatment: Induce vomiting (see page 25) within two hours of ingestion. Call your veterinarian for further instructions. Do not induce vomiting if the product contains a petroleum distillate. With signs of toxicity, proceed immediately to the veterinary clinic.

For topical exposure, remove residual insecticide by bathing the dog in *lukewarm* water and Dawn dishwashing soap or canine shampoo to strip out the chemicals. (*Do not* use flea shampoo.) Rinse very thoroughly. Bathing in hot or cold water may actually increase the rate of absorption or cause hypothermia, which increases toxicity. After bathing, keep the dog warm.

Prevention: Most cases of poisoning occur because of improper application of flea-control products. That may be because the product is being used more often than the instructions call for, or is being combined with another flea-control product. Follow all instructions carefully.

Arsenic

This heavy metal is used in herbicides, insecticides, and wood preservatives. Sodium and potassium arsenate are used in ant poisons. Arsenic has a very rapid action and therefore poses a major risk for accidental poisoning. Death can occur quickly, even before symptoms are observed. Fortunately, the use of arsenic has been greatly curtailed.

Signs of poisoning include thirst, drooling, vomiting, staggering, intense abdominal pain, cramps, diarrhea, paralysis, and death. The breath of the dog has a strong garlic odor.

Treatment: Proceed at once to the nearest emergency veterinary facility. BAL (British Anti Lewisite) is a specific antidote and should be given as soon as the diagnosis is suspected.

GARBAGE AND FOOD POISONS

Dogs who scavenge come into contact with garbage, decomposing food, and carrion, some of which contain endotoxins produced by bacteria and molds. Once ingested, these endotoxins are absorbed and poison the dog.

Signs appear within two to six hours. They include an acute painful abdomen accompanied by vomiting and diarrhea (often bloody). The dog may have noticeably bad breath. Shock and death can occur in severe cases.

Treatment: If you see your dog eating garbage or a dead animal, immediately induce vomiting (see page 25). Follow with liquid Pepto-Bismol; give a dose every 12 hours for two days. Administer by plastic syringe (see page 572 for more information on administration and dosage). If you have trouble getting the liquid into your dog, use the tablets. Try to keep your dog well hydrated.

Mild cases recover in one to two days. If the dog begins to vomit or develops other signs of poisoning, notify your veterinarian.

CHOCOLATE

Most dogs like chocolate, but it can be dangerous. Chocolate contains methylxanthines (made up of caffeine and the alkaloid theobromine). Methylxanthines are not toxic to people in the concentrations found in candy and baked goods, but when ingested by dogs the effects can be lethal. Although some dogs tolerate chocolate far better than others, note that a dog who weighs 5 to 10 pounds (2.3 to 4.5 kg) could die after eating as little as 4 ounces (113 g) of baking chocolate (not candy); a dog who weighs 20 to 40 pounds (9 to 18 kg) after eating as little as 16 ounces (450 g); and a larger dog after eating two pounds (about 1 kg). Dogs have been poisoned by eating an entire pan of brownies or a chocolate cake.

Signs of chocolate toxicity occur within hours after the dog ingests the chocolate. They include hyperexcitability, vomiting, frequent urination, diarrhea, rapid breathing, weakness, seizures, and coma. Death, which is rare, occurs by cardiac arrest.

Treatment: If you know your dog has eaten chocolate within the past six hours and he has not already vomited, induce vomiting (see page 25). Record the type and amount of chocolate ingested (sweet and semisweet chocolate in candy bars is not nearly as toxic as baking chocolate). Then call your veterinarian for further instructions.

Prevention: Use commercial dog products as treats. Keep all chocolate stored securely to prevent accidental ingestion. Make sure everyone in your family, especially the children, understands that chocolate is dangerous for dogs.

Raisins, Grapes, and Other Food Poisons

Dogs who eat raisins and grapes are at risk for acute and possibly fatal kidney failure. Most dogs will vomit some of the raisins or grapes within hours of eating them, but the damage may already be done. Dogs suffering from grape poisoning stop eating, develop diarrhea, and become quiet with signs of abdominal pain. Eventually the blood calcium levels go up and kidney failure follows.

If your dog has eaten raisins or grapes, induce vomiting as soon as you can and take your dog to your veterinarian. He may need to stay for fluid therapy to flush out the toxins.

Macadamia nuts are another food that can be toxic to dogs. Dogs who have eaten these nuts will show mild to severe weakness in the rear legs. So far, dogs seem to recover with time, but treating with activated charcoal hastens recovery.

Onions have sulfur compounds that can lead to a special type of hemolytic anemia. This does not usually cause acute toxicity signs, but will be picked up on blood work. If your dog has ingested onions, induce vomiting and follow that with activated charcoal.

The active yeast in raw bread dough will produce ethanol as the bread rises. This can lead to ethanol poisoning in dogs who ingest it. Unsteady gait and unusual behavior may be the first signs noted. The dog should be taken to your veterinarian, where fluid therapy, along with activated charcoal and possibly the antidote yohimbine, may be administered.

Xylitol is an artificial sweetener used by many diabetic people and people who are dieting. Xylitol can cause a dramatic and rapid drop in blood sugar in dogs, and possibly fatal liver damage. If your dog consumes xylitol, even just in sugar-free gum, induce vomiting and contact your veterinarian.

Corrosive Household Products

Corrosive and caustic chemicals (acids and alkalis) are found in household cleaners, toilet bowl cleaners, dishwasher detergents, anti-rust compounds, alkaline batteries, drain decloggers, and commercial solvents. When ingested, they cause burns of the mouth, esophagus, and stomach. Severe cases cause perforations of the stomach and strictures of the esophagus, which may develop over time due to the tissue damage.

Treatment: *Do not induce vomiting.* Vomiting can result in rupture of the stomach and burns of the esophagus. Rinse the dog's mouth immediately after contact and take him as quickly as possible to the nearest veterinary clinic. If you can't get to the vet very quickly, give the dog water or milk (30 ml per 6 pounds or 2.7 kg of body weight) by plastic syringe to dilute the acid or alkali in the stomach.

The practice of giving an acid to neutralize an alkali and vice versa is no longer recommended, because it causes heat injury to the tissues.

With topical exposure, flush the area with water for 30 minutes. If the substance is in the dog's eyes, see *Burns of the Eyes*, page 179.

PETROLEUM PRODUCTS

Gasoline, kerosene, and turpentine can cause pneumonia if aspirated or inhaled. (Ingesting them usually causes gastrointestinal upset, but is not as serious.) Signs of toxicity include vomiting, rapid labored breathing, tremors, convulsions, and coma. Death is by respiratory failure.

Treatment: *Do not induce vomiting.* Treat as described in the previous section on for corrosive household products (page 34). Flush the mouth with water to remove petroleum residue. Petroleum products are extremely irritating to the skin and must be removed as quickly as possible. Bathe the skin using warm soapy water. For tar in the coat, see *Special Bath Problems*, page 111.

POISONOUS PLANTS

Eating plants and vegetation is not a common cause of poisoning in dogs, but it does occur. Puppies going through the chewing stage are more likely to ingest indoor and outdoor plants. In adult dogs, chewing on plants may be a sign of boredom or frustration associated with separation anxiety or a recent change in the household routine. The variety of potentially poisonous plants and shrubs allows for a wide range of symptoms. Signs include mouth irritation, drooling, vomiting, diarrhea, hallucinations, rapid labored breathing, staggering, muscle tremors, seizures, coma, and death. Some plants cause sudden death without premonitory signs. Other plants contain chemicals that are extremely irritating to the skin.

Milkweed, lily-of-the-valley, laurel, azalea, foxglove, and oleander all contain cardiac glycosides of the digitalis class. Even though these plants have a bitter taste, pets do sometimes eat enough to cause death. Ornamental plants of the nightshade family, including Chinese lantern, Christmas cherry, and ornamental pepper, contain solanines that are toxic to the gastrointestinal system and brain. They, too, are a rare cause of death.

You'll find a list of common toxic plants, shrubs, and trees on pages 36–38, but this list does not include all potentially poisonous plants. If you're not sure about a plant, ask your veterinarian or the local plant nursery. The ASPCA also has a list of poisonous plants on its website (www.aspca.org). Your local Cooperative Extension is often a good source of information about poisonous plants. Note that with some plants, only certain parts are toxic. With others, the whole plant is poisonous.

Treatment: If you suspect your dog has ingested a poisonous plant, induce vomiting (see page 25) and call your veterinarian for further instructions.

Prevention: To prevent houseplant poisoning, determine which plants are toxic and either dispose of them or keep them in a place the dog is unable to reach. Outside, be careful of any sticks you throw for your dog that he may chew on. Fence off dangerous plants so your dog can't reach them.

Indoor Plants with Toxic Effects

Houseplants that cause a skin reaction after contact with the skin or mouth

Chrysanthemum	Poinsettia
Creeping fig	Weeping fig

Irritating plants, some of which contain oxalic acid, which causes mouth swelling, difficulty swallowing, respiratory problems, and gastrointestinal upsets

Arrowhead vine	Malanga
Boston ivy	Marble queen
Caladium	Mother-in-law plant
Calla or arum lily	Neththyis
Dumbcane (diffenbachia)	Parlor ivy
Elephant's ear	Pothos or devil's lily
Emerald duke	Peace lily
Heart leaf (philodendron)	Red princess
Jack-in-the-pulpit	Saddle leaf (philodendron)
Majesty	Split leaf (philodendron)
	Tuberous begonia

Plants that contain a wide variety of poisons—most cause vomiting, an acutely painful abdomen, and cramps; some cause tremors, heart and respiratory and/or kidney problems, which are difficult for owners to interpret

Amaryllis	Ivy species
Asparagus fern	Jerusalem cherry
Azalea	Nightshade
Bird-of-paradise	Pot mum
Creeping Charlie	Ripple ivy
Crown of thorns	Spider mum
Elephant's ear	Sprangeri fern
	Umbrella plant

Outdoor Plants with Toxic Effects

Outdoor plants that can cause vomiting and diarrhea

Bittersweet woody	Indian turnip
Castor bean	Indian tobacco
Daffodil	Larkspur woody
Delphinium	Poke weed
Foxglove	Skunk cabbage
Ground cherry	Soapberry
	Wisteria

Trees and shrubs that may cause vomiting, painful abdomen, and diarrhea

American yew	English yew
Apricot	Horse chestnut
Almond	Japanese plum
Azalea (rhododendron)	Mock orange
Balsam pear	Monkey pod
Bird-of-paradise bush	Peach
Buckeye	Privet
Cherry	Rain tree
English holly	Western black locust yew
	Wild cherry

Outdoor plants with varied toxic effects

Angel's trumpet	Mescal bean
Buttercup	Moonseed
Dologeton	Mushrooms
Dutchman's breeches	Nightshade
Jasmine	Pigweed
Jimsonweed	Poison hemlock
Locoweed	Rhubarb
Lupine	Spinach
May apple	Sunburned potato
Matrimony vine	Tomato vine
	Water hemlock

continued

Outdoor Plants with Toxic Effects (*continued*)	
Hallucinogens	
Locoweed	Nutmeg
Marijuana	Periwinkle
Morning glory	Peyote
Poppy	
Outdoor plants that cause convulsions	
Chinaberry	Nux vomica
Coriaria	Water hemlock
Moonweed	

LEAD

Lead is found in fishing weights and is a base for some artists' paints. Other sources of lead include linoleum, drywall (sheetrock), batteries, plumbing materials, putty, lead foil, solder, golf balls, old paint chips, and tar paper. The use of commercial lead-free paints has significantly reduced the frequency of lead intoxication. Poisoning occurs primarily in puppies and dogs who chew and swallow objects that contain lead. Toxicity usually requires repeated exposure.

Acute lead intoxication is characterized by vomiting and a very painful abdomen. With chronic exposure, a variety of central nervous system signs can develop. They include seizures, uncoordinated gait, excitation, continuous barking, attacks of hysteria, weakness, stupor, and blindness. Chewing and champing fits may be mistaken for the encephalitis of distemper.

Treatment: If you suspect your dog has ingested lead, induce vomiting (see page 25). Seek veterinary attention. Blood tests will be done to check for lead levels. Specific antidotes to bind and remove lead from the dog's system are available from your veterinarian.

ZINC

Pennies made after 1982 have a zinc core. This heavy metal can be toxic to dogs, leading to hemolytic anemia, blood in the urine, and possible kidney failure. If you see your dog ingest pennies, induce vomiting. Many times, clinical signs do not show up for days, as the stomach acid dissolves the metal. Surgery to remove any pennies may be required and your dog may need hospitalization for fluids and to attempt therapy to chelate (remove from the body) the zinc.

TOAD AND SALAMANDER POISONING

There are two species of poisonous toads in the United States: the Colorado River toad, found in the Southwest and Hawaii; and the marine toad, found in Florida. There is one species of poisonous salamander: the California newt, found in California.

All toads, even the ones that aren't poisonous, have a bad taste. Dogs who mouth them slobber, spit, and drool. This does not necessarily mean the dog has been poisoned. Toxicity depends upon the virulence of the toad or salamander venom, the size of the dog, and the amount of poison absorbed. The marine toad, for example, is highly poisonous, causing death in as few as 15 minutes.

Symptoms can vary from slobbering to convulsions, blindness, and death. Puppies and small dogs are more likely to develop toxicity.

Treatment: Repeatedly flush the dog's mouth using a garden hose, if necessary, and induce vomiting (see page 25). Be prepared to administer CPR (see page 8). Dogs with salamander poisoning generally recover quickly.

Insect Stings and Bites

The stings of bees, wasps, and yellow jackets, and the bites of ants all cause painful swelling and redness at the site of the sting, usually on a hairless area such as the nose or feet. The swelling may include the face and neck, even if the dog was not stung on the face. If the dog is stung many times, he could go into shock as a result of absorbed toxins. Occasionally, anaphylactic shock (see page 13) develops in a dog who has been stung in the past.

The bites of black widow and brown recluse spiders are toxic to animals. The first sign is sharp pain at the site of the bite. Later the dog develops intense excitability, fever, weakness, and muscle and joint pains. Seizures, shock, and death can occur, especially with the bite of the black widow spider. An antivenin is available to treat these bites.

The stings of centipedes and scorpions cause a local reaction and, at times, severe illness. These bites heal slowly.

The bites of fleas, ticks, and other common insect parasites are discussed in chapter 4.

Treatment:

1. Identify the insect.
2. If the stinger is found (a small black sac), remove it by scraping it out with your fingernail or a credit card. Do not squeeze or use tweezers, as this can inject more venom. (Only bees leave their stingers behind.)
3. Make a paste of baking soda and water and apply it directly to the sting.

4. Apply an ice pack to relieve the pain and swelling.

5. Apply calamine lotion to relieve the itching.

6. Your veterinarian may prescribe an antihistamine.

If the dog exhibits signs of hypersensitivity to the venom (agitation, face scratching, drooling, vomiting, diarrhea, difficulty breathing, collapse, or seizures), take him at once to the nearest veterinary facility for treatment of anaphylactic shock.

If your dog has a severe reaction to a bee sting, you should consult your veterinarian about keeping an Epi Pen kit available (the Epi Pen is a prepackaged injection of epinephrine used to counteract an anaphylactic reaction) and discuss the proper dose for your dog.

Snakebites

Poisonous and nonpoisonous snakes are widely distributed throughout North America. Ninety percent of snakebites in dogs involve the head and legs.

In the United States there are four types of poisonous snakes: cottonmouths (also called water moccasins), rattlesnakes, copperheads, and coral snakes. The diagnosis of poisonous snakebite is made by the appearance of the bite, the behavior of the animal, and your identification of the species of snake.

In general, bites of nonpoisonous snakes do not cause swelling or pain. They show teeth marks in the shape of a horseshoe, but no fang marks.

Pit Vipers (Rattlesnakes, Cottonmouths, and Copperheads)

You can identify these species by their large size (4 to 8 feet, 1.2 to 2.4 m, long), triangular heads, pits below and between the eyes, elliptical pupils, rough scales, and the presence of retractable fangs in the upper jaw.

The bite: You may see one or two bleeding puncture wounds in the skin; these are fang marks. These marks may not be visible because of the dog's coat. The pain is immediate and severe. The tissues are swollen and discolored due to bleeding at the site of the bite.

Note that 25 percent of poisonous snakebites lack venom and thus do not produce a local reaction. While absence of local swelling and pain is a good sign, it does not guarantee the dog won't become sick. Severe venom poisoning has been known to occur without a local reaction.

The dog's behavior: Signs of envenomation may take several hours to appear because of variables such as time of the year, species of the snake, toxicity of the venom, amount injected, location of the bite, and size and health of the dog. The amount of venom injected bears no relationship to the size of

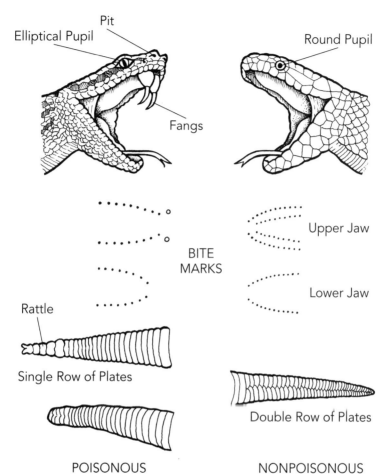

Pit

Elliptical Pupil

Round Pupil

Fangs

BITE MARKS

Upper Jaw

Lower Jaw

Rattle

Single Row of Plates

Double Row of Plates

POISONOUS

NONPOISONOUS

Compare the characteristics of pit vipers and nonpoisonous snakes. Note the elliptical pupil, pit below the eye, large fangs, characteristic bite, and single row of subcaudal plates on the belly of the pit viper.

the snake. Signs of venom poisoning include extreme restlessness, panting, drooling, vomiting, diarrhea, uncoordinated gait, respiratory depression, shock, and sometimes death.

CORAL SNAKES

Identify this snake by its rather small size (less than 3 feet, .9 m, long), small head with black nose, and brightly colored alternating bands (red, yellow, and black) fully encircling the body. The fangs in the upper jaw are not retractable.

The bite: The puncture wounds from a bite are small and the pain is mild. There is little local reaction.

The dog's behavior: Coral snake venom is neurotoxic, meaning it affects the nerves and causes weakness and paralysis. Signs may be delayed for several hours. They include muscle twitching, pinpoint pupils, weakness, difficulty swallowing, shock, and collapse. Death is by respiratory paralysis.

Treating Snakebites

First identify the snake and look at the bite. If the snake is not poisonous, clean and dress the wound as described in the section on *Wounds* (on this page). If it appears the dog has been bitten by a poisonous snake, *proceed at once to the veterinary hospital.* (If the snake has been killed, take it with you for identification. If not, try to describe it as completely as you can.) Some specific precautions:

- *Keep the dog quiet.* Venom spreads rapidly. Excitement, exercise, and struggling increase the rate of absorption. If possible, carry the dog.
- Do not wash the wound, as this increases venom absorption.
- Do not apply ice, as this does not slow absorption and can damage tissue.
- Do not make cuts over the wound and/or attempt to suck out the venom. This is never successful and you could absorb venom.
- Be aware that the snake's fangs may be venomous for up to two hours after it dies, even if you have cut off the head.

Veterinary treatment involves respiratory and circulatory support, antihistamines, intravenous fluids, and species-specific antivenin. The earlier the antivenin is given, the better the results. Because signs of envenomation are often delayed, all dogs who have been bitten by a poisonous snake—even those who don't show signs—should be hospitalized and observed for 24 hours.

If you live in an area where your dog is likely to come in contact with poisonous snakes, you may choose to take him through sensitization training. A skilled professional will use an electric collar to train your dog to fear and avoid snakes.

Wounds

The two most important goals in treating wounds are to stop the bleeding and to prevent infection. Wounds are painful, so be prepared to restrain and muzzle the dog before treating the wound.

Controlling Bleeding

Bleeding may be arterial (bright red blood will spurt out) or venous (dark red blood will ooze out), or sometimes both. Do not wipe a wound that has stopped bleeding, as this will dislodge the clot. Similarly, don't pour hydrogen peroxide on a fresh wound. Peroxide dissolves clots and starts a fresh round of bleeding. It may also damage the tissues and delay healing.

The two methods used to control bleeding in an emergency situation are a pressure dressing and a tourniquet.

Pressure Dressing

The most effective and safest method for controlling bleeding is to apply pressure directly to the wound. Take several sterile gauze squares (or, in an emergency, use any clean cloth such as a thickly folded pad of clothing) and place over the wound. Apply direct pressure for 5 to 10 minutes. Leave the dressing in place and bandage snugly. If material for bandaging is not available, hold the pack in place until help arrives.

Watch for signs of swelling of the limb below the pressure pack (see *Foot and Leg Bandages,* page 47). This indicates impaired circulation. If you see these signs, the bandage must be loosened or removed. Consider adding more bulk to the pack and apply a second bandage over the first. Transport the dog to a veterinary hospital.

Tourniquet

Tourniquets can be used on the extremities and tail to control arterial bleeding that can't be controlled with a pressure pack. *Tourniquets should never be used if bleeding can be controlled by direct pressure.* Always place the tourniquet *above the* wound (between the wound and the heart).

A tourniquet should be used only if bleeding cannot be controlled with a pressure dressing. The tourniquet is looped twice around the leg . . .

. . . and tightened by twisting.

A suitable tourniquet can be made from a piece of cloth, belt, tire, or length of gauze. Loop the tourniquet around the limb as shown in the photo on page 43. Then tighten it by hand or with a stick inserted beneath the loop. Twist the loop until the bleeding stops.

A tourniquet should be loosened every 10 minutes to prevent tissue *hypoxia* and to check for persistent bleeding. If bleeding has stopped, apply a pressure bandage as described in the previous section. If bleeding continues, let the blood flow for 30 seconds and then retighten the tourniquet for another 10 minutes.

TREATING WOUNDS

Nearly all animal wounds are contaminated with dirt and bacteria. Proper care and handling will reduce the risk of tetanus and prevent many infections. Before handling a wound, make sure your hands and instruments are clean. The five steps in wound care are:

1. Skin preparation
2. Wound irrigation
3. Debridement
4. Wound closure
5. Bandaging

Skin Preparation

Remove the original pressure dressing and cleanse the area around the wound with a surgical scrub solution. The most commonly used solutions are Betadine (povidone-iodine) and Nolvasan (chlorhexidine diacetate). Both products are extremely irritating to exposed tissue in the concentrations provided in the stock solutions (Betadine 10 percent, chlorhexidine 2 percent), so be very careful that the solution does not get in the wound while scrubbing the skin around it. Dilute the solution to weak tea color for Betadine or pale blue color for Nolvasan.

Three-percent hydrogen peroxide, often recommended as a wound cleanser, has little value as an antiseptic and is extremely toxic to tissues.

After the scrub, start at the edges of the wound and clip the dog's coat back far enough to prevent any long hairs from getting into the wound.

Wound Irrigation

The purpose of irrigation is to remove dirt and bacteria. The gentlest and most effective method of wound cleansing is by *lavage*, which involves irrigating the wound with large amounts of fluid until the tissues are clean and glistening. Do not vigorously cleanse the wound using a brush or gauze pad because this causes bleeding and traumatizes the exposed tissue.

Tap water is an acceptable and convenient irrigating solution. Tap water has a negligible bacterial count and is known to cause less tissue reaction than sterile or distilled water.

If possible, add chlorhexidine solution or Betadine solution to the tap water for antibacterial activity. Chlorhexidine has the greater residual antiseptic effect, but either antiseptic solution (not soap solutions) is satisfactory when correctly diluted. To dilute chlorhexidine, add 25 ml of the 2 percent stock solution to 2 quarts of water (2 l), making a 0.05 percent irrigating solution. To dilute Betadine, add 10 ml of the 10 percent stock solution to 2 quarts of water to make a 0.2 percent irrigating solution.

The effectiveness of the irrigation is related to the volume and pressure of the fluid used. A bulb syringe is a low-pressure system. It is least effective and requires more fluid to achieve satisfactory irrigation. A large plastic syringe removes a moderate amount of dirt and bacteria. A home Water Pik unit (used by people to clean their teeth) or a commercial lavage unit that provides a high-pressure stream of fluid is the most effective.

A garden hose with a pressure nozzle for the initial lavage, or a kitchen sink spray unit, followed by one of the methods just described to deliver the antiseptic, is a good alternative. You want to flush and clean the wound, not force dirt deeper into the tissues. Angle your flow of liquid to accomplish that and let the fluid pool to bring debris to the surface.

Debridement

Debridement means removing dying tissue and any remaining foreign matter using tissue forceps (tweezers) and scissors or a scalpel. Debridement requires experience to determine the difference between normal and devitalized tissue, and instruments to control hemorrhage and close the wound. Accordingly, wounds that require debridement and closure should be treated by a veterinarian.

Closure

Fresh lacerations on the lips, face, eyelids, and ears are best sutured or stapled to prevent infection, minimize scarring, and speed recovery. Lacerations longer than half an inch (1.25 cm) on the body and extremities probably should be closed, but small lacerations may not need to be. Small V-shaped lacerations heal best if they are closed.

Wounds contaminated by dirt and debris are quite likely to become infected if closed at the time of injury. These wounds should be left open or sutured around a drain that can be used for through-and-through irrigation. Similarly, wounds older than 12 hours should not be closed without drainage. Suturing or stapling should be avoided if the wound appears to be infected (is red, swollen, or has a surface discharge).

Your veterinarian may decide to close a wound that has been left open for several days and has developed a bed of clean tissue. Wounds that are clean after several days are resistant to infection and usually can be closed with

A wound sutured around a drain allows for through-and-through flushing.

impunity. Suturing such a wound is called delayed primary closure.

The length of time sutures or staples should remain in place depends on the wound's location and other characteristics. Most sutures and staples can be removed after 10 to 14 days.

Puncture Wounds

Puncture wounds are caused by bites and pointed objects. Animal bites, in particular, are heavily contaminated with bacteria. Bleeding may occur. There may also be bruising, particularly if the dog was picked up in the teeth of a bigger dog and shaken. Puncture wounds are often concealed by the dog's coat and may be easily overlooked until an abscess develops a few days later.

Treatment of a puncture wound requires a veterinarian. It involves surgically enlarging the skin opening to provide drainage, after which the area is irrigated with a dilute antiseptic surgical solution. These wounds should not be closed. If there is a large, open wound area, parts of the wound may be sutured with a drain left in place to allow air to get in and discharge to drainage. With all animal bites, keep in mind the possibility of rabies. If it is a bite wound from an unknown animal, a rabies booster may be needed.

Antibiotics are frequently prescribed for bite wounds and wounds that are heavily contaminated, such as puncture wounds.

Home Treatment

Small open wounds can be treated at home without sutures or staples. Medicate twice a day with a topical antibiotic ointment such as triple antibiotic. The wound can be left open or covered with a dressing. Make sure the dog is not constantly licking it. You can cover the area with a sock or a T-shirt to keep the dog away from the wound.

Infected wounds that are draining pus require the application of moist sterile compresses. A number of topical antiseptics are effective in treating superficial wound infections. They include chlorhexidine and Betadine (diluted as described in *Wound Irrigation,* page 44), Furacin (both the topical cream and 0.2 percent solution), 1 percent Silvadene cream, and topical antibiotics containing bacitracin, neomycin, and polymyxin B (triple antibiotic). Apply the topical antibiotic directly to the wound or place it first on a gauze pad. Change the dressing once or twice a day to facilitate pus drainage.

Bandaging a Wound

Wounds may be left open or bandaged, depending on their location and other factors. Wounds on the head and neck are often left open to facilitate treatment. Many wounds of the upper body are difficult to bandage and do not benefit greatly from being covered.

Bandaging has the advantage of protecting the wound from dirt and contaminants. It also restricts movement, compresses skin flaps, eliminates pockets of serum, keeps the edges of the wound from pulling apart, and prevents the dog from biting and licking at the wound. Bandaging is most effective for wounds to the extremities. In fact, nearly all leg and foot wounds can benefit from a bandage.

Dressings over draining or infected wounds must be changed once or twice a day. The bandage should be bulky enough to absorb the drainage without soaking through.

Foot and Leg Bandages

To bandage the foot, place several sterile gauze pads over the wound and secure with surgical adhesive tape. Be careful not to make the tape too tight. To secure a foot dressing, you will need to continue the bandage up the leg.

For leg wounds, cover the wound with sterile gauze pads. On top, pad the entire leg with plenty of cotton so the dressing won't become too tight and interfere with the circulation. Wrap first with roll gauze, then wrap the leg with elastic tape or bandage, as shown in the photographs on page 48. Your veterinarian or a veterinary technician can show you the best way to bandage a particular wound.

To bandage a foot with a lacerated pad, first place the foot on several layers of sterile gauze.

Secure the gauze with surgical adhesive tape.

Finish with a leg bandage to hold the foot bandage in place.

Veterinary wraps such as Vet Wrap work well, but you need practice to have the right amount of tension so you don't cut off circulation. Flex the knee and foot several times to be sure the bandage is not too tight and that there is good movement at the joints.

Over the next few hours, check the toes for coolness and observe the feet for swelling. Swelling of the leg below a bandage will be seen in the toes. When the toes are swollen, the nails are spread apart instead of being side by side. If this swelling is not treated by removing the bandage, the foot becomes cold and loses feeling. If there is any question about circulation, remove the bandage.

Put a plastic bag over a leg bandage when the dog goes outside so it will stay clean and dry. Use a sock or a T-shirt to protect the bandage or to cover wounds that are difficult to bandage.

Bandages over clean, healing wounds can be changed every two days, but should be inspected three or four times a day for signs of constriction, limb swelling, slippage, drainage, or soiling. With prolonged bandaging, watch for moisture between the toes. If there are signs of any of these problems, replace the bandage.

Wounds on the foot or leg may be covered with a splint as well as a bandage. The splint minimizes movement of the area and speeds healing. Watch for sores from a splint rubbing on the skin.

To make a leg bandage, apply a gauze square over the wound and pad the leg well.

Wrap the leg with an elastic tape or bandage. Do not stretch the elastic wrap as you apply it, or the dressing will be too tight. Check toes for swelling or redness at least three or four times a day.

The finished dressing; it should be changed every two days.

A many-tailed bandage protects skin from scratching and biting, and is far more comfortable than a restrictive collar.

Many-Tailed Bandage

This type of bandage is used to hold dressings in place and to protect the covered skin from the dog's scratching and biting. It is made by taking a rectangular piece of clean cloth and cutting the sides to make tails. Tie the tails together over the dog's back to hold the bandage in place.

An eye bandage, properly applied.

Eye Bandage

Your veterinarian may prescribe an eye bandage to help treat an eye ailment. Place a sterile gauze square over the affected eye and hold it in place by taping it around the head with one-inch-wide surgical adhesive. Be careful not to wrap the tape too tight. Apply the dressing so that the dog's ears are free. You may have to change the dressing from time to time to apply medication to the eye. Many dogs will need to wear an Elizabethan collar or a BiteNot collar to keep them from rubbing or pawing at the bandage.

C h a p t e r

2

GASTROINTESTINAL PARASITES

Although nearly all dogs are infested with parasites at one time or another, most develop an immunity that keeps the parasite population in check. This immunity can break down, however, under conditions of stress or ill health. When that happens, the worms increase in number and eventually produce signs of intestinal infection, including diarrhea, weight loss, anemia, and blood in the feces.

Dogs develop the highest level of immunity to worms that have a larval phase that migrates in tissue. These are the ascarids, hookworms, and threadworms. Whipworms and tapeworms do not have a migratory phase and thus produce little immunity.

Immunosuppressive drugs such as cortisone have been shown to activate large numbers of encysted hookworm larvae. Stressful events such as pregnancy, surgery, severe illness, trauma, and emotional upsets (such as shipping or going to a new home) can also activate dormant larvae.

Deworming Puppies and Adult Dogs

Although some deworming medications are effective against more than one species of worm, no single medication is effective against them all. A specific diagnosis is necessary to choose the safest and most effective drug. This requires an examination of the dog's stool and determining whether the parasite is in the egg, larval, or adult stage. It is not advisable to deworm a dog suffering from an unexplained illness that is assumed to be caused by "worms."

All *anthelmintics* (medications that act to expel or destroy parasitic worms) are poisons—meant to poison the worm but not the dog. Dogs debilitated by heartworms or some other infestation may be too weak to resist the toxicity of the dewormer. Be sure to check with your veterinarian before using any dewormer. It is also important to give the medication exactly as prescribed.

Deworming agents that are effective against various species of worm are listed in the table on pages 54–55.

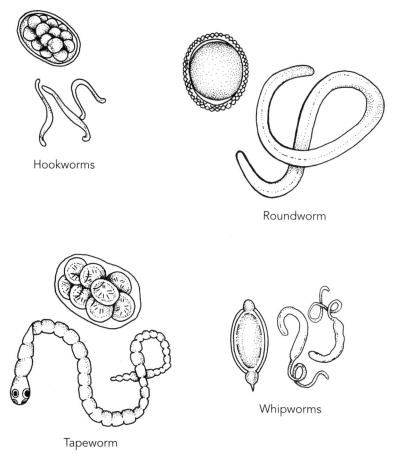

Hookworms

Roundworm

Tapeworm

Whipworms

These drawings show the relative size and appearance of common canine adult worms and eggs. The eggs are magnified 500 times.

Deworming Puppies

Most young puppies are infested with ascarids. Other worm parasites may also be present, but they're not as common. It is advisable to have your veterinarian check your puppy's stool before deworming for ascarids, because if other worms are present, a broad-spectrum deworming agent may be recommended.

Puppies should be dewormed at 2 weeks of age (before ascarid eggs are passed in the stool) and again at 4, 6, and 8 weeks of age. Then, it's prudent to put them on a monthly heartworm preventive for life that also protects the dog against other parsites, or at least continue monthly deworming for six months. This schedule kills all ascarids, whether acquired *in utero*, through infected mother's milk, or by ingesting the eggs. Pyrantel pamoate (Nemex or Strongid) is an excellent choice for ascarids and can be safely given to 2-week-old puppies. It is available as a liquid suspension or tablet (see *How to Give Medications*, page 566).

Worm medications can be harmful to puppies that are ill from a respiratory infection, chilled, crowded in unsanitary surroundings or abruptly weaned from their mothers. Stressful conditions such as these should be corrected before administering the dewormer. Do not deworm a puppy who has diarrhea unless your veterinarian has determined that the diarrhea is caused by the parasite.

DEWORMING ADULT DOGS

Most veterinarians recommend that adult dogs be dewormed only when there is specific reason to do so, such as when eggs or parasites are found during a fecal examination. Dogs can also be kept on a yearlong heartworm preventive that also protects against many of the intestinal parasites. All dogs should have a fecal examination done at least once a year.

Most dogs carry ascarids as encysted larvae, but intestinal infestation by the adult worm is rare in the healthy dog. Hookworms are likely to be a problem in adults only during periods of stress. Only milbemycin (Interceptor) is effective against encysted hookworm larvae.

Whipworms are a frequent cause of acute and chronic diarrhea in adult dogs. They are difficult to diagnose on routine fecal examination. Eradication requires the use of specific agents not commonly used for other worms.

Tapeworms are common in dogs but, fortunately, cause few symptoms. The worm segments are easy to detect in the stool. Threadworms are not common. Very few agents are effective against this parasite.

A brood bitch should have her stool checked before breeding. If parasites are found, she should be dewormed. Deworming during pregnancy should be done only as determined by your veterinarian. Note that some dewormers are contraindicated during pregnancy (see the table on pages 54–55).

How to Control Worms

The life cycle of most worms is such that the possibility of reinfestation is great. To keep worms under control, you must destroy the eggs and larvae *before* they reinfest the dog. This means good sanitation and maintaining clean, dry quarters.

Dogs should not be kenneled with dirt runs, which provide ideal conditions for seeding eggs and larvae. A watertight surface, such as cement, is the easiest to keep clean. Gravel is a good substitute. It provides effective drainage and allows for easy removal of stools. Hose down each kennel or run daily and allow it to dry in the sun.

Remove stools daily from runs and pens. Lawns should be cut short and watered only when necessary. Stools in the yard should be removed every day.

Concrete and gravel surfaces can be disinfected with lime or salt. Lime is an alkaline corrosive, so hose down all pens after disinfecting with lime to

Deworming Agents

Drug	Type of Worm				Comments
	Hook	Ascarid	Whip	Tape	
Canopar (rhenium closylate)	Good	No effect	No effect	No effect	Do not use in nursing puppies or lactating females. Dose is by weight. Avoid in Airedales. May induce vomiting.
Cestex (espisprantel)	No effect	No effect	No effect	Excellent	Do not use in puppies younger than 7 weeks old.
Dichlorvos (many trade names)	Excellent	Excellent	Good	No effect	Do not use if dog is debilitated or has heartworms or liver or kidney disease. May increase the effects of insecticides in coat preparations and flea collars.
Drontal Plus (praziquantel, pyrantel pamoate, febantel)	Excellent	Excellent	Excellent	Excellent	Available in two tablet sizes, depending on the weight of the dog. Broad spectrum. Do not use in pregnant bitches or puppies less than 3 weeks old or weighing less than 2 pounds (.9kg).
Droncit (praziquantel)	No effect	No effect	No effect	Excellent	Single dose. Available as a pill or an injection.
Heartgard Plus (ivermectin, pyrantel pamoate)	Excellent	Excellent	No effect	No effect	Used primarily for heartworm prevention.
Interceptor (milbemycin oxime)	Good	Good	Good	No effect	One tablet a month prevents heartworms and controls hookworms, ascarids, and whipworms. Can be used in puppies 8 weeks and older. Wide margin of safety. Does not cause a problem in Collies. Contraindicated if microfilaria are present in the blood.

Drug					Comments
Ivomec (Ivermectin)	Good	Good	Good	No effect	Approved only for heartworm prevention. Higher doses may cause death in herding breeds and their mixes.
Nemex, Strongid (pyrantel pamoate)	Excellent	Excellent	No effect	No effect	Safe. Can be given to nursing puppies. Available as liquid suspension or tablets.
Panacur (fenbendazole)	Excellent	Excellent	Excellent	Good	Granular formulation. No contraindications.
Piperazine (many trade names)	No effect	Good	No effect	No effect	Inexpensive. Safe. Do not overdose.
Sentinel (milbemycin, lufenuron)	Excellent	Excellent	Excellent	No effect	One tablet a month prevents heartworms; controls hookworms, ascarids, and whipworms; and aids in flea control. Can be used in puppies 8 weeks and older. Wide margin of safety. Does not cause a problem in Collies. Contraindicated if microfilaria are present in the blood.
Telmintic (mebendazole)	Excellent	Excellent	Excellent	Good	Wide range of safety. Give for three days.
Vercom Paste (febantel, praziquantel)	Excellent	Excellent	Excellent	Excellent	Administer to adults by mouth or in food without regard to feeding schedule. Administer to puppies less than 6 months of age only by mouth on a full stomach.

prevent injury to dogs. Borax (1 ounce per 10 square feet, 30 ml per 1 square meter) is another good disinfectant.

Kennels in which the dogs have persistent problems with worms usually have other problems as well, including chronic skin diseases and recurrent respiratory infections. Steps must be taken to improve the management of the kennel, especially the sanitation.

Fleas, lice, cockroaches, beetles, water bugs, and rodents are intermediate hosts of tapeworms and ascarids. To control reinfestation, it is necessary to get rid of these pests (see *Disinfecting the Premises*, page 133).

Many intestinal parasites spend their larval stages in other animals and develop into adults only when the dog eats one of these animals. Preventing dogs from roaming and hunting will reduce their exposure to parasites, as well as toxic substances and poisons. Be sure to thoroughly cook all fresh meat before feeding it to your dog.

Heartworm preventives, such as Interceptor, also prevent and control ascarids, hookworms, and whipworms. Heartgard Plus controls ascarids and hookworms but not whipworms. These agents are given in low dosages. The beneficial effect lasts only as long as you give the medication.

Ascarids (Roundworms)

Ascarids are the most frequent worm parasite in dogs and cats. There are two species that commonly infect dogs: *Toxocara canis* and *Toxascaris leonina*. Adult roundworms live in the stomach and intestines and can grow to 7 inches (18 cm) long. A female may lay 200,000 eggs in a day. The eggs are protected by a hard shell. They are extremely hardy and can live for months or years in the soil.

There are four ways dogs can become infected with roundworms. Prenatal infection occurs when the larvae migrate through the placenta *in utero*. Almost all puppies are infected in this manner before birth. Mother's milk can also transmit ascarids. In addition, puppies and adults can become infected by ingesting eggs in the soil. And finally, dogs can acquire the eggs by ingesting a transport or intermediate host, such as a mouse or other rodent.

The life cycle of *T. canis* in young puppies is as follows: Eggs entering through the puppy's mouth hatch in her stomach. The larvae are carried to the lungs by the circulatory system. Here they break through the capillaries into the air sacs, sometimes causing bouts of coughing and gagging. Once in the lungs, the larvae crawl up the windpipe and are swallowed. Back in the intestines, the larvae develop into adult worms. The adults pass eggs that become infective in soil in three to four weeks.

Dogs older than 6 months develop an acquired resistance to ascarids. Few, if any, larvae complete the life cycle. Most come to rest in various body tissues, where they encyst. While encysted, they are protected against the dog's antibodies and also the effects of most dewormers. (Interceptor is an exception. This dewormer has some effect on encysted larvae.) During pregnancy, however, encysted larvae are activated and migrate to the placenta and mammary glands. Deworming the dam before pregnancy reduces the burden of migrating larvae but does not eliminate all puppy infestations because there are still encysted larvae in the mother's body.

Ascarids rarely cause symptoms in adult dogs; in puppies older than 2 months, they usually produce only mild intermittent vomiting and diarrhea. Worms maybe found in the vomitus or passed in the stool. Typically, they look like white earthworms or strands of spaghetti that may be moving.

In very young puppies, a heavy infestation can result in severe illness or even death. These puppies often fail to thrive, have a dull coat and a pot-bellied appearance, and are anemic and stunted in growth. Such puppies may experience abdominal pain with whimpering and groaning. Rarely, a tangled mass of worms in the small intestines can cause death from intestinal obstruction.

Treatment: Nemex or Strongid (pyrantel pamoate suspension) is an excellent dewormer for nursing pups because it is safe and active against both ascarids and hookworms. This makes it the agent of choice for these youngsters. Pyrantel pamoate dewormers can be obtained from your veterinarian. You do not have to fast your pup before using this medication. Be sure to follow the manufacturer's directions regarding dosage.

Puppies should be dewormed by 2 weeks of age—before they begin to pass ascarid eggs and contaminate the environment. Repeat the treatment at 4, 6, and 8 weeks of age. The purpose of retreating is to kill worms that were in the larval stage during the first dewormings. Subsequent treatments are indicated if eggs or worms are found in the stool.

Drontal Plus, Vercom Paste, Telmintic, and Panacur have a broad spectrum of activity and are all highly effective against ascarids, hookworms, and whipworms. Drontal and Vercom are also highly effective against tapeworms. Panacur is only partially effective against tapeworms. Deworming the brood bitch with Panacur during the last two weeks of gestation and during lactation reduces environmental exposure and helps control puppy infection.

Drontal Plus comes in two tablet sizes: one for small dogs and another for medium and large dogs. The prescribed number of tablets (based on the dog's weight) is given as a single dose. The dose should be repeated in two to four weeks. Drontal Plus cannot be used in dogs who weigh less than 2 pounds (1 kg) or in puppies less than 3 weeks old. A stool sample should be checked following the second course of treatment.

Vercom and Panacur are given daily for three consecutive days. The entire course should be repeated in two to four weeks, followed by a stool check to make sure the worms have been eliminated.

Prevention: Heartworm preventives such as Interceptor prevent and control ascarids as well as hookworms and whipworms. Heartgard Plus controls ascarids and hookworms but not whipworms.

Public health considerations: Ascarids can cause a serious disease in humans called visceral larva migrans. The infection is acquired when the eggs of *T. canis* are ingested by a human. Children 1 to 4 years old are most frequently affected, and often have a history of eating dirt. The frequent use of city parks by pets has resulted in heavy contamination of soil and sandboxes in these areas. One study of parks in a large U.S. city revealed that one out of three soil samples contained *T. canis* eggs.

When a human eats an ascarid egg, larvae develop as in the dog. However, because humans are not a definitive host, the larvae do not progress to adult ascarids. Instead, they burrow into the intestinal wall and migrate to the liver, lungs, and skin. Symptoms, which develop only when the infestation is heavy, include abdominal pain, cough, wheezing, itching, and a skin rash with *papules*. In a very heavy infestation, larvae may reach the heart, kidneys, spleen, brain, eyes, and other tissues. In young children, a syndrome called ocular larva migrans can lead to blindness and necessitate the removal of an eye.

Prevention of human infection is based on recognizing that the vast majority of eggs excreted in the environment are produced by nursing puppies and lactating bitches. This is one reason why it is so important to deworm puppies before eggs appear in the stool.

Older children should be instructed not to put soil and sand in their mouths. Infants and toddlers require parental supervision to prevent this. Infants and young children should not be allowed to play with and handle nursing pups until they have mastered the discipline of washing their hands after petting an animal. Better enforcement of leash laws and pooper-scooper ordinances would reduce environmental contamination. Setting aside separate dog parks or areas for dogs to play can help keep children away from affected areas.

Hookworms (Ancylostoma)

There are three species of hookworms that afflict dogs. These parasites are most prevalent in areas of high temperature and humidity (such as the southern United States), where conditions are favorable for the rapid development and spread of larvae.

Hookworms are small, thin worms about one-quarter to one-half inch (.6 to 1.3 cm) long. They fasten their mouth parts onto the mucosa of the small intestines and suck blood and tissue fluids from the host. This can result in severe blood loss and malnutrition.

There are five routes by which puppies (and adult dogs) can acquire the infection:

- Migration through the placenta *in utero*
- Ingesting larvae in mother's milk

- Ingesting larvae in the soil
- Direct penetration of the skin (usually through the pads of the feet)
- Ingesting an intermediate host

The majority of serious hookworm infestations in puppies occur during the first two months of life and are acquired through the mother's milk. Signs of illness include bloody, wine-dark, or tar-black diarrhea. Progressive blood loss may cause these puppies to rapidly sicken and die. Intensive veterinary management is required.

In adult dogs, the most common routes of infection are ingesting larvae and larvae migrating through the skin. Some larvae encyst in tissues, while others migrate through the lungs to the intestines, where they mature into adults. In two to three weeks the dog begins to pass eggs in her feces. These eggs incubate in the soil. Under proper conditions, the eggs hatch in 48 hours and release larvae that are infective in five to seven days.

Dogs with chronic hookworms often have no symptoms. When symptoms do occur, they include tarry or bloody diarrhea, pale mucous membranes caused by anemia, weight loss and emaciation, and progressive weakness. Symptoms can appear as early as 10 days after exposure. The diagnosis is made by finding eggs in the feces. Because eggs do not appear in the feces for two to three weeks, however, there may be an interval during which a stool examination is negative and the diagnosis must be made on the basis of clinical signs.

Most dogs who recover from hookworms become carriers via larvae encysted in their tissues. During periods of stress or illness, these larvae are released and a new outbreak of bloody diarrhea occurs as worms appear in the intestines.

Treatment: A number of dewormers are highly effective in treating hookworms. They include Nemex, Panacur, Drontal Plus, Telmintic, and Vercom Paste. Treatment should be repeated in one to two weeks, because the initial deworming activates encysted larvae and causes a new crop of adult worms to appear in 10 to 12 days. A follow-up fecal examination is recommended to be sure all parasites have been removed.

Prevention: Good sanitation and periodic stool checks with appropriate deworming will prevent the serious consequences of hookworms. In addition, heartworm preventives such as Interceptor are also effective against hookworms, ascarids, and whipworms. Heartgard Plus controls hookworms and ascarids but not whipworms.

Public health considerations: An itchy disease in humans called cutaneous larvae migrans (creeping eruption) is caused by the hookworm *A. brasiliense*. Larvae present in the soil penetrate the skin, causing lumps and streaks beneath the skin. The condition usually clears up on its own.

Tapeworms

Fresh tapeworm segments are about one-quarter inch (6 mm) long.

Tapeworms live in the small intestines and vary from less than an inch to several feet in length. The head of the worm fastens to the wall of the gut by hooks and suckers. The body is composed of segments that contain the egg packets. To cure tapeworm infection, the head must be destroyed. If it is not, the worm will regenerate.

The body segments containing the eggs are passed in the feces. Fresh, moist segments are about one-quarter inch (6 mm) long and are capable of moving. Occasionally you may see them crawling through the fur near your dog's anus. When dry, they resemble kernels of rice. Some dogs experience anal itching from the segments. Tapeworms will drain nutrition from your dog but not to the extent that ascarids, hookworms, and whipworms will.

The common tapeworm of dogs is *Dipylidium caninum*. Fleas and lice serve as intermediate hosts when they ingest the eggs. A dog must bite or swallow an infected flea or louse to acquire the parasite. A human could also acquire *D. caninum* if they accidentally swallow an infected flea.

Several species of *Taenia*, another type of tapeworm, parasitize dogs. *Taenia* are acquired by eating infected rodents, rabbits, and sheep. *Diphyllobothrium* species are found encysted in the organs of fish. These tapeworms are found in the northern United States and Canada.

Echinococcus tapeworms are uncommon in dogs. Intermediate hosts are deer, elk, goats, sheep, cattle, swine, horses, and some rodents.

Treatment: Droncit, Cestex, Drontal Plus, Telmintic, and Vercom Paste are highly effective against all the common dog tapeworms. Use them under veterinary guidance.

Prevention: The common dog tapeworm can be controlled by eliminating fleas and lice from the environment, as described in *Disinfecting the Premises*, page 133. Dogs should be confined to prevent them from roaming and eating dead animals. Avoid feeding your dog uncooked meat and raw game.

Public health considerations: *Echinococcus granulosa* and *Echinococcus multiocularis* are significant public health problems. Dogs and humans can acquire the infection from eating contaminated uncooked meat, and, in the case of dogs, by feeding on the carcass of an infected animal. Humans can also acquire the disease by ingesting eggs passed in the feces of dogs. Since humans are not the definitive host, adult worms do not develop. Instead, the larvae produce large cysts in the liver, lungs, and brain. These cysts are called hydatids, and they can cause serious illness and even death.

Echinococcus granulosus is found in the southern, western, and southwestern United States—areas where sheep and cattle are common. Although dog-to-human transmission is rare, a number of human cases (presumably from eating uncooked meat) are reported each year. If your dog runs free in a rural area where this tapeworm could be a problem, ask your veterinarian to check her stool for tapeworms twice a year. This species of tapeworm can be identified only after the head has been recovered by effective deworming. Until a definite diagnosis is made, a dog with a tapeworm that could be *Echinococcus* must be handled with extreme care to avoid fecal contamination of hands and food.

Whipworms

The adult whipworm is 2 to 3 inches (50 to 76 mm) long. It is threadlike for the most part, but is thicker at one end, which gives it the appearance of a whip.

The adult worm lives in the last part of the small intestines and the first part of the large intestines, where it fastens to the wall of the gut. The female lays fewer eggs than other worms, and there are long periods during which eggs are not shed. Accordingly, finding eggs in the feces is difficult, even with repeated stool examinations.

Whipworms can cause acute, chronic, or intermittent diarrhea in dogs. Typically, the stool is mucoid and bloody. The diarrhea is often accompanied by urgency and straining (see *Colitis*, page 276). Dogs with a heavy infestation may lose weight, fail to thrive, and develop anemia.

Treatment: A number of preparations are effective against whipworms. They include Panacur, Drontal Plus, Telmintic, and Vercom Paste. However, it is difficult to attain high drug concentrations in the colon, where the whipworms reside, and this makes them difficult to eradicate. To maximize success, follow up the initial deworming with a second deworming three weeks later and a third deworming in three months.

Prevention: Eggs remain infective in the environment for up to five years. In areas such as public parks and backyards, where the ground has been heavily contaminated with whipworm eggs, frequent reinfection is a common problem. It is important to observe pooper-scooper ordinances and remove stools in the yard every day. Dirt runs should be relocated and paved with concrete or new gravel. Use household bleach in a 1:32 dilution to disinfect concrete and gravel runs. It may be necessary to totally change the gravel in gravel runs.

The drug Interceptor, given to prevent heartworms, also controls and prevents whipworms.

Threadworms (Strongyloides)

Threadworms are round worms just 2 mm long that live in the small intestines and infect both dogs and humans. The parasite is found in humid, subtropical regions such as the southeastern United States and Gulf Coast areas.

The life cycle of the threadworm is complex. Eggs and larvae are passed in the feces. Larvae become infective and are either ingested or gain entrance by directly penetrating the skin.

Threadworms are mainly a problem in puppies. Infected pups suffer from a profuse watery or bloody diarrhea that can be fatal. Pneumonia may occur as the larvae migrate through the lungs.

Treatment: The diagnosis is made by finding eggs or larvae on microscopic examination of stool, both fresh and after incubation. A five-day course of Panacur is the treatment of choice. Retreatment in 30 days is recommended. Ivermectin has also been used effectively, although it is not labeled for this purpose.

Public health considerations: Dogs can readily infect humans, and vice versa. Threadworm infection in humans is a debilitating disease accompanied by chronic diarrhea. Accordingly, infected pups must be isolated until treated and cured. Extreme care must be taken to avoid human contact with the feces of dogs infected with threadworms.

Other Worm Parasites
PINWORMS

Pinworms are sometimes a concern to families with pets and children. However, dogs and cats are not a source of human pinworm infection, because they do not acquire or spread these parasites.

TRICHINOSIS

This is a disease acquired by ingesting uncooked pork containing the encysted larvae of *Trichina spiralis*. In humans, only a few cases are reported each year. The incidence is probably somewhat higher in dogs. Prevent trichinosis by keeping your dog from roaming, especially if you live in a rural area. Cook all fresh meat for you *and* your dog.

LUNGWORMS

Lungworms are slender, hairlike parasites about 1 centimeter long. There are several species of lungworm that affect dogs. *Capillaria aerophila* is acquired by ingesting eggs or a transport host, such as snails, slugs, or rodents. These parasites reside in the nasal cavity and upper air passages, producing a mild cough. *Filaroides* species produce a tracheal and bronchial infection that tends to be a kennel-related problem, especially in Greyhounds.

Most dogs with lungworms have mild infections and do not show clinical signs. Heavily infested dogs (usually under 2 years of age) may have a persistent dry cough, weight loss, and exercise intolerance.

Diagnosis is based on clinical signs, a chest X-ray (not always positive), and identification of the eggs or larvae in the stool or in respiratory secretions. *Bronchoscopy* on a dog with a *Filaroides* infection may reveal small nodules in the wall of the trachea. Larvae may be seen peeking out of these growths. Treatment with Panacur (fenbendazole) is often needed for extended periods of time.

LUNG FLUKES

The lung fluke *Paragonimus kellicotti* infects dogs living around the Great Lakes, in the Midwest, and in the southern United States. Flukes are flatworms ranging in size from a few millimeters up to several inches (2.5 to 5 cm) long. The fluke is acquired by eating aquatic snails and crayfish. Cysts develop in the lungs. Rarely, a cyst ruptures and causes a collapsed lung (*pneumothorax*).

The safest and most effective agent for treating all species of lungworms and lung flukes is Panacur. The drug must be given daily for 10 days. Prevent lungworms by cooking fish and restricting your dog's hunting forays.

HEARTWORMS

Heartworms are common in dogs. They are discussed on page 341.

INFECTIOUS DISEASES

Infectious diseases are caused by bacteria, viruses, protozoa, fungi, and rickettsia that invade the body of a susceptible host and cause an illness. They are transmitted from one animal to another by contact with infected urine, feces, and other bodily secretions, or by inhaling pathogen-laden droplets. They may also be acquired by contact with spores in the soil that enter the body through the respiratory tract or a break in the skin. A few are sexually transmitted.

Although pathogens exist everywhere in the environment, only a few cause infection. Fewer still are contagious. Many infectious diseases are species-specific. For example, a dog cannot catch a disease that is specific to a horse, and vice versa. Other infectious diseases are not species-specific, and are capable of causing disease in many animals, including humans. In instances where a disease is *zoonotic*, public health considerations are discussed.

Many infectious agents are able to survive for long periods outside the host animal. This knowledge is important in determining how to contain the spread of infection.

For many diseases, the best way to prevent them is by vaccination. Immunity and vaccinations are discussed at the end of this chapter.

Bacterial Diseases

Bacteria are single-celled microorganisms that are noted for their ability to cause disease.

BRUCELLOSIS

This disease is caused by the bacteria *Brucella canis*. It is a major cause of sterility and spontaneous abortion in dogs. Puppies infected *in utero* are typically aborted at 45 to 59 days after conception. Suspect this disease in any bitch who aborts two weeks before she is due to deliver and whenever a bitch delivers stillborn puppies or puppies who sicken and die.

Dogs with acute infection have enlarged lymph nodes in the groin and/or beneath the jaw. Fever is rare. The testicles of the male may swell in the initial stages, and then become smaller and *atrophic* as the sperm-producing cells are destroyed. Note, however, that this disease can infect a dog or bitch without producing any signs of illness.

In a dog with an acute infection, bacteria are found in the blood, urine, body secretions, and the products of abortion. In a dog with a chronic or inactive infection, bacteria can be transmitted in vaginal secretions during estrus and in semen.

The most common mode of transmission is by contact with infected vaginal discharges following a spontaneous abortion, and by contact with the urine of infected dogs. The disease can spread rapidly throughout a kennel in this manner. Males can acquire the disease through oral and nasal contact with the vaginal secretions of estrus females. Females can acquire the disease through breeding with an infected male. This is of particular concern to breeders, because males can harbor the bacteria for life.

A positive blood culture obtained during an acute infection is the most conclusive diagnostic test. Bacteria can also be cultured from aborted tissue. Blood serum tests will determine if a dog has ever been infected.

Treatment: Brucellosis is difficult to eradicate. A course of intramuscular and oral antibiotics given for a minimum of three weeks will eliminate the disease in 80 percent of dogs. To be considered cured, a dog must be free of the bacteria for at least three months. Since it is difficult to achieve a cure, it is recommended to spay or neuter all infected animals to prevent the transmission of disease to other dogs.

Prevention: All animals should be tested before they are used in a breeding program. Brood bitches should be retested one month before each breeding and, ideally, stud dogs should be retested before every breeding.

Public health considerations: Rare instances of human infection have followed exposure to canine brucellosis. It is important to wear rubber gloves and take proper hygienic precautions when handling all aborted products of conception.

LEPTOSPIROSIS

Canine leptospirosis is caused by an order of bacteria called spirochetes—slender, spirally undulating bacteria. There are at least four species of the leptospira bacteria (or serovars) that can infect dogs: *canicola, icterohemorrhagiae, grippotyphosa,* and *pomona.*

Leptospira are found in wild and domestic animals. The bacteria are spread in the urine, often making their way into water sources and remaining infective in the soil for up to six months. Rats, pigs, raccoons, cattle, skunks, and opossums appear to be the primary reservoirs. With housing spreading into the suburbs, more wildlife are coming into contact with pet dogs. This may be the cause of the upswing in leptospirosis cases. Spirochetes enter a dog's system through a break in the skin or when the dog drinks contaminated water. Dogs who spend a lot of time in the water are at increased risk, as are dogs who drink out of puddles and dogs who spend time in yards that get a lot of runoff or stay wet after it rains.

Most infections are mild and do not show clinical signs. Signs appear 4 to 12 days after exposure. Fever is present in the early stage. Other signs are loss of appetite for several days, vomiting, lethargy, depression, muscle pain, and sometimes diarrhea or blood in the urine. Leptospirosis primarily affects the kidneys and/or the liver.

In severe cases, the whites of the dog's eyes turn yellow (*jaundice*). This indicates hepatitis with destruction of liver cells. Coagulation problems can ensue, with spontaneous bleeding from the mouth and blood in the stools. Following recovery, untreated dogs can become carriers and shed bacteria in their urine for up to a year.

The *canicola* and *gripotyphosa* serovars tend to cause kidney damage, and the *pomona* and *icterohemorrhagiae* serovars most often affect the liver. Young dogs tend to show liver damage with all of the serovars.

The diagnosis can be suspected based on the dog's clinical signs. Tests of kidney and liver function will be abnormal. Spirochetes can be detected in the urine and blood by fluorescent antibody staining. Blood tests are available to confirm the diagnosis.

Treatment: Severely ill dogs should be hospitalized for public health reasons and to provide more intensive care. Antibiotic combinations of penicillin and streptomycin are effective against the disease, although doxycycline is now routinely used as well. Enrofloxacin and ciprofloxacin are also sometimes used. Supportive measures includecontrolling vomiting and diarrhea, correcting dehydration with intravenous fluids, and maintaining nutrition.

Prevention: There is a vaccine for leptospirosis. See page 96.

Public health considerations: Humans can acquire leptospirosis, generally through the same types of exposures that cause the disease in dogs, such as infected water. It can also spread via contact with infected urine, so precautions should be taken if the family dog has leptospirosis. An infected dog who is asymptomatic can still spread the infection.

BORDETELLA BRONCHISEPTICA

Bordetella bronchiseptica bacteria are frequently found in dogs with the kennel cough complex and other respiratory diseases. Signs of upper respiratory illness caused by bordetella include a dry, hacking cough accompanied by a clear nasal or eye discharge. In puppies and immune-compromised adult animals, secondary bacterial invasion of the lower respiratory tract following viral illness may cause life-threatening pneumonia. Dogs who are carrying the organism and may not even be ill themselves, may still cough or exhale the organism into the air. Healthy dogs can then be infected by breathing in that contaminated air.

The bacteria can be cultured from nasal swabs or *transtracheal washings*.

Treatment: Treat all upper respiratory infections by placing the animal in a warm, draft-free environment, humidifying the atmosphere, and avoiding stressful activities that can interfere with a smooth recovery. Antibiotics are indicated if the dog develops fever and a *mucopurulent* nasal discharge. Antibiotics are also indicated for all cases of upper respiratory infection in which bordetella is isolated. Antibiotics given by nebulizer may be more effective than those given orally or by injection. This is because the bacteria attach to the mucosal surface of the respiratory tract and are difficult to reach with systemic antibiotics.

Prevention: Bordetella vaccinations are not routine, but may be advisable for show dogs, boarded dogs, dogs who go to grooming salons or obedience classes, and dogs who live in kennels. (See *Bordetella Vaccine*, page 97.)

SALMONELLA

Several bacteria of the salmonella species are capable of producing acute infectious diarrhea in dogs. Salmonella remain alive for many months or years in soil and manure. In dogs, the disease is acquired by consuming raw or commercially contaminated foods, by eating animal manure, or by making oral contact with surfaces that have been contaminated by the diarrhea of an infected dog. This bacterial infection is a risk in dogs fed a raw diet, unless excellent food-handling hygiene is practiced at all times.

Puppies and young adults are most susceptible, as are dogs whose natural resistance has been compromised by a viral infection, malnutrition, parasites, or being housed in crowded, unsanitary quarters.

Signs of illness include fever, vomiting, and diarrhea. The stool may be bloody and foul smelling. Dehydration develops when vomiting and diarrhea are prolonged. Bacteria in the bloodstream can cause abscesses in the liver, kidneys, uterus, and lungs. The acute illness, which lasts four to ten days, may be followed by a chronic diarrhea that persists for more than a month. Dogs with chronic diarrhea shed salmonella in their feces and are a potential source of infection to other animals and humans.

The diagnosis is made by identifying salmonella bacteria in stool cultures when the dog is in the carrier state, or in the feces, blood, and infected tissues of dogs suffering from acute infection.

Treatment: Mild cases respond well to fluid replacement. Many salmonella species are resistant to common antibiotics. In fact, antibiotics can favor the growth of resistant bacteria and prolong fecal shedding of bacteria.

Accordingly, antibiotics are used only for seriously ill dogs. Sulfa drugs and the quinolones are the antibiotics of choice.

Public health considerations: Salmonellosis is a *zoonotic* disease, so care must be taken to practice excellent hygiene when dealing with a dog with salmonellosis. It is important to wear gloves when cleaning up feces and to disinfect areas where an affected dog has eliminated.

CAMPYLOBACTERIOSIS

Campylobacteriosis is a disease that produces acute infectious diarrhea in puppies. It also occurs in kennel dogs and strays—most of whom are in poor condition and are suffering from other intestinal infections.

The bacteria is acquired by contact with contaminated food, water, uncooked poultry or beef, and animal feces. Campylobacteria can survive for up to five weeks in water or unpasteurized milk.

The incubation period is one to seven days. Signs of acute infection include vomiting and a watery diarrhea that contains mucus and sometimes blood. The disease usually runs its course in five to fifteen days, but may be followed by chronic diarrhea in which bacteria is shed in the feces.

Treatment: Treat mild diarrhea as described in *Diarrhea*, page 283. Keep the dog warm, dry, and in a stress-free environment. More severely affected dogs will require veterinary management with intravenous fluids to correct dehydration. Antibiotics may be advisable. Erythromycin and ciprofloxin are the drugs of choice.

Public health considerations: Campylobacteriosis is a common cause of diarrhea in humans. Most human cases arise from contact with newly acquired kittens and puppies who are suffering from diarrhea. Parents should be aware that puppies with diarrhea may harbor a human pathogen. Good hygiene is essential, especially for young children and people who are immunocompromised.

COLIOBACILLOSIS *(E. COLI)*

Coliobacillosis is an infectious diarrhea caused by the bacteria *E. coli*. There are some strains of *E. coli* that are not part of the normal intestinal flora. When ingested, these strains are capable of producing acute diarrhea. *E. coli* can be acquired from infected drinking water, food, or fecal matter. This bacterial infection is a risk in dogs fed a raw diet, unless excellent food-handling hygiene is practiced at all times.

E. coli is an important cause of puppy *septicemia,* and may also cause urinary tract or reproductive tract infections. In dogs of all ages, a concurrent viral infection of the intestinal tract can allow *E. coli* to become pathogenic and produce a life-threatening illness.

Treatment: Acutely ill dogs must be hospitalized for intensive veterinary management. Dehydration is a serious concern, as is damage from toxins, especially to the kidneys. It is important to maintain strict sanitary precautions when handling infected stool.

Prevention: In humans, outbreaks of severe *E. coli* have occurred after eating undercooked ground beef or contaminated vegetables. Good hygiene is important here as well.

Lyme Disease

Lyme disease is caused by the spirochete bacteria *Borrelia burgdorferi*. The spirochete is acquired through the bite of an infected tick. Lyme disease is now regarded as the most common tick-borne illness in the United States.

This disease was first recognized in 1975, following an outbreak of what appeared to be acute arthritis in several rural communities in southeastern Connecticut, including the town of Old Lyme. Currently, most cases are found in wooded locations in the Northeast, upper Midwest (including much of Wisconsin and Minnesota), northern California, and the Pacific Northwest.

The white-footed mouse is the principal reservoir for the spirochete. Birds can also harbor it. The white-tailed deer supports the tick, but not the spirochete. Lyme disease is spread primarily during tick season (May through August), peaking in the month of July, but ticks can be active any time the temperature is over 32°F (0°C).

Check your dog daily for ticks during tick season. This is an engorged female tick on a dog.

The disease in dogs is most commonly characterized by the sudden onset of lameness. In fact, lameness is often the only sign of infection. One or more joints may become swollen and painful to the touch. Some dogs run a fever and experience weakness, lethargy, loss of appetite, and weight loss. The lameness may last only a few days, but in some cases it becomes chronic and persists or recurs for months.

Kidney problems are the next most common sign. An acute cardiac syndrome is quite rare. Both of these syndromes are usually fatal.

Most dogs exposed to Lyme disease do not become ill. Serological blood tests will indicate whether a dog has been exposed to the disease. Dogs may not test positive until a few weeks after exposure. New serologic tests can distinguish between dogs with vaccine immunity and dogs with natural exposure. A rising antibody titer in the absence of recent vaccination, however, indicates active infection. Western Blot and *ELISA* blood tests are now both used to detect exposure. Many dogs who test positive for Lyme disease will also have other tick-borne diseases, such as ehrlichiosis and babesiosis.

X-rays of swollen joints show fluid without degenerative joint changes. *Synovial fluid analysis* (in which a needle is inserted into a joint to remove fluid for examination) may show spirochetes.

Treatment: Antibiotics are given for a minimum of two to four weeks. Amoxicillin and doxycycline are among the most effective.

Prevention: Ticks must attach for 5 to 20 hours before they are capable of transmitting infection. Accordingly, a daily inspection with removal of ticks will prevent many dogs from becoming infected.

Tick collars such as Preventic, and tick control on the premises, help reduce the occurrence of Lyme disease. Frontline is a flea-control preparation that kills ticks for up to 30 days following a single application. Advantix is another topical product that kills ticks. For more information, see *Ticks*, page 123.

There is a vaccine to prevent Lyme disease in dogs. It may be advisable for dogs at risk for Lyme disease. Discuss this with your veterinarian.

Public health considerations: Lyme disease is a serious illness in humans. Dogs do not transmit Lyme disease to humans, although they can spread the ticks carrying the spirochete. Ticks may transfer to people before feeding on the dog, although this is not common. Once a tick starts feeding on a dog, it will not seek a second host. Dispose very carefully of any ticks you remove from your dog. The best method is to put them in a jar with a bit of alcohol, seal the jar, and throw it away.

Viral Diseases

Viruses are disease-causing organisms that are even more basic than cells. They are simply packages of protein.

DISTEMPER

Distemper is a highly contagious disease caused by a virus similar to the one that causes measles in people. Worldwide, it is the leading cause of infectious disease deaths in dogs, although in the United States it occurs only sporadically. All unvaccinated dogs are at high risk of infection.

Infected animals shed canine distemper virus in all body secretions. Inhaling the virus is the primary source of exposure. The highest incidence of the disease occurs in unvaccinated puppies 6 to 12 weeks of age, at which time maternal antibodies fall below protective levels.

Half the dogs who become infected with canine distemper virus show mild signs of illness or no signs at all. The overall health of the dog has a lot to do with how ill he becomes. The disease is most severe in dogs who are poorly nourished and ill-kept.

The distemper virus tends to attack brain cells and cells that line the surfaces of the body, including the skin, the conjunctiva, the mucous membranes of the respiratory tract, and the gastrointestinal tract. The disease takes a variety of forms. Secondary infections and complications are common, partly attributable to the immunosuppressive effects of the virus.

The first signs of distemper appear six to nine days after exposure, and in mild cases go unnoticed.

First stage is characterized by a fever spike of up to 103° to 105°F (39.4° to 40.5°C). A second fever spike is accompanied by loss of appetite, listlessness, and a watery discharge from the eyes and nose. These symptoms may be mistaken for a cold.

Within a few days, the eye and nasal discharge becomes thick, yellow, and sticky. The dog develops a pronounced dry cough. Pus blisters may appear on the abdomen. Vomiting and diarrhea are frequent and may cause severe dehydration.

During the next one to two weeks, very often the dog seems to be getting better but then relapses. This often coincides with the end of the course of antibiotics and the development of gastrointestinal and respiratory complications due to secondary bacterial invasion.

Second stage occurs two to three weeks after the onset of the disease. Many dogs develop signs of brain involvement (*encephalitis*), characterized by brief attacks of slobbering, head shaking, and chewing movements of the jaws (as if the dog were chewing gum). Epileptic-like seizures may occur, in which the dog runs in circles, falls over, and kicks all four feet wildly. After the convulsive episode the dog appears to be confused, shies away from his owner, wanders about aimlessly, and appears to be blind.

In cases with brain involvement in which the diagnosis is uncertain, a spinal tap and analysis of cerebrospinal fluid may be of assistance. But this is not always diagnostic. Another indication of brain involvement is distemper myoclonus, a condition characterized by rhythmic contractions of muscle groups at up to 60 contractions per minute. The jerking can affect all parts of the body, but is most common in the head. Myoclonus is first seen when the dog is resting or sleeping. Later it occurs both day and night. Pain accompanies myoclonus, and the dog whines and cries. If the dog recovers, the jerking continues indefinitely—but becomes less severe with time.

Hard-pad is a form of distemper in which the virus attacks the skin of the feet and nose, producing thick, horny skin on the nose and calluslike pads on the feet. It first appears about 15 days after the onset of the infection. At one

The thickened, callused pads of a dog with hard-pad, a form of distemper.

time, hard-pad and encephalitis were thought to be separate diseases, but they are now recognized as being caused by different strains of the distemper virus. Hard-pad is much less common than it was in the past, due to better vaccines and increased use of vaccines.

Treatment: Distemper must be treated by a veterinarian. Antibiotics are used to prevent secondary bacterial infections, even though they have no effect on the distemper virus. Supportive treatment includes intravenous fluids to correct dehydration, medications to prevent vomiting and diarrhea, and anticonvulsants and sedatives to control seizures.

The outcome depends on how quickly you seek professional help, the virulence of the distemper strain, the age of the dog, whether he has been vaccinated, and his ability to mount a rapid and effective immune response to the virus.

Prevention: Vaccination against canine distemper is almost 100 percent protective. All puppies should be vaccinated by 8 weeks of age. Brood bitches should be given a DHPP (distemper, hepatitis, parvovirus, and parainfluenza combination) booster shot two to four weeks before breeding. This ensures that high antibody levels will be present in the colostrum. However, some veterinarians believe this additional vaccine booster is not needed.

CANINE HERPESVIRUS INFECTION

Canine herpesvirus is widespread in the dog population and produces a variety of illnesses. It causes a fatal disease in newborn puppies (see *Canine*

Herpesvirus, page 505). It is one of the agents implicated in the kennel cough complex. It causes vaginitis in bitches and infection of the penile sheath in males, and it can be transmitted between males and females during breeding.

Bitches with vaginitis develop hemorrhagic areas and blisterlike lesions of the vaginal mucosa. These lesions may reappear when the bitch comes into heat. Intrauterine infections that progress from the vagina are associated with early embryonic loss, abortions, and stillbirths.

Herpesvirus infection can be confirmed by isolating the virus from infected tissue.

Treatment: There is no effective treatment. A vaccine is not available in the United States at this time, but one is being used in Europe.

Prevention: Most dogs will be exposed to herpes at some time in their lives. As long as it is not during the crucial reproductive periods, it tends to be a mild respiratory infection and is not of consequence. Ideally, bitches should be isolated—not taken to shows or other canine sporting events, or exposed to large numbers of dogs—when they are being used for breeding.

INFECTIOUS CANINE HEPATITIS

Infectious canine hepatitis is a highly contagious viral disease caused by canine adenovirus-1. In the United States the disease is rare and is seen almost exclusively in wild canids and unvaccinated dogs. Most cases occur in puppies under 1 year of age.

Following exposure, the virus multiplies in the dog's tissues and is shed in all body secretions. During this stage, the dog is highly contagious and can spread infection to other dogs who make contact with his infected urine, stool, and saliva. After he has recovered, the dog remains infective and sheds the virus in the urine for up to nine months.

Infectious canine hepatitis affects the liver, kidneys, and lining of the blood vessels, producing a mild infection at one extreme to a rapidly fatal infection at the other. A dog with a mild or subclinical infection loses his appetite and simply appears lethargic. In the fatal form, the dog suddenly becomes ill, develops bloody diarrhea, collapses, and dies within hours. Puppies may die without obvious illness.

A dog with acute infection runs a fever up to 106°F (41.1°C), refuses to eat, passes bloody diarrhea, and, often, vomits blood. The dog has a tucked-up belly caused by painful swelling of the liver. Light is painful to the dog's eyes and causes tearing and squinting. Tonsillitis, spontaneous bleeding beneath the gums and under the skin, and *jaundice* may occur.

Infectious hepatitis can be suspected by the signs and symptoms and confirmed by virus isolation tests. About 25 percent of dogs recovering from infectious canine hepatitis develop a characteristic clouding of the cornea of one or both eyes known as blue eye. In most cases blue eye disappears within a few days.

Treatment: Acute cases must be hospitalized for intensive veterinary treatment.

Prevention: Vaccination is highly effective in preventing infectious canine hepatitis. Infectious canine hepatitis does not cause hepatitis in humans.

RABIES

Rabies is a fatal disease that occurs in nearly all warm-blooded animals, although rarely in rodents. In the United States, vaccination programs for dogs and other domestic animals have been remarkably effective. This has greatly reduced the risk of rabies in pets and their owners.

The major wildlife reservoirs for rabies (with substantial overlap) are the skunk in the Midwest, Southwest, and California; raccoons in New England and the East; foxes in New York, neighboring eastern Canada, Alaska, and the Southwest; and coyotes and foxes in Texas. Bats, which are distributed widely, also carry rabies.

The main source of infection for humans outside the United States continues to be a bite from an infected dog or cat. In India, for example, a country that lacks an effective rabies control program, it is estimated that several thousand people die of rabies each year. Travelers to countries where rabies is endemic should be aware of the risk of dog bites.

The rabies virus, which is present in infected saliva, enters the body at the site of a bite. Saliva on an open wound or disrupted mucous membrane also constitutes exposure. The average incubation period in dogs is two to eight weeks, but it can be as short as one week or as long as one year. The virus travels to the brain along the nerves. The more distant the bite is from the brain, the longer the period of incubation. The virus then travels back along the nerves to the mouth. Entry into the salivary glands occurs less than 10 days before symptoms appear—which means animals can be infectious before they show any signs of rabies (this is unusual but is possible).

Dogs can show either of two versions: the aggressive form, where they attack and act very boldly aggressive; or the "dumb" form, where they are ataxic (an inability to coordinate voluntary muscle movements) and may walk into objects. In both cases, you may notice extensive drooling due to paralysis of the muscles used for swallowing.

Any dog who is bitten by an animal who is not absolutely known to be free of rabies must be assumed to have been exposed to rabies, until proven otherwise. The National Association of State Public Health Veterinarians recommends that if the dog has previously been vaccinated against rabies, revaccinate immediately and observe the dog under leash confinement at home for 45 days. If the dog has not been vaccinated, either euthanize the animal or confine him under strict quarantine without direct handling by

The eyes of this rabid dog show a divergent gaze, protrusion of the nictitating membrane, and a pasty eye discharge.

humans or contact with other animals for six months. Vaccinate him one month before he is released (that is, at five months after the bite). If this seems harsh, keep in mind that it would not have been necessary if the pet had been vaccinated. Different states may have their own specific quarantine and vaccination regulations for dogs who have been exposed to rabies.

Treatment: If you or your dog are bitten by any animal of unknown rabies status, it is extremely important to vigorously cleanse all wounds and scratches, washing them thoroughly with soap and water. Studies in animals have shown that prompt local wound cleansing greatly reduces the risk of rabies. The wound should not be sutured.

Prophylaxis in a previously vaccinated dog consists of a booster shot, which should be given as soon as possible (and certainly within 14 days of the lick or bite). Vaccination is not effective once signs of rabies infection appear.

The introduction of inactivated vaccines grown in human diploid cell cultures has improved the effectiveness and safety of postexposure vaccination for humans. Assuming the human bite victim did not have a preexposure rabies immunization, both passive rabies immune globulin and human origin active diploid cell vaccine should be given.

Prevention: Dogs should be vaccinated against rabies as early as 3 to 6 months of age, with a booster shot a year later and then again every one to three years, depending on the vaccine used and local and state ordinances.

Regardless of the dog's age at the initial vaccination, a second vaccination should be given one year later.

When traveling with your pet, be sure to bring along proof of inoculation against rabies—ideally, a vaccination certificate signed by a veterinarian. If you enter a rabies quarantine area and are unable to prove your dog has been vaccinated, your pet could be impounded. In addition, you could be subject to a heavy fine.

Public health considerations: Do not pet, handle, or give first aid to any dog suspected of having rabies. All bites of wild animals, whether provoked or not, must be regarded as having rabies potential. If your dog is bitten by a wild animal or a domestic animal whose rabies status is unknown, wear gloves when handling your pet to clean his wounds. The saliva from the animal that is in and around the bite wound can infect a person if it gets into a cut or onto a mucous membrane.

Preventive vaccinations are available for high-risk groups of humans, including veterinarians, animal handlers, cave explorers, and laboratory workers.

Early laboratory confirmation of rabies in an animal is essential so that exposed humans can receive rabies prophylaxis as quickly as possible. The animal must be euthanized and his head sent in a chilled (not frozen) state to a laboratory equipped to diagnose rabies. Rabies is confirmed by finding rabies virus or rabies antigen in the brain or salivary tissues of the suspected animal. If the animal cannot be captured and his rabies status can't be verified, you need to consult your physician, who may suggest prophylactic vaccinations.

Whenever you have physical contact with an animal who may conceivably be rabid, *immediately consult your physician and veterinarian*, and also notify the local health department. Biting dogs who appear healthy should be confined and kept under observation for 10 days. *This is true even if the dog is known to be vaccinated for rabies.*

KENNEL COUGH

Kennel cough is, in fact, not one but a group of highly contagious respiratory diseases of dogs that spread rapidly through a kennel or other area where many dogs are kept in close quarters. A harsh, dry cough is the characteristic sign of infection. The cough may persist for many weeks and become a chronic problem as the virus is replaced by secondary bacterial invaders.

A number of viruses, and the bacteria *Bordetella bronchiseptica*, have been implicated in the kennel cough complex.

Treatment: See *Kennel Cough Complex*, page 320.

Prevention: Immunizing your dog with parainfluenza, *bordetella*, and CAV-2 vaccines—incorporated into the routine immunizations—will decrease the prevalence and severity of kennel cough, although it will not entirely prevent it.

CANINE PARVOVIRUS

Canine parvovirus is an acute, highly contagious disease of dogs that was first described in the early 1970s. The virus has a tendency to attack rapidly reproducing cells, such as those lining the gastrointestinal tract.

The virus is shed in large amounts in the stools of acutely infected dogs for up to several weeks following infection. The disease is transmitted by oral contact with infected feces. Parvo can be carried on the dog's hair and feet, as well as on contaminated crates, shoes, and other objects. When the dog licks the fecal material off hair, feet, or anything that came in contact with infected feces, he acquires the disease.

Parvo affects dogs of all ages, but most cases occur in puppies 6 to 20 weeks of age. Doberman Pinschers and Rottweilers appear to acquire the infection more readily and experience more severe symptoms. The reason for lower resistance in these breeds is unknown.

Following an incubation period that averages four to five days, the acute illness begins with depression, vomiting, and diarrhea. Some dog have no fever, while others have high fever (up to 106°F, 41.1°C). Pups with severe abdominal pain exhibit a tucked-up abdomen. Diarrhea is profuse and contains mucus and/or blood. Dehydration develops rapidly.

Heart muscle involvement in neonatal puppies used to be common, but is now quite rare. This is because routine vaccination of brood bitches two to four weeks before breeding boosts maternal antibody levels and provides better protection for puppies.

Suspect parvo in all pups with the abrupt onset of vomiting and diarrhea. The most efficient way to diagnose parvo is to identify either the virus or virus antigens in stools. An in-office blood serum test (*ELISA*) is available for rapid

This puppy has parvovirus infection. Note the tucked-up belly, indicative of abdominal pain. Dehydration developed rapidly, but was corrected with IV fluids. The pup recovered.

veterinary diagnosis. False negatives do occur. Virus isolation techniques are more precise, but require an outside laboratory.

Treatment: Dogs with this disease require intensive veterinary management. In all but the most mild cases, hospitalization is essential to correct dehydration and electrolyte imbalances. Intravenous fluids and medications to control vomiting and diarrhea are often required. More severe cases may require blood plasma transfusions and other intensive care.

Puppies and dogs should not eat or drink until the vomiting has stopped. but require fluid support during that time. This can take three to five days. Antibiotics are prescribed to prevent *septicemia* and other bacterial complications, which are the usual cause of death.

The outcome depends upon the virulence of the specific strain of parvovirus, the age and immune status of the dog, and how quickly the treatment is started. Most pups who are under good veterinary care recover without complications.

Prevention: Thoroughly clean and disinfect the quarters of infected animals. Parvo is an extremely hardy virus that resists most household cleaners and survives on the premises for months. The most effective disinfectant is household bleach in a 1:32 dilution. The bleach must be left on the contaminated surface for 20 minutes before being rinsed.

Vaccinations, starting by 8 weeks of age, will prevent most (but not all) cases of parvovirus infection. During the first weeks of life, puppies are protected by high levels of maternal antibodies. As these levels decline, there is a period lasting from two to four weeks during which puppies are susceptible to infection because vaccinations have not yet fully taken effect. This susceptible period varies from pup to pup, which is why pups anywhere between 6 and 20 weeks age can be especially susceptible to parvo. Nearly all apparent vaccination failures are due to exposure during this susceptible period.

Newer high titer–low passage vaccines are narrowing the window of susceptibility. These modified live virus (see page 91) vaccines contain a higher number of virus particles (high titer), which are less attenuated (low passage; a low passage vaccine contains virus particles that have been less attenuated, or weakened, than those in the average vaccine). That means high titer–low passage vaccines can generally elicit an immune system response in young animals who have a maternal antibody level that would normally prevent them from responding.

Nevertheless, it is still important to isolate young puppies as much as possible from other dogs and from potential sources of infection until they complete the parvo vaccination series at 16 weeks of age.

Currently, recommendations are for a booster a year from the initial vaccine series and then revaccination every three years.

CANINE CORONAVIRUS

Canine coronavirus is a contagious intestinal infection that usually produces a mild disease. However, it can be severe in young puppies and dogs who are stressed by concurrent infections. The distribution is worldwide, and dogs of all ages are affected.

Coronavirus is transmitted by contact with infected oral and fecal secretions. Following infection, the virus is shed in the stool for many months. Symptoms vary from none (the most common form) to outbreaks of acute diarrhea, typically occurring in a community of dogs. Dehydration can occur if the diarrhea is severe.

The early signs of illness are depression with loss of appetite, followed by vomiting and the passage of a foul-smelling, yellow to orange diarrhea that varies from soft to watery. The diarrhea may contain blood. Unlike parvovirus, fever is not common.

There is no readily available test to diagnose coronavirus during the acute illness. A rise in antibody titer in serum tested at the time of illness and two to six weeks later can provide a retrospective diagnosis.

Treatment: Treatment is supportive, and includes maintaining hydration and controlling vomiting and diarrhea, as described for the treatment of parvovirus (page 78). Antibiotics are not prescribed because of the mild nature of most infections.

Prevention: A vaccine is available to control coronavirus. However, because coronavirus is rarely fatal and tends to respond well to treatment, vaccination is not recommended.

Fungal Diseases

Fungi are a large family that includes mushrooms. They live in soil and organic material. Many types of fungi spread via airborne spores. Fungus spores, which resist heat and can live for long periods without water, gain entrance to the body through the respiratory tract or a break in the skin.

Fungal diseases can be divided into two categories. There are fungi that affect only the skin or mucous membranes, such as ringworm and thrush. In the other category, the fungus is widespread and involves the liver, lungs, brain, and other organs, in which case the disease is systemic.

Systemic fungal diseases are not common in dogs. They tend to occur in chronically ill or poorly nourished animals. Prolonged treatment with steroids and/or antibiotics may also change the dog's pattern of resistance and allow a fungal infection to develop. Suspect a fungus when an unexplained infection fails to respond to a course of antibiotics.

Good hygiene is important when handling and caring for a dog with any fungal infection. The risk to humans is low, but these are difficult diseases to treat.

HISTOPLASMOSIS

This disease is found in the central United States near the Great Lakes, the Appalachian Mountains, Texas, and the valleys of the Mississippi, Ohio, and Missouri rivers. These areas have nitrogen-rich soil that facilitates growth of the causative fungus (*Histoplasma capsulatum*). Spores are found in soil contaminated by the dung of bats, and chickens and other birds. Spores are breathed in by dogs, people, or other animals.

In most cases, histoplasmosis is subclinical or inapparent, occasionally producing a mild respiratory infection. There is an acute intestinal form, however, that attacks the small bowel and colon. The principal signs are weight loss and intractable diarrhea. A systemic form is characterized by fever, weight loss, vomiting, muscle wasting, coughing, enlargement of the tonsils and other lymph nodes, as well as involvement of the liver, spleen, bone marrow, eyes, skin, and, rarely, the brain.

The diagnosis is made by chest X-ray, blood studies, and identification of the histoplasma organism in cytology, biopsy, or culture specimens.

Treatment: Oral anti-fungal drugs of the imidazole group, including ketoconazole, itraconazole, and fluconazole, are particularly effective in treating histoplasmosis that is not life-threatening. In dogs with severe infections, amphotericin B is often combined with one of the imidazoles. Amphotericin B is potentially damaging to the kidneys.

Antifungal therapy requires many months of drug use after the symptoms disappear. The disease will reappear if long-term suppression is not maintained. Anti-fungal drugs can be toxic and require close veterinary management.

COCCIDIOIDOMYCOSIS (VALLEY FEVER)

This is the most severe and life-threatening of the systemic fungal diseases. Coccidioidomycosis is found in dry, dusty parts of the southwestern United States, and in California and neighboring Mexico. (Note that coccidioidomycosis is *not* the same disease as coccidiosis, a disease caused by intestinal protozoa.)

Infection occurs by inhaling spores. Most cases are subclinical or inapparent. A severe form affects the lungs and produces acute pneumonia. If the disease becomes systemic, it may involve the long bones (most common), liver, spleen, lymph nodes, brain, and skin. Affected dogs will often have a chronic cough, weight loss, lameness, and fever.

The diagnosis is made by identifying the organism (*Coccidioides immitis*) in cytology, biopsy, or culture specimens.

Treatment: Coccidioidomycosis can be treated effectively using one of the imidazole group of antifungal agents (as described for *Histoplasmosis*, on this page). Prolonged treatment for up to a year is required to try to prevent recurrence. However, relapses are common.

CRYPTOCOCCOSIS

This disease, caused by the yeastlike fungus *Cryptococcus neoformans*, is acquired by inhaling spores found in soil contaminated by bird droppings, especially those of pigeons. In dogs, cryptococcosis involves the brain, eyes, lymph nodes, and skin. About 50 percent of the dogs with this fungus will also show respiratory signs. Signs of brain involvement are an unsteady gait, pressing the head against a hard surface or standing with the head up against a wall, circling, seizures, blindness, and dementia. Involvement of the inner structures of the eyes leads to blindness.

In the less common form that infects the skin, cryptococcosis produces firm nodules, primarily in the head area, that ulcerate and drain pus.

The diagnosis is made by fungal culture and/or tissue biopsy. A cryptococcus latex agglutination test is available.

Treatment: Oral antifungal drugs of the imidazole group (as described for *Histoplasmosis*, page 81) are partially effective when started early in the course of the disease. The response is uncertain and treatment is prolonged. Overall, the prognosis for dogs is guarded to poor.

BLASTOMYCOSIS

This systemic fungal disease occurs along the eastern seaboard, in the Great Lakes region, and the Mississippi, Ohio, and Missouri River valleys. The fungus is associated with moist, rotting organic debris protected from sunlight and enriched with bird droppings, particularly those of pigeons. The disease is acquired by inhaling infected spores. Dogs are considerably more susceptible to blastomycosis than are humans.

Most cases of acute canine blastomycosis involve the respiratory system and cause bronchopneumonia. About 40 percent of cases involve the eyes and skin, producing signs similar to those of cryptococcosis (see above). Weight loss and lameness may also be noted.

Microscopic identification of organisms in *transtracheal washings* or in fluid aspirated from infected tissues is the most efficient way to make the diagnosis. In difficult cases, biopsy and culture may be needed. Serologic tests also are available.

Treatment: A combination of amphotericin B and one of the imidazoles appears to offer the best chance of successful treatment (as described for *Histoplasmosis*, page 81). Months of treatment are required, and some dogs may relapse months to years later.

Public health considerations: Although the hazard to human health is minimal, humans can acquire the fungus from infected bandages and bedding. Use rubber gloves and take hygienic precautions when handling an infected dog.

SPOROTRICHOSIS

This is a skin and subcutaneous infection acquired by contact with spores in the soil. The spores gain access through puncture wounds caused by thorns and splinters; therefore, the disease is seen most often in hunting dogs. Most cases are reported in the northern and central portions of the United States, especially along coastal areas and river valleys.

A nodular, draining, crusted sore forms at the site of the skin wound, usually on the trunk or head. There may be several small firm nodules in the lymph glands that form a chain beneath the skin. On rare occasion the disease becomes systemic and spreads to the liver and lungs. The outlook for these dogs is guarded.

The diagnosis is made by removing a piece of tissue and examining it under the microscope; or more conclusively, by growing the fungus in culture. A fluorescent antibody test can be performed on infected tissue or serum.

Treatment: Response is excellent when the infection is limited to the skin and surrounding tissues. Potassium iodide (a saturated solution) has been used, but care must be taken due to possible toxicity. Antifungals of the imidazole group (as described for *Histoplasmosis*, page 81) are therefore the agents of choice. Treatment needs to be continued for a month after clinical signs are resolved.

Public health considerations: Sporotrichosis is known to infect humans handling animals with infective drainage. It is important to wear rubber gloves and take strict hygienic precautions when handling all animals with draining wounds.

Protozoan Diseases

Protozoa are one-celled animals that are not visible to the naked eye, but are easily seen under the microscope. They are usually carried in water. A fresh stool specimen is required to identify the adult parasite or its cysts (called oocysts).

NEOSPOROSIS

Dogs and herbivores are hosts to Neosporum caninum, with cattle as the intermediate host. Dogs initially acquire the infection by eating infected meat, but once infected, a bitch can pass this on through the placenta to her unborn puppies. The risk to humans is minimal.

Dogs will show nerve and muscle problems, possibly even leading to paralysis. Pneumonia, heart problems, and skin problems may also be seen. Blood tests and muscle biopsies are the main means of diagnosis.

Treatment: Clindamycin, pyrimethamine, and sulfadiazine have been used in treatment.

Prevention: Dogs should not be fed raw or uncooked meat, especially beef. Dogs should also be prevented from defecating in cattle yards and pastures to help prevent exposure. Some veterinarians will attempt treating subsequent litters of affected bitches *in utero*, as it is expected all future puppies will be infected. This must begin after at least two weeks into the pregnancy, to avoid damage to the developing embryos.

TOXOPLASMOSIS

This disease is caused by a protozoan that infects warm-blooded animals. Cats are the definitive host, but other animals, including dogs and humans, can act as intermediate hosts. It is not common in dogs. The principal mode of transmission in dogs and people raw or undercooked pork, beef, mutton, or veal that contains the organism *Toxoplasma gondii*.

Oocysts excreted in the stools of infected cats, or ingesting spores, are other potential sources of infection. Oocysts require one to three days under ideal conditions of warm temperature and high humidity to produce spores. These infective spores can survive in the environment for months or years. Only cats excrete the oocytes in their stool. The dog is therefore not capable of infecting other dogs and humans in this way.

Most dogs with toxoplasmosis experience no symptoms. When symptoms do occur, they include fever, loss of appetite, lethargy, cough, and rapid breathing. Other signs are weight loss, diarrhea, lymph node enlargement, and swelling of the abdomen. Young puppies with toxoplasmosis may show signs of pneumonia, hepatitis, or encephalitis. In brood bitches, intrauterine infection can result in abortion, stillbirths, and the birth of sick puppies who die within the first week of life.

The diagnosis is made by serology. An elevated IgM titer (by *ELISA* tests) is diagnostic for active or recent infection.

Treatment: Antibiotics are available to treat acute toxoplasmosis. Clindamycin is the drug of choice.

Prevention: Prevent the disease by keeping your pet from roaming and hunting. Cook all fresh meat (both yours and your pets') to a temperature of at least 150°F (65.5°C). Wash your hands with soap and water after handling raw meat. Always clean kitchen surfaces that come in contact with raw meat.

COCCIDIOSIS

This disease is caused by a species of coccidia commonly found in the feces of puppies and, occasionally, adult dogs. The main sign is diarrhea. Because infection is mild, symptoms usually do not occur unless the pup's resistance has been lowered by a concurrent disease, malnutrition, or immunosuppression.

Coccidiosis is a particular problem in neonatal puppies who are over-stressed by filth, crowding, chilling, and poor sanitation. Puppies acquire the infection from contaminated premises or from their mother, if she is a carrier. When kennel sanitation is poor, puppies reinfect themselves from their own feces. An outbreak of coccidial diarrhea can also occur in association with roundworm infestation or the trauma of shipping. Coccidiosis is an opportunist. Always look for another precipitating cause.

Five to seven days after ingesting oocytes, infective cysts appear in the feces. The first sign is mild diarrhea that progresses until the feces become mucuslike and tinged with blood. The diarrhea is accompanied by loss of appetite, weakness, and dehydration. Dogs who recover become carriers. Infected dogs and carriers can be identified by finding oocysts in a microscopic slide of fresh stool.

Treatment: Treatment in adult dogs usually is not necessary, due to the mild nature of the diarrhea. Puppies with severe diarrhea may need to be hospitalized for fluid replacement. Antibiotics that are effective against coccidiosis include sulfadimethoxine, trimethoprin-sulfa, furazolidone, and amprolium.

Prevention: Known carriers should be isolated and treated. Wash down infected quarters daily with boiling water and/or dilute bleach or chlorhexidine solution to destroy oocysts. Coccidiosis can be prevented by maintaining clean quarters and providing an appropriate whelping environment, as described in *Caring for the Newborn*, page 490.

TRICHOMONIASIS

This protozoan infection is caused by a species of trichomonas often associated with a mucoid (and occasionally bloody) diarrhea in puppies. Commonly, it is found in association with poor kennel sanitation. Prolonged infection leads to weak, debilitated, stunted puppies with rough coats. The diagnosis is made by finding protozoan cysts in fresh stool.

Treatment: The infection responds well to Flagyl (metronidazole).

GIARDIASIS

This disease is caused by a protozoan of the *giardia* species. Dogs acquire the infection by drinking water from streams and other sources that are contaminated with infective oocysts.

Most infections in adult dogs are subclinical. Young dogs can develop a diarrhea syndrome characterized by the passage of large volumes of foul-smelling, watery, or "cow-pie" stools. The diarrhea maybe acute or chronic, intermittent or persistent, and may be accompanied by weight loss.

Diagnosis is made by finding the protozoan or its characteristics oocysts in saline smears of fresh stool. Smears from rectal swabs are satisfactory. A negative smear does not exclude giardia, as oocysts are shed only intermittently. Three negative fecal smears collected at least two days apart should be obtained before the diagnosis is excluded. Serology tests *(ELISA, IFA)* are now available.

Treatment: Giardiasis responds well to Flagyl (metronidazole). Because Flagyl causes developmental malformations in the fetus, it should not be administered to pregnant bitches. Other effective drugs are available. There is now a vaccine available for giardiasis, but this is rarely recommended because the disease is usually mild and responds well to treatment.

Canine Babesiosis

This is an uncommon disease caused by a protozoan that destroys red blood cells, producing a hemolytic anemia. One mode of transmission is by the bite of a brown dog tick. Natural hosts of this tick are various wild animals, particularly the white-footed mouse and the white-tailed deer. Because these animals are also implicated in Lyme disease, both diseases can occur at the same time. Babesiosis can also be transmitted by blood transfusions from infected animals.

Outside the United States, the disease is found in tropical and subtropical regions throughout the world. For reasons unknown, the Greyhound is particularly susceptible to babesiosis.

Most infections in dogs are subclinical. In dogs with acute illness, the signs are fever, enlargement of the spleen and liver, and abnormal blood tests indicative of hemolytic anemia. The signs of anemia are shortness of breath, exercise intolerance, and pallor of the gums and tongue. The bone marrow and liver can be affected.

Diagnosis is contingent upon finding the protozoan in blood smears. An IFA serum antibody test also is available.

Treatment: Imidocarb is the only drug currently effective against canine babesiosis.

Prevention: Prevent infection by controlling ticks, as described in *Ticks* (page 123).

Canine Hepatozoonosis

This is another protozoan disease transmitted by the brown dog tick. Of the two types of brown dog ticks seen in the United States, *H. americanum* causes a more severe illness than *H. canis*. The geographic distribution of the disease in the United States is limited to Oklahoma, Louisiana, and the Texas Gulf Coast.

In this case, your dog must ingest the tick—perhaps when trying to remove it—to become infected. Illness is most likely to occur in immunosuppressed dogs and pups younger than four months of age. Signs of illness include diarrhea (often bloody), muscle and bone pain with reluctance to move, eye and nasal discharges, and severe loss of weight and body condition.

Treatment: The disease can be treated with a variety of antiprotozoan medications, but a cure has not been established. Most dogs relapse despite treatment, and most die within two years of diagnosis.

Prevention: Hepatozoonosis is best prevented by controlling ticks, as described in *Ticks* (page 123).

AMERICAN TRYPANOSOMIASIS (CHAGAS DISEASE)

Trypanosomiasis is caused by the protozoan *T. cruzi*. A small number of cases have been reported, principally in the southwestern United States, Texas, and California. Raccoons, opossums, armadillos, rats, cats, and dogs serve as the principal reservoirs.

Dogs (and humans) acquire the disease from a family of insects called kissing bugs, so named because they come out of cracks at night and bite the face of sleepers. Infection occurs through contamination of the bug bites by the insects' feces. Another source of infection in dogs is feeding on a host (such as a raccoon) that harbors encysted larvae in its tissues.

Signs include fever, weakness, enlargement of the lymph nodes and spleen, and inflammation of the spinal cord and brain. Trypanosomiasis attacks the heart muscle, causing myocarditis with heart arrhythmias. This can lead to collapse and death. Another complication of myocarditis is congestive heart failure one to three years later.

The diagnosis is made by identifying the protozoan in blood smears. Serology tests also are available.

Treatment: Experimental drugs have been used, but the response is poor.

Public health considerations: Because this often fatal disease can be transmitted to humans through intermediate hosts, euthanizing the animal is recommended. It is essential to take the utmost precautions when handling infected animals, as well as their blood and discharges.

Rickettsial Diseases

Rickettsia are various disease-causing parasites (about the size of bacteria) that are carried by fleas, ticks, and lice. They live within cells. The majority are maintained in nature by a cycle that involves an insect vector, a permanent host, and an animal reservoir.

CANINE EHRLICHIOSIS AND ANAPLASMOSIS

This is a relatively common rickettsial disease caused by the organisms *E. canis* and *E. ewingii*, although several other rickettsia are capable of causing ehrlichiosis. The disease is transmitted by the bite of the brown dog tick and, occasionally, other tick species. Ehrlichiosis occurs mainly in the Gulf Coast area, the eastern seaboard, the Midwest, and California. Outside the United States it is distributed worldwide. Some of the *Ehrlichia* species have been renamed and are now listed in scientific literature as *Anaplasma platys*.

Ticks acquire the rickettsia by feeding on an infected host. A variety of wild and domestic animals serve as reservoirs. Because of its chronic nature, cases of ehrlichiosis are seen year-round, not just during the tick season.

The disease occurs in three phases. During the acute phase, the dog develops fever, depression, loss of appetite, shortness of breath, enlarged lymph nodes, and, occasionally, signs of encephalitis. These symptoms may suggest Rocky Mountain spotted fever, Lyme disease, or canine distemper.

Two to four weeks after the onset of the acute phase, the dog enters a subclinical phase that lasts weeks to months. Some dogs eliminate the infection during the subclinical phase; others progress to the chronic phase. There appears to be a breed disposition for developing chronic ehrlichiosis; German Shepherd Dogs and Doberman Pinschers, for example, are at increased risk.

During the chronic phase, which appears one to four months after the tick bite, the disease attacks the dog's bone marrow and immune system, producing weight loss, fever, anemia, a hemorrhagic syndrome with spontaneous bleeding and nose bleeds, swelling of the limbs, and various neurological signs. These signs may suggest leukemia. Infections of *E. ewingii* usually show arthritis as well.

A serologic blood test (IFA) is sensitive for *E. canis*. However, the test may not be positive until two to three weeks after the tick bite. A new ELISA test has been developed that checks for Lyme disease, ehrlichiosis, anaplasmosis, and heartworm.

Treatment: Tetracycline and doxycycline are highly effective against rickettsiae, and should be given for at least one month. Improvement in the acute phase begins within one to two days. Supportive treatment involves intravenous fluids and blood transfusions. The outlook for recovery is excellent if treatment is started before the dog develops bone marrow suppression.

Prevention: Tick control is the mainstay of prevention (see *Ticks*, page 123). Ticks do not infect dogs until they have been attached for 5 to 20 hours. Therefore, examining pets who have been roaming in tick-infested areas, and promptly removing ticks, can prevent many infections.

Dogs living in areas where the disease is endemic can be protected by giving a low dose of oral tetracycline (1.3 mg per pound or .45 kg of body weight) or doxycycline (0.45 to 0.90 mg per pound or .45 kg of body weight) every 24 hours. However, this is rarely necessary.

Using Frontline or Advantix to control fleas also kill ticks for up to 30 days following a single application. Collars containing amitraz are also effective in controlling ticks.

ROCKY MOUNTAIN SPOTTED FEVER

Rocky Mountain spotted fever is a rickettsial disease caused by *Rickettsia rickettsii* and transmitted by several species of ticks. It is the most significant rickettsial disease in humans. Most cases occur in the southeastern United States, Midwest, Plains States, and Southwest, but it has been seen outside those regions. The Rocky Mountain area, where the disease was first discovered at the turn of the 20th century, now accounts for only a small percentage of cases.

Unlike canine ehrlichiosis, Rocky Mountain spotted fever coincides with the tick season (April through September). The two main reservoirs for Rocky Mountain spotted fever are rodents and dogs. Adult ticks transmit the disease to dogs when they attach and feed.

Signs of acute infection appear during the tick season and include listlessness, depression, high fever, loss of appetite, cough, conjunctivitis, difficult breathing, swelling of the legs, and joint and muscle pains. Ocular signs, such as uveitis, may be present. Rarely, a rash will be noticed around the area of a tick bite. These symptoms may suggest canine ehrlichiosis, Lyme disease, or distemper. Central nervous system signs include unstable gait, altered mental state, and seizures. Inflammation of the heart muscle (myocarditis) can cause cardiac arrhythmias, resulting in sudden death.

One to two weeks after the onset of illness, some dogs develop a hemorrhagic syndrome similar to that seen with canine ehrlichiosis. Various bleeding problems, such as nosebleeds, subcutaneous hemorrhaging, and blood in the urine and stools, may develop. This can cause shock, multiple organ failure, and death.

Rocky Mountain spotted fever should be suspected in a sick dog with a history of tick infestation during April through September. Serologic diagnosis is best achieved by noting a rise in micro-IFA antibody titer in paired serum tests (done at the time of illness and two to three weeks later).

Treatment: Tetracycline and its derivative, doxycycline, are the antibiotics of choice. Enrofloxacin is also effective. Antibiotics should be started as soon as Rocky Mountain spotted fever is suspected, even if the diagnosis is not confirmed. Mortality is high if treatment is delayed. Furthermore, dogs with Rocky Mountain spotted fever respond dramatically in one to two days, which confirms the presumptive diagnosis. Antibiotics are continued for two to three weeks. Supportive treatment is the same as that described for *Canine Ehrlichiosis* (page 87).

Prevention: Tick control is the mainstay of prevention (see *Ticks*, page 123). Using Frontline or Advantix to control fleas has the advantage of also killing ticks for up to 30 days following a single application. Collars containing amitraz are also effective in controlling ticks.

Canine Salmon Poisoning Disease

This is a severe rickettsial disease of dogs and wild canids that requires the presence of several intermediate hosts, including snails, flukes, fish, and mammals. Humans are not affected.

Dogs acquire the infection when they eat raw freshwater or ocean salmon and related species containing encysted flukes that harbor rickettsiae. The disease is limited to the Pacific Northwest. This is because the first intermediate host is a small snail found only in streams along the coasts of Washington, Oregon, and California.

A few days after a dog ingests contaminated fish, the larval fluke matures and attaches to the lining of the dog's intestines, where it inserts the rickettsial organism into the intestinal tissues. The incubation period is 5 to 21 days.

Illness begins with high fever, followed by hypothermia, loss of appetite, vomiting, diarrhea (usually bloody), and generalized lymph node enlargement. These signs are similar to those of canine distemper and parvovirus. However, a history of eating raw fish suggests a diagnosis of salmon poisoning. Diagnosis may include finding fluke ova in a fecal sample.

Treatment: Death usually occurs in 7 to 10 days in untreated dogs. However, the illness does respond well to intravenous tetracycline. Supportive treatment with IV fluids and blood transfusions for hemorrhagic diarrhea may be required. Praziquantel and mebendazole eliminate intestinal flukes.

Prevention: Do not allow dogs to eat raw fish. Thoroughly cooking fish (or freezing it for 24 hours) destroys encysted flukes and rickettsiae.

Antibodies and Immunity

An animal who is immune to a specific pathogen has natural substances in his system called antibodies that attack and destroy that pathogen before it can cause disease.

When a dog becomes ill with an infectious disease, his immune system makes antibodies against that particular pathogen. These antibodies protect the dog against reinfection. The dog has now acquired active immunity. Active immunity is self-perpetuating; the dog continues to make antibodies long after the disease has gone away. Any time the dog is exposed to that particular pathogen, his immune system will produce more antibodies. The duration of active immunity varies, depending on the pathogen and the dog. Following natural exposure, active immunity often persists for life. In general, immunity to viruses lasts longer than immunity to bacteria.

Active immunity also can be induced by vaccination. The dog is exposed to heat-killed pathogens, live or attenuated (antigens that have been treated to make them less infectious) pathogens rendered incapable of causing disease, or toxins and pathogen products that will also stimulate a response by the dog's immune system. As with natural exposure, vaccination stimulates the production of antibodies that are specific for the particular pathogen in the vaccine. However, unlike natural exposure, the duration of protection may be limited. Accordingly, to maintain high levels of protection, booster vaccines are recommended. How frequently a dog will need boosters depends on the antigen used, number of exposures to the pathogens, the dog's own immune response, and the type of vaccination used. Vaccination schedules need to be customized for each individual dog.

Vaccinations may not be successful in all dogs. Rundown, malnourished, debilitated dogs may not be capable of responding to a disease challenge by developing antibodies or building immunity. Such dogs should not be vaccinated at that time, but should be vaccinated when they're in better health. Immunosuppressive drugs, such as cortisone and chemotherapy agents, depress the immune system and also prevent the body from making antibodies.

Another type of immunity is called passive. Passive immunity is passed from one animal to another. The classic example is the antibodies newborn pups absorb from the *colostrum* of their mother. Puppies are best able to absorb antibodies from their mother's milk during the first 24 hours of life. The immunity persists only as long as the antibodies remain in the puppies' circulation. The duration of immunity depends on the concentration of antibodies in maternal milk when the pups were born. Dams vaccinated just before they were bred have the highest antibody levels and are capable of protecting puppies for up to 16 weeks. However, some veterinarians believe this additional booster is unnecessary.

Puppies younger than 3 weeks old may be incapable of developing antibodies in response to vaccination because of physical immaturity or interference by passive maternally acquired antibodies. Maternal antibodies can bind the antigen in the vaccine and keep it from stimulating the immune system. These passive antibodies disappear at between 6 and 16 weeks of age. Therefore, when vaccinating very young puppies, the vaccine must be given more frequently to ensure that the vaccine will stimulate immunity as soon as maternal antibody levels decline and can no longer interfere with the vaccine.

Another source of passive immunity can occur with a transfusion of blood products with antibodies into a dog with a serious infection or immune problem. This is not done frequently, but can be a life-saver for some dogs.

Vaccinations

There are several types of vaccines currently available for use in dogs: modified live virus (MLV), inactivated or killed virus, and the newest recombinant technologies—live vectored, subunit, and DNA vaccines. Modified live virus vaccines are vaccines that contain virus that is alive and will replicate when in a dog, but has been modified so that it shouldn't cause the actual disease. These vaccines tend to generate a quick and full immune response. Killed virus vaccines are vaccines with dead virus, which will not replicate in a dog, so they are incapable of causing disease. Instead, they rely on surface antigens, along with immune stimulants called adjuvants, to stimulate an immune response.

Modified live vaccines are more effective and produce longer-lasting immunity than do killed vaccines. Results for recombinant vaccines indicate that immunity can last as long as MLVs. With all types of vaccines, booster shots are necessary to maintain an adequate level of protection. The frequency of needed boosters shots is very variable, and depends on the disease involved, the individual vaccine, the dog's own immune system, and whether he has been exposed to the disease agent naturally.

Recombinant vaccines are among the newest products in the rapidly emerging biotechnology market. The technology relies on the ability to splice gene-sized fragments of DNA from one organism (a virus or bacteria) and to deliver these fragments to another organism (the dog), where they stimulate the production of antibodies.

For the live vectored version, genes from a canine antigen may be put into a noninfectious virus. Antibodies are stimulated; there is no replication of the antigen. Subunit vaccines stimulate immunity to a part of the antigen of an infectious organism. These are set up to provide the most immunity for the least amount of antigen used. With DNA vaccines—currently experimental for dogs—only a small amount of DNA from the infectious agent is used.

Thus, recombinant vaccines deliver specific antigen material on a cellular level without the risk of vaccination reactions associated with giving the entire disease-causing organism. This represents a truly new development. It is expected that recombinant vaccines will soon replace MLVs and whole killed vaccines for many, if not most, canine infectious diseases.

WHY VACCINES FAIL

Vaccines are highly effective in preventing certain infectious diseases in dogs, but failures do occur. Failures can be due to improper vaccine handling and storage, incorrect administration, inability of the dog to respond because of a depressed immune system, or the presence of neutralizing maternal antibodies.

Stretching out the vaccine by dividing a single dose between two dogs is another reason why a vaccine may not be effective. And if the dog is already infected, vaccinating him will not alter the course of the disease.

Because proper handling and administration of vaccines is so essential, vaccinations should be given by those familiar with the procedure. Anyone giving a vaccine also needs to be ready to handle any adverse reactions. When you go to the veterinarian for your dog's annual physical examination, he will also receive any vaccines that need updating.

THE REVACCINATION DEBATE

A subject of much debate in the field of immunology is the timing of booster injections. Based on a growing body of evidence, recommendations for booster vaccinations have been changing. In general, viral vaccines tend to stimulate longer immunity than bacterial vaccines.

It is now believed that the protective response to vaccines for distemper, parvovirus, and rabies probably persists for several years following a vaccination series, and that booster shots can be given every three years instead of every year. This interval for booster shots may be extended even longer with the newer vaccines and updated research data on the duration of immunity.

On the other side of the scale, evidence also suggests that vaccines for parainfluenza, bordetella bronchiseptica and leptospirosis fail to protect for the full 12 months. These vaccines might need to be given twice a year, rather than annually, especially to dogs who are at increased risk.

The best way to manage vaccinations is to work with your veterinarian to develop a customized vaccination schedule for your dog, based on your own dog's health and risk factors.

CORE AND NONCORE VACCINES

The veterinary community has divided vaccines into two main categories, with a smaller third category. Core vaccines are vaccines that every dog should have at some time in his life. Noncore vaccines are vaccines that only some dogs need, depending on factors such as geographic location and lifestyle. Other vaccines are also available but are generally not recommended for any dogs.

COMBINATION VACCINES

Many canine vaccines are combination or multivalent vaccines. This means a vaccine includes antigens for several diseases all in one injection. At one time, vaccines had as many as seven disease antigens included in one injection. It is now believed that less is better—both because some vaccines simply aren't necessary for all dogs and because you don't want to overwhelm a dog's immune system.

The most common combination vaccines currently are DHPP or DA2PP, both of which are acronyms for distemper, hepatitis, parvovirus, and parainfluenza. Most veterinarians use these minimal multivalent vaccines.

An L added at the end (DHPPL) means the shot also contains leptospirosis vaccine. However, if the dog does require a leptospirosis vaccine, it is now recommended that this be scheduled separately. Rabies vaccine boosters are often staggered as well.

For dogs who have had or are at risk for vaccine reactions, the core vaccines, such as distemper and parvovirus, may be given separately and only boostered as indicated by titers. (Titers measure the immunity present in a dog's system, but more research is needed to determine exactly what minimum titer levels indicate a dog is safe from disease.)

Available Vaccines

Young puppies are highly susceptible to certain infectious diseases and should be vaccinated against them as soon as they are old enough to build immunity. These diseases are distemper, infectious hepatitis, parvovirus, parainfluenza, and rabies. Leptospirosis, giardia, coronavirus, bordetella, bronchiseptica, and Lyme disease vaccinations are optional, depending on the occurrence of these diseases in your area and your dog's individual risk factors.

The American Animal Hospital Association (AAHA) has drawn up guidelines categorizing vaccines as core, noncore, or not recommended, and these categories will be indicated for all the vaccines described in this section. While these guidelines suggest that puppies as young as 6 weeks may be vaccinated, most veterinarians and breeders wait until 7 or 8 weeks of age. Also, vaccine recommendations state that many vaccines do not need boosters beyond 12 weeks of age, but veterinarians, particularly in endemic disease areas, may do a final puppy vaccine at about 16 weeks.

Canine Distemper (Core)

A recombinant distemper vaccine is now available and, ideally, dogs will receive either an MLV or a recombinant version of distemper vaccine.

The first distemper shot should be given shortly after weaning and before a puppy is placed in his new home and is exposed to other dogs. Some veterinarians recommend vaccinating puppies at 5 to 6 weeks of age, using a combination canine distemper-measles-parainfluenza vaccine. The rationale for combining distemper and measles vaccines is that a high percentage of 6-week-old puppies do not get a satisfactory response from the distemper vaccine alone because of maternal antibodies that neutralize the distemper antigen. The measles virus, which is quite similar to the distemper virus, can overcome maternal antibody interference and induce partial distemper protection. Alternatively, if maternal antibodies have actually disappeared in the 6-week-old puppy, the distemper portion of the vaccine will induce complete protection.

The distemper-measles vaccine should be used only once, for the first vaccination, and only in puppies. The newer recombinant distemper vaccine seems to overcome maternal antibodies and is now believed to be a better option than the distemper-measles combination.

Postvaccination encephalitis has occasionally occurred when an MLV distemper vaccine has been used in combination with a parvovirus vaccine in pups younger than 6 to 8 weeks of age. Therefore, parvovirus vaccine should not be given along with the first distemper vaccination in very young puppies. The recombinant distemper vaccine is unlikely to cause encephalitis, and is therefore recommended for young puppies.

Puppies younger than 8 to 9 weeks of age should be revaccinated every four weeks until they are 16 weeks of age. Current recommendations are to revaccinate at 1 year of age or in a year from the last vaccination, and then every three years. This time period may be extended with future research data on duration of immunity.

INFECTIOUS HEPATITIS (CORE)

The infectious hepatitis vaccine is a MLV vaccine containing CAV-2. This vaccine protects against canine hepatitis and two of the adenoviruses involved in the kennel cough complex (CAV-1 and CAV-2).

Hepatitis vaccine is incorporated into the DHPP shot, which is given at 8 to 12 weeks of age and again at 16 weeks of age with a possible booster in between for puppies who were initially vaccinated at 8 weeks of age or younger. It is suggested that a DHPP booster be given at 1 year of age or one year from the last vaccine. Revaccination is currently recommended every three years, although initial immunity may persist for life.

CANINE PARVOVIRUS (CORE)

Commercially available vaccines effectively cross-protect against all the current strains of parvo, including variant strains. The MLV vaccine is much more effective than a killed vaccine in that it produces a faster and stronger immune response.

Because the age at which individual pups can respond to parvovirus vaccination varies, AAHA 2006 guidelines are to give the vaccine at 6 to 8 weeks of age, then every three to four weeks until the dog is 12 to 14 weeks of age, but many veterinarians prefer to wait until a puppy is 7 or 8 weeks of age to start parvo vaccinations and conclude them at 16 weeks.

High titer–low passage vaccines (see page 91) are more effective than older vaccines, even in the presence of maternal antibodies, and have narrowed the window of susceptibility that occurs between declining levels of maternal antibodies and acquired immunity produced by the vaccine. This has resulted in fewer vaccine failures.

Even after a pup has received his first series of vaccinations, he should not be exposed to dogs who may be a source of infection until after he receives his final vaccination at 16 weeks of age. Boosters are recommended every three years to maintain immunity, following an initial booster at one year. This interval may be increased with further research on vaccine efficacy.

In unvaccinated dogs older than 16 weeks, give two doses of vaccine two weeks apart. Brood bitches should be vaccinated two to four weeks before breeding to ensure high levels of antibodies in their colostrum. Some veterinarians believe this booster is unnecessary.

Rabies (Core)

The first rabies vaccination should be given at 3 to 6 months of age, with the first booster shot given one year later (at 15 months of age). Thereafter, give boosters annually or every three years, according to state and local statutes. Rabies vaccination schedules are regulated by law.

Leptospirosis Bacterin (Noncore)

Leptospira bacterins may protect against two or four of the most common subspecies of bacteria that cause leptospirosis. The two-serovar bacterin may be incorporated into a DHPP shot given at 12 weeks of age and again at 14 to 16 weeks of age. Many veterinarians give the four-serovar bacterin as a separate injection as early as 12 weeks and then two to three weeks later.

Leptospira bacterin has been responsible for 70 percent of post-vaccination DHLPP anaphylactic shock reactions. Toy breeds and puppies younger than 12 weeks old seem to have the highest rate of reactions to this bacterin. In addition, the two-serovar vaccines do not protect against the two species that are currently responsible for the majority of cases. Accordingly, routine vaccination is now considered optional. It is still indicated in areas where the risk of the disease is greater than the risk of the vaccination. Leptospirosis is not contained in all the combination vaccines and can be given separately.

Both Fort Dodge and Pfizer have vaccines that now cover all four of the primary serovars of leptospirosis. These are subunit vaccines, so there is less chance of an allergic reaction to the vaccine. With leptospirosis cases on the rise, this vaccine may be recommended in more areas. Immunity following vaccination averages about four to six months. Therefore, if vaccination is important, it may be advisable to revaccinate every six months. Discuss this with your veterinarian.

Canine Parainfluenza (Noncore)

Parainfluenza is the principal virus implicated in the kennel cough complex. Vaccines will decrease the prevalence and severity of the infection, but will not prevent the disease. Parainfluenza is incorporated into the canine distemper-measles-parainfluenza and DHPP shots. The first dose is given at 8 to 12 weeks of age and the second at 16 weeks. AAHA 2006 guidelines are to give the vaccine at 6 to 8 weeks of age, then every three to four weeks until the dog is 12 to 14 weeks of age, but many veterinarians prefer to wait until a puppy is 7 or 8 weeks of age to start vaccinations. An intranasal vaccine that combines the bordetella vaccine is also available.

The injectable parainfluenza vaccine protects dogs but does not eliminate the virus from nasal secretions. That means dogs can still transmit the infection. The intranasal vaccine protects against both disease and infection, thus eliminating the possibility of transmitting the disease to other dogs.

Annual boosters are recommended by the manufacturer. However, evidence suggests that parainfluenza vaccines do not always protect for the full 12 months, and in many cases should be given twice a year, especially for dogs at increased risk. This recommendation is only for the parainfluenza vaccine—not for the other viruses that are often included in a combination vaccine. This is not a core vaccine, so it should only be given to dogs with lifestyles that increase their risk, such as show dogs and dogs who will be boarded.

BORDETELLA (NONCORE)

Bordetella bronchiseptica vaccines are of some help in controlling kennel cough and other respiratory infections caused by this bacteria. Show dogs, boarded dogs, and dogs living in kennels may benefit from this optional protection.

There are two vaccine types available to prevent bordetella. One is an intranasal vaccine and the other is injectable. The intranasal vaccine, which protects against parainfluenza as well as bordetella, gives the most immediate immunity—although either type of vaccine should ideally be given at least one week before possible exposures.

The injectable bacterin must be given twice. The first injection is given at 8 weeks of age and is repeated two to four weeks later. Puppies born in high-risk areas where bordetella is prevalent can be vaccinated with the intranasal vaccine at 3 weeks of age.

Annual boosters are recommended by the manufacturer. But because of the short duration of immunity, semi-annual boosters may be more appropriate.

LYME DISEASE (NONCORE)

Lyme disease (also called *Borrelia burgdorferi*) vaccine is recommended only for dogs in high-risk areas. This includes dogs visiting areas where Lyme disease is prevalent and areas with a high risk of tick exposure.

The killed bacterin version is now out of favor and the subunit vaccine, featuring the OpsA antigen, is recommended if the vaccine is needed. The immunity from this vaccine can be distinguished from a natural exposure. Tick control should be the first line of defense against Lyme disease.

Coronavirus (Not Recommended)

Vaccination against coronavirus does not prevent the disease, but may reduce the severity of the illness. This is a mild disease and is rarely fatal. Accordingly, many veterinarians do not routinely vaccinate against coronavirus.

However, the vaccine may be incorporated into the other vaccines your dog is receiving. This vaccine is not currently recommended, so ask your veterinarian about what is in any combination shots your dog may be receiving.

Giardia (Not Recommended)

There is now a vaccine available for giardiasis, but this is rarely recommended because the disease is usually mild and responds well to treatment.

Porphyromonas (Not Recommended)

Porphyromonas is the most common bacteria involved in periodontitis in dogs (see page 245). A new vaccine purports to protect against with three species of this bacteria: *denticanis*, *gulae*, and *salivosa*. The vaccine is very new, and widespread efficacy tests are now being conducted.

Vaccination Recommendations

The vaccination recommendations on pages 99–100 should be modified under the following circumstances:

- Give bitches a DHPP booster two to four weeks before breeding. (Be aware that some veterinarians believe this booster is unnecessary.)
- Some rabies boosters are required at one-year intervals, others at three years. Follow the instructions of the manufacturer and of your veterinarian. Local statutes often determine when the booster shots should be given.
- Parainfluenza and leptospirosis vaccinations may be necessary twice a year in endemic areas.
- Bordetella may be necessary for show dogs, kennel dogs, dogs who are boarded, and others at high risk for exposure to the kennel cough complex. Boosters may be indicated twice a year in endemic areas.

Vaccination Recommendations

This chart is based on the recommendations of the American Animal Hospital's 2006 Vaccine Guidelines. Be aware that an individual vaccine schedule should be customized for each dog and that booster recommendations are changing frequently, with longer intervals becoming more common.

	Puppy Vaccines	Boosters
CORE VACCINES *These vaccines are recommended for all dogs*		
Rabies Required by law	1 dose at 3 to 6 months of age	1 year later, then annually or every 3 years, as dictated by local law
Canine Distemper Important for every dog	First given at 6 to 8 weeks of age, then every 3 to 4 weeks until 12 to 14 weeks of age	At 1 year of age, then every 3 years, unless circumstances dictate otherwise
Canine Parvovirus Important for every dog	First given at 6 to 8 weeks of age, then every 3 to 4 weeks until 12 to 14 weeks of age	At 1 year of age, then every 3 years, unless circumstances dictate otherwise
Canine Adenovirus 2 Important for every dog	First given at 6 to 8 weeks of age, then every 3 to 4 weeks until 12 to 14 weeks of age	At 1 year of age, then every 3 years, unless circumstances dictate otherwise

continued

Vaccination Recommendations (*continued*)

	Puppy Vaccines	Boosters
NONCORE VACCINES *Depending on individual circumstances, these vaccines may or may not be important for your dog*		
Distemper/Measles For puppies under 12 weeks who did not get good passive immunity	1 dose at between 4 and 12 weeks of age	Never in younger puppies or older dogs
Parainfluenza	First given at 6 to 8 weeks of age, then every 3 to 4 weeks until 12 to 14 weeks of age	At 1 year of age, then every 3 years, unless circumstances dictate otherwise
Bordetella Bronchiseptica	1 dose at 6 to 8 weeks of age and a second dose at 10 to 12 weeks of age	Annually
Combined Intranasal Parainfluenza and Bordetella	1 dose at as early as 3 weeks of age, then a second dose 2 to 4 weeks later for best results	Annually
Borrelia Burgdorferi (Lyme Disease)	1 dose at 8 weeks of age and a second dose at 12 weeks of age	Annually
Leptospirosis Not recommended for Toy breeds unless the risk is very high	1 dose at 12 weeks of age and a second dose at 16 weeks of age	Annually

NOT RECOMMENDED
These vaccines are not recommended due to mild disease and/or inadequate efficacy

Canine Coronavirus

Giardia

THE SKIN AND COAT

Skin disease is a common problem in dogs. The condition of the skin can also tell you a great deal about your dog's general health. A dog's skin is thinner and more sensitive to injury than human skin. It is easily damaged by rough handling with the wrong type of grooming equipment, and once the surface of the skin is broken and disturbed by trauma or some other disorder, the condition tends to spread rather easily and become a major problem.

The outer layer of skin is the epidermis, a scaly layer that varies in thickness over different parts of the body. For example, it is thick and tough over the nose and foot pads, and thin and most susceptible to injury in the creases of the groin and armpits.

The layer beneath the epidermis is the dermis. The dermis gives rise to the skin appendages: hair follicles, sebaceous glands, nails, and sweat glands. Sweat glands are found only in the foot pads of dogs.

Hair follicles produce three types of hair. Primary hair is exemplified by the long guard hair that makes up the top coat. Generally, each guard hair grows from its own follicle, but in some breeds more than one hair may grow from a single follicle. Muscles connected to the root of each guard hair enable the hair to stand erect, as happens when a dog raises her hackles.

Within each guard hair follicle is a cluster of accessory hair that composes the undercoat. The function of the undercoat is to provide warmth and protection. Whiskers and eyelashes make up a third type of hair, which is modified to serve the sense of touch.

Sebaceous glands are located in the dermis, and are linked to the hair follicles. Sebaceous glands secrete an oily substance called sebum, which collects in the hair follicles and coats each strand of hair. This adds shine and, more important, enables the hair to shed water. Water-going breeds depend upon sebum to waterproof their coats. Sebum is also responsible for the characteristic doggy odor apparent in some dogs with oily coats.

The color of a dog's skin can vary from pink to light brown, or it may be dark with patches of black. The dark pigment in the skin is called melanin. It is produced by cells in the dermis called melanocytes.

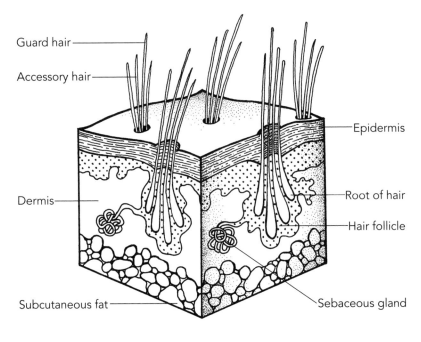

Cross-Section of the Skin

The Dog's Coat

The quality of a dog's coat is controlled by a number of factors, including hormone concentrations, nutrition, general health, parasite infestations, genetics, and the frequency of grooming and bathing. Dogs who live outdoors in cold weather grow a heavy coat for insulation and protection.

Hormonal disorders such as hypothyroidism, hyperestrogenism, and Cushing's syndrome slow or suppress hair growth, making the coat appear thin or sparse. A protein deficiency caused by parasites, poor diet, or ill health may cause the coat to be dull, dry, brittle, and thin.

If your dog's coat is below par, have her checked by your veterinarian. Poor coat quality is often an indication of a *systemic* disease.

HAIR GROWTH AND SHEDDING

Dog hair grows in cycles. Each follicle has a period of rapid growth (the anagen phase), followed by slower growth and then a resting phase (the catagen phase). During the resting phase, mature hair remains in the follicles and eventually detaches at the base. When the dog sheds her coat (the telogen phase), a young hair pushes out the old hair and the cycle begins anew. The average dog takes about four months to grow a coat, but there are individual and breed variations. The Afghan Hound, for example, grows her coat in about 18 months.

There are "hairless" dog breeds, such as the Chinese Crested (which has hair on the head, tail, and legs) and the Xoloitzcuintal (which is normally hairless except for a single tuft on the head and some long hairs on the tail). Both of these breeds have coated versions as well. The hairless condition in these dogs is due to a genetic mutation, not a health problem.

Most dogs shed or "blow" their coat at least once a year. Dams often blow their coat six to eight weeks after delivering puppies. Major shedding may follow a bitch's heat cycle as well, due to the hormonal swings.

Many people assume that temperature changes govern when a dog sheds her coat. In fact, the seasonal length of daylight exerts the major influence. Longer periods of daylight in spring activate a shedding process that lasts four to six weeks. In fall, as the daylight hours grow shorter, many dogs may again shed their coat. Sensitivity to ambient light is most pronounced in dogs who live outdoors. Dogs who live primarily indoors are exposed to artificial light and a rather fixed photoperiod. These dogs may shed and grow new coats all year long.

Some breeds, such as Poodles, Bedlington Terriers, and Kerry Blue Terriers, have what is called a nonshedding curly coat. These breeds do not shed loose hair into your house. Instead, their loose hair tends to collect into mats that remain on the body. Dogs with corded coats, such as the Puli and Komondor, have similar coats, but their hair works itself into cords.

Some dogs have a double coat comprised of long, coarse outer guard hairs and a soft, fine, wooly undercoat. When a dog with a double coat begins to shed, the appearance of the coat can be quite alarming. The undercoat is shed in a mosaic or patchy fashion, giving the dog a moth-eaten appearance that may suggest a skin disease.

When shedding begins, remove as much of the irritating dead hair as possible by daily brushing. In breeds with a thick double coat, a bath will loosen the dead hair and make it easier to remove. Always brush out a dog before bathing to help prevent the formation of mats.

Avoiding Coat and Skin Problems
GROOMING

Grooming at regular intervals will keep your dog's coat and skin in good condition and prevent many problems. Even hairless breeds require some grooming for healthy skin. Establish a grooming schedule during puppyhood and stick to it throughout the dog's life. Initially, keep the sessions brief and make grooming a pleasurable experience. If the puppy grows to dislike the basic grooming routine, a simple procedure will become most difficult.

How often to groom depends on the dog's coat type, breed, and the purpose for which she is being groomed. Show dogs, for example, usually require daily grooming. Longhaired dogs should be brushed frequently to prevent the coat from tangling and matting. Certain breeds require braiding or tying up, plucking, and clipping. For these dogs it is a good idea to consult a breeder or professional pet groomer.

These are some useful grooming tools. The ones you will use most will depend upon your dog's breed and the nature of her coat.

- **Grooming table.** It should be solid with a nonslippery surface. Adjust the table to a height at which you can work without bending. Use for all grooming sessions that last more than a few minutes.
- **Bristle brush.** This is a brush for all breeds. It removes loose hair and surface dirt and dresses the top coat. A brush with natural bristles produces less static electricity.
- **Pin brush.** This brush has long pins protruding from a rubber cushion. It's especially effective for longhaired breeds.
- **Slicker brush.** This is a rectangular board with thin, bent wire teeth and a handle. A slicker brush is used to remove loose hair. Brush in short, deep strokes. This brush may be too harsh to use on shorthaired dogs.
- **Hound glove (palm brush).** Intended for shorthaired breeds, this is a glove or pouch that you slip over your hand and then use to wipe down. It may have small rubber nubs or a sisal pad that does the actual grooming. The glove removes dead hair and gives a polish to the coat.
- **Comb.** A standard wide-tooth metal comb with smooth, round teeth is used for areas where the hair is short and to hold up hair for scissors. A fine-tooth comb is used to unsnarl fine hair. Many utility combs, such as the Greyhound comb, combine both features: the teeth are one-quarter inch (6mm) apart on one side of the comb and one-eighth inch apart (3mm) on the other. A flea comb is a very fine-tooth comb with 30 to 36 teeth per inch.
- **Scissors.** These are used to trim the coat, trim long hair on the feet in most breeds, and cut out mats. Dogs with long hair may need the hair trimmed around the rectum. The tips should be blunt or rounded. Thinning shears are scissors with spaces between the teeth that thin out hair but don't cut all of it.
- **Rake.** Long- and short-toothed rakes are used to remove loose, dead hair during shedding. They will damage healthy hair if used too vigorously.
- **Mat splitter.** This single- or multi-bladed tool is used to break up mats into smaller and smaller strands.

Clockwise from the top center: metal comb, electric clipper (blades are in the center), Dremel tool, rake, flea comb, scissors, thinning shears, nail clipper, and slicker brush.

- **Electric clipper.** This is used for trimming or to shave down a matted coat. Different size blades are used on different types of coats. Care must be taken not to cut the dog's skin.
- **Nail clipper.** Nail clippers come with either two cutting edges or a single blade that clips down like a guillotine.
- **Dremel tool or nail grinder.** A Dremel can be used to carefully grind nails down to an acceptable length.
- **Nail file.** Handy after cutting nails to round the edges.
- **Towel.** Toweling shorthaired breeds will remove loose dead hair. A wipe with a damp towel may be all the grooming your hairless breed needs. Rubbing with a towel tends to tangle long hair, though.

It is important that the bristles on the brush and the teeth on the comb be the right length for the dog's coat. For example, if the coat is thick and the bristles and teeth are too short, the top coat may look smooth for a time but the undercoat will mat. Eventually the top coat becomes involved and the dog may have to be shaved. On the other hand, if the dog has a thin undercoat, grooming with tools that have long bristles and teeth can scratch and injure the skin.

BRUSHING AND COMBING TECHNIQUES

A dog's coat is easily damaged by rough handling and improper grooming techniques. Each strand of hair has tiny scales that lie flat against the hair shaft. As the hair is pulled and stretched (which is not desirable), the scales project out like barbs. Adjacent hairs become snarled and eventually break during the unsnarling process.

Dry hair attracts static electricity, which causes individual hairs to stick together. It is a good practice to use an antistatic coat conditioner before brushing. A number of popular products are available as pumps, aerosols, and rub-on creams. You can also simply spray the coat lightly with water.

The coat should be brushed with tools that pass smoothly through the hair. In general, a pin brush can be used safely without stretching the hair. To avoid stretching, do not pull forcefully on a rake, slicker brush, or comb—except when removing dead hair during the shedding stage. If you find that you are pulling hard, you are either trying to groom too deep into the coat with each stroke or you are using a grooming tool with teeth or bristles that are too stiff or too close together.

With longhaired dogs, insert the bristle or pin brush all the way into the coat and twist it slightly. Using short strokes, brush *against* the lay of the hair. Avoid using long strokes, as this can break the hair. You can also line brush—working up the side of your dog, brushing short sections at a time. You push the hair up, then brush small sections down at a time. This way, the hair underneath is brushed out as well as the top coat. It always makes sense to talk to your dog's breeder about the best grooming techniques for the breed.

For shorthaired breeds, brush *with* the lay of the hair, starting at the head and working back toward the tail. In all breeds, pay particular attention to the hindquarters and backs of the thighs, where dead hair is likely to mat. Carefully check behind the ears, as the soft hair there may also mat.

If the dog is blowing her undercoat, remove loose hair with a rake. Start on the underside of the dog and work layer by layer up to the topside.

Hairless dogs can be wiped with a damp towel, then carefully dried. They may need a bath to remove excess skin oils and to prevent the buildup of sunscreen (necessary to prevent sunburn).

REMOVING MATS

Mats are solid clumps of fur that can form anywhere on the body but are usually found behind the ears, in the folds of the armpits, around the anus, on the backs of the thighs, in the groin area, and between the toes. Mats are evidence of neglected grooming or grooming with the wrong tools. Dogs with softer hair are more prone to develop mats.

To remove mats, first saturate the clumps of hair with coat conditioner for several minutes. This rehydrates the hair and closes the barbs. Then separate as much of the mat as you can with your fingers.

Some mats can be removed with the tip of a comb. However, most require the use of scissors, an electric clipper, or a mat splitter. Cutting into mats with scissors must be done with extreme care, because a dog's skin is not attached to the underlying muscle and tents up as the mat is pulled. Do not slide the scissors beneath the mat and attempt to remove it flush with the skin. You will almost certainly remove a piece of skin. When possible, slide a comb beneath the mat as a barrier between the scissors and the skin. Then hold the scissors *perpendicular* to the comb and carefully snip into the fur ball in narrow strips. Similar care must be taken with electric clippers. Tease the mat out gently. After the mat has been removed, comb out residual snarls.

This technique also works for removing burdocks and tangled plant material. Nonstick cooking sprays may help to ease the plant material out of the hair without cutting any coat.

To remove gum, put an ice cube on the gum first, then try to slide it off. If that doesn't work, you will need to carefully cut it out.

Beyond the Brush

A good canine care and maintenance program should include a schedule for examining the ears, cleaning the teeth, clipping the nails, and, if necessary, emptying the anal sacs.

Be sure to groom beneath the ear flaps and inspect the openings of the ear canals at least once a month, and whenever your dog has been running in tall grass, weeds, and brush. Plant matter can enter the ear canals by first clinging to the hair around the openings.

Inspect the ear canals for dirt, debris, excess wax, and a disagreeable odor. If any of these are present, clean as described in *Cleaning the Ears*, page 207. If the ear canals are clean, leave them alone, as excessive cleaning can interfere with local immune defense mechanisms. Any discharge should be brought to the attention of your veterinarian.

Routinely inspecting and cleaning the teeth will prevent the build-up of tartar and calculus. For more information, see *Taking Care of Your Dog's Teeth*, page 248.

Inspecting the anal sacs may disclose a buildup of secretions. To empty the anal sacs, see *Anal Sacs*, page 290.

TRIMMING THE NAILS

Most dogs wear down their nails through activity. If they are not worn down naturally, however, they can become extremely long and damage carpets and

This neglected dewclaw has grown around and into the pad.

upholstery. Excessively long nails can splay the toes and interfere with traction by preventing the foot pads from making contact with the ground. Long nails should be trimmed.

Nails are also trimmed to prepare a dog for show. If trimming is done twice a month, the quick (the bundle of nerves and blood vessels inside the nail) will recede toward the base of the nail and the nail will remain permanently shorter.

Dogs with dewclaws must have these nails looked at frequently. Dewclaws are remnants of fifth toes and are found high on the inside of each foot. In many breeds the dewclaws are removed shortly after birth. In other breeds, such as Briards and Great Pyrenees, the presence of dewclaws is required by the breed standard. These nails do not contact the ground and thus can grow around in a circle and pierce the skin. Dewclaws should be trimmed regularly. This is particularly true for dogs with dewclaws on the rear legs. If you have a puppy with dewclaws, it is important to get her used to having them trimmed, even though trimming may not yet be necessary.

Some nail clippers for dogs have two cutting edges, while others of the guillotine type have one. Either type is satisfactory. Nail clippers designed for humans do not work well because a dog's nails are not flat the way a person's are.

Begin by lifting the dog's paw and extending the nail. Identify the quick (the pink part running down the center), which contains the nerves and blood vessels. If the nails are white, it's easy to see the quick. Be sure to trim

The correct angle for trimming the nail.

Quick

Nail

Cutting line

Trim the nails parallel to the toe pads.

the nail in front of (but close to) the quick. When using a guillotine cutter, the blade should slice upward from the underside of the nail. If the nails are dark and the quick is invisible, a good rule is to cut the nails parallel to the toe pads, so that the nails just clear the floor.

If you accidentally cut into the quick, the dog will feel a brief moment of pain and the nail will begin to bleed. Hold pressure over the end of the nail with a cotton ball. The blood will clot in a few minutes. If bleeding persists, pack with styptic powder or use a styptic pencil. In a pinch, cornstarch will also do.

To use a Dremel tool, you need to put on a sanding drum and carefully pull any hair away from the nail you are working on. Then carefully hold the tool against the nail with a slight pressure, removing just a small amount if you cannot see the quick. Do not push the sanding drum against the foot, just hold it lightly against the surface of the nail. You need to be careful that the tool is not getting warm and heating your dog's toe.

Do not trim back into the quick. Rather, follow the guideline about trimming nails parallel to the toe pads.

Bathing

There are no firm guidelines for how often to bathe a dog. The quality and texture of the dog's hair (whether it's long, silky, curly, smooth, or wiry) will determine how much dirt it collects and how frequently the dog should be bathed. Your dog's lifestyle and activities will also influence how often she gets dirty and needs a bath. If you own a dog with special coat requirements, you may wish to consult a breeder or a professional groomer for specific recommendations.

The usual reasons for bathing a dog are to remove accumulated dirt and debris, to facilitate the removal of dead hair at shedding time, to eliminate doggy odor in dogs with oily coats, and to improve the appearance of the coat. Routine bathing is not necessary for the health of the coat or the dog. In fact, frequent bathing can rob the coat of its natural sheen and make it harsh and dry. For most dogs, regular brushing will keep the coat and skin in good condition and eliminate the need for frequent baths.

Before bathing a dog, brush out all snarls and tangles and remove mats. If this step is omitted, the wet, matted hair will set and be most difficult to manage.

It is important to select a shampoo labeled "for dogs." The pH of canine skin is neutral (7 to 7.4). Most shampoos for humans are on the acid side and are therefore unsuitable for dogs. There are a number of good commercial dog shampoos on the market for white dogs and dogs with other coat colors. Do not use human hair dyes or coloring agents on dogs.

Household disinfectants must never be used on dogs. These chemicals are absorbed through the skin and can cause death.

Except on warm, sunny days, baths should be given indoors using a bathtub or basin. Place a rubber mat on the bottom of the tub or basin to keep the dog from slipping and panicking. Plug her ears with cotton to keep water out—wet ear canals are predisposed to infection.

Add some lukewarm water to the tub, then place the dog in the tub. Begin by washing her face with a damp cloth. Lift up the ear flaps and wipe the undersurface to remove dirt, wax, and dead skin. Using a bath sprayer, wet the dog thoroughly with warm water. If necessary, bury the nozzle into her hair to get to the skin.

Then work the shampoo in by hand, one section at a time. Be sure to lather all of the dog—not only her back and sides, but also her neck, chest, belly, legs, feet, and tail. If the coat is badly soiled, rinse lightly and then repeat the sudsing process.

Remove the shampoo by rinsing the coat with the bath sprayer. Don't forget between the toes. It is essential to rinse and rinse until all the soap is out of the coat. Residual soap makes hair dull and tacky. It may also cause contact dermatitis (see page 141) if left on the skin.

Commercial coat conditioners are often used to bring out the beauty of the coat for show purposes. Do not use vinegar, lemon, or bleaches; they are either too acid or too alkaline and will damage the coat. Some exhibitors add Alpha-Keri bath oil to the final rinse to give luster to the coat. The concentration is 1 teaspoonful (5 ml) per quart (1 l) of water.

After the dog has been thoroughly rinsed, squeeze out as much water as you can by hand. Allow the dog to shake, and then blot her dry with towels. You can encourage your dog to shake by blowing gently at her ear.

You can complete the drying process with a good air blower. Commercial dog-drying units are very effective when used as directed. Do not use your own hair dryer on high heat. This damages the coat and may burn the dog's skin. Use handheld dryers only on low heat and slant them to keep the column of air from blowing directly on the dog's skin. Some dogs may be frightened by the noise and blowing air. If this is the case, do not force the dog to submit, as this can lead to trauma and problems later on.

After the bath, keep the dog indoors until her coat is completely dry. This can take several hours.

DRY SHAMPOOS

Maintaining a clean coat between baths is highly desirable, especially for dogs with oily coats that are prone to collecting dirt. A number of household products have been used successfully as dry shampoos. Calcium carbonate, unscented talcum or baby powder, and cornstarch are all effective. They can be used frequently without damaging the coat or skin.

Work the substance into the coat and leave it in for 20 minutes to absorb oils. Then remove the powder with a soft bristle brush. If you're showing your dog, remember that all traces of powder must be removed from the coat before entering the conformation ring for judging.

Commercial waterless shampoos (they require no rinsing) are sprays for quick cleaning problem spots. When used as an all-over spray, they are an excellent bath substitute. Apply and towel off.

SPECIAL BATH PROBLEMS

See *Removing Mats*, page 106, for advice on removing burdocks and chewing gum.

De-Skunking

The old remedy for removing skunk oil involved soaking the affected parts in tomato juice and then giving the dog a bath. What you usually ended up with was a pink dog who stilled smelled faintly of skunk. A new recipe appeared in *Chemical & Engineering* magazine and has been widely quoted on the Internet. It is far more effective and does not require repeated use. It can be used on cats as well as dogs. The recipe is as follows:

1 quart (1 l) 3 percent hydrogen peroxide (from the drug store)

¼ cup (55 g) baking soda (sodium bicarbonate)

1 teaspoon (5 ml) liquid dish soap

Bathe the pet and work the solution into the coat. Follow with a tap water rinse. In longhaired dogs, most of the challenge is getting the solution down to the skin.

Discard any unused formula because the release of oxygen caused by the chemical reaction could make the container explode.

Tar and Paint

When feasible, trim away any hair that contains tar, oil, or paint. To remove residual substances, saturate the effected parts with vegetable oil. Leave for 24 hours, then wash the coat with soap and water or give the dog a complete bath.

Do not use petroleum solvents such as gasoline, kerosene, or turpentine to remove any substance from a dog's coat. These products are extremely harmful to the skin and are highly toxic if absorbed.

Sorting Out Skin Diseases

The tables on pages 113 to 117 serve as an introduction to skin diseases and suggest where to look to find the cause of a problem.

The itchy skin diseases in the first table are characterized by constant scratching, biting at the skin, and rubbing up against objects to relieve the itch.

The next two tables list diseases characterized by hair loss with few if any other signs. Hair loss can mean impaired growth of new hair. It may involve the entire coat, or you may see patches of hair loss on certain parts of the body. In general, hair loss caused by hormonal diseases is symmetric (the same on both sides of the body), while that caused by parasites and other causes is asymmetric.

The fourth table lists diseases in which the predominant sign is skin infection or *pyoderma*. Pyoderma is characterized by *pus*, infected sores, scabs, *ulcers of the skin*, *papules*, *pustules*, *furuncles*, *boils*, and skin *abscesses*. The skin infection is often secondary to some other skin disease, particularly an itchy skin disease that causes the dog to attack her own skin.

The table after that lists *autoimmune* and *immune-mediated* skin diseases, characterized by *blebs*. Blebs, also called *vesicles*, are blisters that contain clear fluid. Large ones are called *bullae*. All tend to progress through rubbing, biting, and scratching, eventually producing skin erosions, ulcers, and crusts. Look for these changes to appear first on the face, nose, muzzle, and ears.

During the course of grooming, playing with, or handling your dog, you may discover a lump or bump on or beneath the skin. To learn what it may be, see the last table on lumps or bumps on or beneath the skin. Chapter 18, "Tumors and Cancers," contains more information.

Itchy Skin Diseases

Allergic contact dermatitis: Same as contact dermatitis, but rash may spread beyond the area of contact. Requires repeated or continuous exposure to allergen (such as wearing a flea collar).

Canine atopy: Severe itching that occurs in young dogs and begins in late summer and fall. Caused by seasonal pollens. Occurs in mixed breeds as well as purebreds. Common. Tends to get worse each year. May start with face rubbing and foot chewing.

Chiggers: Itching and severe skin irritation between the toes and around the ears and mouth. Look for barely visible red, yellow, or orange chiggers.

Contact dermatitis: Red, itchy bumps and inflamed skin at the site of contact with a chemical, detergent, paint. or other irritant. Primarily affects feet and hairless parts of the body. Can also be caused by rubber or plastic food dishes, with hair loss on the nose.

Damp hay itch (pelodera): Red pimplelike bumps on skin. Severe itching. Occurs in dogs bedded on damp hay and similar grass. Caused by a parasite.

Flea allergy dermatitis: Red, itchy pimplelike bumps over the base of the tail, back of rear legs, and inner thighs. Scratching continues after fleas have been killed.

Fleas: Itching and scratching along the back, and around the tail and hindquarters. Look for fleas, or black and white gritty specks in hair (flea feces and eggs).

Fly-bite dermatitis: Painful bites at tips of erect ears and bent surfaces of floppy ears. Bites become scabbed and crusty black, and bleed easily.

Food allergy dermatitis: Nonseasonal itching with reddened skin, papules, pustules, and wheals. Found over the ears, rump, back of the legs, and undersurface of the body. Sometimes confined just to the ears with moist, weeping redness.

Grubs/Cuterebra: Inch-long fly larvae that form cystlike lumps beneath the skin with a hole in the center for the insect to breathe. Often found beneath the chin, by the ears, or along the abdomen.

Lice: Two-millimeter-long insects, or white grains of "sand" (nits) attached to the hair. Not common. Found in dogs with matted coats. May have bare spots where hair has been rubbed off.

Lick granuloma (acral pruritic dermatitis): Red, shiny skin ulcer caused by continuous licking at wrist or ankle. Mainly in large, short-coated breeds.

Maggots: Soft-bodied, legless fly larvae found in damp matted fur or wounds that aren't kept clean.

Scabies (sarcoptic mange): Intense itching. Small red spots that look like insect bites on the skin of the ears, elbows, and hocks. Typical crusty ear tips.

Ticks: Large or very small insects attached to the skin. May swell up to the size of a pea. Found beneath the ear flaps and where hair is thin. May or may not induce itching.

Walking dandruff (cheyletiella mange): Occurs in puppies 2 to 12 weeks of age. Large amounts of dry, scaly, flaky skin over the neck and back. Itching is variable.

Hormone-Related Diseases with Hair Loss

Cortisone excess: Symmetric hair loss over trunk and body. Abdomen is pot-bellied and pendulous. Seen with Cushing's syndrome. In some cases, the dog is taking steroids.

Growth hormone-responsive alopecia: Bilaterally symmetric hair loss, mainly in male dogs. Begins around puberty. More prevalent in certain breeds, including Chow Chows, Keeshonds, Pomeranians, Miniature Poodles, Airedales, and Boxers.

Hyperestrogenism (estrogen excess): Occurs in females and males. Bilateral symmetric hair loss in perineum and around genitals. Enlarged vulva and clitoris; in males, pendulous prepuce.

Hypoestrogenism (estrogen deficiency): Occurs in older spayed females. Scanty hair growth and thinning coat, initially around vulva and later over entire body. Skin is smooth and soft, like a baby's.

Hypothyroidism: Most common cause of bilaterally symmetric hair loss without itching. Coat is thin, scanty, and falls out easily. Involves the neck beneath the chin to the brisket, sides of body, backs of thighs, and top of tail.

Other Diseases with Hair Loss

Acanthosis nigrans: Mainly in Dachshunds. Hair loss begins in armpit folds and on ears. Black, thick, greasy, rancid-smelling skin.

Color mutant alopecia (blue Doberman syndrome): Loss of hair over the body, giving a moth-eaten look. Papules and pustules may appear in areas of hair loss. Also affects other breeds.

Demodectic mange: Localized—Occurs in puppies. Hair loss around eyelids, lips, and corners of mouth, occasionally on the legs or trunk, giving a moth-eaten look. Fewer than five patches, up to 1 inch (25 mm) in diameter. Generalized—Numerous patches that enlarge and coalesce. Severe skin problem complicated by pyoderma. Primarily affects young adults. Generalized form is associated with immune deficiencies.

Nasal solar dermatitis (Collie nose): Loss of hair at junction of nose and muzzle. Can lead to severe ulceration. Affects dogs with lightly pigmented noses. May be part of an autoimmune problem.

Pressure sore (Callus): Gray, hairless, thickened pad of wrinkled skin, usually over elbows but may involve other pressure points. Caused by lying on hard surfaces. Mostly seen in large and giant breeds.

Ringworm: A fungal infection. Scaly, crusty circular patches ½ to 2 inches (12 to 50 mm) across. Patches show central hair loss with a red ring at the periphery. Some cases show widespread involvement.

Sebaceous adenitis: Seen mainly in Standard Poodles, but does occur in other breeds, including Akitas. Symmetrical loss of hair over face, head, neck, and back. Dandrufflike scales and hair follicle infection can develop.

Seborrhea: Dry type—Similar to heavy dandruff. Greasy type—Yellow-brown greasy scales that adhere to hair shafts; rancid odor. May occur secondary to other skin problems.

Vitiligo: Some hair loss, but mostly pigment loss that causes hair to change color. Mostly seen on the face and head. Seen most often in Rottweilers and Belgian Tervuren.

Zinc-responsive dermatosis: Crusty, scaly skin with hair loss over the face, nose, elbows, and hocks. Cracked feet. Caused by zinc deficiency. Arctic or Northern breeds are most susceptible.

Skin Diseases with Pus Drainage

Actinomycosis and nocardiosis: Uncommon skin infections with abscesses and draining sinus tracts that discharge pus and respond slowly to treatment.

Acute moist dermatitis (hot spots): Rapidly advancing patches of inflamed skin from which the hair falls out. The skin is covered with a wet exudate of pus. Progresses through self-chewing and results in pyoderma. Often occurs under ear flaps of dogs with drop ears, such as Newfoundlands and Golden Retrievers. May be associated with an underlying skin disease, but can also occur in hot, humid weather if dogs swim or are bathed and don't dry thoroughly.

Cellulitis or abscess: Painful, warm, reddened skin or pockets of pus beneath the skin. Look for a cause, such as a foreign body, bite wound, or self-trauma from irritative skin disease.

Folliculitis (hair pore infection): Hair shaft protrudes through the center of a pustule. Superficial—Similar to impetigo, but extends to involve armpit folds and chest. Deep—Pustules become larger and firmer. Pus, crusts, and draining tracts in the skin.

Impetigo: Pustules and thin brown crust on hairless skin of abdomen and groin. Occurs in young puppies. May also be called puppy acne.

Interdigital cysts: A swelling between the toes that may open and drain pus.

Mycetoma: Painful swelling at the site of a puncture wound, usually on the legs or feet. Pus drains through sinus tracts deep in the mass. Usually caused by a fungus, but can be bacterial.

Puppy acne: Purplish red bumps on the chin and lower lip. Not painful. Also called impetigo.

Puppy strangles (juvenile pyoderma): Painful swelling of the face (lips, eyelids, ears), followed by rapid appearance of pustules and draining sores. Swollen lymph nodes around the head and neck. Occurs in puppies under 4 months of age.

Skin fold pyoderma (skin wrinkle infection): Red, inflamed skin with a foul odor in a lip fold, nose fold, vulvar fold, or tail fold.

Autoimmune and Immune-Mediated Skin Diseases

Bullous pemphigoid: Similar to pemphigus vulgaris, but usually begins at the junction of the skin and the mucous membranes. The mouth is commonly involved.

Discoid lupus erythematosus: Affects the flat surface of the nose. Ulceration and depigmentation are characteristic.

Erythema multiforme: Acute eruption of the skin and mucous membranes. Often caused by drugs. Characteristic targetlike eruptions with red rims and blanching at the center.

Pemphigus erythematosus: Similar to pemphigus foliaceus, but restricted to the face, head, and foot pads.

Pemphigus foliaceus: Red skin patches (macules) that progress rapidly to pustules and then to dry yellow crusts. Usually limited to the face (nose, muzzle, around the eyes and ears). Crusts adhere to underlying skin and hair. Often becomes generalized. Depigmentation seen in late stages. The feet can become thickened and cracked. Occasionally only the foot pads are involved.

Pemphigus vegetans: Flat-topped pustules involving skin folds. Heals with wartlike growths.

Pemphigus vulgaris: Vesicles and bullae that ulcerate and form thick crusts. Usually found around the lips and in the mouth, but may be generalized. Ulceration of foot pads and shedding of nails are common.

Nodular panniculitis: Multiple lumps (like marbles beneath the skin) over the back and along the sides. Lumps open and drain, then heal by scarring.

Systemic lupus erythematosus: Skin involvement similar to pemphigus foliaceus. First sign may be wandering lameness. Ulceration of foot pads is common.

Toxic epidermal necrolysis: Severe, painful skin disease. Blebs and ulcers involve the skin, mucous membranes, and foot pads. Large sections of skin are shed as in a burn injury.

Lumps and Bumps on or Beneath the Skin

Abscess: A painful collection of pus at the site of a bite or puncture wound.

Basal cell tumor: Solitary nodule, usually on a narrow base or stalk. Round, normally hairless, and may be ulcerated. Found on the head, neck, and shoulders of older dogs.

Ceruminous gland adenoma: A pinkish-white dome-shaped growth in the ear canal less than 1 centimeter in size. May become ulcerated and infected.

Epidermal inclusion cyst: A firm lump beneath the skin. May discharge cheesy material and become infected.

Hematoma: A collection of clotted blood beneath the skin; often involves the ear flaps.

Histiocytoma: Rapidly growing dome-shaped (buttonlike) growth found anywhere on the body, usually in young adults.

Lipoma: Smooth round or oblong growth beneath the skin; feels somewhat soft.

Mast cell tumor: Solitary or multiple growths usually found on the trunk, perineum, and legs. More prevalent in certain breeds, including Boxers, Golden Retrievers, Bulldogs, and Boston Terriers.

Melanoma: A brown or black pigmented nodule found in areas of dark skin. Growths in mouth and nailbeds usually are malignant.

Perianal gland tumor: A solitary or multinodular growth in the perineum around the anus. Occurs most often in older intact males.

Sebaceous adenoma: Also called sebaceous cyst. Smooth, pink, wartlike growth less than 1 inch (2.5 cm) in diameter. Most common on the eyelids and limbs. Occurs in older individuals (average age 10). Very common in Poodles and Cocker Spaniels.

Skin papillomas: These grow out from the skin and may look like a wart. Not painful or dangerous

Soft-tissue sarcomas: Ill-defined or well-demarcated masses of varying size and location. Often slow growing.

Squamous cell carcinoma: A nonhealing gray or reddish-looking ulcer found on the belly, scrotum, feet, legs, lips, or nose. May resemble a cauliflowerlike growth.

Transmissible venereal tumors: Ulcerated, often multiple cauliflower-like growths on the genitalia of both sexes.

Fleas

The ordinary cat flea (*Ctenocephalides felis*) is the leading cause of itching and scratching in dogs and cats. Fleas survive by jumping onto a host animal, cutting open their skin, and feeding on the blood. In many dogs, the bites cause only a mild itch, but a heavy infestation in a puppy or small dog can cause severe anemia and even death.

Some dogs develop a marked hypersensitivity to the saliva of fleas and experience intense itching which results in skin abrasions, hair loss, and secondary *pyoderma* (see *Flea Allergy Dermatitis*, page 137). Fleas are also an intermediate host for tapeworms.

Flea infestation can be diagnosed by finding fleas on the dog or by seeing black-and-white, salt-and-pepper-like grains in the coat. These particles are flea feces (the "pepper") and flea eggs (the "salt"). Fecal material is made up of digested blood. When brushed onto a wet paper, it turns a reddish brown.

The adult flea is a small dark brown insect about 2.5 millimeters in size and can be seen with the naked eye. Although fleas have no wings and cannot fly, they do have powerful back legs and can jump great distances. Fleas move through the hair rapidly and are difficult to catch. Run a fine-tooth flea comb through the hair to look for fleas on your dog's back, in the groin, and around the tail and hindquarters. Itching is most pronounced in these areas.

The Flea Life Cycle

An effective flea-control strategy requires an understanding of the flea life cycle. Fleas need a warm, humid environment to flourish and reproduce. The higher the temperature and humidity, the more efficient their reproduction. The adult flea can live up to 115 days on a dog, but only one or two days off her.

After taking a blood meal, fleas mate on the skin of the dog. The female lays eggs within 24 to 48 hours, and may produce up to 2,000 eggs in a four-month life span. The eggs fall off and incubate in your home beneath furniture and in carpets, cracks, and bedding. Deep pile and shag carpets make an ideal environment for egg development.

In 10 days the eggs hatch into larvae that feed on local debris. Larvae spin a cocoon and go into a pupal stage that lasts for days or months. Under ideal temperature and humidity conditions, fleas can emerge rapidly. After hatching, immature adult fleas have two weeks to find a host.

At any given time, about 1 percent of the flea population is composed of adult fleas, while 99 percent remain in the invisible egg, larval, and pupal stages. An effective flea-control program must eliminate this large reservoir.

New Methods of Flea Control

New products such as Program, Advantage, Advantix, and Frontline have practically replaced the use of oral Proban (a twice weekly tablet or liquid used to kill fleas and ticks that bite your dog) and dips, powders, sprays, and shampoos to treat and prevent fleas. The new products are more effective and safer than the traditional insecticides. They are also easier to administer.

Program (the brand name for lufenuron) was the first and remains one of the most popular agents for controlling fleas on dogs. Program is a tablet given once a month with a meal. The active ingredient accumulates in the dog's subcutaneous tissue and requires that the flea bite the dog in order to work.

Program works by inhibiting flea eggs from growing and hatching. This leads to a steady drop in the number of new fleas in the environment. Its affect is limited to the hard outer shell of the flea, making it completely harmless to mammals. However, because mature fleas are not affected, it can take 30 to 60 days or longer for the adult fleas on the dog to die of old age before you notice a reduction in itching and scratching.

For more immediate results, and especially if the dog is suffering from flea allergy dermatitis, Program should be combined with a flea shampoo or some other topical insecticide treatment. Advantage or Frontline can be added to

Program to kill adult fleas within one to two days. It may be necessary to eliminate fleas on the premises using insecticides, as well (see *Eliminating Fleas on the Premises*, page 122).

Program should not be used on puppies younger than 6 weeks of age, but is safe to use on pregnant and lactating bitches.

Sentinel combines Program with the heartworm preventive Interceptor. This broad-spectrum preventive not only controls fleas, but also protects against heartworms, ascarids, hookworms, and whipworms.

Advantage (imidacloprid) is a once-a-month liquid preparation that kills fleas by direct contact. Fleas don't have to bite the dog for the preparation to work. Advantage comes in a tube and is applied to the dog's skin between the shoulder blades (you must carefully part the hair to make sure you get the liquid on the skin) and to three or four additional sites along the dog's back for larger dogs. The amount to apply depends on the size of the dog, and will be prescribed by your veterinarian. One application protects a dog for up to 30 days.

Advantage kills fleas on direct contact and may reduce hatching eggs and larvae. Following application, 98 to 100 percent of adult fleas are killed within 12 hours. Thus, any new fleas that infest the dog should be killed before they have a chance to lay eggs. This breaks the flea life cycle and eventually eliminates fleas in the environment. Advantage is not absorbed into the dog's system, and therefore is nontoxic. Humans do not absorb the chemical after petting a treated dog. **Advantix** is a new formulation that also acts against ticks.

One drawback of Advantage is that it loses some of its effectiveness if the dog's coat becomes thoroughly wet more often than once a week. If this happens, the dog can be retreated as often as once a week.

Advantage should not be used on puppies under 7 weeks of age, or on pregnant or lactating females.

Frontline and **Frontline Spray** contain the active ingredient fipronil, which kills fleas on contact within 24 to 48 hours. The fleas do not need to bite the dog to be killed. Frontline is a liquid that comes in tubes and is applied as described for Advantage. The effectiveness of Frontline is not diminished if the dog's coat becomes wet. The product has a residual effect that lasts up to 90 days in some dogs. Like Advantage, Frontline is not absorbed and thus appears to be nontoxic. One additional benefit is that it also kills ticks for up to 30 days. Frontline should not be used on puppies under 10 weeks of age.

Frontline Plus has (S) methoprene, which is labeled to kill adult fleas, flea eggs, and larvae. It also treats chewing lice and is used as part of a program to control sarcoptic mange. Frontline Plus is labeled for puppies 8 weeks of age. It is also labeled for use on breeding, pregnant, and lactating bitches.

The heartworm preventive **Revolution** (selamectin) is a once-a-month liquid preparation applied to the skin of the dog's neck between the shoulder

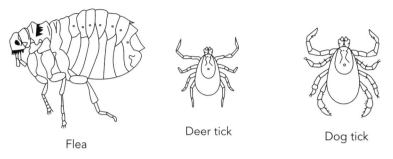

Flea

Deer tick

Dog tick

These pests are not drawn to scale, but the ticks are in relative proportion to one another.

blades, as described for Advantage. It also controls adult fleas and prevents flea eggs from hatching. It is discussed in the section on *Heartworms*, page 341.

TOPICAL INSECTICIDES FOR FLEA CONTROL

A variety of insecticide products are available to control fleas, but there are differences in safety and effectiveness. Be sure to read the label to make sure the product is specifically intended to control fleas on dogs. Better yet, consult your veterinarian and use the products he or she recommends. *Do not* use flea products made for dogs on cats or rabbits!

Flea shampoos kill only when they are on the pet. Once rinsed off, they have no residual effect. They are best used for mild to moderate flea infestations when the environment has also been thoroughly treated. In general, pyrethrin-based shampoos are safest, especially on puppies.

Powders and dusts have more residual killing activity, but must be worked thoroughly through the hair coat down to the skin. They tend to leave the coat dry and gritty. Dusting must be repeated two to three times a week, or as recommended by the manufacturer. Dogs who lick or chew on themselves may swallow toxic doses of these chemicals.

Sprays, foams, and dips have the most effective killing action and are the best choices for severe flea infestations and for dogs with flea allergy dermatitis if you are not using a topical preventive such as Advantage or Frontline. Sprays and foams work best on dogs with short coats. Sprays come in pressurized cans and trigger-activated bottles. The hiss of the pressurized can may frighten some dogs, in which case the foam is preferable. Most sprays have a residual killing action that lasts up to 14 days.

Water-based sprays are preferable to alcohol-based sprays, which are flammable and can dry the coat. When using a spray, begin near the back of the dog's head and work toward the tail. This prevents fleas on the body from escaping the treatment by moving up onto the face.

Sprays and foams should not be used on puppies under 2 months of age, unless the manufacturer's label says it is safe to do so. Always use these chemicals exactly as directed, because some can be toxic if the dog licks or chews them off the hair.

Insecticide flea dips applied to the coat and allowed to dry are extremely effective in getting rid of fleas. Dips penetrate the hair coat and have the most immediate killing action and the longest residual activity. They also have the greatest potential for toxicity. Before using a dip, read the instructions carefully. Use according to the manufacturer's recommendations. If your dog shows signs of toxicity, bathe or rinse her right away. Excess drooling, weakness, or instability in walking are all signs of mild toxicity. For information on how to use a flea dip, see *Insecticide Dips,* page 132.

Flea collars aid in flea control but do not eradicate all fleas. Most collars contain dichlorvos, which turns onto a vapor that surrounds the dog. If the dog sleeps outdoors, the collar will not be as effective. Flea collars lose their potency over time and must be changed every two months, or as recommended by the manufacturer. *Dog flea collars should never be used on cats.*

Dogs can become sensitive to the chemicals in flea collars and develop contact dermatitis. This can be prevented to some extent by airing the collar for 24 hours when you first take it out of the package and applying it loosely. The collar should fit so that you can get at least two fingers between it and the dog's neck.

Using a dichlorvos flea collar along with a dichlorvos-containing dewormer could result in the dog absorbing a toxic concentration of dichlorvos. Remove the collar one week before deworming and replace it one week after deworming. Also, do not allow the dog to eat or chew on her collar, as it can be toxic. Initial signs of toxicity may include excess drooling, *ataxic* gait, and diarrhea.

A Suggested Flea-Control Program

Start your dog on a monthly flea-prevention protocol (if possible, before the fleas attack), using a product such as Program or Sentinel, Advantage, Advantix, or Frontline Plus. Prevention is the key to success.

If fleas have already become established, it is essential to kill them on the dog and prevent them from coming back. One way to do this is to shampoo or dip the dog to immediately eliminate the fleas. Thoroughly vacuum the environment and wash all dog bedding. Twenty-four to 48 hours later, apply Frontline or Advantage to kill new fleas hatching from eggs on the premises. Some veterinarians combine Frontline or Advantage with Program or Sentinel for more rapid results, and to minimize development of resistance. Because all of these products prevent fleas from reproducing, they eventually rid the environment of fleas.

For this approach to be successful, it is essential to treat all the dogs and cats in the family, as well as any ferrets or house rabbits. Note that many products that are safe for dogs are not safe for these other pets. Any product that contains permethrin, even if it is labeled as safe for cats, is potentially toxic.

The following protocol for eliminating fleas can be used *only if your dog is not on a monthly flea-control program.*

- All dogs, cats, ferrets, and rabbits must be treated.
- Dip all pets every other week using a solution containing chlorpyrifos or permethrin. It is important to be sure the product is labeled as safe for the pet in question. (If you are unable to treat every animal in the home, substitute sprays and foams at the maximum frequency allowed by the manufacturer.)
- Alternatively, use sprays or foams containing pyrethrins and/or permethrin every other week. Apply to the pet's skin surface, not just the hair.
- For unaffected pets, a dip or a spray application (not both) twice a month is sufficient.
- Physically removing fleas using a flea comb (32 teeth per inch or per 2.5 cm) is effective on shorthaired pets. The pet must be combed at least every other day. Comb the face as well as the body. Kill fleas on the comb by immersing it in alcohol or liquid detergent.
- Flea collars should not be used as the sole source of flea control.

ELIMINATING FLEAS ON THE PREMISES

If you are using a monthly flea-control product such as Program, Sentinel, Advantage, Advantix, or Frontline, the fleas in the environment should eventually be eliminated as they fail to reproduce. For this to be effective, all pets must be treated with the flea-control product.

To immediately reduce fleas in the house or for severe infestations, thoroughly clean the entire house and then apply insecticides in the form of carpet shampoos and house sprays. On carpeted floors, electrostatically charged sodium polyborate powder (Rx for Fleas is the brand name) is most effective and lasts up to a year.

In households with cats and/or young children, the safest insecticides are the pyrethrins (this includes pyrethroids and permethrin), and the insect growth regulators methoprene and fenoxycarb. Insect growth regulators prevent eggs and larvae from developing into adult fleas. Methoprene must come into contact with the flea egg within 12 hours after it is laid to be completely effective, while fenoxycarb can contact the egg any time during its development to be effective.

Insecticides must be applied monthly to all floor surfaces. If pyrethrins are used alone, weekly spraying for the first three weeks is necessary.

Foggers generally contain permethrin or synergized natural pyrethrins (pyrethroids). Some contain insect growth regulators. One disadvantage of foggers is that the mist settles on top of carpets and may not settle into the cracks in upholstery and beneath furniture. Flea larvae and pupae, however, burrow deep into the nap and also seek out cracks and crevices. To offset this disadvantage, shampoo carpets and spray beneath furniture before activating the fogger.

Do not use foggers in rooms where toddlers and young children live or play. Although labels on these products say that rooms should be vacated for one to three hours, studies show that high residue levels can remain for a week or longer. Especially dangerous are exposed plastic toys and stuffed animals, which seem to attract the pesticide.

Mechanical cleaning and insecticide applications must be repeated at three-week intervals. It may take nine weeks to eliminate all visible fleas. With a heavy infestation, it may be advisable to enlist the services of a professional exterminator.

Outdoor control involves treating the yard, kennel, pens, runs, and favorite resting spots. For more information, see *Disinfecting the Premises*, page 133.

Ticks

Ticks are found in nearly all parts of the country and are especially prevalent in spring and fall. Ticks are vectors for several diseases in dogs, including:

- Rocky Mountain spotted fever
- Canine ehrlichiosis
- Canine babesiosis
- Canine hepatozoonosis
- Lyme disease

In the case of Lyme disease and Rocky Mountain spotted fever, these diseases can also spread to humans and cats. And ticks can carry different forms of ehrlichiosis, babesiosis, and hepatozoonosis that can affect humans and other animals.

The saliva of ticks can also produce an allergic hypersensitivity reaction and, in the case of the female wood tick, lone star tick, and Gulf Coast tick, a disease called tick paralysis. The most common ticks, such as the dog tick, have males about the size of a match head and females that expand to the size of a pea after a blood meal. Deer ticks are much smaller—about the size of a pinhead.

Deer Tick

Dorsal View   Ventral View

Dog Tick

Dorsal View   Ventral View

The abdomen edges are smooth on the dorsal view of this deer tick. On the ventral view, the anal opening is near the edge of the tick and is surrounded by a ridge of tissue.

Note that there are no ridges around the abdomen on the dorsal view of the dog tick. On the ventral view, you can see the anal opening near the middle of the tick.

Ticks begin as eggs that hatch into six-legged larvae. The larvae live and feed on animals for about a week before detaching and then molting. After the molt, the larvae become eight-legged nymphs. Nymphs feed on animals, engorge for 3 to 11 days, detach, and molt again into an adult tick.

Ticks do not run and jump as fleas do, but scuttle around slowly. They climb up grass and plants and hold their legs up to sense passing hosts. When a warm-blooded animal walks by, the adult tick crawls onto them and begins feeding.

Ticks can fasten to any part of the dog's skin, but are commonly found around the ears, between the toes, and sometimes in the armpits. A severely infested dog may have hundreds of ticks all over her body. The ticks insert their mouths, attach to their prey, and engorge themselves with a blood meal. During feeding, tick saliva can get into the host's body and blood stream; this is how diseases are transmitted.

Males and females mate on the skin of the dog, after which the female takes a blood meal and then drops off to lay her eggs. This usually occurs 5 to 20 hours after the dog acquires the ticks. Thus, prompt removal of ticks is an effective method of preventing tick-borne diseases.

Ticks may drop off a dog and transfer to people, although this is not common. Once a tick starts feeding on a dog, it will feed until it is engorged and will not seek a second host.

Treatment: Always examine your dog after hiking in tick-infested areas. If you find only one or two ticks, the easiest thing to do is remove them. Keep in mind that the blood of ticks can be dangerous to people. Therefore, do not crush or squeeze a tick with your bare fingers. Before removing the tick, put on disposable rubber or plastic gloves.

Ticks that are not attached to the skin are easily removed with a pair of tweezers. There are also special tick removing devices that are widely available, including Ticked Off, Protick Remedy, and Tick Nipper. Once removed, the tick can be killed by putting it in rubbing alcohol.

You must be careful if you find a tick with its head buried in the skin, because the head may detach and remain behind. Grasp the tick firmly with tweezers or a tick removal device, as close to the dog's body as possible without pinching her skin, and lift it off.

Use the tweezers to place the tick in a jar or plastic dish with a little alcohol, Seal it well and dispose of the container in an outdoor garbage can. Don't flush it down the toilet, because the tick will survive the trip and infect another animal. Wash the tweezers thoroughly with hot water and alcohol.

Before you dispose of the tick, it can be a good idea to ask your veterinarian if they think it is important to bring the tick in for identification and to see if it is carrying any disease.

If the head or mouth parts remain embedded in the skin, redness and swelling is likely to occur at the site of the bite. In most cases, this reaction clears up in two to three days. A dab of antibiotic ointment will help prevent most skin infections. However, if it does not—or if the redness seems to be getting worse—consult your veterinarian.

If the dog has many ticks, treatment involves an insecticide dip containing natural or synthetic pyrethrins labeled for ticks, or an organophosphate dip such as Paramite. For information on how to use a dip, see *Insecticide Dips,* page 132.

With a heavy infestation, dip the dog every week for four to six weeks. Be sure to eliminate all ticks from the dog's sleeping quarters (see *Disinfecting the Premises,* page 133).

Ticks can work their way deep into the ear canals. These ticks should be removed by a veterinarian.

Prevention: Ticks must attach for several hours before they can transmit diseases. Therefore, if you remove all ticks promptly after your dog has been running in the fields or woods, you can prevent many tick-borne infections.

This tick has just attached itself to the dog and buried its head into the skin.

An engorged tick.

Preventic tick collars containing amitraz are quite effective in controlling ticks. These collars are effective for up to three months, but should not be used on puppies under 12 weeks of age and should not be used on household dogs where young children may come in contact with the collar. Frontline, used to control fleas, kills or disables most ticks for up to 30 days following a single application. Consider using this product along with an amitraz tick collar during the tick season. Advantix is another topical product that can repel and kill some species of ticks.

For outdoor control, cut tall grass, weeds, and brush. Treat the yard with an insecticide labeled as safe for use with animals. Use according to directions.

Other External Parasites
Scabies (Sarcoptic Mange)

Scabies, tiny spiderlike mites, are highly contagious and are transmitted primarily by direct contact and through contaminated grooming equipment and kennels. These mites are also transferable to humans and other pets.

Probably no other skin disease will cause your dog to scratch and bite at her skin with such intensity. The severe itching is caused by female mites tunneling a few millimeters under the skin to lay their eggs. The eggs hatch in 3 to 10 days. The immature mites develop into adults and begin to lay eggs of their own. The entire life cycle occurs on the dog's skin, and takes just 17 to 21 days.

Scabies attacks the skin of the ears, elbows, hocks, and the underside of the chest and face. The onset is abrupt with scratching, hair loss, and inflamed skin in these areas. Crusty ear tips are characteristic. A classic test for scabies is to rub the ear flap between your fingers and watch the dog scratch on the same side. In the later stages the skin becomes thick, crusted, scaly, and darkly pigmented.

Scabies in people can produce an itchy rash, typically found at the belt line. This rash is caused by insects that have transferred from the dog. Scabies mites, however, do not live on human skin for longer than three weeks. If the problem does not disappear in three weeks, look for a continuing source of infestation.

The diagnosis is made by examining skin scrapings under a microscope. In some cases the mites may not be identified. If the dog's symptoms strongly suggest scabies, your veterinarian may decide to begin treatment as a diagnostic test. A positive response to the treatment confirms the diagnosis of scabies.

Treatment: Scabies must be treated under veterinary supervision. Clip the hair away from scabies-affected areas on medium- and longhaired dogs and bathe the entire animal using a benzoyl peroxide shampoo (such as OxyDex or Pyoben). The shampoo loosens scales and makes it possible for an insecticide dip to penetrate the hair pores.

Scabies mites have developed resistance to a number of organophosphate dips. Two dips that remain active against them are amitraz (brand name Mitaban) and 2 to 4 percent lime-sulfur (LymDyp). Only lime-sulfur is licensed by the FDA to treat scabies in dogs. However, LymDyp has an unpleasant odor, stains white coats, and can irritate the skin.

Dip the dog once a week for six consecutive weeks (or until the symptoms resolve), using the dip recommended by your veterinarian. Continue treatment for two more weeks after the dogs appears to be cured. When using any dip, carefully follow the instructions on the label. For information on how to dip, see *Insecticide Dips*, page 132. It is important to treat all dogs who have come into contact with the affected individual.

Oral ivermectin is effective against scabies and is frequently used as a diagnostic test when skin scrapings have been negative. Ivermectin, in doses used for scabies, has produced central nervous system problems and deaths in Collies, Shetland Sheepdogs, Old English Sheepdogs, Australian Shepherds, and other herding breeds and their crosses. The drug is contraindicated in these breeds at the higher dosages. Dogs of these breeds made be tested for the MDR 1 (multi-drug resistance) gene by having your veterinarian send a cheek swab to Washington State University College of Veterinary Medicine.

Always have the heartworm status of your dog checked before giving ivermectin, because it may cause a reaction in dogs who are positive for the heartworm larvae. Recent reports suggest that Interceptor (milbemycin oxime) may also be effective against scabies mites, and could be used instead of ivermectin in breeds in which Ivermectin is contraindicated. Revolution (selamectin) is also labeled to help in preventing and treating sarcoptic mange in dogs.

Corticosteroids relieve severe itching and may be required for the first two to three days of treatment. Infected skin sores require oral and topical antibiotics. Adult mites can live for 21 days off the host.

Treatment of the indoor environment (as described in *Eliminating Fleas on the Premises*, page 122) is advisable to prevent recurrence.

CHEYLETIELLA MANGE (WALKING DANDRUFF)

Cheyletiella mange is a highly contagious skin disease that affects young puppies. It is caused by large reddish mites that infest kennels and pet shops. These mites live on the surface of the skin and die within 10 days when off their host. Cheyletiella mange is becoming less prevalent because of the widespread use of flea-control preparations that also kill cheyletiella mites. Also, the mite tends to live in straw and animal bedding, which is not used as frequently as it once was.

Cheyletiella mites are usually found along the back, but occasionally infest other parts of the body. The signs are a red bumpy rash along with a large

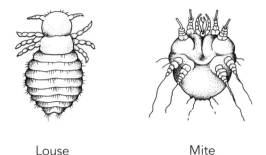

Louse   Mite

amount of flaky skin in the hair coat. The condition is also called walking dandruff because when you look at these skin flakes, you may see them moving. The movement is actually caused by the mites moving around under the scales of skin.

Suspect this condition if you find heavy dandruff over the neck and back of a recently acquired puppy or kitten. Itching may be intense or completely absent.

The diagnosis is made by finding mites or eggs in dandruff scrapings collected with a flea comb or sticky tape. In some cases the mites or eggs cannot be seen, and the diagnosis depends on the animal's response to therapy.

Cheyletiella mites can infect humans, producing an itchy papular rash (small red pumps with areas of central *necrosis*) found most often on the arms, trunk, and buttocks. This rash, like that of scabies, should disappear when the pet is successfully treated.

Treatment: All animals who have been in contact with the affected dog must be treated to eliminate mites from the kennel and household. Pyrethrin shampoos and 2 percent lime-sulfur dips (LymDyp) are effective in killing cheyletiella mites. Follow the directions on the label (see *Using Insecticides*, page 131). Treat weekly for six to eight weeks. If the mites are resistant, seek veterinary consultation; other treatments are available.

Clean and spray the dog's quarters with a residual insecticide appropriate for killing adult fleas. Repeat every two weeks during the treatment period.

CHIGGERS (TROMBICULID MITES)

Chiggers, also called harvest mites or red bugs, live as adults in decaying vegetation. Only their larval forms are parasitic. Dogs acquire the infestation while prowling in forest grasslands and fields in late summer and fall, when chiggers are reproducing.

Chigger larvae appear as red, yellow, or orange specks, barely visible to the naked eye but easily seen with a magnifying glass. They tend to clump in areas where the skin is thin, usually between the toes or about the ears and mouth. The larvae feed by sucking on the skin. The result is severe itching and the formation of sores and scabs. The diagnosis is made by identifying the mites by visual inspection or by microscopic examination of skin scrapings.

Treatment: Chiggers respond well to a single application of a lime-sulfur dip (LymDyp) or a pyrethrin shampoo. Corticosteroids may be required for two or three days to control the intense itching. If the ear canals are involved, treat with thiabendazole drops (brand name Tresaderm). Prevent reinfestation by keeping your dog out of fields and grasses during the chigger season.

LICE (PEDICULOSIS)

Lice are not common in dogs. They are found primarily on dogs who are run-down and poorly kept. Lice are usually found beneath matted hair around the ears, head, neck, shoulders, and in the perineal area. Because of the severe itching and constant irritation, bare spots may be seen where the hair has been rubbed off.

There are two species of lice: biting lice, which feed on skin scales, and sucking lice, which feed on the dog's blood and can cause severe protein deficiency and anemia.

Adult lice are wingless, pale-colored insects about 2 to 3 millimeters long. Sucking lice move slowly; biting lice move quickly. The eggs, called nits, look like white grains of sand firmly attached to the hair. The diagnosis is made by visual identification of adult lice or nits. Nits may look something like flaky skin (dandruff), but inspection with a magnifying glass reveals the difference.

On dogs, lice are most often found around the head and ears and beneath matted hair.

Treatment: Lice show little resistance to treatment and do not live long off their host. They are easily killed with most insecticides, including lime-sulfur, pyrethrins, and pyrethroids. The infected dog and all animals who have been in contact with her should be treated every 10 to 14 days for four weeks with an insecticide shampoo, dip, or powder. Infected bedding should be destroyed or thoroughly cleaned (lice do not live long off the host), and the dog's sleeping quarters and grooming equipment disinfected.

Severely anemic dogs may require a blood transfusion or vitamins and iron supplements.

Prevention: Frontline Plus is labeled for control of lice.

Pelodera Dermatitis (Damp Hay Itch)

This disease is caused by the larvae of a threadlike worm found in decaying rice hulls, straw, marsh hay, and other grasses that are in contact with damp soil. The larvae burrow into the skin of the dog's chest, abdomen, and feet, causing intense itching and pimplelike bumps. Later, you may see raw, crusted, inflamed areas where the dog has scratched and chewed the skin.

The condition is found in dogs who are bedded on damp hay and straw. The diagnosis is made by finding the worm larvae on microscopic examination of skin scrapings.

Treatment: Bathe the dog with a benzoyl peroxide shampoo such as OxyDex or Pyoben to remove scales and crusts. Follow with an organophosphate insecticide dip such as Paramite (see *Using Insecticides*, page 131). Repeat the dip in one week if the dog continues to itch. Apply topical antibiotic ointment to inflamed skin areas three times a day.

Clean out old hay and straw. Wash the dog's bedding and spray the sleeping area with an organophosphate insecticide containing malathion or diazinon. Change the bedding from hay to cedar shavings or shredded paper, or provide the dog with a fabric-covered sleeping pad that is washed frequently.

Flies

Adult flies may deposit their eggs on raw or infected wounds, or in soil where larvae can penetrate the dog's skin.

Maggots

A maggot infestation, called myiasis, is a seasonal, warm-weather condition most often caused by the bluebottle or blow fly, which lays its eggs on open wounds or on badly soiled, matted fur. Debilitated dogs and old dogs who are unable to keep themselves clean are susceptible to maggots.

The eggs hatch within three days. Over the next two weeks, the larvae grow into large maggots that produce a salivary enzyme that digests the dog's skin, causing "punched-out" areas. The maggots then penetrate the skin, enlarge the opening, and set the stage for a bacterial skin infection. With a severe infestation, the dog could go into shock. The shock is caused by enzymes and toxins secreted by the maggots. This is a medical emergency and requires immediate veterinary attention.

Treatment: Clip the affected areas to remove soiled and matted hair. Remove all maggots with blunt-nosed tweezers. Wash infected areas with Betadine solution and dry the dog. Then spray or shampoo the dog using a nonalcohol-based product that contains pyrethrins. Repeat as described for *Fleas* (page 117) and check closely for remaining maggots.

Dogs with infected wounds should be treated with oral antibiotics. If the dog is debilitated, her health and nutrition must be improved to bring about a cure.

Grubs (Cuterebriasis)

Grubs are the larvae of a large botfly that has a wide seasonal distribution in the United States. This fly lays its eggs near the burrows of rodents and rabbits. Dogs acquire the disease by direct contact with infested soil.

Newly hatched larvae penetrate the skin to form cystlike lumps with small openings, which allow the grubs to breathe. Several grubs may be found in the same area of the dog's body. In such cases, they form large nodular masses. Typical infestation locations are along the jaw, under the belly, and along the flanks. Inch-long (2.5 cm) grubs may protrude from these breathing holes. In about one month, the grubs emerge and drop to the ground.

Treatment: Veterinary assistance is best. The veterinarian will clip away hair to expose the breathing holes. Grasp each grub with a fine-tipped forceps and gently draw it out. Do not crush or rupture the grub. This can produce anaphylactic shock in the dog.

If the veterinarian is unable to grasp the grub, a small incision must be made under local anesthesia to remove the parasite. Grub wounds are slow to heal and often become infected. Antibiotics may be required.

Using Insecticides

Dealing effectively with fleas, lice, mites, ticks, and other external parasites often involves using insecticides on your pets, your home, and your yard. Insecticides are incorporated into powders, sprays, dusts, and dips. They are used both on the dog and to disinfect bedding, houses, kennels, runs, gardens, garages. and other spots where a dog could become reinfested.

There are four classes of insecticides in current use. In order of decreasing toxicity, they are:

1. Chlorinated hydrocarbons
2. Organophosphates and carbamates
3. Pyrethrins (natural and synthetic)
4. Natural insecticides, such as d-limonene

In addition, there are insect growth regulators that, although not insecticides, act to prevent insect reproduction. Because their action is limited to insects with a hard outer shell, they do not affect mammals.

Insecticides can be dangerous if not used properly, so it is important to follow all directions on the label and to use with them care. The diagnosis and treatment of insecticide poisoning is discussed in *Poisoning*, page 31. For a discussion of insecticides used in flea control, see *Topical Insecticides for Flea Control*, page 120. If your dog has open wounds or damaged skin, check with your veterinarian before applying any form of insecticide.

When you purchase an insecticide, be sure it is labeled as safe for use on dogs. Preparations manufactured for sheep and livestock can irritate the skin of dogs and even cause death.

Insecticides are poisons! *Before using any insecticide, be sure to read and follow the directions of the manufacturer.* This will prevent accidental poisoning from improper use.

INSECTICIDE DIPS

Dips are insecticide solutions that are sponged or rinsed onto the body and allowed to dry on the hair and skin. Use a dip that is recommended by your veterinarian or, if you decide to use a commercial preparation, read the label to be sure the product is effective against the parasite in question. If you are not sure which parasite your dog has, or if she may have more than one, consult with your veterinarian. If your dog has recently been dewormed, check with your veterinarian before using a dip.

Before dipping, plug the dog's ears with cotton to keep the insecticide out of the ear canals. Begin by washing the dog with a gentle commercial dog shampoo, or, if prescribed by your veterinarian, a shampoo that loosens crusts and scales. Squeeze out all excess water from the coat to keep it from diluting the dip.

Make up the dip according to the directions on the package. Then apply as directed. Protect the dog's eyes from contact with the shampoo or dip to avoid eye bums (see *Burns of the Eyes*, page 179).

If your dog has a very thick coat, she may need to be clipped first to make sure the preparation reaches all the way down to the skin.

Most dips must be repeated one or more times at intervals of 7 to 10 days to rid the dog of the parasite in question. Consult the label for recommended frequency. *Do not* exceed this frequency. Many dips should not be used on young puppies. Make sure to read the label. Do not used dips approved for dogs on any other pets.

DISINFECTING THE PREMISES

The goal here is to prevent reinfestation by ridding the environment of insects, eggs, larvae, and other intermediate stages of the parasite. This is accomplished by physically cleaning and then applying insecticides.

Indoor Control

To eliminate all sources of reinfestation, it is essential to treat all animals in the household. Destroy infected bedding or thoroughly clean it with insecticides. Blankets and rugs on which the dog regularly sleeps should be washed weekly at the hottest setting. Scrub all the places the dogs rests and sleeps with a strong household disinfectant. To be effective, these areas should receive at least two thorough cleanings, followed by the application of an insecticide, spaced three weeks apart.

A thorough housecleaning involves vacuuming carpets, curtains, and furniture. Vacuum cleaner bags must be discarded immediately after use in an outside trash can, as they provide an ideal environment for fleas to hatch. Floors should be mopped, giving special attention to cracks and crevices where eggs are likely to incubate.

Steam cleaning carpets is highly effective in killing eggs and larvae. Insecticides can be used in the water of the steam cleaner. Specific products are available where you rent the equipment. With a heavy infestation, consider enlisting the services of a professional exterminator.

Insecticides are applied in the form of carpet shampoos and premise sprays (see *Eliminating Fleas on the Premises*, page 122). Remove all pets and children before you begin, and read all instructions carefully.

Additional products that can help eliminate fleas in the house include boric acid compounds such as Fleabusters and Fleago, which dehydrate fleas. Diatomaceous earth works in the same way. This is available as Fleas Away.

Outdoor Control

For outdoor control, first remove all decaying vegetation. Mow, rake, and discard the debris in tightly sealed bags.

For disinfecting kennels, runs, and other areas, the liquid application of chlorpyrifos, permethrin, or diazinon is preferred. Follow the directions for mixing, preparation, and application. When applying sprays, give special attention to the dog's favorite sleeping spots, such beneath the porch or in the garage. Be sure the ground is dry before allowing pets outside.

Repeat the application twice at three-week intervals, or as recommended by the manufacturer. The residual activity of outdoor insecticides depends on weather conditions. In dry weather, they may remain effective for a month; in wet weather, for only one to two weeks.

Some insecticide dips can be used as sprays on gardens, lawns, and kennels. Use according to the instructions on the label.

Diatomaceous earth, including the product Fleas Away, can be spread in areas of the yard where your dog likes to stay. You can also explore the use of beneficial nematodes that feast on flea larvae and help to keep your yard flea free.

Discourage rodents such as squirrels, chipmunks, and mice that may be reinfesting your yard with fleas. You may need to trap them, or at a minimum, remove any bird feeders in the hopes the rodents will move elsewhere. Don't leave pet food outdoors, because it attracts strays and wildlife. And be sure to securely cover all garbage cans.

Lick Granuloma (Acral Pruritic Dermatitis)

A lick granuloma is an open sore, usually at the ankle or wrist, perpetuated by constant licking. It is seen most often in large, shorthaired dogs such as Doberman Pinschers, Great Danes, Labrador Retrievers, and bird dogs.

At one time, lick sores were thought to be *psychogenic* in origin and related to boredom and inactivity. It now appears that many cases are preceded by an itchy skin disease (such as canine atopy) that starts the lick cycle. Other possible initiating causes include demodectic mange, a bacterial or fungal infection, prior trauma, and underlying joint disease. The precipitating event focuses the dog's attention on the area. The licking then becomes a habit that may be perpetuated by psychological events, so behavior may still be a factor.

As the dog licks at her wrist or ankle, the hair is rubbed off and the surface of the skin becomes red and shiny. Eventually, the skin becomes raised, thick, hard, and insensitive to pressure. However, it remains fresh-looking from the constant licking. Some dogs will lick long enough and hard enough to cause breaks in the skin and serious wounds.

Treatment: It is important to review the course of events in an attempt to identify the precipitating cause. If a disease such as canine atopy is diagnosed, medical treatment is directed toward that condition.

Local treatment may involve the use of topical and injectable steroids, radiation therapy, bandaging, surgical removal, cryotherapy, and acupuncture. Some dogs will require antibiotics due to secondary infections. Results are variable. The lick granuloma is one of the most difficult skin problems to treat successfully.

A lick granuloma near the ankle. The hair is rubbed off and the ulcer is clean and shiny.

Because lick sores are perpetuated by *psychogenic* factors, a change in the dog's routine or lifestyle should be part of the treatment program. For example, some arrangement may need to be made to provide company for the dog when the owner is away. A new puppy in the house may provide companionship and entertain an older dog. Behavior-modifying drugs may be beneficial in some cases.

Allergies

The number of dogs with allergies has increased dramatically in recent years. It is now estimated that one in seven dogs suffer from allergic symptoms. According to Veterinary Pet Insurance, skin allergies are now the most common reason dog owners take their dog to the veterinarian. Heredity plays a role. Although certain breeds appear to be more allergy prone, all breeds and their mixes can be affected.

An allergy is in an unpleasant reaction caused by exposure to a food, inhalant, or something in the dog's environment. What the dog is exposed to is called the *allergen*. The way in which the dog's immune system responds to the allergen is the allergic or hypersensitivity reaction.

Before a dog can have an allergic reaction, she must be exposed to the allergen at least twice. The first exposure causes the immune system to manufacture antibodies to the allergen. A later exposure triggers an allergen-antibody reaction that releases histamine, the chemical mediator responsible for the reaction.

While humans tend to experience upper respiratory symptoms when an allergy is triggered, the target organ in dogs is usually the skin, with intense itching being the principal sign. Dogs with allergies often scratch continuously and are miserable, snappish, and generally unpleasant to be around.

There are two kinds of hypersensitivity. The immediate type occurs minutes after exposure and usually produces hives. The delayed response occurs hours or days later and causes intense itching. Anaphylactic shock (see page 13) is a severe hypersensitivity reaction of the immediate type, accompanied by diarrhea, vomiting, weakness, difficulty breathing with *stridor*, collapse, and, if untreated, death.

Canine allergies fall into four categories:

1. Those caused by fleas and other biting insects (flea allergy dermatitis)
2. Those caused by inhaled allergens such as dust mites, grasses, molds, and tree and weed pollens (canine atopy)
3. Those caused and by foods and drugs (food allergies)
4. Those caused by irritants that have direct contact with the skin (contact allergies)

HIVES

Hives are an allergic reaction characterized by the sudden appearance of raised, circular, itchy *wheals* on the skin of the face and elsewhere. The hair sticks out in little patches. Frequently, the eyelids will also swell. Hives generally appear within 30 minutes of exposure and disappear within 24 hours.

Insect bites are a common cause of hives. Hives can occur after a vaccination. Penicillin, tetracycline, and other antibiotics can produce hives. Topical insecticides and soaps are other causes. Hives that come and go usually are caused by an allergen in the dog's environment.

Treatment: When possible, identify the allergen and prevent further exposure. When a food allergy is suspected, modify the dog's diet (see *Food Allergy*, page 140). In the case of an acute reaction, you can give a dose of Milk of Magnesia to speed removal of the food from the intestinal tract (see *Over-the-Counter Drugs for Home Veterinary Use*, page 572).

When hives appear shortly after a shampoo or application of a topical insecticide, bathe the dog and rinse thoroughly to remove the chemical from the dog's coat and skin.

Hives usually respond well to an antihistamine such as Benadryl (see *Over-the-Counter Drugs for Home Veterinary Use*, page 571, for dosage). Cortisone may be needed to control a severe case. Consult your veterinarian.

Flea Allergy Dermatitis

This is the most common allergy in dogs. It is caused by a hypersensitivity reaction to one or more substances in the saliva of fleas. Flea allergy dermatitis is an allergic reaction of both the immediate and delayed type; itching begins immediately and tends to persist long after fleas have been eliminated. One bite is enough to trigger this reaction. Symptoms are worse in midsummer during the flea season. However, dogs who live in the house may suffer all year long if fleas are present.

Flea allergy dermatitis is characterized by severe itching with inflamed skin and red *papules* found where fleas are heavily concentrated—over the rump and base of the tail, under the legs, and on the groin and belly. Dogs chew and rub at these areas. Hair falls out and the skin becomes dry and scaly. In some cases the skin breaks down and develops raw areas that become crusted and infected. In time, the skin becomes thick and darkly pigmented.

The diagnosis can be suspected by finding fleas on the dog and seeing the characteristic skin rash. Check for fleas by standing your dog over a sheet of white paper and brushing the coat. White and black grains of sandy material that drop onto the paper are flea eggs and feces. An allergic response to flea saliva can be confirmed with an intradermal skin test.

Treatment: The majority of dogs with flea allergy dermatitis can be cured by eliminating fleas on the dog and controlling fleas in the environment. All pets in the household, even those who are not affected, must be treated simultaneously to eliminate fleas. Antihistamines and/or corticosteroids may be required for two to three days to control itching. A medicated bath may also help to make your dog more comfortable. *Pyoderma* requires topical and oral antibiotics. Seek veterinary attention for these problems.

Prevention: The monthly application of a flea-control product, such as Frontline Plus or Advantage, will kill adult fleas before they bite the dog. Program inhibits reinfestation by preventing fleas from reproducing. The combination of Program with Frontline or Advantage should eventually eliminate fleas, but for a more rapid response it may be necessary to treat the environment as described in *Eliminating Fleas on the Premises*, page 122.

Hair loss over the rump, thighs, and belly due to excessive itching, scratching, and rubbing caused by flea bites.

ATOPIC DERMATITIS (CANINE ATOPY)

Atopic dermatitis is a disease in which there is an inherited tendency to develop IgE antibodies in response to exposure to *allergens* that are inhaled or absorbed through the skin. This extremely common allergic skin disease is second only to flea allergy dermatitis in frequency, and affects about 10 percent of dogs.

Atopy begins in dogs 1 to 3 years of age. Susceptible breeds include Golden Retrievers, Labrador Retrievers, Lhasa Apsos, Wire Fox Terriers, West Highland White Terriers, Dalmatians, Poodles, English Setters, Irish Setters, Boxers, and Bulldogs, among others, although any dog may be affected. Even mixed breeds may suffer from atopy.

Signs generally first appear at the same time as the weed pollens of late summer and fall. Later, other pollens begin to influence the picture: tree pollens in March and April; then grass pollens in May, June, and early July. Finally, the dog starts to react to wool, house dust, molds, feathers, plant fibers, and so forth. With prolonged exposure and multiple allergens, the condition becomes a year-round affair. Some dogs have indoor allergies (usually house dust, grain, mites, or molds), so they may react all year-round from the start.

In early canine atopy, itching is seasonal and the skin looks normal. Dogs scratch at the ears and undersides of the body. The itching is often accompanied by face-rubbing, sneezing, a runny nose (known as allergic rhinitis), watery eyes, and licking at the paws (which leaves characteristic brown stains on the feet). In many dogs the disease does not progress beyond this stage.

When it does progress, an itch-scratch-itch cycle develops with deep scratches (called *excoriations*) in the skin, hair loss, scabs, crusts, and secondary bacterial skin infection. These dogs are miserable. In time, the skin

The brown stains on the dog's feet from licking at the paws are characteristic of canine atopy.

becomes thick and darkly pigmented. A secondary dry or greasy seborrhea with flaky skin often develops in conjunction with the skin infection.

Ear canal infections may accompany these signs, or may be the sole manifestation of atopy. The ear flaps are red and inflamed, and the canals are filled with a brown wax that eventually causes bacterial or yeast otitis (see *Ear Allergies*, page 209).

Canine atopy, especially when complicated by *pyoderma*, can be difficult to distinguish from flea allergy dermatitis, scabies, demodectic mange, food allergies, and other skin diseases. The diagnosis can be suspected based on the history, location of skin lesions, and seasonal pattern of occurrence. Skin scrapings, bacterial and fungal cultures, skin biopsy, and a trial hypoallergenic test diet should be considered before embarking on an involved course of treatment for atopy. It is important to treat and eliminate

This dog has severe allergic dermatitis with a surface skin infection, in this case caused by canine atopy.

fleas. The majority of dogs with canine atopy are allergic to fleas and may have an associated flea allergy dermatitis complicating the picture.

The preferred method of diagnosing canine atopy is through intradermal skin testing, which means injecting small amounts of many known allergens and observing the skin reaction. This can be time consuming and expensive, because it requires many trips to the veterinarian. To be accurate, all supportive drugs must be withdrawn during the testing period. If intradermal skin testing is not available, a serologic blood test (*ELISA*) designed to detect group-specific IgE antibody may assist in making the diagnosis.

Treatment: The most effective long-term solution is to change the dog's living circumstances to avoid the allergen. The atopic dog is usually allergic to many different allergens, however, and often it is not possible to avoid exposure to them all.

Most dogs with atopy respond well to treatment. A first and most important step is to reduce the threshold for scratching by treating and eliminating all associated irritative skin problems, such as fleas, seborrhea, and *pyoderma*. Wipe the dog down with a damp towel when she comes in from outdoors, which helps remove pollens picked up in the coat.

Antihistamines control itching and scratching in 20 to 40 percent of atopic dogs. Corticosteroids are the most effective anti-itch drugs, but also have the most serious side effects. They are best used intermittently in low doses and for a limited time. Preparations containing hydrocortisone with Pramoxine are often prescribed for treating local areas of itching. Pramoxine is a topical anesthetic that provides temporary relief from pain and itching.

Derm Caps and other essential omega-3 fatty acid products derived from fish oils have produced good results in some dogs. They are used as nutritional supplements in conjunction with other therapies. A variety of shampoos are available and may be prescribed by your veterinarian to rehydrate the skin, treat bacterial infection, and control seborrhea.

Dogs who do not respond to medical treatment can be considered for immunotherapy with hyposensitization. This involves skin testing to identify the allergen(s) and then desensitizing the dog to the specific irritants through a series of injections given over a period of 9 to 12 months or longer. Some dogs will require periodic boosters during times when allergens are heavy.

Some dogs with atopy benefit from switching to a higher-quality dog food, even if they don't have a food allergy. And if they are allergic to house dust mites, they often cross-react with grain mites and will benefit from a canned food or kibble that has no grain.

Food Allergy

Food allergy is the third most common cause of allergic itching and scratching in dogs. It occurs in dogs of all ages. Unlike canine atopy, food allergy is not seasonal. Dog can develop allergies to chicken, milk, eggs, fish, beef, pork, horse meat, grains, potatoes, soy products, or dietary additives. A dog must have been exposed to the allergen one or more times to become allergic. Typically, the dog has been on the same diet for at least two years.

The principal sign is severe itching, sometimes accompanied by the appearance of small red bumps, *pustules*, and raised patches of skin. Characteristically, the rash involves the ears, feet, backs of the legs, and underside of the body.

Since food allergy is less common than canine atopy and flea allergy dermatitis, the dog is often thought to be suffering from one of those diseases. Many dogs will start by showing signs just in their ears, with a red, moist rash.

Treatment: The diagnosis is made by placing the dog on a hypoallergenic test diet and watching for a definite reduction in itching and scratching. A hypoallergenic diet is one that has a very limited number of ingredients. It should contain no added coloring, preservatives, or flavorings. Most important, it should contain ingredients that the dog is unlikely to have encountered in the past. Your veterinarian can prescribe an appropriate hypoallergenic diet after carefully reviewing the composition of the dog's current diet. Switching from one commercial food to another is not an adequate test, as these nonprescription diets contain too many ingredients and the dog is likely to have eaten some of them in the past.

The test diet usually consists of a commercial hypoallergenic prescription diet such as salmon and rice or duck and potato, available through Hill's Pet Products, Purina, and Waltham. Once a good commercial hypoallergenic diet is found, the dog can be left on that diet indefinitely. Eliminate all treats and chews, and switch from a chewable tablet heartworm preventive to one that comes in a different form.

A reduction in itching may occur within a few days of starting the test diet, but in many cases it takes several weeks. The test diet should be continued for at least 10 weeks. Once improvement is noted, various foods can be added one by one until the offending allergen is identified by noting that it causes an increase in the amount of itching and scratching.

Purina has tried a new way to attack food allergies. Instead of simply substituting novel proteins, their HA Hypoallergenic Diet uses modified and denatured proteins of small molecular weight to render them nonallergenic. If protein is the culprit, this kind of diet can be effective in controlling the allergy.

IRRITANT AND ALLERGIC CONTACT DERMATITIS

Irritant contact dermatitis is caused by the direct effect of a chemical or irritant on the skin. It occurs in areas where the skin is not well protected by hair, such as the feet, chin, nose, hocks, stifles, and the undersurface of the body, including the scrotum. Irritant contact dermatitis can occur after a single exposure or repeated exposure.

Irritant contact dermatitis produces itchy red bumps and inflammation of the skin. You may notice moist, weepy spots, blisters, and crusts. The skin becomes rough and scaly and hair is lost. Excessive scratching damages the skin and sets the stage for secondary *pyoderma*.

Chemicals that can cause irritant dermatitis include acids and alkalis, detergents, solvents, soaps, and petroleum byproducts.

Less commonly, the skin becomes sensitized to a certain chemical and a delayed type of hypersensitivity reaction develops. This is allergic contact dermatitis. This rash is indistinguishable from that of irritant contact dermatitis, but appears after repeated exposure and often spreads beyond the site of contact.

Allergic contact dermatitis can be caused by chemicals found in soaps, flea collars, shampoos, wool and synthetic fibers, leather, plastic and rubber dishes, grasses and pollens, insecticides, petrolatum, paint, carpet dyes, and rubber and wood preservatives. Chemicals used to clean your carpet are a frequent source of irritation. Neomycin, found in many topical medications, can produce allergic contact dermatitis, as can other drugs and medications.

Plastic and rubber food dish dermatitis affects the nose and lips (see *Plastic Dish Nasal Dermatitis*, page 226).

Flea collar dermatitis is an allergic contact dermatitis. The signs include itching, redness, hair loss, and the development of *excoriations*, scabs, and crusts beneath the collar. It can be prevented to some degree by airing the collar for 24 hours and applying the collar loosely. The flea collar should fit so that you can get at least two fingers beneath the ring. However, if your dog develops flea collar dermatitis, the best course of action is not to use a flea collar.

Treatment: Consider the area of involvement and identify the chemical or skin allergen causing the problem. Prevent further exposure. Treat infected skin with a topical antibiotic ointment such as triple antibiotic. Topical and oral corticosteroids prescribed by your veterinarian can relieve itching and inflammation.

Disorders with Hair Loss

The distinguishing feature of this group of skin diseases is hair loss without itching or scratching. Later, the initial problem can become complicated by seborrhea (see page 150) and *pyoderma*.

Hormone diseases are among those associated with hair loss. Although these diseases involve many systems, the skin and coat changes provide visual evidence that may lead to early recognition and treatment. Hormone skin disorders cause bilateral hair loss and skin changes that are symmetrical—one side of the body being the mirror image of the other.

Hypothyroidism

This is a disease of thyroid deficiency. The thyroid gland sits on the throat below the larynx. Its function is to produce the hormones thyroxine (T4) and triiodothyronine (T3), which control the rate of metabolism. Thus, dogs with hypothyroidism have metabolic rates below normal. Hypothyroidism, in most cases, is caused by autoimmune thyroiditis (also called lymphocytic thyroiditis), which results in destruction of thyroid tissue. Autoimmune thyroiditis is known to be an inherited disease. Idiopathic thyroid gland atrophy is a rare cause of hypothyroidism. The cause of both types of thyroid gland atrophy is unknown, but environmental and dietary factors are possible contributing factors.

The disease occurs most often in middle-aged dogs of medium and large breeds, but has been seen in virtually every breed and in mixed breeds as well. The breeds most commonly affected are the Golden Retriever, Doberman Pinscher, Irish Setter, Miniature Schnauzer, Dachshund, Shetland Sheepdog, Cocker Spaniel, Airedale Terrier, Labrador Retriever, Greyhound, Scottish Deerhound, and others. Hypothyroidism is the most common endocrine skin disease in dogs—but it is still less common than other skin diseases. Coat and skin changes are bilateral and symmetrical. A typical sign is poor hair regrowth, which is most noticeable after the dog has been clipped.

It is also common to see hair loss that involves the front of the neck down to the chest, the sides of the body, the backs of the thighs, and the top of the tail. The hair is excessively dry and brittle, and falls out easily. The exposed skin is dry, thick, puffy, and darkly pigmented. Some dogs develop secondary seborrhea.

Other signs of hypothyroidism include weight gain, intolerance to cold, a slow heart rate, absence of heat cycles, lethargy, and a variety of nonspecific symptoms that could be due to a number of other diseases. Hypothyroid dogs may develop blepharitis, corneal ulcers, deafness, adult-onset megaesophagus, chronic constipation, and anemia. Hypothyroidism has been found in association with dilated cardiomyopathy, strokes, coronary artery disease (rare in dogs), von Willebrand's disease, and myasthenia gravis. At least two-thirds of hypothyroid dogs have high serum cholesterol levels. Finding elevated serum cholesterol on routine blood screening warrants a workup for hypothyroidism. Behavior changes, including aggression, have also been noted in hypothyroid dogs, particularly German Shepherd Dogs.

The recommended blood test for screening purposes is the total T4. This test is indicated for dogs who have findings suggestive of hypothyroidism on physical examination. A normal T4 is fairly conclusive evidence that the dog does not have hypothyroidism. However, a low-normal or below-normal level does not mean the dog is hypothyroid, because concentrations below normal are common for many reasons other than hypothyroidism.

To avoid overdiagnosing and overtreating the disease, it is important to confirm the significance of a low T4 using a more accurate thyroid function test, such as the FT4 by equilibrium dialysis. Other blood tests are also available for diagnosing hypothyroidism. One is an assay for thyroglobulin autoantibodies; these autoantibodies are present in about 50 percent of dogs with autoimmune thyroiditis. This test must be sent to a special laboratory for analysis.

Treatment: Hypothyroidism is permanent, but can be effectively treated with daily or twice-daily thyroid hormone replacement using synthetic L-thyroxine (L-T4). The initial dose is based on the dog's weight. This should be adjusted for individual circumstances. Monitoring is done by physical examination and measuring the total T4. This must be done frequently, particularly early in the course of treatment. Hair loss and other signs of hypothyroidism usually reverse with treatment. A few dogs will need T3 supplementation as well.

The Orthopedic Foundation for Animals (OFA) maintains a hypothyroid registry to identify dogs as normal for breeding (see appendix D). A certificate and breed registry number is issued to all dogs found to be normal at 12 months of age, based on the results of FT4, cTSH, and thyroid autoantibody screening by an OFA-approved laboratory. Screening and registration is of value for dogs at risk of inherited hypothyroidism. If the test is positive, these dogs should not be used for breeding.

Michigan State University also has a thyroid registry and keeps statistics on thyroid function in dog breeds.

HYPERADRENOCORTICISM (CUSHING'S SYNDROME)

The adrenal glands are small, paired structures located just above each kidney. The outer zone of the adrenal gland (the cortex) is composed of glandular cells that manufacture and release corticosteroids. There are two types of corticosteroids: mineralocorticoids and glucocorticoids. Mineralocorticoids regulate electrolyte concentrations. Glucocorticoids reduce inflammation and suppress the immune system. Glucocorticoids are the type of corticosteroids used in nearly all steroid medications. The output of corticosteroids from the adrenal glands is controlled by the pituitary gland through the production of adrenocorticotropic hormone (ACTH).

Cushing's syndrome is a disease caused by long-term exposure to high levels of glucocorticosteroids, either manufactured by the body or given as medications.

Tumors of the pituitary gland that secrete ACTH stimulate the adrenal glands to produce large amounts of adrenal hormones. This sustained overproduction in response to pituitary stimulation accounts for 85 percent of cases of spontaneous Cushing's syndrome. The remaining 15 percent are caused by corticosteroid-producing tumors of the adrenal glands themselves.

Spontaneous Cushing's syndrome occurs primarily in middle-aged and older dogs, although dogs of all ages can be affected. Poodles, Boston Terriers, Dachshunds, and Boxers have the highest incidence.

A number of cases of Cushing's syndrome are caused by long-term therapy with drugs that contain corticosteroids. This is called *iatrogenic* Cushing's syndrome.

Excess cortisone can cause hair loss over the body in a symmetric pattern, with darkening of the underlying skin. The remaining hair is dry and dull. Small blackheads may be found on the abdomen. The abdomen is pendulous, distended, and pot-bellied. Other signs include lethargy with reduced activity, infertility in females, testicular atrophy and infertility in males, loss of muscle mass, and weakness. Excessive thirst and frequent urination also occur.

Dogs with hyperadrenocorticism lose body condition and develop severe problems such as hypertension, congestive heart failure, and diabetes mellitus. Other complications include increased susceptibility to infections, blood clots in the circulatory system (*thromboembolism*), and central nervous system signs including behavioral changes and seizures.

The diagnosis of Cushing's syndrome is based on laboratory tests, especially those that measure serum cortisol concentrations before and after the injection of ACTH and dexamethasone. Advances in CT *scans* and magnetic resonance imaging (*MRI*) techniques have made it possible to visualize small tumors of the pituitary and adrenal glands. Ultrasound can also be used to measure the size and symmetry of the adrenal glands.

Treatment: Spontaneous Cushing's syndrome is treated with mitotane. The medication acts on the adrenal cortex to selectively suppress the production of glucocorticoids. The drug protocol is complex and requires close veterinary monitoring. The prognosis is guarded. The average life span with medical treatment is about two years, although longer survival is possible. Benign and malignant tumors of the adrenal glands can be surgically removed in some cases. Iatrogenic Cushing's syndrome is often reversible if the causative drug can be tapered and, preferably, discontinued. If your dog is on long-term corticosteroids for a medical condition and develops signs of hyperadrenocorticism, your veterinarian may be able to reduce the dosage or find a substitute medication.

Anipryl (deprenyl) has been approved for treating spontaneous Cushing's syndrome of that originates in the pituitary gland. It appears to be effective in improving some of the symptoms of Cushing's syndrome, particularly the reduced activity level. Pituitary tumors often respond to radiation therapy, but the availability of equipment is limited and the cost is high.

HYPERESTROGENISM (ESTROGEN EXCESS)

Hyperestogenism is caused by the overproduction of estrogen from the ovaries or testicles. In females, it is associated with granulosa cell tumors and cysts of the ovaries. In males, it is caused by testicular tumors. These subjects are discussed in chapter 18.

Signs of hyperestrogenism are feminization with enlargement of the mammary glands and nipples in both sexes, enlargement of the vulva and clitoris in females, and the development of a pendulous prepuce in males. Females may have irregular heat cycles, false pregnancy, and pyometra.

Skin and coat changes begin in the perineum around the genital areas and proceed to the underside of the abdomen. Typically, the hair becomes dry and brittle, falls out easily, and fails to regrow. Later the skin becomes darkly pigmented. A dry, flaky seborrhea often

In this dog with hyperestrogenism, excess estrogen causes enlargement of the vulva.

develops, particularly in females. The coat and skin changes follow a symmetrical pattern.

The cause of the hyperestrogenism should be determined by physical examination, ultrasound, endocrine blood tests, and, if necessary, laparoscopy or exploratory surgery.

Treatment: Hyperestrogenism in both sexes responds well to neutering.

Growth Hormone–Responsive Alopecia

This is a rare cause of bilateral symmetrical hair loss. Growth hormone (somatotropin) is secreted by the pituitary gland. In some cases, for unknown reasons, the pituitary does not manufacture or release adequate concentrations of growth hormone, resulting in coat and skin changes similar to those described for hyerperestrogenism. Symptoms generally appear at puberty, but may occur at any age.

This disease has been observed in Pomeranians, Chow Chows, Poodles, Samoyeds, Keeshonds, and American Water Spaniels. It occurs predominantly in male dogs.

Treatment: It is important to exclude other hormone-dependent causes of hair loss. The treatment of choice for growth hormone–responsive alopecia is neutering. If the coat does not improve, the dog may respond to growth hormone administered subcutaneously three time a week for four to six weeks. Dogs receiving growth hormone must be monitored for the development of diabetes mellitus.

Hypoestrogenism (Estrogen Deficiency)

This mild skin condition occurs in some older females who were spayed as puppies. There is gradual loss of hair due to lack of new growth over the undersurface of the belly and around the vulva. Later, it involves the lower chest and neck. The skin becomes soft, smooth, and nearly hairless. Affected females shed very little, do not collect much dirt, and make excellent house pets.

Treatment: This is not a serious disease and can be left untreated. If treatment is desired, estrogen can be given under veterinary supervision. The hormone must be given at least twice a week to affect hair growth.

Note that estrogens may cause bone marrow suppression in dogs. This can be fatal if not recognized in time. Accordingly, all dogs receiving estrogen must be monitored with frequent blood counts.

Traction Alopecia

Hair loss with baldness occurs in dogs who have had barrettes, rubber bands, and other devices used to tie up their hair. When these accessories are applied too tightly or for too long a time, traction on the hair effects the hair follicles, causing the roots to stop growing. This results in an area of hair loss that may be permanent.

Treatment: The only treatment for a permanent bald spot is to remove it surgically. This would only be done for cosmetic reasons. Alopecia can be prevented by using hair ties loosely and for short periods—or preferably, not using them at all.

ACANTHOSIS NIGRANS

Acanthosis nigrans literally means "thick, black skin." Primary acanthosis nigrans is seen principally in Dachshunds. The age of onset is less than 1 year. The exact cause is unknown. Secondary acanthosis nigrans occurs in all breeds in association with endocrine skin diseases, itchy skin diseases, and obesity.

In Dachshunds, the disease affects the armpit folds, the ears, and the skin folds of the groin. As the disease progresses, you will see extreme black pigmentation and a greasy, rancid discharge on the surface of the skin. Secondary bacterial infections are common. Eventually the disease extends over a considerable area, covering the brisket and legs. This disease causes considerable distress to the dog and her owner.

Treatment: Primary acanthosis should be treated by a veterinarian. The disease is controllable but not curable. Most dogs can be kept comfortable with potent topical (and occasionally, oral) corticosteroids. Melatonin and vitamin E have been effective in some cases. Antibiotics are used to treat secondary skin infections. Use antiseborrhea shampoos to remove excess oil and bacteria (see *Seborrhea*, page 150). Weight reduction to reduce skin fold friction is desirable.

Secondary acanthosis nigrans responds to treatment of the underlying skin problem.

VITILIGO

Vitiligo is a condition in which pigment is lost from the skin and hair of the nose, lips, face, and eyelids. Black pigment is present early in life in affected dogs, but it gradually fades to a chocolate brown or even to white. There do not appear to be health problems related to the loss of pigment. Rottweilers are one of the breeds in which this problem is seen.

The exact cause of vitiligo in dogs has not yet been determined, but it is believed it may have a genetic predisposition and/or be an *autoimmune* problem.

Treatment: There is no definitive treatment, though omega-3 fatty acids and antioxidants such as vitamin C may help with this problem.

ZINC-RESPONSIVE DERMATOSIS

Zinc is a trace mineral required for hair growth and maintenance of the skin. A deficiency of zinc causes thinning of the hair and a scaly, crusty dermatitis over the face, most noticeable on the nose and around the eyes, ears, and mouth. Crusts also appear over pressure points such as the elbows and hocks. The feet become callused and crack easily.

Siberian Huskies, Alaskan Huskies, Doberman Pinschers, Great Danes, and Alaskan Malamutes are predisposed to zinc-responsive dermatosis. A genetic defect involving zinc absorption from the intestines has been identified in Siberian Huskies, Alaskan Huskies, and Malamutes. In these breeds the disease may occur even when the dog is eating a well-balanced diet.

Diets high in fiber and calcium may precipitate zinc deficiency by binding zinc in the gastrointestinal tract. A zinc deficiency syndrome occurs in large-breed puppies fed diets that are oversupplemented with vitamins and minerals (particularly calcium). A closely related condition has been observed in dogs fed dry, generic dog foods that are deficient in zinc.

Treatment: The diagnosis is confirmed by the response to therapy. Regardless of the cause, the dermatosis responds rapidly to zinc sulfate (10 mg per kilo of body weight, daily) or zinc methionine (1.7 mg per kilo of body weight, daily). Improvement begins almost at once. Affected Alaskan Malmutes, Alaskan Huskies, and Siberian Huskies usually require zinc supplements for life.

Puppies with an acquired zinc deficiency respond to zinc supplements and a nutritionally balanced diet.

Crusty dermatitis over the face of a Siberian Husky, caused by zinc deficiency.

COLOR MUTANT ALOPECIA (BLUE DOBERMAN SYNDROME)

This hereditary skin disease is seen most often in fawn and blue-coated Doberman Pinschers, and occasionally in blue Great Danes, blue Newfoundlands, Chow Chows, Whippets, Italian Greyhounds, and other breeds with dilute coat colors.

Affected dogs are born with a healthy hair coat. At 6 months of age or later, the coat becomes thin, brittle, and dry and takes on a moth-eaten appearance. The skin becomes rough and scaly. Blackheads, *papules*, and *pustules* appear on the involved areas. Some blue Dobermans do not manifest the disease before 3 years of age.

Treatment: There is no cure. Treatment is directed toward relieving the surface condition, which involves shampoos that rehydrate the skin, remove scales, and flush the hair follicles. These must be prescribed by your veterinarian. Because the affected hair is fragile and comes out easily, vigorous brushing and the use of harsh or inappropriate shampoos aggravates the problem and should be avoided.

The coat mutation has a genetic basis. Affected dogs should not be bred.

BLACK HAIR FOLLICLE DYSPLASIA

This syndrome shows up very early in a dog's life and may manifest as complete lack of hair in areas with black coloration. Only the areas that would have had black hair are affected. This condition is most often seen in Papillons and Bearded Collies, but is not common in either breed. It can occur in dogs of any breed and in mixed breed dogs.

Treatment: At present there is no treatment.

SEBACEOUS ADENITIS

This is an inherited skin disease controlled by an autosomal recessive gene that adversely affects the development of sebaceous glands. Predisposed breeds include the Standard Poodle, Akita, Samoyed, and Vizsla. Signs usually appear in the first four years of life, but may develop later.

Longhaired breeds such as the Standard Poodle have areas of symmetrical hair loss involving the muzzle, top of the head, ear flaps, and the top of the neck, trunk, and tail. The skin develops a scaly seborrhea, and in advanced cases a bacterial infection of the hair follicles. Shorthaired breeds such as the Vizsla have circular areas of hair loss with scaling on the head, ears, trunk, and legs.

Treatment: The diagnosis is confirmed by skin biopsy. Treatment involves corticosteroids, Accutane (isotretinoin), and a number of antiseborrhea and antifollicular drugs and shampoos that can be prescribed by your veterinarian.

The institute for Genetic Disease Control in Animals maintains a registry for sebaceous adenitis in Standard Poodles (see appendix D). OFA has taken over much of the sebaceous adenitis data and registry. Dogs with sebaceous adenitis and those identified as carriers should not be bred.

Seborrhea

Seborrhea is a condition in which flakes of dead skin are shed from the epidermis and hair follicles. These flakes may be dry and dandrufflike, or oily and greasy. Oily seborrhea is due to excessive production of sebum by the sebaceous glands. Sebum is responsible for the rancid doggy odor that accompanies oily seborrhea.

Primary and secondary seborrhea are two different diseases.

Primary Seborrhea

This common disease is seen most often in American Cocker Spaniels, English Springer Spaniels, West Highland White Terriers, Basset Hounds, Irish Setters, German Shepherds, Labrador Retrievers, Chinese Shar-Pei, and other breeds. Affected dogs may have dry flaky skin, greasy scaly skin, or a combination of both. The flakes of dry seborrhea are easy to lift off the skin. The scales of oily seborrhea stick to the hair. In oily seborrhea the hair follicles can become plugged and infected, resulting in the development of folliculitis (see page 158).

The elbows, hocks, front of the neck down to the chest, and hair along the borders of the ears are commonly involved. With oily seborrhea, wax may accumulate in the ear canals, producing a condition called ceruminous otitis.

Treatment: Primary seborrhea is incurable but treatable. Therapy is directed toward controlling scale formation using shampoos and rinses. A number of commercial antiseborrheic products are available. The choice of shampoos and rinses and frequency of application vary with the specific problem, and should be determined by your veterinarian.

For mild dry flaking, moisturizing hypoallergenic shampoos and rinses that contain no dyes, fragrances, or other added ingredients can help rehydrate the skin. These products can be used frequently without causing harm.

For severe dry flaking, shampoos containing sulfur and salicylic acid are recommended to remove scales. For oily seborrhea, shampoos containing coal tar are effective and retard further scale production. Benzoyl peroxide shampoos have excellent hair-pore flushing activity and aid in removing greasy scales that adhere to hair shafts.

Therapeutic shampooing may be more effective when preceded by a warm water shampoo. Rinse thoroughly and follow with the medicated shampoo. Leave on for 15 minutes or as directed, then rinse thoroughly.

Systemic antibiotics are used to treat folliculitis and other skin infections. A short course of oral corticosteroids may be prescribed during periods of severe itching. Dietary supplements containing omega-3 essential fatty acids derived from fish oil are said to be beneficial for seborrhea and certainly can do no harm.

Secondary Seborrhea

This condition occurs when some other skin disease triggers the seborrheic process. Diseases often associated with secondary seborrhea include scabies, demodectic mange, canine atopy, food hypersensitivity dermatitis, flea allergy dermatitis, hypothyroidism, hormone-related skin diseases, color mutant alopecia, pemphigus foliaceus, and others. *Primary seborrhea should not be diagnosed until secondary seborrhea has been ruled out.*

Treatment: Secondary seborrhea is managed in the same way as primary seborrhea. It usually disappears with control of the underlying skin disease. Always look for a primary cause when faced with a dog with seborrhea.

RINGWORM

Ringworm is a fungal infection that invades the hair and hair follicles. Most cases are caused by *Microsporum canis*. Ringworm in dogs is primarily a disease of puppies and young adults. Typical areas of involvement are the face, ears, paws, and tail.

The dry, flaky skin of secondary seborrhea, triggered by long-standing atopic dermatitis.

Ringworm on the muzzle of a Cocker Spaniel.

Ringworm is transmitted by spores in the soil and by contact with the infected hair of dogs and cats, typically found on carpets, brushes, combs, toys, and furniture. Humans can acquire ringworm from pets, and vice versa. Children are especially susceptible.

Ringworm takes its name from its classic appearance: a spreading circle of hair loss with scaly skin at the center and a red ring at the periphery. Note, however, that many cases of circular hair loss thought to be ringworm are actually localized demodectic mange or hair follicle infection. Black fly bites in the groin area in the spring will also have this ringed appearance. Atypical ringworm is common, with irregular areas of hair loss associated with scaling and crusting.

Ringworm by itself is not an itchy skin condition, but secondary bacterial infection with scabs and crusts can provoke licking and scratching. Ringworm can invade the nails. This results in nails that are dry, cracked, brittle, and deformed.

A kerion is a round, raised, nodular lesion that results from a ringworm fungus in combination with a bacterial infection that invades the roots of the hair. In most cases the fungus is *Microsporun gypseum* and the bacteria is a type of *Staphylococcus*. Kerions occur on the face and limbs. Therapy involves treating the bacterial component, as described in *Folliculitis* (page 158).

Ringworm mimics many other skin diseases, so an accurate diagnosis is essential. Hair infected by *Microsporum canis* may fluoresce green under an ultraviolet light (called a Wood's light), but false positive and false negative results are common. Ultraviolet light is used as a screening tool only. Microscopic examination of hairs plucked from areas that fluoresce can sometimes provide an immediate diagnosis, but the most reliable method of diagnosing ringworm is by fungal culture. Some hairs from the abnormal area are plucked and placed on a special medium to grow out any fungus that is present. Results may take up to two weeks.

Treatment: Although mild cases resolve spontaneously in three to four months, all cases of ringworm should be treated to prevent progression and spread to other pets and people in the household.

With only one or two areas of involvement, apply a topical antifungal agent containing miconazole 2 percent cream or 1 percent lotion twice a day in the direction of the lay of the hair. Continue treatment until the skin is healed. Be ready to treat the dog for at least four to six weeks.

When several sites are involved, repeat the treatment just described, and add an antifungal shampoo containing miconazole or another shampoo labeled for the treatment of ringworm. Continue to treat for two weeks beyond apparent cure. Longhaired dogs may need to be shaved for effective treatment.

In difficult cases your veterinarian may prescribe an antifungal drug called Griseofulvin. Ketoconazole, itraconazole, and other drugs of the imidazole group are also effective, but may not be approved by the FDA for treating ringworm in dogs. Griseofulvin, itraconazole, and ketoconazole have serious possible side effects and should not be given to pregnant bitches because they may cause birth defects. Antifungal drugs require close veterinary counseling and supervision.

Prevention: Ringworm spores can survive for up to one year and should be eliminated from the environment. Discard the dog's bedding. Sterilize grooming equipment in a 1:10 dilution of bleach. Vacuum the carpets at least weekly to remove infected hair. Mop and wash hard surfaces (floors, countertops, dog runs) using diluted bleach. Technical Captan can be used as a spray in a dilution of 1:200 in water to treat a kennel.

Kerions are deep-seated skin infections caused by a ringworm fungus in combination with a bacteria.

There is a vaccine for cats for ringworm, primarily used in catteries with longstanding problems, but nothing for dogs at this time.

Strict hand-washing precautions are necessary to prevent human contamination. Children should not be allowed to handle pets with ringworm. Wash contaminated clothing and fabrics with bleach.

DEMODECTIC MANGE

Demodectic mange is caused by a tiny mite, *Demodex canis,* too small to be seen with the naked eye. Nearly all dogs acquire mange mites from their mother during the first few days of life. These mites are considered normal skin fauna when present in small numbers. They produce disease only when an abnormal immune system allows their numbers to get out of control. This occurs primarily in puppies and in adult dogs with lowered immunity. A high incidence of mange in certain bloodlines suggests that some purebred dogs are born with an inherited immune susceptibility.

Demodectic mange occurs in localized and generalized forms. The diagnosis is made by taking multiple skin scrapings and looking for the mites. Demodectic mites are usually easy to find.

Localized Demodectic Mange

This disease occurs in dogs under 1 year of age. The appearance of the skin is similar to that of ringworm. The principal sign is thinning hair around the eyelids, lips, and corners of the mouth, and occasionally on the trunk, the legs, and the feet. The thinning progresses to patches of ragged hair loss about 1 inch (2.5 cm) in diameter. In some cases the skin becomes red, scaly, and infected.

Localized mange usually heals spontaneously in six to eight weeks, but may wax and wane for several months. If more than five patches are present, the

Localized demodectic mange with moth-eaten hair loss around the dog's right eye and on the forehead. The skin is red and inflamed.

disease could be progressing to the generalized form. This occurs in approximately 10 percent of cases.

Treatment: A topical ointment containing either benzoyl peroxide gel (OxyDex or Pyoben), or a mild topical preparation used to treat ear mites can be massaged into affected areas once a day. This may shorten the course of the disease. The medication should be rubbed with the lay of the hair to minimize further hair loss. Treatment may cause the area to look worse for the first two to three weeks.

There is no evidence that treating localized mange prevents the disease from becoming generalized. The dog should be checked again in four weeks.

Generalized Demodectic Mange

Dogs with the generalized disease develop patches of hair loss on the head, legs, and trunk. These patches coalesce to form large areas of hair loss. The hair follicles become plugged with mites and skin scales. The skin breaks down to form sores, crusts, and draining tracts, presenting a most disabling problem. Some cases are a continuation of localized mange; others develop spontaneously in older dogs.

When generalized demodectic mange develops in dogs under 1 year of age, there is a 30 to 50 percent chance that the puppy will recover spontaneously. It is uncertain whether medical treatment accelerates this recovery.

In dogs older than 1 year, a spontaneous cure is unlikely but the outlook for improvement with medical treatment has increased dramatically in recent decades. Most dogs can be cured with intense therapy. Most of the remaining cases can be controlled if the owner is willing to commit the necessary time and expense.

Treatment: Generalized demodectic mange must be treated under close veterinary supervision. Therapy involves the use of medicated shampoos and dips to remove surface scales and kill mites. Shave or clip hair from all affected areas to facilitate access to the skin.

The FDA protocol involves first bathing the dog with a medicated benzoyl peroxide shampoo (OxyDex or Pyoben) to remove skin scales. Allow the shampoo to remain on the dog for 10 minutes before rinsing it off. Completely dry the dog.

Generalized demodectic mange with extensive areas of hair loss, crusts, and sores. Treatment takes a long time but is usually successful.

Amitraz (brand name Mitaban) currently is the only miticide approved by the FDA for use on dogs. Make up an amitraz dip by adding Mitaban to water, according to the directions on the label. Be sure to treat the dog in a well-ventilated area and wear rubber or plastic gloves to keep the chemical off your skin. Sponge on the dip over a 10-minute period, allowing the dog's feet to soak in the rinse. Allow the dip to dry on the dog. Repeat every two weeks, or as directed by your veterinarian. Try to keep the dog from getting her coat and feet wet between dips. Continue this protocol for 60 days beyond the day when skin scrapings first became negative.

Side effects of Mitaban include drowsiness, lethargy, vomiting, diarrhea, dizziness, and a staggering gait. Puppies are more susceptible than adults to these effects. If such a reaction occurs, immediately remove the miticide by thoroughly rinsing the coat and skin.

If the FDA protocol is not completely effective, your veterinarian may suggest an alternative treatment. Oral milbemycin and ivermectin have been used as *off-label* treatments, and require close cooperation between your veterinarian and you since they are not officially approved for treating this problem.

Secondary skin infections should be treated with antibiotics, based on culture and sensitivity tests. Corticosteroids, often used to control severe itching, lower the dog's immunity to the mites and should not be used to treat this disease.

Because of an inherited immune susceptibility, dogs who recover from generalized demodectic mange should not be bred.

Pressure Sores (Calluses)

A callus is a gray, hairless, wrinkled pad of thickened skin overlying a bony pressure point. It is caused by lying on a hard surface. Calluses tend to occur in

A callus on the outside of the back leg, caused by lying on a cement surface.

heavy dogs and dogs who are kenneled on cement floors. The most common site is the elbow. Other sites are the outside of the hocks, the buttocks, and the sides of the legs.

If the callus goes unchecked, the surface breaks down, forming an ulcer or abscess that can become infected. This then becomes a most difficult problem to treat.

Treatment: Provide the dog with a soft sleeping surface, such as a dog mattress or foam pad covered with fabric, to take pressure off the callus. An infected ulcer over bone must be treated by a veterinarian.

Pyoderma (Skin Infections)

Bacterial infections often develop in skin that has been traumatized and abraded by excessive rubbing, chewing, and scratching. Pyoderma is therefore a frequent complication of other skin diseases, particularly those that cause intense itching. Antibiotics and medicated shampoos may be included in treatment plans.

PUPPY DERMATITIS (IMPETIGO AND ACNE)

Impetigo and acne are mild surface skin infections that occur in puppies under 1 year of age. Impetigo presents with pus-filled blisters on the hairless parts of the abdomen and the groin. The blisters rupture, leaving thin brown crusts. Puppies housed in unsanitary quarters are most likely to be infected.

Acne occurs in puppies 3 months of age and older. It can be identified by purplish red *pustules* and blackheads that come to a head and drain *pus*. These lesions are found on the chin and lower lip, and occasionally in the genital area, perineum, and groin. Blockage of hair follicles by skin scales and sebum

Pyoderma of the side of the face, caused by excessive scratching. The dog has a severe itchy ear disorder. A hot spot would have a similar appearance.

is a predisposing cause. Acne is more common among Doberman Pinschers, Golden Retrievers, Boxers, Great Danes, and Bulldogs, but can occur in any puppy.

Treatment: Topical therapy for impetigo and mild acne involves bathing the puppy with a benzoyl peroxide shampoo (OxyDex or Pyoben) twice a week for two to three weeks. Correct any predisposing causes, such as unsanitary puppy quarters.

Acne is often a deep-seated skin infection and may not respond to topical therapy alone. Your veterinarian may add a course of oral antibiotics that are effective against *Staphylococcus*. Acne usually resolves spontaneously at sexual maturity.

FOLLICULITIS

Folliculitis is an infection that begins in the hair follicles. In mild folliculitis you typically will find many small *pustules* with a hair shaft protruding through the center of each. Dogs with mild cases may have rings of scales around the follicles. Once the follicles become infected, the infection can bore deeply into the dermis, forming large pustules and *furuncles* that rupture, discharge pus, and crust over. Draining sinus tracts develop in cases of deep folliculitis.

These small, pimplelike pustules on the abdomen are typical of folliculitis.

Folliculitis usually involves the undersurface of the body, especially the armpits, abdomen, and groin. A condition called Schnauzer comedo syndrome is common in Miniature Schnauzers. Dogs suffering from this disease have many large blackheads running down the middle of their back.

Folliculitis often occurs as a secondary complication to scabies, demodectic mange, seborrhea, hormonal skin disease, and other problems. Some cases are caused by vigorous grooming, which traumatizes the hair follicles.

Treatment: It is important to identify and treat the underlying cause as well as the folliculitis.

Mild cases should be treated as described for acne. Deep folliculitis requires vigorous topical and systemic therapy. Clip away the hair from infected skin on longhaired dogs (don't clip shorthaired dogs), and bathe the dog twice a day for 10 days with a povidone-iodine shampoo such as Betadine or one with chlorhexidine such as Nolvasan. As the skin infection improves, switch to a benzoyl peroxide shampoo such as Stiff OxyDex, OxyDex, or Pyoben, used once or twice a week. Continue until healing is complete.

The dog should also be placed on an oral antibiotic selected on the basis of culture and sensitivity tests. Continue oral antibiotics for six to eight weeks, including at least two weeks beyond apparent cure. Treatment failures occur when antibiotics are stopped too soon or used at too low a dosage. The prolonged use of corticosteroids should be avoided in dogs with folliculitis.

SKIN FOLD PYODERMA

When skin surfaces rub together, the skin becomes wet and inflamed. This creates ideal conditions for bacterial growth. An infection of the skin folds can take a variety of forms. It occurs as lip fold pyoderma in spaniels, setters, St. Bernards, and other breeds with heavy lips; as face fold pyoderma in Pekingese and Chinese Shar-Pei; as vulvar fold pyoderma in obese females;

An English Bulldog with skin fold pyoderma of the neck.

and as tail fold pyoderma in breeds with corkscrew tails, such as Bulldogs, Boston Terriers, and Pugs.

The signs of skin fold pyoderma anywhere on the body are the same: irritation and inflammation of the skin. The moist skin also gives off a foul odor.

Treatment: The most effective treatment is to eliminate the skin fold by corrective surgery. When this is not feasible, the condition can be controlled by cleansing the infected skin fold with a benzoyl peroxide shampoo such as Sulf OxyDex, OxyDex, or Pyoben. Dry the skin and then apply OxyDex or Pyoben gel twice a day for 10 to 14 days. An antibiotic-steroid cream (such as Panolog) can be used twice a day for two or three days to control inflammation and itching. There are also medical wipes available for cleaning the skin folds.

Once the infection has been successfully treated, use benzoyl peroxide gel as needed to prevent recurrence. Medicated powders applied to cleaned and dried areas will also assist in controlling this condition.

Acute Moist Dermatitis (Hot Spots)

A hot spot is a warm, painful, swollen patch of skin 1 to 4 inches (2.5 to 10 cm) across that exudes pus and gives off a foul odor. Hair in the area is lost rapidly. The infection progresses when the dog licks and chews the site. These circular patches appear suddenly and enlarge quickly, often within a matter of hours.

Hot spots can occur anywhere on the body, often in more than one spot. One very typical location is under the ear flaps in large breeds with heavy, hairy ears, such as Newfoundlands and Golden Retrievers. Hot spots occur most often in breeds with heavy coats, and tend to appear just before shedding, when moist, dead hair is trapped next to the skin. Fleas, mites, and other skin parasites, skin allergies, irritant skin diseases, ear and anal gland infections, and neglected grooming are other factors that can initiate the itch-scratch-itch cycle.

Treatment: Hot spots are extremely painful. The dog usually will need to be sedated or anesthetized for the initial treatment. Your veterinarian will clip away hair to expose the hot spot, then gently cleanse the skin with a dilute povidone-iodine shampoo (Betadine) or a chlorhexidine shampoo (Nolvasan) and allow the skin to dry. An antibiotic steroid cream or powder (Panolog or Neocort) is then applied twice a day for 10 to 14 days. Oral antibiotics are usually prescribed. Predisposing skin problems must be treated as well.

Your veterinarian may also prescribe a short course of oral corticosteroids to control severe itching. Prevent the dog from traumatizing the area by using an Elizabethan collar or a BiteNot collar (see page 5).

In hot, humid weather, always be sure to dry your heavy-coated dog thoroughly after bathing her and after she swims. Otherwise, the conditions are perfect for a hot spot to develop.

CELLULITIS AND SKIN ABSCESS

Cellulitis is an infection involving the skin and subcutaneous tissue. Most cases are caused by puncture wounds, deep scratches, bites, and lacerations. Cellulitis can often be prevented by properly treating wounds, as described in *Wounds*, page 42.

An area affected by cellulitis will be tender to pressure, feel hotter than normal, not be as soft as it would normally be, and appear redder than normal. As infection spreads out from the wound, you may feel tender cords beneath the skin, which are swollen lymphatic channels. Regional lymph nodes in the groin, armpit, or neck may enlarge to contain the infection.

A skin *abscess* is a localized pocket of pus beneath the epidermis. Pimples, *pustules, furuncles*, and boils are examples of small skin abscesses. A large abscess feels like fluid under pressure.

Treatment: Localize the infection by clipping away the hair. Apply warm soaks for 15 minutes three times a day. Saline soaks (1 teaspoon, 10 g, of table salt to 1 quart, 1 l, of water), or Epsom soaks (¼ cup, 33 g, of Epsom salts to 1

This dog has a skin infection with cellulitis and draining abscesses due to staphylococcus.

quart, 1 l of water) are useful. Splinters and foreign bodies beneath the skin are a continuing source of infection and must be removed.

Pimples, pustules, furuncles, boils, and abscesses that do not drain spontaneously may need to be lanced by your veterinarian. If there is a sizeable cavity, your veterinarian may ask you to flush it once or twice a day using a dilute antiseptic surgical solution such as chlorhexidine until healing is complete. Your veterinarian may place a drain in a large abscess to help speed healing.

Oral and injectable antibiotics may be prescribed to treat wound infections, cellulitis, abscess, and other *pyodermas*.

Juvenile Pyoderma (Puppy Strangles)

Juvenile pyoderma occurs in puppies 4 to 16 weeks of age and often affects several puppies in the same litter. It can be recognized by a sudden swelling of the lips, eyelids, ear flaps, or face, along with the rapid development of *pustules*, crusts, skin erosions, and ulcers. The lymph nodes beneath the chin may become swollen and enlarged. These pups are quite sick and must be seen promptly by a veterinarian.

Although bacteria have been implicated in some cases of puppy strangles, this is the exception rather than the rule. Most cases are considered to be an inflammatory immune process of unknown cause.

Treatment: Apply warm, moist packs for 15 minutes three times a day. Further treatment involves the use of oral corticosteroids and antibiotics for 14 days. Antibiotics alone are not effective.

Do not attempt to express the pus from the sores. This increases the likelihood of scarring.

Puppy strangles can cause pustules and swollen lymph nodes beneath the chin.

MYCETOMA

A mycetoma is a tumorlike mass caused by several species of fungi that enter the body through wounds. This condition typically appears as a lump on the feet or legs beneath the skin, with a tract to the surface that drains granular material. The granules are white, yellow, or black, depending on the type of fungus involved. The condition resembles a chronic abscess that resists healing, despite prolonged treatment with antibiotics.

Treatment: Complete surgical removal is the treatment of choice. This is not always possible. Some of the newer antifungal drugs (such as ketoconazole and itraconazole) show promise in treating difficult cases. Treatment must be continued for at least two months beyond apparent cure.

INTERDIGITAL CYSTS AND PODODERMATITIS

An interdigital cyst is an inflammatory reaction between the toes, and not a true cyst. It appears as a swelling that may open and drain pus. The causes are numerous, and include trauma, contact irritants, foreign bodies such as thorns and plant awns, and the bites of ticks and other external parasites.

Treatment: Treatment may involve long-term antibiotics. Try to remove any primary cause, such as a foreign body. Warm compresses may be helpful; alternatively, soak the affected feet in a medicated solution of betadine or nolvasan for 5 to 10 minutes. Further diagnostics may be needed to find the underlying cause.

ACTINOMYCOSIS AND NOCARDIOSIS

These bacterial skin infections, acquired by contact with infected soil, generally occur in hunting dogs. Both types of bacteria can produce a systemic infection that involves the lymph nodes, brain, chest cavity, lungs, and bones.

This interdigital cyst has ruptured and formed a draining tract.

Subcutaneous abscesses with draining sinus tracts appear at the site of a puncture wound or break in the skin, usually in the head and neck area. The wound discharge often resembles tomato soup and/or contains material that looks like sulfa granules. Norcardiosis can be associated with gingivitis and mouth ulcers.

Treatment: The diagnosis is made by culturing the wound drainage. Treatment involves surgically opening infected abscesses and draining body cavities. Norcardiosis responds to sulfa drugs; actinomycosis to penicillin. Prolonged antibiotic treatment is necessary. If the infection has spread deeper than the skin, the dog may not survive.

Autoimmune and Immune-Mediated Skin Diseases

Autoimmune skin diseases are caused by a specific antibody directed against a normal component of the skin. The antibody (called an autoantibody) destroys the cohesiveness of skin cells, resulting in the development of *blebs*, *pustules*, and other skin changes typical of the disease. Pemphigus is an example of an autoimmune skin disease.

Immune-mediated skin diseases (exemplified by lupus erythematosus) are systemic diseases in which the immune reaction may be stimulated by an outside influence, such as a drug. The autoantibody reacts with the *antigen* (the substance that stimulates this reaction), and the two form a complex that is deposited in various locations in the body, including the kidneys, the blood vessel walls, and the skin. The deposited complexes trigger an inflammatory response that destroys the tissue.

PEMPHIGUS COMPLEX

In pemphigus, the autoantibody is directed against the walls of the skin cells. These cells lose their ability to remain attached and separate, forming *blebs*, *vesicles*, and *pustules*. The exact stimulus for the pemphigus antibody is unknown. Four types of pemphigus are seen in dogs. All are best diagnosed by skin biopsy. Serologic blood tests are helpful, but false positives and false negatives are common.

Pemphigus foliaceus is the most common autoimmune skin disease of dogs. It generally occurs in dogs 2 to 7 years of age. Predisposed breeds include Akitas, Bearded Collies, Newfoundlands, Chow Chows, Dachshunds, Doberman Pinschers, Finnish Spitz, and Schipperkes.

Pemphigus foliaceus is a pustular dermatitis that begins with red skin patches that involve the face and ears, but often becomes generalized. The patches rapidly progress to blisters and pustules, which then become dry,

This Akita has pemphigus foliaceus, showing extensive face involvement.

yellow crusts. The crusts adhere to the underlying skin and hair. Areas of depigmentation occur as the disease progresses.

Pemphigus foliaceus can involve the feet, causing thickening and cracking of the foot pads, and pain when the dog puts weight on her feet. In some cases the disease involves only the foot pads. Pemphigus foliaceus should be considered whenever a dog with a painful limp has thickened or cracked foot pads.

Pemphigus erythematosus is a localized variant of pemphigus foliaceus with involvement limited to the face, head, and foot pads. Collies and German Shepherds appear to be at greatest risk. The disease is easily confused with discoid lupus erythematosus (see page 166).

Pemphigus vulgaris is an uncommon disease in which blisters and ulcers form at the junction of the skin and the mucous membranes. It involves the lips, nostrils, and eyelids. It can also attack the nailbeds, with subsequent shedding of the nails.

Pemphigus vegetans is an extremely rare form of pemphigus vulgaris. It is characterized by flat-topped pustules in the skin folds of the armpits and groin. Characteristically, the lesions heal with wartlike growths.

Treatment: There is no cure for any form of pemphigus, but more than 50 percent of dogs with pemphigus foliaceus and pemphigus erythematosus can be kept relatively free of symptoms using corticosteroids alone, or corticosteroids in combination with immunosuppressive drugs such as cyclophosphamide, azathioprine, or chlorambucil. Treatment is life long. Sunscreen applied to the depigmented skin of the nose helps to prevent ultraviolet injury (see *Collie Nose*, page 224).

Pemphigus vulgaris and pemphigus vegetans respond less well to treatment.

BULLOUS PEMPHIGOID

This is an uncommon autoimmune skin disease in which blisters, *bullae*, and ulcerative erosions are found on the skin of the trunk, groin, armpits, and abdomen. Collies and Doberman Pinschers appear to be predisposed. This disease also affects the foot pads, and 80 percent of cases ultimately involve the mouth.

Treatment: Treatment is similar to that for pemphigus foliaceus (page 164). The outlook for improvement is poor.

LUPUS ERYTHEMATOSUS COMPLEX

Lupus erythematosus is an immune-mediated disease in which the antigen-antibody complex lodges in the small vessels of many organs, including the skin. The exact stimulus for the antigen-antibody reaction is unknown. Two types of lupus occur in dogs.

Systemic Lupus Erythematosus

This is a complex disease affecting several body parts, including the skin, kidneys, heart, and joints. The first indication may be a stilted gait or lameness that wanders from joint to joint. Eventually, the lungs, nervous system, lymph nodes, and spleen may be involved.

Skin involvement is especially evident about the face and over the nose and muzzle, but may be found elsewhere. An erosive dermatitis, characterized by *vesicles* and *pustules*, develops in these areas, and is followed by crusting, oozing, and hair loss. The mucous membranes of the mouth are often involved. The foot pads can become thickened and ulcerated and may eventually shed. Anemia and bleeding problems may develop. Secondary pyoderma is a major cause of death.

The diagnosis is difficult, but is aided by a skin biopsy and an antinuclear antibody (ANA) test. This test is positive in 90 percent of cases.

Treatment: Treatment depends on what organs are involved. Most cases require chemotherapy. Secondary pyoderma must be treated aggressively. The outlook for long-term control is guarded.

Discoid Lupus Erythematosus

This is the second most common autoimmune skin disease, after pemphigus foliaceus. It is considered to be a milder form of systemic lupus and is limited to the face. Depigmentation of the nose is usually followed by the appearance of open sores and crusts. Collies, German Shepherds, Siberian Huskies, Shetland Sheepdogs, Brittanys, and German Shorthaired Pointers are most often affected. The typical appearance and location of discoid lupus, and the absence of other sites of skin involvement, make the diagnosis almost certain.

Ulceration of the skin of the nose, with open sores and crusts, is typical of discoid lupus erythematosus.

Treatment: Discoid lupus can be successfully managed with oral and/or topical corticosteroids. Oral vitamin E in a dose of 400 IU given every 12 hours, two hours before or after meals, is reported to be beneficial. Apply topical sunscreens during periods of exposure to sunlight (see *Collie Nose,* page 224). Sunblock may help as a preventative measure, as well. Ultraviolet injury severely aggravates this problem.

TOXIC EPIDERMAL NECROLYSIS

Toxic epidermal necrolysis is a rare, ulcerative skin disease that appears to be triggered by various drugs, internal cancers, infections, and unknown factors. *Blebs,* ulcers, and erosions develop suddenly and progress rapidly. The mouth and foot pads are frequently involved.

This is an extremely painful skin disease. The dog is severely depressed and refuses to eat. The death rate approaches 30 percent.

Treatment: Treatment involves stopping all suspect medications and correcting any underlying cause. Corticosteroids, intravenous fluids, and antibiotics are required during the acute phase of illness to support the circulation. Recovery takes two to three weeks.

ERYTHEMA MULTIFORME

Erythema multiforme is an acute eruption of the skin and mucous membranes. The characteristic skin lesion is a round or oval targetlike skin eruption with a red rim and central blanching. There is an association with drugs, infections, tumors, and connective tissue diseases. Erythema multiforme tends to be less severe than toxic epidermal necrolysis.

Treatment: Many cases recover spontaneously, especially if the predisposing cause can be found and corrected. Immunosuppressive medications and corticosteroids may be needed.

Nodular Panniculitis

This is an uncommon inflammatory condition of subcutaneous fat in which lumps appear over the back and along the sides of the body, much like marbles beneath the skin. These lumps are more apparent in shorthaired breeds. As the disease progresses, the lumps ulcerate and drain, then heal by scarring. The dog usually runs a fever and appears lethargic. The cause of the disease is unknown. Biopsy of a nodule confirms the diagnosis.

Treatment: Surgical excision is the treatment of choice for a solitary nodule. With multiple nodules, treatment involves corticosteroids and/or vitamin E. The outlook for long-term recovery is good.

THE EYES

The eye is an organ with several parts, each uniquely adapted to meet the special needs of the dog. The eyeball is seated in a bony socket and protected by a cushion of fat. Muscles surrounding the eyeball close the eyelids tightly in response to pain, irritation, and objects approaching the eye. This makes it difficult to inspect the surface of the eye for injuries and foreign bodies.

The large, clear window at the front of the eye is the cornea. Bordering it is a narrow rim of white connective tissue called the sclera, which is much less conspicuous in dogs than it is in humans. The sclera surrounds and supports the entire eyeball. In certain breeds the sclera may be pigmented or spotted.

The round opening at the center of the eye is the pupil. Around the pupil is a sphincterlike muscle called the iris. Like a shutter on a camera, the iris opens and closes to regulate the amount of light that enters the eye. The iris contains the pigment that gives the eye its color. While most dogs have eyes that are a shade of brown, blue eyes are normal for some breeds and colors and have normal vision. In some Northern breeds and dogs with the *merle* pattern, odd eyes (one brown and one blue) are not uncommon.

A pinkish membrane called the conjunctiva covers the white of the eye and doubles back to cover the inner surface of the eyelid. This membrane contains blood vessels and nerve endings. When inflamed, the conjunctiva appears red and swollen.

The eyelids are tight folds of skin that support the front of the globe. Eyelashes are always present on the upper eyelids, but not on the lower eyelids. There are small hairs on the edge of the lower lids.

The dog has an important third eyelid, the nictitating membrane, located at the inner corner of the eye. This third eyelid is normally inconspicuous, but when it extends across the surface of the eye, it looks as if the eyeball has rolled back into its socket.

Tears are secreted by the lacrimalglands. Each eye has two lacrimalglands: one beneath the bony ridge at the top of the eye socket and the other incorporated into the third eyelid. Tears are conveyed to the surface of the eye by small ducts that empty behind the lids. Tears prevent the cornea from drying

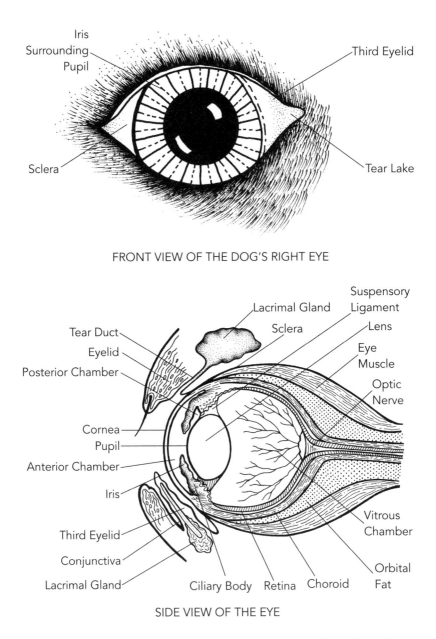

Iris
Surrounding
Pupil

Third Eyelid

Sclera

Tear Lake

FRONT VIEW OF THE DOG'S RIGHT EYE

Lacrimal Gland

Suspensory
Ligament

Sclera

Lens

Tear Duct

Eyelid

Eye
Muscle

Posterior Chamber

Optic
Nerve

Cornea
Pupil

Anterior Chamber

Iris

Vitrous
Chamber

Third Eyelid

Conjunctiva

Orbital
Fat

Lacrimal Gland

Ciliary Body   Retina   Choroid

SIDE VIEW OF THE EYE

out. They also contain substances that fight infections. Tears help flush out any irritating substances or foreign bodies that come in contact with the eye. Tears gather at the inner corner of the eye and are carried by the nasolacrimal ducts into the nasal cavity near the front of the nose. The inner eye has three fluid-filled chambers. The anterior chamber is found between the cornea and the iris. The small posterior chamber lies between the iris and front of the lens. The large vitreous chamber, containing a clear jelly, fills the cavity behind the lens and in front of the retina.

The lens is held in place by a series of strands called the suspensory ligaments. These attach to the ciliary body, a structure composed of muscle, connective tissue, and blood vessels. The ciliary body secretes the fluid that fills the anterior and posterior chambers. Contraction of the ciliary muscles changes the curvature of the lens, which enables images of objects at different distances to be focused onto the retina.

Light enters the eye by passing through the cornea and anterior chamber and then through the pupil and lens. It then travels through the vitreous and is received by the retina. The retina is a layer of photoreceptor cells that convert light into electrical impulses. These impulses are then carried to the brain via the optic nerves.

How Dogs See

Dogs have relatively poor vision in some areas when compared with people. Dogs are nearsighted and *accommodate* poorly. Most dogs see at about 20/75—remember that for people normal eyesight is 20/20. Accommodation is the process during which the lens changes shape to focus light on the retina. Dogs accommodate poorly because the ciliary muscles that change the shape of the lens are relatively weak.

The dog's retina contains a small number of cone cells that distinguish between blue, yellow, and gray. However, the canine retina lacks photoreceptors for red and green, and thus is similar to the retina of people who are red-green colorblind. While dogs do perceive some colors, it is believed that the ability to perceive subtle shades of gray is the most important function of the cone cells. Dogs can detect degrees of brightness.

On the positive side, dogs have large pupils and a wide field of vision, making them adept at following moving objects. Dogs also have an abundance of rods in the retina, which are the cells that detect light. Along with the cone cells that distinguish shades of gray, the rods enable dogs to see very well in relative darkness. Dogs also have a fair degree of binocular vision and depth perception. Furthermore, any shortcoming dogs may have in eyesight is more than made up for by their superior senses of hearing and smell.

Visual abilities vary somewhat with breed, head shape, and eye shape. A dog with a long muzzle will have "visual streaks," which are areas in the retina with extra cells for vision over a wide area and for detecting up motion. Many of the sighthounds fit that description. A dog with a short muzzle and prominent eyes will have an "area centralis." This is a central spot on the retina with extra cells to pick up details. These are the dogs who tend to watch television more closely.

What to Do if Your Dog Has an Eye Problem

If your dog has matter in his eye or if the eye waters, if the dog blinks, squints, paws at the eye, and gives evidence that the eye is painful, or if the eye appears red, the dog has an eye problem. You must examine the eye and attempt to determine the cause.

Signs of Eye Ailments

Eye diseases are accompanied by a number of signs and symptoms. The most serious is pain. A *dog with a painful eye should be taken to the nearest veterinary hospital as soon as you notice the condition.* Irreversible damage can occur in a matter of hours.

- **Eye pain.** Signs of pain include excessive tearing, squinting, tenderness to the touch, and sensitivity to light. Other signs of a painful eye are loss of appetite, lethargy, whining, and crying. The nictitating membrane often protrudes in response to pain. The dog may paw at the eye. The most common causes of severe eye pain are acute glaucoma, uveitis, keratitis, and corneal injuries.

- **Discharge.** The appearance of discharge helps to define the cause of the problem. A clear discharge with no other signs suggests a problem with the tearing mechanism. A painless discharge accompanied by redness is typical of conjunctivitis. Any discharge accompanied by signs of pain should alert you to the possibility of corneal or inner eye problems. A thick green or yellow discharge, often mucoid, can indicate infection or a foreign body. This may build up on the lids or on the hairs around the eye.

- **Film over the eye.** An opaque or whitish membrane that moves out over the surface of the eyeball from the inner corner of the eye is a protruded nictitating membrane. Causes are discussed in *The Nictitating Membrane,* page 182.

- **Cloudiness.** Loss of clarity or transparency, accompanied by signs of pain, suggests keratitis, glaucoma, or uveitis. Corneal edema, the buildup of fluid in the normally clear cornea, will give the eye a uniform blue-gray appearance. This is usually associated with signs of pain. Cataracts are the most likely cause when the eye is not painful. If the eye is entirely opaque you might think the dog is blind, but this is not necessarily the case.

- **Hard or soft eye.** Changes in eye pressure and firmness of the eyeball are caused by diseases of the inner eye. A hard eye with a dilated pupil indicates glaucoma. A soft eye with a small pupil indicates uveitis.

- **Irritation of the eyelids.** Diseases that cause swelling, crusting, itching, or hair loss are discussed in *Eyelids*, page 177.

- **Bulging or sunken eye.** A bulging eye occurs with glaucoma, tumors and abscesses behind the globe, and with an eye out of its socket. A sunken eye occurs with dehydration, weight loss, eye pain, and tetanus. Some breeds, such as Pugs, have eyes that normally bulge somewhat.

HOW TO EXAMINE THE EYE

An eye examination can be performed easily and does not require any technical expertise. It will provide you with the type of information you need to determine if this is an emergency. When in doubt, consider any change in the eye to be an emergency.

How to examine the surface of the eyeball. Note the third eyelid in the bottom of the eye. It contains a tear gland that produces about half the tear volume.

The examination is best done in a dark room using a single light source, such as a flashlight. A magnifying glass will help you see fine details on the surface of the eye. Have an assistant restrain the dog, as described in *Restraining for Examination and Treatment*, page 2.

First compare one eye to the other. Are they the same size, shape, and color? Are the pupils equal in size? (Remember, if you shine a light directly into an eye, the pupil will shrink.) Is there a discharge, and if so, is it watery or mucoid? Is the dog squinting? Is the nictitating membrane visible? Does the cornea look smoky, hazy, or cloudy? Is it painful to the dog when you press gently on the eyeball through closed eyelids?

To examine the surface of the eyeball, place one thumb against the skin of the cheek below the eye and the other thumb against the ridge of bone above. Gently draw down with the lower thumb and apply counter traction with the other. Because of the mobility of the skin of the dog's face, the lower eyelid will sag out and you can look in and see the conjunctival sac and most of the cornea behind it. Reverse the procedure to examine the eye behind the upper eyelid. Flash a light across the surface of the cornea to see if it is clear and transparent. Any dull or dished-out spot is an indication of corneal abrasion or ulcer.

Press gently on the surface of the eye through the closed eyelids to see if one eye feels harder or softer than the other. If the eye is tender, the dog will give evidence of pain.

To test the dog's vision, cover one eye and make a movement as if you are about to touch the other eye with your finger. If the dog has vision in that eye, he will blink as he sees your finger approaching.

Do not neglect minor eye ailments. If there is any doubt about the diagnosis, and particularly if the eye has been treated at home but has not shown improvement in 24 hours, call your veterinarian. Eye problems can go from minor to serious in a very short time.

HOW TO APPLY EYE MEDICINES

Place ointments into the space behind the lower eyelid (the conjunctival sac). Drops can be applied directly to the eyeball.

To apply ointment, steady your dog's head with one hand and draw down on the lower eyelid with your thumb to expose the conjunctival sac. Rest the hand containing the applicator against the dog's forehead, as shown in the photos on this page. This way, if the dog jerks his head your hand will move with it, preventing the applicator from poking the eye. Slowly squeeze out a ribbon of ointment. Then gently close the eyelids, massaging a bit to spread the ointment over the entire eyeball.

To instill drops, steady the hand holding the dropper against the side of the dog's head. Tilt the dog's muzzle up; then drop the medication into the eye. Eye drops tend to wash out with tears and must be applied several times a day.

Drops are applied directly to the eyeball.

Apply ointment to the inner surface of the lower lid.

Only use drops and ointments that are specifically labeled for ophthalmic use. Be sure to check the expiration date on the product's label. Note that prolonged administration of antibiotics in the eye may lead to resistant infections. Your veterinarian may recommend flushing or cleaning the eye with artificial tears before putting in a new dose of medication.

An eye out of its socket is an emergency.

The Eyeball
EYE OUT OF ITS SOCKET

This is an emergency. Dislocation of one or both eyeballs is a common problem in dogs with large, bulging eyes such as Boston Terriers, Pugs, Pekingese, Maltese, and some spaniels. It is generally caused by dog bites and other types of trauma. Struggling with these dogs while attempting to hold and restrain them for any reason can cause the eye to bulge out so far that the eyelids snap shut behind the eyeball. This prevents the eyeball from returning to its socket and may pull on and damage the optic nerve

Treatment: A dislocated eyeball is an extremely serious condition that may cause loss of vision. Shortly after the eye dislocates, swelling behind the eye makes it extremely difficult to return the eyeball to its normal position. *Proceed at once to the nearest veterinary hospital.* Carry the dog, if possible. Cover the eye with a wet cloth. Prevent the dog from pawing at the eye.

If it appears that veterinary help will not be available within 30 minutes, consider attempting to reposition the eyeball yourself. This requires at least two people: one to restrain and hold the dog and the other to reposition the eye. Lubricate the surface of the eye with K-Y or petroleum jelly and lift the eyelids out and over the eyeball, while maintaining gentle inward pressure on the globe with a wad of moist cotton. If you're not successful, make no further attempt. Seek professional assistance. Even if you can replace the eyeball, you should visit your veterinarian for follow-up care, because the delicate tissues may be damaged.

After the eye has been replaced, your veterinarian may suggest a surgical procedure to prevent a recurrence.

OTHER CAUSES OF A BULGING EYE

Abscesses, hematomas, and tumors in the retrobulbar space behind the eye can push the globe forward and cause bulging.

A retrobulbar abscess (an abscess behind the eyeball) is an extremely painful condition that comes on rapidly. The face around the eye is swollen and the globe is extremely tender to finger pressure. Dogs experience great difficulty opening and closing their mouths. A retrobulbar abscess must be surgically drained.

Retrobulbar hematomas (blood clots behind the eyeball) also develop suddenly. They occur with head injuries and can appear spontaneously in conjunction with some bleeding disorders.

Tumors in the retrobulbar space produce a gradual bulging. Unlike the two conditions just described, they are relatively painless.

Chronic glaucoma can lead to increased eye size and protrusion.

Enophthalmos (Sunken Eye)

When an eye recedes, the third eyelid usually slides out over the surface of the eyeball and becomes visible. The treatment of a sunken eye is directed toward the underlying cause.

Both eyeballs may recede when there is loss of substance in the fat pads behind the eyes. This occurs with severe dehydration or rapid weight loss.

There is a retractor muscle, which, when it goes into spasm, pulls the eyeball back into its socket. Tetanus produces spasms of the retractor muscles of both eyeballs, along with the characteristic appearance of the third eyelids.

When only one eye is involved, the most likely cause is a painful eye. Nonpainful causes include nerve damage following a neck injury or a middle ear infection. With this condition, called Horner's syndrome, the pupil is small on the affected side. Finally, after a severe eye injury, the eye can become smaller and sink into its socket.

Severe squinting and shutting the eye is indicative of a painful eye.

Dermoid Cyst (Hair Growing from the Eyeball)

Dermoid cysts are congenital growths usually found at the outer corners of the eyes. These cysts contain hair that often appears to be growing out of the surface of the eye. The dermoid is not a malignant tumor, but it should be removed because of the irritating effect of the hair. This is most often seen in German Shepherd Dogs but is not a common problem.

Eyelids

BLEPHAROSPASM (SEVERE SQUINTING)

Severe squinting with spasms of the muscles around the eye is a symptom of a painful eye. Any painful eye condition can cause squinting. The tightening of the muscles rolls the eyelids in against the eye. Once rolled in, the rough edges of the lids and the hairs rub against the eyeball, causing further pain and spasms.

Treatment: Anesthetic drops can be applied to the eyeball to relieve the pain and break the cycle. The relief is temporary, unless the irritating factor is identified and removed.

BLEPHARITIS (INFLAMED EYELIDS)

Bacterial blepharitis is a condition in which the eyelids become thick, reddened, inflamed, and encrusted. Mucuslike pus may adhere to the lids. Blepharitis in puppies occurs primarily in association with puppy strangles. In older dogs it can be associated with various skin diseases, including canine atopy, demodectic mange, autoimmune diseases, and hypothyroidism.

Staphylococcal blepharitis occurs in both puppies and adults. It is identified by small white pimples on the edges of the eyelids. The pimples rupture

Treatment: Blepharitis is treated with oral and topical antibiotics. To remove adherent crusts, use a washcloth soaked in warm water as a daily compress over the eyelids. Three or four times a day, apply a topical ophthalmic ointment or solution containing neomycin, bacitracin, or polymyxin D. Your veterinarian may prescribe an ophthalmic ointment that contains corticosteroids.

Blepharitis is difficult to cure. Some dogs require long-term treatment. Dogs with chronic blepharitis should be checked for hypothyroidism. Any primary cause will need to be treated.

This dog shows the thickened, inflamed, and encrusted eyelids characteristic of blepharitis.

Chemosis (Allergic Blepharitis)

Sudden swelling of the eyelids is an allergic reaction, most often to insect bites or ingredients in foods. The lids appear fluid-filled, soft, and puffy, and the dog itches and rubs his face. The reaction may be accompanied by hives in which the hair stands out erect in little patches all over the body.

This is not a serious problem. It is of short duration and improves when the *allergen* is removed.

Treatment: Simple cases can be treated with eye drops or ointments containing a corticosteroid prescribed by your veterinarian. Your veterinarian may also suggest an oral antihistamine to reduce the allergic response.

Foreign Bodies in the Eyes

Foreign material such as grass seeds, dirt, and specks of vegetable matter can adhere to the surface of the eye or become trapped behind the eyelids. Dogs who ride in the open bed of a pickup truck and in the cars with their head out the windows are at high risk for getting dirt and debris in the eyes. Thorns, thistles, and splinters can also penetrate the cornea. This is most likely to happen when a dog is running through dense brush and tall weeds.

Signs of a foreign body in the eye are tearing and watering, blinking, squinting, and pawing. The third eyelid may protrude to protect the painful eye.

Examine the eye as described on page 172. You may be able to see dirt or plant material on the surface or behind the upper and lower eyelids. If not, the foreign body may be caught behind the third eyelid. In that case, the dog will need a topical eye anesthetic before it can be removed.

Treatment: To remove foreign material on the surface of the eye or behind the eyelids, restrain the dog and hold the eyelids open as described in *How to Apply Eye Medicine*, page 174. Flush the eye for 10 to 15 minutes using cool water, or preferably a sterile saline eyewash or artificial tears. To flush the eye, soak a wad of cotton in the solution and squeeze it into the eye repeatedly. If you have a bottle of artificial tears on hand, you can flush the eye directly from the bottle.

If the foreign body cannot be removed by irrigation, you may be able to remove it by gently touching it with a wet cotton-tipped swab. The foreign body may adhere to the cotton tip. Foreign bodies that penetrate the surface of the eye must be removed by a veterinarian. Restrain the dog from pawing at the eye while you drive to the veterinary hospital.

If the dog continues to squint or tear after the foreign body has been removed, have him checked by your veterinarian to see if the cornea has been damaged.

BURNS OF THE EYES

Chemical injuries to the conjunctiva and cornea can occur when acids, alkali, soaps, shampoos, or topical insecticides are splashed into the eyes. Toxic fumes can also irritate and injure the eyes. The signs are tearing, squinting, and pawing at the eye.

Treatment: Flush the eyes with cool water, artificial tears, or a sterile saline solution, as described in *Foreign Bodies in the Eyes* (page 178). This must be done immediately after exposure to prevent damage to the eye. Flush for a full 15 minutes. After you have completed the flushing, take your dog to the veterinarian for further evaluation and treatment.

Be sure to protect the eyes from shampoos and insecticides when bathing and dipping your dog.

STIES AND CHALAZIONS

The eyelid contains hair follicles and meibomian glands. The meibomian glands secrete an oil that acts as a barrier to prevent the evaporation of tears. Infection in either a hair follicle or a meibomian gland produces a sty, also called a hordeolum, which is a small abscess that comes to a head.

An uninfected meibomian gland may become plugged, resulting in the development of a nontender swelling on the eyelid called a chalazion. Chalazions tend to occur in older dogs. They remain relatively static and only require treatment if they are getting larger.

Treatment: A dog with a sty should be placed on oral and topical antibiotics, as described for blepharitis (page 177). Applying warm compresses to the eyelid three or four times a day is beneficial in bringing the sty to a head. If the sty does not rupture on its own, your veterinarian may puncture it with a sterile needle or a scalpel.

Chalazions are removed surgically. Do not squeeze the chalazion in an attempt to express its contents. If the chalazion ruptures into the eyelid, the oily contents set up a severe inflammatory reaction that is very difficult to treat.

DISTICHIASIS (EXTRA EYELASHES)

This is a congenital condition in which an extra row of eyelashes grows from the eyelid and is directed inward, rubbing against the surface of the eye. If left untreated, the constant irritation leads to corneal abrasion. The condition may not be noticed until the puppy is grown.

Extra eyelashes are seen most often in Poodles, Cocker Spaniels, Golden Retrievers, and Pekingese, but all breeds can be affected.

Dogs with long hair around the face are subject to eye irritation.

Aberrant eyelashes that grow inward on the upper and lower eyelids produce the same type of problem.

Treatment: The offending eyelashes should be removed and their roots destroyed through *cryotherapy* (chemical freezing), electrolysis, or surgery. Plucking them with blunt-nosed tweezers provides temporary relief, but the eyelashes grow back in about four weeks. Dogs who have had their eyelashes permanently removed cannot be shown in conformation.

FACIAL HAIR

Hair in the nasal folds may grow up against the eyeball and rub against the cornea. This tends to be a problem in Poodles, Maltese, Yorkshire Terriers, and in short-nosed breeds such as Pekingese, Shih Tzu, Lhasa Apsos, and Bulldogs. In Old English Sheepdogs and other breeds with long facial hair, a similar problem can occur. The involved hair will be stained reddish-brown by tears.

Treatment: The offending hairs should be removed by clipping, or, if the hair is in the nasal folds, by surgery.

ENTROPION

This condition, in which the eyelids roll inward, is the most common congenital defect of the eyelids. It can also be caused by injury and long-standing eyelid infections that cause scarring. The abnormal eyelids produce irritation with tearing and squinting. Corneal injuries are common from abrasion by the hairs.

It may be difficult to distinguish entropion from blepharospasm (see page 177). The best way to tell them apart is to administer a topical eye anesthetic. If the inverted eyelids are caused by blepharospasm, temporarily blocking the eye pain causes the inversion to disappear.

Breeds most commonly affected by entropion are the Chinese Shar-Pei, Chow Chow, Great Dane, Great Pyrenees, St. Bernard, Bulldog, and the hunting breeds. Most cases involve the lower eyelids. In dogs with large heads and loose facial skin, such as Chinese Shar-Pei, Bloodhounds, and St Bernards, the upper eyelids may be involved.

Treatment: Entropion requires surgical correction. Note that dogs who have had corrective surgery on their eyelids cannot be shown in conformation.

Many Shar-Pei puppies suffer from a condition called neonatal entropion. These puppies should have their eyelids everted with temporary sutures at 3 to 5 weeks of age. If they do not outgrow the problem, plastic surgery on the eyelids can be performed at a later date.

This Shar-Pei puppy's eyelids have been everted with temporary sutures. This may correct the entropion without the need for plastic surgery.

ECTROPION

In dogs with this condition, the lower eyelid rolls out from the surface of the eye. This exposes the eye to irritants and leads to a high incidence of chronic conjunctivitis and corneal injury. Foreign bodies may get caught in the pocket created by the loose eyelid. Ectropion occurs in dogs with loose facial skin, such as scenthounds, spaniels, and St Bernards. It is also seen in older dogs whose facial skin has lost its tone. It can occur temporarily in hunting dogs, after a long day in the field.

Treatment: Mild ectropion that causes no symptoms needs no treatment. But in most cases, ectropion should be corrected by a surgical procedure that tightens the eyelids.

Ectropion exposes the eyes to irritants and leads to chronic eye infections and corneal injuries.

These growths on the eyelids are meibomian gland adenomas.

EYELID TUMORS

The most common tumor of the eyelid is a meibomian gland adenoma. Meibomian glands are found only on the eyelids. These glands secrete an oil that acts as a barrier to prevent the evaporation of tears. Meibomian gland adenomas have a cauliflowerlike appearance and may be single or multiple.

Among other eyelid tumors, the most common is the sebaceous adenoma. Most are benign, and are found in older dogs.

Papillomas are wartlike tumors caused by the canine oral papilloma virus. These tumors also grow on the surface of the eye.

Treatment: Eyelid tumors should be removed to prevent injury to the cornea. The tumors mentioned here are not usually malignant tumors.

The Nictitating Membrane (Third Eyelid)
FILM OVER THE EYE

An opaque third eyelid, normally not seen, may become visible across the front of the eye, in which case the nictitating membrane is protruding. The appearance of the third eyelid indicates that the eyeball has sunken into its socket (see *Enophthalmos*, page 176), or that the eyeball has been pulled back into its socket by spasm of the retractor muscles in response to severe eye pain.

A dog may be born with visible third eyelids, called haws. In the show ring this is often considered undesirable, because it gives the animal a somewhat

The nictitating membranes protrude on this dog, showing the haws.

haggard look. Most breed standards (if they mention it at all) require that the haws be scarcely apparent. The haws are a concern only because they give the dog an unsightly appearance. There is no medical reason to remove the third eyelid just because the haws are visible.

EVERSION OF THE CARTILAGE

This is a congenital condition among Weimaraners, Great Danes, Golden Retrievers, St Bernards, and other breeds. The third eyelid appears to roll back upon itself like a dry leaf. Corneal irritation may occur.

Treatment: This can be treated surgically if it is causing a problem.

CHERRY EYE

There is a tear gland wrapped around the cartilage of the third eyelid that is a major source of tears for the eye. In a dog with cherry eye, the fibrous attachments to the undersurface of the third eyelid are weak. This allows the gland to prolapse, or bulge out from beneath the eyelid, exposing a cherrylike growth that is really a normal-size tear gland. This growth can irritate the surface of the eye and produce recurrent conjunctivitis.

Cherry eye is a congenital defect that occurs most commonly in Cocker Spaniels, Beagles, Boston Terriers, and Bulldogs.

Treatment: Removing the third eyelid or the tear gland seriously interferes with tear production and may result in a dry eye syndrome in breeds so disposed (see *The Tearing Mechanism*, page 186). If the gland is removed, your dog may require artificial tears daily for life. Instead, surgery can be performed that repositions the third eyelid and the tear gland. This corrects the problem while maintaining tear production.

Cherry eye (on the right side in the photo) is a prolapse of the tear gland of the third eyelid.

The Outer Eye
CONJUNCTIVITIS (RED EYE)

Conjunctivitis, sometimes called red eye or pink eye, is an inflammation of the conjunctival membrane that covers the back of the eyelids and the surface of the eyeball, up to the cornea. It is one of the most common eye problems in dogs.

The classic signs of conjunctivitis are a red eye with a discharge. Conjunctivitis is not usually painful. If the eye is red and the dog is squinting and shutting the eye, consider the possibility of keratitis, uveitis, or glaucoma. Any delay in treating these conditions can lead to blindness.

When the discharge involves both eyes, suspect an allergy or a systemic disease such as canine distemper. When it involves only one eye, consider a local predisposing cause such as a foreign body in the eye or hair rubbing on the eye.

The eye discharge in conjunctivitis may be clear (*serous*), mucuslike (*mucoid*), or puslike (*purulent*). A stringy, mucoid discharge suggests the dog may have inadequate tear volume, a problem associated with keratoconjunctivitis sicca (see page 187). In fact, this is the most common cause of conjunctivitis in dogs.

Serous conjunctivitis is a mild condition in which the membranes look pink and somewhat swollen. The discharge is clear and watery. Serous conjunctivitis is caused by physical irritants such as wind, cold, dust, and various allergens such as those that cause allergic blepharitis. Allergic conjunctivitis is often accompanied by itching, and the dog will rub his face. Some viral agents will cause a clear discharge as well.

Follicular (mucoid) conjunctivitis is a condition in which the small mucous glands (follicles) on the underside of the nictitating membrane react to an eye irritant or infection by forming a rough, cobblestone surface that irritates the eye and produces a mucoid discharge. After the inciting factor has been treated, the follicles may persist and the rough surface acts as a chronic irritant.

Purulent conjunctivitis is serous conjunctivitis that becomes infected. The usual culprits are the bacteria *Streptococcus* and *Staphylococcus*. The conjunctiva is red and swollen. The eye discharge contains mucus and pus. Thick secretions may crust the eyelids.

Treatment: Any underlying cause of conjunctivitis should be corrected. Dogs with recurrent or persistent conjunctivitis should be tested for keratoconjunctivitis sicca.

Serous conjunctivitis can be treated at home. Flush the eye three or four times a day with an over-the-counter sterile saline eyewash or artificial tears. Notify your veterinarian if the eye appears to be getting worse.

Mild cases of follicular conjunctivitis respond to antibiotic and corticosteroid eye ointments prescribed by your veterinarian. In resistant cases, the follicles may need to be destroyed by chemical cauterization.

Purulent conjunctivitis requires veterinary examination and treatment. It is important to remove mucus and pus from the eyes, as well as pus and crusts that adhere to the eyelids. Moisten a cotton ball with sterile eyewash and gently cleanse the eye. Warm, moist packs may help loosen crusts. Repeat as necessary and apply topical antibiotics as prescribed by your veterinarian (see *How to Apply Eye Medicines*, page 174). Continue topical antibiotics for several days beyond apparent cure.

Note that corticosteroids and eye medications containing corticosteroids should not be used in dogs with purulent conjunctivitis because they impair the local inflammatory response that fights infection. Bacterial culture and sensitivity tests are indicated if the conjunctivitis does not improve.

This dog has chronic purulent conjunctivitis. The discharge is thick and tenacious. This condition is difficult to clear up.

NEONATAL CONJUNCTIVITIS

The eyes of newborn puppies open at 10 to 14 days of age. Infection behind the eyelids, called neonatal conjunctivitis, can occur before or after the eyelids separate. This form of conjunctivitis is caused by bacteria that gain

In puppies with neonatal conjunctivitis, the eyelids should be gently separated to evacuate the pus and treat the infection.

access to the space behind the eyelids during or shortly after birth.

There is a condition called anky-loblepharon in which the eyelids do not open as widely as they should. This predisposes a puppy to neonatal conjunctivitis. Neonatal conjunctivitis may affect several puppies in the same litter.

Suspect this problem if the eyelids appear swollen and/or the eyelids bulge. A purulent discharge may be present if the infection occurs when the eyes are beginning to open. The discharge may cause the eyelids to stick together.

Treatment: Notify your veterinarian immediately if you suspect neonatal conjunctivitis. Delay in treatment can lead to corneal damage and blindness.

The eyelids (if still fused) should be opened to allow pus to escape. With puppies older than seven days, this can usually be done by gently pulling the eyelids apart. In puppies younger than seven days, your veterinarian may need to open the eyelids with a surgical instrument.

Once the lids are open, the surface of the eye and the eyelids should be cleaned to remove purulent discharge, as described for purulent conjunctivitis (page 185). Repeat as necessary. Eyelids that stick together should be manually separated to facilitate drainage. Solutions or ointments prescribed by your veterinarian that contain broad-spectrum antibiotics should be instilled into the eyes several times daily. Artificial tears should also be used frequently, as newborns do not make tears before their eyes would naturally open. The artificial tears prevent drying of the cornea.

The Tearing Mechanism

Each eye has two lacrimal glands: one beneath the bony ridge at the top of the eye socket and the other incorporated into the third eyelid. Each produces approximately half the aqueous tear volume. Excess tears are collected at the inner corner of the eye and drained by the nasolacrimal duct into the nasal cavity near the front of the nose.

The tear film actually comprises three layers. The outer layer is a lipid or oily layer produced by meibomian glands in the eyelids. This layer acts as a barrier and prevents tears from evaporating and spilling over the eyelids. The middle or aqueous layer consists of the watery tears produced by the lacrimal glands. The inner layer is composed of *mucus* secreted by the conjunctiva. Mucus is a wetting agent and holds the aqueous layer against the surface of the eye.

Diseases of the tearing mechanism produce either a dry eye or a watery eye.

KERATOCONJUNCTIVITIS SICCA (DRY EYE)

Keratoconjunctivitis sicca is a disorder of the tear glands that results in insufficient aqueous tear production and a correspondingly dry cornea. The tear film contains less of the aqueous layer and more of the mucus layer. In consequence, the classic sign of dry eye is a thick, stringy, *mucoid* to *mucopurulent* discharge. Since this type of discharge can also be seen with conjunctivitis, dogs with dry eye may be mistakenly treated for chronic conjunctivitis for long periods with little or no improvement.

In a dog with dry eye, the bright, glistening sheen normally seen in the eye is replaced by a lackluster appearance in which the cornea is dry, dull, and opaque. Recurrent bouts of conjunctivitis are typical. Eventually the cornea becomes ulcerated or develops keratitis. Blindness may ensue.

Dry eye can have several causes. *Immune-mediated* diseases appear to play a major role. Other cases are *idiopathic*—that is, the cause is not known. Breeds predisposed to dry eye include Bulldogs, Cocker Spaniels, Lhasa Apsos, West Highland White Terriers, and others.

Some specific conditions that predispose a dog to dry eye include:

- Injury to the nerves that innervate the lacrimal glands. A branch of the facial nerve that activates the tear glands passes through the middle ear. Infections in the middle ear can damage this branch, affecting the tear glands as well as the muscles on that side of the face. In this case, the opposite eye is not affected.

- Injury to the tear glands themselves. Partial or complete destruction of tear glands can follow *systemic* diseases such as canine distemper, Addison's disease, and immune-mediated diseases such as rheumatoid arthritis. Bacterial blepharitis or conjunctivitis can destroy the tear glands or occlude the small ducts that carry the tears into the eye. A number of sulfonamide drugs are toxic to tear glands. Tear gland injuries may be partially reversible if the underlying cause is eliminated.

- Congenital absence of the tear glands is rare, but may occur in the smaller breeds.

- Removal of the third eyelid or the lacrimal gland attached to it.

The diagnosis of dry eye is made by measuring the volume of tears. The Schirmer tear test involves placing a commercial filter paper strip into the tear pool at the inner corner of the dog's eye and leaving it for one minute to see how much of the strip is wetted. Normally the strip should be wet to a distance of 20mm. In dogs with dry eye, the strip wets less than 10mm (often less than 5mm).

Treatment: For many years, the frequent application of artificial tears was the only treatment available for dry eye. But FDA approval of ophthalmic cyclosporin has revolutionized treatment and greatly improved results. Cyclosporin is an immunosuppressive drug that reverses immune-mediated destruction of the lacrimal glands.

Cyclosporin ointment is applied to the surface of the involved eye. The frequency of application must be determined by your veterinarian. The effect is not immediate. Artificial tears and topical antibiotics should be continued until the Schirmer tear test indicates that the volume of tears is adequate.

Treatment is life-long. Interrupting cyclosporin for as little as 24 hours causes symptoms to reappear in 90 percent of dogs. This can be reversed by resuming treatment.

When damage to the lacrimal glands leaves little or no functioning tissue, cyclosporin is not likely to be effective. Artificial tears (drops and ointments) prescribed by your veterinarian must then be instilled into the dog's eyes several times a day for life. Ointments are less expensive and do not need to be applied as frequently as drops. Saline drops should not be used because they aggravate the problem by washing away the lipid layer of the tear film.

A topical mucolytic agent containing acetylcystine may be recommended to reduce heavy mucus accumulation. Topical antibiotics are indicated whenever the mucus discharge becomes *purulent*. Topical corticosteroids may be prescribed by your veterinarian in some circumstances to decrease inflammation. In the presence of corneal ulceration, corticosteroids are contraindicated because they predispose a dog to rupture of the cornea.

Surgical treatment can be considered as a last resort when medical management fails. The operation involves transplanting the duct of the parotid salivary gland up into the corner of the eye. The saliva takes the place of the tears. The operation has several significant disadvantages. One is that the volume of tears may be more than the drainage system can handle. This can result in a watery eye and the accumulation of mineral deposits on the cornea and face.

EPIPHORA (WATERY EYE)

There are many conditions in which a watery or mucus discharge overflows the eyes and runs down the face. With a severe watery eye there is constant wetness and the skin may become inflamed and infected, adding to the dog's unsightly appearance and physical discomfort.

Epiphora is primarily a cosmetic problem unless it causes inflammation or is a symptom of a painful eye. For example, entropion, conjunctivitis, foreign bodies, corneal ulcers, anterior uveitis, and acute glaucoma are all accompanied by excessive tearing. Excessive tearing may also be caused by eye irritation due to extra eyelashes or facial hairs that rub on the surface of the eye.

Treatment: For treatment of epiphora, see *Poodle Eye*, page 190.

NASOLACRIMAL OCCLUSION

This is a blockage of the tear drainage system. The tear drainage system is composed of a nasolacrimal duct that collects tears at the tear lake and empties them into the nasal cavity near the front of the nose. The duct branches at the corner of the eye into two smaller collecting ducts—the upper and lower canaliculi—whose openings (called punctums) are located in the upper and lower eyelids.

A puppy can be born with a defective tear drainage system. In one condition, called imperforate inferior punctum, the duct system is normal except for a conjunctival membrane across the punctum of the lower eyelid. The problem occurs most often in Cocker Spaniels.

Other causes of nasolacrimal occlusion include entropion, in which the eyelid rolls inward and blocks the punctum; scarring of a punctum following a bout of purulent conjunctivitis; infection in a duct that causes cellular debris to plug the duct; and foreign bodies such as grass seeds that lodge in the ducts. These conditions usually cause tearing in only one eye.

The drainage system is first tested to see if it is open by staining the pool of tears with fluorescein dye. If the dye does not appear at the nostril, the system is blocked on that side. Nasolacrimal probes can be inserted into the ducts and various flushing techniques used to establish the point of obstruction. The flushing often removes the blockage and opens the duct.

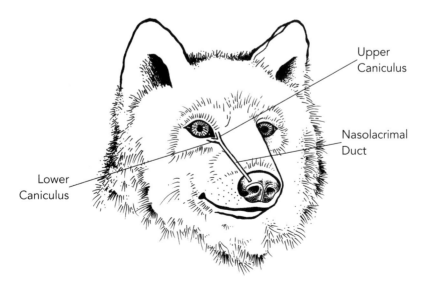

Upper Caniculus

Nasolacrimal Duct

Lower Caniculus

The Nasolacrimal Duct System

Treatment: Nasolacrimal duct infection is treated with antibiotics, in some cases by instilling them directly into a duct. The dosage, type, and route of administration must be determined by your veterinarian.

A minor operation on a duct opening may be needed to clear a blockage. Follow-up treatment includes topical antibiotics and topical corticosteroids to reduce inflammation.

Poodle Eye

This problem, in which brown stains appear at the corner of the eye, is common to several toy breeds, including Toy Poodles, Lhasa Apsos, Maltese, Pomeranians, Pekingese, and others.

The exact cause of tear overflow in these breeds is unknown. One theory is that susceptible breeds have a pooling space that is too small to collect a lake of tears. Tears contain chemicals that react with light to produce reddish-brown stains. The staining will be more apparent in dogs whose haircoat is light colored or white. This is primarily a cosmetic problem.

Treatment: Poodle eye often improves when the dog is given a course of tetracycline, which is secreted in the tears and binds the photochemicals that cause the staining. The face remains wet but is not discolored. Tetracycline is given orally for three weeks. If the staining returns after the antibiotic is stopped, long-term antibiotics can be considered. One option is to add low-dose tetracycline to the dog's daily food.

Surgery is another alternative. The operation involves removing part of the tear gland of the third eyelid. While this reduces tear volume and makes a better tear lake, it does carry the risk of producing a dry eye, as discussed in *Cherry Eye* (page 183). Removal of the tear gland should be considered only if the Schirmer tear test shows that the strip wets more than 15mm per minute (see *Keratoconjunctivitis Sicca,* page 187). After the surgery, dogs may still develop keratoconjunctivitis sicca later in life.

The dog's appearance can be improved for cosmetic purposes by plucking the stained hairs or clipping them close to the face. Daily cleaning alone will decrease, but not eliminate, the discoloration. Stains can be removed by bathing the area with a dilute solution of hydrogen peroxide (1:10). Be sure peroxide does not get into the eyes. A minor problem can be improved with a piece of white chalk. Do *not* get chalk dust in the eye itself. If you are planning to show the dog, note that all powder or chalk must be removed from the hair before the dog is brought into the conformation ring for judging.

Do not use chlorine bleach for eye stains! The fumes are painful and may cause chemical conjunctivitis. Commercial grooming wipes are also available to help with tear stains.

The Cornea

The cornea is the clear part of the eye. Corneal injuries are extremely painful and require immediate veterinary attention. Affected dogs will squint, tear, and avoid light. The third eyelid often comes out to protect the injured eye. Breeds with bulging eyes, such as the Pekingese, Maltese, Boston Terriers, Pugs, and some spaniels, are particularly susceptible to corneal injuries.

Corticosteroids, which are incorporated into many common eye preparations used in treating conjunctivitis, should not be used in an eye suspected of having a corneal injury because of the danger the cornea will rupture into the anterior chamber.

CORNEAL ABRASION

The cornea is covered by a protective surface layer of epithelial cells. Any irritation, such as a scratch or foreign body, damages this surface layer. Swelling at the site of the injury, as well as *edema*, causes the area to appear hazy and opaque when viewed under magnification. The opaque area also stains positive with fluorescein dye.

Corneal abrasions in the upper part of the cornea may be caused by misdirected eyelashes. Lower corneal opacities suggest an imbedded foreign body. Abrasions near the inner corner of the eye suggest a foreign body beneath the third eyelid.

A corneal abrasion usually heals in about three to five days by a process in which the adjacent epithelial cells enlarge and migrate over the defect. The injury will not heal, however, if a foreign body is imbedded in the cornea or beneath one of the eyelids. It is important to check for a foreign body in all cases of corneal abrasion.

Note the opaque area on the surface of the cornea at the site of a healed corneal abrasion.

Corneal abrasions and ulcers are diagnosed using a special fluorescein dye that is applied to the eye. Damaged tissues will pick up the dye.

Treatment: All corneal injuries must be seen and treated by a veterinarian to avoid complications, including keratitis and corneal ulcer. Broad-spectrum topical antibiotic drops or ointments are prescribed every four to six hours to prevent infection.

A topical atropine preparation is used to keep the pupil dilated, which reduces eye pain. Keep your dog out of bright light, including bright sunlight, when the pupil is dilated. The atropine has a bad taste and many dogs will foam at the mouth if they get some in their mouths while you are medicating them. This will pass in a minute or two.

The eye is examined periodically to monitor progress. Treatment is continued until the abrasion is healed.

Corneal Ulcer

An ulcer is similar to a corneal abrasion, except that an ulcer is deeper and involves the middle and sometimes the inner layer of the cornea.

Most corneal ulcers are caused by trauma, but some are associated with keratoconjunctivitis sicca, corneal dystrophy, diabetes mellitus, Addison's disease, or hypothyroidism.

Corneal ulcers are extremely painful and cause severe tearing, squinting, and pawing at the eye. Dogs frequently avoid light. Large ulcers are visible to the naked eye as dull spots or dished-out depressions on the surface of the cornea. Small ulcers are best seen after the eye has been stained with fluorescein.

Treatment: Early veterinary consultation and treatment is vital to prevent serious complications and even loss of the eye. Medical treatment is similar to that described for a corneal abrasion (page 191), except that ulcers take more time to heal. Your veterinarian may recommend injecting antibiotics directly into the eye beneath the conjunctiva.

Surgical treatment involves suturing the third eyelid or a flap of conjunctiva over the surface of the eye to protect the cornea during healing. Soft contact lenses and collagen shields are other methods of protecting a damaged cornea. The advantage of a contact lens is that it can be changed weekly to observe and treat the ulcer. Collagen shields need to be replaced periodically because they degrade and disappear within a few days. Your dog may need to wear an Elizabethan or BiteNot collar while the eye is healing to prevent rubbing or pawing at the eye.

Rupture of the eye into the anterior chamber can be anticipated if the cloudy central portion of a deep ulcer begins to clear, or the endothelial layer protrudes like a bulging tire. This can be recognized by your veterinarian. It is an emergency. Immediate surgery is necessary to prevent loss of the eye.

A large corneal ulcer of the type often seen in Boxers.

INDOLENT CORNEAL ULCERS IN BOXERS

A specific type of slow-healing (indolent) ulcer is found in Boxers and some other breeds, including the Samoyed, Dachshund, Miniature Poodle, Pembroke Welsh Corgi, Wire Fox Terrier, and Shetland Sheepdog. Most affected dogs are neutered males or females over the age of 6.

The indolent ulcer is caused by lack of a binding substance normally present in the basement membrane of the cornea. (The basement membrane is a thin layer of cells between the outer and middle layers of the cornea.) When this binding "glue" is missing, the epithelium peels away, leaving a concave ulcer.

Treatment: The treatment is prolonged—often six to eight weeks or more. It involves paring away the poorly adherent corneal epithelium and treating the ulcer as described in *Corneal Ulcer,* page 192. Your veterinarian will need to do this. Expect your dog to be on frequent doses of eye medications and wearing an Elizabethan or BiteNot collar.

KERATITIS (CLOUDY EYE)

Keratitis is inflammation of the cornea in which the cornea becomes cloudy, resulting in loss of transparency. The signs are excessive tearing, squinting, pawing at the eye, avoiding light, and protrusion of the third eyelid. There are different types of keratitis; all are serious diseases and can lead to partial or complete blindness. All types of keratitis must be treated by a veterinarian.

Ulcerative keratitis is a painful corneal inflammation that occurs as a complication of keratoconjunctivitis sicca or corneal ulcer. The cornea appears dull and hazy, then cloudy, and finally milky white and relatively opaque. Treatment is similar to that described for *Corneal Ulcer* (page 192).

Infectious keratitis occurs when a bacterial infection complicates ulcerative keratitis, keratoconjunctivitis sicca, or corneal ulcer. The most common invading bacteria are *Staphylococcus, Streptococcus,* and *Pseudomonas.* In addition to eye pain, infectious keratitis is characterized by a purulent discharge from the eye. The eyelids are swollen and matted. This might, at first, suggest conjunctivitis (which could seriously delay diagnosis and treatment), but recall that conjunctivitis is not usually accompanied by signs of a painful eye.

Treatment is similar to that described for *Corneal Ulcer* (page 192). It is important to use topical antibiotics selected following culture and sensitivity tests.

Fungal keratitis is uncommon in dogs, but may occur with the prolonged use of topical antibiotics. The diagnosis is made by fungal culture. It is treated with antifungal drugs.

Interstitial keratitis (blue eye) is a corneal inflammation in which a bluish-white film appears over the clear window of the eye. It is caused by the same virus that causes infectious hepatitis, and at one time it occurred after vaccination with CAV-1 (vaccines with this version of the hepatitis virus are no longer used). Signs appear 10 days after exposure. The eyes begin to water and the dog squints and avoids light. Most dogs recover completely within a few weeks. In some cases the eye remains permanently clouded.

Vascular keratitis is caused by neovascularization—the process by which the transparency of the cornea is lost due to an ingrowth of blood vessels and connective tissue. You can see blood vessels growing onto the cornea with your naked eye.

Pigmentary keratitis results when melanin pigment is deposited in the cornea. This is a separate process, but is often associated with vascular keratitis. Both conditions interfere with vision and may progress to blindness.

Vascular and pigmentary keratitis may, in some cases, be the result of a chronic corneal irritation such as that caused by entropion or lagophthalmos (inability to completely close the eyes). Removing the initiating process may reverse the keratitis.

Blood vessels are growing on the surface of this dog's eye (pigmentary keratitis), in this case caused by lack of tears (keratoconjunctivitis sicca).

This German Shepherd Dog has pannus. Note the blood vessels and pigment in the cornea and the thickening of the third eyelid.

Pannus is a specific type of nonpainful pigmentary keratitis found in German Shepherd Dogs and their crosses, and also in Belgian Tervurens, Border Collies, Greyhounds, Siberian Huskies, Australian Shepherds, and other breeds. It occurs in dogs over 2 years old. An *immune-mediated* disease is suspected to be the cause. Pannus may be associated with dogs who live at high altitudes, due to the decreased ozone layer. A distinguishing feature of pannus is redness and thickening of the third eyelid, but this may not always be present.

Treatment: Vascular and pigmentary keratitis that are not related to chronic eye irritation are progressive and incurable. The goal of treatment is to arrest the disease and maintain remission.

Neovascularization responds well to high-dose topical corticosteroids. These preparations must be monitored closely by your veterinarian, because prolonged use of corticosteroids in the eyes can lead to a mild form of Cushing's syndrome and other problems. Improvement begins in two to six weeks. Treatment is life-long. Stopping the eye drops even for a short time is followed by relapse. Only a low dose may be needed for maintenance.

Ophthalmic cyclosporine instilled into the eyes twice daily may reduce the deposition of melanin pigment.

CORNEAL DYSTROPHY

Corneal dystrophies are diseases of the cornea that occur in both eyes, are not related to inflammation, and are inherited. In most cases a dystrophy appears as a gray-white crystalline or metallic opacity in the substance of the cornea. These opacities are usually oval or round. They often become progressively larger, but in some cases remain the same size. Rapid progression usually leads to blindness. Slow progression may or may not lead to blindness.

Corneal dystrophy is a genetic disorder that affects many breeds, including the Collie, Siberian Husky, Cavalier King Charles Spaniel, Beagle, Airedale

Terrier, Cocker Spaniel, Alaskan Malamute, Bearded Collie, Bichon Frise, German Shepherd Dog, Lhasa Apso, Shetland Sheepdog, Chihuahua, Miniature Pinscher, Weimaraner, Pointer, and Samoyed. The age of onset, rate of progression, appearance, and location of the opacities and mode of inheritance vary with the breed and the individual dog. In some breeds, such as the Siberian Husky, the disease is evident as early as 4 months of age; in others, such as the Chihuahua, it appears as late as 13 years. In the Airedale the problem is sex linked, with males affected and generally showing signs by 1 year of age.

Some cases of corneal dystrophy are complicated by the development of a corneal ulcer.

Treatment: There is no effective treatment. A corneal dystrophy that threatens eyesight can be removed surgically. This may temporarily improve vision, but the opacity will re-form.

Prevention: Corneal dystrophies can be identified by veterinary eye examination. Affected individuals should not be used for breeding. The mode of inheritance has been determined for some breeds. This may make it possible to project which dogs in the pedigree are carriers. For more information, see *Retinal Diseases*, page 201.

The Inner Eye
BLINDNESS

Any condition that blocks light from getting to the retina impairs a dog's vision. Corneal diseases and cataracts fall into this category. Glaucoma, uveitis, and retinal diseases are other important causes of blindness in dogs.

Most causes of blindness will not be evident on general observation of the eye itself. But there are some signs that suggest a dog may not be seeing as well as before. For example, a visually impaired dog may step high or with great caution, tread on objects that normally are avoided, bump into furniture, and carry his nose close to the ground. Dogs who normally catch well may suddenly start to miss objects thrown to them. The inactivity of older dogs is often attributed simply to old age, but failing eyesight may also be a cause.

Shining a bright light into the dog's eye to test for pupil constriction is not an accurate test for blindness, because the pupil can become smaller from a light reflex alone. This doesn't tell you whether the dog is able to form a visual image.

One way to test eyesight is to observe the dog in a dark room in which the furniture has been rearranged. As the dog begins to walk about, see if he moves with confidence or hesitates and collides with the furniture. Turn on the lights and repeat the test. A completely blind dog will perform the same way on both tests. A dog with some sight will show more confidence when the lights are on. Performance tests such as these give qualitative information about eyesight, but the degree of impairment can only be determined by veterinary examination.

A diagnosis of blindness or irreversible vision loss is not a catastrophe. The fact is that most dogs, even those with normal eyesight, do not really see very well. They rely to a greater extent on their keen senses of hearing and smell. These senses take over and actually become more acute as eyesight fails. This makes it relatively easy for visually impaired dogs to get around in areas they know. However, a blind dog should not be turned loose in unfamiliar surroundings or he could be injured. In the house, try to avoid moving furniture, because your dog will have a "mental map" of where things are. When left outdoors, confine a visually impaired dog to a fenced yard or run. Walking on a leash is safe exercise. The dog learns to rely on his owner as a "seeing-eye person."

It is important to be aware of impending blindness while the dog is still able to see. This allows time for retraining in basic commands such as "stop," "stay," and "come." When the dog actually does go blind, obedience training can be a lifesaver.

CATARACTS

A cataract is a loss of normal transparency of the lens. Any opaque spot on the lens, regardless of its size, is technically a cataract. A cataract that is visible to the naked eye appears as a milky gray film behind the pupil.

The majority of cataracts in dogs are genetically determined, but the mode of inheritance varies among breeds. Congenital cataracts (also called juvenile cataracts) have been described in more than 75 breeds, including Cocker Spaniels, Bichons Frises, Boston Terriers, Wire Fox Terriers, West Highland White Terriers, Miniature Schnauzers, Standard Poodles, Siberian Huskies, Golden Retrievers, Old English Sheepdogs, and Labrador Retrievers. Juvenile cataracts appear in dogs before they are 6 years of age and usually involve both eyes, although not necessarily at the same time. A genetic test for some of the affected breeds is under development through VetGen (see appendix D).

This dog has a juvenile cataract in the left eye.

An acquired cataract associated with a displaced lens.

Acquired cataracts occur as a consequence of aging and other eye diseases, most notably uveitis. Dogs with diabetes can develop cataracts in a matter of weeks. Puppies fed milk-replacement formula that is deficient in arginine can develop bilateral cataracts. Newer formulas have been adjusted for this problem.

Senile cataracts are a major cause of blindness in dogs 6 to 8 years of age and older. These cataracts begin at the center of the lens and gradually spread out toward the periphery like the spokes of a wheel. When the lens becomes uniformly opaque, the cataract has reached its mature stage. Senile cataracts often occur in both eyes, but seldom develop at the same rate. One cataract generally matures before the other.

Senile cataracts should be distinguished from nuclear sclerosis, a normal aging of the lens in which new fibers are continually forming at the periphery of the lens and pushing inward toward the center. These changes cause a bluish haze in the lenses of older dogs. This haze does not interfere with vision.

Treatment: Senile cataracts do not need to be treated unless both eyes are involved and the degree of blindness is such that the dog is having difficulty getting around. Visual impairment can be corrected by surgery— removing the lens, either by extraction or preferably by an operation called phacoemulsification, which first breaks down the lens. Without a lens, the image the dog sees is blurred and the edges are indistinct, but objects can be seen. Replacement with an artificial lens (intraocular lens replacement) is an option.

Some juvenile cataracts will be spontaneously reabsorbed, usually within one year of their appearance. Complete resorption results in vision comparable to that of successful lens surgery. If the cataract is breaking down on its own, as in resorption, surgery should not be done.

Prevention: Hereditary cataracts can be prevented by not breeding affected dogs and those who carry the gene. Dogs with congenital cataracts can be identified by annual eye examinations carried out by veterinary ophthalmologists affiliated with the Canine Eye Registry Foundation (see appendix D and *Retinal Diseases*, page 201).

ANTERIOR UVEITIS (SOFT EYE)

This disease is caused by an inflammation of the iris and ciliary body. The iris is the shutter that controls the size of the pupil. The ciliary body produces the fluid that nourishes the structures in front of the lens and maintains intraocular pressure.

Most cases of anterior uveitis are caused by autoimmune complexes that gain access to the anterior chamber. Thus, anterior uveitis may occur with a long list of bacterial infections and systemic diseases in dogs. Local diseases associated with anterior uveitis include corneal ulceration, rupture of the lens, and trauma to the eye. In some cases of uveitis the cause is unknown.

Anterior uveitis is painful and is accompanied by a red eye, severe tearing and squinting, avoidance of light, and protrusion of the third eyelid. The pupil is small and reacts sluggishly to light. It may appear hazy or cloudy due to inflammation in the anterior chamber. A distinguishing feature of anterior uveitis (but one that is not always present) is that the affected eye feels softer than the normal eye.

The diagnosis is made by a complete veterinary eye examination. It is important to measure intraocular pressure to rule out glaucoma.

Treatment: Any systemic or local disease must be identified and treated. The treatment of uveitis is complex and involves the use of local and systemic corticosteroids, *NSAIDs*, immunosuppressants, and drugs that dilate the pupil. Problems that can occur along with or after an episode of anterior uveitis include secondary glaucoma, cataracts, sunken eye, and blindness. The likelihood of such complications can be minimized by early diagnosis and treatment.

Anterior uveitis is a painful eye condition, causing the dog to tear and squint.

Glaucoma

Glaucoma is a serious eye disease that often leads to blindness. There is a continuous (although very slow) exchange of fluid between the chambers of the eye and the systemic venous circulation. Fluid in the eye is produced by the ciliary body and leaves the eye at the angle formed by the iris and the cornea. Glaucoma occurs when fluid in the eye is produced faster than it can be removed. This leads to a sustained increase in intraocular pressure. High intraocular pressure causes degenerative changes to the optic nerve and the retina. Glaucoma is described as primary or secondary.

Primary glaucoma is a hereditary disease that affects Beagles, Cocker Spaniels, Basset Hounds, Samoyeds, and other breeds. In 50 percent of cases the second eye is involved within two years of the first.

Secondary glaucoma is a complication of another eye disease such as uveitis, displacement of the lens, or trauma to the eye. Treatment of secondary glaucoma is directed toward the underlying eye problem.

Glaucoma may also be acute or chronic, depending on how quickly the signs develop and how long the glaucoma has been present. An eye with acute glaucoma is exquisitely painful, with tearing and squinting. The affected eye feels harder than the normal eye and has a fixed, blank look due to the hazy and steamy appearance of the cornea and enlarged pupil.

Glaucoma in the chronic stage is associated with enlargement of the globe and protrusion of the eyeball. The eye may be tender to pressure and feel harder than the unaffected eye. In nearly all cases the affected eye is blind.

The diagnosis of glaucoma can be made only by a veterinary eye examination and measurement of intraocular pressure.

Treatment: *Acute glaucoma is a veterinary emergency that can produce blindness in a matter of hours.* This is one reason why it is so important to take your dog to a veterinary hospital *immediately* on suspicion of a painful eye. Medical treatment involves the use of drugs to rapidly lower intraocular pressure.

The initial drug of choice has been intravenous mannitol. Other veterinarians will start with prostaglandins, such as Xalatan, and give carbonic anhydrase inhibitors orally. Mannitol increases serum osmotic pressure and draws fluid out of the anterior chamber into the circulatory system. Other drugs used in treating glaucoma include carbonic anhydrase inhibitors that block the enzyme that produces the intraocular fluid. Topical medications increase outflow of fluid by constricting the pupil. This widens the angle between the iris and the cornea.

If medical treatment is not effective, a surgical procedure such as cyclodestructive surgery or filtering surgery may be done. These reduce fluid production in the eye. Some veterinarians use cryosurgery, which involves freezing and destroying a portion of the ciliary body to reduce the production of intraocular fluid. The operation can also be done with a laser, but this requires referral to a special canine eye center.

In chronic glaucoma the affected eye is blind and thus susceptible to corneal injuries and other problems, including intense pain. If these develop, the eye should be removed. If desired, a prosthesis can be inserted for cosmetic reasons.

This dog has chronic glaucoma with enlargement of the globe and protrusion of the eyeball. Note an associated cataract.

Prevention: Eye examinations (such as the CERF exam discussed in *Retinal Diseases*, on this page) will detect small increases in intraocular pressure, thereby allowing sufficient time to start preventive treatment before glaucoma develops. Annual eye examinations should be performed on all dogs with a hereditary predisposition to primary glaucoma.

A dog with glaucoma in one eye must be watched carefully for signs of glaucoma in the other eye. Intraocular pressure should be measured every four months in these high-risk individuals. Dogs with primary glaucoma should not be used for breeding. There is now evidence that pulling on a neck collar increases intraocular pressure. Dogs with increased intraocular pressure, weak or thin corneas, or full-blown glaucoma should therefore be walked with a harness rather than a collar.

Retinal Diseases

The retina is a thin, delicate membrane that lines the backs of the eyes. It is supported and nourished by the choroid, a layer of pigmented vascular tissue behind the retina.

In dogs, the retina has a layer of reflective cells behind it called the tapetum lucidum. This layer reflects light back to the front of the eye—causing the glowing eyes in photos of dogs. This reflective layer helps dogs see better in poor light, because the retina gets two chances to absorb the light. In dogs with retinal diseases, the retina loses some or all of its capacity to perceive light. The majority of retinal diseases in dogs are inherited and are transmitted when an affected or carrier dog is used for breeding. Therefore, to control the prevalence of retinal disease, it is important to determine *before a dog is used for breeding* whether that dog is affected. Inherited eye disease can often be identified at an early age by a routine eye examination performed by a veterinary ophthalmologist, most of whom are affiliated with the Canine Eye Registry Foundation (CERF).

CERF was established in 1974 with two purposes:

* To screen purebred dogs for inherited eye diseases and issue certificates to those free of disease.
* To collect research data on the incidence of various inherited eye diseases.

In 1989, the activities of CERF were combined with those of the Veterinary Medicine Data Bank at Purdue University. More recently, the Canine DNA Registry has been added to the Data Bank.

Dogs are screened for all types of hereditary eye diseases during a CERF examination. There are more than 260 board-certified veterinary ophthalmologists affiliated with CERF throughout the United States and Canada. A dog receives a certification based on the appearance of the eyes at the time of the examination. Because some inherited eye diseases develop later in life, certification is good for only one year and must be repeated annually. Furthermore, certification does not imply clearance for the carrier state. Dogs who are unaffected by disease may or may not be carriers of the gene that causes that disease.

CERF maintains a website that contains the names of all dogs who have a current CERF certification. The site is updated at the beginning of each month. The American Kennel Club now incorporates CERF certification on pedigrees. This will only tell you which dogs were checked and found to be normal, but it is important information. OFA now has access to CERF records as well. Your veterinarian can refer you to a veterinary ophthalmologist affiliated with CERF in your area, or you can contact CERF directly (see appendix D).

Because the CERF registry is closed (that is, the identity of affected dogs remains confidential), CERF information cannot be used to determine which ancestors in a dog's pedigree may have been affected. The Institute for Genetic Disease Control in Animals (GDC) also maintains a registry for hereditary eye diseases. This open registry allows breeders to share the results of eye examinations on all dogs registered with the GDC, including those who are found to be affected by genetic eye diseases. Knowing which ancestors are affected makes it possible to determine which progeny may be carriers. This knowledge can be of value in selecting breeding animals who are at low risk for transmitting the disease. For information on the GDC, see appendix D.

COLLIE EYE ANOMALY SYNDROME

This disease was originally described in Collies, but also affects Shetland Sheepdogs, Australian Shepherds, Border Collies, and some other breeds. The disease attacks the choroid that nourishes the retina. Eye abnormalities include retinal degeneration and retinal detachment—both of which cause loss of vision.

Collie eye can be detected by a veterinary ophthalmologist in puppies as young as 4 to 8 weeks of age, after the bluish puppy film disappears from the eye. The retina is graded 1 to 5, depending on the degree of degeneration. Grades 1 and 2 do not affect eyesight; grades 3, 4, and 5 are associated with increasing visual impairment. The grade does not change as the dog grows older, but retinal detachment with sudden blindness can occur at any time. There is no treatment.

Prevention: The inheritance of Collie eye anomaly has been investigated in the breed and found to be a simple recessive genetic trait. Genetic tests from OptiGen are now available for Collie eye anomaly in many of the affected breeds.

PROGRESSIVE RETINAL ATROPHY

Progressive retinal atrophy (PRA; also known as PRCD, progressive rod and cone degeneration) was first discovered in the Gordon Setter in 1911 and is now recognized in more than 86 breeds. PRA includes several specific inherited types of the diseases. In most instances the mode of inheritance is an autosomal recessive gene. In all cases there is destruction of retinal cells in both eyes, leading to blindness. There is no treatment for PRA.

The initial sign of PRA is night blindness. The dog hesitates to go out at night and won't jump on or off furniture in a dark room. As vision loss progresses, the dog develops other signs of impairment. For example, the dog may go up but not down a flight of stairs. Other behavioral changes also suggest loss of vision.

Early onset slow progression PRA causes night blindness during the first year of life but dogs may retain daylight vision for a year or longer. Breeds affected by this type of PRA include the Akita, Miniature Schnauzer, Norwegian Elkhound, Tibetan Terrier, Dachshund, and Gordon Setter.

Early onset rapid progression PRA causes visual impairment beginning during the first year of life and progressing to complete blindness in a matter of months. Breeds affected by this type include the Collie, Irish Setter, and Cardigan Welsh Corgi.

Late onset PRA causes night blindness that is noted after 2 years of age. Complete blindness occurs by age 4. This variant affects the Afghan Hound, Border Collie, Cocker Spaniel, and Labrador Retriever.

Sudden acquired retinal degeneration is a disease of unknown cause found most often in healthy, middle-aged female dogs 6 to 14 years of age. It produces rapid and complete loss of vision in both eyes in a matter of hours to several days.

An electroretinogram (ERG), which measures the retina's response to light using a corneal electrode and neutral electrodes placed on the skin around the eye, may be done to definitively diagnose PRA after a CERF exam has suggested this diagnosis.

Prevention: It is important to certify all breeding stock and register all off-spring with CERF or the GDC. Breed only those dogs who are free of PRA and are at low risk for carrying and transmitting the gene. Carrier dogs can be identified by pedigree analysis—if it is known which ancestors in the pedigree had PRA. For example, knowing that a dog has PRA (an autosomal recessive trait) automatically tells you that both parents were at least PRA carriers and may even have been affected. Pedigree information may be available through open registries such as the GDC or through those sponsored by breed clubs; or in specific instances from conscientious breeders who keep meticulous records and are willing to share the information.

For many breeds there are now genetic tests that can identify affected, normal, and carrier dogs at an early age. VetGen and Optigen are two companies that offer this type of testing.

CENTRAL PROGRESSIVE RETINAL ATROPHY

Central progressive retinal atrophy (CPRA) is a degenerative retinal disease that affects both eyes. It is less common than PRA and occurs in older dogs. CPRA affects the pigment cells at the center of the retina. It is recognized in Labrador Retrievers, Golden Retrievers, Shetland Sheepdogs, Border Collies, Rough Collies, Redbone Coonhounds, and other breeds.

Because the central part of the retina (where the dog sees best) is the primary target of the disease, a dog with CPRA is unable to see stationary objects well, especially in bright light. However, the dog is still able to see moving objects because motion is perceived at the periphery of the retina. Although vision decreases as the disease progresses, complete blindness is rare.

This is another problem that can be diagnosed on a CERF exam and also through genetic testing. There is currently no treatment.

CONGENITAL STATIONARY NIGHT BLINDNESS

This is a degenerative disease of the retina seen in Briards and also in people. This inherited eye disorder principally affects the rod photoreceptors in the retina, impairing night vision. There may also be moderate to high myopia (shortsightedness). Under good lighting conditions, there is usually no visual deficit.

The disorder is diagnosed by electroretinography. Eventually it leads to blindness.

Veterinarians at Cornell University's College of Veterinary Medicine have used gene therapy to restore the vision to affected dogs. While gene therapy is certainly a hope for the future of individual dogs, it is still best to have a CERF exam and use genetic testing to screen breeding dogs to prevent producing puppies with this defect.

6

THE EARS

Hearing is one of the dog's keenest senses. Dogs can hear sounds too faint for us to detect, and can also hear noises pitched at a much higher frequency. They can detect very slight changes in tones of sounds much better than we can. Because their hearing is so acute, dogs rely much more on their hearing than on their eyesight to navigate the world.

Dogs' ears come in all sizes and shapes, and can be carried erect, bent, or flopped over. The outside of the ear flap is covered by hair that matches the rest of the coat. Hair is also present on the inside of the ear flap, although it is sparsely distributed in most breeds. Some breeds, such as Cocker Spaniels and Poodles, will have a great deal of hair both on the flap and down into the ear canal. The skin on the inside of the ear flap is light pink in some breeds and spotted in others.

Sound, which is really vibrations of the air, is collected by the ear flap, or pinna, and directed down the comparatively large ear canal. (In puppies, there is no opening to the ear canal until some time between 1 and 2 weeks of age, so they are virtually deaf until then.) The ear canal descends in a vertical direction and then angles horizontally to end at the eardrum (tympanic membrane). This shape is the cause of many ear problems, since moisture or debris that goes into the ear is often trapped down there. Movements of the tympanic membrane are transmitted via a chain of small bones (the auditory ossicles) to the bony canals of the inner ear.

Within the bony canals lies the cochlea. The cochlea, which is the receptor organ for hearing, contains a lymphlike fluid that converts sound vibrations into fluid waves. The fluid waves are transformed into nerve impulses and conducted by the cochlear nerve to the auditory nerve.

Within the bony canals also lies the vestibular apparatus, an organ of balance composed of the semicircular canals, the utricle, and the saccule. The purpose of the vestibular apparatus is to synchronize eye movements and maintain posture, balance, and coordination. The vestibular nerve joins the cochlear nerve to form the auditory nerve that connects to the hearing and balance centers in the brain.

ANATOMY OF THE EAR

Also found in the middle ear is the opening of the auditory tube. The auditory tube connects the middle ear cavity to the nasopharynx. The purpose of the auditory tube is to equalize air pressure on each side of the eardrum.

Basic Ear Care
AVOIDING EAR PROBLEMS

Ear problems are the second most common reason dog owners take their dog to the veterinarian, according to a survey by Veterinary Pet Insurance.

Wet ear canals can predispose a dog to ear infections. When bathing your dog, keep water out of her ears by inserting cotton wadding into the ear canals. Similarly, it is important to dry your dog's ears after she has been swimming. If water gets into an ear, wipe the opening gently with a cotton ball. If you know from prior visits to your veterinarian that your dog's eardrums are intact, you can instill an ear solution that contains a drying agent (see *How to Apply Ear Medicines*, page 208). Commonly used drying solutions include ClearX, Panodry, and Vet Solutions Swimmers Ear Astringent. A drop of white vinegar will also help prevent "swimmer's ear."

Foreign material in the ears causes irritation and, later, infection. Grass seeds and awns frequently cling to the hair surrounding the ear openings and then drop into the canals. Because the ear canal has an L shape, foreign bodies can become lodged down in the canal and it can be difficult to thoroughly clean the ear without sedation. To avoid this, always groom under the ear flaps, especially after your dog has been running in tall grass, weeds, and brush.

It is common in professional grooming parlors to pluck hair out of the ear canals. Serum then oozes from the hair pores. The serum makes an excellent medium for bacterial growth. This may be one reason why ear infections are more common among Poodles, Schnauzers, and other breeds that are professionally groomed. It is recommended that you do not allow hair to be plucked from this area unless there is a medical reason to do so. In some cases, the hair forms a wad that obstructs air flow and keeps the ear canals moist; avoiding this would be a valid medical reason to remove the offending hair.

Mats in the hair at or above the external opening should be removed as described in *Removing Mats* (page 106). Wads of hair that are actually in the ear canals should be removed by a veterinarian.

CLEANING THE EARS

Routine ear cleaning is not required. A small amount of light brown waxy secretion in the ear canals is normal, and some ear wax is necessary for the health of the ears. However, the insides of the ear flaps should be cleaned whenever there is a accumulation of wax, dirt, or debris. Gently wipe the skin with a cloth that has been dampened with mineral oil, or better yet, with an

Clean the ears with a damp cotton ball. Do not insert cotton-tipped swabs into the ear canals.

ear cleansing solution such as Oti-Clens, Epi-Otic, or a similar product. Ear cleaners can be purchased at pet supply stores or through your veterinarian. Do not use alcohol, ether, or other irritating solvents; they can cause intense pain and inflame the tissues.

If there is an excessive accumulation of wax in the ear canals that appears to be the blocking air flow; if the ear appears to be red, inflamed, and moist; or if there is discharge from the ear, take your dog to the veterinarian for treatment. The ears are either infected or likely to become so.

After an initial cleaning at the veterinary clinic, you may be instructed to instill a cleansing solution at home. Apply a few drops of cleaning solution to the canal and massage the base of the ear to loosen wax and debris. Then gently wipe out the ear canal with cotton balls.

Never insert cotton-tipped applicators or swabs down into the ear canals, because this pushes wax and cellular debris further into the ear. This is a common cause of ear infection. However, cotton-tipped applicators and swabs can be used to clean the skin folds of the outer ear.

How to Apply Ear Medicines

Ear medicines should be applied only to clean, dry ear canals. Some ear preparations come in tubes with long nozzles; others use medicine droppers. Restrain the dog so that the tip of the applicator does not accidentally tear the wall of the ear canal (see *Restraining for Examination and Treatment,* page 2). Fold the ear flap over the top of the dog's head. Insert the end of the nozzle or medicine dropper into the ear canal only as far as you can see. Squeeze in the amount of ointment or number of drops recommended by your veterinarian.

Most infections involve the part of the ear canal next to the eardrum. It is important that the medicine reach this area. Massage the cartilage at the base of the ear for 20 seconds to disperse the medicine. This makes a squishy sound.

Do not use ear preparations or drying solutions unless you know for sure that the eardrums are intact, as determined by a veterinary exam using an otoscope. If a preparation is inserted into an ear canal with a perforated eardrum, it will enter the middle ear and damage structures essential to hearing.

Antibiotics for the Ear

Ear medications should be instilled once or twice daily, or as directed by your veterinarian. Antibiotics commonly prescribed to treat external ear infections include Panolog (neomycin, nystatin, cortisone), Liquichlor (chloramphenicol), Tresderm (neomycin, thiabendazole, cortisone), and Gentocin Otic (gentamicin). Gentamicin can cause ototoxicty or hearing loss, especially if your dog has a ruptured ear drum. Only use this medication under

To apply ear medication, fold the ear flap over the top of the dog's head and insert the tip of the applicator into the canal only as far as you can see.

veterinary guidance. Preparations containing miconazole and clortrimazole are also available for treating yeast and fungal infections. Allergic skin reactions can occur with any of these products.

Prolonged use of antibiotics in the ear predisposes the dog to development of antibiotic-resistant bacterial infections and the overgrowth of yeast and fungi. When bacterial and fungal cultures are needed, your dog must be off antibiotics for at least three days.

The Ear Flap

The ear flap, or pinna, is a sheet of cartilage covered on both sides by a layer of skin and hair. The pinna is often involved in diseases as part of a generalized process, especially in the case of allergic and autoimmune skin diseases, as discussed in chapter 4.

BITES AND LACERATIONS

It is not uncommon for the pinna to be injured during fights with other animals.

Treatment: Control bleeding and treat the wound as described in *Wounds* (page 42). Apply a topical antibiotic ointment such as triple antibiotic or Neosporin. Leave the ear uncovered, unless your dog shakes her head and reopens the wound so that bleeding restarts; in that case, you may need to bandage the ear to the head. Wounds caused by animal bites are often complicated by infection and must be watched carefully.

Large lacerations, and those involving the edges of the ears or the ear cartilage, should receive prompt veterinary attention. Surgical repair is necessary to prevent scarring and deformity. Your veterinarian may decide to bandage the ear to the head to keep it still for faster healing.

Allergic Otitis (Ear Allergy)

Dogs with canine atopy and food hypersensitivity dermatitis are predisposed to develop inflamed ears. In fact, ear involvement may be the only indication of an allergy. In dogs with ear allergies, an itch-scratch-itch cycle develops, resulting in excoriations, hair loss, scabs, and crusts about the ears. The ear canals are filled with a brown wax or, alternately, may appear very red, inflamed, and moist.

An allergic contact dermatitis can develop in ear canals that have been medicated with an ear preparation. The antibiotic neomycin is a frequent cause of this problem.

Treatment: Any underlying allergic skin disease must be treated to eliminate the ear symptoms. Treatment for itching involves the use of antihistamines and topical and oral corticosteroids. Discontinue any ear preparation that may be allergenic. An allergic otitis is often complicated by a bacterial or yeast infection that must also be treated.

Swollen Ear Flap

Sudden swelling of the ear flap can be caused by an *abscess* or *hematoma*. Abscesses frequently occur after dog fights. A hematoma is an accumulation of blood beneath the skin. One cause of hematoma is violent head shaking and scratching at the ear. The area will feel warm and slightly soft to the touch. It may be painful. Look for an underlying itchy ear disorder.

Treatment: Blood must be released from a hematoma to prevent scarring and ear deformity. Removing it with a needle and syringe (something your veterinarian must do) is effective in about 20 percent of cases. If serum accumulates in the drained blood pocket, treatment involves removing a window of skin to provide open and continuous drainage. Sutures are then made through both sides of the ear to pull the skin down and eliminate the pocket.

Sometimes a drain will be installed under the skin of the ear to serve this same purpose. If the blood is not removed, the cartilage will curl down and deform the ear as the clot retracts inside.

The treatment of abscess is discussed in *Cellulitis and Skin Abscess*, page 161.

FLY BITE DERMATITIS

Biting flies can attack the face and ears of dogs, sucking blood and inflicting painful bites over the tips or bent folds of the ears. These bites are typically scabbed and crusty black, and they bleed easily. German Shepherd Dogs and other breeds with erect ears are most susceptible.

Treatment: Keep the dog indoors during the day until the wounds are healed. If you are unable to do so, apply insect repellant to the ear tips. Products approved for use around horses' eyes work well, such as Farnam's Fly Off Ointment. Keep the ears clean and dry to discourage flies. Infected ear tips should be treated with a topical antibiotic ointment such as triple antibiotic.

FROSTBITE

Frostbite affects the ear tips of dogs left outdoors in severe winter weather, particularly under conditions of high wind and humidity. The ears are especially vulnerable to frostbite because they are so exposed.

Initially, the skin of frostbitten ears appears pale or even blue. All the frost bitten tissue may survive, or a sharp line of demarcation may develop between normal skin and black, dead skin. This demarcation line may not be obvious right away—it can take days to know what tissue will survive. If this happens, seek veterinary help.

The emergency treatment of frostbite is discussed in *Frostbite*, page 18.

EAR FISSURE

Ear fissure occurs in breeds with floppy ears. It results from intense scratching along with violent head shaking, which causes the ears to snap. The ear tips are denuded of hair and often become bloody. With continued trauma, the tips of the ears split and a crack in the skin, called a fissure, appears.

Treatment: The underlying irritation, often an external otitis (see page 212), should be sought and treated to eliminate the head-shaking. Treat the ear tips by applying an antibiotic-steroid ointment such as Panolog once or twice daily. If the fissure does not heal, it may need to be surgically repaired. Bandaging techniques that prevent ear movement may help speed up healing.

MARGINAL SEBORRHEA

This is a skin disease caused by a buildup of skin oil (sebum) on the hair along the edges of the ear flaps. The hair has a greasy feel. When rubbed with a thumbnail, the hair falls out. The disease is most common in Dachshunds.

Treatment: Marginal seborrhea is incurable, but it can be controlled by bathing the ears with benzoyl peroxide or a sulfur-tar shampoo (see *Seborrhea*, page 150). Soak the ear margins in warm water (using compresses) before shampooing. Put cotton balls in the ear canal to prevent any water from dripping down into the ear. Repeat every 24 to 48 hours until all the greasy material has been removed. Use a moisturizer to keep the ears soft and pliant. Repeat the treatment as necessary. If the skin is severely inflamed, apply 1-percent hydrocortisone ointment.

The Ear Canal
EXTERNAL OTITIS

External otitis is an infection of the ear canal. The ear canals are delicate structures and are easily infected. Eighty percent of infections occur in breeds with long, dropped ears. This is a function of lack of air circulation; open, erect ears dry out more easily than dropped ears and therefore provide less favorable conditions for bacterial growth.

Many factors contribute to the development of external otitis. Some breeds (such as the Chinese Shar-Pei) are predisposed because of narrow or *stenotic* ear canals. Other breeds may be predisposed because they have an abundance of hair that blocks the circulation of air. Many dogs with allergic skin diseases, particularly canine atopy and food hypersensitivity dermatitis, are predisposed to ear infections as part of the generalized skin response. Similarly, dogs with primary and secondary seborrhea often have ear canal involvement characterized by a buildup of yellowish oily wax that provides an excellent medium for bacterial growth. Foreign bodies such as grass seeds and foxtails, and growths in the ear canal, are other predisposing causes. Ear mites (see page 214) can precede bacterial otitis.

Iatrogenic causes of infection include using cotton-tipped applicators to clean the deep recesses of the ears, allowing water to get into the ears during bathing, excessive and improper cleaning of the ears, and a grooming routine that calls for plucking or clipping hair in the external ear canals.

Signs of external otitis are head-shaking and scratching and rubbing at the affected ear. The ear is painful. The dog often tilts or carries her head down on the painful side and cries or whines when the ear is touched. An examination reveals redness and swelling of the skin folds. There usually is a waxy or *purulent* discharge with a bad odor. Hearing can be affected.

This dog has severe external otitis with a swollen, inflamed ear canal. Note the skin abrasions from scratching at the ear.

Ceruminous otitis occurs with primary seborrhea (see page 150). There is an extensive buildup of oily, yellowish wax in the ear canals, which provides an excellent medium for bacteria and yeast. Treatment is directed toward control of the seborrhea. Regularly cleaning the ear canal may be necessary until this problem is controlled.

Bacterial otitis, in its acute form, is usually caused by *Staphylococci*. The discharge is moist and light brown. Chronic infections usually are caused by *Proteus* or *Pseudomonas* bacteria. The discharge is generally yellow or green, although there are exceptions. More than one species of bacteria may be involved, which complicates antibiotic treatment.

Yeast or fungal infections may follow antibiotic treatment of bacterial otitis. Yeast infections also occur commonly in dogs suffering from atopic dermatitis, food hypersensitive dermatitis, and seborrheic skin diseases. A brown, waxy discharge with a rancid odor is sometimes seen, or a very red, inflamed, moist ear with minimal discharge. These infections tend to persist until the underlying disease is controlled.

Treatment: Because external ear infections often progress to the middle ear, *it is extremely important to take your dog to a veterinarian as soon as you suspect an ear problem.* Veterinary examination of the deep portions of the ear canal using an otoscope is the most important step in making the diagnosis and planning the treatment.

Otoscopic examination cannot be attempted if the canal is dirty and filled with wax and purulent debris. First, the ear must be cleaned. This may require sedation or anesthesia.

It is essential to know whether the eardrums are intact, since it is not safe to medicate the ears with certain medications if the drums are perforated. It is also important to be sure the problem is not caused by a foreign body or tumor. A specimen of waxy material is taken with a cotton-tipped applicator, rolled onto a glass slide, and examined under the microscope looking for bacteria, yeast, ear mites, and any other predisposing factors. Your veterinarian may need to do a culture and sensitivity test on the discharge, especially if this is a recurring problem. A correct and definite diagnosis of the cause helps to determine the most appropriate and best treatment.

The first step in treatment is to clean and dry the ear canals. This requires ear-cleaning solutions, a syringe, an ear curette, and cotton balls. It should be done at the veterinary clinic. Cleaning creates a less favorable environment for bacteria to grow and allows the medication to treat the surface of the ear canal. Medication can't penetrate the debris in a dirty ear.

Follow-up care at home involves medicating the ear with a preparation prescribed by your veterinarian (see *How to Apply Ear Medicines*, page 208). If the ear continues to produce wax and exudate, a cleansing and flushing solution such as Oti-Clens or Epi-Otic, and/or a drying solution such as ClearX or Panodry, may be recommended. These solutions are used immediately before medicating the ear with an antibiotic or antifungal medication. Topical and/or oral corticosteroids may be recommended to control pain and decrease swelling and inflammation. Some dogs may need oral antibiotics as well for severe infections.

Bacterial infections that continue to progress produce thickening and narrowing of the ear canal and chronic pain. These ears are difficult to clean and treat. As a last resort, your veterinarian may advise a surgical procedure called an ear resection that reestablishes air circulation and promotes drainage.

OTODECTIC MANGE (EAR MITES)

Otodectic mites are tiny insects that live in the ear canals and feed by piercing the skin. They are highly contagious to cats and dogs, but not to humans. Ear mites are the most common cause of ear symptoms in puppies and young adult dogs. Suspect ear mites when both of the dog's ears are involved.

Ear mites should not be confused with the mites that cause sarcoptic mange. This is an entirely different disease, but one whose signs can include crusty ear tips (see *Scabies*, page 126).

It takes only a few ear mites to produce a severe hypersensitivity reaction that leads to intense itching with scratching and violent head shaking. The ear flaps become red, excoriated, crusted, and scabbed. The canals contain a dry, crumbly, dark brown, waxy discharge that looks like coffee grounds and may have a bad odor due to secondary infection.

Ear mites can be identified by removing a specimen of wax with a cotton-tipped applicator and looking at it under a magnifying glass against a black background. Mites are white specks, about the size of the head of a pin, that move.

Treatment: Once the diagnosis has been made, all dogs and cats in the household should be treated to prevent reinfestation. If you have a house bunny or ferret, check their ears as well. The ears must be cleaned as described for external otitis (page 212). This is *essential*. Dirty ear canals provide wax and cellular debris that shelter mites and make it difficult for ear medications to contact and destroy them.

After cleaning, medicate the ears using a miticide ear preparation prescribed by your veterinarian. Most preparations contain pyrethrins and thiabendazole. Commonly used ones are Nolvamite, Cerumite, Mitox, Acarex, and Tresaderm. Tresaderm contains a miticide, an antibiotic, and a steroid to relieve itching. Use according to the manufacturer's instructions.

Revolution is a flea control product that is also effective against ear mites and approved for use in treatment and prevention. Ivermectin may be used as an *off-label* medication for treating tough cases of ear mites.

It is important to complete the entire course of treatment. If treatment is stopped too soon, a new crop of mites will reinfest the dog.

During treatment, mites escape from the ear canals and temporarily take up residence elsewhere on the dog, causing itching and scratching. In addition to treating the ear canals, the entire dog and all animals that come in contact with her should be treated weekly for four weeks using a pyrethrin-based shampoo, a pyrethrins-based flea powder, or Revolution (see *Fleas*, page 117).

Mite infections are often complicated by secondary bacterial otitis. When present, treat as described for external otitis (page 212).

FOREIGN BODIES AND TICKS IN THE EAR

Foreign bodies in the ear canal cause irritation and, later, infection. Most are grass seeds and awns that first cling to hair surrounding the ear opening and then drop down into the canal. Always examine the ears after a dog has been running in tall grass, weeds, and brush.

Foreign bodies near the opening can be removed with blunt-nosed tweezers, taking care not to push them deeper into the ear canal. Foreign bodies in the deep recesses of the ear generally go undetected until they produce external otitis and are found and removed during veterinary examination.

Ticks may be found on the ear flaps or in the ear canals. When a tick is accessible, remove it as described in *Ticks* (page 123). Recall that ticks carry diseases; they should not be squeezed or crushed with your bare fingers. Ticks deep in the ear canal should be removed by a veterinarian.

CERUMINOUS GLAND TUMORS

These tumors arise from wax-producing glands in the ear canal. They are pinkish-white dome-shaped growths, less than 1 centimeter across. Most are pedunculated (on a stalk), with the base attached to the wall of the ear canal. The length of the stalk allows the tumor to extend outward and become visible. Ceruminous gland tumors may become infected and bleed.

Small tumors tend to be benign. Large tumors are usually malignant and invasive. Cocker Spaniels seem to be predisposed to these tumors.

Treatment: Surgical removal is the treatment of choice. Surgery, combined with radiation therapy, is recommended for invasive tumors.

The Middle Ear
Otitis Media (Middle Ear Infection)

Otitis media is an infection of the eardrum and the cavity of the middle ear, including the three bony ossicles. Most cases are caused by an outer ear infection that involves the eardrum and then progresses to the middle ear. In fact, about 50 percent of cases of chronic external otitis are associated with otitis media. Bacteria can also gain entrance to the middle ear through the opening of the auditory tube that connects the middle ear to the nasopharynx. Occasionally, the infection is blood-borne.

The early signs of otitis media are the same as those of external otitis (page 212). However, as the middle ear becomes infected the pain increases dramatically. The dog often tilts her head down on the affected side, holds it as still as possible, and exhibits increased pain sensitivity when her head is touched or her mouth is opened. Hearing can be affected, but the loss may not be noticed unless both ears are involved.

Horner's syndrome can be caused by otitis media. This dog shows the protruding third eyelid and drooping upper eyelid characteristic of Horner's.

An otoscopic examination performed after the dog has been sedated or anesthetized reveals a bulging eardrum. If the drum is ruptured, pus may be seen draining from the middle ear. X-rays occasionally show fluid or inflammatory tissue in the middle ear cavity.

Injury to a branch of the facial nerve that crosses the eardrum causes drooping of the upper lip and ear on the affected side. Another sign of facial nerve injury is Homer's syndrome, a symptom complex of the eye that consists of a small pupil, drooping upper eyelid, protrusion of the nictitating membrane, and retraction of the eyeball into the orbit.

Treatment: This involves thoroughly cleansing and flushing the ear, as described for external otitis (page 212). If the eardrum is intact but bulging, pus and fluid in the middle ear can be aspirated by your veterinarian using a syringe and needle. This reduces pressure and relieves pain.

The exudate is cultured. Oral antibiotics are started and can be changed pending the results of sensitivity reports. Antibiotics are continued for at least three weeks, or until the problem resolves. Recurrent or chronic otitis media may require middle ear surgery.

Prevention: Most cases of otitis media can be prevented by treating ear canal infections at an early stage. This is why it is so important to take your dog to a veterinarian as soon as you suspect an ear problem.

The Inner Ear
INTERNAL OTITIS (INNER EAR INFECTION)

Internal otitis is an inflammation and infection of the inner ear. Most cases are preceded by outer ear infections. Suspect internal otitis if the dog suddenly develops signs of labyrinthitis, as described on page 217.

Treatment: This is an emergency. Take your dog to the veterinarian. Treatment is similar to that described for otitis media (page 215).

LABYRINTHITIS

Diseases of the inner ear are characterized by labyrinthitis, or dizziness. The labyrinth is part of a complex organ of balance composed of the semicircular canals, the utricle, and saccule (see the drawing *Anatomy of the Ear*, page 206). The labyrinth is like a gyroscope. Its purpose is to synchronize eye movements and maintain posture, balance, and coordination. The most common cause of labyrinthitis is inner ear infection.

A dog with labyrinthitis will often assume an abnormal posture, with her head tilted down on the affected side. Dizziness, lack of coordination, and loss of balance are evident. The dog circles and leans toward the affected side and may exhibit rapid jerking movements of the eyeballs, a condition called nystagmus. Some dogs vomit.

Idiopathic vestibular syndrome is a disease of unknown cause that affects middle-aged and older dogs. It is the second most common cause of labyrinthitis. The onset is sudden. The dizziness, staggering, and vomiting can be incapacitating. Vomiting may last for several days, in which case the dog may require intravenous fluids. Signs peak in 24 hours, but some degree of imbalance persists for three to six weeks. Recovery occurs in almost all cases. After recovery, some dogs experience a slight but permanent head tilt.

The prolonged administration of aminoglycoside and neomycin antibiotics can produce labyrinthitis, as well as deafness. Most ear preparations are capable of causing labyrinthitis and ear damage if they make contact with the

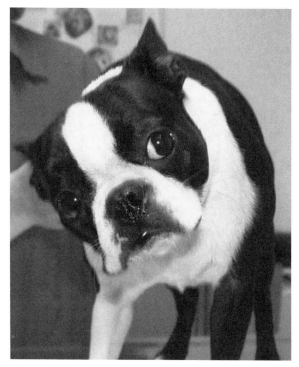

This Boston Terrier shows the typical posture of a dog with labyrinthitis. The head is tilted down on the affected side.

sensitive structures of the inner ear. This is why the ears should never be flushed or medicated without first making sure that the eardrums are intact.

Other causes of labyrinthitis include head trauma, brain tumor, poisoning, and drug intoxication. Suspect one of these if your dog develops labyrinthitis without having had a prior ear infection.

Treatment: The underlying cause must be diagnosed and treated. Supportive care and medications to relieve the symptoms assist in recovery.

Deafness

For a dog to hear, the cells that transmit sounds must be intact, as must the brain cells that interpret the sounds. Hearing loss can be caused by congenital deafness, changes of old age, middle and inner ear infections, head injuries, wax and debris blocking the ear canals, tumors of the middle ear, and certain drugs and poisons. The antibiotics streptomycin, gentamicin, neomycin, and kanamycin can damage the auditory and vestibular nerves, causing both deafness and labyrinthitis. Hypothyroidism can be associated with a type of deafness that may respond to treatment with thyroid hormone.

Congenital deafness is caused by developmental defects in the hearing apparatus. Although present from birth, it is not evident until puppies are old enough to respond to sound. This happens from 11 days onward. Deafness may involve one or both ears. If only one ear is affected, you may not notice the deafness.

There is a connection between hereditary deafness and a gene for coat color. Dogs with predominantly white coats, and those with *merle* coats, are at increased risk for congenital deafness. The highest incidence occurs in Dalmatians, but at least 60 breeds and their crosses are affected. The deafness is due to a lack of pigment or melanin in the "hair cells" that detect sounds. If these dogs with merle or white coats have pigmented cells in their inner ears, even though the rest of their haircoat is lacking pigment, they can hear normally.

Senile deafness develops gradually, beginning at about 10 years of age. It is seldom total. Old dogs with deafness often retain some ability to hear high-pitched sounds, such as a dog whistle. The deafness may not be particularly noticeable unless there is also loss of vision.

A dog with significant hearing loss is less active, moves more slowly, is difficult to arouse from sleep, and fails to respond to commands. Shouting, clapping loudly when the dog is not looking, blowing a whistle, and other attention-getting sounds can be used to test the dog's hearing.

Stamping on the floor attracts a deaf dog's attention, because she can feel the vibrations. Always do this before waking or touching a deaf dog, so that you do not startle her.

Hearing tests can be done on puppies and adult dogs. Hearing is tested using an electroencephalogram (*EEG*) to record the brain waves produced in response to sounds of different frequencies. If the brain wave pattern remains unchanged, the sound was not heard. This procedure, called a brain stem auditory evoked response (BAER) test, is particularly useful for screening puppies who are at risk for congenital deafness. It is available at referral centers.

The Institute for Genetic Disease Control in Animals (GDC) maintains an open registry for inherited deafness. Results are used to better understand the mode of inheritance and develop data that can help in selecting normal breeding animals. Testing is done at a minimum age of 35 days, according to a BAER protocol. Most of GDC's operation has been transferred to OFA, so search there for deafness registry information, as well (see appendix D).

THE NOSE

A dog's nose is made up of the nostrils (also called nares) and the nasal cavity, which runs the length of the muzzle. The nasal cavity is divided by a midline partition into two passages, one for each nostril (see the figure *Anatomy of the Head*, page 232). These passages open into the throat behind the soft palate. The dog has two major sinuses that connect with the nasal cavity: the maxillary and the frontal.

The nasal cavity is lined by a mucous membrane called the mucociliary blanket, which is abundantly supplied with blood vessels. This blanket acts as a defense against infection by trapping bacteria and foreign irritants and conveying them to the back of the throat through the actions of tiny hairlike structures called cilia. At the back of the throat, foreign particles are trapped in mucus and either coughed out or swallowed. Dehydration or exposure to cold air stops the motion of the cilia and thickens the layer of mucus. This reduces the effectiveness of the mucociliary blanket.

The nasal cavity is extremely sensitive and bleeds easily when traumatized. An otoscope and nasal forceps are used to remove foreign bodies. Instruments passed into the nasal passages cause violent sneezing, however, so heavy sedation or anesthesia is required to conduct a thorough examination.

Most dogs have darkly pigmented noses, but brown, pink, and spotted noses are normal for some breeds. In some dogs with pink noses, the nose will darken in summer and then lighten up again in winter. This is normal (see *Snow Nose*, page 225).

The moisture at the tip of the nose is secreted by mucous glands in the nasal cavity. A dog's nose is normally cool and moist, but may be warm and dry, depending on the dog's activity and state of hydration, and the temperature and humidity. A warm, dry nose does not necessarily indicate that a dog has a fever. If you suspect fever, confirm it with a rectal thermometer.

There is a rich supply of nerves in the nasal cavity of dogs—far greater than in most other animals. These nerves ultimately connect with the highly developed olfactory center in the dog's brain. The abundant nerve supply and the large olfactory center account for the dog's keen sense of smell—perhaps 100 times greater than ours.

Dogs are able to keep track of multiple scents at once and do not experience nasal fatigue, as humans do (our noses quickly become accustomed to a scent and then ignore it). Dogs are trained to sniff out narcotics, track people, detect cancers and metabolic problems, and indicate the presence of pests from termites to bed bugs.

Dogs use scent as their primary sense to identify friend from foe. While many older dogs will lose some vision and hearing, the sense of smell normally stays with a dog for his entire life.

Signs of Nasal Irritation
Nasal Discharge

A runny nose indicates an irritant in the nasal passages. Because irritants also produce sneezing, these two signs tend to occur together.

Excited and nervous dogs often secrete a clear, watery mucus that drips from the nose. This type of discharge is not accompanied by sneezing and disappears when the dog relaxes.

Any nasal discharge that persists for several hours is significant. A clear, watery discharge is typical of allergic and viral rhinitis, while a thick discharge suggests a bacterial or fungal infection. A nasal discharge accompanied by gagging and retching indicates a postnasal drip. A discharge from one nostril only is seen with oral nasal fistulas and foreign bodies and tumors in the nose.

Foreign bodies, tumors, and chronic bacterial and fungal infections can erode the mucous membranes and produce a blood-streaked mucus discharge or a nosebleed. Nosebleeds also occur with bleeding disorders such as von Willebrand's disease and hemophilia. Trauma, such as banging the nose, may also lead to some bloody discharge. If you see blood in the nasal discharge, notify your veterinarian.

Human cold viruses don't affect dogs. However, dogs are afflicted by a number of serious respiratory diseases that initially produce symptoms similar to those of the human cold. A runny nose, along with an eye discharge and coughing and sneezing, is an indication that you should seek veterinary attention for your dog. A yellowish discharge along with coughing and fever could indicate canine influenza (see page 325) and you should contact your veterinarian immediately.

Sneezing

Sneezing is an important early sign of nasal irritation. Occasional sneezing is normal, but if the sneezing is violent, uninterrupted, or accompanied by a nasal discharge, it's a serious condition and you should consult your veterinarian. Some dogs will sneeze if your house has a new carpet or new cleaning agents are used. Perfumes, cigarette smoke, hairspray, and even scented candles may cause your dog to sneeze.

Sneezing with a watery nasal discharge and rubbing the face with the paws is typical of canine atopy (see page 138). A sudden bout of violent sneezing, along with head shaking and pawing at the nose, suggests a foreign body in the nose. Nosebleeds can occur after particularly violent bouts of sneezing.

Prolonged sneezing causes swelling and congestion of the nasal membranes. The result is a sniffling or noisy character to the dog's breathing.

MOUTH BREATHING

Dogs are nose breathers and usually do not breathe through their mouths except when panting. Mouth breathing indicates that both nasal air passages are blocked. In these dogs, no air is moving through the nose—only through the mouth. This may not be obvious until the dog becomes excited or begins to exercise.

The Nose
STENOTIC NARES (COLLAPSED NOSTRILS)

Collapsed nostrils occur in puppies of the brachycephalic breeds, including Pugs, Pekingnese, Bulldogs, Boston Terriers, Shih Tzu, and others. In these puppies, the nasal cartilages are soft and floppy, so that as the puppy breathes in the nostrils come together and obstruct the nasal openings. This causes various degrees of respiratory obstruction, which can seriously compromise the puppy's health and development.

Collapsed nostrils are a congenital problem often accompanied by other manifestations of the brachycephalic syndrome described on page 313.

Collapsed nostrils is a common problem in short-nosed breeds, such as these Pugs. These dogs snort, sniffle, and have a foamy nasal discharge.

Nasal Solar Dermatitis (Collie Nose)

This is a weepy, crusty dermatitis that affects Collies, Australian Shepherds, Shetland Sheepdogs, and related breeds. It is seen most commonly in sunny regions such as Florida, California, and the mountainous regions of the West. It is caused by lack of pigment on the nose and prolonged exposure to the ultraviolet rays in sunlight. Lack of pigment is hereditary in some dogs, but it can be acquired through skin diseases and scarring.

Initially, the skin appears normal except for the lack of black pigment. With exposure to sunlight, the skin at the border between the muzzle and nose becomes irritated. As the irritation continues, hair falls out and the skin begins to ooze and crust. With continued exposure, the skin breaks down. In advanced cases, the whole surface of the nose becomes ulcerated and the tip itself may disappear, leaving unsightly tissue that bleeds easily. Skin cancer may develop.

Nasal solar dermatitis must be distinguished from discoid lupus erythematosus, pemphigus foliaceus, and zinc responsive dermatosis—skin diseases discussed in chapter 4. All three diseases produce a skin reaction similar to nasal solar dermatitis. A distinguishing feature of nasal solar dermatitis is that pigment was lacking *before* the disease developed. In the other three, the pigment disappears as the disease progresses. Note that once depigmentation occurs in dogs with these diseases, the damaging effects of sunlight add to the problem.

Treatment: Prevent further exposure by keeping your dog indoors as much as possible when the sunlight is the most intense—between 9 a.m. and 3 p.m. Letting the dog out on cloudy days does not address the problem, because ultraviolet rays penetrate clouds. Sunscreens are of some aid in protecting

These crusts and ulcerations of the skin on the nose were caused by nasal solar dermatitis.

dogs who spend time outdoors. Use products containing an SPF greater than 15. Apply the sunscreen 30 to 60 minutes before exposure and again later in the day.

Treat an irritated nose with a skin preparation such as Cortaid that contains 0.5 to 1.0 percent hydrocortisone.

NASAL DEPIGMENTATION

Nasal depigmentation, also called Dudley nose, is a syndrome of unknown cause that may be a form of vitiligo. A nose that is solid black at birth gradually fades to a chocolate brown, or in the case of complete depigmentation, to pinkish white. Some dogs experience a remission in which the nose spontaneously becomes darker. Depigmentation primarily affects the skin of the nose where hair is absent. It tends to occur in Afghan Hounds, Samoyeds, white German Shepherd Dogs, Doberman Pinschers, Irish Setters, Pointers, and Poodles.

Snow nose is a separate but common condition in which dark pigment on the nose fades during the winter months and darkens again in spring and summer. Complete depigmentation does not occur. Snow nose is seen in Siberian Huskies, Golden Retrievers, Labrador Retrievers, Bernese Mountain Dogs, and other breeds.

Treatment: Lack of pigment on the nose is primarily a cosmetic problem and is considered to be a conformation fault in the show ring. A number of home remedies have been advocated, but their success is questionable. Sunscreen, as described for nasal solar dermatitis, helps prevent ultraviolet injury to dogs who lack pigment.

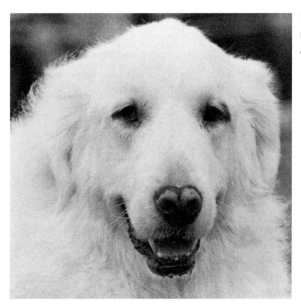

Depigmentation of the nose, as seen here, can be a seasonal abnormality.

PLASTIC DISH NASAL DERMATITIS

This is a localized form of depigmentation that affects the nose and lips. It is caused by eating out of plastic and rubber dishes that contain the chemical p-benzylhydroquinone. This chemical is absorbed through the skin and inhibits the synthesis of melanin, the substance that produces dark pigment in the skin. The involved skin may also become irritated and inflamed.

Treatment: The problem can be corrected by switching to glass, ceramic, or stainless steel bowls for all the dog's food and water.

HYPERKERATOSIS (NASAL CALLUS)

This disease occurs in old dogs. The cause is unknown. The skin of the nose becomes dry, thickened, and hornlike. The callused nose may crack and develop fissures, then become irritated and infected. Hyperkeratosis can also occur in association with zinc-responsive dermatosis, pemphigus foliaceus, and discoid lupus erythematosus (all described in chapter 4).

Hard pad is a related condition involving the nose and foot pads; it occurs as a sequel to canine distemper. As the dog recovers from distemper, the nose often regains its normal appearance.

Treatment: There is no cure for idiopathic nasal callus. Control is aimed at softening the nasal callus with wet dressings and keeping the nose well lubricated with mineral oil, aloe, or petroleum jelly. Local infection is treated with topical antibiotics, such as triple antibiotic ointment.

The Nasal Cavity
EPISTAXIS (NOSEBLEEDS)

Nosebleeds are caused by foreign bodies, trauma, infections, tumors, or parasites that erode the nasal mucous membranes. Some are caused by lacerations of the nostrils or puncture wounds from objects such as thorns or barbed wire. Nosebleeds are often accompanied by bouts of sneezing that aggravate the bleeding.

A spontaneous nosebleed may be a manifestation of a generalized clotting disorder such as hemophilia or von Willebrand's disease. Vitamin K deficiency is another cause of spontaneous bleeding. It occurs most often with poisoning by rodenticide anticoagulants.

Treatment: Keep the dog as quiet as possible. Apply an ice pack wrapped in cloth to the bridge of the nose. If the nostril is bleeding and the bleeding site is visible, apply steady pressure with a gauze square.

Most nosebleeds subside rather quickly when interference is kept to a minimum. If the bleeding does not stop, or if there is no obvious cause, take your dog at once to the veterinary clinic.

FOREIGN BODY IN THE NOSE

Foreign bodies that may work their way into the nasal cavity include blades of grass, grass seeds, awns, and bone and wood splinters. The principal sign is a sudden bout of violent sneezing, accompanied by pawing at the nose, and occasionally, bleeding from one nostril. The sneezing is first continuous and later intermittent. When a foreign body has been present for hours or days, there is a thick discharge (often bloody) from the involved nostril.

Treatment: A foreign body may be visible close to the opening of the nostril, in which case it can be removed with tweezers. In most cases it will be located farther back. If the foreign body is not removed in a short time, it tends to migrate even deeper into the nasal cavity. Do not poke blindly in your dog's nose, as this causes further injury. Take your dog to the veterinarian. Removal of most foreign bodies requires heavy sedation or general anesthesia.

After the foreign body has been removed, your veterinarian may prescribe an oral antibiotic to treat any secondary bacterial infection.

ORAL-NASAL FISTULA

In this condition, food and water regurgitate out the nose when the dog eats and drinks. The most common congenital cause is cleft palate (see page 507). An infected tooth is the most common acquired cause. The canine teeth and fourth premolars in the upper jaw lie beneath the nasal passages. An abscessed tooth (usually a canine tooth) can rupture into the nasal cavity. The tooth falls out and the space it once occupied opens a passage through the hard palate that allows food to pass from the mouth into the nose.

The signs of oral-nasal fistula are a unilateral nasal discharge accompanied by sneezing, especially after eating.

Treatment: The problem is treated surgically by taking a flap of mucous membrane from the inside of the mouth and suturing it across the defect. Long-term antibiotics may be needed to clear up any infections.

Prevention: Proper dental care and prompt attention to any dental problems while they are still minor will help prevent oral-nasal fistula caused by tooth decay.

ALLERGIC RHINITIS

An allergic nasal discharge occurs in dogs with canine atopy (see page 138). Signs are the abrupt onset of sneezing with a clear nasal discharge. Itching around the eyes may cause the dog to rub his face on the carpet or furniture. With repeated exposure to different allergens, the allergic response becomes a year-round problem.

Treatment: An episode of allergic rhinitis responds well to an antihistamine such as Benadryl (see *Over-the-Counter Drugs for Home Veterinary Use,* page 571, for dosage). Definitive treatment is directed toward the underlying atopy.

RHINITIS AND SINUSITIS

The frontal and maxillary sinuses are extensions of the nasal cavity and are lined by a mucous membrane similar to the one that lines the nose. Accordingly, infections in the nasal cavity may spread to the sinuses, and vice versa. A nasal infection is called rhinitis and a sinus infection is called sinusitis.

The signs of rhinitis and sinusitis are sneezing, nasal discharge and gagging or retching from a postnasal drip. The discharge is thick, creamy, and foul smelling.

In young dogs, bacterial rhinitis and sinusitis usually do not occur unless the mucous membrane has been damaged by an upper respiratory infection, foreign body in the nasal cavity, or trauma to the nose. Respiratory infections caused by the herpesvirus, adenovirus, or parainfluenza virus are the most common causes of acute rhinitis. These infections may be followed by secondary bacterial involvement.

Canine distemper is a serious cause of secondary bacterial rhinitis. The discharge is *mucoid* and *purulent.* Other signs of distemper will be present.

In older dogs, tumors and infected teeth are the most common causes of rhinitis and sinusitis. Both are characterized by a chronic, long-standing *purulent* discharge from one nostril, along with sneezing and sniffling. Tumors and abscessed teeth may cause a blood-streaked discharge.

The diagnosis of rhinitis or sinusitis is based on X-rays, cultures, direct visualization of the nasal cavity using a flexible endoscope, and, in some cases, tissue biopsy.

Treatment: Bacterial rhinitis following upper respiratory infection is treated with broad-spectrum antibiotics that are continued for at least two weeks. Fungal infections usually respond to one of the newer antifungal agents, such as itraconazole or fluconazole. Antifungal drugs are given for six to eight weeks.

Chronic infections are difficult to clear up. Inflammatory debris builds up, causing further obstruction of air flow. Treatment involves using an antibiotic selected on the basis of sensitivity tests. In some cases, exploratory surgery will be required to clean out the nasal cavity and/or an infected sinus.

NASAL MITES

Nasal mites (*Pneumonyssoides caninum*) can cause sneezing, coughing, and head shaking in infested dogs. These uncommon mites are spread directly from dog to dog and are seen more often in large breed dogs. Diagnosis may be made by seeing mites with an *endoscope* or flushing the nose with saline and examining the fluid.

Treatment: There are no drugs currently approved for treating nasal mites in dogs, but ivermection and milbemycin have been successfully used *off-label*.

NASAL POLYPS AND TUMORS

A polyp is a growth that begins as an enlargement of one of the mucous glands in the nose. It looks something like a cherry on a stalk. It is not cancer. Polyps cause symptoms by bleeding and blocking the flow of air. They can be removed by your veterinarian. Recurrence is possible.

Other tumors are found in the nasal cavity and sinuses. Most are malignant. They tend to occur in older dogs. Breeds reported to be at increased risk include the Airedale Terrier, Basset Hound, Old English Sheepdog, Scottish Terrier, German Shepherd Dog, Keeshond, and German Shorthaired Pointer. The main signs are discharge or bleeding through one nostril, accompanied by sneezing and sniffling.

The diagnosis is suspected on X-rays and confirmed by biopsy of the tumor through an endoscope. A CT scan may be useful in evaluating the extent of bone involvement. Large tumors can make one side of the face protrude. If they extend behind the eye, the eye will bulge. These tumors are far advanced.

Treatment: Benign tumors are cured by complete surgical removal. Malignant tumors are invasive and generally are not curable, but survival can sometimes be prolonged using a combination of surgery and radiation therapy.

THE MOUTH AND THROAT

The oral cavity is bounded on the front and sides by the lips and cheeks, above by the hard and soft palate, and below by the tongue and muscles of the floor of the mouth. Four pairs of salivary glands drain into the mouth, the two largest being the parotid and mandibular glands.

The saliva of dogs is alkaline and contains antibacterial enzymes. There is also a normal flora of bacteria in the mouth that keep harmful bacteria from gaining a foothold. These factors reduce the frequency of mouth infections in dogs. Still, a dog's saliva is not sterile and doesn't have magical healing powers.

The pharynx is a space where the nasal passages join with the back of the mouth. Food is prevented from entering the respiratory tree by the epiglottis, a flaplike valve that closes over the larynx as the dog swallows.

How to Examine the Mouth

Most mouth problems can be identified by inspecting the lips, gums, teeth, and throat. To open the mouth, slip a thumb into the space behind the canine tooth and press upward on the roof of the mouth. As the mouth begins to open, press down on the lower jaw with the opposite thumb. To see the throat and tonsils, depress the tongue with a finger.

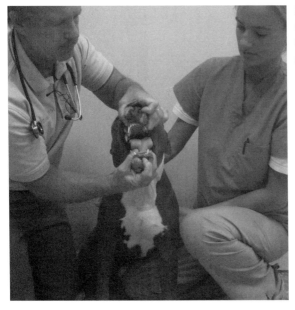

Place your thumbs in the spaces behind the canine teeth and open the dog's mouth to examine it.

Another method is to gently squeeze in from the top of the dog's muzzle, right behind the whiskers, with your thumb and forefinger. As the mouth opens, separate the top and bottom jaws with your fingers.

To examine the dog's bite (also known as occlusion), close the mouth and raise the upper lip while drawing down on the lower lip with your thumb. The bite is determined by seeing how the upper and lower incisor teeth come together (see *Malocclusion*, page 242).

Raising the lips also exposes the mucous membranes of the gums. The appearance of the gums gives an indication of anemia and the state of circulation. This is easiest to evaluate in dogs with pink gums (as opposed to pigmented gums).

Signs of Mouth and Throat Disease

An important sign of mouth pain is a change in eating behavior. A dog with a tender mouth eats slowly and selectively, dropping food that is particularly coarse and large. A dog with pain on one side of the mouth often tilts her head and chews on the opposite side. With an extremely painful mouth, the dog stops eating altogether.

Excessive drooling is common in all painful mouth diseases. It is often accompanied by bad breath. Any form of halitosis is abnormal. Periodontal disease and gingivitis are the most common causes of halitosis in dogs.

Sudden gagging, choking, drooling, and difficulty swallowing suggest a foreign object in the mouth or throat.

Difficulty opening and closing the mouth is characteristic of head and neck abscesses, nerve damage, or jaw injuries.

The Mouth
Cheilitis (Inflammation of the Lips)

Cheilitis usually results from an infection inside the mouth that extends to involve the lips. In hunting dogs, chapped lips can be caused by contact with weeds and brush. Dogs with canine atopy may irritate their lips by constantly rubbing and pawing the face.

Cheilitis can be recognized by the serum crusts that form at the junction of the haired and smooth parts of the lips. As the crusts peel off, the skin becomes raw and denuded and is sensitive to touch. Involvement of the hair follicles produces a localized folliculitis.

Treatment: Clean the lips daily using benzoyl peroxide shampoo (OxyDex or Pyoben), or hydrogen peroxide diluted 1:5 with water. Then apply an antibiotic-steroid cream such as Neocort. As the infection subsides, apply petroleum jelly or aloe to keep the lips soft and pliable. Chapstick may also be used. Periodontal disease or canine atopy, if present, should be treated to prevent recurrence.

Lip Fold Pyoderma

In breeds with pendulous lips, folds on the lower lip that make contact with the upper teeth may become inflamed and infected. This tends to occur in St. Bernards, Cocker Spaniels, setters and some scenthounds. The lower skin folds often form pockets with the overlying skin folds of the upper lips, which

This inflammation of the lips is characteristic of cheilitis.

trap food and saliva, creating a constantly wet environment that favors bacterial growth. When the folds are flattened, a raw surface is visible. The foul odor is often the reason for seeking medical attention.

Treatment: Treat as described for *Skin Fold Pyoderma*, page 159.

MOUTH LACERATIONS

Lacerations of the lips, gums, and tongue are common. Most occur during fights with other animals. Occasionally a dog accidentally bites her own lip or tongue, usually because of a badly positioned canine tooth. Dogs can cut their tongues picking up and licking sharp objects, such as the top of a food can.

An unusual cause of tongue trauma is freezing to metal in extremely cold weather. When the tongue pulls free, epithelium strips off, leaving a raw, bleeding surface.

Treatment: Control lip bleeding by applying pressure to the cut for 5 to 10 minutes. Grasp the lip between the fingers using a clean gauze dressing or a piece of linen. Bleeding from the tongue is difficult to control with direct pressure. Calm the dog and proceed to the nearest veterinary clinic.

Minor cuts that have stopped bleeding do not need to be sutured. Stitching should be considered when the edges gape open, when the laceration involves the lip border, or when bleeding persists after the pressure dressing is removed. Cuts into the muscle of the tongue will need suturing, as well.

During healing, clean the dog's mouth twice a day with an antiseptic mouth wash, as described in the treatment of stomatitis (page 235). Feed a soft diet for one week.

If the laceration was caused by a poorly positioned tooth, the tooth should be extracted or realigned.

MOUTH BURNS

Electrical burns of the mouth are caused by chewing on electric cords (see *Electric Shock*, page 21). Most heal spontaneously, but in some cases a grayish ulcer develops at the site of the burn. The ulcer may need to be surgically removed.

Chemical burns of the mouth are common. They are caused by licking a corrosive substance such as lye, phenol, phosphorus, household cleaners, or alkalis. If the dog swallows the chemical, her esophagus or stomach may also be burned.

Treatment: For emergency treatment of oral chemical burns, sponge and rinse the mouth with copious amounts of tap water. Then transport the dog as quickly as possible to the nearest veterinary clinic for treatment of poisoning. If there must be a delay, follow the instructions for *Corrosive Household Products* (page 34). The aftercare for burns of the mouth is the same as that described on this page for stomatitis.

Stomatitis (Sore Mouth)

Stomatitis is inflammation of the mouth, gums, and tongue. It is usually caused by periodontal disease or foreign bodies caught between the teeth or embedded in the tongue. Occasionally, it follows mouth lacerations and burns of the mucous membranes.

Stomatitis is an extremely painful condition accompanied by drooling, bad breath, refusal to eat, difficulty chewing, and reluctance to permit an examination of the mouth. The inside of the mouth is red, inflamed, and sometimes ulcerated. The gums often bleed when rubbed.

Stomatitis can be a local manifestation of a systemic disease. It is seen in dogs with kidney failure and uremia, diabetes mellitus, hypoparathyroidism, leptospirosis, distemper, and autoimmune skin diseases.

Trench mouth (St. Vincent's stomatitis; necrotizing ulcerative stomatitis) is an exceptionally painful stomatitis caused by a variety of bacteria. There is a characteristic serious mouth odor, accompanied by brown, *purulent*, slimy saliva that stains the front of the legs. The gums are beefy red and bleed easily. Ulcerations occur in the mucous membranes. Some cases are initiated by periodontal disease.

Thrush (yeast stomatitis) is an uncommon stomatitis seen chiefly in dogs who are receiving broad-spectrum antibiotics that destroy normal bacterial flora and allow the growth of yeast. Thrush also occurs in dogs with compromised immunity associated with chronic illness. The mucous lining of the gums and tongue are covered with soft white patches that coalesce to produce an adherent white membrane. Painful ulcers appear as the disease progresses.

Recurrent stomatitis occurs where jagged, broken, or diseased teeth make repeated contact with the mucous lining of the lips, cheeks, or gums, causing traumatic ulcers of the mouth. A bacteria and a fungus are quite commonly cultured from these ulcers.

Treatment: In most cases periodontal disease is present as a cause or a contributing factor. Your veterinarian may recommend a thorough cleaning of the dog's mouth under anesthesia. This affords the opportunity to treat dental calculus, decayed roots, and broken teeth—treatments that are all essential to cure the problem. The dog is then placed on an appropriate antibiotic.

This dog's tongue is covered by the soft white patches that are characteristic of thrush.

It is important to diagnose and treat any systemic cause of the stomatitis.

Aftercare at home involves rinsing the mouth with a 0.1 or 0.2 percent chlorhexidine solution (Peridex or Nolvadent) once or twice a day. Soak a cotton ball and gently swab the gums, teeth, and oral cavity. You can use a plastic syringe and squirt the mouth wash directly onto the gums.

Feed a soft diet consisting of canned dog food diluted with water to a mushy consistency. Buffered or enteric-coated aspirin helps to control pain (see *Over-the-Counter Drugs for Home Veterinary Use*, page 571, for dosage), or your veterinarian may prescribe a pain medication such as Etogesic or Deramax. B-complex vitamins that contain niacin may be of benefit.

Thrush is treated with topical Nystatin or an antifungal drug such as keto-conazole or itraconazole.

ORAL PAPILLOMAS

Oral papillomas are painless warts that grow on the lips and in the mouths of dogs younger than 2 years old. They are caused by the canine oral papilloma virus. Initially, papillomas are small and pink. Over four to six weeks, they increase in size and take on a rough, grayish-white, cauliflowerlike appearance. As many as 50 to 100 papillomas may be present.

Skin papillomas caused by the same virus are common and occur on the surface of the eyelids and the skin of the body.

Treatment: Oral papillomas usually disappear spontaneously in 6 to 12 weeks. If they fail to do so, they can be removed by surgery, freezing, or electrocautery. Chemotherapy is effective in dogs with numerous lesions. The dog's immune system makes antibodies that prevent reinfection.

FOREIGN OBJECTS IN THE MOUTH

Foreign objects in the mouth include bone splinters, slivers of wood, sewing needles and pins, porcupine quills, fish hooks, and plant awns. Sharp objects can penetrate the lips, gums, and tongue. Other objects can get caught between the teeth or wedged across the roof of the mouth. Pieces of string can become wrapped around the teeth and tongue.

A common place for a penetrating foreign body is beneath the tongue. On lifting the tongue, you may see a grapelike swelling or a draining tract. This means the foreign body has been present for some time.

In areas where cockle and sand burrs are prevalent, many small spines can become embedded in the tongue and gums as the dog grooms burrs from her coat and feet.

The signs of a foreign body are pawing at the mouth, rubbing the mouth along the floor, drooling, gagging, licking the lips repeatedly, and holding the mouth open. When a foreign object has been present for a day or longer, the principal signs may be lethargy, bad breath, and refusal to eat.

Treatment: Obtain a good light source and gently examine your dog's mouth, as described earlier in this chapter. A good look may reveal the cause. It is possible to directly remove some foreign bodies. Others will require a general anesthetic, which means a trip to the veterinarian.

A thread attached to a needle should not be pulled out, because it can be used to locate the needle.

Foreign bodies present for a day or longer are difficult to remove and may cause infection. They must be removed, and the dog evaluated, by a veterinarian. After removal, the dog is placed on an antibiotic for one week.

Fish Hook

To remove a fish hook from the lip, if the barb is visible, cut the shank next to the barb with wire cutters and remove the hook in two pieces. If the barb is embedded in the lip, determine which direction the barb is pointed and push the hook through until the barb is free. *Do not* try to pull the barbed end back through the tissue! Then cut the hook and remove it. Treat the puncture wound as described in *Wounds* (page 42).

Do not attempt to remove a fish hook embedded in the mouth or one that has been swallowed with the line attached. Take your dog to the veterinarian at once.

Porcupine Quills

Porcupine quills can penetrate the face, nose, lips, oral cavity, feet, and skin of the dog. Always check carefully between the toes, as dogs may get quills stuck there from their face as they paw at them. The decision to remove quills at home is based on the number of quills, their location, how deeply they are embedded, and whether professional help is readily available. Quills inside the mouth are difficult to remove without anesthesia.

To remove quills at home, restrain the dog as described in *Restraining for Examination and Treatment* (page 2). Using a surgical hemostat or needle-nose pliers, grasp each quill near the dog's skin and draw it straight out on the long axis of the quill. If the quill breaks off, a fragment will be left behind, causing a deep-seated infection that requires prompt veterinary treatment.

After removing quills, observe your dog for about one week, looking for signs of infection, *abscess*, or deeply embedded quills working their way out.

Dogs with many quills will need anesthesia to be sure all the quills are removed. Your veterinarian may prescribe antibiotics for a large number of quills. Broken-off quill fragments can migrate in the tissues and cause serious deep-seated infections.

String Around the Tongue

Swelling and bluish discoloration of the tongue may be caused by a rubber band or a string around the base. Occasionally a dog swallows one end of a string and the other end loops around the tongue. The harder the dog swallows, the more the string cuts into the tongue. Depending on how tightly the tongue is constricted, the venous and/or arterial blood supply may be cut off, resulting in irreversible tissue damage.

Signs of tongue strangulation are similar to those of a foreign object in the mouth. It is easy to overlook a constriction because the band cuts into the tissue. A close inspection may be necessary to find the string and divide it, then cut it off using blunt-nosed baby scissors. If the dog is struggling, take her to the veterinarian right away to have it done.

GROWTHS IN THE MOUTH

A common tumor in the mouth is the epulis, seen most often in Boxers and Bulldogs. These benign tumors grow from the periodontal membrane in response to gum inflammation. They appear as growths on a flap of tissue. There are often multiple growths. Rarely, an epulis becomes malignant.

Gingival hyperplasia is a condition in which the gums grow up alongside or over the teeth. A familial inheritance has been identified in Boxers, and is suspected in Great Danes, Collies, Doberman Pinschers, and Dalmatians. The enlarged gums can interfere with eating and are easily traumatized. They also predispose the dog to periodontal disease. If any of these occur, the enlarged gums should be surgically removed.

Malignant tumors in the mouth are rare. In order of frequency, they include melanoma, squamous cell carcinoma, and fibrosarcoma. These tumors tend to occur in older dogs. Biopsy is required to make an exact diagnosis.

Dogs with oral tumors may drool, have trouble eating, and/or have a very foul odor to their breath. The drool may be bloody.

Treatment: Early, aggressive treatment of mouth tumors, with wide local excision and/or radiation therapy, offers the best chance for a cure. Surgery may involve removing part of the upper or lower jaw.

In many cases the tumor is already too far advanced for treatment. The prognosis is best for squamous cell carcinomas. Fifty percent of treated dogs survive a year or longer.

A string from a piece of baloney became wrapped around the base of this dog's tongue, causing ulceration. It was not seen until the tongue was raised.

A melanoma is growing on the inside of the upper lip.

Teeth and Gums
DECIDUOUS AND ADULT TEETH

With rare exceptions, puppies are born without teeth. The first teeth to erupt are the incisors, at 2 to 3 weeks of age. Next are the canines and premolars. The last premolar erupts at about 8 to 12 weeks of age. As a rule, the teeth of larger breeds erupt sooner than those of smaller breeds.

The average puppy has 28 deciduous (temporary or baby) teeth. These are the incisors, canines, and premolars. Puppies don't have molars.

The deciduous teeth remain for only three to seven months. Beginning at about 3 months of age, the baby incisors are shed and replaced by adult incisors. By 5 months, a puppy should have all her adult incisors. The adult canines, premolars, and molars come in between 4 and 7 months of age. Thus, by 7 to 8 months of age, a puppy should have all her adult teeth. Knowing this teething sequence can give you an approximate idea of the age of a puppy.

The average adult dog has 42 teeth: 22 in the mandible or lower jaw, and 20 in the maxilla or upper jaw. In each jaw there are 6 incisors, 2 canines, and 8 premolars. There are 6 molars in the lower jaw and 4 in the upper jaw. The wear on the incisors is used to judge the age of the adult dog.

How Dogs' Teeth Reveal Their Age

In adult dogs, approximate age can be determined by checking the wear on the incisors. This method is relatively reliable up to about 6 years of age, but individual variations do occur. Beyond 7 years, using the teeth to determine age is unreliable.

The edges of the incisors are called the cusps. The amount of wear on the cusps is the most important factor in determining the age of the dog. The chart on 241 explains how wear patterns typically occur (upper and lower

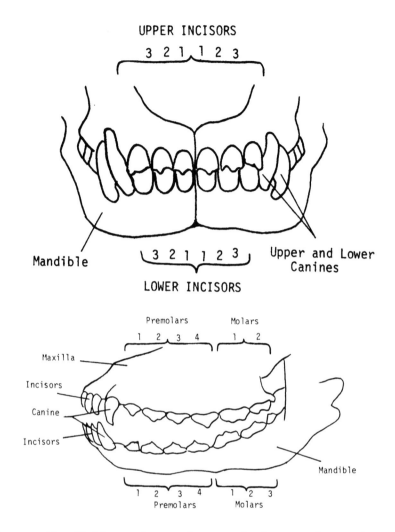

UPPER INCISORS

3 2 1 1 2 3

Mandible

3 2 1 1 2 3   Upper and Lower
                          Canines

LOWER INCISORS

Premolars   Molars

1 2 3 4   1 2

Maxilla

Incisors

Canine

Incisors

Mandible

1 2 3 4   1 2 3
Premolars   Molars

incisors are identified by numbers, as shown in the figure on this page). Wear patterns are described for each age, but individual variations do occur. Dogs who chew on metal, such as crate or fence wires, or chew on abrasive materials such as tennis ball coverings, will wear down their teeth more quickly.

RETAINED BABY TEETH

Normally, the roots of the baby teeth are reabsorbed as the adult teeth take their place. When this fails to happen, you will see what appears to be a double set of teeth. Toy breeds, in particular, tend to retain baby teeth as their adult teeth erupt. The adult teeth are then pushed out of line, producing a malocclusion or bad bite.

Typical Wear Patterns of Canine Teeth

Age	Wear Pattern
1 year	Cusps are worn off lower incisors #1; tartar begins to form on the canines.
2 years	Cusps are worn off lower incisors #2; tartar is quite noticeable on the canines.
3 years	Cusps are worn off upper incisors #1.
4 years	Cusps are worn off upper incisors #2.
5 years	Cusps are worn slightly (at the corner) on lower incisors #3; the canines begin to show wear.
6 years	Cusps are worn off lower incisors #3; the canines are becoming blunted.

Treatment: Puppies 3 to 4 months of age should be checked from time to time to see that their adult teeth are coming in normally. Whenever baby teeth interfere with adult teeth, the baby teeth should be pulled. If this is done by 4 to 5 months of age, the bite should correct spontaneously.

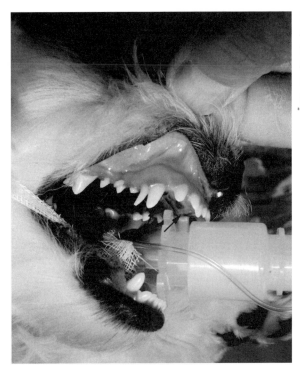

Retained baby teeth, such as the ones indicated by the arrows, can force the adult teeth out of line, causing malocclusion and gum injury.

ABNORMAL NUMBER OF TEETH

The standard of 42 teeth is normal for all adult dogs, whether large or small. An exception is the hairless breeds, such as the Chinese Crested, because the hairless gene also modifies dentition. And in Bulldogs and other *bracycephalic* breeds, the last molars may be absent because of the short jaw.

Some dogs carry a genetic mutation for missing teeth. Doberman Pinschers may have fewer than the normal eight premolars. This is considered a show fault but has no real significance in terms of the dog's health, unless the missing teeth shift the bite. Genetic variations of this type usually are hereditary.

You may find that your dog has more teeth than normal. This occurs most often in spaniels and sighthounds (especially Greyhounds). The extra teeth may crowd, twist, or overlap the normal teeth. The offending teeth should be removed.

MALOCCLUSION (INCORRECT BITE)

A dog's bite is determined by how the upper and lower incisor teeth meet when the mouth is closed. The ideal occlusion is one in which the upper incisors just overlap and touch the lower incisors. This is called the scissors bite. In the even or level bite, the incisors meet edge to edge. This is a common occlusion, but is not considered ideal because the edge-to-edge contact wears the teeth. The correct bite for any given breed is described in the standard for that breed.

An incorrect bite causes breeders more concern than any other mouth problem. Bad bites interfere with the dog's ability to grasp, hold, and chew food. Teeth that are out of alignment may injure the soft parts of the mouth.

Most malocclusions are hereditary, resulting from genetic factors that control the rate of growth of the upper and lower jaws. Some incorrect bites are caused by retained baby teeth, which push the erupting adult teeth out of line.

Overshot bite occurs when the upper jaw protrudes beyond the lower jaw, causing the upper teeth to overlap the lower teeth without touching. This condition is also called prognathism. Some breeds, such as German Shepherd Dogs, will go through a normal stage as puppies in which the bite is overshot. The overshot bite may correct itself spontaneously in young puppies if the gap is no greater than the head of a wooden match. Improvement may continue until the puppy is 10 months old, at which time the jaws stop growing.

Puppies with severe overshot bites may have problems, because as the adult teeth come in they can injure the soft parts of the mouth. This requires treatment.

Undershot bite is the reverse of the overshot bite; the lower jaw protrudes beyond the upper jaw. It is considered normal for *brachycephalic* breeds, such as Bulldogs and Pugs. Undershot bite is also called brachygnathism.

Wry mouth is the worst of the malocclusion problems. In a dog with wry mouth, one side of the jaw grows faster than the other, twisting the mouth. This can be a severe handicap in grasping and chewing food.

Treatment: Puppies should be examined by the veterinarian at 2 to 3 months of age to identify bite problems. In most cases treatment will not be necessary. If there is overcrowding

An overshot bite in an adult dog.

or displacement of permanent teeth, however, the problem should be corrected by tooth extractions or orthodontic procedures such as crown-height reductions or the use of spacers. Interventional orthodontics will disqualify your dog for conformation competition.

The overshot bite is definitely hereditary and may be passed on to members of the next generation. The undershot bite is hereditary in some breeds. Dogs with hereditary dental malocclusions should be eliminated from breeding programs. This does not apply to brachycephalic dogs, in which malocclusion is a breed characteristic.

When a dog has an undershot bite, the teeth can injure the soft tissues of the mouth.

Unstable Jaw

This condition, seen in Pekingese, Chihuahuas, and some other toy breeds, occurs when the cartilage that joins the two sides of the lower jaw at the chin fails to calcify. The lower incisors that are set in this soft cartilage become loose and unstable. Infection descends to the roots of these teeth and destroys the cartilage. This allows the two sides of the jaw to detach and move independently. This condition can be caused by an incorrect calcium to phosphorous ratio in the dog's diet.

Treatment: The unstable jaw can be treated by removing the diseased teeth, administering antibiotics, and stabilizing the joint with wires or screws. If diet is a contributing factor, the diet must be corrected as well.

Periodontal Disease

Periodontal disease is one of the most common problems seen in veterinary practice. It occurs in two forms: The first is gingivitis, a reversible inflammation of the gums. The second is periodontitis, an inflammation of the deeper structures supporting the teeth.

Gingivitis

Gingivitis develops when bacteria build up between the teeth and gums, leading to irritation, inflammation, and bleeding. The edges of healthy gums fit tightly around the teeth. In a dog with gingivitis, rough dental calculus builds up in an irregular fashion along the gum line, producing points at which the gum is forced away from the teeth. This creates small pockets that trap food and bacteria. In time, the gums become infected.

Dental calculus (also called tartar) is composed of calcium salts, food particles, bacteria, and other organic material. It is yellow-brown and soft when first deposited. At the soft stage it is called plaque. The plaque quickly hardens into calculus. Calculus collects on all tooth surfaces, but is found in the greatest amounts on the cheek side of the upper premolars and molars.

This buildup of calculus on the teeth is the primary cause of gum inflammation. This occurs to some extent in all dogs over the age of 2. Certain breeds, such as Poodles, and smaller dogs seem to form calculus more readily. Dogs who eat dry kibble and chew on bones or dog biscuits have less calculus buildup than dogs who eat only soft, canned foods.

A characteristic sign of gingivitis is bad breath. The halitosis may have been present for some time—even accepted as normal. The gums appear red and swollen, and bleed easily when touched. Pressing on the gums may cause pus to ooze from the gum line.

Treatment: Treatment is directed toward preventing gingivitis from progressing to periodontitis and delaying the progress of periodontitis once it is established.

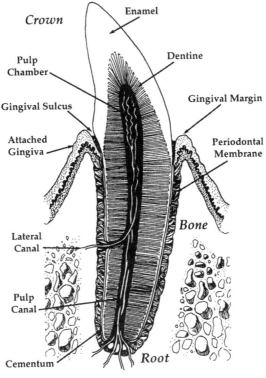

Crown

Enamel

Pulp
Chamber

Dentine

Gingival Sulcus

Gingival Margin

Attached
Gingiva

Periodontal
Membrane

Bone

Lateral
Canal

Pulp
Canal

Cementum

Root

STRUCTURE OF A TOOTH

The teeth should be professionally cleaned, scaled, and polished to remove all plaque and calculus. Many veterinarians now use ultrasonic dental units, similar to the ones used on people, for cleaning dogs' teeth. For optimum results, the dog should be heavily sedated or given a general anesthetic.

The cleaning should be followed with a regular regimen of home oral care. Oxyfresh washes and rinses are also helpful. See *Taking Care of Your Dog's Teeth* (page 249) for suggestions on how to prevent plaque and tartar buildup.

Periodontitis

Periodontitis develops as a continuation of gingivitis. The teeth are held in their bony sockets by a substance called cementum and a specialized connective tissue called the periodontal membrane. As the gum infection attacks the cementum and periodontal membrane (see above the figure *Structure of a Tooth*), the roots become infected, the teeth begin to loosen, and eventually they detach. This is a painful process. Although the dog's appetite is good, she may sit by her food dish, eat reluctantly, and drop food from her mouth. Drooling is common. A root abscess can rupture into the maxillary sinus or nasal cavity, producing a *purulent* unilateral nasal discharge, an oral-nasal fistula (see page 227), or a swelling below the eye.

This dog has severe periodontal disease with swollen, infected gums and heavy calculus deposits on the teeth.

Treatment: The teeth should be professionally cleaned, as described for gingivitis (page 244). Severe infections may necessitate removing a portion of the diseased gum (a procedure called gingivectomy). In a dog with advanced periodontitis, it may be necessary to extract some or all of the teeth before healing can begin. Once the gums are healed, a dog without teeth is able to eat surprisingly well. Antibiotics are given for one to three weeks, depending on the severity of the disease.

Aftercare at home involves rinsing the mouth with 0.2 percent chlorhexidine solution (Peridex or Nolvadent) once or twice a day. Soak a cotton ball and gently swab the gums and teeth, or use a plastic syringe and squirt the antiseptic directly onto the teeth and gums. You can also brush the dog's teeth with a dog tooth brush and a toothpaste made especially for dogs that contains chlorhexidine. Massage the gums with your finger, a piece of linen, or a soft gauze pad, using a gentle circular motion, while pressing on the outside surface of the gums. Continue the mouth washes and massages until the gums are healthy. Feed a soft diet consisting of canned dog food mixed with water to make a mush. Once healing is complete, switch to a good home dental program.

A product called Stomadhex, available through your veterinarian, may prove to be an effective substitute for the aftercare just described. Stomadhex is a small adhesive patch that sticks to mucous membranes. The patch is applied to the inside surface of the upper lip. It stays in place for several hours and slowly releases chlorhexidine and a vitamin called nicotinamide that promotes oral hygiene. The sustained release delivery system helps to prevent dental plaque and tartar and aids in controlling bad breath. The patch is applied daily for 10 days following a dental procedure, or as recommended by your veterinarian.

Pfizer has just released a new vaccine aimed at the primary bacteria found in cases of periodontitis: *Porphyromonas denticanis, gulae* and *salivosa.* The vaccine is aimed at preventing and helping in the treatment of periodontitis. It is currently undergoing more efficacy tests and is not recommended at this time.

CAVITIES

Cavities are not common in dogs. When present, they usually form at the gum line and are related to periodontal disease. They can also occur on the crown of a molar. They appear as a black spot on the tooth. Cavities are painful and eventually lead to root abscesses.

Treatment: The quickest and easiest way to treat a cavity is to extract the tooth. The cavity can be filled and the tooth saved, but most veterinarians do not have the supplies and the equipment to fill cavities and will refer the dog to a veterinarian who specializes in dentistry.

Root canal therapy is also being done for dogs who have deep cavities that expose the tooth pulp. Root canals are fairly common today and can be especially useful for dogs with fractured canine teeth.

ABSCESSED ROOTS

Root abscesses can affect any of the teeth, but the ones most commonly involved are the canines and the upper fourth premolars. Tooth abscesses are extremely painful and are accompanied by fever, reluctance to eat, and depression. You may see pus oozing around the tooth. X-rays confirm the diagnosis and show whether bone is involved.

An abscessed upper fourth premolar causes a characteristic swelling of the face below the eye. Eventually the abscess breaks through the skin and drains pus over the side of the face. A diseased tooth may break through the skin of the lower jaw and produce a similar condition. An abscessed tooth can result in an oral-nasal fistula (see page 227).

Treatment: The abscessed tooth is extracted under anesthesia and the tooth cavity is cleaned and drained. In some cases the tooth can be saved by doing a root canal or endodontic procedure. Antibiotics are used to treat infection. Aftercare at home involves the use of chlorhexidine mouthwashes, as described for periodontitis (page 245).

This dog has a ruptured abscess involving the root of the upper fourth premolar, with pus and blood draining over the side of the face.

BROKEN TEETH

Broken teeth are common. They are caused by chewing on hard objects, such as stones and hard bones, by catching the teeth on the wire of kennels and cages, or by trauma.

Treatment: If the fracture involves only the enamel, the tooth is not painful and no treatment is necessary. However, a break in the crown that extends into the dental pulp can be extremely painful, and the dog may become depressed and refuse to eat. Restorative dentistry or extraction of the tooth will be necessary to prevent an abscessed root. Along with a root canal, a crown may be made to replace the damaged tooth. These can be made of metal or a new ceramic. This is most commonly done for working dogs such as police dogs. Dogs may not compete in conformation competition with a crowned tooth.

ENAMEL HYPOPLASIA OR DAMAGE

Some dogs will have damage to the enamel covering of their teeth. This may be developmental, or may be associated with disease, such as distemper or other diseases that cause fevers when a pup's teeth are still growing. The teeth will show areas of discoloration, often in a band.

The enamel covering the tooth may also be damaged from chewing on metal fences or crate wires and even from chewing on abrasive material, such as tennis ball coverings, over the long term.

Treatment: Normally, some enamel loss is not a problem. If your dog is experiencing problems due to the enamel loss, it can be restored with new ceramics.

Taking Care of Your Dog's Teeth

Most dogs should receive professional dental care by age 2 to 3 years. The frequency of dental examinations, scaling, and polishing depends on how quickly calculus forms on the dog's teeth. A good program of home dental care will cut down on how often your dog's teeth need to be professionally cleaned.

In fact, dental disease in dogs can be almost completely avoided by following these guidelines:

- Feed a dry kibble diet. Dry foods are abrasive and keep the teeth clean. Feed once or twice a day rather than allowing the dog to nibble all day. If you prefer to feed canned dog food, offer some dry biscuits, such as Milk Bones, daily. Science Diet and Eukanuba offer foods that help prevent the buildup of plaque and tartar.
- Brush the teeth and gums at least three times a week using a toothpaste made for dogs. Start the program when the dog is young and her gums are still healthy. If the dog develops periodontal disease, you will need to brush the teeth every day.
- Avoid giving your dog objects to chew that are harder than her teeth. High-impact rubber balls and rawhide chew toys are less likely to split or break teeth than knuckle bones. Some chews are specially treated to help diminish plaque and tartar. Cheweeze and Dentabones are examples. Avoid feeding chicken bones and long bones that splinter. They provide no benefit and may cause constipation and other problems. In fact, it is best to avoid all bones.
- Schedule annual veterinary visits for cleaning and scaling. A yearly checkup is the best prevention against dental problems.
- The Veterinary Oral Health Council has a list of products proven to aid the dental health of your dog. You can find it at www.vohc.org (click on "Products Awarded the VOHC Seal").

BRUSHING THE TEETH AND GUMS

There are a number of good toothpastes and dental products designed for pets. Some contain abrasives such as calcium and silicates. An example is CET Dentifrice. Others use oxygenating substances to limit the growth of anaerobic bacteria (CET dental products and Oxyfresh). Nolvadent and Peridex contain chlorhexidine, which is both antibacterial and antiviral. MaxiGuard contains zinc ascorbate, which promotes healing of diseased gums. Your veterinarian may suggest that you use one of these products, particularly if your dog has gum disease.

Even with regular home dental care, professional scaling and polishing is sometimes needed.

For routine cleaning, a satisfactory toothpaste can be made by mixing 1 tablespoon (14 g) of baking soda with 1 teaspoon (5 ml) of water. If the dog is on a salt-restricted diet, substitute a salt replacer (such as potassium chloride) for the baking soda. Most dogs prefer flavored toothpastes made especially for dogs, such as poultry or mint. Dog toothpastes also have enzymes that clean more thoroughly than just the normal abrasive action of baking soda.

Do not use toothpaste made for humans. Its foaming action is unpleasant to dogs, and they cannot spit and rinse after using it. Swallowing the fluoride in many human toothpaste is also not good for them.

The gums and teeth can be brushed with a finger or a soft nylon toothbrush with a 45-degree angle to the head. Toothbrushes designed specifically for dogs are available at pet supply stores. Finger brushing is done with a terrycloth washcloth or a piece of gauze wrapped around the finger. Denta Clean, Petrodex, and DDS all offer finger brushes and/or wipes to clean your dog's teeth. Apply the toothpaste to your wrapped finger. Lift the lips to expose the outside surface of the teeth. Gently rub the teeth and gums in a circular motion. With a toothbrush, apply the toothpaste, then hold the brush at a 45-degree angle, parallel to the gums. Brush in small circles, overlapping the teeth and gums.

It is not necessary to open the mouth, as the self-cleaning action of the tongue will keep the inside surface of the teeth relatively free of calculus. The most important part to brush is the gingival sulcus, where the gum attaches to the tooth (see the figure on page 245). Bleeding may occur with vigorous brushing. This indicates gum disease. Daily brushing should tighten the gums and stop the bleeding in one to two weeks.

The Throat
PHARYNGITIS (SORE THROAT) AND TONSILLITIS

These two conditions have a common cause and thus often occur together. In fact, sore throats usually do not occur in dogs as isolated infections, the way they do in people. Most sore throats are associated with infections in the mouth, sinuses, or respiratory tract. They can also occur with systemic diseases such as parvovirus, distemper, herpesvirus, and pseudorabies. Dogs with an anal gland infection may also have a sore throat from spreading the infection while licking at their glands.

The signs of sore throat are fever, coughing, gagging, pain on swallowing, and loss of appetite. The throat looks red and inflamed. A *purulent* drainage may be seen coating the back of the throat.

The group A streptococcal sore throat (commonly known as strep throat) that occurs in young children can produce mild or unapparent sore throat in dogs and cats, who may then harbor the bacteria in the respiratory tract. Although dogs usually get the infection from human members of their family, and not vice versa, to eliminate the bacteria in households with recurrent strep throat, consider treating pets as well as family members.

The tonsils are aggregates of lymph tissue located at the back of the throat in dogs, as they are in people. They may not be visible unless they are inflamed. This generally occurs as a secondary symptom of a sore throat.

Primary bacterial tonsillitis is rare. It occurs in young dogs of the smaller breeds. Symptoms are similar to those of a sore throat, except that fever is more pronounced (over 103°F) and the dog appears depressed. The tonsils are bright red and swollen. Localized abscesses may be visible as white spots on the surface of the tonsils.

Chronic tonsillitis with tonsil enlargement is caused by persistent infection or by mechanical irritation from prolonged coughing, retching, or regurgitation of stomach acid into the throat. Any dog showing signs of tonsillitis should also be checked for anal gland problems, as grooming and licking the anal glands can spread the infection to the mouth.

Treatment: Acute pharyngitis and tonsillitis respond to treatment of the underlying condition. When a primary cause cannot be identified, treatment involves giving a broad-spectrum antibiotic for 10 days. Feed a soft diet consisting of canned dog food mixed with water to make a mush. Aspirin relieves pain (see *Over-the-Counter Drugs for Home Veterinary Use*, page 571, for dosage).

Enlarged tonsils must be distinguished from lymphoma and squamous cell carcinoma—the most common cancers of the tonsil. This is done by biopsy. Tonsillectomy for chronically inflamed tonsils is seldom necessary.

Foreign Body in the Throat (Gagging)

Dogs gag on small rubber balls and other objects that can lodge in the back of the throat. Bones that lodge sideways in the throat are another cause of gagging. The signs of a foreign body in the throat are sudden anxiety, pawing furiously at the mouth, drooling, gagging, and attempting to vomit.

Foreign bodies in the throat should be distinguished from objects in the larynx. Objects in the larynx cause coughing, choking, and respiratory distress.

Treatment: Soothe and quiet the dog. Proceed directly to the nearest veterinary clinic. If the dog is coughing and choking—or has fainted—the object has moved from the throat into the larynx and is blocking the airway. Administer emergency treatment as described for *Choking* (page 316).

Salivary Glands

The dog has four pairs of salivary glands that drain into the mouth. Only the parotid gland, located below the dog's ear on the side of the face, can be examined from the outside. The salivary glands secrete an alkaline fluid that lubricates the food and aids in digestion.

Hypersalivation (Drooling)

Some degree of drooling is normal in dogs, particularly in breeds with loose, pendulous lips. Excessive drooling is called hypersalivation. Hypersalivation is commonly triggered by psychological events such as fear, apprehension, and nervous anxiety, as well as anticipation of food treats.

Drooling also occurs in response to mouth pain caused by periodontal disease, abscessed teeth, and stomatitis. A dog who drools excessively and acts irrationally should be suspected of having rabies. Distemper, pseudorabies, and heat stroke are other diseases associated with drooling. Another common cause of drooling is motion sickness.

Tranquilizers cause drooling, as do many poisons. When a dog drools for no apparent reason and appears healthy, look for a foreign body in the mouth.

Treatment: This depends on the cause of the drooling.

Salivary Gland Cysts, Infections, and Tumors

The salivary glands can be injured as a result of fights and lacerations of the head and neck. The damaged duct or gland may leak saliva into the surrounding tissue, forming a fluid-filled cyst called a mucocele. This occurs most often in the mandibular glands, located in the floor of the mouth. Mucoceles in this location are known as a honey cysts or ranulas. A ranula presents as a large, smooth, rounded swelling in the floor of the mouth on the right or left side of the tongue.

Mucoceles cause problems when they become large enough to interfere with eating or swallowing. If a needle is inserted into the swelling, a thick, mucuslike, honey-colored material is extracted. This may eliminate the problem, but more often surgery is required. It involves draining the cyst into the mouth. If this is not successful, the salivary gland can be removed.

Salivary gland infection is uncommon. Most cases are associated with pre-existing mouth infections. The zygomatic gland, located beneath the cheek bone, is the gland most often involved. The signs of zygomatic gland infection are a bulging eye, tearing, and pain on opening the mouth. Treatment involves removing the gland.

Tumors of the salivary glands are rare. Most are malignant. They appear as slowly enlarging lumps or masses located beneath the tongue or on the side of the face. Small tumors can be cured with surgical removal.

The Head

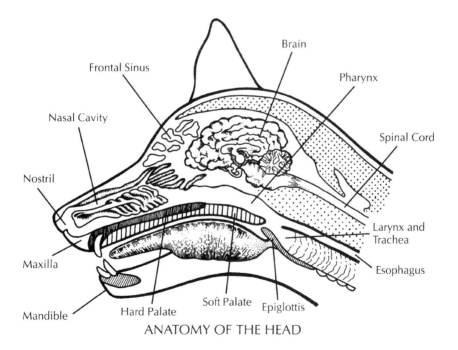

ANATOMY OF THE HEAD

HEAD AND NECK ABSCESSES

Head and neck abscesses are caused by infected animal bites and sharp objects that work their way back into the soft tissues, such as wood splinters, pins, chicken bones, and quills. Some are preceded by a sore throat, tonsillitis, mouth infection, or abscessed tooth.

Head and neck abscesses appear suddenly and are accompanied by fever. They are extremely tender and may give a lopsided look to the head, face, or neck. Opening the mouth may cause extreme pain. Affected dogs refuse to eat and drink.

A retrobulbar abscess occurs in the space behind the eyeball. It is accompanied by tearing and protrusion of the eye. A submandibular abscess is a swelling in the floor of the mouth that extends beneath the jaw bone. An abscess in the frontal sinus causes swelling beneath the eye.

Treatment: Head and neck abscesses should receive immediate veterinary attention. You may be asked to apply warm, moist packs for 15 minutes four times a day to bring the abscess to a head. Antibiotics help to localize the infection. Once the swelling becomes soft, it is ready to be drained by a veterinarian.

After incision and drainage, a wick may be used to keep the edges apart so that the abscess cavity can heal from below. Aftercare is similar to that described for *Cellulitis and Skin Abscess* (see page 161).

CRANIOMANDIBULAR OSTEOPATHY (SWOLLEN JAW)

This condition of unknown cause occurs predominantly in young West Highland White Terriers, Scottish Terriers, and Cairn Terriers, and has also been reported in Boston Terriers, Boxers, Labrador Retrievers, Great Danes, and Doberman Pinschers. A recessive mode of inheritance has been described.

The disease begins in puppies 4 to 10 months of age. It is characterized by the deposition of excess bone along the underside of the lower jaw and on other parts of the jaw and skull. The swollen jaw is extremely painful. The hinge joints of the jaw may be involved, making it extremely difficult for the dog to open her mouth. Fever, drooling, and loss of appetite are characteristic. When the mouth is forcefully opened, the dog cries in pain.

Treatment: There is no effective treatment for the abnormal bone deposits. Tube feeding may be required during periods of appetite loss to support nutrition. Pain is controlled with buffered aspirin or other NSAIDs. The disease usually stabilizes at 1 year of age. Partial or complete regression of the excess bone may then occur. Although complete recovery is uncommon, most dogs are able to eat and maintain their weight.

Dogs who have suffered from craniomandibular osteopathy should not be bred. OFA and the GDC maintain craniomandibular osteopathy registries for terriers, in an attempt to diagnose and track the disease. (For information on contacting these organizations, see appendix D.)

THE DIGESTIVE SYSTEM

The digestive tract begins at the mouth and ends at the anus. The lips, teeth, tongue, salivary glands, mouth, and pharynx are considered in other chapters of this book. The remaining digestive tract organs are the esophagus, stomach, duodenum (the first part of the small intestine), jejunum and ileum (also parts of the small intestine), colon, rectum, and anus. The organs that aid in digesting and absorbing foodstuffs are the pancreas, gall bladder, and liver. The pancreas is located next to the duodenum. The pancreatic enzymes drain into the pancreatic duct, which joins the bile duct from the liver; both ducts empty into the duodenum.

The esophagus is a muscular tube that carries food down to the stomach through a series of rhythmic contractions. The esophagus runs along the neck and into and through the chest cavity, on its way to the stomach. The lower esophagus enters the stomach at a sharp angle, which prevents food and liquids from refluxing back up into the esophagus.

Food can remain in the stomach for up to eight hours before passing through the pylorus into the duodenum and rest of the small intestine. Digestive juices from the pancreas and small intestine break the food down into amino acids, fatty acids, and carbohydrates. The products of the meal are absorbed into the intestinal circulation and are carried to the liver, where they are converted to stored energy.

Fiber and undigested food continue on through the small intestine into the colon. The function of the colon is to remove water and store waste material as feces.

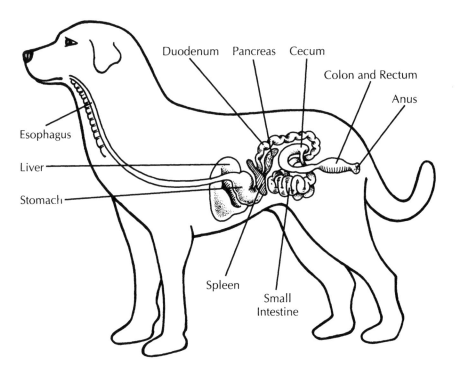

Duodenum Pancreas Cecum

Colon and Rectum

Anus

Esophagus

Liver

Stomach

Spleen

Small
Intestine

ANATOMY OF THE DIGESTIVE SYSTEM

Endoscopy

An endoscope is an instrument used for viewing the interior of a body canal or a hollow organ such as the stomach or colon. Its use as a diagnostic tool is invaluable for digestive tract disorders, and more veterinary hospitals and clinics have acquired endoscopes.

While the dog is under general anesthesia, the flexible endoscope is inserted into the mouth or anus and fed through the gastrointestinal tract. A powerful light and a fiber optic cable are used to view the interior of the bowel. Tiny instruments passed through the scope are used to take biopsies and perform other procedures.

GASTROSCOPY

Gastroscopy, also called esophagogastroduodenoscopy or *EGD*, is the endoscopic procedure for exploring and biopsying the upper gastrointestinal (GI) tract. It is the best way to diagnose gastritis, stomach and duodenal ulcers, tumors, and foreign bodies. The endoscope is inserted into the mouth and passed through the esophagus into the stomach and duodenum. Foreign bodies, if encountered during the examination, can sometimes be removed from the esophagus and stomach using specially made instruments. Large objects may require open surgery.

COLONOSCOPY

Colonoscopy is a procedure in which the endoscope is passed through the anus into the rectum and colon. The ability to visualize the interior of the lower GI tract and biopsy the intestine has greatly simplified the diagnosis of colitis and other colon diseases.

The Esophagus

The esophagus is a muscular tube that propels food and water into the stomach. This is accomplished by a series of rhythmic contractions called peristaltic waves, which are coordinated with the act of swallowing.

Signs of esophageal disease include regurgitation, painful swallowing (dysphagia), drooling, and weight loss.

REGURGITATION

Regurgitation is the relatively effortless expulsion of undigested food, without retching. It occurs because the esophagus is physically blocked or because it lacks peristaltic activity. In either case, the food accumulates until the esophagus is overloaded, after which the food is passively expelled.

Regurgitation should not be confused with vomiting. Vomiting is the forceful expulsion of stomach contents, preceded by drooling and retching. The material vomited is usually sour smelling, partly digested, and stained with yellow bile.

The sudden onset of regurgitation in a previously healthy dog is almost certainly due to a foreign body caught in the esophagus. Constant drooling indicates that the dog cannot swallow saliva.

Chronic regurgitation (the kind that comes and goes but seems to be getting worse) suggests a partial obstruction caused by megaesophagus, stricture, or tumor.

A serious complication of regurgitation is aspiration pneumonia, in which the lungs become infected as a result of food being aspirated into them. When regurgitated food ends up in the lungs, aspiration pneumonia is the result. Another potentially serious complication is nasal cavity infection. This occurs when food is regurgitated into the nose.

Dysphagia (Difficult, Painful Swallowing)

A dog with a painful esophagus eats slowly, stretches his neck, and makes repeated efforts to swallow the same mouthful. As the condition becomes more painful, the dog stops eating and begins to lose weight.

Difficult, painful swallowing indicates a partial blockage caused by an esophageal foreign body, stricture, or tumor. Pain on swallowing also occurs with mouth infections, sore throat, and tonsillitis.

Megaesophagus (Enlarged Esophagus)

Megaesophagus means enlarged esophagus. When the esophagus is partially obstructed over a period of time, it gradually enlarges like a balloon and becomes a storage organ. This process, called megaesophagus, is accompanied by regurgitation, loss of weight, and recurrent episodes of aspiration pneumonia.

There are two causes of megaesophagus. The first is a failure of the esophagus to contract and propel food into the stomach. This impaired motility occurs as a hereditary disorder in puppies and as an acquired disease in adults. The second cause of megaesophagus is a physical blockage, such as a foreign body or a developmental problem with abnormal blood vessels that encircle the esophagus.

Congenital megaesophagus is a hereditary form of the disease that occurs in puppies. It is caused by a developmental disorder involving the nerve plexus in the lower esophagus. Peristaltic activity stops at the level where the esophagus is paralyzed, and food can go no further. In time, the esophagus above the inert segment enlarges and balloons out. This can be seen by lifting the puppy by his back legs and looking for a bulging out of the esophagus at the side of the neck.

Congenital megaesophagus has been described in German Shepherd Dogs, Golden Retrievers, Great Danes, Irish Setters, Greyhounds, Labrador Retrievers, Newfoundlands, Miniature Schnauzers, Chinese Shar-Pei, and Wire Fox Terriers. Hereditary myopathies (see page 363) are other causes of congenital megaesophagus.

Puppies with congenital megaesophagus show signs at weaning, when they begin to eat solid foods. Characteristically, they approach the food dish with enthusiasm but back away after a few bites. They often regurgitate small amounts of food, which they eat again. After repeatedly eating the food, it becomes quite liquid and passes into the stomach. Repeated inhalation of food causes bouts of aspiration pneumonia.

Another type of congenital megaesophagus is caused by retained fetal arteries in the chest. The arteries produce a constriction around the esophagus (known as vascular ring anomaly) that prevents swallowing. The most common anomaly is a persistent right aortic arch. Regurgitation and difficulty swallowing appear at 4 to 10 months of age. These puppies are stunted and malnourished.

Adult-onset megaesophagus is an acquired condition that occurs with several rare neuromuscular diseases, including myasthenia gravis. Other known causes are hypothyroidism, hypoadrenocorticism, esophagitis, autoimmune diseases, and heavy metal poisoning. In most cases the cause is unknown.

A chest X-ray may show an enlarged esophagus, opaque material in the esophagus, or aspiration pneumonia. The diagnosis can be confirmed by administering a barium meal and then taking an X-ray of the chest. Ultrasound will also detect megaesophagus.

Treatment: The primary goals are maintaining nutrition and preventing complications. Divide a puppy's daily ration into four or more small meals. *It is important to provide food and water from raised bowls to maximize the effects of gravity.* A semiliquid or gruel mixture is easier for some dogs to swallow. Others do better with solids. This should be determined by trial and error. If possible, the dog should remain standing up—that is, front feet on a stepstool or ladder—for 15 to 30 minutes after eating so gravity will help move the food into the stomach.

Even with dedicated care, many dogs with megaesophagus will remain somewhat stunted and have bouts of aspiration pneumonia. Episodes of aspiration pneumonia require antibiotics, selected after culture and sensitivity tests. Signs of pneumonia are coughing, fever, and rapid, labored breathing (see *Pneumonia*, page 324).

Puppies with congenital megaesophagus may eventually outgrow the condition. Surgical correction of some vascular ring anomalies is possible. Dogs with congenital megaesophagus should not be used for breeding.

Adult-onset megaesophagus is irreversible, but some dogs do well for many years with careful attention to feeding and prompt treatment of respiratory infections.

FOREIGN BODY IN THE ESOPHAGUS

Foreign bodies in the esophagus are common. Bones and bone splinters are seen most often. Other objects that obstruct a dog's esophagus include string, fishhooks, needles, wood splinters, and small toys. Suspect a foreign body in the esophagus when a dog suddenly begins to gag, retch, drool, and regurgitate. A history of regurgitation and difficulty swallowing for several days or longer suggests a partial obstruction.

Sharp foreign bodies are particularly dangerous, because they can perforate the esophagus. A dog with a perforated esophagus exhibits fever, cough, rapid breathing, difficulty swallowing, and a rigid stance.

The diagnosis can usually be made by taking X-rays of the neck and chest. Ingesting a contrast material such as Gastrografin, followed by an X-ray of the esophagus, may be required.

Treatment: An esophageal foreign body is an emergency. Take your dog to a veterinarian at once.

Many foreign bodies can be removed by gastroscopy. The dog is given a general anesthetic, after which an endoscope is passed through the mouth and into the esophagus. The object is located visually and removed with a grasping instrument. If the object cannot be withdrawn, it can often be pushed down into the stomach and removed surgically from the abdomen. Foreign bodies that cannot be dislodged using the endoscope require open esophageal surgery. The same is true for esophageal perforations.

ESOPHAGITIS

A mucosal injury caused by a foreign body, or a burn caused by ingesting a caustic liquid (see *Corrosive Household Products*, page 34), can cause inflammation of the esophagus, known as esophagitis. Gastroesophageal reflux (similar to acid reflux in humans) is the other possible cause.

Gastroesophageal reflux is the process in which stomach acid backs up into the esophagus, resulting in chemical burns of the mucosal lining. This can occur when a dog is tilted in a head-down position during general anesthesia. It may also occur with the use of a stomach tube, after chronic vomiting, and with a hiatal hernia.

With this type of hernia, the stomach protrudes through an abnormally large esophageal opening in the diaphragm. The opening allows part or all of the stomach to slide up into the chest. Hiatal hernias are not common in dogs. Most of them are congenital, with an increased incidence among Chinese Shar-Pei. The major concern with hiatal hernia is that it causes gastroesophageal reflux.

Signs of moderate to severe esophagitis are *dysphagia*, repeated swallowing, regurgitation, and drooling. With chronic esophagitis the dog loses appetite and weight. The diagnosis is made by *gastroscopy*, which reveals an inflamed, swollen esophageal mucosa.

Treatment: This is directed toward correcting the underlying condition. Hiatal hernias can be surgically repaired. Medications used to treat chronic gastroesophageal reflux in people are also effective in dogs.

ESOPHAGEAL STRICTURE

A stricture is a circular scar that forms after an injury to the wall of the esophagus. Most injuries are caused by esophageal foreign bodies. Swallowed caustic liquids and gastroesophageal reflux are other causes. Tumors of the esophagus can produce a stricturelike narrowing.

The principal sign of esophageal stricture is regurgitation. The diagnosis can be made by X-ray after the dog has been given a barium solution, or by an esophageal *endoscopy*. The stricture appears as a fibrous ring that narrows the esophagus.

Treatment: Early strictures can be treated by stretching the wall of the esophagus with a balloon catheter passed through the endoscope. When this is not successful, surgery may be considered to remove the strictured segment. The operation is difficult and has a high complication rate. After successful surgery, most dogs are able to swallow normally. Those who continue to have problems may have developed a motility disorder due to enlargement of the esophagus (see *Megaesophagus,* page 258).

GROWTHS

Primary tumors of the esophagus are rare and most are malignant. A common benign tumor is a leiomyoma. Tumors that have spread to lymph nodes around the esophagus can also press on the esophagus, creating a physical obstruction.

Growths on the esophagus caused by a worm parasite (*Spirocerca lupi*) occur in the southwestern United States. The disease is uncommon. A few of these growths can transform into cancers.

Treatment: Surgical removal of benign tumors (and malignant tumors that have not spread) offers the best chance for cure. Worm parasites are treated with anthelmintics.

The Stomach

Stomach problems are often associated with vomiting. Since vomiting is so common in dogs, it will be discussed in separate section (see page 270).

STOMACH AND DUODENAL ULCERS

Stomach and duodenal ulcers are being diagnosed more frequently in dogs due to the wider use of gastroscopy. Seen through the endoscope, superficial ulcers are patches of inflamed and eroded mucosa covered by white or yellow pus. Deep ulcers are punched-out areas involving all layers of the stomach wall. Ulcers can be single or multiple, and can range in size from less than 1 inch (2.5 cm) to several inches in diameter. Ulcers occur more often in the stomach than in the duodenum.

Bacteria are often the cause of ulcers in humans, but ulcers in dogs are not generally believed to be caused by stomach bacteria—although *Helicobacter* species have been found in dogs. The usual cause in dogs is corticosteroids or nonsteroidal anti-inflammatory drugs (*NSAIDs*), such as aspirin and ibuprofen. Dogs are even more susceptible than people to the ulcer-producing effects of these drugs.

Other conditions that predispose a dog to ulcers include all forms of liver disease, kidney failure, extreme stress (from severe illness or major surgery), chronic gastritis (particularly the eosinophilic type), and shock.

Mast cell tumors of the skin (see page 533) can cause ulcers. This is because these tumors produce and release histamine, which is a powerful stimulant to acid secretion. In fact, ulcers occur in up to 80 percent of dogs with mast cell tumors.

The principal sign of an ulcer is sporadic or chronic vomiting. Dogs may also lose weight and be anemic. In dogs with nonspecific signs, such as chronic vomiting, the diagnosis is made by *gastroscopy*.

Occasionally the vomitus contains old blood (which looks like coffee grounds) or fresh blood and blood clots, although the bleeding in many ulcers is microscopic. With rapid bleeding the dog goes into shock and passes black, tarry stools. Stomach and duodenal ulcers can rupture into the abdomen, causing peritonitis.

Treatment: Perforated ulcers require emergency surgery. Dogs with gastrointestinal bleeding should be hospitalized for observation and further tests. Severe anemia is treated with blood transfusions. It is important to identify and eliminate predisposing causes. Discontinue all ulcer-producing medications.

Ulcer drugs used in people are effective in dogs. They include the histamine blockers Tagamet (cimetidine), Pepcid (famotidine), and Zantac (ranitidine); the mucosal protectants Carafate (sucralfate) and Cytotec (misoprostol); Prilosec (omeprazole); and antacids such as Mylanta, Maalox, and Amphogel. These drugs are best taken in combination (an antacid along with a histamine blocker), several times a day. A veterinarian should determine the most effective drug combination and schedule. Treatment is continued for at least three to four weeks. A follow-up gastroscopy is advisable to ensure that healing is complete.

GASTRIC OUTFLOW OBSTRUCTION

At the outlet of the stomach is the pyloric canal. Scarring and contraction of the pyloric canal prevents the stomach from emptying. Stomach and duodenal ulcers close to the pyloric canal are the most common causes of inflammation and scarring. Other causes of scarring and contraction include hypertrophic and eosinophilic gastritis (see *Chronic Gastritis*, page 268), and gastric tumors. Foreign bodies and *bezoars* are other causes of gastric outflow obstruction (see *Gastrointestinal Foreign Bodies*, page 276).

Gastric outflow obstruction can be partial or complete. Dogs with partial obstruction vomit intermittently, often 12 to 16 hours after eating. The vomitus usually contains undigested food and, occasionally, blood. When obstruction is complete, vomiting occurs immediately after eating and is often projectile. Other signs of gastric outflow obstruction include loss of appetite, weight loss, bloating, and belching.

The diagnosis can sometimes be made by an X-ray of the abdomen or an ultrasound showing an enlarged, fluid-filled stomach. *Gastroscopy* or an upper GI series may be required for more complete diagnosis.

Treatment: The blockage must be surgically removed.

GASTRIC TUMORS

A stomach tumor should be considered in an older dog with sporadic vomiting. The vomitus often contains old, partially digested blood. Anemia and weight loss are frequently found. Tumors in the pyloric canal region often cause gastric outflow obstruction.

Adenocarcinoma is the most common malignant tumor of the stomach. Benign tumors such as leiomyomas and polyps also occur. The diagnosis is made by *gastroscopy* and biopsy of the tumor.

Treatment: Surgical treatment involves removing the part of the stomach containing the tumor. The prognosis for dogs with benign tumors is excellent. Malignant tumors are difficult to cure.

GASTRIC DILATATION VOLVULUS (BLOAT)

Bloat is a life-threatening emergency that affects dogs in the prime of life. The mortality rate for gastric volvulus approaches 50 percent. Early recognition and treatment are the keys to survival.

Anatomy of Bloat

Bloat actually refers to two conditions. The first is gastric dilatation, in which the stomach distends with gas and fluid. The second is volvulus, in which the distended stomach rotates on its long axis. The spleen is attached to the wall of the stomach, and therefore rotates with the stomach.

Gastric dilatation may or may not be complicated by volvulus. If volvulus occurs, the stomach may twist 180 degrees or less (technically called a torsion). An actual volvulus is a twist of 180 degrees to 360 degrees or more.

During volvulus, the pylorus is pulled out of position and becomes displaced to the left of the gastroesophageal junction (as shown in the figure on page 264). This pinches off the duodenum and prevents fluid and air from escaping from the stomach through the pyloric canal. Simultaneously, the gastroesophageal junction becomes twisted and obstructed, preventing the dog from belching and vomiting. Gas and fluid are trapped in the closed-off stomach, which becomes hugely distended as the material ferments. Interference with blood circulation results in *necrosis* of the wall of the stomach.

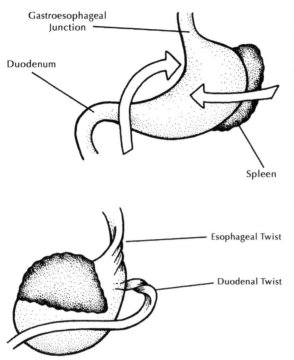

In a dog with volvulus, the stomach (shown here in its normal position) rotates. The arrows show the direction of the rotation.

The twists at the gastro-esophageal junction and duodenum trap gas and fluids in the stomach. The dog is unable to belch or vomit.

This sequence produces a number of other problems, including acute dehydration, bacterial *septicemia*, circulatory shock, cardiac arrhythmias, gastric perforation, peritonitis, and death.

Bloat can occur in any dog at any age, but typically occurs in middle-aged to older dogs. There may be a familial association. Large-breed dogs with deep chests are anatomically predisposed. These breeds include the Great Dane, German Shepherd Dog, St. Bernard, Labrador Retriever, Irish Wolfhound, Great Pyrenees, Boxer, Weimaraner, Old English Sheepdog, Irish Setter, Collie, Bloodhound, and Standard Poodle. Chinese Shar-Pei and Basset Hounds have the highest incidence among midsize dogs. Small dogs are rarely affected, with the exception of Dachshunds, who are also deep-chested.

Bloat develops suddenly, usually in a healthy, active dog. The dog may have just eaten a large meal, exercised vigorously before or after eating, or drank a large amount of water immediately after eating. There is no evidence that the protein or soy content in the diet contributes to bloat; research has shown that the majority of gas associated with bloat is due to swallowed air.

Signs of Bloat

The classic signs of bloat are restlessness and pacing, salivation, retching, unproductive attempts to vomit, and enlargement of the abdomen. The dog may whine or groan when you press on his belly. Thumping the abdomen produces a hollow sound.

Unfortunately, not all cases of bloat present with typical signs. In early bloat the dog may not appear distended, but the abdomen usually feels slightly tight. The dog appears lethargic, obviously uncomfortable, walks in a stiff-legged fashion, hangs his head, but may not look extremely anxious or distressed. Early on it is not possible to distinguish dilatation from volvulus.

Late signs (those of impending shock) include pale gums and tongue, delayed *capillary refill time*, rapid heart rate, weak pulse, rapid and labored breathing, weakness, and collapse.

If the dog is able to belch or vomit, quite likely the problem is not due to a volvulus, but this can only be determined by veterinary examination.

Treating Bloat

In all cases where there is the slightest suspicion of bloat, take your dog to a veterinary hospital immediately. Time is of the essence.

Gastric dilatation without torsion or volvulus is relieved by passing a long rubber or plastic tube through the dog's mouth into the stomach. This is also the quickest way to confirm a diagnosis of bloat. As the tube enters the dog's stomach, there should be a rush of air and fluid from the tube, bringing relief. The stomach is then washed out. The dog should not be allowed to eat or drink for the next 36 hours, and will need to be supported with intravenous fluids. If symptoms do not return, the diet can be gradually restored.

Passing a stomach tube is a procedure normally done by a veterinarian. In extreme circumstances when professional help is not available, you may be asked to perform the procedure at home. If you live in a remote location where fast access to veterinary services is limited, you may wish to acquire a stomach tube and add it to your home emergency medical kit.

To pass a stomach tube, first mark the tube by measuring the distance from the dog's nose to his last rib. Then lubricate the tube with K-Y or petroleum jelly. It is helpful to put a roll of adhesive tape in the dog's mouth to pass the tube through, so the dog can't bite down on the tube. Insert the tube behind one of the canine teeth and advance it into the throat until the dog begins to swallow. If the dog gags, continue to advance the tube. If the dog coughs, the tube has entered the trachea. Withdraw the tube a few inches and start again. *If the tube will not pass into the stomach, discontinue further attempts*, as it is possible to harm the dog.

If you do not have a tube available, a fairly large gauge sterile needle, such as an 18-gauge needle from a syringe, may be used to poke directly through the body wall into the distended area to release gas and relieve pressure on the abdominal tissues. This is only a stopgap measure to buy you time to reach your veterinarian, and should only be done in a serious emergency in which

Before passing a tube into the stomach, the tube is marked by measuring the distance from the nose to the last rib.

no veterinarian is available, because the needle could damage other tissues as it is pushed through the body wall.

If you can pass a tube, you should still try to reach your veterinarian for follow-up treatment to prevent a recurrence. Being able to pass a tube does not always rule out volvulus. Occasionally, the tube passes even though the stomach is twisted.

A diagnosis of dilatation or volvulus is best confirmed by X-rays of the abdomen. Dogs with simple dilatation have a large volume of gas in the stomach, but the gas pattern is normal. Dogs with volvulus have a "double bubble" gas pattern on the X-ray, with gas in two sections separated by the twisted tissue.

Emergency therapy is directed toward correcting shock and dehydration with intravenous fluids and corticosteroids. Antibiotics may be needed to control infection. Ventricular arrhythmias are common. They require heart monitoring and the use of anti-arrhythmic drugs.

If the dog has a volvulus, emergency surgery is required as soon as the dog is able to tolerate the anesthesia. The goals are to reposition the stomach and spleen, or to remove the spleen and part of the stomach if these organs have undergone *necrosis*. Future recurrence can often be prevented by suturing the wall of the

The tube is inserted in back of the canine teeth and advanced to the mark just measured.

stomach to the abdominal wall (a procedure called gastropexy). This important step keeps the stomach in position and prevents it from twisting.

Preventing Bloat

Dogs who respond to nonsurgical treatment have a 70 percent chance of having another episode of bloat. Some of these episodes can be prevented by following these practices:

- Divide the day's ration into three equal meals, spaced well apart.
- Do not feed your dog from a raised food bowl. (Raised food bowls were once recommended to avoid bloat, but research has found that that they actually make things much worse.)
- Avoid feeding dry dog food that has fat among the first four ingredients listed on the label.
- Avoid foods that contain citric acid.
- Restrict access to water for one hour before and after meals.
- Never let your dog drink a large amount of water all at once.
- Avoid strenuous exercise on a full stomach.
- Be aware of the early signs and seek prompt veterinary attention whenever you suspect bloat.

ADDISON'S DISEASE (HYPOADRENOCORTICISM)

The adrenal glands, found in the abdomen above the kidneys, are important in the production of corticosteroids and other hormones that regulate body functions. Addison's disease is caused by inadequate production of corticosteroids and mineralocorticoids.

In some cases, this uncommon condition arises after other illness, including infections, tumors, and toxic drugs, destroy the adrenal glands. An *autoimmune* reaction, in which antibodies are directed against the cells of the adrenal cortex (the part of the adrenal gland that produces corticosteriods), may be responsible for cases in which the cause is not known. There may be a genetic predisposition in Bearded Collies, Portuguese Water Dogs, and Standard Poodles.

An *iatrogenic* form of Addison's disease occurs after corticosteroids are administered to treat a medical condition. The corticosteroids have the side effect of putting the adrenal glands at rest. An abrupt withdrawal of the drug can produce a temporary deficit of hydrocortisone and cause an acute Addisonian crisis with shock and circulatory collapse. Another common iatrogenic cause of Addison's disease is the use of mitotane to treat Cushing's syndrome (see page 144).

The signs of Addison's disease are lethargy, muscle weakness, intermittent vomiting and diarrhea, and slow pulse. The disease should be considered when a dog unaccountably collapses. The diagnosis is made by an ACTH stimulation test. In a positive test, the adrenal cortex does not respond to an injection of ACTH by increasing the concentration of cortisol in the serum.

Treatment: Shock associated with acute adrenal insufficiency responds rapidly to corticosteroids and intravenous fluids. Chronic adrenal insufficiency can be controlled by giving an oral cortisone preparation such as prednisone daily, along with fludrocortisone acetate for mineralocorticoid replacement. Treatment is life-long. The dosage varies with the severity of the disease and must be determined by your veterinarian.

ACUTE GASTRITIS

Acute gastritis is an irritation of the lining of the stomach that comes on suddenly. The principal sign is severe and continuous vomiting. Keep in mind that persistent vomiting is also associated with life-threatening diseases such as intestinal obstruction and peritonitis. Seek professional consultation in all cases where the cause of persistent vomiting is not known.

Common stomach irritants include spoiled food and garbage, stools, grass, plastic wrappings, hair, and bones. Certain drugs (notably aspirin, virtually all NSAIDs, cortisone, butazolidine, and some antibiotics) produce gastric irritation. Common poisons that may cause vomiting are antifreeze, fertilizers, plant toxins, and crabgrass killers. If poisoning is suspected, contact your veterinarian.

A dog with acute gastritis vomits shortly after eating. Later the dog appears lethargic and sits with his head hanging over the water bowl. The dog's temperature remains normal unless he is suffering from acute infectious enteritis, a disease that also causes diarrhea.

Treatment: Acute nonspecific gastritis is self-limiting and usually resolves in 24 to 48 hours if the stomach is rested and protected from excess acid. Follow the instructions in *Home Treatment of Vomiting* (page 272).

CHRONIC GASTRITIS

Dogs with chronic gastritis vomit from time to time over a period of days or weeks. These dogs appear lethargic, have a dull hair coat, and lose weight. The vomitus sometimes contains foreign material and food eaten the day before.

A common cause of chronic gastritis is a food allergy (see page 140). Other causes are persistent grass eating; repeated consumption of drugs, chemicals, or toxins; and ingesting cellulose, plastic, paper, or rubber products. Also consider the possibility of hairballs. Hair is shed more heavily in the springtime and is swallowed as the dog licks and pulls it out. Hair and other foreign materials can be incorporated into a hard mass called a *bezoar*. Bezoars may grow to a size that makes it impossible for them to pass out of the stomach (see *Gastrointestinal Foreign Bodies*, page 276). Note that in many cases of chronic vomiting the cause is not known.

Hypertrophic gastropathy is a thickening of the mucous membranes of the lower half of the stomach, which can lead to gastric obstruction and food retention. Vomiting occurs three to four hours after eating. Hypertrophic gastropathy occurs most often in middle-aged dogs of the small breeds. It may also be seen as a congenital problem called pyloric stenosis in *brachycephalic* breeds such as Bulldogs and Boston Terriers. The cause is unknown in older dogs, but may be related to histamine release from mast cell tumors in some dogs.

Chronic atrophic gastritis involves a thinning of the stomach wall. This is primarily seen in Norwegian Buhunds, and may develop from an immune problem.

Eosinophilic gastritis is a chronic condition characterized by the accumulation of *eosinophils* (a type of white blood cell) in the mucous lining of the stomach, along with thickening and scarring of the stomach wall. The cause is unknown, although a food allergy or parasites have been proposed. Eosinophilic gastritis is more likely than other types of gastritis to be associated with ulcers and bleeding.

Stomach and duodenal ulcers also produce sporadic vomiting. Finally, if there is no obvious explanation for the sporadic vomiting, the dog may be suffering from a systemic disease, such as liver or kidney failure, which can be diagnosed by blood tests.

Treatment: Dogs with chronic vomiting should be seen by a veterinarian. Gastroscopy with a biopsy of the stomach wall is the quickest way to make a diagnosis of chronic gastritis.

Treatment involves switching to a bland, high-carbohydrate diet such as Hill's Prescription Diet i/d. Alternatively, you can feed a homemade diet of boiled rice and cottage cheese. Offer frequent small feedings and avoid large meals. As the dog recovers, gradually introduce a high-quality commercial premium dog food, or consult a veterinary nutritionist for a balanced homemade meal you can cook.

Histamine blocking agents, such as Tagamet (cimetidine), Pepcid (famotidine), and Zantac (ranitidine), may help in cases of hypertrophic gastropathy. While not approved for use in dogs, they can be used safely under the guidance of your veterinarian.

Eosinophilic gastritis responds well to a course of corticosteroids, but sometimes the dog needs other immunosuppressive drugs and a hypoallergenic diet prescribed by your veterinarian. Gastritis associated with gastric outflow obstruction is treated as described for *Stomach and Duodenal Ulcers* (page 262).

Motion Sickness

Many young dogs become sick when traveling by car, boat, or air. The signs are restlessness followed by salivation, yawning, nausea, and then vomiting. Motion sickness is caused by overstimulation of the labyrinth in the inner ear.

Treatment: If your dog is susceptible to motion sickness, your veterinarian may prescribe a drug such as dimenhydrinate (brand names Dramamine and Gravol; see *Over-the-Counter Drugs for Home Veterinary Use*, page 571, for dosage), to control the symptoms. Give the first dose one hour before traveling. Remember, do not medicate your dog on the day of a dog show, because dimenhydrinate causes drowsiness. Cerenia is a new drug that is said to relieve vomiting in dogs, including motion sickness. It is currently undergoing efficacy studies.

Ginger, even a ginger snap cookie, may also relieve motion sickness.

Dogs travel best on an empty stomach, so it is best to withhold food and water before taking a trip. Try to keep the car cool, choose travel routes on smooth roads, and minimize stops and turns. Most dogs with motion sickness become accustomed to riding in the car and eventually outgrow the problem.

Vomiting

Vomiting is common in dogs. All vomiting is the result of activating the vomiting center in the brain. The vomiting center is well developed in dogs, so dogs vomit more readily than most other animals. As a dog perceives a need to vomit, he becomes anxious and may seek attention and reassurance. He then begins to salivate and swallow repeatedly.

Vomiting begins with a simultaneous contraction of the muscles of the stomach and abdominal wall. There is an abrupt increase in intra-abdominal pressure. The lower esophagus relaxes, allowing the stomach contents to travel up the esophagus and out the mouth. The dog extends his neck and makes harsh gagging sounds. This sequence should be distinguished from the passive act of regurgitation (see page 257).

Causes of Vomiting

The most common cause of vomiting is eating indigestible substances, such as grass, that irritate the lining of the stomach. Another cause of vomiting is overeating—dogs who eat more than their daily amount of food, perhaps because they have gotten into the dog food bag. Also, puppies who gobble their food and exercise immediately after are likely to vomit. This after-meal vomiting is frequently caused by feeding a group of puppies from a common food pan. Since they are all competing for food, each one eats as much as he possibly can. Separating puppies, or feeding them frequent small meals, eliminates the problem of gorging.

Dogs may vomit when they are upset, excited, or suffering from a phobia (for example, during a thunderstorm). Phobic dogs also drool, whine, paw, and tremble. Puppies with heavy loads of roundworms may vomit up some worms.

Vomiting occurs with most acute infectious diseases. It also occurs with many chronic diseases, including kidney and liver failure, Cushing's syndrome, Addison's disease, and diabetes mellitus.

To determine the cause of vomiting, note whether it is repeated, and if so, whether it is sporadic or persistent. How soon after eating does it occur? Is it projectile? Inspect the vomitus for blood, fecal material, and foreign objects.

Persistent Vomiting

If the dog vomits or retches repeatedly, bringing up a frothy, clear fluid, this suggests a stomach irritation such as acute gastritis. However, persistent vomiting also occurs with life-threatening diseases such as acute pancreatitis, gastric outflow obstruction, intestinal obstruction, and peritonitis.

Persistent retching without bringing up any vomitus is typical of bloat. Repeated vomiting along with diarrhea suggests acute infectious enteritis.

Sporadic Vomiting

Sometimes a dog vomits off and on over a period of days or weeks. There is no relationship to meals. The appetite is poor. The dog has a haggard look and appears listless. Suspect liver or kidney disease, or an illness such as chronic gastritis, stomach or duodenal ulcer, a heavy worm infestation, or diabetes mellitus.

A foreign body in the stomach is another possibility. In an older dog, suspect a gastric or intestinal tumor. A veterinary checkup is in order.

Vomiting Blood

Red blood in the vomitus indicates active bleeding somewhere between the mouth and the upper small bowel. (Blood from the nasopharynx and esophagus may be swallowed.) Common causes are stomach and duodenal ulcers, gastrointestinal foreign bodies, and gastric tumors. Material that looks like coffee grounds is old, partially digested blood. This also indicates a bleeding point between the mouth and upper small bowel. Any dog who vomits blood should be seen by a veterinarian.

Vomiting Feces

A dog who vomits foul material that looks and smells like feces is most likely suffering from intestinal obstruction or peritonitis. Seek immediate professional treatment. Dogs who eat feces may also do this, but it will be an isolated incident.

Projectile Vomiting

Projectile vomiting is forceful vomiting in which the stomach contents are ejected a considerable distance. Typically it occurs in a dog with gastric outflow obstruction. Diseases that cause pressure on the brain (tumors, encephalitis, blood clots) also cause projectile vomiting.

Vomiting Foreign Objects

Dogs may also vomit foreign objects, including rubber balls, pieces of toys, sticks, and stones. Puppies with a heavy roundworm infestation may vomit adult worms. These pups should be treated as described in *Ascarids*, page 56.

HOME TREATMENT OF VOMITING

If there is any question about the cause or seriousness of the vomiting, seek veterinary help. Vomiting dogs can rapidly become dehydrated as they lose body fluids and electrolytes. Home treatment is appropriate only for normal, healthy adult dogs who show no signs other than vomiting. Puppies, dogs with preexisting health conditions, and old dogs are less able to tolerate dehydration and should be treated by a veterinarian.

An important initial step is to rest the stomach by withholding food and water for a minimum of 12 hours. If the vomiting stops with stomach rest, the dog can be permitted to lick a few ice chips every three to four hours. If the vomiting has stopped, offer ¼ to ½ cup of water (63 to 125 ml), depending on the size of the dog, every two to three hours. A pediatric electrolyte solution (see *Home Treatment of Diarrhea*, page 285) can be given in small amounts, in addition to the water.

After 12 hours with no vomiting, start the dog on a bland diet such as two parts boiled rice mixed with one part ground beef or chicken. (Boil the meat to remove the fat—fat delays stomach emptying.) Other bland foods that may be substituted are cottage cheese, canned mackerel, strained meat baby food, chicken noodle soup, and chicken and rice soup. Begin by offering small amounts (1 or 2 tablespoons, 15 to 30 ml, at a time) every two to three hours. Increase the volume over the next two days and gradually return the dog to his customary diet.

Stop all food and water and obtain immediate veterinary assistance when:

- Vomiting persists despite the fact that the dog has received no food or water for several hours.
- Vomiting recurs during attempts to reintroduce food and water.
- Vomiting is accompanied by diarrhea.
- The dog vomits fresh blood or material that looks like coffee grounds (partially digested blood).
- The dog becomes weak and lethargic or shows other signs of systemic illness.

Small and Large Bowels

Problems in the small and large bowels are associated with three common symptoms: diarrhea, constipation, and passing blood. Diarrhea is by far the most common, and will be discussed in a separate section (see page 283).

INFLAMMATORY BOWEL DISEASE

This is a group of diseases of the small and large intestines, characterized by chronic and protracted diarrhea, malabsorption, weight loss, anemia, and malnutrition. They are all treatable, but are seldom cured. In each specific disease, a different type of inflammatory cell is found in large numbers in the lining of the small and/or large intestines. These cells distinguish the specific diseases. Diagnosis is made by *endoscopy* and biopsy of the intestine wall, or by exploratory surgery.

Lymphocytic-Plasmacytic Enterocolitis

This is the most common inflammatory bowel disease in dogs. Lymphocytic-plasmacytic enterocolitis has been associated with giardiasis, food allergy, and overgrowth of intestinal bacteria. Lymphocytes and plasma cells are the target cells seen on biopsy.

Certain breeds are predisposed, suggesting a genetic influence. They are the Basenji, Soft Coated Wheaten Terrier, German Shepherd Dog, and Chinese Shar-Pei. In the Basenji, the disease is known to be related to an *autoimmune* disorder. While signs can show up in younger dogs, most dogs are middle-aged when diarrhea starts.

Lymphocytic-plasmacytic enterocolitis produces a small bowel type of diarrhea (see page 283). Vomiting is common. Involvement of the colon produces signs of colitis.

Treatment: This is an illness for which the realistic goal is control, not cure. Hypoallergenic diets bring about partial or complete resolution of symptoms in some dogs. The Purina h/a and d/d veterinary diets may be useful, as well as Hill's z/d and z/d Ultra, and Royal Canin IVD. Antibiotics are used to treat bacterial overgrowth and giardiasis. Immunosuppressant drugs such as azathioprine (Imuran) and/or prednisone are used if other treatments are not successful.

Eosinophilic Enterocolitis

This is a relatively uncommon form of inflammatory bowel disease in dogs. On biopsy, *eosinophils* may be found in the stomach, small intestine, or colon, and the eosinophil count in the blood may be elevated. Some cases are thought to be associated with food allergy or the tissue migration of round-worms and hookworms.

Treatment: High-dose corticosteroids are used to treat this disease. They are tapered off as symptoms diminish. The dog should be tested for intestinal parasites and placed on a hypoallergenic diet.

Granulomatous (Regional) Enteritis

This is a rare disease, similar to Crohn's disease in humans. There is thicken-ing and narrowing of the terminal small bowel due to inflammation of sur-rounding fat and lymph nodes. Macrophages, which are cells found in tissues that fight infections, are found on biopsy of the colon. The diarrhea is the chronic large bowel type (see page 284), containing mucus and blood. Biopsies are processed with special stains to exclude histoplasmosis and intes-tinal tuberculosis.

Treatment: This involves the use of corticosteroids and immunosuppres-sive drugs to reduce inflammation and scarring. A course of metronidazole may be of benefit. A strictured bowel requires surgery.

Neutrophilic Enterocolitis

This inflammatory bowel disease produces acute and chronic large bowel diar-rhea (see page 284). The inflammatory infiltrate is composed of mature white cells in the tissues and blood vessels. Diagnosis is based on a colon biopsy and stool cultures to exclude bacterial infection.

Treatment: Antibiotics and/or corticosteroids are used to control the disease.

Histiocytic Ulcerative Colitis

This inflammatory bowel disease occurs almost exclusively in Boxers. Signs usually appear before age 2. Affected dogs develop severe, unrelenting diar-rhea that contains mucus and blood, and corresponding weight loss. The diag-nosis is based on a colon biopsy.

Treatment: Treatment is similar to that described for lymphocytic-plasma-cytic enterocolitis (see page 273).

ACUTE INFECTIOUS ENTERITIS

Enteritis is an infection of the gastrointestinal tract characterized by the sud-den onset of vomiting and diarrhea, rapid pulse, fever, apathy, and depression. The vomitus and diarrhea may contain blood. Dehydration occurs rapidly. Dogs under 1 year of age and those over 10 are particularly susceptible to the effects of dehydration and shock.

The most common cause of infectious enteritis in dogs is parvovirus (see page 78). *Salmonella, E. coli, camphylobacter,* and other bacteria are also responsible for some cases.

The bacteria *Clostridium perfringens* produces canine hemorrhagic gastroenteritis. This disease begins suddenly with vomiting, followed in two to three hours by a profuse, bloody diarrhea. Small breeds, particularly Miniature Schnauzers and Toy Poodles, have a predisposition for hemorrhagic gastroenteritis.

Garbage poisoning and ingesting poisons and toxic chemicals produces signs and symptoms similar to those of acute enteritis. When diarrhea and vomiting occur together, the dog's condition is serious and warrants an immediate trip to the veterinarian.

Treatment: This is directed toward prompt replacement of fluids and electrolytes. Intravenous fluids may be necessary. Antibiotics that are effective against the causative bacteria may be administered. Medications to control vomiting and/or diarrhea may also be needed.

MALABSORPTION SYNDROME

Malabsorption is not a specific disease, but occurs as a consequence of some underlying disorder of the small bowel or the pancreas. In malabsorption syndrome, the dog either does not digest food or does not absorb the products of digestion from the small intestine. Dogs suffering from malabsorption are underweight and malnourished despite a voracious appetite. Diarrhea occurs three or four times a day. The stools are typically large, rancid smelling, and contain a great deal of fat. The hair around the anus may be oily or greasy.

Predisposing causes of malabsorption include exocrine pancreatic insufficiency, permanent damage to the intestinal mucosa following infectious enteritis, inflammatory bowel disease with inflamed or destroyed intestinal mucosa, surgical removal of a major portion of the small bowel, and primary diseases of the small intestine. Soft Coated Wheaten Terriers may suffer from a protein-losing enteropathy, where they don't properly digest and absorb protein (also see *Lymphocytic-Plasmacytic Enteritis*, page 273).

Idiopathic villous atrophy is one of the primary diseases of the small intestine. Villi are microscopic hairlike structures that make up the absorptive surface of the small bowel. In a dog with villous atrophy these structures are blunted and poorly developed. Idiopathic villous atrophy occurs most often in German Shepherd Dogs. A similar hereditary disease is wheat-sensitive or gluten-sensitive enteropathy, described in Irish Setters.

Small intestinal bacterial overgrowth has been identified as another important cause of malabsorption. German Shepherd Dogs, Basenjis, and Chinese Shar-Pei have an increased incidence. Affected dogs develop an abundant and abnormal bacterial flora in the small intestine, which causes foul-smelling diarrhea. Some cases have been associated with exocrine pancreatic insufficiency, inflammatory bowel disease, or stagnant loops of bowel caused by intestinal surgery. In German Shepherd Dogs and Chinese Shar-Pei, the condition may be related to a specific immune deficiency. In the majority of cases the cause of the bacterial overgrowth is unknown. In many cases the cause of malabsorption can be identified through special diagnostic tests, including stool analysis and an intestinal biopsy.

Treatment: Treatment is directed toward the specific disease. Dogs with villous atrophy are managed with gluten-free prescription diets. Small intestinal bacterial overgrowth usually responds to one or more courses of an oral broad-spectrum antibiotic. The addition of probiotics and live culture yogurt products may help in treatment.

COLITIS

Colitis is an inflammation of the colon. It is responsible for about 50 percent of cases of chronic diarrhea in dogs. The signs of colitis are painful defecation, prolonged squatting and straining, flatulence, and passing many small stools mixed with blood and mucus. These signs can easily be mistaken for constipation.

The usual cause of colitis is one of the inflammatory bowel diseases (see page 273). Whipworms are another frequent cause. Fungal colitis is uncommon. It targets dogs with immune deficiency and lowered resistance. Prototheca colitis is a rare disease caused by an algae. It produces a severe form of colitis and can become systemic. Treatment has not been successful.

Colitis is diagnosed by *colonoscopy* and colon biopsy. Stool specimens are examined for parasites and fungi.

Irritable bowel syndrome describes a diarrhea motility disorder often associated with stress. It tends to occur in high-strung, nervous dogs. Dogs with irritable bowel syndrome have frequent small stools, often mixed with mucus. The diagnosis is based on the exclusion of other causes of colitis.

Treatment: Treatment is directed toward the underlying condition, often an inflammatory bowel disease. Irritable bowel syndrome can be helped by a high-fiber diet (see *Constipation*, page 280). Bacterial causes of colitis, such as salmonella, campylobactor, and clostridium, will respond to appropriate antibiotics.

GASTROINTESTINAL FOREIGN BODIES

Dogs have been known to swallow bones, toys, sticks, stones, pins, needles, wood splinters, cloth, rubber balls, rawhide, leather, string, peach pits, and other objects. With string, one end often knots up while the other gets caught in food. Tension on the string then causes it to cut through the wall of the bowel. Swallowing pennies will not usually cause an obstruction, but can lead to zinc toxicity as the metal leaches out of the coins. Batteries can also cause toxicity when swallowed.

The esophagus of the dog is larger than the outlet of his stomach. Thus, dogs may swallow objects that are too large to pass out of the stomach. Gastric foreign bodies are therefore associated with chronic gastritis and episodes of gastric outflow obstruction.

If an object makes it into the small intestine, it may pass through the entire GI tract without causing problems. Those that do cause an obstruction usually do so at the ileocecal valve or in the colon and rectum. Foreign bodies in the rectum cause anorectal obstructions. Sharp objects such as pins, splinters, and bone chips can lodge anywhere in the GI tract and obstruct or perforate the bowel, causing intestinal obstruction or peritonitis.

Unless it also causes indigestion, a swallowed foreign body will go unnoticed until it produces symptoms. Many foreign bodies can be seen on X-rays of the abdomen if they are radio-opaque. A contrast study may be needed to identify foreign bodies that are not visible on X-rays.

Treatment: Foreign bodies that produce symptoms should be removed. This usually involves abdominal surgery. Gastric foreign bodies can sometimes be removed through an endoscope.

INTESTINAL OBSTRUCTION

Any problem that interferes with the passage of intestinal contents through the GI tract results in a blocked bowel. The most common cause is a gastrointestinal foreign body. The second most common cause is intussusception—a situation in which the bowel telescopes in upon itself, like a sock pulled inside out. Most cases of intussusception occur at the cecum, where the small bowel joins the colon. As the small bowel inverts into the cecum and colon, the lead point travels a considerable distance, dragging the small intestine after it. Intussusceptions generally occur in puppies and young dogs.

Other causes of intestinal obstruction are tumors and strictures, adhesions following abdominal surgery, and navel and groin hernias that trap loops of bowel in the hernia sac. In young puppies, heavy infestations of roundworms may obstruct the bowel.

An intestinal obstruction can be partial or complete. Partial obstructions cause intermittent vomiting and/or diarrhea, which tend to occur over several weeks. Complete obstructions produce sudden abdominal pain and vomiting that continues without relief. When the blockage is in the upper small bowel, the vomiting may be projectile. Blockages in the lower GI tract cause abdominal distension and the vomiting of brown, fecal-smelling material. Dogs with complete obstruction pass no stool or gas.

Intestinal strangulation occurs when the obstruction interferes with the blood supply to the bowel. Within hours the bowel becomes gangrenous. The dog's condition deteriorates rapidly (see *Peritonitis*, page 279).

The diagnosis of intestinal obstruction is made by abdominal X-rays or ultrasound showing distended, gas-filled loops of bowel.

Treatment: Obstructions require immediate veterinary attention. Surgical exploration and relief of the blockage is necessary. Gangrenous bowel is resected back to viable bowel, and intestinal continuity is restored with end-to-end suturing of the bowel.

FLATULENCE (PASSING GAS)

Dogs who pass often gas can embarrass or distress their owners. The most common cause of flatulence is swallowing large amounts of air while gulping food. The next is eating highly fermentable foods such as onions, beans, cauliflower, cabbage, and soybeans. Flatulence also occurs with malabsorption syndromes. The excess gas is related to incomplete digestion of carbohydrates. Boxers are renowned for flatulence problems.

A sudden bout of flatulence, accompanied by abdominal discomfort, loss of appetite, or diarrhea, is an indication to seek veterinary attention.

Treatment: It's important to first rule out any malabsorption syndrome. Change the dog's food to a highly digestible, low-fiber diet, and avoid giving table scraps. Feed three small meals instead of one large meal to keep the dog from gulping food and swallowing air. If this does not stop the flatulence, consider switching to a prescription diet such as Hill's i/d or Hill's k/d, available from your veterinarian.

If further treatment is desired, simethicone can be given to absorb intestinal gas. Simethicone is available over the counter for people as a liquid or tablets. The dose for dogs is 40mg once or twice a day after meals. Charcoal-based treats and biscuits, and supplements that contain yucca, may also assist with gas.

COPROPHAGIA (EATING STOOL)

Coprophagia is the name given to the habit of eating stools—either the dog's own or another animal's. Cats' stools seem particularly tempting to dogs.

Most dogs with coprophagia are well nourished and show no evidence of a nutrient deficiency that would account for the compulsion to eat stools. These individuals may have acquired a taste preference for stools beginning in puppyhood. Other reasons sometimes suggested for stool eating include boredom and confinement in close quarters, such as a kennel. Scolding the dog for a housetraining accident may also cause him to want to eat the evidence. Whatever the cause, once established, the habit is difficult to break.

A minority of dogs have a medical reason for coprophagia. Dogs with malabsorption syndrome, in particular, have a ravenous appetite and eat stools in an attempt to acquire additional calories. Coprophagia has also been described in dogs on corticosteroid therapy and those with Cushing's syndrome, diabetes mellitus, hyperthyroidism, and intestinal parasites.

Stool eating is undesirable, not only for aesthetic reasons but because ingesting animal feces can bring in intestinal parasites. Dogs who eat large amounts of horse manure can develop severe vomiting and diarrhea. Dogs who eat the feces of large animals that were wormed recently may develop toxicity from the worm medication residue present in the stools.

Treatment: Veterinary examination is warranted to check for parasites and other medical problems. Management includes removing stools from the environment as quickly as possible, making cat litter boxes inaccessible to dogs, and distracting the dog by providing extra exercise and interaction with pets and humans. Providing suitable chew toys may also help prevent coprophagia caused by boredom. Sometimes, giving the dog canned food to provide a similar texture may help.

A number of ingredients have been suggested as additives to the dog's food to improve digestion or to render the stools unappetizing. A partial list includes meat tenderizers, crushed pineapple, Viokase, B-complex vitamins, sulfur, glutamic acid, monosodium glutamate, sauerkraut, and canned pumpkin. Forbid is a frequently recommended product made from alfalfa that gives the stool a disagreeable odor and taste. There are no scientific studies to prove or disprove the effectiveness of any of these additives, but anecdotal reports suggest they may be of benefit in some cases.

PERITONITIS

Inflammation of the cavity containing the abdominal organs is called peritonitis. Peritonitis occurs when digestive enzymes, food, stool, bacteria, blood, bile, or urine leak into the peritoneal cavity. Common causes are bloat, ruptured ulcers, perforations caused by gastrointestinal foreign bodies, intestinal obstructions, rupture of the uterus, rupture of the bladder, acute pancreatitis, penetrating wounds of the abdomen, and breakdown of suture lines following intestinal surgery.

Peritonitis can be localized or diffuse. In localized peritonitis an apron of fat (called the omentum) seals off and contains the source of contamination. In diffuse or generalized peritonitis, the infection spreads rapidly throughout the abdominal cavity.

Dogs with generalized peritonitis have severe abdominal pain and are reluctant to move. Vomiting is common. Pressing on the abdomen causes the dog to groan. The abdomen has a tucked-up appearance and feels rigid or boardlike, owing to reflex spasms of the abdominal wall muscles.

Dehydration, infection, and shock rapidly ensue. The pulse is weak and thready, breathing is rapid and labored, and the gums are cool and pale. The *capillary refill time* is prolonged more than three seconds. Collapse and death occur in a matter of hours.

Treatment: Immediate veterinary treatment is essential for survival. Intravenous fluids and broad-spectrum antibiotics are given to treat dehydration and shock. Surgical exploration is needed as soon as the dog is able to tolerate general anesthesia.

After the source of the peritonitis is repaired, the peritoneal cavity is repeatedly flushed to remove all foreign material. The surgeon may decide to pack the abdominal wound open with gauze pads to facilitate drainage of infected peritoneal fluid. An incision left open can be closed at a later date.

Localized peritonitis may respond to fluid replacement and antibiotics alone.

CONSTIPATION

Constipation means absent, infrequent, or difficult defecation. Most healthy dogs have one or two stools a day. This varies with the individual and the diet. A day or even two without stools is not a cause for concern, if the stools remain normal in size and pass without difficulty. But when feces are retained in the colon for two or three days, they become dry and hard, and require forceful straining to pass.

Note that straining also occurs in dogs with colitis, obstructed bladder, and anorectal obstructions. It is important to be sure the dog is not suffering from one of these other problems before treating him for constipation. Colitis, in particular, is often confused with constipation. Remember that a dog with colitis will pass many small stools that contain mucus and/or blood.

Causes of Constipation

Many middle-aged and older dogs are prone to constipation. A common predisposing cause is failure to drink enough water. With mild dehydration, water is withdrawn from the colon, which dehydrates the feces.

Ingesting foreign materials such as bone chips, hair, grass, cellulose, cloth, paper, and other substances is a well-recognized cause of acute and chronic constipation. The indigestible material mixes with feces to form rocklike masses in the colon.

Many drugs commonly used in dogs cause constipation as a secondary side effect. Discuss this possible correlation with your veterinarian. Hypothyroidism is an occasional cause of chronic constipation.

The urge to defecate can also be voluntarily overridden. Dogs develop such inhibitions during housetraining. When left alone in the house for long periods, they often override the urge to defecate. Dogs may also be reluctant to empty their bowels when hospitalized, boarded, or taken on a trip.

Dogs with constipation of recent onset should be examined by a veterinarian. Other reasons to seek veterinary consultation are painful defecation, straining during defecation, and passing blood or mucus.

Treating Constipation

Eliminate or control predisposing causes. Be sure to provide access to clean, fresh water at all times. Constipation associated with ingesting foreign materials such as bone chips can be corrected by eliminating the source and giving dog biscuits to chew on instead. Older dogs with reduced bowel activity can be helped by soaking the kibble with equal parts of water and letting the mixture stand for 20 minutes.

Dogs who voluntarily retain their stool can be helped by providing frequent opportunities for the dog to eliminate. Take the dog outside several times a day, preferably to an area where he is accustomed to going. A mild laxative may be needed when the dog is traveling.

Laxatives

A number of laxatives are available for treating constipation. Osmotic laxatives draw water into the intestines and liquefy the feces. Products containing lactulose, which must be prescribed by your veterinarian, are among the safest and most effective. A mild osmotic laxative effect can also be obtained by adding milk to the diet in amounts that exceed the capacity of the intestinal enzyme lactase to break down lactose into absorbable sugars—in other words, enough milk to cause diarrhea in a dog who is not constipated. The lactose molecule pulls fluid into the bowel and stimulates intestinal motility.

The mild saline laxative magnesium hydroxide (milk of magnesia) acts in a manner similar to osmotic laxatives (see *Over-the-Counter Drugs for Home Veterinary Use*, page 571, for dosage). Magnesium hydroxide is contraindicated in dogs with kidney failure.

Stimulant laxatives increase the force of intestinal peristalsis. They are highly effective in treating constipation, but repeated use can interfere with colon function. A commonly used stimulant laxative is bisacodyl (Dulcolax). The dose for dogs is 5 mg to 20 mg per day.

These laxatives are used for treating constipation only. If they are given to dog with an obstruction, they can do serious damage. They are not the laxatives of choice for preventing constipation and should not be used every day. Consult your veterinarian before you give your dog any laxative.

Preventing Constipation

Good hydration, a nonconstipating diet, and regular exercise are the best preventives, along with adding fiber to the diet, if needed. A convenient way to provide the fiber is to feed a commercial food formulated for senior dogs. You can also obtain a high-fiber diet, such as Hill's Prescription w/d, from your veterinarian.

Another way to provide additional fiber is to add a bulk-forming laxative daily to the dog's food. Bulk laxatives soften the feces and promote more frequent elimination. Commonly used bulk laxatives are unprocessed wheat bran (1 to 5 tablespoons, 15 to 75 ml per day) and Metamucil (1 to 5 tea-spoons, 5 to 25 ml per day). Plain canned pumpkin (1 tablespoon to ½ cup, 100 ml) depending on the size of the dog, can also help. Bulk laxatives or pumpkin can be fed indefinitely without causing problems.

Emollient laxatives containing docusate are indicated when the feces are dry and hard, but should not be used if the dog is dehydrated. Examples are Colace (50 to 200 mg per day), Surfak (100 to 240 mg per day), and Dialose (100 mg per day). These products promote water absorption into the feces, thereby softening the stool. They can be used daily.

Mineral oil is a lubricant laxative that facilitates the passage of hard stool through the anal canal. However, mineral oil interferes with the absorption of fat-soluble vitamins, so daily or frequent administration may cause vitamin deficiency. Mineral oil also reacts adversely with docusate and thus should not be used in conjunction with Colace and the other emollient laxatives. The best way to give mineral oil is to add it once or twice a week to the dog's meal at a dose of 1 to 25 ml, depending on the weight of the dog. Never administer mineral oil by syringe because it is tasteless and can be inhaled into the lungs.

Medications can also be given that influences intestinal motility, such as cisapride. These medicines should only be used under veterinary guidance.

FECAL IMPACTION

A fecal impaction is a mass of hard stool in the rectum and colon. There may be a predisposing condition, such as an enlarged prostate, that compresses the rectal canal (see *Anorectal Obstructions*, page 287).

Dogs with fecal impactions pass little or no stool despite repeated and forceful straining, are lethargic, have no appetite, experience abdominal distension and vomiting, and may have a hunched-up appearance. Digital rectal examination reveals a large, tubular mass.

Treatment: Veterinary examination and treatment is needed. A severe fecal impaction requires rehydration with intravenous fluids prior to removal. Most will need to be removed under general anesthesia using finger extraction and forceps.

Mild fecal impactions may respond to a combination of an osmotic or stimulant laxative (see *Constipation*, page 280) and a small enema. (Be careful when giving an enema; if done improperly, you could perforate the rectum.) A safe and effective small enema is warm tap water administered at 2.5 to 5.0 ml per pound of body weight. Tap water enemas can be repeated every few hours.

Tap water enemas are given through a rubber catheter connected to a plastic syringe or enema bag. Lubricate the tip of the catheter and insert it 1 to 2 inches (2.5 to 5 cm) into the rectum. Administer the enema. After the enema has been expelled, administer 10 to 20 ml mineral oil (5 to 10 ml for a small dog) into the rectum through the catheter to facilitate passage of the remaining stool.

Packaged saline laxative enemas that contain sodium phosphate (such as Fleet) also are effective for treating constipation and fecal impactions. Phosphate, however, has the potential to cause toxicity in small dogs and dogs with kidney disease, and should not be used in these individuals. Fleet enemas are safe to use in midsize and large dogs with normal kidney function. The recommended dose is one-half unit of a Fleet enema, or one unit of a Fleet Children's enema. Do not repeat. There are special enemas made for pets that are quite safe. Enemas come in plastic bottles equipped with nozzles. Always lubricate the tip of the nozzle before attempting to insert it into your dog's rectum. Insert it far enough into the anal canal to retain the fluid. Squeeze the bottle to administer the enema. Make sure you have help to restrain the dog in case he resists. Most dogs will defecate within a few minutes of receiving an enema.

Diarrhea

Diarrhea is the passage of loose, unformed stools. In most cases there is a large volume of stool and an increased number of bowel movements. The two most common causes of diarrhea in dogs are dietary indiscretion and intestinal parasites. Many canine infectious diseases are also associated with acute diarrhea. Diarrhea in puppies is discussed in *Dehydration*, page 493.

Food takes about eight hours to pass through the small intestines. During that time, the bulk of the food and 80 percent of the water is absorbed. The colon concentrates the remainder. At the end, a well-formed stool is evacuated. A normal stool contains no mucus, blood, or undigested food.

With rapid transit through the bowel, food arrives at the rectum in a liquid state, resulting in a loose, unformed bowel movement. This type of rapid transit accounts for the majority of temporary diarrhea in dogs.

Dietary indiscretion is a common cause of rapid transit. Dogs are natural scavengers and tend to eat many indigestible substances, including garbage and decayed food, dead animals, grass, wild and ornamental plants, and pieces of plastic, wood, paper, and other foreign materials. Many of these are irritating to the stomach as well as to the bowel, and are partially eliminated through vomiting.

Food intolerance can also cause rapid transit. Foods that some dogs seem unable to tolerate can include beef, pork, chicken, horsemeat, fish, eggs, spices, corn, wheat, soy, gravies, salts, spices, fats, and some commercial dog foods. Note that food intolerance is not the same as food allergy (see page 140), which causes dermatitis and possibly vomiting, but rarely causes diarrhea.

Some adult dogs are unable to digest milk and milk byproducts because of a lactase deficiency. Lactase is an intestinal enzyme that breaks down the lactose in milk into small-chain sugars. Undigested lactose cannot be absorbed and remains in the bowel, and holds water with it. This increases motility and causes large-volume diarrhea.

Characteristics of Diarrhea

	Likely Cause	Likely Location
COLOR		
Yellow or greenish	Rapid transit	Small bowel
Black, tarry	Upper GI bleeding	Stomach or small bowel
Red blood or clots	Lower GI bleeding	Colon clots
Pasty, light	Lack of bile	Liver
Large, gray, rancid	Inadequate digestion	Small bowel or absorption
CONSISTENCY		
Watery	Rapid transit	Small bowel
Foamy	Bacterial infection	Small bowel
Greasy, often with oily hair around the anus	Malabsorption	Small bowel, pancreas
Glistening or jellylike	Contains mucus	Colon
ODOR		
Foodlike, or smelling like sour milk	Rapid transit and inadequate digestion or absorption (suggests overfeeding, especially in puppies)	Small bowel
Rancid or foul	Inadequate digestion with fermentation	Small bowel, pancreas
FREQUENCY		
Several small stools in an hour, with straining	Colitis	Colon
Three or four large stools a day	Inadequate digestion or absorption	Small bowel, pancreas
CONDITION OF THE DOG		
Weight loss	Inadequate digestion or absorption	Small bowel, pancreas
No weight loss, normal appetite	Large bowel disorder	Colon
Vomiting	Enteritis	Small bowel, rarely colon

Intestinal parasites are a common cause of acute and chronic diarrhea in puppies and adults. The greatest problems are caused by roundworms, hookworms, whipworms, threadworms, and giardia.

Diarrhea is a common side effect of many drugs and medications, particularly the *NSAIDs*, which include aspirin. Some heart medications, some dewormers, and most antibiotics also can cause diarrhea.

Dogs can experience diarrhea when they're excited or upset—for example, when they're going to the veterinary hospital or a dog show. In fact, any sudden change in a dog's diet or living circumstances may cause emotional diarrhea.

In trying to figure out the cause of a diarrhea, it is important to decide whether the diarrhea originates in the small bowel or the large bowel. The characteristics of the diarrhea, as well as the condition of the dog, will help make this determination. The chart on the previous page details what to look for.

Diarrhea can be classified as acute or chronic, depending on its duration. Acute diarrhea comes on suddenly and is finished in a short period. Chronic diarrhea often comes on gradually and persists for three weeks or longer, or has an episodic pattern of recurrence.

Chronic diarrhea requires veterinary investigation. Routine tests include stool examinations for parasites (hookworms, whipworms, giardia), bacteria (*Salmonella, Camphylobacter, Clostridia*) and occasionally fungi (histoplasmosis, aspergillosis, candida). A number of immune assays and fecal absorption tests are available for diagnosing maldigestion and malabsorption syndromes.

Colonoscopy, with direct visualization of the interior of the colon, is an important diagnostic test for large bowel diarrhea. Liquid stool can be aspirated for culture and *cytology*, and biopsies taken of the bowel wall or any suspicious lesions. *Gastroscopy* with biopsy of the duodenum and sampling of small bowel secretions helps in diagnosing small bowel diarrhea. Ultrasound is another diagnostic tool that may help to pinpoint the cause of diarrhea.

HOME TREATMENT OF DIARRHEA

Diarrhea that does not cause dehydration and contains no blood can be treated at home. Adult dogs with no fever will drink enough water to remain hydrated if moderate to severe diarrhea does not persist for more than 24 hours. Young puppies and elderly dogs with acute diarrhea are at risk for dehydration and should be seen by a veterinarian. Dogs who are vomiting as well as suffering from diarrhea are at greater risk for dehydration.

Acute Diarrhea

The most important step in treating acute diarrhea is to rest the GI tract by withholding all food for 24 hours. The dog should be encouraged to drink as much water as he wants. With persistent diarrhea, consider giving a supplemental electrolyte solution such as Pedialyte, available over the counter in pharmacies and grocery stores. Dilute it by one-half with water and add it to the dog's drinking bowl. Custom canine electrolyte solutions and sport drinks are also available, such as K9 Thirst Quencher. These are flavored to encourage the dog to drink. If the dog won't drink the electrolyte solution, offer only water. A low-salt bouillon cube dissolved in the water can help encourage him to drink.

With persistent diarrhea, an antidiarrheal drug is a good way to slow intestinal motility. Pepto-Bismol and Kaopectate are safe and effective when used as directed (see *Over-the-Counter Drugs for Home Veterinary Use*, page 571, for dosage).

Acute diarrhea usually responds within 24 hours to intestinal rest. Start the dog out on an easily digestible diet that's low in fat. Examples are boiled hamburger (one part drained meat to two parts cooked rice) and boiled chicken with the skin removed. Cooked white rice, cottage cheese, cooked macaroni, cooked oatmeal, and soft-boiled eggs are other easily digestible foods. Feed three or four small meals a day for the first two days. Then slowly switch the diet back to the dog's regular food.

Obtain immediate veterinary care if:

- The diarrhea continues for more than 24 hours
- The stool contains blood or is black and tarry
- The diarrhea is accompanied by vomiting
- The dog appears weak or depressed or has a fever

Chronic Diarrhea

The first step is to find and treat the underlying cause. Diarrhea resulting from a change in diet can be corrected by switching back to the old diet and then making step-by-step changes to pinpoint the cause. When lactase deficiency is suspected, eliminate milk and dairy products from the diet, particularly as they are not required for adult dogs.

Diarrhea caused by overeating (characterized by large, bulky, unformed stools) can be controlled by tailoring the diet more accurately to the caloric needs of the dog and feeding his daily ration in three equal meals.

Chronic, intermittent diarrhea that persists for more than three weeks requires veterinary attention.

The Anus and Rectum

The signs of anorectal disease are pain on defecation, straining to pass stool, rectal bleeding, scooting, and biting and licking at the rear. Dogs with anorectal pain often attempt to defecate from a standing position.

Bleeding from the anal canal is recognized by finding blood on the outside of the stool rather than mixed in with it.

Scooting is rubbing the bottom along the ground. It indicates anal itching. Anal itching can be caused by flea bites, inflammation of the anal skin, anal sac disease, or tapeworms.

ANORECTAL OBSTRUCTIONS

A common cause of an anorectal obstruction is an enlarged prostate that bulges backward and compresses the rectum. This occurs in older male dogs. Foreign bodies that pass through the upper GI tract may obstruct the rectum. Pelvic fractures that have healed improperly can narrow the rectum, causing a blockage. Boston Terriers and Bulldogs are predisposed to this, and any dog born with a screw tail may have a rigid extension of the tail that pushes down upon the anal canal, pinching it against the pelvic floor. Other causes of blockage are fecal impactions, matted stool around the anus, rectal strictures, perianal gland tumors, perineal hernias, and rectal polyps and cancers.

Rectal strictures result from perianal infections, fistulas, and surgical attempts to treat them. Perineal hernias are bulges that occur alongside the anus. They weaken the muscular support of the rectum and interfere with the mechanics of elimination. The bulge becomes larger as the dog strains. Perineal hernias primarily occur in elderly, unneutered males.

The principal sign of anorectal obstruction is straining to defecate. The stool may be flat or ribbonlike. The dog may or may not pass blood. The diagnosis is made by digital rectal examination and, occasionally, by *colonoscopy*.

Treatment: It varies with the cause of the obstruction. Most foreign bodies can be removed by digital extraction under sedation or anesthesia. Neutering is the treatment of choice for an enlarged prostate (see page 418). Perineal hernias are repaired with a surgical procedure plus neutering, or by neutering alone. Strictures are corrected with surgery. Perianal gland tumors and polyps are discussed later in this chapter (page 293). Constipation associated with the screw tail usually requires surgical correction of the tail.

For conditions for which surgical treatment is not feasible, the goal is to maintain normal defecation using laxatives and stool-softening diets (see *Constipation*, page 280).

PSEUDOCONSTIPATION (MATTED STOOL AROUND THE ANUS)

When hair around the anus becomes densely matted with dried stool and forms a barrier to defecation, pseudoconstipation results. It occurs in longhaired dogs, usually following a bout of diarrhea. The skin becomes irritated, painful, and infected. This introduces an element of voluntary retention, as well.

Dogs with pseudoconstipation are restless and bite and lick at the anus. Other signs are scooting, whining, and attempting to defecate while standing. There is an extremely offensive odor.

Treatment: Clip away the matted hair to remove the cause of the blockage. If the area is painful, this is best done under a general anesthetic by your veterinarian. Keep the area clean and apply a topical ointment such as triple antibiotic or Cortaid to the inflamed skin.

If the dog strains and does not eliminate easily, see *Constipation* (page 280). Dogs who are prone to pseudoconstipation should have the hair around the anus regularly trimmed or clipped short.

PROCTITIS (INFLAMED ANUS AND RECTUM)

Inflammation of the anal skin can be caused by pseudoconstipation. Repeated bouts of diarrhea, especially in puppies, can cause an inflamed anus. Other causes are insect bites and worms. Irritation of the anal canal is caused by the passage of bone chips and hard stools.

Straining is a common sign of proctitis. Other signs are scooting, licking, and biting at the rear.

Treatment: Irritated anal skin can be soothed by applying an ointment such as that described for pseudoconstipation (see page 287). Clean the area thoroughly first with warm water and a mild soap. Treat constipation and diarrhea as described earlier in this chapter.

ANORECTAL PROLAPSE (PROTRUSION OF ANAL TISSUE)

Anorectal prolapse is the protrusion of rectal tissue through the anus. It occurs after forceful and prolonged straining. Conditions associated with forceful straining include severe constipation, fecal impaction, diarrhea, an anorectal obstruction, labor and delivery, an obstructed bladder, and heavy parasite loads, especially in puppies.

A mucosal *prolapse* is confined to the lining of the anal canal. It appears as a red, swollen, doughnut-shaped ring of tissue. This might be mistaken for prolapsed hemorrhoids, but dogs don't get hemorrhoids. In a complete rectal prolapse, a segment of rectum several inches long protrudes through the anus, appearing as a pink or red cylindrical mass.

Treatment: A mucosal prolapse disappears spontaneously when the underlying cause of straining is corrected. The dog should be placed on a stool softener such as Colace and fed a highly digestible, low-residue diet until symptoms resolve.

A rectal prolapse requires veterinary management to reduce the prolapse. A temporary purse-string suture may be made around the anal opening to prevent immediate recurrence. If the prolapsed bowel is necrotic (the tissue is

A dog with complete rectal prolapse.

dead), it will have to be surgically removed. Bowel continuity is restored with end-to-end suturing. Postoperative care includes stool softeners, a low-residue diet, and possibly medications to adjust intestinal motility.

MALFORMATION OF THE ANUS

Imperforate anus is a rare congenital condition in which the anus, or the anus and rectum, do not develop. In female puppies there may be a passage between the colon and the vagina called rectovaginal fistula.

Newborn puppies without an anus are unable to pass gas or meconium—the dark green fecal material that is usually excreted at birth. Abdominal distention and vomiting appear during the first 24 hours. If the colon opens into the vagina, gas and stool may pass out through the vulva, temporarily averting a bowel obstruction.

Treatment: Imperforate anus and rectovaginal fistula require surgical correction or the pups will not survive.

ANAL SAC DISEASE

The dog has two anal sacs or glands located at five and seven o'clock in reference to the circumference of the anus. They can be seen by drawing down on the skin of the lower part of the anus and looking in those locations.

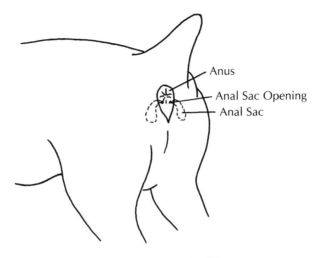

THE ANAL SACS

The anal sacs are similar to scent glands. In skunks they serve a defensive purpose. In dogs they produce an odor that identifies the individual and marks his stool to establish territory. This is why dogs greet each other by sniffing at the rear.

The anal sacs are emptied by the pressure of stool passing through the anus. They can also be emptied by forceful contractions of the anal sphincter—something that may happen when a dog is frightened or upset.

Anal sac disease is a cycle that begins with impaction and progresses through infection to abscess and rupture. Dogs with anal problems may develop tonsillitis from licking at the rear area.

Anal Sac Impaction

Impaction is the accumulation of pasty secretions in the anal sacs. The sacs become distended and mildly tender. The expressed secretions are thick and dark brown or grayish brown. The sacs become impacted when they don't empty completely. This may be due to insufficient pressure on the sacs during defecation because of small, soft stools; inadequate sphincter pressure; or blockage of the openings by thick, dry secretions. Impactions tend to occur most often in small-breed dogs and in overweight dogs.

Treatment: Impaction is treated by manually expressing the secretions. Dogs with recurrent anal sac impactions should have their sacs emptied at regular intervals. Place the dog on a high-fiber diet or a bulk laxative to increase the size of the stools (see *Constipation*, page 280).

How to Empty the Anal Sacs

Manually emptying the anal sacs is called expressing them. It is not necessary to express the anal sacs unless the dog has an anal sac disease, or when frequent

The anal sacs can be emptied by squeezing the skin surrounding the sacs between the thumb and forefinger.

When impacted, the anal sacs are best emptied with a finger in the anal canal and a thumb on the outside.

malodor poses a problem. Begin by putting on a disposable latex or plastic surgical glove. Raise the dog's tail and locate the openings as shown in the figure on this page. If they're full, the anal sacs can be felt as small, firm lumps in the perianal area at the five and seven o'clock positions.

Grasp the skin surrounding the sacs between your thumb and forefinger and squeeze. When an anal sac is impacted (blocked), it usually is best to empty the sacs with a finger in the anal canal and a thumb on the outside.

As the sac empties, you may smell a strong odor. Wipe the secretions with a damp cloth or gently hose the dog's rectal area. Normal secretions are liquid and brown. If the discharge is yellow, bloody, or puslike, the sac is infected and you should seek veterinary attention.

Sacculitis (Anal Sac Infection)

Anal sac infection complicates impaction. Infection is recognized by a painful swelling on one or both sides of the anus. The anal secretions are thin, yellowish, or blood-tinged. The dog will scoot, lick, and bite at his rear.

Treatment: Begin by expressing the anal sacs. Repeat in one to two weeks. For recurrent infection, empty the sacs weekly. After emptying, an antibiotic is instilled into the sacs. This procedure should be done by your veterinarian.

Dogs with recurrent anal sac infections should have their anal sacs surgically removed. This is best done during a period between infections.

Anal Sac Abscess

Abscess is recognized by fever and the signs of anal sac infection. The swelling, usually on one side, is red at first, then later turns a deep purple.

Enlarged, inflamed anal sac   Ruptured anal sac abscess

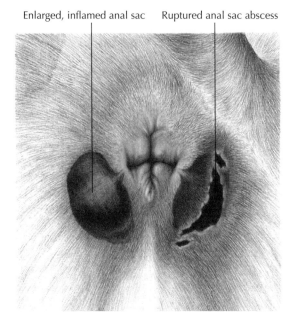

Unlike anal sac infection, the swelling of an abscess cannot be reduced by emptying the sac. An abscess often ruptures through the adjacent skin, producing a draining tract.

Treatment: If the abscess has not ruptured spontaneously, it should be lanced by your veterinarian when it becomes soft and fluidlike. The cavity is flushed repeatedly and the dog is placed on an oral antibiotic. Your veterinarian may ask you to flush the cavity twice a day with a topical antiseptic such as dilute Betadine solution for one to two weeks, and apply warm compresses to the area.

PERIANAL FISTULAS

Fistulas are draining tracts in the perianal skin caused by infection of the skin glands in and around the anus. Initially they appear as draining puncture holes. Later they coalesce to form open sores and draining tracts. The discharge is foul-smelling. Occasionally fistulas connect internally with the anal sacs.

Perianal fistulas occur most often in German Shepherd Dogs, but are found in Irish Setters, English Setters, Labrador Retrievers, and other breeds. There may be an association with breeds that have a low-slung, broad-based tail.

Symptoms are similar to those of anal sac infection (page 291). There may be a foul-smelling discharge. The diagnosis is made by visual inspection of the perianal area.

Treatment: Surgery is the most effective treatment and may include tail amputation. Cyclosporine and other immune-mediating medications may also be helpful in treating perianal fistulas. Perianal fistulas are difficult to cure and are associated with postoperative complications and recurrences. Early treatment offers the best chance for recovery. *Cryotherapy* and laser treatments have been used with success. Unfortunately, many surgical treatments may leave the dog with a degree of fecal incontinence.

RECTAL POLYPS AND CANCERS

Polyps are benign, grapelike growths that occur in the rectum and may protrude from the anus. They are not common, but when present they should be removed.

Adenocarcinoma is the most common malignant colorectal growth, followed by lymphoma. Adenocarcinomas are slow-growing gastrointestinal tumors found predominantly in older dogs, usually in the lower colon and rectum. These tumors can obstruct, ulcerate, and bleed. The diagnosis is made by *colonoscopy* and *biopsy* of the tumor.

Cancers can also arise from the anal sacs. This occurs primarily in older females. Anal sac adenocarcinomas have the unique property of producing parathyroid hormone, and thus may be associated with a severe form of hypercalcemia (see *Hyperparathyroidism,* page 407). These tumors vary in size from small lumps that are barely palpable to large masses protruding from the rectum.

Treatment: Surgical resection is the treatment of choice for colon and rectal cancers. Lymphomas can be treated with chemotherapy. Anal sac adenocarcinomas are best treated by surgical excision. Chemotherapy is a consideration for large tumors. Radiation may also be part of the treatment regimen.

PERIANAL GLAND TUMORS

These common tumors, often multiple, arise from glands located around the anus and at the base of the tail. They occur primarily in intact males over 7 years of age, and require the presence of testosterone. Adenomas can be recognized by their typical location and rounded, rubbery appearance. A minority undergo malignant transformation to adenocarcinomas. These cancerous neoplasms can grow to a large size, break through the skin, become infected, and cause anorectal obstruction. Metastases to the lungs occur frequently.

Treatment: The diagnosis is confirmed by tissue *biopsy.* For small tumors, this is best done by completely excising the tumor. If the tumor is found to be malignant, a chest X-ray should be taken to rule out metastatic spread.

Perianal gland tumors may regress completely following removal of the testicles. Thus, all dogs with perianal tumors, whether benign or malignant, should be neutered. Benign tumors should be removed with a rim of normal tissue. Malignant tumors should be removed as widely as possible at the time of neutering, providing the operation can be performed without causing rectal incontinence. Radiation and chemotherapy are other treatment options.

The Liver

The liver performs many vital functions, including synthesizing enzymes, proteins, and metabolites; removing ammonia and other wastes from the bloodstream; manufacturing blood-clotting factors; and detoxifying the blood of drugs and poisons.

LIVER FAILURE

The early signs of liver disease are nonspecific. They include loss of appetite, weight loss, and chronic intermittent vomiting and diarrhea. Vomiting is more common than diarrhea. Drinking and urinating more often than normal may be the first signs, and the principal reason for seeking medical attention.

In the early stages of liver disease the liver swells and enlarges. As the disease progresses, the liver cells die and are replaced by scar tissue. The liver then becomes rubbery and firm. This condition is called cirrhosis. It is not reversible. Before the liver reaches this terminal stage, it can recover from damage and heal itself to the point where your dog has normal liver function. This is possible if proper treatment is instituted early on; the extent of recovery depends on the exact cause of the liver damage. Eighty percent of liver cells must die before the liver begins to fail. The signs of liver failure are jaundice, hepatic encephalopathy, ascites, spontaneous bleeding, and dependent edema—swollen lower limbs. Treatment of liver failure is directed toward treating the liver disease that is causing it.

Jaundice

With impaired liver function, bile accumulates in the blood and tissues, staining the tissues yellow. This can be seen in the yellow appearance of the white of the eyes and in the mucous membranes of the gums and tongue. The inside of the ears is another area where yellow pigment can be detected. Bile excreted in the urine turns the urine dark brown (the color of tea).

Jaundice may also result from the breakdown of large numbers of red blood cells, such as in acute hemolytic anemia (see page 350). Post hepatic bile duct obstruction can also cause jaundice.

Hepatic Encephalopathy

This is a type of brain dysfunction caused by high levels of ammonia and other toxins in the blood. Ammonia is a byproduct of protein metabolism, and is normally removed from the bloodstream by a healthy liver. When the liver is sick, ammonia accumulates to toxic levels and exerts a poisonous effect on the brain.

Dogs with hepatic encephalopathy develop incoordination, sporadic weakness, disorientation, head-pressing, behavioral changes, drooling, stupor, and mental dullness. Symptoms tend to wax and wane. They become more severe after a high-protein meal. Seizures and coma occur when hepatic encephalopathy is advanced.

Ascites

Ascites is the accumulation of fluid in the abdomen. In a dog with liver disease, it is caused by low serum proteins and increased pressure in the veins that supply the liver. A dog with ascites has a swollen or bloated look. Thumping on the abdomen produces a dull, flat sound.

Bleeding

Spontaneous bleeding occurs in dogs with advanced liver disease. Common sites of bleeding are the stomach, intestines, and urinary tract. Blood may be noted in the vomitus, stools, or urine. Punctate (pinhead-size) hemorrhages may be seen on the gums. Bruises can appear under the lips and skin. Major blood loss from spontaneous bleeding is relatively uncommon, but uncontrollable bleeding can be a serious problem if the dog is injured or requires surgery.

Dependent Edema

Swelling of the abdominal wall and lower legs is related to malnutrition and low serum protein levels. It is not as common in dogs with liver disease as it is in those with congestive heart failure.

CAUSES OF LIVER DISEASE

A number of diseases, chemicals, drugs, and toxins can damage the liver. The liver is directly affected by infectious canine hepatitis and leptospirosis. It is frequently involved in heartworm infection, Cushing's syndrome, and diabetes mellitus. Primary and metastatic tumors are a major cause of liver failure in dogs.

Chemicals known to produce liver toxicity include carbon tetrachloride, insecticides, and toxic amounts of lead, phosphorus, selenium, arsenic, and iron. Drugs capable of damaging the liver include anesthetic gases, antibiotics, antifungals, dewormers, diuretics, analgesics (including NSAIDs), anticonvulsants, testosterone preparations (Cheque drops), and corticosteroids. Most drug reactions are associated with excessive dosage and/or prolonged use.

Some plants and herbs can also cause liver failure; these include ragwort, certain mushrooms, and blue-green algae. Molds such as aflatoxin, which grows on corn and may contaminate foods, can cause severe liver damage.

A blockage of the bile duct by gallstones, liver flukes, tumors, or pancreatitis is uncommon, but becomes a consideration when a dog has unexplained jaundice.

Treatment: Blood tests, including bile acid assay, ultrasound, and CT scan, provide useful information, but the only definitive test is biopsy of the liver. The prognosis for recovery depends on how long the dog has been ill, the extent of liver damage, and whether the disease can be surgically cured or controlled with medications.

Infectious diseases respond to treatment of the underlying condition. Drugs and poisons frequently exert temporary effects that are reversed when the exposure is stopped. Bile duct obstructions and some primary tumors of the liver can be corrected by surgery.

In addition to treating the liver disease, it is important to control and prevent complications, particularly hepatic encephalopathy and bleeding. This may involve feeding a special diet that is low in protein, lowering blood ammonia levels, maintaining blood-clotting factors, preventing seizures, correcting electrolyte abnormalities, and administering antacids to prevent stomach and duodenal ulcers. Supplements such as SAM-e and milk thistle are useful in both restoring and maintaining normal liver function.

Liver Shunt

Liver shunts, also called portosystemic shunts, are abnormal veins that enable blood from the intestines to bypass the liver. Ammonia and other toxins are not metabolized or removed from the circulation, resulting in signs of hepatic encephalopathy.

The majority of portosystemic shunts are congenital. Multiple shunts outside the liver may be congenital but are more often caused by cirrhosis. Dogs of a variety of breeds have been identified with liver shunts, but Miniature Schnauzers, Maltese, and Yorkshire Terriers appear to be at increased risk for congenital shunts that develop outside the liver. Large-breed dogs, such as Irish Wolfhounds, are at increased risk for shunts inside the liver that occur because a fetal vein that normally closes at birth fails to do so. Most dogs with congenital liver shunts develop symptoms of hepatic encephalopathy by 6 months of age, although some dogs may not develop symptoms until middle age or older. The diagnosis is confirmed by X-ray studies where contrast dyes are injected into the liver circulation, and by bile acid assays. Ultrasound may also be useful. These studies are available at referral centers.

Treatment: The treatment of choice for liver shunts is partial or complete surgical ligation of the shunt. This is not always possible. Medical management is directed toward controlling hepatic encephalopathy. Dogs with liver shunts should not be bred.

Idiopathic Chronic Hepatitis

This is not one disease, but a group of poorly understood liver diseases that culminate in cirrhosis. With the exception of copper-associated hepatitis, these diseases appear to have an *autoimmune* basis: The dog's immune system is somehow stimulated to manufacture antibodies against its own liver. This establishes an inflammatory process that progresses to liver failure. The basis for the autoimmune reaction is unknown.

Treatment: This involves the use of corticosteroids and immunosuppressants such as azathioprine (Imuran). Supplements such as SAM-e, antioxidants, and milk thistle are often helpful. The prognosis varies. Some dogs respond well and can be taken off medications; others require life-long treatment. Dogs who respond poorly generally have advanced liver disease with cirrhosis.

Copper-Associated Hepatitis

Hepatitis related to high levels of copper occurs in Doberman Pinschers, Bedlington Terriers, West Highland White Terriers, and Skye Terriers. In Bedlingtons and Westies there is an inherited defect in copper metabolism that enables toxic concentrations of copper to accumulate in the liver.

In Dobermans, copper concentrations are increased in most but not all affected dogs. It is unclear in the Doberman (and Skye Terrier) whether high copper levels are the cause of the hepatitis or the result. Copper can accumulate in the liver as a consequence of hepatitis alone. As a rule, the higher the copper concentration, the more likely it is that copper is the cause. Genetic testing for copper toxicosis in Bedlington Terriers and for Doberman Pinschers is available through VetGen.

Treatment: Treatment varies with the affected breed. Medications can be given to move copper out of the liver into the circulation, where it can be excreted in the urine. The absorption of copper can be decreased by giving oral zinc products that bind copper in the gut. Dogs with inherited defects in copper metabolism should not be bred.

The Pancreas

The pancreas has two functions. The first is to provide digestive enzymes; the second is to make insulin for sugar metabolism. Digestive enzymes are manufactured by the acinar cells and insulin by the islet cells.

PANCREATITIS

Pancreatitis is inflammation and swelling of the pancreas. It can occur in a mild or severe form. The cause of spontaneous pancreatitis in dogs is not well understood. Dogs taking corticosteroids are at increased risk. There is a higher incidence of pancreatitis in dogs with Cushing's syndrome, diabetes mellitus, hypothyroidism, and idiopathic hyperlipemia (a disease of Miniature Schnauzers). These diseases are associated with high serum lipid levels. Pancreatitis is also more prevalent in overweight spayed females and dogs on high-fat diets. An attack may be triggered by eating table scraps or a fatty meal.

Acute pancreatitis is characterized by the abrupt onset of vomiting and severe pain in the abdomen. The dog may have a tucked-up belly and assume a prayer position. Abdominal pain is caused by the release of digestive enzymes into the pancreas and surrounding tissue. Diarrhea, dehydration, weakness, and shock may ensue.

The diagnosis can be suspected based on a physical examination. It is confirmed by blood tests showing elevated amylase and/or lipase levels, along with a new serum test called canine pancreatitis lipase immuninol reactivity and TAP (trypsinogen activation peptide). Abdominal ultrasonography may reveal an enlarged and swollen pancreas.

Mild pancreatitis produces loss of appetite, depression, intermittent vomiting, and diarrhea and weight loss.

Fulminant necrotizing pancreatitis is an acute, extremely severe, usually fatal form of pancreatitis. In hours, your dog will go into shock. Dogs may vomit or simply show signs of severe abdominal pain. If you suspect this problem, get your dog to the veterinarian immediately!

Following an attack of pancreatitis, the pancreas may be permanently damaged. When it is, the dog may develop diabetes mellitus if the islet cells have been destroyed or may develop exocrine pancreatic insufficiency if the acinar cells have been destroyed.

Treatment: Dogs with acute pancreatitis require hospitalization to treat shock and dehydration. The most important step in treating pancreatitis is to rest the gland completely. This is accomplished by giving the dog nothing by mouth for several days and maintaining fluid and electrolyte balance with intravenous saline solutions. Antibiotics are used to prevent secondary bacterial infections. Pain is controlled with narcotics. Cardiac arrhythmias, if present, are treated with anti-arrhythmic drugs.

Dogs who do not respond to medical treatment may require surgery to drain an infected pancreas. The prognosis for dogs with shock and spreading peritonitis is poor.

Dogs who recover from pancreatitis are susceptible to recurrent attacks, which can be mild or severe. These episodes can be prevented, in part, by eliminating predisposing factors. For example, place overweight dogs on a weight-loss program (see *Weight Reduction*, page 308). Feed the total daily ration in two or three small servings to avoid overstimulating the pancreas. Do not feed table scraps. Dogs with high serum lipid levels (determined by your veterinarian) should be placed on a fat-restricted diet. If scarring has damaged the acinar or islet cells, your dog may need supplemental treatment such as enzymes or insulin (see *Exocrine Pancreatic Insufficiency*, on this page, and *Diabetes Mellitus*, page 300).

EXOCRINE PANCREATIC INSUFFICIENCY

The acinar cells in the pancreas manufacture digestive enzymes that empty into the duodenum in response to the stimulation of a meal. Without them, food cannot be adequately digested and nutrients therefore cannot be adequately absorbed. For reasons that are unknown, the acinar cells may *atrophy* and stop producing enzymes. This condition is called pancreatic acinar cell atrophy (PAA), and is one of the major causes of pancreatic insufficiency.

PAA begins in dogs under 2 years of age. All breeds are affected, but there is a predisposition in large breeds, particularly German Shepherd Dogs, in whom the disease may be inherited as an autosomal recessive trait.

A less common cause of pancreatic insufficiency is pancreatitis. Following a bout of inflammation, the pancreas may become scarred and contracted. This produces the same effect as acinar cell atrophy. This form of pancreatic insufficiency tends to affect middle-aged and older dogs of the small breeds.

Dogs with pancreatic insufficiency lose weight despite a voracious appetite and increased food consumption. The unabsorbed food produces a diarrhea with large, gray, semi-formed cow-pie stools with a rancid odor (see *Malabsorption Syndrome*, page 275). The hair around the anus is often oily from undigested fat. Intense hunger may cause the dog to eat his own stool.

The diagnosis of pancreatic insufficiency can be suspected from the appearance of the stool and other observations. The best and most accurate test is the serum trypsinlike immunoreactive assay (TLI), available to veterinarians through special mail-out laboratories. Folate and vitamin B12 levels may also be used as diagnostic aids.

Treatment: Most dogs respond well to having the missing enzymes added to their meals. Powered pancreatic extracts (Viokase-V and Pancrezyme) are superior to enteric-coated and uncrushed tablets. Divide the daily food intake into two or three meals. Add 1 or 2 teaspoons (5 to 10ml) of powdered extract to each meal just before feeding, as directed by your veterinarian. As the diarrhea comes under control, reduce the enzyme replacement to the minimum effective maintenance dose. One teaspoon added to each of two daily meals is adequate for most dogs.

Dogs who do not respond completely to pancreatic enzymes may do so when the maintenance diet is switched to a highly digestible, fat-restricted diet such as Hill's Prescription Diet i/d. An acid-blocker such as cimetidine

(Tagamet) or ranitidine (Zantac) may be prescribed by your veterinarian to prevent destruction of the pancreatic enzymes by acid in the stomach.

Vitamin absorption is reduced in dogs with pancreatic insufficiency. Vitamin supplements (oral and subcutaneous) may be advisable, at least for the first three months. Discuss this with your veterinarian.

Diabetes Mellitus (Sugar Diabetes)

Diabetes mellitus, sometimes called sugar diabetes, is a common disease in dogs. Golden Retrievers, German Shepherd Dogs, Miniature Schnauzers, Keeshonden, and Poodles have the highest incidence, but all breeds can be affected. Females with the disease outnumber males by three to one. The average age of onset is 6 to 9 years.

Diabetes is a result of inadequate production of insulin by the islet cells in the pancreas. There may be a genetic predisposition for this in some dogs. Islet cell destruction also occurs in some cases of pancreatitis. Insulin enables glucose to pass into cells, where it is metabolized to produce energy for metabolism. Insulin deficiency results in hyperglycemia (high blood sugar) and glycosuria (high urine sugar). Glucose in the urine causes the diabetic animal to excrete large volumes of urine. In turn, this creates dehydration and the urge to drink large amounts of water.

Initially, dogs who do not metabolize enough sugar have an increase in appetite and a desire to consume more food. Later, with the effects of malnourishment, the appetite drops.

In summary, the signs of early diabetes are frequent urination, drinking lots of water, a large appetite, and unexplained loss of weight. The laboratory findings are high glucose levels in the blood and urine.

In more advanced cases there is lethargy, loss of appetite, vomiting, dehydration, weakness, and coma. Cataracts are common in diabetic dogs. Ultimately, diabetes is a disease that affects all organs. Diabetic dogs will have enlarged livers, be susceptible to infections, and often develop neurological problems if not treated.

Diabetic ketoacidosis is a condition associated with severe hyperglycemia in which ketones (acids) build up in the blood. Ketones are byproducts of the metabolism of fat. In diabetic ketoacidosis, fats are metabolized for energy because sugar is unavailable. Diabetic ketoacidosis can be recognized by weakness, vomiting, rapid breathing, and the odor of acetone on the breath (it smells like nail polish remover). Diabetic ketoacidosis is a life-threatening emergency. If you suspect diabetic ketoacidosis, take your dog at once to the veterinarian.

Treating Diabetes

Dietary control and daily injections of insulin can regulate most diabetic dogs, allowing them to lead active, healthy lives. Oral hypoglycemic agents used for treating diabetes in people have not been effective in dogs, but research is continuing in this area.

Insulin requirements cannot be predicted solely on the basis of the dog's weight, because the degree of pancreatic failure is different in every dog. The daily insulin dose must be established for each individual. In the newly diagnosed diabetic, insulin therapy is started at home. After a week of treatment, the dog is brought back to the clinic and a blood glucose curve (a series of blood sugar tests drawn over 12 to 24 hours) is obtained to see when the blood glucose peaks and hits its lows. Refinements are then made in the dosage and timing of the injections. How to prepare and inject the insulin will be explained to you by your veterinarian. You may be asked to monitor urine glucose levels by collecting urine samples and using a test strip (a small piece of paper that indicates the glucose levels in urine).

Dietary Management

Obesity greatly reduces tissue responsiveness to insulin and makes diabetes difficult to control. Accordingly, an overweight diabetic dog should be put on a high-fiber, high-carbohydrate diet until he reaches an ideal weight. Examples of such diets are Hill's Prescription Diets r/d and w/d, Purina OM, and Fit and Trim Dry. Avoid soft-moist foods and treats, which are high in sugar. (Also see *Weight Reduction*, page 308.)

Hyperglycemia is less likely to occur if the dog is fed canned and dry kibble foods containing high concentrations of fiber and complex carbohydrates. Both of these components slow absorption and help minimize fluctuations in blood sugar after eating. Some commercially available diets meeting these requirements are Hill's Prescription Diets w/d and r/d (canned and dry), Purina OM, and Fit and Trim Dry.

Daily caloric requirements are determined by the weight and activity level of the dog. Once those are established, the amount to feed is determined by dividing the daily caloric requirement by the amount of calories per cup or can of food. It is important to keep the number of calories constant from day to day, because insulin requirements are computed on that basis.

It is equally important to maintain a strict schedule for insulin injections. To prevent severe hyperglycemia after eating, do not give all the day's calories at one sitting. Divide the ration into equal parts and feed two or three meals a day, or as directed by your veterinarian. Diabetic dogs do best on a very regimented schedule with feedings and insulin injections being given at the same times each day. Ideally, your dog should have the same levels of exercise and activity.

A thin dog who has lost weight should be fed a low-fiber diet (low-fiber diets have higher caloric density) such as Alpo Light (canned) or Iams Less Active (dry) until weight is regained.

Insulin Overdose

An overdose of insulin causes the blood sugar to drop to levels well below normal. This is called hypoglycemia. Suspect this if your dog appears confused, disoriented, drowsy, shivers, staggers about, collapses, falls into a coma, or has seizures. Insulin overdoses are associated with improper administration, using the wrong syringe (resulting in too high a dose), or changing the type of insulin. To treat an insulin overdose, see *Hypoglycemia*, page 507.

Feeding and Nutrition

Dogs have fewer taste buds than humans do (about 2,000, compared with our 12,000), and thus have relatively insensitive palates. Dogs can discern sweetness, sourness, bitterness, and saltiness. It is probably accurate to describe a dog's sense of taste as being able to discern pleasant, unpleasant, and indifferent.

Nonetheless, dogs do show a preference for certain foods. In side-by-side comparisons of various dog foods, 80 percent of dogs showed definite likes and dislikes. Incidentally, the more expensive foods were not necessarily the tastiest.

PROTEIN AND DOG FOOD

Pet food manufacturers have made feeding your dog a relatively simple task. You need only decide which brand to buy, how much to feed, and whether the dog likes the food. The cost is often the final consideration, but don't let that override nutritional quality.

Federal law requires that all pet food manufacturers provide a list of ingredients on the package. However, a list by itself gives only a rough idea of the quality of the food. For example, protein in dog food is derived from meat and poultry, meat byproducts, poultry byproducts, fish byproducts, soybean meal, and cereal grain such as corn or wheat. These various protein sources are not all of the same quality and digestibility. The mere fact that beef or some other protein is mentioned on the package is no guarantee of quality—it may indicate levels as low as 3 percent.

However, if the product's name contains the words "beef," "chicken," "lamb," "fish," and so on, 95 percent of the dry weight of the product must be derived from that protein source—although in a variety of forms, including byproducts and digest. (If the product's name is something like "beefy chunks," it means the manufacturer has sidestepped the 95 percent requirement.)

A high-quality diet should furnish a proper balance of essential amino acids. Ten amino acids cannot be manufactured by the dog and are considered dietary essentials. These ten essential amino acids are arginine, histidine, isoleucine, leucine, lysine, methionine, phenylalanine, threonine, tryptophan, and valine. The quality of the protein in the food depends on the right combination of essential amino acids. In general, a good balance of amino acids is created using a combination of proteins from plant and animal sources, because the amino acids deficient in one source are usually present in the other.

Symptoms of amino acid deficiency include depressed appetite, impaired growth, gray haircoat in a dog who should be dark, low hemoglobin levels, immune deficiency, and lowered reproductive performance.

COMMERCIAL DOG FOODS

Brands of commercial dog foods can be classified as generic, popular, or premium. Generic foods are less expensive than popular ones, and premium foods are the most expensive.

Generic dog foods do not carry a brand name. Closely related to generics are the private-label pet foods that carry the names of the stores in which they are sold. These foods provide a list of ingredients as required by law, but most cannot make claims that the food is nutritionally balanced or complete. Generic products are less expensive than popular and premium brands, because the food is manufactured using low-cost ingredients. Furthermore, the ingredients vary from package to package, depending on which nutrient sources were available at the time the food was manufactured. In feeding trials, many of the generic products were found to have lower digestibility, due to the addition of indigestible fibers.

Popular dog foods are the recognizable brands from major food manufacturers. They are available at most supermarkets and grocery stores. These companies spend a good deal of time and energy testing and advertising their products.

To show that their foods contain all the protein, fat, vitamins, and minerals dogs need to grow and thrive, popular dog food makers cite one of two established standards on the label. Both standards are set by the Association of American Feed Control Officials (AAFCO), a nonprofit association of federal and state officials that develops guidelines for the production, labeling, and sale of animal foods. One standard requires that the food meet an AAFCO profile that is based on a calculation of all the nutrients dogs are theoretically known to require to maintain health and fitness. The other standard involves feeding trials that demonstrate dogs can live and thrive on the product.

The calculation approach is limited in its usefulness because current knowledge is not firm for all the nutrients dogs require. In addition, there is no guarantee that the dog can digest and absorb all the nutrients in a specific food. Feeding trials are superior to the calculation method because they show that the product actually works and delivers the desired results. The drawbacks are that only a six-month feeding trial and only a small number of test dogs are required for a manufacturer to make the claim. Nevertheless, for a pet food company to represent its product as "complete," "balanced," "perfect," "scientific," or "formulated for growth, pregnancy, or lactation," the product must conform to one of the AAFCO profiles for that stage of life. Any food marketed as "for all life stages" must have the extra protein and calories needed to support growing young puppies as well as maintain elderly dogs. Because of these constraints, the nutrient content of these products remains fairly constant even though different sources may be used in the formulation.

Premium dog foods are available only through veterinarians, pet supply stores, feed stores, and the Internet. In general, the ingredients used in these products are highly digestible and have good to excellent nutrient availability. In contrast to popular brands, premium foods are produced using fixed formulas. The ingredients used do not change in response to availability or market price. Manufacturers of these foods validate their claims through AAFCO feeding studies (not calculations). Because these products contain high-quality food sources that are easily digested, dogs can be fed smaller amounts. Therefore, even though a bag may cost more, the cost per serving may be comparable to many popular brands.

Dog food is available as canned, semimoist, and dry kibble. It makes little difference from a nutritional point of view which of these you choose. Semimoist foods have more preservatives, however, and many dog owners try to avoid those. Some dogs find canned food more palatable because it generally has a higher percentage of moisture and fat. Dry kibble is least expensive and has the advantage of maintaining the health of the teeth and gums. You can leave dry food out all day for free-choice consumption—but only if your dog is not overweight or having housetraining problems. Canned food should be left out only for short periods because it spoils quickly. Any unused portion should be refrigerated.

Commercial foods contain instructions on the label about how much to feed, based on the weight of the dog. The manufacturer's recommended serving size is often more than many dogs require. Follow the directions at first, but monitor your dog's weight. Feed more if the dog starts to lose weight and less if he gains weight or leaves food in the dish. Each dog really needs a customized diet based on his individual size, health, age, and activity level.

In summary, while the standards set by AAFCO do have some limitations, they still provide the best guidelines available for selecting a dog food. Look on the package for the AAFCO statement that the nutritional adequacy of the product has been confirmed by a feeding trial. This shows that the product is complete and balanced for the intended life stage. Avoid generic and private-label foods that do not contain the AAFCO feeding trial statement.

Once you have narrowed the field, select a product that your dog finds especially tasty. Premium foods may be more digestible and consistent from batch to batch, but these considerations may not be significant for some dogs.

FEEDING GROWING PUPPIES

Most breeders supply a diet sheet with a new puppy, detailing what the pup has been fed, how much, and at what times of the day. Follow this, at least for the first few days, since an abrupt change in diet can cause digestive upsets.

The caloric requirements of growing puppies are shown in the table on page 499. Pups up to 6 months of age require twice as many calories per pound of body weight per day as do adults. Protein requirements are also higher. After six months, these requirements begin to decline as the puppy's growth rate decelerates.

These requirements are best met by feeding a product labeled "for growth of puppies." The information on the label should show that on a dry matter basis the product:

- Has at least 25 percent protein
- Has at least 17 percent fat
- Has less than 5 percent fiber
- Has 1.0 to 1.8 percent calcium
- Has 0.8 to 1.6 percent phosphorus
- Is 80 percent digestible
- Provides 1,750 metabolizable calories per pound (.45 k) of food

Labels provide recommended daily feeding amounts. They are useful as guidelines, but are not applicable for every pup, nor for every stage of the puppy's life.

Puppies should be fed at least three times a day from weaning to 6 months of age. After 6 months, puppies can be fed twice a day. Do not feed puppies snacks between meals, as this will unbalance the diet. Feeding regular meals will also help with housetraining.

Overfeeding is a much more common problem than underfeeding. Do not leave a bowl of food down all day for puppies! Overfeeding can lead to obesity and may worsen the symptoms of hip dysplasia and other inherited bone diseases. Overfeeding is particularly undesirable in heavy-boned, rapidly growing puppies of the large breeds. In fact, in larger breeds a slower growth rate has been found to be healthier, because it allows the muscles and tendons to develop at the same rate as the bones.

If you own a large-breed puppy, you may want to feed somewhat less than the amount recommended on the package. Some packages have instructions for feeding large-breed puppies. These may be more accurate than following general guidelines. Special formulas for large-breed puppies that are lower in calories, fat, and calcium are available through your veterinarian. Feed as prescribed.

FEEDING ADULTS

When a puppy reaches 1 year of age, his diet should be changed to one that is appropriate for maintaining an adult dog. Your veterinarian may recommend making this change earlier, depending on the growth rate of your individual dog. Adult foods generally have less protein and fat than puppy foods.

From a nutritional point of view, there is no harm in leaving an adult dog on a puppy food as long as the amount fed is trimmed back to be appropriate for adult maintenance. Failure to reduce the daily caloric intake is one of the main reasons for excessive weight gain in early adulthood.

Although feeding once a day is fine for many dogs, dividing the daily ration into two equal servings is healthier and more satisfying. If you are feeding dry kibble, you can leave the food out during the day for free-choice consumption, unless your dog tends to be overweight, in which case the dog should be fed carefully measured meals. When you leave food down all day you won't get an accurate picture of whether your dog is eating every day and how much he is consuming, either. Discard unused food at the end of the day. Canned and semimoist products should be fed twice daily, at the same time each day, and the unused portion should be picked up after 15 minutes and refrigerated. Feeding regular meals is the best way to manage your dog's diet.

Caloric requirements differ from dog to dog, but in general, dogs need fewer calories as they grow older. They also need less in warm weather and during periods of inactivity. Once again, feeding instructions on dog food packages should be taken as guidelines only. These instructions are only rough estimates and are not always applicable to a specific breed or individual. The goal is to maintain normal body weight. Feed the dog whatever is necessary to maintain his ideal weight. Purina provides a body condition scoring table (see appendix D for the Purina web site) that can help you decide if your dog is overweight or underweight. Hard-working dogs require a highly digestible diet with increased fat content to maintain stamina and body condition. This is one area where a premium dog food formulated for working dogs may be particularly beneficial. In the off season when the dog is not working, feed less of the high-calorie food or gradually change to a less nutrient-dense dog food.

Feeding during pregnancy and lactation is discussed in *Care and Feeding During Pregnancy*, page 469. Feeding the elderly dog is discussed in *Diet and Nutrition*, page 554.

RAW AND HOMEMADE DIETS

Raw diets or BARF (bones and raw foods) have become popular recently. These diets consist of raw meat with some fruits, vegetables, and occasionally grains mixed in, along with meaty raw bones.

There are numerous serious problems that can arise with feeding a diet like this. Getting a correct nutritional balance can be tricky. Raw meats must be handled very carefully to prevent bacterial disease such as salmonella—which can affect people as well as dogs. Careful storage and thawing and superb hygiene in handling are essential to prevent health problems. Parasites can be a serious problem in raw meat. Chewing bones could lead to splinters if the dog isn't observed carefully, and even ground bones can cause an impaction.

The average dog owner does not have the time or nutritional background to feed a diet like this successfully and safely. If you choose to go with a raw diet, you need to consult a veterinary nutritionist for guidance. The same rules and need for guidance apply if you choose to cook homemade meals for your dog.

TABLE SCRAPS AND EXTRAS

Table scraps and "people food" compete with dog food for a dog's appetite. Calories obtained from extra foods may or may not be of the same quality as those obtained through the dog's regular food. If you are feeding a high-quality commercial food, additional calories will unbalance the food and lead to obesity. Vegetables can make good low-calorie treats, as can bits of rice cakes or Cheerios.

Attacks of pancreatitis have occurred after a dog eats table scraps. Feeding table scraps can also lead to unwanted behavior problems, such as begging or stealing food from the table.

If you decide to feed your dog people food or treats, limit the amount to no more than 5 to 10 percent of the dog's daily caloric intake. Do not offer him greasy leftover scraps that you would not eat. Meats, fish, and poultry should be well cooked and all bones should be removed. Note that many adult dogs are lactose intolerant. Feeding dairy products such as milk and cheese may result in diarrhea. These foods should be avoided.

SUPPLEMENTS

Calcium, phosphorus, iron, microminerals, and vitamins are supplied in ample quantities in good-quality dog food. Vitamin and mineral supplements are not necessary and can be detrimental to a dog's health. They are not recommended unless there is a medical indication for their use. However, supplements such as glycosaminoglycans and chondroitin sulfate for joint health may be recommended by your veterinarian and can be beneficial. Other supplements can be helpful for dogs with specific health conditions. Always ask your veterinarian before giving your dog any supplements.

DIETS FOR HEALTH PROBLEMS

Great progress has been made in developing diets that are helpful in treating and/or controlling health problems in dogs. Many of these are available only by prescription or through your veterinarian. These diets are customized to be ideal for certain health problems. Examples are the Eukanuba, Purina, and Hill's diets for dogs with allergies, kidney problems, and certain types of urinary stones. Do not start your dog on one of these diets without veterinary supervision, as they may cause problems for a dog with normal health.

SWITCHING DIETS

Dogs do not seem to object to eating the same food day after day. But if you believe, as many people do, that variety is the spice of life, you may wish to change your pet's diet from time to time. Note that when you change flavors you may change the nutritional value of the food as well. The new flavor (because of the flavor additive) may contain more or less protein, fat, or fiber.

A change in diet may be indicated for medical reasons, in which case the new diet will be prescribed by your veterinarian.

When changing diets, gradually mix the new diet in with the old over 7 to 10 days. Observe how well your dog eats the new diet. A change in the appearance of the stool (loose or increased bulk) suggests that the new diet may not agree with the dog as well as the old one did.

WEIGHT REDUCTION

It has been estimated that up to 40 percent of dogs in the United States are overweight. Obesity is due to overfeeding, particularly feeding snacks and treats between meals, failing to reduce the caloric intake of puppies when they reach adulthood, and inadequate exercise. Adding people food to a nutritionally balanced diet is another cause of weight gain. Some breeds of dogs are more prone to obesity, such as Beagles and Labrador Retrievers.

Obesity greatly complicates many diseases, including diabetes, hypertension, heart disease, arthritis, and other musculoskeletal problems. It also shortens the quality and duration of the pet's life. For these reasons it is important to prevent excessive weight gain and to return an overweight dog to a more normal body condition.

Determine your dog's body condition by his appearance and the amount of fat distributed over the ribs. You should be able to feel the ribs as individual structures. From above, you should see a well-defined narrowing or waistlike effect below the rib cage and above the hips. If you are unable to feel the individual ribs and the dog has lost his waist, he is carrying too much fat.

Breed standards give the ideal weight for males and females of each breed. If your dog is of the typical height, he or she should fall within the standard range for weight.

The two dietary approaches to weight reduction are to feed less of the current food or to feed another food that is less dense in calories. A disadvantage of feeding less of the maintenance food is that it can lead to nutritional deficiencies. This is because maintenance foods meet daily nutrient requirements only if the dog consumes the amount recommended. Furthermore, because the dog is eating less, he doesn't feel as full and is more apt to beg or steal food.

Special reducing dog foods that are less dense in calories are advantageous because the volume of food does not need to be significantly reduced. Commercial dog foods marketed as "lean," "light," or "low-calorie" that conform to AAFCO feeding trial standards supply all the nutrient requirements when fed as directed. Nutrient deficiencies should not occur.

These reducing foods provide fewer calories by reducing the amount of fat. This is accomplished by replacing some of the fat with either digestible carbohydrates or indigestible fiber. Those that use carbohydrates are preferable to those that use fiber. Diets with even stricter calorie restrictions than commercial products can be obtained through your veterinarian.

To begin a reduction program, weigh your dog to establish his current weight. Chart the weight at weekly intervals. Compute the amount to feed based on the dog's ideal weight—not his current weight. The dog should lose no more than 2 percent of his body weight per week. Use the feeding directions on the package as a good reference, but adjust the size of the meals to maintain gradual weight loss. *Avoid feeding snacks or treats.* After the dog reaches his ideal weight, feed a balanced ration to maintain that weight. If you use treats for training, simply switch to using the dog's regular food as a treat and deduct that amount from his daily ration.

Combine weight-reducing diets with more exercise. Increase the length of the exercise gradually, to avoid overtaxing the dog. Walking is an ideal way for dogs to exercise more. Swimming is another good form of exercise and reduces strain on the joints.

Splentrol is a new drug that was developed as an aid to weight loss in dogs. Along with the drug, a reduced-calorie diet and increased exercise are recommended. Efficacy tests on this drug are ongoing.

THE RESPIRATORY SYSTEM

The upper respiratory system is made up of the nasal passages, throat, larynx, and trachea (see the figure *Anatomy of the Head* on page 232). The bronchi and lungs make up the lower respiratory tract. The breathing tubes branch into progressively smaller passages until they open into the air sacs (alveoli). The lungs are composed of the bronchi, air sacs, and blood vessels. The ribs and muscles of the chest, along with the diaphragm, function as a bellows, moving the air into and out of the lungs.

Abnormal Breathing
RAPID, LABORED BREATHING

A dog at rest takes about 10 to 30 breaths per minute. Breathing at a faster rate suggests fever, pain, anxiety, or a problem with the lungs or chest. Rapid breathing should be distinguished from panting. Panting is the primary way a dog lowers her body temperature; water evaporates from the mouth, tongue, and lungs, and warm air in the body is exchanged for cooler air in the atmosphere.

Rapid breathing, when accompanied by labored or difficult breathing, is a sign of distress. Dogs with congestive heart failure and/or lung disease often have rapid, labored breathing at rest or with only mild exertion. Other causes of rapid, labored breathing are shock, heat stroke, dehydration, and ketoacidosis associated with diabetes, kidney failure, and some kinds of poisoning.

Dogs with rapid, labored breathing should be seen by a veterinarian.

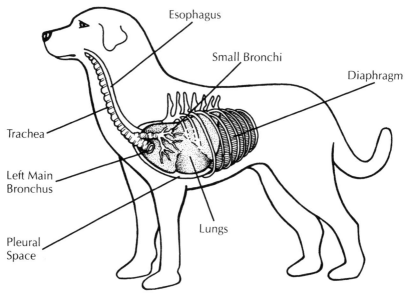

Esophagus

Small Bronchi

Diaphragm

Trachea

Left Main
Bronchus

Lungs

Pleural
Space

ANATOMY OF THE RESPIRATORY SYSTEM

Noisy Breathing

Noisy breathing indicates an obstruction in the nasal passages, the back of the throat, or the larynx. Snorting and snoring are typically heard with the brachycephalic syndrome discussed on page 313. If your dog normally breathes quietly but suddenly develops noisy breathing, this is a cause for concern. She should be checked by a veterinarian.

Stridor (Croupy Breathing)

Croupy breathing, or *stridor*, is a high-pitched raspy sound caused by air passing through a narrowed voice box. It may be heard only when the dog exercises. When the onset is sudden, the most likely cause is a foreign body in the voice box. When croupy breathing has been present for some time, laryngeal paralysis is a possible cause.

Wheezing

A wheeze is a whistling sound heard when the dog inhales or exhales, or both. Wheezing indicates spasm or narrowing in the trachea or bronchi. Wheezes in the lungs are best heard with a stethoscope. Some causes of wheezing are chronic bronchitis, congestive heart failure, and tumors of the larynx, trachea, and lungs.

SHALLOW BREATHING

Shallow breathing is seen in dogs with broken ribs and severe bruising of the chest wall. Blood, pus, or serum in the chest cavity (called *pleural effusion*) restricts breathing by interfering with the range of motion of the chest and expansion of the lungs. A dog with shallow breathing compensates by breathing more rapidly.

BRACHYCEPHALIC SYNDROME

Bulldogs, Pugs, Pekingese, Shih Tzu, English Toy Spaniels, Boston Terriers, Chow Chows, and other dogs with broad skulls and short muzzles frequently show some degree of airway obstruction, known as brachycephalic syndrome, manifested by mouth breathing, snorting, and snoring. These difficulties become more pronounced when the dog is exercising or is overheated, and tend to get worse as the dog grows older.

The obstructed breathing in these dogs is caused by deformities that include collapsed nostrils, an elongated soft palate, and eversion of the laryngeal saccules. These deformities often occur together. Collapsed nostrils and elongated soft palate are congenital. Eversion of the laryngeal saccules is acquired.

Stenotic Nares (Collapsed Nostrils)

In puppies with stenotic nares, the nasal openings are small and the nasal cartilage is soft and floppy, causing the nostrils to collapse as the puppy breathes in. This produces varying degrees of airway obstruction, manifested by mouth breathing, noisy breathing, and occasionally a nasal discharge. In severe cases the chest is flattened from front to back. These pups fail to thrive and are poorly developed.

Treatment: Stenotic nares can be treated successfully by surgically enlarging the nasal openings. This is accomplished by removing a wedge of nasal skin and cartilage. Not all dogs with stenotic nares require surgery. In some dogs the cartilage firms up satisfactorily by 6 months of age. If there is no urgency in symptoms, your veterinarian may delay treatment to see if this happens.

Elongated Soft Palate

The soft palate is a flap of mucosa that closes off the nasopharynx during swallowing (see the figure *Anatomy of the Head*, page 232). Normally, it touches or slightly overlaps the epiglottis. In dogs with an elongated soft palate, the palate overlaps the epiglottis to a considerable degree, partially obstructing the airway during breathing. This is manifested by snorting, snoring, *stridor*, gurgling, and gagging. The obstruction is worse with exercise. In time, stretched ligaments in the larynx lead to labored breathing and laryngeal collapse.

Treatment: An elongated soft palate is treated by surgically shortening the palate so that the edge opposes or slightly overlaps the epiglottis. Results are good if the operation is done before destructive changes occur in the larynx.

Eversion of the Laryngeal Saccules

Laryngeal saccules are small mucosal pouches that project into the larynx. In long-standing upper airway obstruction the saccules enlarge and turn out (eversion), narrowing the airway even further.

Treatment: Everted laryngeal saccules often accompany an elongated soft palate. If present, they should be removed. This operation is done at the same time as shortening of the palate. Your veterinarian may refer you to a surgical specialist for these surgeries.

The Larynx (Voice Box)

The larynx is an oblong box of tissue located in the throat above the windpipe (trachea). Just above the larynx is the epiglottis, a leaflike flap of cartilage that closes over the larynx and protects the airway during swallowing.

The larynx is composed of cartilage held together by ligaments. Within the larynx are the vocal cords, which is why the larynx is sometimes called the voice box. A dog's vocal chords are thick and prominent, enabling them to

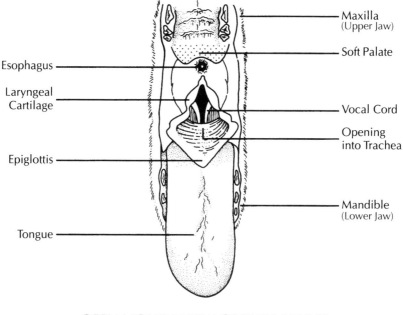

OPEN MOUTH VIEW OF THE LARNYX

bark loudly. The interior of the larynx is lined with a mucous membrane. The mucosa of the larynx, unlike the rest of the respiratory tract, does not contain cilia—hairlike structures that help move things through the passage. Therefore, mucus tends to pool in the larynx. Exaggerated throat-clearing is required to bring up the phlegm.

The larynx is the most sensitive cough area in the respiratory tract. Pressure over the larynx, such as that caused by a tight choke collar, can cause episodes of explosive coughing.

Diseases of the larynx cause hoarseness and progressive loss of the ability to bark. Choking, gagging, and coughing may be observed, especially while eating or drinking. Laryngeal obstructions such as those caused by laryngeal collapse, vocal cord paralysis, or a foreign body in the airway produce shortness of breath on exertion, *stridor, cyanosis*, and collapse.

LARYNGITIS

Laryngitis is inflammation and swelling of the vocal cords and surrounding laryngeal mucosa. The signs are hoarseness and the inability to bark. The most common cause of laryngitis is voice strain caused by excessive barking or coughing. In the absence of these, suspect vocal cord paralysis. Laryngitis can accompany tonsillitis, throat infections, kennel cough, or tumors in the throat.

Treatment: Laryngitis due to excessive barking usually responds to removing the stimulus for the barking (see *Excessive Barking*, page 318). When voice strain is due to prolonged coughing, take your dog to the veterinarian to investigate and eliminate the cause of the coughing.

LARYNGEAL EDEMA

Sudden swelling of the larynx and vocal cords can result in marked narrowing or complete obstruction of the airway. Signs are *stridor*, rapid labored breathing, *cyanosis*, and collapse.

Insect bites can cause an anaphylactic reaction with sudden swelling of the larynx. Another cause of laryngeal edema is excessive panting, particularly when it is associated with heat stroke. Similarly, any process that results in forced breathing across a narrowed airway (such as vocal cord paralysis) can lead to swelling that exacerbates the original disease.

Treatment: Sudden stridor and difficulty breathing is an acute emergency. Proceed as quickly as possible to the nearest veterinary clinic. Corticosteroids are given to reduce swelling and inflammation. Adrenalin is a specific antidote for an allergic reaction (see *Anaphylactic Shock*, page 13). Antihistamines also are beneficial. Sedatives help to relieve anxiety and panting.

Choking (Foreign Body in the Larynx)

The sudden onset of forceful coughing, pawing at the mouth, and respiratory distress in a healthy dog suggest a foreign body caught in the larynx. This is an emergency! If the dog is conscious and able to breathe, proceed at once to the nearest veterinary clinic.

If your dog is gagging and retching but is not experiencing difficulty in breathing, assume a foreign object such as a bone splinter or rubber ball is caught in her mouth or in the back of her throat. These subjects are discussed in *Foreign Body in the Throat*, page 252.

Fortunately, a foreign body in the larynx is not common. Most objects are expelled by the forceful coughing that results from laryngeal stimulation.

Treatment: If the dog collapses and is unable to breathe, place her on her side with her head down. Open her mouth, pull out her tongue as far as you can, sweep your fingers from side to side, grasp the object, and remove it. Then administer artificial respiration or CPR as necessary (see *CPR*, page 7).

If the object cannot be easily removed, do not try to get around it with your fingers. This will force it further down the throat. Instead, proceed to the Heimlich Maneuver.

The Heimlich Maneuver

1. **Abdominal compressions.** It may be easiest to hold the dog upside down in your lap, with her back against your chest and her head highest, but facing down. Place your arms around the dog's waist from behind. Make a fist and grasp it with the other hand. For a small dog, you may have to just use two fingers. Place your fist or fingers in the dog's upper mid-abdomen close to the breast bone at the apex of the V formed by the rib cage.

   Compress the abdomen by forcefully thrusting up and in with the fist or fingers four times in quick succession. This maneuver pushes the diaphragm upward and forces a burst of air through the larynx. This usually dislodges the object. Proceed to step 2.

2. **Finger sweeps.** Pull out the tongue and sweep the mouth. Remove the foreign body and proceed to step 5. If you are unable to dislodge the object, proceed to step 3.

3. **Artificial respiration.** Give five mouth-to-nose respirations. Even a small volume of air getting past the obstruction is beneficial. Proceed to step 4.

4. **Chest thumps.** Deliver a sharp blow with the heel of your hand to the dog's back between the shoulder blades. Repeat the finger sweeps. If the object is still not dislodged, repeat steps 1 through 4 until the object is dislodged.

5. **Ventilation.** Once the object is dislodged, check for breathing and heart rate; administer artificial respiration and CPR if necessary. When the dog revives, proceed to the veterinary hospital for further treatment.

LARYNGOSPASM (REVERSE SNEEZING)

This uncommon condition can be alarming because it sounds as if the dog can't catch her breath. During an attack, the dog produces a loud snorting noise caused by violent attempts to draw in air. This may occur several times in succession. After the attack, the dog appears completely normal.

Reverse sneezing is believed to be caused by a temporary spasm of the muscles of the larynx, possibly the result of a drop of mucus that falls on the vocal cords from the soft palate. The attack can be ended by making the dog swallow. This is accomplished by massaging the front of the neck in the region of the pharynx just beneath the jaw. Alternatively, place your hand over the dog's nostrils for an instant.

If the attack does not stop and the dog collapses, suspect a foreign body in the larynx. Reverse sneezing is commonly seen in Corgis and Beagles. (See *Choking*, page 316.)

LARYNGEAL PARALYSIS (VOCAL CORD PARALYSIS)

This is an acquired disease that occurs in older dogs of the large and giant breeds, particularly Labrador Retrievers, Golden Retrievers, Irish Setters, St. Bernards, and Great Pyrenees. In Siberian Huskies, Bouviers des Flandres, Bull Terriers, and Dalmatians it occurs as a hereditary defect. In these breeds, dogs with this problem should not be bred.

Laryngeal paralysis results from damage to the nerves that control the movement of the larynx. Trauma and age may be factors. Hypothyroidism may also contribute to this problem.

A classic sign of laryngeal paralysis is a characteristic croupy or "roaring" noise heard as the dog inhales. Initially it appears during or after exercise. Later it occurs at rest. Another sign is progressive weakening of the bark, which ends in a croaky whisper. In time the dog develops noisy breathing, labored breathing, reduced exercise tolerance, and fainting spells. Laryngeal edema may develop and further compromise the airway, causing respiratory collapse and even death.

The diagnosis is made by examining the vocal cords with a laryngoscope. Paralyzed vocal cords come together in the middle instead of remaining well apart. This produces a tight air passage through the larynx.

Treatment: A number of surgical procedures have been used to enlarge the airway. The technique used most often involves removing both the vocal cords and their supporting cartilage. This relieves the obstruction, but the dog is unable to bark. Surgery may also predispose the dog to aspiration pneumonia, so usually medical therapy is tried first (keep dog calm and cool, and have sedatives and corticosteroids on hand).

Laryngeal Trauma

Choke chain injuries, tight slip collars, or any rope around the neck can fracture the hyoid bone and/or cause compression damage to the nerves of the pharynx and larynx. Other causes of trauma to the larynx include bite wounds and sharp foreign objects such as bones and pins that penetrate the larynx. Dogs with laryngeal injuries often breathe normally at rest but show respiratory distress during exertion.

Treatment: Treatment of laryngeal trauma involves confining and resting the dog and administering anti-inflammatory medications. If the larynx is severely traumatized, a *tracheostomy* (an operation in which an opening is made through the skin into the trachea to establish a new airway) may be required. Choke chain injuries can be prevented by using a buckle collar, head halter, or chest harness.

Laryngeal Collapse

This is a late stage in airway obstruction. Pressure changes in the upper airway caused by stenotic nares, an elongated soft palate, laryngeal paralysis, or everted laryngeal saccules stretch the ligaments that support the laryngeal cartilages. These cartilages gradually collapse inward and block the airway. At this stage any change in the dog's need for air can cause acute respiratory insufficiency and cardiac arrest.

Treatment: The first step is to surgically correct predisposing factors. If symptoms persist, the dog may benefit from a permanent *tracheostomy*.

Debarking and Barking Problems

Some dogs simply seem to enjoy barking. But constant shrill barking can lead to problems with neighbors and a dog being dropped off at the local shelter.

Debarking surgery removes some of the vocal chord tissue. This can be done through the mouth or through the throat. Lasers are sometimes used for this surgery. After debarking, dogs can still bark but it is a quieter, hoarse sound. If the dog develops scar tissue, she may recover the ability to bark normally. Too much scar tissue may interfere with breathing. Postoperative care is important, because any swelling in this area could cause acute breathing problems. You may need to search for a veterinarian experienced with this surgery.

Before doing debarking surgery, you should try behavior training and/or eliminate the cause of the excessive barking. Using a citronella or electronic bark collar may also work. These deliver a negative response when your dog barks, either with a spray of citronella or a mild shock.

Coughing

Coughing is a reflex initiated by an irritation in the airway. Coughs are caused by respiratory infections, congestive heart failure, chronic bronchitis, respiratory tract tumors, collapsing trachea, pressure from tight collars, and inhaled irritants such as grass seeds, fumes, and food particles.

Coughs are self-perpetuating. Coughing dries out the mucous membranes and irritates the breathing tubes—leading to further coughing.

DIAGNOSING A COUGH

The type of cough often suggests the diagnosis:

- A deep, dry, hacking cough made worse by exercise or excitement is characteristic of kennel cough.
- A moist, bubbling cough indicates fluid or phlegm in the lungs and suggests pneumonia.
- A high, weak, gagging cough, followed by swallowing and licking the lips, is characteristic of tonsillitis and sore throat.
- A spasm of prolonged coughing that occurs at night or while lying on the sternum suggests heart disease.
- A "goose-honk" cough in a toy breed dog indicates a collapsing trachea.

The diagnostic workup of a dog with a chronic cough includes a chest X-ray and *transtracheal washings*. Washings are cells obtained by flushing the trachea with saline solution. This can be done with a sterile tube passed down the trachea while the dog is sedated, or by direct penetration of the trachea through the skin of the neck using a needle and catheter. The washings are processed for *cytology* and bacterial culture. The information usually leads to a specific diagnosis.

Bronchoscopy is particularly useful in the investigation of chronic coughs and coughs with the production of mucus and blood. The procedure requires sedation or general anesthesia. A rigid or flexible endoscope is passed into the trachea and bronchi. This enables the veterinarian to see the interior of the respiratory tract. Biopsies can be taken with accuracy, and washings collected for examination and culture. Bronchoscopy is also the procedure of choice for removing bronchial foreign bodies.

Treating a Cough

Only minor coughs of brief duration should be treated at home. Coughs accompanied by labored breathing, a discharge from the eyes or nose, or the production of bloody sputum should be seen and treated by a veterinarian.

It is important to identify and correct any contributing factors. Eliminate any irritating atmospheric pollutants, such as cigarette smoke, aerosol insecticides, strong cleaners, house dust, and perfumes, from the home environment.

Breaking the cough cycle is an important part of treating irritant coughs. A variety of children's cough medicines are available over the counter. Children's Robitussin is an effective cough medicine that contains an expectorant called guaifenesin. It does not suppress the cough reflex, but does liquefy mucus secretions so that they can be brought up more easily. Robitussin is safe to use for all coughs.

Robitussin-DM and Benylin Expectorant, also available over the counter, contain the cough suppressant dextromethorphan. (The correct dosage for all these cough preparations is given in the table *Over-the-Counter Drugs for Home Veterinary Use*, page 571.) When stronger cough suppressants are needed, preparations containing the narcotics hydrocodone bitartrate (Hycodan) and butorphanol tartrate (Torbutrol, Torbugesic) are available by prescription from your veterinarian.

Cough suppressants should be used selectively and only for short periods. Although they decrease the frequency and severity of the cough, they do not treat the condition causing it. Overuse may delay diagnosis and treatment. Cough suppressants (but not expectorants) should be avoided in dogs with bacterial infections and when phlegm is being brought up or swallowed. In these cases, productive coughs are clearing unwanted material from the airway.

Dogs with a dry cough can be helped by keeping them in the bathroom while you shower and not using the fan. The added moisture may loosen secretions. Using a humidifier can also be helpful.

Trachea and Bronchi
Acute Tracheobronchitis (Kennel Cough Complex)

The kennel cough complex is a group of highly contagious respiratory diseases in dogs. The name comes from the fact that the infection tends to spread rapidly, especially among dogs in boarding kennels or dogs who have been to places where large numbers of dogs congregate, including dog shows and dog parks. Several viruses and bacteria, alone or in combination, can cause the disease. The organisms most frequently involved are canine parainfluenza virus and the bacteria *Bordetella bronchiseptica* (both are discussed in chapter 3). Canine adenovirus types CAV-1 and CAV-2, as well as canine herpesvirus, canine distemper, and mycoplasma, are other causes of kennel cough.

A harsh, dry, hacking cough is the characteristic sign of tracheobronchitis. The cough is unproductive and is often accompanied by gagging and retching. Except for the cough, the dog is bright and alert, and has a good appetite and a normal temperature. In most cases kennel cough is a mild disease. With rest and a stress-free environment, most adult dogs recover completely in 7 to 14 days. Keeping the dog quiet will speed recovery.

Kennel cough may be complicated by secondary bacterial pneumonia. This is most likely to occur in dogs with bronchitis, collapsing trachea, or diseases that lower their resistance to infection. In puppies, kennel cough can be accompanied by nasal congestion. These puppies require frequent care to loosen thick secretions, improve breathing, and prevent pneumonia. This is also true for toy breeds.

A severe form of tracheobronchitis that can lead to pneumonia is characterized by low-grade fluctuating fever, loss of appetite, and depression. These dogs have a moist productive cough, nasal discharge, exercise intolerance, wheezing, and rapid breathing. This form of kennel cough requires hospitalization.

Treatment: Kennel cough should be treated by a veterinarian. Isolate dogs to prevent spreading the disease. The quarters should be warm, dry, and well-ventilated. Humidification is beneficial. A cool mist vaporizer offers some advantage over a heat vaporizer, because it is less likely to add excessive heat to the atmosphere. If one is not available, having the dog in the bathroom while you shower can help.

Moderate daily exercise is beneficial to the extent that it assists bronchial drainage. Strenuous exertion off leash should be avoided. If the dog drags against her collar, use a harness or head halter.

Antibiotics are routinely used to treat kennel cough. The drugs of choice are the tetracyclines and trimethoprimsulfa. Continue the antibiotics for 7 to 10 days. Excessive coughing is controlled with cough suppressants.

Dogs with severe tracheobronchitis or pneumonia must be hospitalized and treated intensively with intramuscular or intravenous antibiotics and drugs that dilate the breathing passages.

Prevention: The intranasal Bordetella vaccine is useful but may have to be given twice annually. There is also an intramuscular Bordetella vaccine. CPI and CAV-2 vaccines—incorporated into routine immunizations—will decrease the prevalence and severity of kennel cough. Show dogs, boarded dogs, and dogs who go to grooming salons may benefit from the optional bordetella vaccination (For more information, see *Vaccinations*, page 92.)

FOREIGN BODY IN THE LUNGS

Grass seeds and food particles are the most common foreign materials inhaled by dogs that are big enough to lodge in the smaller breathing tubes. Most of these are quickly coughed up. If the object becomes fixed in the airway, it causes intense irritation and swelling of the air passage. Mucus collects below the obstruction and forms an ideal medium for bacterial growth and infection. Objects that remain in the lungs for several weeks can cause pneumonia.

Sudden attacks of coughing that occur immediately after vomiting or after a dog has been running in tall grass and weeds suggest inhalation of a foreign body. Lungworms in the bronchi also cause severe coughing spasms.

Treatment: Unexplained coughing should be investigated by a veterinarian. Avoid cough medicines, unless prescribed by your veterinarian, since they delay treatment. *Bronchoscopy* is usually successful in locating and removing bronchial foreign bodies, particularly if the procedure is done within two weeks of inhalation.

COLLAPSING TRACHEA

This condition occurs primarily in older dogs of the toy breeds, particularly Chihuahuas, Pomeranians, and Toy Poodles, and occasionally in young dogs as a congenital defect.

Collapsing trachea occurs because the C-shaped tracheal rings do not possess normal rigidity. As a result, the involved wall of the trachea collapses as the dog inhales. Obesity is a predisposing factor, as is chronic bronchitis.

The principal sign of collapsing trachea is a characteristic goose-honk cough. The cough is made worse by stress and exertion, including pulling against a collar. Coughing may also occur when the dog eats or drinks. Respiratory insufficiency develops as the disease progresses.

Treatment: Examination by a veterinarian is the first step. Diseases of the heart and lungs should be ruled out before making the diagnosis. Dogs with mild to moderate symptoms respond to proper nutrition and a low-stress routine that avoids situations that trigger episodes of coughing. Moderate exercise is beneficial. Using a harness or head halter instead of a collar is important.

Overweight dogs should be put on a weight-loss diet, as described for chronic bronchitis (page 323). Eliminate cigarette smoke and other atmospheric pollutants that can trigger coughing.

NORMAL TRACHEA   PARTIAL COLLAPSE   COMPLETE COLLAPSE

Collapsing tracheal cartilages lack rigidity and are drawn into the airway when the dog inhales.

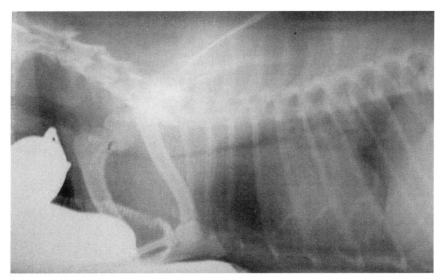

This chest X-ray shows an enlarged air column (dark shadow) in the neck, indicating a normal-sized trachea, and a narrow air column in the chest, indicating a collapsing trachea.

Bronchodilator drugs such as aminophylline, theophylline, or albuterol are beneficial for many small dogs. Mild low-dose sedatives during stressful periods also are helpful. Cough suppressants and corticosteroids may be prescribed when the coughing is particularly severe. Respiratory infections require prompt treatment with antibiotics.

Surgery can be considered in severe cases. It involves suturing plastic rings around the trachea, which then keep the airway open. Complications are possible.

CHRONIC BRONCHITIS

This disease affects middle-aged dogs of both sexes. It is characterized by an acute inflammatory reaction of the interior of the smaller airways. Chronic bronchitis should be considered whenever a cough persists for more than two months.

In most cases the cause is unknown. Although some cases are preceded by kennel cough, infectious agents usually do not play a role except as secondary invaders. House dust, cigarette smoke, and other atmospheric irritants contribute to bronchial inflammation.

The hallmark of chronic bronchitis is a harsh, dry cough that may or may not be productive. Coughing is triggered by exercise and excitement. Episodes often end with gagging, retching, and the expectoration of foamy saliva. This can be mistaken for vomiting. The dog's appetite and weight are well maintained.

Unchecked chronic bronchitis damages the airways and leads to the accumulation of infected mucus and pus in dilated bronchi. This is called bronchiectasis. Chronic coughing can also lead to enlargement of the alveoli (lung air sacs), a condition called emphysema. These two diseases are not reversible and gradually progress to chronic lung disease and congestive heart failure.

The diagnostic workup for bronchitis is the same as that described in *Diagnosing a Cough*, page 319.

Treatment: General measures include eliminating atmospheric pollutants such as dust and cigarette smoke. Minimize stress, fatigue, and excitement. Overweight dogs should be put on a weight-loss diet (see *Weight Reduction*, page 308). Walking on a leash is good exercise, but don't overdo it. To avoid pressure on the larynx, switch from a collar to a chest harness or head halter.

Medical management is directed toward reducing bronchial inflammation. Your veterinarian may prescribe a course of corticosteroids for 10 to 14 days. If this is beneficial, the dog may be placed on a maintenance dose given daily or every other day. Bronchodilators such as theophylline or albuterol relax the breathing passages and reduce respiratory fatigue. They are beneficial for dogs with associated wheezing and airway spasms.

If the cough gets worse there is probably a secondary bacterial infection. Seek veterinary attention, because antibiotics will be required. Cough suppressants are beneficial for episodes of exhaustive coughing, but should be used only for short periods, as they interfere with host defenses and prevent the elimination of *purulent* secretions. Expectorants can be used as often as needed.

The response to treatment varies. Some dogs make a near-normal recovery, while others require frequent medication adjustments.

The Lungs
Pneumonia

Pneumonia can be caused by viruses, bacteria, fungi, or parasites. Bacterial and viral pneumonia are often preceded by an infection in the nasopharynx or airways.

Pneumonia is uncommon in healthy adult dogs. It tends to target the very young and the very old, and those whose immune systems have been compromised as a result of corticosteroid therapy, chemotherapy, or chronic illness. Dogs with chronic bronchitis, collapsing trachea, or foreign bodies in the lower airway frequently develop bacterial pneumonia.

Inhalation or aspiration pneumonia occurs with megaesophagus, gastroesophageal reflux, paralysis of the swallowing mechanism, and reflux of gastric contents into the lungs during general anesthesia or vomiting. Chemical pneumonia is caused by inhaling smoke or ingesting hydrocarbons such as gasoline or kerosene.

Signs of pneumonia are cough, fever, depression, rapid breathing, rapid pulse, and occasionally a nasal discharge that is thick with mucus. The cough is moist and bubbling, indicating fluid in the lungs. Dogs with severe pneumonia frequently sit with their head extended and elbows turned out to allow for greater expansion of the chest.

The diagnosis is made by chest X-ray and blood tests. Bacterial culture and sensitivity tests aid in selecting the most effective antibiotic.

Treatment: Dogs with fever and signs of respiratory infection should receive urgent veterinary care. Take the dog to the hospital immediately. *Do not give cough suppressants.* Coughing is beneficial because it clears the airway and facilitates breathing.

Bacterial infection responds well to antibiotics selected specifically for the bacteria causing the disease. Your veterinarian will select the most appropriate drug. The antibiotic should be continued for at least three weeks, or until the follow-up chest X-rays show clearing.

Any predisposing causes, such as gastroesophageal reflux or a bronchial foreign body, should be treated to prevent recurrence.

PULMONARY INFILTRATES OF EOSINOPHILS

Pulmonary infiltrates of eosinophils (PIE) is an uncommon respiratory disease in dogs, caused by the presence of numerous *eosinophils* (a type of white blood cell) in the blood, respiratory secretions, and lungs. Eosinophils usually indicate a hypersensitivity reaction. Accordingly, an allergic basis for PIE has been proposed. What the dog is allergic to is usually unknown.

Before a diagnosis of PIE can be made, other causes of eosinophilia, such as heartworms, lungworms, migrating intestinal parasites, fungal infections, and lymphosarcoma, must be excluded.

The signs of PIE are fever, cough, rapid breathing, and weight loss. Listening to the chest with a stethoscope reveals dry, crackling sounds. The diagnosis is made by finding eosinophils in the blood and *transtracheal washings.*

Treatment: Treatment involves large doses of corticosteroids that are tapered off gradually over several weeks. Many dogs recover fully, but relapses can occur.

CANINE INFLUENZA

This respiratory virus first was isolated from racing Greyhounds in 2004. The virus appears to have mutated from the equine influenza virus. It has been found in dogs of all breeds and mixes and across North America.

Affected dogs will have a high fever, a soft, gagging cough (unlike the goose-honk cough of kennel cough), and may have a nasal discharge. While 80 percent of dogs have a mild course of disease when exposed to this new pathogen, some will go on to develop pneumonia. Mortality is about 5 to 8 percent, with most fatalities in puppies, old dogs, and dogs with compromised immune systems. Some dogs will shed the virus either before becoming ill or chronically.

To differentiate this problem from "standard" kennel cough will require laboratory tests. Treatment should start immediately, however.

Treatment: Isolate the dog, because this disease is contagious and is spread through the air. Supportive care is important, with antibiotics used if a secondary bacterial infection develops. Many dogs require fluids and hospitalization if they develop pneumonia. There is no vaccine at this time.

PLEURAL EFFUSION

A pleural effusion is an accumulation of serum or blood in the chest. The most common cause is congestive heart failure. Other causes include liver disease, kidney failure, pancreatitis, and primary and metastatic tumors of the lungs. Bacterial pneumonia can extend to the pleural space, producing an infected pleural effusion called empyema. Blood in the pleural space (called hemothorax) occurs with chest trauma, malignant lung tumors, and spontaneous bleeding disorders. Chylothorax is a buildup of lymphatic fluid in the chest that can occur with lung torsions, tumors, and a blockage of lymphatic flow. Afghan Hounds have a breed predisposition to this, and possibly Shiba Inus.

Large pleural effusions press on the lungs and cause respiratory distress. Severely affected dogs have rapid, labored breathing and often stand or sit with elbows out, chest fully expanded, and head and neck extended. Breathing is open-mouthed. The lips, gums, and tongue may appear blue. The least bit of effort can cause collapse.

Treatment: *Urgent veterinary attention is required.* The fluid in the lungs must be removed as soon as possible to facilitate breathing. This is done by inserting a needle or catheter into the pleural space and withdrawing the fluid by syringe. The dog should be hospitalized to discover and treat the cause of the problem.

Tumors of the Larynx, Trachea, and Lungs

Benign and malignant tumors occur in the larynx, trachea, bronchi, and lungs. The diagnosis of laryngeal, tracheal, and lung tumors is based on chest X-rays, ultrasound, *bronchoscopy* and/or *transtracheal washings* and *cytology* (see *Diagnosing a Cough*, page 319). Tissue biopsy provides an accurate diagnosis and helps in planning treatment.

Laryngeal tumors are uncommon and occur in middle-aged to older dogs. Most are malignant (squamous cell carcinomas). Signs are noisy breathing, change in voice, and loss of bark. A characteristic *stridor* may be heard when the dog inhales. Sudden death can occur from respiratory obstruction.

Tracheal tumors are rare. In older dogs they tend to be malignant (osteosarcomas). In young dogs they are more likely to be benign (osteochondromas). The most common sign is a productive cough. Stridor on inhalation may be noted during exercise or panting. *Cyanosis* and collapse can occur when the tumors get very large and cause severe respiratory obstruction.

Lung tumors account for about 1 percent of all *neoplasms* in dogs. Most arise from cells lining the bronchi. They tend to occur in older dogs of both sexes. Lung tumors in dogs may be associated with exposure to cigarette smoke.

Most primary lung tumors are malignant and will have already spread to other parts of the body by the time they are diagnosed.

A harsh, nonproductive cough is the most common sign. *Pleural effusion* may occur as a late complication.

Metastatic lung tumors—that is, tumors that spread to the lungs from other parts of the body—are more common than primary lung tumors. Tumors that metastasize to the lungs include mammary gland cancers, osteosarcomas, thyroid cancers, melanomas, and squamous cell carcinomas.

Treatment: Surgical exploration and removal of small tumors offers the best chance for cure. Larger tumors usually cannot be cured, but may respond to chemotherapy. The advanced age of many dogs with respiratory tract tumors usually makes aggressive treatment impractical.

THE CIRCULATORY SYSTEM

The circulatory system comprises the heart, the blood, and the blood vessels.

The heart is a pump made up of four chambers: the right atrium and right ventricle, and the left atrium and left ventricle. The two sides of the heart are separated by a muscular wall. In a dog with normal anatomy, blood cannot get from one side of the heart to the other without first going through the general or pulmonary circulation. Four heart valves keep blood flowing in one direction. When the valves are diseased, blood can leak backward, creating difficulties.

In a dog with normal circulation, blood is pumped out of the left ventricle, through the aortic valve, and into the aorta. It passes through arteries of progressively smaller size until it reaches the capillary beds of the skin, muscles, brain, and internal organs. In these capillary beds, oxygen is exchanged for carbon dioxide. From the capillaries blood is carried back through veins of progressively larger diameter, finally reaching two large veins called the anterior and posterior vena cavae.

From these large veins, the blood enters the right atrium. It passes from the right atrium through the tricuspid valve and into the right ventricle. As the right ventricle contracts, the pulmonary valve opens, allowing the blood to enter the main pulmonary artery. The pulmonary artery branches into smaller vessels and finally into capillaries around the air sacs of the lungs. It is here that carbon dioxide is exchanged for oxygen. The blood then returns via the pulmonary veins, passes through the mitral valve, and into the left ventricle. As the left ventricle contracts, the aortic valve opens and blood is pumped into the general circulation—thus completing the cycle.

The beating of the heart is controlled by its own internal electrical system, but also responds to outside influences. Thus, the heart beats faster when a dog exercises, becomes frightened, is overheated, or requires greater blood

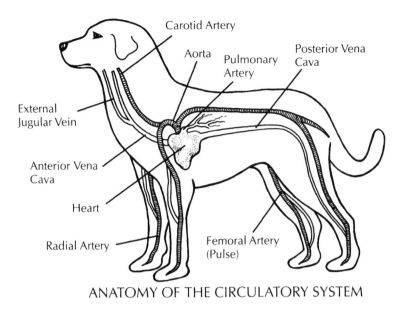

ANATOMY OF THE CIRCULATORY SYSTEM

flow to the body. The arteries and veins can expand or contract to maintain correct blood pressure.

The Normal Heart

There are outward physical signs that help determine whether a dog's heart and circulatory system are working normally. Familiarize yourself with what is normal so you can recognize any abnormality.

PULSE

The pulse, a transmitted heartbeat, is easily detected by feeling the femoral artery, located in the groin. With your dog standing, or preferably lying on his back, feel along the inside of the thigh where the leg joins the body. Press with your fingers until you locate the pulse.

You can also feel a dog's pulse by pressing against the rib cage over his heart. Feel the heartbeat just below and behind the elbow joint. If the heart is enlarged or diseased, you may be able to detect a buzzing or vibration over the chest wall.

The pulse rate is determined by counting the number of beats per minute. Most adult dogs at rest maintain a rate of 60 to 160 beats per minute. In large dogs the rate is somewhat slower and in toy dogs it's somewhat faster. In young puppies the heart rate is about 220 beats per minute.

Feel for the femoral pulse in the thigh, where the leg joins the body.

Another way to take the pulse is to feel the heart-beat behind the left elbow.

HEART SOUNDS

Veterinarians use a stethoscope to listen to the heart. You can listen to your dog's heart by placing your ear against his chest. The normal heartbeat is divided into two sounds. The first is a *lub*, followed by a slight pause and then a *dub*. Put together, the sound is *lub-dub, lub-dub* . . . in a steady, evenly spaced rhythm.

The heartbeat should be strong, steady, and regular. A slight alteration in rhythm as the dog breathes in and out is normal. An exceedingly fast pulse can indicate anxiety, fever, anemia, blood loss, dehydration, shock, infection, heat stroke, or heart (and lung) disease. A slow pulse can indicate heart disease, pressure on the brain, or an advanced morbid condition causing collapse of the circulation.

An erratic, irregular or disordered pulse indicates a cardiac *arrhythmia*. Many arrhythmias are associated with a sudden drop in blood pressure as the arrhythmia begins. The corresponding decrease in blood flow to the muscles and brain is accompanied by sudden weakness or collapse, often giving the impression of a fainting spell.

When the heart sounds can be heard all over the chest, the heart is probably enlarged.

Heart murmurs are common. Murmurs are caused by turbulence in the flow of blood through the heart. Serious murmurs are caused by heart disease or anatomical defects.. Anemia can cause a heart murmur.

Not all murmurs are serious. Some are said to be innocent; that is, there is no disease, just a normal degree of turbulence. To determine whether a murmur is serious or innocent, your veterinarian may request diagnostic studies such as a chest X-ray, an electrocardiogram (*ECG* or *EKG*), and an *echocardiogram*.

Thrills are caused by turbulence of such a degree that you can feel a buzzing or vibration over the chest. This suggests an obstruction to the flow of blood—for example, a constricted valve or a hole in the wall between two chambers of the heart. A thrill indicates a serious heart condition.

CIRCULATION

You can determine the adequacy of your dog's circulation and the presence or absence of anemia by examining the gums and tongue. A deep pink color is a sign of good circulation and a normal red blood cell volume. A pale color indicates anemia. A gray or bluish tinge is a sign of insufficient oxygen in the blood (called *cyanosis*). With severe circulatory collapse, the mucous membranes are cool and gray. However, some dogs, such as Chows Chows, have pigmented lips, gums, and even tongues. These will normally appear bluish, purple, or even black all the time. Know what is normal for your dog.

The adequacy of the circulation can be tested by noting how long it takes for the gums to "pink up" after being firmly pressed with a finger. This is called *capillary refill time*. The normal response is one second or less. More than two seconds suggests poor circulation. When the finger impression remains pale for three seconds or longer, the dog is in shock.

THE VALVES AND CHAMBERS OF THE HEART

Heart Disease

The leading cause of heart failure in dogs is chronic valvular disease. Next is dilated cardiomyopathy, followed by congenital heart disease and heartworms. More infrequent causes include bacterial endocarditis and myocarditis. Coronary artery disease is rare in dogs. It occurs only in dogs with severe hypothyroidism accompanied by extremely high serum cholesterol levels.

CHRONIC VALVULAR DISEASE

This common heart disease of unknown cause affects 20 to 40 percent of dogs. It occurs most often in toy and small breed dogs, particularly Cavalier King Charles Spaniels, Miniature and Toy Poodles, Chihuahuas, Lhasa Apsos, Yorkshire Terriers, Schnauzers, and Cocker Spaniels.

Chronic valvular disease is characterized by degenerative changes in the heart valves. The mitral valve is affected in nearly all cases; the tricuspid valve in about one-third of cases. The valve leaflets become thickened and distorted so that the free edges of the valves no longer make contact. The cords that attach the valve leaflets to the lining of the heart may rupture, allowing the valve to flap in the bloodstream.

These changes result in loss of valve function and a fall in cardiac output. When the ventricles contract, some blood is ejected backward into the corresponding atrium. This is called regurgitation. Regurgitation increases the blood pressure in the atrium and causes it to enlarge. Because the mitral valve is invariably involved, chronic valvular disease is also sometimes called mitral valve disease or mitral regurgitation.

The hallmark of chronic valvular disease is a loud heart murmur heard over the left side of the chest. A chest X-ray, *ECG*, and *echocardiogram* may show an enlarged left atrium, thickened valves, or a ruptured cord (muscle band). If the tricuspid valve is involved, there will be a loud heart murmur heard over the right side of the heart. It is important to exclude heartworms as a cause of a right-sided heart murmur.

Signs of congestive heart failure can be attributed to low cardiac output and lung congestion. They include a cough that occurs after exercise and/or is worse at night; lethargy and tiring easily; and fainting spells often related to cardiac arrhythmias.

Treatment: Many dogs with uncomplicated heart murmurs associated with chronic valvular disease remain asymptomatic for years. The disease, however, is chronic and progressive. Treatment should be started at the first signs of impending heart failure (coughing, easy tiring). The outlook depends on how far the disease has progressed and the general health and age of the dog. (For more information on treatment, see *Congestive Heart Failure*, page 339.)

DILATED CARDIOMYOPATHY

Dilated cardiomyopathy is a disease in which the heart chambers enlarge and the walls of the ventricles become thin. The heart muscle weakens and begins to fail.

Dilated cardiomyopathy is the most common cause of congestive heart failure in large and giant breed dogs. It is rare in toy breeds and small dogs. A high incidence is found in Boxers, Doberman Pinschers, Springer Spaniels, and American and English Cocker Spaniels. Other breeds affected include German Shepherd Dogs, Great Danes, Old English Sheepdogs, St. Bernards, and Schnauzers. Most dogs are 2 to 5 years of age at the onset of symptoms. The majority are males.

In most cases the cause of dilated cardiomyopathy is unknown. Myocarditis, an inflammation of the heart muscle, may precede dilated cardiomyopathy in some dogs. Hypothyroidism has been associated with dilated cardiomyopathy. A genetic or familial basis has been proposed for giant and large breed dogs. Cardiomyopathy related to taurine and/or carnitine deficiency is seen in American Cocker Spaniels, Boxers, and possibly Golden Retrievers, Newfoundlands, and other breeds.

The signs of dilated cardiomyopathy are the same as those of congestive heart failure and cardiac arrhythmias. Weight loss can occur in a matter of weeks. Affected dogs are lethargic, tire easily, breathe rapidly, and cough frequently, sometimes bringing up bloody sputum. Coughing is especially

This dog's swollen abdomen is associated with dilated cardiomyopathy and congestive heart failure.

common at night. A swollen abdomen (called *ascites*) may be noted. Cardiac arrhythmias can cause weakness and collapse.

The diagnosis of dilated cardiomyopathy is based on *ECG* changes showing cardiac arrhythmias, a chest X-ray showing enlarged heart chambers, and an *echocardiogram* showing the characteristic pattern of a failing heart muscle.

Treatment: Treatment is directed at improving the force of the heart muscle, controlling arrhythmias, and preventing the buildup of fluid in the lungs and abdomen (see *Congestive Heart Failure*, page 339). Many dogs benefit from the addition of taurine and/or carnitine to their diet. The prognosis for long-term survival is guarded. With excellent medical control, some dogs may live for a year or more. Death usually occurs as the result of a sudden cardiac arrhythmia. Some dogs will drop dead without any noticeable signs beforehand.

Congenital Heart Disease

All forms of congenital heart disease occur in dogs. The most common defects are valve malformations (called dysplasias), valve narrowing (stenosis), abnormal openings between the heart chambers (septal defects), patent ductus arteriosus, and Tetralogy of Fallot.

Patent ductus arteriosus is a persistent arterial connection between the aorta and pulmonary artery that normally closes at birth or shortly thereafter. In the uterus, the ductus plays an important role in shunting blood away from the nonfunctioning lungs. Many large and small breeds are affected by patent ductus arteriosus. This murmur can often be felt through the body wall—it feels like a washing machine churning.

Tetralogy of Fallot is a congenital defect of the heart consisting of four abnormalities that result in insufficiently oxygenated blood pumped to the body.

Most dogs with severe congenital heart defects die within the first year of life. Dogs with moderate defects may survive but usually exhibit exercise intolerance, fainting episodes, and stunted growth. In these individuals, heart failure can occur suddenly and unexpectedly. Dogs with mild valvular disease or small septal defects are often asymptomatic; the only indication of a congenital heart defect is a heart murmur discovered on physical examination.

The diagnosis of congenital heart defect is based on ECG, chest X-rays and *echocardiogram*. An ultrasound study called Doppler echocardiography measures the velocity and direction of blood flow in the heart chambers. This information makes the diagnosis of congenital heart defects extremely accurate. You may need to be referred to a specialty clinic for this test.

Cardiac catheterization with angiocardiography was once the "gold standard" for diagnosing congenital heart defects, but it carries a small risk and is often available only at referral veterinary hospitals. Doppler echocardiography, being accurate and noninvasive, has largely replaced cardiac catheterization for routine diagnosis.

Treatment: Dogs with minor heart defects have a good prognosis and do not benefit from surgery. However, many dogs benefit from surgery to correct more severe defects. Many of these surgeries will require referral to a large veterinary center.

Patent ductus arteriosus is an example of a defect that does benefit from surgery. Without surgery, 60 percent of affected puppies die within the first year. With surgery, the death rate is less than 10 percent.

Moderate atrial and ventricular septal defects can be repaired surgically with varying degrees of success. This requires open-heart surgery and cardiopulmonary bypass.

Valve dysplasias and large septal defects have a poor prognosis, regardless of the method of treatment. Affected dogs are at risk of congestive heart failure and sudden death.

The treatment of congestive heart failure and cardiac arrhythmias is discussed later in this chapter.

Prevention: Most congenital heart defects have a hereditary basis. Breeds with a known predisposition for specific congenital heart defects are shown in the accompanying chart. This list is by no means comprehensive, and individuals of other breeds and mixed breeds may also show these defects.

Breed Predispositions for Congenital Heart Defects	
Atrial septal defects	Samoyed
Ventricular septal defects	Bulldog
Aortic and subaortic stenosis	Newfoundland, Golden Retriever, German Shepherd, Rottweiler, Boxer, German Shorthaired Pointer, Samoyed
Tricuspid dysplasia	Labrador Retriever, Great Dane, Weimaraner, German Shepherd Dog
Mitral dysplasia	Great Dane, German Shepherd Dog, Bull Terrier
Patent ductus arteriosus	Poodle, Pomeranian, Collie, Shetland Sheepdog, German Shepherd Dog, Cocker Spaniel, English Springer Spaniel
Pulmonic stenosis	Beagle, Labrador Retriever, Cocker Spaniel, Schnauzer, Newfoundland, Rottweiler
Tetralogy of Fallot	Keeshond, English Bulldog, Miniature Poodle, Miniature Schnauzer

It is important to identify affected individuals when treatment is most likely to be successful and before the dog is used for breeding. The best time to screen puppies for congenital heart defects is when they are 6 to 8 weeks of age, before being released to their new homes. Screening is done by carefully listening for murmurs with a stethoscope over the four valve areas. The examination is best performed by a veterinarian who is experienced in recognizing heart murmurs. Murmurs heard at this age may not be associated with disease; some will disappear as the pup matures. If the murmur is present at 16 weeks, however, the puppy should be screened using cardiac ultrasound.

OFA maintains a cardiac registry to gather data on congenital heart defects. (See appendix D for information on how to contact OFA.) Dogs are screened at 12 months of age or later by a board-certified veterinary cardiologist, and if they are found to be unaffected, they are issued a certificate and a registration number. For bloodlines with an increased incidence of congenital heart defects, it is highly desirable to seek OFA certification before selecting breeding animals.

BACTERIAL ENDOCARDITIS

Bacterial endocarditis is an infection of the heart valves and the lining of the heart. The disease is not common. It is caused by bacterial species that gain entrance to the circulation system through wounds and infections elsewhere in the body. In many cases the actual source of infection is unknown. Dogs on corticosteroids and immunosuppressant drugs are at increased risk, as are mid-size and large dogs.

As the bacteria invade the heart valves, they produce ulcerations and small wartlike bumps called vegetations. The effects on the valves are similar to those of chronic valvular disease. In addition, parts of infected vegetation can break off and spread the infection to other organs. This seeding process causes a variety of signs, including fever, shaking, chills, swollen joints, lameness, spontaneous bleeding, blindness, behavioral and personality changes, unstable gait, stupor, and seizures. These signs are nonspecific and may suggest a number of other diseases.

The presence of a heart murmur, particularly a new or changing murmur, suggests a diagnosis of bacterial endocarditis. This can be confirmed by ECG, chest X-rays, and *echocardiography*. Blood cultures identify the causative bacteria.

Treatment: Antibiotics must be selected based on blood culture and sensitivity tests. To eliminate vegetations, long-term antibiotic therapy (two to four months) is required. The dog should be monitored closely for signs of congestive heart failure, which may appear suddenly, and for the development of antibiotic-resistant organisms.

Dogs with less severe valve disease may recover with only mild permanent damage. The prognosis is guarded for dogs with mitral valve involvement and poor for those with aortic valve involvement.

MYOCARDITIS

Myocarditis is an inflammation of the heart muscle. It is an uncommon cause of heart disease in dogs. Myocarditis occurs with American trypanosomiasis, Lyme disease, viral diseases including distemper, and bacterial, fungal, and protozoan infections. Parvovirus produces a fatal form of myocarditis in neonatal puppies. It is rarely seen now because of the practice of routinely immunizing brood bitches against parvo.

One of the first signs of myocarditis is weakness and fainting caused by cardiac arrhythmias. It can also be suspected by the sudden appearance of congestive heart failure, along with abnormal findings on an ECG and *echocardiogram*. If necessary, the diagnosis can be confirmed by a heart muscle biopsy. This must be done at a medical center.

Treatment: Treatment and prognosis are similar to those described for dilated cardiomyopathy (page 334). If a specific cause is found, it should be treated.

Arrhythmias

Arrhythmias are irregular or erratic heartbeats. Normally the heart beats at a steady, regular pace. This changes with activity or rest, but is almost always a regular rhythm. Abnormal rhythms may be slower than normal (called bradycardia) or faster than normal (called tachycardia). Sometimes the speed or rate may be normal but the heartbeats follow an abnormal path through the heart muscle.

Many things may cause irregular heart rates and rhythms, including increased potassium, hormonal influences, certain cancers such as hemangiosarcoma, and heart diseases such as cardiomyopathy. Affected dogs may show anxiety, weakness, lethargy or even faint.

To diagnose these problems, your dog will need an *EKG* (electrocardiogram, sometimes also called ECG) and possibly a cardiac ultrasound evaluation. Your veterinarian may decide to have your dog wear a special heart monitor for 24 hours if the abnormality is infrequent.

Treatment: This may include various drugs to regulate the heart rate or rhythm. Some dogs benefit from having a pacemaker implanted.

Congestive Heart Failure

Congestive heart failure is the inability of the heart to provide adequate circulation to meet the body's needs. It is the end result of a weakened heart muscle. The health of the liver, kidneys, lungs, and other organs is impaired by the circulatory failure, resulting in a problem involving multiple organs.

A diseased heart can compensate for many months or years without signs of failure. When failure does occur, it may appear suddenly and unexpectedly—sometimes immediately after strenuous exercise, when the heart is unable to keep up with the body's demands.

In toy and small-breed dogs, chronic valvular disease with mitral regurgitation is the most common cause of congestive heart failure. In large-breed dogs it is dilated cardiomyopathy.

The early signs of congestive heart failure are tiring easily, a decrease in activity level, and intermittent coughing. The coughing occurs during periods of exertion or excitation. It also tends to occur at night, usually about two hours after the dog goes to bed. Dogs may be restless—pacing instead of quickly settling down to sleep.

These early signs are nonspecific and may even be considered normal for the dog's age. As heart failure progresses the dog develops other signs, such as lack of appetite, rapid breathing, abdominal swelling, and a marked loss of weight.

Because the heart no longer pumps effectively, blood backs up in the lungs, liver, legs, and other organs. Increased pressure in the veins causes fluid to leak into the lungs and peritoneal cavity. Fluid in the lungs is the cause of the coughing. A rapid accumulation of fluid in the small airways can cause the dog to cough up a bubbly red fluid, a condition called pulmonary edema. Pulmonary edema indicates failure of the left ventricle.

With failure of the right ventricle, fluid leaks into the abdomen, giving the belly a characteristic swelling or potbellied appearance (called *ascites*). This

This dog suffers from right-sided congestive heart failure with ascites and dependent leg edema.

may be accompanied by swelling of the legs (dependent *edema*). An accumulation of fluid in the chest cavity (*pleural effusion*) also occurs with right-sided heart failure.

In the late stages of congestive heart failure the dog sits with his elbows spread and his head extended. Breathing is labored. The pulse is rapid, thready, and often irregular. The mucous membranes of the gums and tongue are bluish-gray and cool. A thrill may be felt over the chest. Fainting can occur with stress or exertion.

An accurate diagnosis is established through chest X-rays, *ECG, echocardiography*, and other tests (such as a heartworm antigen test) as indicated.

Treatment: It is important to correct any underlying cause whenever possible. Heartworms, bacterial endocarditis, and some forms of congenital heart disease are potentially curable if they are treated before the heart is damaged.

Treatment of congestive heart failure involves feeding the dog a low-salt diet, restricting exercise, and giving appropriate medications to increase heart function and prevent cardiac arrhythmias.

Most commercial diets contain excessive amounts of salt. Your veterinarian may prescribe a low-salt prescription diet such as Hill's h/d, Purina CV, or Royal Canin EC. In dogs with mild symptoms, salt restriction may be the only treatment required.

Exercise is beneficial, but only for dogs who are not symptomatic. If symptoms such as easy tiring, coughing, or rapid breathing appear with exercise, *do not allow your dog to engage in activities that elicit these symptoms*.

Various drugs are available that increase the force and contraction of the heart muscle or decrease the workload. They include the digitalis glycosides, calcium channel blockers, angiotensin-converting enzyme (ACE) inhibitors, beta blockers, and anti-arrhythmics. These are the same drugs used in people. ACE inhibitors such as enalapril maleate (Enacard) and benazepril (Fortekor) may prolong the life of dogs with valvular heart disease and cardiomyopathy, and are commonly used in dogs with these diseases. Fluid accumulation in the lungs and elsewhere is managed by diuretics such as furosemide (Lasix). Potassium supplements may be necessary when giving certain diuretics. A diuretic that spares the potassium the body needs is spironolactone (Aldactone).

Dogs with congestive heart failure may benefit from vitamin-B supplements and taurine or carnitine. Coenzyme Q is another supplement that may help dogs with cardiac problems.

When treating cardiac arrhythmias, it is important to search for and correct any underlying electrolyte or metabolic problems that might trigger an attack. A number of cardiac drugs, including digitalis, lidocaine, diltiazem, procainamide, atropine, and propanalol (Inderal), are used to control arrhythmias in dogs. Dogs whose primary problem is an arrhythmia may be able to have a pacemaker implanted to help control the heart rate.

With proper treatment, a dog with congestive heart failure can live a longer and more comfortable life. However, heart disease requires close monitoring. You will need to return to your veterinarian regularly for checkups.

Heartworms

Heartworm disease, so named because the adult worms live in the right side of the heart, continues to be a major problem for many species of animals. Heartworms are spread by mosquitoes, and thus are found throughout the world. In the United States the prevalence is highest along the southeastern Atlantic and Gulf Coasts, but heartworm has been found in all 50 states. The disease is less prevalent at higher elevations.

The highest infection rates (up to 45 percent) in dogs not maintained on heartworm preventive are observed within 150 miles of the Atlantic Coast from Texas to New Jersey and along the Mississippi River and its major tributaries. Other areas of the United States have lower incidence rates (5 percent or less) of canine heartworm disease, while some regions have environmental, mosquito, and dog population factors that combine for a higher incidence of heartworm infection. The infection rate in male dogs is as much as four times that of female dogs, and dogs housed outdoors are four to five times more likely to be infected than indoor dogs.

Although there are differences in frequency of infection for various groups of dogs, all dogs in endemic regions should be considered at risk and placed on prevention programs.

Heartworm Life Cycle

A knowledge of the life cycle of this parasite (*Dirofilaria immitis*) is needed to understand how to prevent and treat it. Infection begins when L_3 infective larvae in the mouthparts of a mosquito enter the dog's skin at the site of a bite. The larvae burrow beneath the skin and undergo two molts that eventually lead to the development of small immature worms. The first molt (L_3 to L_4) occurs one to 12 days after the dog is bitten by the mosquito. The larvae remain in the L_4 stage for 50 to 68 days, and then molt into the L_5 stage (immature worms).

It is only during the brief L_3 stage, 1 to 12 days after the larvae enter the dog's body, that they are susceptible to the killing effects of diethylcarbamazine. However, throughout the L_3 and L_4 stages the larvae are susceptible to three other drugs: ivermectin, selamectin, and milbemycin.

Immature worms make their way into a peripheral vein and are carried to the right ventricle and the pulmonary arteries. Approximately six months after entering the dog's body, they mature into adults. Adults can grow to 4 to 12 inches (10 to 30 cm) long and live up to five years. As many as 250 worms may be found in a heavily infested dog.

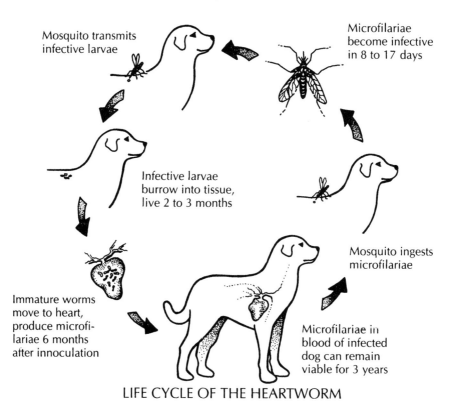

Mosquito transmits infective larvae

Microfilariae become infective in 8 to 17 days

Infective larvae burrow into tissue, live 2 to 3 months

Mosquito ingests microfilariae

Immature worms move to heart, produce microfilariae 6 months after innoculation

Microfilariae in blood of infected dog can remain viable for 3 years

LIFE CYCLE OF THE HEARTWORM

This model shows heart-worms in the right atrium and right ventricle.

Sexual reproduction occurs if worms of both sexes are present. Females give birth to live young called microfilaria; 5,000 microfilariae can be produced in one day by a single worm. Microfilaria are able to remain alive in the dog's circulatory system for up to three years.

Before the microfilariae can become infective to another dog, the L_i larvae must go into a secondary host, the mosquito. This occurs when the mosquito bites the dog. The L_1 larvae in the mosquito molt to L_3 larvae. In warm southern climates this process takes less than 10 days; in northern climates it can take up to 17 days. The L_3 larvae then move to the mouthparts of the mosquito and are ready to infect a new host.

HEARTWORM DISEASE

When there are fewer than 50 adult worms in the average-size dog, the worms live primarily in the pulmonary arteries and the right ventricle of the heart. When the numbers are greater than 75, the worms usually extend into the right atrium. With a heavier infestation, the worms may migrate into the superior and inferior vena cavae and the veins of the liver.

Worms in the lungs can migrate into the terminal branches of the pulmonary arteries, where they obstruct the flow of blood and cause the vessels to clot. This is known as pulmonary thromboembolism. Even after treatment, dead worms can be carried by the bloodstream into the pulmonary circulation, resulting in a similar severe and sometimes fatal reaction. Chronic pulmonary thromboembolism causes loss of lung tissue and right-sided congestive heart failure. Dogs with thromboembolism may cough up bloody sputum.

Worms entwined about the heart valves can interfere with the mechanics of the heart and produce effects similar to those of chronic valvular disease.

Worm clumps in the vena cava or hepatic veins are responsible for a condition called vena cava syndrome, which causes liver failure with jaundice, *ascites*, spontaneous bleeding, and anemia. Collapse and death can occur in two to three days.

DIAGNOSIS

The signs of heartworm disease depend on the number of worms and the size of the dog. Dogs with a light infestation involving only a few worms may remain asymptomatic.

The typical early signs of heartworm infestation are tiring easily, exercise intolerance, and a soft, deep cough. As the disease progresses these symptoms become more severe and the dog loses weight, breathes more rapidly, and may cough after exercise to the point of fainting. The ribs become prominent and the chest starts to bulge. Acute vena cava syndrome or episode of thromboembolism can lead to collapse and death.

A number of blood tests are available to diagnose heartworms. The most accurate is the heartworm antigen test, which identifies an antigen produced by the adult female heartworm. False negatives occur in dogs with early infections (before the appearance of mature worms), in light infections with fewer than five adult worms, and in infections in which only males are present. False positives are rare.

Another important heartworm test is the microfilarial concentration test, in which parasites in a sample of blood are identified under the microscope. Although a positive test definitely indicates heartworms, a negative test does not rule out the diagnosis because typically 10 to 25 percent of infected dogs do not have microfilariae circulating in the peripheral blood.

Dogs with a negative microfilarial concentration test who do have heartworms are said to be suffering from an *occult* infection. There are a number of explanations for occult infection. One is that the dog is receiving a heartworm preventive. Preventives kill microfilaria but not adult worms. Thus these dogs will have a positive heartworm antigen test and a negative microfilarial concentration test. Also, a dog could be infected with adult heartworms of just one sex, which means no reproduction is taking place.

There is yet another type of microfilaria that can be present in dogs tested for heartworms. It is called *Dipetalonema*. It is a harmless worm living under the skin. Its importance lies in the fact that its microfilaria may be mistaken for those of heartworm. This can be differentiated from heartworm microfilaria by careful examination under a microscope.

A chest X-ray is the best test for determining the severity of the infection. Dogs with a heavy burden of worms in the pulmonary artery have X-rays that show enlargement of the right ventricle and/or pulmonary arteries.

An *ECG* may show right ventricular enlargement and cardiac arrhythmias. An *echocardiogram* may show worms in the main pulmonary artery or the right ventricle. In dogs with vena cava syndrome, heartworms can be seen in the vena cava. Blood and urine samples are obtained to check for anemia and assess kidney and liver function.

TREATING HEARTWORM DISEASE

When and how to treat depends on the number of heartworms, their location, any medical complications (such as congestive heart failure or liver or kidney disease), the age and condition of the dog, and the presence of circulating microfilariae. After a thorough medical examination, your veterinarian will discuss these options and recommend a treatment program based on the findings.

For dogs with uncomplicated heartworm disease, the objectives are to eliminate all adult worms, kill the microfilariae (if present), and initiate preventive measures. At the same time, it is important to avoid complications associated with drug toxicity and the passage of dead worms into the lungs. Some veterinarians may choose to reduce the microfilaria numbers first, then go after the adult worms.

If you and your veterinarian decide to eliminate the adult worms first, the first step in dealing with uncomplicated heartworm infection is to administer an agent that will poison the worms. Two drugs that are FDA-approved and commonly used are thiacetarsamide (Caparsolate) and melarsamine (Immiticide). Both contain arsenic. Caparsolate is given intravenously twice a day for two days. Significant toxic reactions can occur, and include loss of appetite, vomiting, diarrhea, jaundice, kidney failure, and death. Caparsolate does not always kill all the worms. Immature worms, especially females, are relatively resistant. Treatment with Caparsolate must be followed by treatment for microfilaria. The drug is not safe to use on high-risk dogs with congestive heart failure, liver failure, or kidney impairment.

Immiticide eliminates more than 90 percent of worms, making it more effective than Caparsolate. It has a higher margin of safety and can be given to dogs at high risk. Immiticide is given by intramuscular injection once a day for two days. If the dog is severely debilitated by heartworms, the drug can be given in divided doses 30 days apart. Complications are similar to those of Caparsolate, but occur less often. Both drugs can cause a local reaction at the site of injection. Thromboembolism is a complication associated with the death of adult worms, and can occur with either drug.

Approximately 10 percent of dogs are poor candidates for immediate drug treatment because of severe pulmonary artery infestation and congestive heart failure. These dogs will benefit from complete rest and confinement for a minimum of two to three weeks before and after drug therapy. Aspirin, a mild anticoagulant, is given to help prevent respiratory failure due to worm thromboembolism.

Elderly dogs with heartworms are at high risk of death from therapy to kill the adult worms. Some old dogs may be better off without treatment. An acceptable alternative is to restrict exercise and administer a low dose of aspirin daily to prevent further damage to the lungs. Give the dog a monthly heartworm preventive to prevent new worms from being acquired.

Surgical removal of worms is reserved for critically ill dogs with vena cava syndrome who are not candidates for drug therapy because of the risk of liver failure or thromboembolism. To remove the worms this way, an incision is made over the jugular vein in the neck. The vein is opened and a long grasping instrument is passed down through the superior vena cava into the right atrium and the inferior vena cava. The worms are grasped one by one and removed. The procedure requires X-ray equipment and special skills. Residual worms are eliminated with drug therapy after the dog improves.

A heartworm antigen test should be performed three to five months after drug therapy. If all worms have been eliminated, the test will be negative. If the test is positive, consider retreatment.

The next step is to kill circulating microfilaria. This step is omitted if parasites are not found on a microfilaria concentration test. Most veterinarians wait four weeks to allow the dog to recover from the effects of killing the adult worms before beginning therapy to kill the microfilaria. Currently there are four drugs used—although none is licensed for this purpose. They are ivermectin, selamectin, moxidectin, and milbemycin. Ivermectin is considered the most effective and has the fewest complications, except in dogs with drug sensitivity (see page 349).

Currently many veterinarians choose to simply give the monthly preventive drugs to dogs with circulating microfilaria, knowing that the microfilaria will slowly die off over six to nine months. Since the dogs are heartworm carriers during that time, they should be kept indoors during times of high mosquito activity and wear bug repellant when outside.

If the veterinarian decides the microfilaria must be eliminated as quickly as possible, the dog is admitted to the hospital on the morning of treatment. Ivermectin is given orally and the dog is observed for 10 to 12 hours for signs of toxicity, including vomiting, diarrhea, lethargy, weakness, and shock. Most reactions are mild and respond to intravenous fluids and corticosteroids. Shock and death have occurred in Collies, Shetland Sheepdogs, Australian Shepherds, Old English Sheepdogs, and other herding breeds and their crosses with the genetic defect that allows these drugs to pass into the brain (see *Ivermectin Sensitivity*, page 349). Ivermectin should not be used in these dogs.

Dramatic declines in microfilaria counts occur over the next few days. Ninety percent of dogs are free of all microfilaria at three weeks. At this time the dog should return for a microfilaria concentration test. If positive, the protocol is repeated. If negative, begin heartworm prevention.

A positive microfilaria concentration test after two treatments strongly suggests that adult worms are still present in the dog. Confirm this with a heartworm antigen test and treat accordingly.

HEARTWORM PREVENTION

As the previous section on treatment illustrates, treating a heartworm infestation is difficult and dangerous. It is far easier and more effective to prevent the problem in the first place. In theory, the best way to prevent heartworms is to keep your dog from being bitten by a mosquito. Unfortunately, preventing mosquito bites can never be 100 percent effective. Dogs can be reasonably protected if they remain indoors in the late afternoon and evening, when mosquitoes are feeding.

Areas of most frequent heartworm infestation are along coastal regions, where swamps or other brackish water provide ideal conditions for mosquitoes to breed. Since mosquitoes have a flight range of one quarter mile, spraying around the yard and kennel and removing standing water can be partially effective, but they will never eliminate the threat.

If you live or travel with your dog in an area where heartworm is endemic, your dog should be on a heartworm prevention program. Ask your veterinarian about local prevalence and follow their recommendations for prevention. Most dogs should be on a heartworm preventive program.

A prevention program should be started at 6 to 8 weeks of age in endemic areas, or as soon thereafter as climate conditions dictate. In the Deep South, where mosquitoes are a year-round problem, dogs should be kept on preventive drugs all year long. In areas where it is not necessary to administer the drug year round, start one month before the mosquito season and continue one month beyond the first frost (generally from May or June to November or December). Heartworm prevention is important for the dog's whole life. Some owners may elect to give heartworm preventives year round for zoonotic parasite protection and to reduce the risk of breakthrough heartworm disease in case they miss a monthly dose. All dogs 7 months and older should have an antigen test for heartworms before starting a prevention program. If the test is positive, a microfilaria concentration test should be performed. The antigen test should be repeated annually or as frequently as your veterinarian recommends—even if the dog is on a heartworm prevention program. Many heartworm preventives can cause illness if given to a dog with circulating microfilaria.

There are a number of drugs currently in use as heartworm preventives. They include ivermectin (Ivomec, Heartgard), milbemycin oxime (Interceptor), and selamectin (Revolution).

Heartgard is an effective preventive that is given once a month. This drug acts on the L_4 larvae. It has the advantage that dogs do not have to be heartworm-free to initiate therapy; dogs infected for as long as two months before treatment will not develop heartworms. If a monthly dose is missed, restart the drug and obtain a heartworm antigen test seven months later. Heartgard is marketed in chewable tablets of different sizes, depending on the weight of the dog. The recommended dose is generally considered to be safe to use on Collies and other herding breeds. However, with safer alternatives available, most owners avoid this for the breeds with the genetic defect that causes sensitivity to ivermectin.

Heartgard Plus is a popular chewable tablet that combines ivermectin with pyrantel pamoate. This combination prevents heartworms and also controls roundworms and hookworms.

Interceptor (milbemycin oxime) is another orally administered once-a-month heartworm preventive that also acts on the L_4 larvae. Like Heartgard, this drug is marketed in different dosages based on the weight of the dog. Interceptor also controls hookworms, roundworms, and whipworms. This drug is safer to use on Collies and Collie crosses.

The injectable form of ProHeart, called ProHeart 6, was considered to provide protection for six months. However, it has been removed from the market due to potential side effects. The FDA is still considering a final decision about this medication.

Selamectin (Revolution) is a once-a-month liquid heartworm preventive applied to the skin of the dog's neck between the shoulder blades. It is available from your veterinarian in premeasured doses based on the dog's size and age. A principal advantage of selamectin is that it also controls adult fleas and prevents flea eggs from hatching for one month. In addition, it treats ear mites and the mites that cause scabies.

Diethylcarbamazine (DEC) has proven over many years to be extremely safe and effective when given daily. It is less convenient than the drugs just described, and unlike them it does not protect if two or three days are missed. DEC is currently unavailable because so many dog owners have switched to the convenient monthly medications. If it should become available again, the following precautions must be taken.

Dogs over 6 months of age *must be tested for microfilaria before starting on DEC.* If microfilaria are found in the blood, the drug should not be given because anaphylactic reactions of varying severity, including death, may develop.

DEC kills L_3 infective larvae before they molt to L_4. Since molting can occur in as little as 24 hours, DEC must be given daily to be effective. If more than two days of treatment are missed, stop the drug and consult your veterinarian for further instructions.

Medications containing DEC have an extremely bitter taste and need to be mixed with flavoring agents to be given in chewable form.

Ivermectin Sensitivity

Some breeds show an increased susceptibility to the potential toxicity of ivermectin and similar drugs. In these dogs, there is a defect of the gene MDR-1. This is a multi-drug transporter gene that influences the movement of drugs across the blood brain barrier. Dogs who are homozygous for this autosomal recessive trait will have severe, potentially fatal reactions to some drugs, including ivermectin. Dogs who are heterozygous may be able to safely take the medications, but may pass on the defective trait to their offspring.

A genetic test for this defect is available through Washington State University's Veterinary Laboratory of Clinical Pharmacology. A cheek swab can be sent to determine if your dog has the gene. This testing is recommended for Collies, Border Collies, Shetland Sheepdogs, Australian Shepherds, Old English Sheepdogs, and longhaired Whippets. In breeds such as the Collie, more than 70 percent of the dogs tested are either homozygous for this defect or carry it.

Anemia and Clotting Disorders

Anemia is a defined as a deficiency of red blood cells (*erythrocytes*) in the circulatory system. Adult dogs are anemic when the concentration of red cells in whole blood is less than 37 percent by volume. The normal range is 39 to 60 percent. Red cells are produced by the bone marrow and have an average life span of 110 to 120 days. Old red cells are trapped by the spleen and removed from the circulation. The iron they contain is recycled to make new erythrocytes.

The purpose of red blood cells is to carry oxygen. Thus, the symptoms of anemia are caused by insufficient oxygen in the organs and muscles. Signs include lack of appetite, lethargy, and weakness. The mucous membranes of the gums and tongue become pale pink to white. In dogs with severe anemia, the pulse and respiratory rate are rapid and the dog may collapse with exertion. A heart murmur may be heard.

Anemia can be caused by blood loss, hemolysis, or inadequate red blood cell production.

BLOOD-LOSS ANEMIA

In adult dogs the most common causes of blood loss are trauma, slow gastrointestinal bleeding associated with stomach and duodenal ulcers, parasites, and tumors in the gastrointestinal tract. Chronic blood loss also occurs through the urinary system (see *Blood in the Urine*, page 412). Hookworms and fleas are common causes of chronic blood loss in puppies.

Treatment: Treatment must be directed toward the cause of the anemia. Gastrointestinal bleeding can be detected by checking the stools for microscopic traces of blood. Urinalysis will pick up traces of blood in the urine that may not be visible to the naked eye. Other tests can also be used to determine the cause of the *occult* (microscopic) bleeding.

HEMOLYTIC ANEMIAS

Hemolysis is an acceleration in the normal process of red blood cell breakdown. Red blood cells break down to form bile and hemoglobin. With severe hemolysis, these breakdown products accumulate in the body. Accordingly, in a dog experiencing an acute hemolytic crisis you would expect to see *jaundice* and *hemoglobinuria* (passing dark-brown urine that contains hemoglobin). In addition, the dog appears weak and pale and has a rapid pulse. The spleen, liver, and lymph nodes may be enlarged.

Causes of hemolysis include immune-mediated hemolytic anemia, congenital hemolytic anemia, infectious diseases (such as canine babesiosis and leptospirosis), drug reactions to medications such as acetaminophen, and poisonous snake bites. A number of bacteria produce toxins that destroy red blood cells, so hemolysis can also occur with severe infections.

Neonatal isoerythrolysis is a hemolytic disease of newborn puppies; it is discussed on page 503.

Immune-Mediated Hemolytic Anemia

This is the most common cause of hemolysis in adult dogs. Red blood cell destruction is caused by *auto-antibodies* that attack antigens present on the surface of the cells, or by antigens from medications or organisms attached to the red blood cell walls. The weakened cells are trapped in the spleen and destroyed.

Poodles, Old English Sheepdogs, Irish Setters, and Cocker Spaniels are predisposed to immune-mediated hemolytic anemia, but all breeds are susceptible. Affected dogs are usually between 2 and 8 years of age; females outnumber males four to one.

Most cases of immune-mediated hemolytic anemia are idiopathic. That is, the reason why the auto-antibodies developed in that particular dog is unknown. In some cases there is a history of recent drug therapy. An immune-mediated hemolytic anemia also occurs with systemic lupus erythematosus.

The diagnosis is made by microscopic examination of blood smears, looking for specific changes in the appearance of the erythrocytes and other blood elements; and by serologic blood tests.

Treatment: Treatment of idiopathic immune-mediated hemolytic anemia is directed toward preventing further red cell destruction by blocking the antigen-antibody reaction using corticosteroids and immunosuppressants.

Severe anemia is corrected with blood transfusions. Splenectomy (removal of the spleen) may be beneficial, but only when tests prove that the spleen is contributing to the hemolytic process.

The response to treatment depends on the rate of hemolysis and whether an underlying cause can be found and corrected. The outlook is guarded; even with appropriate medical treatment, the mortality rate is close to 40 percent.

Congenital Hemolytic Anemia

Several inherited abnormalities in the structure of red blood cells can result in their premature destruction. Phosphofructokinase deficiency is an autosomal recessive trait that occurs in English Springer Spaniels and Cocker Spaniels. A deficiency of this enzyme results in changes in the pH of red blood cells, causing the cells to periodically fragment and produce bouts of hemoglobinuria. There is no effective treatment.

Pyruvate kinase deficiency is another red blood cell enzyme deficiency caused by an autosomal recessive gene. This disease is recognized in several breeds, including Basenjis, Beagles, and West Highland White Terriers. Puppies usually develop the hemolytic anemia at 2 to 12 months of age. Death by age 3 is the usual outcome.

Genetic tests for phosphofructokinase and pyruvate kinase deficiency are available through the University of Pennsylvania at PennGen, and from OptiGen and VetGen.

OFA maintains a voluntary diagnostic service and registry for dogs with phosphofructokinase deficiency, and Basenjis with pyruvate kinase deficiency, in cooperation with the respective national breed clubs (see appendix D).

INADEQUATE RED BLOOD CELL PRODUCTION

When the metabolic activity of the bone marrow is depressed, new red blood cells are not manufactured as fast as old ones are destroyed. This results in an anemia due to inadequate red blood cell production. A common cause of bone marrow depression is chronic illness, especially associated with kidney and liver disease.

Iron, trace minerals, vitamins, and fatty acids are all incorporated into red blood cells. Thus a deficiency of one or more of these nutrients could slow down or stop cell production. This is an unusual cause of anemia in dogs, because commercial dog foods contain more than adequate amounts of essential vitamins and minerals.

Iron deficiency is an exception. It occurs when iron is lost from the body faster than it can be replaced through the diet. The two situations in which this is most likely to happen are chronic gastrointestinal bleeding and a heavy infestation of blood-sucking insects (such as fleas, ticks, or lice).

Red blood cell production can be depressed by certain drugs. Estrogen is an important cause of bone marrow depression. This includes estrogens given for medical purposes as well as those produced by testicular and ovarian tumors. Other drugs that depress the bone marrow include chemotherapy agents, chloramphenicol, butazolidin, thiacetarsamide, quinidine, and trimethoprim-sulfadiazine.

Primary and metastatic cancer can invade the bone marrow and crowd out normal cells, also depressing red blood cell production.

The diagnosis of inadequate red cell production is made by bone marrow biopsy.

Treatment: Treatment is directed toward eliminating the cause of the bone marrow deficiency. The dog should be screened for kidney and liver disease. Iron deficiency anemia warrants stool examination and a further medical workup. Estrogen-producing tumors of the ovary or testicle should be sought and treated. Many drug-related causes of bone marrow depression reverse when the drug is stopped.

Erythropoietin is a substance that stimulates red blood cell production. It is normally manufactured by the kidneys and, to a much lesser extent, by the liver. Recombinant erythropoietin can be helpful in dogs if the bone marrow is capable of responding. Human erythropoietin has been used for the most part, but the dog eventually develops antibodies against it. A new canine recombinant version will be available soon.

CLOTTING DISORDERS

Clotting disorders are caused by an absence of one of the coagulation factors needed to complete the clotting sequence. Severe deficiencies are associated with spontaneous bleeding. Blood in the urine or stools may be associated with a spontaneous bleeding disorder.

Von Willebrand's Disease

Von Willebrand's disease (vWD) is the most common inherited bleeding disorder in dogs. It has been described in more than 50 breeds. Both males and females can transmit and express the genetic trait. The disease is inherited as an autosomal dominant gene with variable expression. That is, the severity of the bleeding is related to the degree to which the gene is expressed.

The bleeding is caused by a deficiency of a plasma protein called the von Willebrand factor, which is critical for normal platelet function in the early stages of clotting.

In most cases the bleeding in vWD is mild or inapparent, and lessens with age. Severe problems include prolonged nosebleeds, bleeding beneath the skin and into the muscles, and blood in the stool and urine. There is often a history of bleeding from the gums following tooth eruptions, and oozing from wounds following tail docking and dewclaw removal.

Breeds at risk for vWD in which bleeding is likely to be mild include the Doberman Pinscher, Golden Retriever, Standard Poodle, Pembroke Welsh Corgi, Manchester Terrier, Miniature Schnauzer, Akita, and others. Breeds in which bleeding is likely to be more severe include the Scottish Terrier, Shetland Sheepdog, German Shorthaired Pointer, and Chesapeake Bay Retriever.

Hypothyroidism is common in dogs with vWD, and may contribute to the bleeding risk.

The diagnosis is made by specific blood tests, including a bleeding time. In this test, a small cut is made and the amount of time it takes for bleeding to stop on its own is measured. From a nail cut too short, two to six minutes is normal, while from a cut on the gums, two to four minutes is normal. A quantitative test for von Willebrand's disease involves measuring the vWD antigen. Dogs with vWD antigen levels below the normal range are at risk for expressing and/or carrying the trait.

OFA maintains a vWD registry for many of the breeds mentioned here. A DNA test to identify affected dogs and carriers is available through VetGen and is the most accurate diagnostic test.

Hemophilia

This is a sex-linked recessive trait that occurs only in males who inherit a maternal X chromosome carrying a defective gene. Females always inherit two X chromosomes, at least one of which usually contains a normal dominant gene. Thus females can carry the trait but do not develop the disease—the exception being a female who inherits two recessive genes: one from a hemophiliac father and the other from a mother who is either a hemophiliac or a carrier. This is extremely rare.

Hemophilia produces bleeding into the chest and abdominal cavities, muscles, and subcutaneous tissues. Bleeding into the joints is common.

Hemophilia A (the most common type) is a deficiency of coagulation factor VIII. Hemophilia B is a deficiency of factor IX. Hemophilia occurs in all breeds, with a predisposition among German Shepherd Dogs, Airedale Terriers, and Bichons Frises.

Other coagulation deficiencies involve factors VII, X, XI, and prothrombin. These deficiencies are inherited as single-factor autosomal traits and affect males and females alike. They are less common than hemophilia. Affected breeds include the Boxer, English and American Cocker Spaniel, English Springer Spaniel, Beagle, and Kerry Blue Terrier.

The diagnosis of a coagulation factor deficiency is based on a number of clotting tests, plus an analysis for the specific factor that is deficient. PennGen offers genetic tests for factor VII and factor XI.

Disseminated Intravascular Coagulation

This is an acquired bleeding disorder triggered by shock and infection, certain tumors (particularly hemangiosarcomas, osteosarcomas, and cancers of the prostate and mammary glands), and severe injuries such as crush wounds and burns. Disseminated intravascular coagulation (DIC) is characterized by intravascular clotting throughout the entire capillary circulation, followed by spontaneous bleeding when all the clotting factors have been consumed. The bleeding associated with DIC involves the nose, mouth, gastrointestinal tract, and body cavities. Dogs with DIC are extremely ill and often die.

Another acquired bleeding disorder is caused by vitamin K deficiency. It is discussed in *Rodent Poisons* (page 27).

Treating Clotting Disorders

Successful treatment of spontaneous bleeding requires rapid diagnosis. Dogs with severe blood loss are given fresh, whole blood containing red cells, platelets, and active coagulation factors. Dogs with less severe blood loss who don't require a blood transfusion are given fresh-frozen plasma or concentrates containing the missing coagulation factor. Blood banks are available in some areas to provide canine blood and clotting factors.

Treating vWD hypothyroid dogs with thyroid replacement therapy may prevent subsequent bleeding episodes.

An important additional step in treating DIC is to control the underlying cause of the intravascular coagulation. While it may seem contradictory, these dogs may need heparin to limit the clotting taking place.

Dogs with inherited coagulation disorders, and those who may be carriers, should not be bred.

THE NERVOUS SYSTEM

The brain comprises the cerebrum, cerebellum, midbrain, and brain stem. The cerebrum is the largest part of the brain, and is the center of learning, memory, sensory input, behavior, and voluntary movement. Diseases affecting the cerebrum are characterized by depression, alterations in personality and behavior, and seizures.

The cerebellum has two lobes. Its primary functions are to integrate motor pathways, coordinate movements, and maintain balance. Diseases of the cerebellum result in lack of coordination, unstable gait, and muscle tremors.

In the midbrain and brain stem are the centers that control the respiratory rate, heartbeat, blood pressure, and other vital functions. At the base of the brain and closely connected to the midbrain and brain stem are the hypothalamus and pituitary glands. These structures are important in regulating the dog's body temperature and hormone systems. They are also the centers for primitive responses such as hunger, thirst, anger, and fright.

The spinal cord passes down a bony canal formed by the arches of the vertebrae. The cord sends out nerve roots that combine with one another to form the peripheral nerves. Diseases of the spinal cord produce varying degrees of weakness and paralysis.

The cauda equina is the termination of the spinal cord. Diseases of the cauda equina can produce paralysis of the tail, loss of bladder and bowel control, and paralysis of the anal sphincter.

The paired cranial nerves, 12 total, arise from the midbrain and brain stem and pass directly out into the head and neck through openings in the skull. The optic nerves to the eyes, the otic nerves to the ears, and the olfactory nerves to the nasal cavity are examples of paired cranial nerves.

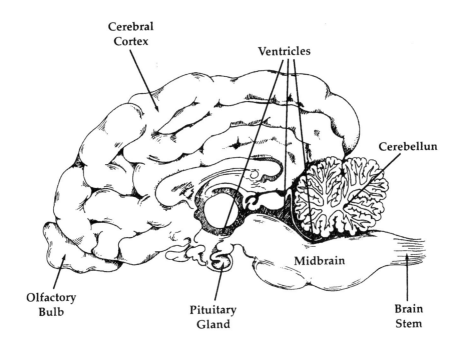

Cerebral
Cortex

Ventricles

Cerebellun

Olfactory
Bulb

Pituitary
Gland

Midbrain

Brain
Stem

CROSS-SECTION OF THE BRAIN

Neurological Evaluation

A complete health history is of paramount importance in diagnosing unexplained neurological symptoms. Your veterinarian will want to know if the dog has been in an accident. Did she receive a blow to the head? Is she taking any medications? Has she been exposed to other dogs who exhibit similar signs? Could she have gotten into any toxic substances? When did you first notice the symptoms? Did they come on suddenly or gradually? Have they progressed? If so, has the progression been rapid or gradual? The age, sex, and breed of the dog are important, because some neurological diseases are genetically determined and appear in certain breeds or at certain ages. Special tests are used in addition to a standard physical examination for a dog with a possible neurological problem. Your veterinarian will manipulate your dog to check her balance, motor control, and sensory perceptions.

Diagnostic tests used in evaluating neurological function include X-rays of the skull and vertebral column, electroencephalography (EEG), and muscle and nerve conduction studies. A spinal tap is a procedure in which a needle is inserted into the spinal canal to remove cerebrospinal fluid for laboratory analysis. A myelogram is a spinal tap in which dye is introduced into the spinal canal so signs of spinal cord compression will be visible on X-rays.

Computer-assisted tomography (*CAT scan*) and magnetic resonance imaging (*MRI*) enable a radiologist to see a computerized image of the structures in the brain, spinal canal, and body cavities. These examinations are now available at veterinary schools and many large veterinary hospitals.

Head Injuries

A dog's head can be injured in many ways, including a car accident, a fall, a blow to the head, or a gunshot wound. Since the brain is encased in bone and surrounded by a layer of fluid, it takes a major blow to the head to fracture the skull and injure the brain.

SKULL FRACTURES

A skull fracture can be linear, star shaped, compound (a compound fracture opens to outside the body), or depressed (forming a depression). Skull fractures often extend into the middle ear, nasal cavity, or sinuses, creating pathways for bacteria to gain access to the brain and cause infection. In general, the larger the skull fracture, the greater the likelihood of brain injury. However, the brain can be injured even if the skull is not broken.

OPEN FONTANEL

The skull is formed by three bone plates, and the area at the top of the skull where they come together is called the fontanel. Usually these plates fuse when a puppy is about 4 weeks old, but sometimes they never completely fuse, leaving a hole at the top of the skull called an open fontanel, or molera. The open area can range in size from a 50-cent piece to a penny.

Most of the time an open fontanel will close over by the time the dog is 1 year of age, but sometimes it will remain open throughout the dog's lifetime. These areas can be susceptible to trauma but are generally not a problem. In some dogs this condition may be associated with hydrocephalus (see page 367).

Congenital open fontanel is seen primarily in Chihuahuas, but the condition can be found in all the toy breeds. Since it's likely a hereditary problem, dogs with an open fontanel should not be bred.

BRAIN INJURIES

Injuries severe enough to fracture the skull are often associated with bleeding into and around the brain. Brain injuries are classified according to the severity of brain damage.

Contusion (Bruising)

With a contusion, there is no loss of consciousness. After a blow to the head the dog remains dazed, wobbly, and disoriented. The condition clears gradually.

Concussion

By definition, a concussion means the dog was knocked unconscious. With a mild concussion there is only a brief loss of consciousness, while with a severe concussion the dog may be unconscious for hours or even days. When she returns to consciousness, the dog exhibits the same signs as for a contusion.

A severe concussion causes the death of millions of neurons. Recent information indicates that brain cell death does not cease within a few hours of the injury, but can continue for weeks or months.

Seizures

Seizures can occur at the time of injury or at any time thereafter. Seizures at the time of injury are particularly detrimental because they increase pressure in the skull and compromise blood flow. This worsens the effects of the injury. Seizures that occur weeks after the injury are caused by scars that form in areas where brain tissue has died.

Brain Swelling and Bleeding

Severe head injuries result in brain swelling and bleeding into and around the brain. Brain swelling, technically called cerebral edema, is always accompanied by a depressed level of consciousness and often coma. Since the brain is encased in a rigid skull, as the brain swells the cerebellum is slowly forced down through the large opening at the base of the skull. This squeezes and compresses the vital centers in the midbrain. Death occurs from cardiac and respiratory arrest.

Blood clots can form between the skull and the brain or within the brain itself. A blood clot produces localized pressure that does not, at least initially, compress the vital centers. Like cerebral edema, the first indication is a depressed level of consciousness. One pupil may be dilated and unresponsive to a light shined in the eye. Another sign is weakness or paralysis involving one or more limbs.

TREATING HEAD INJURIES

Treating shock takes precedence over managing the head injury (see *Shock*, page 7). If the dog is unconscious, establish an open airway by extending the head and pulling the tongue forward as far as you can beyond the level of the canine teeth.

Signs of death are no pulse, no effort to breathe, dilated pupils, and soft eyes. Usually it is impossible to tell at the time of an accident whether such signs are reversible. Accordingly, begin administering CPR immediately if you suspect the dog is dead (see *CPR*, page 9).

At the scene of the head injury, before transporting the dog to the nearest veterinary hospital, be sure to:

- Handle the dog with extreme care and gentleness. Pain and fright deepen the level of shock. Cover the dog with a warm blanket.
- Control bleeding as described in *Wounds*, page 42.
- Place the dog on a flat stretcher as described in *Spinal Cord Injuries,* page 375.
- Stabilize all fractures, if possible (see *Broken Bones*, page 15).
- Record a baseline neurological exam (level of consciousness, limb movements, pupil size).
- Transport the dog with her head higher than her hindquarters; this helps lower intracranial pressure.

Signs of cerebral edema can appear at any time during the first 24 hours after a blow to the head. The most important thing to observe is the dog's level of consciousness. An alert dog is easily aroused (no apparent brain swelling). A semi-comatose dog is sleepy but arousable (mild to moderate brain swelling). A comatose dog cannot be aroused (severe brain swelling).

Cerebral edema is treated with intravenous corticosteroids, oxygen, and diuretics such as mannitol or furosemide. Seizures are controlled with an intravenous or oral anticonvulsant such as diazepam (Valium).

Open skull fractures require surgical cleansing and removal of devitalized bone. Depressed bone fragments may need to be elevated to relieve pressure on the brain. Antibiotics are often necessary with open fractures to prevent infection.

Only dogs who are fully alert, are not having seizures, and exhibit no neurological signs should be permitted to return home. Awaken the dog every two hours for the first 24 hours at home to check her level of responsiveness. Any change from an alert status is an indication to return at once for veterinary evaluation. In addition, be sure to check the dog's pupils. They should be of equal size. An enlarged pupil that does not constrict when light is shined in the eyes indicates pressure on the brain. Also notify your veterinarian if the dog's breathing becomes rapid or irregular, if she exhibits any form of muscle weakness, or if she has a seizure.

The prognosis for recovery depends upon the severity of the brain injury. When the dog remains in a coma for more than 48 hours, the outlook is poor. However, if the dog steadily improves throughout the first week, the outlook is good.

Dogs who recover may exhibit a posttraumatic syndrome that can include seizures, behavior changes, head tilt, and blindness.

Brain Diseases
Encephalitis (Brain Infection)

Encephalitis is an inflammation of the brain. Symptoms include fever, depression, behavior and personality changes (especially aggression), uncoordinated gait, seizures, stupor, and coma.

Canine distemper is the most common cause of encephalitis in dogs. Signs develop two to three weeks after the onset of the disease. Other causes of viral encephalitis include rabies, pseudorabies, and herpesvirus. Rabies is a very serious disease, but with present-day vaccination programs the disease is not common among domesticated animals. Canine herpesvirus produces an encephalitis in puppies younger than 2 weeks of age.

Bacterial encephalitis is caused by organisms that enter the brain via the circulatory system, such as bacterial endocarditis, or by direct extension from an infected sinus, nasal passage, or an abscess in the head or neck. Migrating foreign bodies such as porcupine quills or grass awns may get into the central nervous system. Fungal brain infections (caused by cryptococcosis, blastomycosis, or histoplasmosis) are rare causes of encephalitis, as are protozoan infections. Tick-borne rickettsial diseases, notably Rocky Mountain spotted fever and canine ehrlichiosis, are infrequent causes. These diseases may also involve the spinal cord.

Postvaccination encephalitis is rare with modern vaccines. It was most likely to occur when modified live virus distemper vaccine was administered at the same time as modified live parvovirus vaccine in puppies less than 6 to 8 weeks old. This is not usually seen with current vaccines and vaccination schedules.

Lead encephalitis is seen primarily in young dogs who chew on materials that contain lead, such as paint and drywall, especially in older buildings. Lead alters brain metabolism and causes inflammation and swelling. Central nervous system signs are often preceded by vomiting, diarrhea, or constipation. The diagnosis is confirmed by an elevated blood lead level.

Meningitis is an infection of the surface of the brain and spinal canal. It is caused by infected bite wounds about the head and neck and bacterial infections that travel to the brain from the sinuses, nasal passages, or middle ears. Aseptic meningitis is a nonbacterial disease of unknown cause. It affects large-breed dogs 4 to 24 months of age.

The diagnosis of encephalitis or meningitis is based on analysis of cerebrospinal fluid obtained by spinal tap. Serologic tests may identify the cause of the inflammation.

Treatment: Corticosteroids are used to reduce inflammation and swelling of the brain. Seizures are controlled with anticonvulsants. Antibiotics are used to treat bacterial infections. Rickettsia are extremely sensitive to tetracycline and doxycycline. Dogs who recover from encephalitis may develop seizure disorders and other neurological symptoms. Rabies is almost always fatal.

GRANULOMATOUS MENINGOENCEPHALITIS

This common inflammatory brain disease in dogs is abbreviated GME. The cause is unknown. Female dogs of small breeds, especially terriers, Dachshunds, Poodles, and Poodle crosses, are predisposed. Although GME can occur at any age, most affected dogs are 2 to 6 years of age.

A chronic form of GME called Pug encephalitis occurs as an inherited disease in Pugs between the ages of 9 months and 4 years. It often begins with seizures, confusion, and loss of memory. This form of the disease has also been seen in Yorkshire Terriers and Maltese.

GME can affect all parts of the brain (the disseminated form), or only specific areas (the focal form). There is a rare ocular form that targets the optic nerves of the eyes.

The disseminated disease appears suddenly and progresses over a matter of weeks. It is characterized by incoordination, stumbling, falling, circling, head tilt, seizures and, dementia.

The focal disease begins with symptoms such as those of a brain tumor. Behavior and personality changes may predominate. The focal disease progresses to the disseminated disease over a period of 3 to 6 months.

The ocular disease is characterized by sudden blindness with a dilated pupil. It progresses to the disseminated disease more slowly than does the focal disease.

GME can be suspected when a toy dog such as a Poodle inexplicably develops confusion, disorientation, seizures, or other neurological signs that progress rapidly over a matter of weeks. A spinal tap with analysis of cerebrospinal fluid helps confirm the diagnosis. A *CAT scan* or *MRI* is useful in determining the form and location of the disease.

Treatment: Corticosteroids and immunosuppressive drugs may slow the progression of GME and provide temporary relief for several months. However, GME is almost invariably a progressive and fatal disease.

BRAIN TUMORS AND ABSCESSES

Brain tumors are not common. They tend to occur in middle-aged and older dogs. The highest incidence is found in the short-nosed breeds that have large-domed heads, including the Boxer, Bulldog, and Boston Terrier. Tumors that can *metastasize* to the brain include cancers of the mammary glands, prostate, and lungs, as well as hemangiosarcoma.

Symptoms depend on the tumor's location and rate of growth. Tumors in the cerebrum produce seizures and/or behavioral changes. The dog may exhibit a staggering gait, head tilt, nystagmus (rhythmic movement of the eyeballs), and limb weakness or paralysis. These signs are progressive and continue to worsen. Late signs are stupor and coma.

A brain *abscess* is a collection of pus in or around the brain. The signs are similar to those of a brain tumor. These dogs will often have a fever. There may be a prior infection in the oral cavity, inner ear, or respiratory tract.

Treatment: The diagnosis of tumor or abscess is made by neurological examination and special tests, including *EEG*, cerebrospinal fluid analysis, and *CAT scan* or *MRI*. Surgical removal of benign brain tumors may be possible in some cases. Chemotherapy and radiation therapy have not proven to be effective against most brain tumors in dogs. There may be temporary improvement with corticosteroids and anticonvulsants.

Abscesses are treated with high doses of antibiotics. Corticosteroids are usually contraindicated. The outlook for recovery is guarded.

STROKE

Strokes are not common in dogs. A stroke can be caused by bleeding into the brain, obstruction of an artery caused by an embolus, or clotting of a cerebral artery. An embolus is a clot that develops at another site and travels through the vascular system to a smaller vessel, where it becomes lodged and interrupts blood flow to the area served by that artery. This results in death of tissue in the affected area, a condition called infarction. Most strokes in dogs are caused by emboli.

Bleeding in the brain is seen with ruptured cerebral blood vessels and brain tumors. Spontaneous bleeding may occur with coagulation disorders. Disseminated intravascular coagulation is a cause of both bleeding and infarction. Some hemorrhagic strokes occur for unknown reasons.

Infarctions can occur with Rocky Mountain spotted fever, hardening of the arteries associated with hypothyroidism, and for unknown reasons.

The onset of stroke is sudden. The signs depend on the location and extent of the bleeding or brain infarction. They include behavioral changes, disorientation, seizures, weakness or paralysis on one side of the body, stupor, and coma. Large strokes are often accompanied by cardiac arrhythmias and collapse. The diagnostic workup is similar to that for a brain tumor.

Treatment: Treatment involves the use of corticosteroids to prevent brain swelling and anticonvulsants to control seizures. Dogs who survive the first few days have a good prognosis for recovery. The long-term outlook depends on controlling or eliminating the underlying disease.

Hereditary Diseases

Hereditary nervous system diseases are not common. Most run in families. Affected individuals should not be bred.

HEREDITARY MYOPATHIES (MUSCULAR DYSTROPHY)

Muscular dystrophy is actually a group of genetically determined diseases in which there is a progressive degeneration of skeletal muscle (the muscles that are attached to the skeleton). Nerves and muscles work hand in hand, so damaged nerves will lead to damaged muscles. Weakness is the predominant sign. The diagnosis can be suspected by finding high serum CPK levels.

Many of these problems will require a muscle biopsy for an accurate diagnosis. One of the best places to send samples is the Comparative Neuromuscular Laboratory of the University of California at San Diego. Some of the more common disorders are listed here.

Hereditary Myopathy of Labrador Retrievers

This disease is inherited as an autosomal recessive trait. Signs of weakness begin at between 6 weeks and 7 months of age. There is a marked decrease in exercise tolerance. An affected pup may have difficulty holding up her head, bunny hop when running, and collapse after brief exertion. The disease may affect the muscles involved in chewing and swallowing, resulting in drooling and the development of megaesophagus. Exposure to cold greatly exacerbates the symptoms.

Treatment: Diazepam (Valium) given twice a day benefits some puppies. It is important to prevent stress and chilling, and to warm a pup quickly if she is exposed to cold. The disease often stabilizes or improves by 6 to 12 months of age. Many dogs are able to live a normal life. If drooling and megaesophagus develop, however, the outlook is guarded.

Breeding dogs can be tested by the Alfort School of Veterinary Medicine in Maisons-Alfort, France, to see if they carry this defect.

Sex-Linked Muscular Dystrophy

This disease affects Golden Retrievers, Irish Terriers, Samoyeds, Rottweilers, Belgian Tervurens, and Miniature Schnauzers. It is transmitted on the X chromosome from the dam. Affected pups are weak at birth and often die. Those who survive develop a stilted gait, drooling, muscle wasting, and stunted growth. The condition may stabilize temporarily by 6 months of age, but later progresses.

Treatment: There is no effective treatment and the long-term prognosis is poor. If these dogs survive to middle age, many will die of cardiomyopathy.

Bouvier des Flandres Myopathy

This disease affects only the muscles of swallowing, resulting in regurgitation and megaesophagus. Signs appear at about 2 years of age. With severe megaesophagus the outlook is guarded.

Treatment: The only treatment is to tend to the symptoms of *Megaesophagus* (see page 258).

Distal Myopathy of Rottweilers

This disease affects the legs and feet, producing an abnormal stance with splayed toes and weak hocks.

Treatment: There is no treatment.

Myotonia

This disease affects Chow Chows, Staffordshire Terriers, Rhodesian Ridgebacks, Cavalier King Charles Spaniels, Great Danes, Golden Retrievers, and Irish Setters. Signs appear when the pups begin to walk. They include stiffness upon rising and walking. This is followed by a progressive stiffening of the gait as the dog exercises.

Treatment: *Off-label* use of the drug procainimide may help with signs in some dogs.

DEGENERATIVE MYELOPATHY

This is a degenerative disease of the spinal cord that appears to run in families. It occurs primarily in middle-aged German Shepherd Dogs but has been diagnosed in many breeds. It is the most common cause of hindquarter weakness in German Shepherds and their crosses. The Siberian Husky, Old English Sheepdog, Rhodesian Ridgeback, Weimaraner, and other large breeds are also affected. Among smaller dogs, older Pembroke Welsh Corgis are seen with this problem.

The disease manifests itself as a slowly progressive weakness or paralysis of the hind limbs, along with an unsteady gait suggestive of hip dysplasia. The toenails on the hind feet may show abnormal wear from dragging on the ground. This disease appears to be *autoimmune* in nature and similar to multiple sclerosis in people.

Treatment: Treatment with corticosteroids and/or vitamin supplements has not proven to be effective in curing or reversing the problem. Still, about 50 percent of dogs will show some improvement when given the medications aminocaproic acid and n-acetylcysteine. Dietary supplements are also helpful—tofu, vitamins C and E, coenzyme Q (Q 10), and green tea for their antioxidant properties. A regular exercise program, customized for each dog's capabilities, is also helpful.

INHERITED NEUROPATHIES

There are a number of rare diseases in which sensory and motor nerves degenerate. With loss of sensation and motor function, an affected dog does not feel the position of her limbs, is unable to position them correctly to prevent stumbling, and fails to withdraw a leg from a painful stimulus.

The diagnosis is made by sensory and motor nerve conduction studies. There is no cure, but because of the slow progression of the disease some dogs live comfortably for many years. Most of these neuropathies are inherited as autosomal recessive traits. Some of the most common ones are noted here.

Neuropathy of German Shorthaired and English Pointers is first noted at 3 to 4 months of age. The pup with this sensory neuropathy begins to lick and bite at her paws, which become swollen, reddened, ulcerated, and eventually mutilated. Loss of sensation can extend up the limb and involve the trunk. The mode of inheritance is autosomal recessive.

Dachshund sensory neuropathy begins in longhaired Dachshunds at 2 to 3 months of age. It is characterized by uncoordinated gait, urinary incontinence, and loss of sensation over the entire body. Self-mutilation of the penis may be the first sign in males.

Global cell leukodystrophy is caused by an enzyme deficiency that results in degeneration of nerve cells. It occurs in West Highland White Terriers, Cairn Terriers, Beagles, Pomeranians, and Poodles. Signs are unsteady gait, head tremors, nystagmus (a rhythmic movement of the eyeballs), and blindness.

Scotty cramp is an autosomal recessive disease in Scottish Terriers where puppies show increased muscle tone when excited, stressed, or exercising vigorously. They show a stiff, hyper gait. Diazepam (Valium) helps, and most of these dogs can be comfortable pets.

Hypertrophic neuropathy in Tibetan Mastiffs begins at 7 to 12 weeks of age and is characterized by hind-limb weakness that progresses to generalized weakness and, ultimately, an inability to stand. Some dogs maintain a degree of strength. This is an autosomal recessive disease.

Polyneuropathy in Alaskan Malamutes shows up at about 12 to 18 months of age. Initially, dogs show exercise intolerance but this can progress to paralysis. Some dogs may stabilize, but most dogs continue on a downward trend. Treatments have not been effective.

Hypomyelination diseases manifest when myelin, which forms a sheath around nerve fibers, is not completely developed at birth. The result is that nerve impulses are conducted very slowly. Hypomyelination occurs in Chow Chows, Weimaraners, Samoyeds, and Bernese Mountain Dogs. One form, called the shaking puppy syndrome, is a sex-linked recessive trait that affects only males.

The characteristic sign of hypomyelination is muscle tremors involving the limbs, trunk, head, and eyes of newborn puppies. The tremors get worse with activity and disappear with sleep. Severely affected puppies show uncoordinated body movements and are unable to stand. There is no cure for the disease. Tremors in Chow Chows and Weimaraners may improve gradually and disappear by 1 year of age.

WHITE DOG SHAKER SYNDROME

This syndrome occurs primarily in adult dogs with white coats, although dogs with other coat colors are occasionally affected. The disease occurs most often in small breeds, including West Highland White Terriers, Maltese, Bichons Frises, and Toy and Miniature Poodles.

It is characterized by the sudden appearance of tremors, sometimes accompanied by wild and random movements of the eyes. The disease affects the cerebellum, which coordinates muscle movement. Sudden trembling that involves the entire body and head is the main sign. The dog does not shake while sleeping, but the more she moves, the worse the tremor gets. These tremors can be disabling.

The cause is unknown, but an autoimmune basis has been suggested.

Treatment: See your veterinarian if your small dog suddenly develops a tremor that seems to get worse. Corticosteroids reverse the shaking within a few days. Some dogs require extended treatment. About 25 percent of dogs retain some degree of tremor for life. With refractory cases, diazepam (Valium) may be added to control tremors.

CEREBELLAR DISEASES

Cerebellar degeneration is a slowly progressive disease in which the nerve cells in the cerebellum die. The disease has been described in numerous breeds, including the Kerry Blue Terrier, Gordon Setter, rough-coated Collie, Great Dane, Labrador Retriever, Golden Retriever, Cocker Spaniel, Airedale Terrier, Samoyed, Cairn Terrier, and Bullmastiff.

Affected puppies appear normal for the first two months of life, but then begin to show uncoordinated body movements such as jerking, stumbling, falling, and overreaching with the paws. Although there is no cure, cerebellar degeneration stabilizes in some puppies, allowing them to remain active.

Cerebellar hypoplasia is a condition in which the cerebellum is abnormally small at birth. A hereditary form has been reported in Airedales, Gordon Setters, and Chow Chows. A nonhereditary form has been described in Bull Terriers, Weimaraners, Dachshunds, and Labrador Retrievers. Signs are similar to those of cerebellar degeneration, but are observed shortly after birth when puppies first begin to crawl. Some puppies compensate and make good pets.

Lissencephaly is a condition seen rarely in Lhasa Apsos, Irish Setters, Wire Fox Terriers, and Samoyeds. The brain is smooth without the gyri or folds normally seen. Affected dogs may show behavioral abnormalities, including difficulty housetraining and sometimes seizures.

HYDROCEPHALUS

Hydrocephalus is caused by the excessive accumulation of cerebrospinal fluid in the *ventricles* of the brain. The enlarged ventricles damage the cerebral cortex by compressing it against the skull. Most cases are congenital. Some are acquired through trauma, brain infections, or tumors.

Breeds with an increased risk of congenital hydrocephalus include the Maltese, Yorkshire Terrier, Chihuahua, Lhasa Apso, Pomeranian, Toy Poodle, Cairn Terrier, Boston Terrier, Pug, Pekingese, and Bulldog.

Hydrocephalus causes seizures, partial or complete blindness, and *dementia*. The diagnosis is made by skull X-rays, ultrasound of the ventricles and, in difficult cases, by *CT scan* or *MRI*. A characteristic enlargement of the dome of the skull occurs in congenital hydrocephalus, but this may not be seen until the puppy is several months old.

An increase in ventricular size without clinical signs has also been noted. This is called subclinical hydrocephalus. In certain lines of toy breeds with a high incidence of clinical and subclinical hydrocephalus, EEG screening and breeding only dogs with normal EEGs has reduced the incidence of hydrocephalus.

Treatment: This is directed toward decreasing the production of cerebrospinal fluid with corticosteroids and diuretics. Surgery has been beneficial is some cases. The long-term prognosis is favorable if diagnosis and treatment is begun before the brain is damaged. Nonetheless, affected dogs often appear dull and have a limited ability to learn.

Seizure Disorders

A seizure is caused by an abnormal burst of electrical activity within the brain, commonly in one of the cerebral hemispheres. The electrical activity sometimes spreads out and involves other areas, including the midbrain.

A typical grand mal seizure is preceded by a period of altered behavior, called the aura. During the aura dogs may be restless and anxious, cry out, demand affection, or seek seclusion. The actual seizure normally lasts less than two minutes, and is characterized by collapse with rigid extension of the legs. The dog becomes unconscious and may stop breathing for 10 to 30 seconds. This is followed by rhythmic jerking of the legs (which resembles running or paddling). Some dogs also chomp, chew, drool, or urinate and defecate. As the dog regains consciousness there is a postseizure state characterized by disorientation and confusion. The dog may stumble into walls and appear blind. The postseizure state can persist for minutes or hours. Grand mal seizures are typical of epilepsy.

A focal motor or partial seizure is one in which the jerking or twitching is limited (at least initially) to a particular part of the body. A focal seizure usually indicates a specific brain lesion, such as a scar, tumor, or abscess.

Seizures are commonly associated with brain injury, encephalitis, heat stroke, brain abscess, brain tumor, stroke, poisoning, kidney failure, or liver failure. Seizures associated with a concussion frequently occur weeks or months after the head injury and are caused by a focus of scar tissue in the brain.

Postencephalitic seizures occur three to four weeks after the onset of encephalitis. Distemper, in particular, is characterized by attacks that begin with chomping, tongue chewing, foaming at the mouth, head shaking, and blinking, all followed by a dazed look.

Postvaccination seizures have been described in puppies under 6 weeks of age following inoculation with a combined distemper-parvovirus vaccine. This is extremely rare with current vaccines.

A bitch may develop low blood calcium levels after whelping and have seizures. A sudden drop in blood sugar (hypoglycemia) can also trigger a seizure. This occurs in newborn pups with cardiopulmonary syndrome (discussed in *Why Puppies Die*, page 494). It can also occur in small-breed puppies who have not been fed adequately. A common cause of hypoglycemia is giving too much insulin to a diabetic dog.

Common poisons that cause seizures are animal baits such as strychnine, antifreeze (ethylene glycol), lead, insecticides (organophosphates), and chocolate. Seizures caused by organophosphates are preceded by drooling and muscle twitching. Exposure to a spray, dip, or premise treatment suggests the diagnosis.

There are a number of conditions that, while not true seizures, are often mistaken for them. Bee stings, for example, can cause frenzied barking followed by fainting or collapse. Cardiac *arrhythmias* can be mistaken for seizures because they cause loss of consciousness and collapse.

Treatment: If the dog is in a dangerous location at the time of the seizure, move her to a safe site. Otherwise, do not disturb the dog during or after the seizure, as this may trigger further seizures. Despite the old wives' tale, do not pull out the dog's tongue or wedge something between her teeth. Dogs can't swallow their tongue.

Note the length of the seizure. As soon as the seizure is over, notify your veterinarian, because he or she will want to examine the dog to diagnose and treat the underlying cause.

Seizures lasting more than five minutes (status epilepticus seizures) or cluster seizures (several seizures one after the other without a return to consciousness) are emergencies. They must be stopped with intravenous Valium or other anticonvulsants to prevent permanent brain damage or death. Seek immediate veterinary attention. Status epilepticus has a poor prognosis, because it is usually caused by poisoning or a serious brain disease.

EPILEPSY

Epilepsy is a recurrent seizure disorder that may be *idiopathic* or acquired. Acquired epilepsy has an identifiable cause, such as a mass of scar tissue in the brain following a head injury. Idiopathic epilepsy occurs in up to 3 percent of dogs and accounts for 80 percent of recurrent seizures. The cause is unknown, although an imbalance in chemicals that transmit electrical impulses in the brain has been suggested. Seizures, usually of the grand mal type, begin between 6 months and 5 years of age.

Breeds in which the condition is inherited include Beagles, Dachshunds, Keeshonden German Shepherd Dogs, Belgian Tervurens, and others. Breeds with a high incidence, but in which inheritance has not yet been established, include Cocker Spaniels, Collies, Golden Retrievers, Labrador Retrievers, Irish Setters, Poodles, Miniature Schnauzers, St. Bernards, Siberian Huskies, and Wire Fox Terriers. Even mixed breeds can be afflicted with epilepsy.

If the diagnosis is truly epilepsy, the attacks must be recurrent and similar. Epileptic seizures usually become more frequent with time. Your veterinarian will ask you to keep a log of the frequency of seizures and to provide a description of the dog's behavior before, during, and after each seizure.

A typical epileptic seizure has three phases: an aura, a generalized grand mal seizure, and a postseizure state—as described in the previous section. All three phases may not be seen, because many seizures occur while the dog is resting or asleep. Furthermore, in some cases the seizure is atypical. Instead of a classic grand mal convulsion, the dog exhibits strange behavior such as frenzied barking, licking or chewing at herself, staring into space, or snapping at invisible objects. This is called a psychomotor seizure and is believed to arise from a center lower in the brain (not the cerebrum).

Focal motor seizures, as already discussed, indicate a lesion in the brain. An abnormal neurological exam or *EEG* during a period when there have been no recent seizures also indicates a lesion in the brain. These findings eliminate the diagnosis of epilepsy. Further diagnostic tests include a spinal tap with cerebrospinal fluid analysis, skull X-rays, and a *CT scan* or *MRI*.

Treatment: A number of newer drugs are available for treating epilepsy. However, anti-epileptic drugs, either singly or in combination, are not 100 percent effective. The best one can hope for is that treatment will significantly decrease the number and severity of the seizures while increasing the seizure-free interval between them. In general, treatment is indicated if there are two or more seizures a month, or more than 10 to 12 seizures a year. Cluster seizures and status epilepticus are other indications to start treatment.

Phenobarbital continues to be the single most effective drug for treating epilepsy in dogs. Its principal initial side effect is sedation. Most dogs, however, develop a tolerance to the sedative effects within a few weeks. In some dogs, it can cause liver damage. Potassium bromide can also be used to treat epilepsy. More dogs respond to phenobarbital than to potassium bromide alone, but potassium bromide has no potential to cause liver damage. Rarely, it will cause hind leg stiffness, but this is reversible if the drug is stopped. Many dogs are best controlled by a combination of phenobarbital and potassium bromide. A few dogs are well controlled on potassium bromide alone.

If seizures cannot be controlled with phenobarbital and potassium bromide, other drugs, such as Clonazepam, Valproic acid, Clorazepate, and many others can be added. The dosages and rates of action of all anticonvulsants are variable. Regular monitoring of serum drug levels is essential—both to control seizures and to avoid toxicity. Liver enzymes are monitored as well. The two common causes of treatment failure are not maintaining adequate drug levels and not giving the drugs as often as directed. A missed dose of an anticonvulsant can precipitate a seizure. *It is important to work closely with your veterinarian.*

Acupuncture and dietary changes may also help to reduce the number and extent of seizures.

Research is under way to identify the defective gene or genes responsible for epilepsy so that dogs can be identified as carriers before being bred. Affected dogs may not have their first seizure until 3 to 5 years of age, by which time they may have already been bred. No dog known to seizure from suspected epilepsy should be bred.

NARCOLEPSY AND CATAPLEXY

Narcolepsy and cataplexy are uncommon disorders of the sleep mechanism in which a dog is excessively sleepy all day (narcolepsy) or experiences sudden muscle paralysis and collapse (cataplexy). Between attacks the dog is completely normal. Narcolepsy can occur without cataplexy, and vice versa, although narcolepsy alone is difficult to recognize in dogs.

A dog may have one or many episodes of collapse in a day, each lasting a few seconds or up to 30 minutes. The attacks can usually be reversed by petting the dog or making a loud noise.

Treatment: There are several effective drugs available to prevent narcolepsy and cataplexy. Dogs afflicted with the inherited form (mainly Doberman Pinschers, Dachshunds, and Labrador Retrievers) often improve as they grow older. This is an autosomal recessive problem in these three breeds. OptiGen has a DNA test to identify carriers before dogs are bred.

COMPULSIVE BEHAVIORS

There are some unusual behaviors in dogs that may, in fact, be partial seizures. These include fly biting and tail chasing/spinning. In the fly biting situation the dog may be sitting quietly and suddenly starts to bite at imaginary flies. These dogs can usually be distracted and never lose consciousness. Cavalier King Charles Spaniels are one breed in which this behavior is seen.

In the tail biting/spinning sequence, the dog is intent on trying to catch her tail and spins rapidly. These dogs may become so intent that it is difficult to break their concentration. Bull Terriers and German Shepherd Dogs may have an inherited component to this behavior.

Treatment: For dogs with these disorders, veterinary behaviorists work with a variety of behavior-modulating drugs, along with behavior modification. These are *off-label* uses of these drugs, so you need to work closely with your veterinarian and do not give your dog any of these medications without veterinary guidance. Clomipramine and fluoxetine are two drugs that are sometimes prescribed; clomipramine is approved for use in dogs.

AGGRESSIVE BEHAVIORS

Some syndromes in dogs, such as rage syndrome and sudden-onset aggression, may have a physiological basis such as seizures or a metabolic disturbance in serotonin levels. These dogs may suddenly switch from acting normally to viciously attacking whomever or whatever is nearest. Minutes later, the dogs often act as if nothing happened.

English Springer Spaniels and Cocker Spaniels may have an inherited predisposition to these problems. Aggressive behavior has also been associated with hypothyroidism in Golden Retrievers, German Shepherd Dogs, and Shetland Sheepdogs. Thyroid levels should be checked in any dog with newly appearing aggressive behavior.

Treatment: Whether this is truly a physical problem or a behavioral one has not been fully determined. Any dog showing these signs should be worked up for a physical problem and also seen by a veterinary behaviorist. Using behavior modification and behavior modifying medications, some of these dogs can become relatively safe pets. If there is an underlying physical problem that can be treated, it should be.

Coma

Coma is a depressed level of consciousness. It begins with confusion, progresses through stupor, and ends up with complete loss of consciousness. A dog in a coma is insensitive to pain and cannot be awakened. Coma occurs with oxygen deprivation, brain swelling, brain tumor, encephalitis, and poisoning. Many diseases that cause seizures progress to coma. Following a head injury with cerebral concussion, coma can occur without progressing through the earlier stages.

Low blood sugar (hypoglycemia) is a common cause of coma. It tends to occur in toy-breed puppies and adult hunting dogs after a long day in the field. A common *iatrogenic* cause is giving too much insulin to a diabetic dog (see *Diabetes Mellitis*, page 300). Another cause of coma is prolonged hypothermia (see *Cold Exposure*, page 17).

Coma related to high fever and heat stroke is a serious complication that leads to permanent brain damage and is usually preceded by seizures. Vigorous efforts must be made to bring down the fever (see *Heat Stroke* page 22). Coma is also especially ominous when it is associated with brain trauma or when it occurs in the late stages of kidney or liver disease.

Common poisons that may cause coma are ethylene glycol (antifreeze), barbiturates, kerosene, turpentine, arsenic, cyanide, organophosphates, plants, chocolate, and lead. A dog found in a coma in a closed car or in an air-tight space may have smothered or developed carbon monoxide poisoning (see *Drowning and Suffocation*, page 20).

Treatment: First determine the level of consciousness and whether the dog is alive. If the dog shows no signs of life, begin CPR (as described on page 9). An unconscious dog can choke on her vomitus, so pull out the tongue and clear the airway with your fingers. If the dog has a foreign body, such as a piece of meat, obstructing the airway, treat as described for *Choking*, page 316. Wrap the dog in a blanket and proceed at once to your veterinarian.

Weakness or Paralysis

There are several diseases—none of them very common—that attack the motor nerves, causing weakness and paralysis but leaving the sensory nerves intact. These diseases resemble one another and are difficult to tell apart.

Tick Paralysis

The saliva of a variety of ticks contains a toxin that affects the motor nerves, producing weakness and paralysis. Signs appear about one week after a dog has been bitten by the tick. Over the next 48 to 72 hours, the dog grows progressively weaker. Sensation to a pin prick is normal. In time, the paralysis reaches a level where the dog collapses and is unable to lift her head. Death can occur from respiratory arrest.

Treatment: Presence in a wooded area suggests the diagnosis. Seek veterinary attention whenever a dog exhibits unexplained weakness. Tick paralysis can be prevented by removing ticks promptly from the dog and using the methods of tick control described in *Ticks*, page 123. Most dogs show dramatic improvement with tick removal, but may need supportive care for a while.

BOTULISM

Botulism is a paralytic disease caused by neurotoxins produced by the bacteria *Clostridium botulinum*. The disease is acquired by eating infected carcasses or improperly canned vegetables and meats.

Treatment: The outlook for recovery is good if the disease does not progress rapidly. Antitoxins are available. Mildly affected dogs recover without treatment.

COONHOUND PARALYSIS

The cause of this disease is unknown. It is believed to be an *immune-mediated* disease with antibodies directed at the dog's own peripheral nerves. The agent triggering the immune reaction may be a virus or a bacteria. It occurs most often in hunting dogs one to two weeks after having had contact with a raccoon. The illness is not limited to Coonhounds.

Paralysis begins as weakness in the hindquarters and progresses forward until the dog is unable to stand. During this time the dog remains anxious but alert. The paralysis can affect the muscles involved in respiration and swallowing. It reaches its peak at about 10 days. Muscle atrophy may be dramatic.

Treatment: Good nursing care is the main treatment. Full recovery may take weeks or months.

MYASTHENIA GRAVIS

This is a rare disease caused by a deficiency of acetylcholine receptors, normally present at the junction of nerve endings and muscle cells. When an animal decides to move a muscle, the nerve endings release acetylcholine, which is a neurotransmitter. The acetylcholine carries the nerve impulse across the junction, where acetylcholine receptors respond and send the nerve impulse on its way. A reduction in the number or function of these receptors produces generalized muscle weakness, made worse by exercise. Weakness is most apparent in the hindquarters. Dogs with myasthenia gravis have difficulty getting up and exhibit a swaying or staggering gait.

There is a focal form of myasthenia gravis that affects only the muscles involved in swallowing. The dog is unable to swallow solid food and develops enlarged, dilated megaesophagus. Aspiration pneumonia often follows.

A congenital form of myasthenia gravis is inherited as an autosomal recessive trait. It occurs in Jack Russell Terriers, Springer Spaniels, and Smooth Fox Terriers.

An acquired form of myasthenia gravis occurs in all breeds, but is seen most often in Golden Retrievers, German Shepherd Dogs, Labrador Retrievers,

Dachshunds, and Scottish Terriers, often occurring at 1 to 4 years of age or 9 to 13 years of age. Acquired myasthenia gravis is an *immune-mediated* disease in which auto-antibodies are directed at and destroy the acetylcholine receptors.

Hypothyroidism can occur at the same time as autoimmune myasthenia gravis. Occasionally, myasthenia gravis is related to a tumor of the thymus gland, but this is rare.

The diagnosis of myasthenia gravis is based on neurological examination. One test involves injecting a drug called edrophonium chloride. This drug blocks the enzyme that breaks down acetylcholine, resulting in higher concentrations of this neurotransmitter at the receptor sites. The test is positive if muscle strength improves after the injection. A serologic test for diagnosing autoimmune myasthenia gravis is available.

Treatment: Drugs are available that increase the concentration of acetylcholine at receptor sites, thereby reversing muscle weakness. These drugs can be given as a syrup or by injection. The dose varies according to the dog's activity and stress levels. Close veterinary monitoring is required. Drugs to counter immune responses may also be helpful.

Megaesophagus is treated as described on page 258. Thymus gland tumors are removed surgically. Hypothyroidism responds to thyroid replacement therapy (see page 142). With appropriate treatment, the outlook for complete recovery and the return of normal swallowing is good.

HYPOKALEMIA (LOW SERUM POTASSIUM)

Hypokalemia, a condition in which the dog has low serum potassium, is a metabolic cause of generalized muscle weakness. Loss of potassium occurs with severe vomiting. It also occurs with the long-term use of diuretics that cause the kidneys to excrete potassium, such as Lasix (furosemide). Other causes of hypokalemia include bloat, diabetic ketoacidosis, and Cushing's syndrome.

Treatment: The diagnosis is made by measuring serum potassium levels. Weakness disappears as potassium is replaced and the underlying cause is corrected. Close veterinary supervision is required until normal levels are restored.

Spinal Cord Diseases

Injuries and diseases of the spinal cord generally produce weakness and paralysis in one or more limbs and/or the tail. Spinal cord diseases do not cause seizures, nor do they produce changes in personality or behavior. This sets them apart from brain diseases. However, injuries to peripheral nerves may be difficult to distinguish from spinal cord injuries.

SPINAL CORD INJURIES

Spinal cord injuries are associated with ruptured discs and vertebral fractures and dislocations caused by accidents such as automobile accidents, gunshot wounds, and falls.

Immediately after a spine injury, there may be neck or back pain, weakness or paralysis of the legs, a stumbling gait, loss of feeling in the limbs, and urinary or fecal incontinence. Signs that get worse after an injury are often caused by tissue swelling, which interferes with the blood supply to the spinal cord and may cause permanent paralysis.

A pelvic fracture can be mistaken for a spinal fracture. In both cases the dog is unable to bear weight on her hindquarters and shows pain when handled in the injured area. Thus it might appear as if the outlook is poor, even though a dog with a broken pelvis often makes a complete recovery.

Treatment: Dogs with spinal cord trauma usually have life-threatening injuries that take precedence and require immediate attention (see *Treating Head Injuries*, page 358). All dogs who are unconscious or unable to stand should be considered to have spinal cord injuries until proven otherwise. Handle these animals with extreme care to protect the spine. Vertebral fractures are unstable. Flexing the neck or back may compress the spinal cord and worsen the injury.

Transport a dog with a back injury on a flat surface. Duct tape over the shoulders and hips prevents this dog from moving his back.

At the scene of the accident, move the dog as gently as possible onto a flat surface, such as a piece of plywood, and transport to the nearest veterinary clinic. Sliding the dog onto a blanket and lifting the corners is an acceptable way to transport her if a makeshift stretcher is not available.

Spinal cord injuries are treated with corticosteroids and diuretics such as mannitol to prevent further swelling at the site of the injury. Good nursing care and physiotherapy are extremely important in preventing complications and hastening recovery. Surgery may be necessary to relieve pressure on the spinal cord or to stabilize a fractured vertebra.

A dog with mild bruising of the spinal cord begins to recover in a few days. However, if the cord has been lacerated or severely damaged, paralysis or death may be the result.

INFECTIONS AND TUMORS

Infections of the vertebrae, discs, and spinal cord are uncommon. Most bacterial infections occur after trauma or from infected wounds close to the spine. Viral, fungal, rickettsial, and protozoan diseases that cause encephalitis can also cause spinal cord infections (known as myelitis). The diagnosis of myelitis is made by spinal tap and cerebrospinal fluid analysis.

Tumors can involve the spinal cord, nerve roots, or structures around the cord. Symptoms are caused by the compression of the cord or the nerves coming out from the cord. Benign neoplasms such as meningiomas, and bony growths called osteophytes (see *Spondylosis,* page 380), may also cause compression. Malignant tumors include osteosarcomas and lymphosarcomas.

Treatment: Treatment of myelitis involves the long-term use of antibiotics, selected after culture and sensitivity tests. Surgery may be necessary to remove a foreign body, drain an abscess, obtain material for testing, or relieve pressure on the spinal cord.

Some benign tumors can be removed surgically. Malignant tumors usually are not removable but may respond temporarily to radiation and/or chemotherapy.

RUPTURED DISCS

A disc is a cushion of cartilage that sits between the vertebrae and acts as a shock absorber. It is composed of a rim of tough, fibrous connective tissue that surrounds a gel-like center called the nucleus. When a disc ruptures, one of two things may happen. The first is that the fibrous capsule breaks, allowing the inner nucleus to push out through the opening and impinge on the spinal cord or a nerve root. This type of rupture is called a Hansen Type 1. The second is

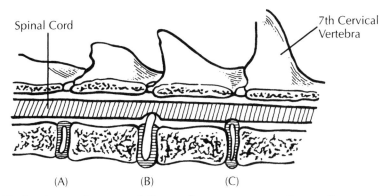

Spinal Cord

7th Cervical Vertebra

(A)   (B)   (C)

In this drawing, (A) is a normal disc; (B) is an acute Hansen Type 1 disc rupture; (C) is a Hansen Type 2 disc rupture.

that the entire disc, surrounded by an unbroken capsule, can bulge outward. This is called a Hansen Type 2.

The diagnosis of ruptured disc is made by neurological examination and imaging studies including spine X-rays, a *myelogram,* and possibly a *CT scan* or *MRI.*

Ruptured discs in the back of the Hansen Type 1 occur in small breeds such as the Dachshund, Beagle, Cocker Spaniel, Pekingese, and small mixed breeds. In fact, ruptured discs are more frequent in Dachshunds than in all other breeds combined.

The capsule begins to degenerate at about 2 to 9 months of age, and signs of impingement on the spinal cord appear at 3 to 6 years of age. About 80 per cent of Type 1 ruptured discs occur in the lower back between the last thoracic and the first two lumbar vertebrae. Most of the remainder occur in the neck. There is often a history of mild trauma, such as jumping off a sofa, but normal movements are sufficient to cause a Type 1 rupture. Occasionally, more than one disc becomes ruptured.

The symptoms of a Type 1 rupture usually come on gradually but can appear with sudden explosiveness. The main sign is pain. The dog holds her back stiffly and may cry or whine when patted or handled in the injured area. She usually refuses to walk up stairs or jump into a car. Neurological signs include weakness, lameness, and a wobbly gait. A dog experiencing the severe back pain of an acute rupture will have a hunched-up position and a tight abdomen. The dog may pant and tremble. Sudden disc ruptures can produce complete hindquarter paralysis.

Hansen Type 2 discs ruptures occur in the larger breeds, including German Shepherd Dogs and Labrador Retrievers. The entire disc, surrounded by its capsule, gradually impinges on the spinal canal. Symptoms appear in dogs 5 to 12 years of age. Because the process is gradual, symptoms progress slowly.

Both these dogs suffer from hindquarter paralysis caused by a Type 1 back disc rupture.

Ruptured discs in the neck of the Hansen Type 1 cause a dog to carry her head low and rigidly, making the neck look shorter. This type of injury is extremely painful. A dog will often cry out when patted on the head and refuse to lower her head to eat and drink. Weakness and lameness involve the front legs. Complete paralysis of all four legs does occur but is rare.

Hansen Type 2 neck discs occur with the wobbler syndrome discussed on page 379.

Treatment: A dog with a sudden onset of symptoms of paralysis requires immediate veterinary evaluation. If surgery is indicated, the best outcome is when it is performed within 24 hours.

Most disc problems involving pain or mild paresis improve with rest and medication. The dog should be closely confined for two to four weeks to allow the disc to return to its former position. Corticosteroids reduce swelling and inflammation. Analgesics relieve pain.

Dogs with neck disc problems should be walked with a chest harness rather than a collar.

Disc injuries that cause paralysis require special handling and transporting, as described for *Spinal Cord Injuries,* page 375. The most common surgery is called a laminectomy. It involves opening the spinal column and removing the extruded disc material. Dogs undergoing surgery will still need a period of careful rehabilitation afterward.

A newer method is to use of proteolytic enzymes to dissolve the disc material. This is called chemonucleolysis. This may only be appropriate for dogs who are in pain without neurologic deficits. If there are neuological signs, surgery is often the better option because it relieves pressure on the spinal cord more quickly.

Acupuncture and physical therapy may be incorporated into treatment protocols.

FIBROCATILAGINOUS EMBOLIC MYELOPATHY

This problem occurs when small emboli of disc material break off and block spinal cord blood vessels. Dogs often show a short period of pain followed by weakness ranging from mild *ataxia* to paralysis. Signs may be on only one side. This problem is seen more often in large to giant breed dogs, but also Shetland Sheepdogs and Miniature Schnauzers.

Treatment: Most dogs show at least a partial recovery after treatment with corticosteroids.

WOBBLER SYNDROME

Wobbler syndrome is a disease that results from compression of the spinal cord in the neck. The compression is caused by vertebral instability related to either a malformed cervical vertebrae or a ruptured Hansen Type 2 neck disc. Both may be accompanied by *hypertrophy* (enlargement) of the ligament that runs down the vertebral canal beneath the vertebrae. Ligament enlargement is believed to be a reaction to instability of the spine.

Most cases of wobbler syndrome occur in Doberman Pinschers over 5 years of age, and to a lesser extent in Great Danes under 2 years of age, but other breeds can also be affected. Ruptured discs are more common in Doberman Pinschers, while vertebral malformations predominate in Great Danes. The malformed vertebrae may be related to the long neck and rapid rate of growth in Great Danes.

The principal sign of both conditions is a progressive loss of coordination in the rear legs, accompanied by a peculiar, wobbly gait. Weakness or partial paralysis affects the front legs as the disease progresses. Manipulating the neck up and down is painful and may exacerbate the paralysis. The diagnosis is made by X-rays of the cervical spine and by a *myelogram*.

Treatment: Medical treatment is similar to that described for ruptured discs. Dogs with mild symptoms may respond to medical management. More severely affected dogs respond best to a surgical procedure that decompresses the spinal cord and stabilizes the vertebral column. Dogs will require extensive rehabilitation after the surgery. Acupuncture and cervical collars may help.

Breed factors and genetic influences appear to contribute to the wobbler syndrome. Until more is known about the exact cause, affected individuals should not be bred.

CAUDA EQUINA SYNDROME

The cauda equina is composed of nerves that form the terminal extension of the spinal cord. Injuries to the cauda equina can be caused by ruptured discs, spina bifida (a developmental defect in the bones of the lower back), infections of the spinal cord and disc spaces, spinal cord tumors, and lumbosacral vertebral canal stenosis.

Lumbosacral vertebral canal stenosis is an acquired disorder in which there is instability of the spine in the lower back. There may be a congenital component that produces narrowing of the bony canal. German Shepherd Dogs are most often affected.

The early signs of the cauda equina syndrome include pain in the lower back (lumbosacral area), difficulty getting up, and recurring lameness in one or both hind legs. Testing for sensation in the lumbosacral area reveals an increased sensitivity to touch and pinprick. This is the key to early diagnosis.

In more advanced cases there is weakness or partial paralysis in the hind limbs and urinary and/or fecal incontinence. The anal sphincter may be completely relaxed.

Treatment: Medical management is similar to that described for ruptured discs. It is most successful when symptoms are mild. Surgical decompression and bone fusion can be considered for dogs who do not respond to medical management and for those with progressive hind limb weakness. Dogs with a paralyzed bladder or rectum are unlikely to benefit from treatment.

SPONDYLOSIS (BONE SPURS)

Spondylosis is characterized by the presence of osteophytes—bone spurs that form around intervertebral discs as a dog ages. They usually do not produce symptoms. On rare occasions, spurs project into the spinal canal and cause symptoms similar to those of a ruptured disc. A fusion of the osteophytes, called spondylosis deformans, restricts movement of the vertebral column and causes pain and stiffness. Large-breed dogs are most often affected.

Treatment: Dogs with the pain and stiffness of spondylosis deformans respond well to analgesics. Surgery to remove osteophytes and decompress the spinal cord may be benefit dogs who are not helped by analgesics. Acupuncture and physical therapy will help some dogs, as well.

Peripheral Nerve Injuries

An injury to a nerve results in loss of sensation and/or muscle movement in the structures affected by that nerve. With complete paralysis the leg hangs limply. With partial paralysis, the dog stumbles when attempting to put weight on the leg. Common injuries are stretches, tears, and lacerations.

Stretches involving the brachial and radial nerves are usually caused by auto accidents or falls in which the front leg is jerked away from the trunk. A similar stretching of the femoral or sciatic nerves can cause a paralyzed back leg. Nerves can be crushed when a vehicle rolls over the leg. Bone fractures and muscle injuries often occur at the same time.

Another cause of nerve paralysis (usually temporary) is the injection of an irritating medication into the tissue surrounding a nerve. This problem does not occur frequently, but can be a cause of concern when it does. The correct procedure for giving injections is described on page 567. (Also see *Horner's Syndrome*, page 176.)

Treatment: Lacerated nerves do not regenerate. The paralysis is permanent. Stretched nerves may (but do not always) return to normal. Those that do recover begin to improve in three weeks and may continue to improve for 12 months. If recovery does not occur, the dog may benefit from amputation of the paralyzed leg. Electroacupuncture to stimulate nerves may encourage healing.

DEAD TAIL OR LIMBER TAIL

This condition has been seen in Labrador Retrievers, Pointers, Setters, Foxhounds, and Beagles. The dogs will hold their tails totally limp or out away from their body three to four inches, then hanging limply. Most often this occurs after a strenuous day of hunting or swimming—especially if the water is cold.

Dogs may act as if the tail is painful. It appears to be a sprain or strain of the tail muscles and nerves after working much harder than usual.

Treatment: Rest and anti-inflammatory medications usually result in a normal tail in just a few days.

THE MUSCULOSKELETAL SYSTEM

The dog's skeleton is made up of 319 bones—about 100 more than humans have. Although the number of bones is roughly the same in all breeds, there is considerable variation in the size and shape of individual bones, as the result of selective breeding.

The place where two bones meet is called a joint, or articulation. In some joints there is a cushioning pad of cartilage interposed between the bones. This pad is called a meniscus. A damaged meniscus can deteriorate and inflame the joint. Abnormal wear and tear on joint surfaces and joint cartilages leads to arthritis. In many cases the abnormal wear and tear is the result of poor joint conformation associated with inherited orthopedic abnormalities such as hip dysplasia.

Joint position is maintained by the ligaments, the tendons, and a tough fibrous capsule surrounding the joint. Together, these structures provide stability and hold the joint together. Joint looseness (called laxity) is caused by stretching of these support structures. Laxity enables the ends of the bones to slip partly out of position. When the joint capsule ruptures, the bones slip completely out of position. This is called dislocation.

The skeletal anatomy of humans and dogs has much in common, including similar terminology. However, there are significant differences in the angles, lengths, and position of the bones. The dog's hock, for example, is actually the heel bone in humans. While people walk on the soles of their feet, dogs walk on their toes. Humans carry all their weight on their hips. Dogs carry 75 percent of their weight on their shoulders and front legs.

Veterinarians, dog breeders, and dog show judges use specific terms to describe a dog's overall composition and structure. *Conformation* is how the various angles, shapes, and parts of the dog's body conform to the breed standard. Standards for purebred dogs describe the ideal conformation for each breed. These standards are based, to a certain extent, upon aesthetic considerations, but they also take into account the breed's original purpose as a working dog.

Most breed standards provide some information on the desired angle or slope of the bones of the shoulders, pelvis, and limbs. These angles are determined using imaginary lines drawn horizontally and vertically through the plane of the standing dog.

Another term used to judge the physical attributes of a dog is *soundness*. When applied to the musculoskeletal system, it means that all the bones and joints are in correct alignment and are functioning as intended. In particular, in a dog with good skeletal conformation the alignment of the legs allows equal distribution of weight, equal bone pressure, and equal strain on the supporting ligaments when the dog is standing naturally or moving at a trot.

Limping or Lameness

Limping indicates a structural problem, pain, or weakness in the involved leg. It is a common sign of bone and joint disease, but it also occurs with muscle and nerve injuries.

Determining the Cause

Consider the history and circumstances surrounding the appearance of lameness. Did the lameness appear spontaneously or was there an injury? Which leg is involved? A dog often holds up the paw or places less weight on a painful leg, especially one that has been recently injured. A dog usually takes shorter steps on a painful or weak leg. You may notice that his head bobs or drops as his weight comes down on the painful leg. With chronic lameness, the dog may simply take very short strides with no obvious limp. This is also true if more than one leg is injured or hurts. The dog's head bobs up on the painful side and down on the side with the sound leg.

Having identified which leg is involved, try to identify the specific site and possible cause. First examine the foot and look between the toes. Many cases of lameness are due to foot injuries such as sprains, pad lacerations, broken nails, and penetrating puncture wounds caused by thorns and splinters. Carefully feel the leg from the toes up. Locate areas of tenderness by applying gentle pressure. You may also feel areas of swelling. Next, flex and extend all joints from the toes to the shoulder looking for resistance (lack of easy movement). Resistance is a sign of joint pain, which will be evident when the dog attempts to pull the leg free. If you aren't sure if something you feel is normal, check the dog's other leg. You have one for a comparison for both front and rear leg problems.

Having located the site of pain, the next step is to try to determine the cause of the pain. Consider the following:

- **Infected areas** are red, warm, and tender, and are often associated with skin lacerations or bite wounds. There may be *purulent* drainage from the wound. The limp grows steadily worse. An abscess may be developing. The dog may have a fever. Dogs often lick at abscessed or wounded areas.

- **Sprains and strains** occur suddenly and are often accompanied by swelling and bruising. Usually the dog is able to bear some weight on the leg. The lameness may persist for days or weeks.

- **Fractures and dislocations** cause severe pain and the dog is unable to bear weight on the leg. There is some degree of deformity. The tissues are swollen and discolored from bleeding.

- **Inherited orthopedic diseases** generally come on gradually. Young to middle-aged dogs are commonly affected. There may be few local findings to explain the lameness. Swelling, if present, is often slight. The lameness persists and grows worse with time.

- **Degenerative joint disease,** also called arthritis or osteoarthritis, is the most common cause of lameness in older dogs. The lameness is worse when the dog wakes up and improves as he moves about.

- **Spinal cord injuries and peripheral nerve injuries** (discussed in chapter 12) produce weakness or paralysis without pain in one or more limbs.

- **Bone tumors** are evidenced by a firm mass or swelling with or without signs of inflammation (see page 538). Pressure over a bone tumor causes varying degrees of pain. Consider this diagnosis in a mature dog with an unexplained limp. Bone tumors are more common in large-breed dogs.

Diagnostic Tests

X-rays of the bones and joints are used to diagnose fractures and dislocations. They are also helpful in distinguishing bone growths from soft tissue swellings. Note that many cases of lameness occur without positive findings on conventional X-rays.

A bone scan (also called nuclear scintigraphy) is an imaging technique that uses radioactive isotopes injected into the body and X-ray equipment to form a picture of the bone and surrounding tissue. These scans are especially useful in diagnosing bone cancers and determining the extent of their spread. Because of the cost and the restrictions on using radioactive isotopes, bone scans are performed only at medical centers and schools of veterinary medicine.

A CT scan or MRI may be of benefit in special circumstances, particularly with tendon, ligament, and muscle damage, but their availability and cost of these studies limit their usefulness.

Synovial fluid is a viscous joint lubricant that contains hyaluronic acid. The fluid can be removed using a sterile needle and syringe. Analyzing this fluid helps determine the cause of joint swelling. Normal synovial fluid is clear and pale yellow. Blood in the fluid indicates recent joint injury. Pus indicates joint infection (septic arthritis).

Bone and Joint Injuries

Emergency treatment for fractures is discussed in *Broken Bones,* page 15. A fracture (or even a suspected fracture) is always an emergency and requires immediate veterinary attention.

Osteomyelitis (Bone Infection)

Bacterial contamination and subsequent infection is a hazard whenever bone is exposed. It occurs most often with open fractures. Other causes are gunshot wounds and animal bites that become infected and progress to adjacent bone. In rare cases osteomyelitis is caused by blood-borne bacteria or fungi. This occurs in dogs receiving chemotherapy and those suffering from illnesses that impair immunity.

Signs of acute osteomyelitis are excessive pain, lameness, fever, and swelling. In dogs with chronic osteomyelitis there is an intermittent *purulent* discharge through the sinus tracts connecting the bone to the skin. The diagnosis is confirmed by X-rays and a culture of the bone.

Treatment: Bone infection is a most difficult problem to treat. It is essential to remove all devitalized bone and leave the wound open for daily dressing changes and wound irrigation. Bacterial cultures of the infected bone aid in selecting appropriate antibiotics.

Osteomyelitis associated with nonhealing fractures is treated by stabilizing the fracture with plates and screws and implanting a sterile bone graft.

SPRAINS

A sprain is an injury caused by sudden stretching or tearing of the ligaments in and around the joint, or the joint capsule itself. Signs are pain over the joint, swelling of the tissues, and temporary lameness.

Treatment: If the dog is unable to put weight on the leg, seek veterinary consultation to rule out a fracture or dislocation. This is true for any injury that fails to improve in 24 hours. X-rays should be taken.

It is most important to prevent further injury by resting the affected part. Restrict activity by confining the dog in a small area. Apply cold packs to the injured joint for 15 to 30 minutes, three or four times a day for the first 24 hours. Use a chemical cold pack or put crushed ice in a plastic bag. Wrap the pack in a towel and secure it in place over the injured joint with a loose gauze wrap. An alternative method is to run cold water over the affected leg for 5 to 10 minutes, three or four times a day.

After the first 24 hours, switch to warm, moist compresses for 15 to 30 minutes, three times a day for the next two to three days. Apply as described for cold packs. Avoid hot compresses, which can burn the skin.

Analgesics may be prescribed by your veterinarian to relieve pain (see *Over-the-Counter Drugs for Home Veterinary Use*, page 571). One disadvantage of pain relievers is that they may allow the dog to begin using the leg while the injury is still fresh. This can delay healing, but if the dog's activity is restricted this is not a problem. Anti-inflammatories may hasten healing by reducing swelling and inflammation around the area. Keep the dog off the leg by confining him in a small, closed area. Take him out on a leash only to eliminate. Allow at least three weeks for successful healing. Incomplete healing is associated with prolonged lameness and the later development of degenerative arthritis in the joint.

TENDON INJURIES

Tendons can be stretched, partly torn, or ruptured. Strained tendons follow sudden wrenching or twisting injuries. The tendons of the forepaws (front and back) are strained most often. The signs of tendon injury are lameness, pain on bearing weight, and painful swelling over the course of the tendon.

Rupture of the Achilles tendon at the hock joint can be caused by sudden and extreme flexion of the hock. This injury tends to occur in Greyhounds and sporting and performance breeds. The Achilles tendon is the one most often severed in dog fights and car accidents. Rupture of the Achilles tendon causes a dropped hock.

The Achilles tendon in the heel is the one most often ruptured in dogs.

Inflammation of a tendon is called tendonitis. This injury follows strenuous field or road work and overuse of the limb.

Treatment: This is the same as described for sprains (see page 387). A ruptured Achilles tendon should be surgically repaired. Surgery will be followed by a long course of rest and rehabilitation.

Muscle Strains

Muscle strains are caused by stretching or tearing the muscle fibers or by overuse of a muscle following strenuous field or road work. Signs are lameness, swelling of the muscle, tenderness over the injured part, and bruising. Bruising may be difficult to see beneath the fur.

Treatment: Initial treatment is similar to that described for sprains (see page 387). The dog should be rested for at least three weeks.

Luxation (Dislocated Joint)

A strong force is necessary to rupture a joint and displace the bones. Such injuries are usually caused by auto accidents and falls from a height. Signs of a dislocated joint are sudden pain and inability to use the limb. The elbow or knee may be bent, with the leg pointing either toward or away from the body. The affected leg may be either shorter or longer than the opposite leg.

When the bone is removed from the joint it belongs in, it is important to realize that the soft tissues, such as ligaments, tendons, and muscles, are often torn or damaged as well. Simply replacing the bone may not be enough, because the support tissues that hold the joint together also need to heal.

Subluxations (also called luxations) are dislocations in which the bones are only partly out of joint. Some subluxations are congenital, but most are caused by trauma. The limb does not shorten and joint deformity is minimal.

Dislocations and subluxations affect the hips, stifles, shoulders, elbows, and the small joints that make up the hocks and wrists. Subluxations of these smaller joints can be caused by a sudden force, such as jumping from a height.

Treatment: Veterinary examination is necessary to rule out fractures and to replace the dislocated bones—a procedure that requires anesthesia. The treatment of other life-threatening injuries may take precedence. After reduction (replacement of the dislocated joint), the limb is immobilized in a sling or splint.

This dog shows subluxation of the left hip, with outward rotation of the knee and inward rotation of the heel.

Depending on the extent of the injury, the dog is placed on strict crate rest or allowed limited exercise on a short leash. Physical therapy with exercises that move the joint passively through a limited range of motion, and activities such as swimming, help the dog recover strength and joint flexibility.

Joint surgery is necessary for dislocations that cannot be reduced by manipulating the limbs. Surgery gives the best results for recurrent dislocations and for subluxations of the wrists and hocks. Surgery may also be required to repair associated soft tissue injuries.

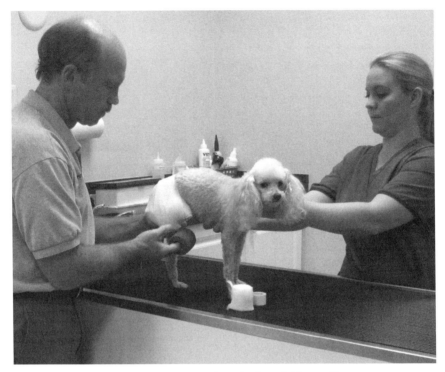

A restriction bandage is used to immobilize the leg of this Poodle.

Stifle Injuries

The stifle joint is stabilized by a number of ligaments. The two large ligaments that cross in the middle of the joint are the cranial and caudal cruciates. The ligaments that stabilize the sides of the joints are the medial and lateral collaterals. The meniscus is a cushion of cartilage between the femur and the tibia and fibula.

Rupture of the cranial cruciate is a common and serious injury of the stifle. It occurs in all breeds at all ages, but is more likely to occur in younger, active dogs. There may be a congenital or developmental predisposition in some dogs (see *Osteochondrosis*, page 400). If one tears, unless it is repaired, the ligament in the other knee also eventually tears.

The sudden onset of rear leg lameness suggests a rupture. The lameness may disappear with rest, then recur with exercise. In some cases the presenting sign is persistent lameness in one or both hind legs. The diagnosis is confirmed by palpating the stifle joint. In many cases the medial collateral ligament is also damaged.

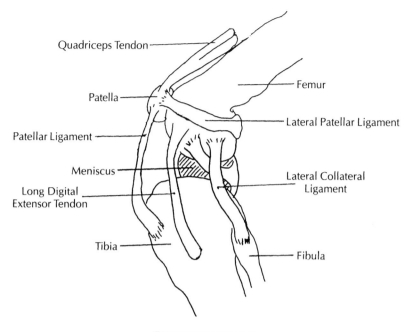

Quadriceps Tendon

Patella

Patellar Ligament

Meniscus

Long Digital
Extensor Tendon

Tibia

Femur

Lateral Patellar Ligament

Lateral Collateral
Ligament

Fibula

THE STIFLE JOINT

Rupture of the medial or lateral collateral ligament usually is caused by a severe blow to the side of the joint or a twisting motion, especially at speed. The affected ligament may be stretched, partially torn, or completely severed. Diagnosis is made by manipulating the joint and looking for a degree of looseness. Severe blows to the stifle may also cause joint fractures. Dogs may need to be anesthetized for a thorough evaluation of the stifle.

Injuries to the meniscus are associated with injuries to the cruciates. If a cruciate injury goes untreated, secondary damage to the meniscus occurs in the weeks and months that follow. The end result is degenerative arthritis and permanent lameness. Isolated meniscus injuries are rare in dogs.

Treatment: The treatment of choice for ruptured cruciate ligaments is surgical repair. If this is not done, the joint becomes unstable and is subject to further damage. Following surgical repair, physical therapy and restricted exercise (as described for *Luxation,* page 388) are important for successful recovery. The complete rehabilitation program may take months for dogs to return to near full athletic performance levels.

Collateral ligaments that have been stretched but not torn usually heal satisfactorily with rest and restricted activity.

Meniscal injuries respond well to surgical removal of the damaged part of the cartilage.

Inherited Orthopedic Diseases

Inherited bone and joint diseases have a genetic basis, despite the fact that only a certain number of offspring will be affected. If, after a careful veterinary examination, one of these conditions is diagnosed in your dog, do not breed the animal.

Hip Dysplasia

Hip dysplasia is the most common cause of rear leg lameness in dogs. The highest incidence occurs in large-breed dogs, including St. Bernards, Newfoundlands, Rottweilers, Chesapeake Bay Retrievers, Golden Retrievers, German Shepherd Dogs, Labrador Retrievers, and many others. Smaller breeds are also affected, but are less likely to show symptoms.

Hip dysplasia is a polygenic trait. That is, more than one gene controls the inheritance. Environmental factors such as diet are also involved. The hip is a ball-and-socket joint; the ball is the head of the femur and the socket is the acetabulum of the pelvis. In a dysplastic hip, the head of the femur fits loosely into a poorly developed, shallow acetabulum. Joint instability occurs as muscle development lags behind the rate of skeletal growth. As the stress of weight-bearing exceeds the strength limits of the supporting connective tissue and muscle, the joint becomes loose and unstable. This allows for free play of the femoral head in the acetabulum, which promotes abnormal wear and tear.

Feeding a very high-calorie diet to growing dogs can exacerbate a predisposition to hip dysplasia, because the rapid weight gain places increased stress on

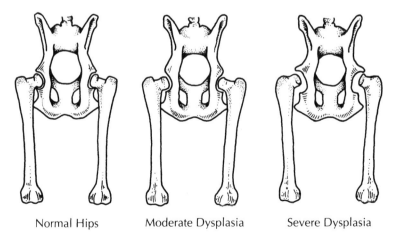

Normal Hips   Moderate Dysplasia   Severe Dysplasia

Hip dysplasia, showing progressive increase in the joint space and increasing joint wear.

Normal Hip

Severe Dysplasia with Upward Dislocation

Upward displacement is the most common type of subluxation in canine hip dysplasia.

the hips. Being overweight supports the genetic potential for hip dysplasia, as well as other skeletal diseases. A diet with an imbalance of calcium and phosphorous is bad for bone development.

Another factor that can bring on the symptoms of hip dysplasia is inappropriate exercise during the period of rapid bone growth. Young dogs should be discouraged from jumping up and down from heights in situations where they land on their back legs (such as jumping up to catch a ball), and from standing up on their back legs (which dogs do when they stand up against a fence or window to get a better view). They should also avoid running on pavement.

Dogs with hip dysplasia are born with hips that appear normal but progressively undergo structural changes. The age of onset is 4 to 12 months. Affected puppies may show pain in the hip, walk with a limp or a swaying gait, bunny hop when running, and experience difficulty in the hindquarters when getting up. Pressing on the rump can cause the pelvis to drop. With the puppy on his back, the rear legs may not extend into the frog-leg position without causing pain.

An X-ray of the hips and pelvis is the only reliable way of determining whether a dog has hip dysplasia. Good X-rays require heavy sedation or anesthesia. The standard view is taken with the dog lying on his back with his rear legs parallel and extended. The knees (stifles) are rotated internally. Care is taken to be sure the pelvis is not tilted.

Hip dysplasia is graded according to the severity of X-ray findings. In ideal hips, the femoral head fits tightly into a well-formed hip socket with a minimum of space between the head of the femur and the acetabulum. The hip ball is almost completely covered by the socket.

Normal hips are rated Excellent, Good, or Fair, depending on how closely they match the ideal. Dysplastic hips are rated Mild, Moderate, or Severe. If the findings are not clear, the hips are rated Borderline.

In a dog with mild hip dysplasia, the X-rays will show mild subluxation (increased space in the joint) with the hip ball partway out of the socket. There are no changes associated with degenerative arthritis.

An X-ray of normal hips. The femoral heads fit tightly into well-formed sockets.

Moderate dysplasia. These loose hips are partly out of their sockets and the femoral heads are beginning to flatten.

Severe dysplasia with degenerative arthritis. Note bilateral subluxations and bone spurs on the femoral heads and rims of the sockets.

In a dog with moderate hip dysplasia, the hip ball is barely seated into a shallow acetabulum. Arthritic changes begin to appear. These include wear and flattening of the femoral head, a rough appearance to the joint surfaces, and the beginning of bone spurs.

In a dog with severe hip dysplasia, the head of the femur is completely out of the joint and arthritic changes are marked. Once arthritis is noted, the condition is irreversible. But even with arthritis, some dogs are not lame. The onset of lameness is unpredictable, and some dogs may go most of their lives with dysplastic hips but no lameness. Others develop lameness as puppies.

The OFA maintains a hip dysplasia registry for purebred dogs (see appendix D). An OFA-certified radiologist will review hip X-rays taken by your veterinarian and, if the conformation of the hips is normal for the breed, certify the dog as Excellent, Good, or Fair and assign him an OFA number. As an optional step, you can have the OFA number added to your dog's AKC registration papers.

Dogs must be 24 months of age or older to be tested. Some female dogs will show subluxation when X-rayed around an estrus cycle, so OFA recommends not X-raying females around a heat period or within three to four weeks of weaning a litter.

The OFA registry is closed. That means if the dog is found to have hip dysplasia, the information remains confidential unless the owner marks off on the application that all results may be made public.

Dog breeders often request preliminary evaluations on hip status before selecting puppies for show and breeding stock. The OFA accepts preliminary X-rays for puppies as young as 4 months of age. Their own analysis reveals that these evaluations are about 90 percent accurate when compared with follow-ups at 24 months of age.

Another method of evaluating hips was developed at the University of Pennsylvania Veterinary School and is now administered by PennHip via the University of Pennsylvania (see appendix D). PennHip X-rays are taken using the traditional OFA views, but additional views are also required. Distraction pressure is applied with special techniques to look for joint laxity by seeing how much the joint can be distracted (pulled apart). This is done very carefully and to a set standard. These views are used to gauge joint laxity, which can be measured in puppies, starting at 16 weeks of age. The joint laxity does not change as the dog ages.

Dogs X-rayed for PennHip measurements are compared only to other dogs of the same breed. Your dog then receives a joint laxity distraction index (DI) number, ranging from 0.0 (perfect) to 1.1 (severely dysplastic). PennHip suggests that only dogs in the top half for their breed with respect to joint laxity (that is, those with the tightest joints) be used for breeding. Those dogs who fall into the lower half, which are the ones with the loosest hips, have a greater chance of developing hip dysplasia in the future. In general, dogs with a DI of .3 or less are unlikely to develop degenerative joint disease.

Finally, the Institute for Genetic Disease Control (GDC) in Animals maintained a separate hip dysplasia registry for some time, although its database has now been merged with OFA's (with the exception of some eye and tumor problems). The GDC certifies dogs starting at 12 months of age. The GDC's registry is open. That is, the GDC provides information on affected as well as normal dogs to anyone making an inquiry.

The GDC requests that veterinarians palpate the stifle joints for patella *luxation* at the time the hip X-rays are taken. They also request that copies of pedigrees be submitted with X-rays.

A genetic test for hip dysplasia that is applicable for a number of breeds is under development through VetGen. However, the mode of inheritance is still not clearly understood, making it difficult to develop a test.

Treatment: Hip dysplasia is treated both medically and surgically. Medical treatment includes restricting activity and giving an NSAID analgesic such as

Rimadyl, and a joint chondroprotectant such as Cosequin or Adequan to relieve pain and inflammation and to repair damaged cartilage. Weight loss and moderate exercise are also important. These agents are discussed in more detail in *Degenerative Joint Disease*, page 401.

It is important to exercise lame dogs on a leash and not allow them to run, jump, or play as long as they exhibit pain. Swimming is an excellent exercise that improves muscle mass and joint flexibility without overstressing the hips.

After reviewing the X-rays, your veterinarian may recommend hip surgery. Early surgery in selected puppies can prevent some cases of degenerative joint disease. Surgery is also indicated for dogs who continue to experience pain and lameness despite medical treatment.

There are five surgical options; technical factors govern the choice. Triple pelvic osteotomy and femoral osteotomy are two operations performed on puppies who do not have degenerative joint changes. The goal of both is to position the femoral head more deeply in the acetabulum. Normal joint function is thus maintained and arthritis may not develop, although this is not always the case.

Pectineus myectomy is a relatively simple operation in which all of the pectineus muscle is removed on both affected sides. This operation does not slow the progress of joint disease but does relieve the pain for some time.

Femoral head and neck excision arthroplasty is an effective operation that provides relief for intractable hip pain. The head of the femur is removed, allowing a fibrous union to replace the ball-and-socket joint. The operation is usually reserved for dogs who weigh less than 36 pounds. Total hip replacement is the most effective procedure for dogs 9 months and older who have disabling degenerative joint disease in one or both hips. The operation removes the old joint and replaces it with a new, artificial joint. The procedure requires special equipment and is usually performed by an orthopedic specialist. Good results are obtained in more than 95 percent of cases.

Dorsal acetabular rim arthroplasty—building up the acetabular rim with bone from other sites in the body to create a deeper socket—is another surgical option that is currently the subject of investigational studies.

Prevention: Preventing excessive weight gain in puppyhood and keeping the puppy from placing undue stress on the hips will delay the onset of hip dysplasia in many dogs with a genetic predisposition. It may also lead to a less severe form of the disease. Feed puppies a quality food in amounts appropriate for normal (but not accelerated) growth. Puppies at risk for hip dysplasia should be fed a calorie-controlled diet, as described in *Feeding Weaned Puppies*, page 510. Overweight puppies should be given a calorie-restricted diet. Discuss this with your veterinarian. Vitamin and mineral supplements have no proven benefit in preventing or treating hip dysplasia, and may even be detrimental if given in excess.

Preventing hip dysplasia in a bloodline is based on selective breeding practices. Hip dysplasia is a moderately heritable condition. It is twice as common among littermates who have one dysplastic parent. Experience shows that repeatedly using only dogs with normal hips for breeding stock significantly reduces the incidence of hip dysplasia in susceptible bloodlines.

Information on breed risk is available through the OFA and PennHip. In breeds in which hip dysplasia is a particular problem, prospective puppy buyers are advised to check pedigrees for OFA, PennHip, or GDC certifications, particularly for sires and dams. Ideally, you will also be able to find evaluations of littermates of the sires and dams, as well as the grandparents.

Legg-Perthes Disease

Legg-Perthes disease is caused by a vascular necrosis of the femoral head. Avascular necrosis means death of bone in the head of the femur resulting from an interruption in the blood supply. It is not clear what causes this, but genetic factors may be involved.

The disease occurs most often in toy-breed puppies between 4 and 11 months of age. Large breeds are occasionally affected. Avascular necrosis occurs in both hips in about 15 percent of cases. Occasionally, it is the result of a traumatically dislocated hip caused by trauma such as an auto accident or a fall from a height.

Weight bearing causes the dead bone beneath the cartilage of the femoral head to collapse. This fractures the cartilage and causes a gradual destruction of the hip joint.

Signs are severe lameness and sometimes the inability to bear weight on the leg. Muscle wasting is pronounced and the joint loses some range of motion. The affected leg may be shorter than the opposite normal leg. A standard X-ray of the hips and pelvis establishes the diagnosis.

Treatment: Medical therapy involves restricting activity and administering analgesics. Some dogs may improve, but surgery generally produces the best results. Surgery involves either a femoral head and neck excision arthroplasty or a total hip replacement, as described in *Hip Dysplasia,* page 392. It is difficult to do hip replacement surgery on very small dogs.

The GDC maintains a Legg-Perthes registry, which is now merged with OFA, for breeds in the Terrier Group. OFA also has a Legg-Perthes registry for a variety of breeds. The determination can be made from standard hip X-rays.

Luxating Patella (Slipping Kneecap)

The patella, or kneecap, is a small bone that protects the front of the stifle joint on the rear leg. The patella is anchored in place by ligaments and slides in a groove in the femur called the trochlea. If the groove is too shallow, the patella will slip out when the knee bends. When the patella slips out to the inside of the knee joint, it's called medial luxation. When it slips out to the outside, it's called lateral luxation.

Luxating patella is usually an inherited developmental defect. Rarely, it is acquired through trauma.

Medial luxation is more common. It occurs in toy, miniature, and large breeds, and is apparent in some puppies when they begin to walk. In others it appears later. The patella may slip in and out of place, resulting in a gait that is sometimes normal and sometimes not. When the patella is out of place, the affected leg is usually carried with the stifle joint bent and the foot turned inward. The condition is bilateral in about 25 percent of cases.

Lateral luxation occurs in large and giant breeds at 5 to 6 months of age. A knock-kneed stance is the most noticeable sign. The foot often twists outward as weight is placed on the limb. Both knees are almost always involved.

In the early stages, luxating patella may not be painful. But pain can increase as the grooves are polished smoother by the slipping action of the kneecap and as arthritis develops in the joint.

The diagnosis of luxation is made by attempting to push the patella out of the trochlear groove. The degree of luxation is graded 1 to 4, depending on how easy it is to dislocate the patella and whether the patella returns spontaneously to the trochlear groove. This manipulation should only be done by breeders or veterinarians experienced in this technique. Preliminary veterinary screening for medial patella luxation should be done on dogs of toy and small breeds at 6 to 8 weeks of age, before these pups are sent to their new homes.

Treatment: A Grade 1 luxation may never worsen, and these dogs may need only medical treatment to deal with any pain that develops. For other dogs, though, surgery to deepen the trochlear groove and repair any loose or torn ligaments is usually recommended. The specific operation depends on the age of the dog and the type of luxation.

The OFA maintains a patellar luxation registry and issues certificates to all dogs who palpate normal at 12 months of age or older. The GDC maintains a medial patella luxation registry for breeds in the Terrier Group and also issues certificates to dogs who palpate normal at 12 months of age or older. The GDC is attempting to accumulate information on patella luxation based on palpating patellas when dogs are X-rayed for hip dysplasia. This GDC registry is now merged with OFA.

Dogs with genetically determined patella luxation should not be bred.

Elbow Dysplasia

Elbow dysplasia is a common cause of front-leg lameness in large-breed dogs. Breeds predisposed to elbow dysplasia include the Golden Retriever, Labrador Retriever, English Setter, English Springer Spaniel, Rottweiler, German Shepherd, Bernese Mountain Dog, Chow Chow, Chinese Shar-Pei, Newfoundland, and others.

The elbow joint is composed of the humerus, which articulates with the radius and ulna, and those two bones. The anconeal process unites with the ulna at about 6 months of age. It forms a curved depression in the ulna. The coronoid process forms part of the lower curved bone of the ulna.

Dogs with elbow dysplasia have one or more of the following inherited developmental defects, which may occur singly or in combination: ununited anconeal process, fragmented medial coronoid process, osteochondritis dissecans of the medial condyle of the head of the humerus, and incongruity of growth rate between the radius and ulna resulting in curvature of the radius. The first three defects are related to osteochondrosis (discussed on page 400). The fourth is related to an enlargement of the epiphyseal growth plate at the head of the radius.

Signs of elbow dysplasia usually appear in puppies at 4 to 10 months of age, but some dogs may not show signs until adulthood, when degenerative joint disease starts. The signs consist of varying degrees of front-leg lameness that worsens with exercise. Characteristically, the elbow is held outward from the chest and may appear swollen.

The diagnosis is made using detailed X-rays of the elbow joint, taken in extreme flexion. Radiologists are particularly interested in the appearance of the anconeal process of the ulna. In a dog with elbow dysplasia, the anconeal process has a rough, irregular appearance due to arthritic changes. Another sign of dysplasia is widening of the joint space associated with a loose, unstable joint. X-rays may be difficult to interpret before a pup is 7 months of age. A *CT scan* may be required to demonstrate a fragmented coronoid process.

The OFA evaluates X-rays and maintains registries for dogs with elbow dysplasia. Dogs must be 24 months of age or older to be certified by OFA, although it accepts preliminary X-rays on growing pups for interpretation only.

The wide stance and swollen elbow joints of a dog with bilateral elbow dysplasia.

Treatment: Medical treatment is similar to that described for *Hip Dysplasia*, page 392. Surgery is the treatment of choice for most dogs. Several factors, including the age of the dog and the number and severity of the defects, govern the choice of surgical procedure. The more defects in the elbow, the greater the likelihood that the dog will develop degenerative arthritis—with or without surgery.

OSTEOCHONDROSIS

Bone lengthening is a continuous process in which rapidly growing cartilage at the ends of bones becomes calcified and is gradually incorporated into the bone. Osteochondrosis is a disease caused by a defect in the calcification process of this growing cartilage. In a dog with osteochondrosis, the cartilage is calcified in an irregular instead of a uniform fashion. This creates areas of uncalcified, defective cartilage over the ends of the bones. With stress on the joint, the defective cartilage breaks into loose fragments called joint mice. This process, which is accompanied by joint pain and swelling, is called osteochondritis dissecans.

Osteochondrosis most often involves the head of the humerus in the shoulder joint. It also occurs in the elbow, where it is responsible for many of the defects of elbow dysplasia. Osteochondrosis occurs less commonly in the stifle and hock joints. In the stifle, osteochondrosis involves the femur at its articulation with the tibia. Symptoms of intermittent lameness may look like luxating patella. In the hock, osteochondrosis involves the articulation between the tibia and the talus (the first bone of the hock).

Osteochondrosis is a common disease of rapidly growing large-breed puppies. The first signs show up at between 4 and 8 months of age. The symptoms may resemble those of panosteitis (see this page), another disease that causes lameness in growing puppies. The typical presentation is gradual lameness that seems to stem from the shoulder, elbow, stifle, or hock in a young dog of one of the large breeds. Lameness often gets worse with exercise. Symptoms may appear following a traumatic episode such as jumping down stairs. Pain is present on flexing and extending the joint. X-rays may show fragmentation of joint cartilage or a loose piece of cartilage in the joint. The diagnosis may not be made definitively until the dog is 18 months of age.

Treatment: Medical treatment involves restricting activity and prescribing analgesics and chondroprotectants, as described for the treatment of degenerative joint disease, page 401. Preparations that contain polysulfated glycosaminoglycan (such as Adequan) may be of benefit in limiting further cartilage degeneration and relieving pain and inflammation.

In most cases surgery will be required to scrape away defective cartilage and remove any joint mice. The best results are obtained in the shoulder and elbow joints. The results are less favorable for the hock, which is a small joint, and for the stifle, which is a more complex joint. In the hock and stifle, degenerative joint disease is likely to occur over time.

PANOSTEITIS (WANDERING LAMENESS)

Panosteitis is a disease of large, rapidly growing puppies between 5 and 12 months of age. The disease has been described in German Shepherd Dogs,

Doberman Pinschers, Great Danes, Irish Setters, St. Bernards, Airedale Terriers, Basset Hounds, Miniature Schnauzers, and other breeds. The cause is unknown, but an inherited polygenic trait is suspected. Males are affected four times more often than females. Suspect this disease if your puppy exhibits intermittent lameness in one or more legs that is unrelated to trauma.

A characteristic sign is the tendency for pain and lameness to shift from one limb to another over the course of several weeks or months. That's why this disease is sometimes called wandering leg lameness. Pressure over the shaft of an affected bone elicits pain. X-rays show a characteristic picture of increased density in the affected long bone. Panosteitis must be distinguished from other causes of lameness in growing puppies, including osteochondrosis, elbow dysplasia, and hip dysplasia.

Treatment: The disease is self-limiting, but lameness may persist for several months. Symptoms usually disappear by the time the dog is 20 months old. Analgesics prescribed by your veterinarian can be given to relieve pain. If the dog is severely affected, restrict exercise.

Arthritis

Arthritis is a degenerative condition that affects one or more joints. Most cases occur in dogs with an inherited orthopedic disease such as osteochondrosis or hip dysplasia, or those with a joint injury. Some cases of arthritis are related to an immune-mediated joint disease or a joint infection.

OSTEOARTHRITIS (DEGENERATIVE JOINT DISEASE)

Osteoarthritis is a common disease that affects one out of five dogs during their lifetime. The problem isn't confined to older dogs. Hip dysplasia, ruptured cruciate ligaments, patella luxation, joint trauma, and other joint conditions can cause degenerative arthritis, even in young dogs. Large-breed dogs are affected more often than small dogs. Heavy dogs are more likely to experience symptoms because of the extra strain placed on ligaments and joints.

Dogs with degenerative arthritis experience varying degrees of lameness, stiffness, and joint pain, which is more apparent in the morning and after getting up from a nap. They often exhibit irritability and behavioral changes associated with increasing disability. Cold and damp surroundings increase pain and stiffness. Degenerative arthritis is progressive, and in time makes the dog's life miserable.

The diagnosis is made by joint X-rays that show bone spurs at points where the ligaments and the joint capsule attach to the bone. There may be varying degrees of joint space narrowing and increased density of bone around the joint.

Treating Osteoarthritis

Degenerative joint disease is incurable, but treatment can substantially improve the dog's life. Treatment involves physical therapy and weight control, the use of analgesics and corticosteroids to relieve pain and improve function, and the use of *chondroprotective* agents to repair joint cartilage and prevent further damage. Acupuncture is another therapy that has shown good results for arthritic dogs. All of these should be used at the same time. (See the chart on pages 404–405 for an overview of medications used to treat osteoarthritis.)

Acupuncture and physical therapy are alternative or additional ways to make arthritic dogs comfortable.

In severe cases, surgical fusion of painful joints, such as the hock or elbow, relieves pain and restores limb movement in some dogs.

Physical Therapy

Moderate exercise is beneficial because it maintains muscle mass and preserves joint flexibility. Excessive exercise, however, is counterproductive. Arthritic dogs should not be allowed to jump up and down and should never be encouraged to stand up on their back legs. Dogs with pain and lameness should be exercised on a leash or a harness. There are veterinary physical therapists who can help design an exercise (and weight loss) program.

Swimming is an excellent exercise that improves muscle mass without overstressing the joints. Exercise can be increased as the dog improves with the use of medications.

Overweight dogs should be encouraged to lose weight, as described in *Weight Reduction*, page 308. Being overweight seriously complicates the treatment of osteoarthritis.

Nonsteroidal Anti-Inflammatory Drugs

These are anti-inflammatory medications, but they do not repair or heal cartilage. Ideally, they would be used along with supplements and given with food. These do provide rapid relief from pain.

A few NSAIDs have chondroprotective characteristics, which means they protect against the breakdown of cartilage. Others, such as aspirin, actually destroy cartilage in the dosage required for pain relief. This is one reason why aspirin is used less frequently for treating osteoarthritis.

The NSAIDs most often recommended are prescription medications. Newer medications have been developed that offer significant advantages over aspirin and the older NSAIDs. Rimadyl (carprofen) is an excellent drug with a low incidence of gastrointestinal side effects that has proven itself over time. It must be given daily. Rimadyl provides good pain relief and seems to slow the arthritic process. There are no detrimental effects on cartilage. Labrador Retrievers, and possibly a few other breeds, may show a higher predisposition for liver toxicity with Rimadyl. Etogesic (etodolac) is another newer NSAID. It requires only one dose a day. This drug may prove as effective as Rimadyl. These drugs are available through your veterinarian by prescription. See the chart *Osteoarthritis Medications* (pages 404–405) for other drugs that may be used. Note that many over-the-counter NSAIDs used for pain control in people are dangerous when given to dogs. *Do not use any drugs without veterinary approval, and never use more than one NSAID at the same time.*

Due to potential serious side effects, dogs on these drugs should have blood work first to assess liver and kidneys. The drugs may prolong bleeding times and interfere with clotting, and have the potential to cause life-threatening liver and kidney problems and gastrointestinal ulcerations. Nausea and vomiting may be the first indication of trouble. Blood work should be rechecked every six months, or sooner if there are problems. These drugs should not be combined or given with steroids.

The most common side effect is GI bleeding. This can be difficult to diagnose and quite extensive before signs become apparent (see *Stomach and Duodenal Ulcers*, page 261). Misoprostol (Cytotec) is a drug that prevents ulceration and helps heal ulcers caused by NSAIDs. Sulcrafate (Carafate) is another drug that protects against mucosal damage. Your veterinarian may prescribe one of these stomach protectants if your dog is taking an NSAID for chronic arthritis.

Steroids

Oral glucocorticoids (corticosteroids) are used for their anti-inflammatory effects. Low dosages appear to protect cartilage, while high dosages (those needed to relieve pain) destroy cartilage. Future formulations may have better protective effects and a wider margin of safety.

Unfortunately, dogs are unusually sensitive to the adverse effects of both the NSAIDs and glucocorticoids. Glucocorticoids are best used for short periods in dogs with osteoarthritis who have failed to respond to NSAIDs. Long-term therapy should be reserved for dogs with immune-mediated arthritis.

Steroids are regarded as highly dangerous medications with many side effects. These can range from interfering with cartilage repair to causing increased drinking and eating (with the associated increased elimination). Long-term use can lead to liver and adrenal problems. Still, steroids can provide quick relief for many conditions, and for immune problems they may be the drug of choice. They should not be combined with any of the NSAIDs.

Most steroids, such as prednisone, are given orally, but long-lasting injections may also be used. Dosing schedules will vary greatly and usually work on a decreasing dose schedule to wean the dog off the medication, if possible, and minimize side effects.

Chondroprotectants

These compounds appear to modify the progression of osteoarthritis by preventing further breakdown of cartilage. Breakdown of cartilage is the first step in the development of degenerative joint disease. Chondroprotectants are most effective when used early in the course of osteoarthritis.

Adequan (a polysulfated glycosaminoglycan similar to glucosamine) is a chondroprotective given by intramuscular injection twice a week for four or more weeks. It can be used as a preventive in dogs who are at high risk of developing degenerative joint disease, such as those with hip dysplasia.

Other chondroprotective agents are *nutraceuticals*—products that lie somewhere between a nutrient and a drug. Nutraceuticals are believed to have medical value based on subjective evidence of their effectiveness, although clinical evidence based on controlled studies is lacking for many of these. Unlike drugs, nutraceuticals do not undergo an approval process and are not regulated by a federal agency. Numerous controlled studies in humans, limited studies done on dogs, and canine anecdotal reports suggest these substances do have medical value for arthritic dogs. Many of the supplements mentioned in the chart on pages 404–405 are used based on anecdotal information, not clinical studies. So far, however, these compounds appear to be both safe and effective.

Osteoarthritis Medications

Nonsteroidal Anti-Inflammatory Drugs

Generic Name	Brand Name	Dosing	Special Side Effects
Aspirin	Many	Variable, best given with food	Gastrointestinal tract ulceration, prolonging bleeding times
Carprofen	Rimadyl, Novox	Once or twice daily (has a chewable form)	Possible idiosyncratic reaction in Labrador Retrievers, can cause liver problems within 3 weeks
Deracoxib	Deramaxx	Once daily with food	
Etodolac	Etogesic	Once daily with food	Possible association with dry eye
Firocoxib	Previcox	Once daily (has a chewable form)	
Meloxicam	Metacam	Once daily with food (liquid)	
Phenylbutazone	Butazolidine	Three times daily with food	
Piroxicam	Feldene	Daily or every other day, with food	Possible cancer prevention
Tepoxalin	Zubrin	Once daily with food (rapid disintegration tablet)	

Chondroprotectants and Other Supplements

Supplement	Use	Side Effects
Perna cannaliculus, green lipped mussel	Cartilage protection and repair	Minimal
Sea cucumber, sea jerky	Cartilage protection and repair	Minimal
Chondroitin sulfate	Cartilage production and repair, prevents damage, controls pain	Minimal
Glucosamine	Cartilage production and repair	Minimal
Methylsulfonylmethane, MSM	Sulfur supplement, controls pain	Minimal
Polysulfonated glycosaminoglycan (must be given by injection)	Cartilage protection and repair	Minimal
Omega-3 fatty acids	Anti-inflammatory	Minimal
Vitamins C and E	Antioxidants	Minimal, but excessively high doses can result in toxicity
Boswellia	Anti-inflammatory herb	Minimal
Yucca	Anti-inflammatory herb containing steroidal saponins	Minimal

Most nutraceuticals used to treat osteoarthritis contain glucosamine, polysulfated glycosaminoglycans, and chondroitin sulfates—compounds known to be involved in the synthesis and repair of joint cartilage. Examples include Cosequin and Glycoflex. These compounds are given orally and can be considered as follow-up therapy after Adequan, or in any condition in which joint damage is anticipated or expected, such as trauma, surgery, degenerative joint disease, or immune-mediated arthritis.

Chondroprotectives may be given along with an NSAID. The combination reduces pain and alleviates joint inflammation. The chondroprotectants can also be used to help prevent the development of osteoarthritis. There are now some prescription diets that include chondroprotectants in their formulation. Always check with your veterinarian before adding any supplements to avoid adverse interactions with medications your dog may be on. Supplements generally take a month or so to show positive effects. Dosages will vary greatly, so consult your veterinarian.

IMMUNE-MEDIATED ARTHRITIS

This is an unusual group of diseases in which antibodies are directed against the dog's own connective tissue, resulting in either an erosive or nonerosive arthritis. In erosive arthritis, cartilage and joint surfaces are destroyed. In nonerosive arthritis, there is inflammation but no tissue destruction.

Rheumatoid arthritis is an erosive arthritis that occurs primarily in toy breeds and other small breeds, such as Shetland Sheepdogs, at approximately 4 years of age. It is characterized by morning stiffness, shifting lameness, and swelling of the smaller joints, particularly the wrists and hocks. Fever, loss of appetite, and lymphadenopathy are accompanying features.

Nonerosive arthritis tends to occur in midsize and large-breed dogs at about 5 to 6 years of age. The cause is unknown. Signs are intermittent fever, loss of appetite, joint swelling, and a lameness that often shifts from limb to limb. A form of nonerosive arthritis occurs with systemic lupus erythematosus.

The diagnosis of immune-mediated arthritis is made by joint X-rays and specific laboratory tests. *Synovial fluid analysis* helps distinguish immune-mediated arthritis from infectious arthritis and osteoarthritis.

Treatment: Immune-mediated arthritis responds to anti-inflammatory and immunosuppressive drugs, including corticosteroids and chemotherapy agents. Treatment must be continued for eight weeks or longer. Your veterinarian may use several drugs or drug combinations before determining which protocol works best for your dog. Rheumatoid arthritis is less responsive than nonerosive arthritis to drug therapy.

Light to moderate activity is beneficial, but vigorous exercise, which is most likely during periods of remission, can injure the joints and should be restricted. Overweight dogs should be placed on a calorie-restricted diet. In fact, it may be advantageous if the dog is somewhat lean. Discuss this with your veterinarian.

INFECTIOUS ARTHRITIS

Infectious diseases can produce arthritis. Rickettsial arthritis is seen with Rocky Mountain spotted fever and canine ehrlichiosis, and spirochetal arthritis with Lyme disease. (All of these are tick-borne diseases.) Fungal arthritis is a rare complication of a systemic fungal infection.

Septic arthritis is caused by bacteria that gain access to joints through open wounds, soft-tissue infections around joints, and via the bloodstream. Injecting steroids into a joint carries a small risk of introducing bacteria.

Treatment: This involves opening the joint and removing all infected and devitalized tissue. This is followed by a long-term course of antibiotics. Most of the tick-borne diseases respond to doxycycline or tetracycline. Some dogs will have permanent joint damage.

Metabolic Bone Diseases

Hyperparathyroidism

The parathyroids are four small glands in the neck located near the thyroid gland. The parathyroid glands secrete the hormone PTH, which is essential to bone metabolism and blood calcium regulation.

Primary Hyperparathyroidism

This disease is rare in dogs. It is caused by tumors of the parathyroid glands that cause them to secrete excessive amounts of PTH. Middle-aged and older dogs are affected. The average age of onset is 10. Keeshonds seem to have a breed predisposition to this problem.

Signs are nonspecific and include loss of appetite, lethargy, excessive thirst, and frequent urination. Constipation, weakness, vomiting, muscle twitching, and a stiff gait have all been reported. The disease may not be suspected until a chemistry panel reveals a high serum calcium.

A primary parathyroid hyperplasia syndrome, in which all four parathyroid glands are enlarged, has been identified in German Shepherd Dog puppies. This is an inherited autosomal recessive trait.

Anal sac adenocarcinomas have the unique property of producing PTH, and thus are a rare cause of pseudohyperparathyroidism (see *Anal Sacs*, page 289).

The diagnosis of primary hyperparathyroidism can be confirmed by measuring PTH. The serum PTH is above normal in dogs with this disease.

Treatment: Surgical removal of the affected glands is the only possible treatment.

Renal Secondary Hyperparathyroidism

This is the end result of long-standing kidney disease that causes the body to retain phosphorus. The high serum phosphorus and low serum calcium stimulates the parathyroids to produce PTH. Symptoms similar to those of primary hyperparathyroidism are usually overshadowed by the kidney problem.

Treatment: Treatment is directed toward correcting the kidney disease, as described in *Kidney Failure*, page 423.

Nutritional Secondary Hyperparathyroidism

This disease (now rare) is caused by an excess of phosphorus or a deficiency of calcium in the diet. Vitamin D is required for calcium to be absorbed from the small intestine. Thus, a deficiency of vitamin D produces a deficiency of calcium. This can cause the parathyroid glands to produce more PTH.

One cause of nutritional secondary hyperparathyroidism is feeding a diet that consists primarily of organ meats, such as hearts, livers, or kidneys. Such diets are too high in phosphorus and too low in calcium and vitamin D. Other diets low in calcium are all-vegetable diets, corn bread diets, and diets containing leftover table scraps. *The disease does not occur in dogs who eat a nutritionally balanced diet.*

In puppies and young dogs, signs suggest skeletal problems and include lameness, bone pain, stunted growth, and spontaneous fractures. In adult dogs, nutritional secondary hyperthyroidism produces periodontal disease. Thinning of the jaws exposes the roots of teeth. The teeth then loosen and fall out.

Treatment: Correct the diet by feeding a high-quality balanced food—in the case of puppies, one advertised as supporting growth. Vitamin and mineral supplements should not be given unless prescribed by a veterinarian.

Affected puppies should be kept quiet and confined for the first few weeks to prevent fractures. Older dogs with advanced periodontal disease or intractable eating habits may not eat enough of their balanced food. These dogs need restorative dentistry and may require dietary supplements.

Hypertrophic Osteodystrophy

Hypertrophic osteodystrophy is a developmental disease that affects large- and giant-breed dogs 2 to 8 months of age. The cause is unknown.

Hypertrophic osteodystrophy targets the long bones close to the growth plates at the wrists and hocks. These areas become painful and give rise to lameness. The lameness ranges from mild to incapacitating. It often affects both front or both rear limbs. The bones are extremely warm, swollen, and painful to the touch. Affected dogs are reluctant to move. Some dogs develop high fever, depression, loss of appetite, and weight loss.

Bone X-rays show enlargement of the affected growth plate and increased density of bone adjacent to the growth plate. These findings distinguish hypertrophic osteodystrophy from panosteitis and other causes of lameness in growing pups.

Treatment: There is no specific treatment for hypertrophic osteodystrophy. Symptomatic therapy involves resting the dog and giving an NSAID, available through your veterinarian. Many pups do well with on antibiotics, and some are treated with prednisone as well.

Review the pup's diet with your veterinarian to be sure he is not being overfed; if he is, reduce caloric intake. Discontinue all vitamin supplements. Most affected puppies have one to two episodes of hypertrophic osteodystrophy and then recover, but permanent bone changes and physical deformities may develop.

Vitamin and Mineral Supplements

Contrary to popular belief, puppies do not need vitamin or mineral supplements for their normal growth and development. Modern name-brand commercial puppy foods are formulated to supply all the nutrients required to sustain normal growth—provided the puppy or young dog consumes the puppy food as the sole or main source of calories. More vitamins and minerals added to the diet will not add more substance or coat to the growing dog.

When calcium, phosphorus, and vitamin D are given in excess of a dog's capacity to use them, growth and development can be adversely affected. Overdosing with vitamin D causes bones to calcify in an uneven fashion. In addition, calcium may be deposited in the lungs, heart, and blood vessels.

Vitamin and mineral supplements are most effective when given to elderly dogs with poor eating habits who may have developed a specific deficiency. The appropriate dose of any supplement should be determined by your veterinarian.

THE URINARY SYSTEM

The urinary tract is made up of the kidneys, ureters, bladder, urethra, and, in the male, the prostate. (The male genitourinary system is shown below and the female system is shown on page 460.) There are two kidneys—one on either side of the backbone just behind the last rib. Each kidney has a renal pelvis, or funnel, that siphons the urine into a ureter. The ureters transport urine to the bladder. The bladder empties into the urethra. The opening of the urethra is found at the tip of the penis in the male and between the folds of the vulva in the female. In the male, the urethra also serves as the channel for semen. The prostate envelops the urethra just below the bladder. The top surface of the prostate can be felt by rectal examination.

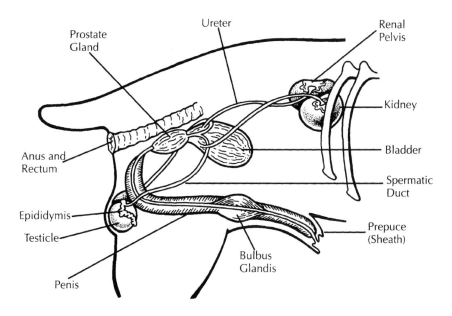

THE MALE GENITOURINARY SYSTEM

The chief functions of the kidneys are to regulate fluid, electrolyte, and acid-base balance, and to excrete the wastes of metabolism. This is accomplished by millions of nephrons, the basic working units of the kidneys. A nephron is composed of a globe of blood vessels (called the glomerulus) that filters waste from the blood plasma and passes it through a system of tubules that reabsorb water and electrolytes. This concentrates the waste liquid, which is now urine. Urine is normally yellow and clear. However, its appearance can be altered by the state of hydration and various drugs and diseases.

The decision to void or urinate is under the conscious control of the brain. Teaching a dog when to void is the basis for successful housetraining. Once the dog decides to urinate, the actual mechanism of emptying the bladder is carried out by a complicated spinal cord reflex.

Signs of Urinary Tract Disease

Most urinary tract disorders cause some disturbance in the normal pattern of voiding. There are a number of signs to look for.

Dysuria (Painful Urination)

Signs of dysuria are obvious distress during urination with straining, dribbling, licking at the penis or vulva, crying out in pain, voiding frequently in small amounts, squatting but not passing urine after many tries, and/or passing mucus, blood clots, or bloody urine. These signs indicate a disorder of the bladder, urethra, or prostate.

Pain and swelling in the lower abdomen suggest an overdistended bladder. A dog who does not pass urine after prolonged squatting or lifting of the leg is obstructed. This is usually caused by a stone, but could also be due to a tumor obstructing the urine flow.

Hematuria (Blood in the Urine)

Blood in the first portion of urine that clears with voiding indicates a problem in the urethra, penis, prostate, uterus, or vagina. Blood that appears at the end of voiding suggests a disease of the bladder or prostate. A uniformly bloody urine is seen with diseases of the kidneys, ureters, and bladder.

Bleeding without pain suggests kidney disease. Vaginal bleeding may give a false impression of hematuria. Microscopic hematuria means finding red blood cells on microscopic examination of urine that appears normal to the naked eye.

POLYURIA (EXCESSIVE URINATION)

Frequently passing large volumes of urine suggests kidney disease. The dog compensates by drinking large amounts of water. You may notice the increased thirst (polydipsia) first.

Other common causes of polyuria include diabetes mellitus, Cushing's syndrome, a pituitary tumor, hyperparathyroidism, and some types of poisoning. Polyuria should be distinguished from dysuria and urinary incontinence.

URINARY INCONTINENCE

Incontinent dogs void inappropriately, in many cases because they have lost voluntary control. Characteristic signs are wetting the bedding or floor where the dog has been sleeping, dribbling, sometimes frequent voiding, and voiding urine when excited or stressed. Incontinence is discussed on page 416.

Diagnosing Urinary Tract Diseases

Because of overlapping symptoms and the fact that more than one organ may be involved, it is difficult to make an exact diagnosis based on the symptoms alone. Laboratory tests can be of considerable help. Routine tests are urinalysis, which tells your veterinarian whether your dog has a urinary tract infection, and blood chemistries, which provide information about the function of the kidneys. Blood chemistries may include a BUN (blood urea nitrogen, which measure the efficiency of the kidney's filtering mechanisms. However, this value can be influenced by diet and other factors. Creatinine is another kidney function test.

Your veterinarian may ask you to bring in a urine specimen, which you can easily obtain by collecting a sample midstream in a plastic specimen container as the dog voids. These "free catch" samples may have some contamination from the dog's hair and penis or vulva. Sterile urine specimens are obtained by aspirating urine from the bladder with a sterile needle and syringe, called cystocentesis, or by passing a sterile catheter into the bladder through the urethra. This will be done by your veterinarian when it is important to culture the urine. A valuable urine test, called the UPC ratio, determines the urine protein:creatinine ratio—again showing the efficiency of the kidneys. The proportion of protein may also reflect inflammation or disease elsewhere in the body.

X-ray films of the abdomen are particularly useful in diagnosing stones. Abdominal ultrasonography is an excellent, noninvasive test that provides images of the kidneys, ureters, and bladder. An intravenous pyelogram (IVP) is an X-ray examination in which a dye is injected into a vein. The dye is excreted by the kidneys and outlines the renal pelvis and ureters. Other selective studies include *CT scan* and surgical exploration and biopsy of the kidneys or the bladder.

Diseases of the Bladder and Urethra

There are four basic problems, often interrelated, in the lower urinary tract. They are infection, obstruction, stones, and urinary incontinence.

CYSTITIS (BLADDER INFECTION)

Cystitis is a bacterial infection of the lining of the bladder. Urethral infections in both males and females often precede bouts of cystitis. Other predisposing causes include increasing age, diabetes mellitus, and being on long-term corticosteroid therapy. In sexually intact males there may be a preexisting prostatitis. Dogs who go long periods of time without eliminating have a greater risk of developing bladder infections.

Urinary stones can occur as a result of cystitis. The bacteria form a nidus (a central point) around which the stone develops.

The principal sign of cystitis is frequent, painful urination. The urine may appear cloudy and have an abnormal odor. Females with cystitis may lick at the vulva and have a vaginal discharge. The diagnosis is confirmed by a urinalysis showing bacteria, white blood cells, and often red blood cells in the urine.

Treatment: Cystitis should be treated promptly to prevent kidney infection. Your veterinarian will prescribe an oral antibiotic that is effective against the bacteria in question. Antibiotics are administered for two to three weeks, after which the urine should be checked again to be sure the infection has been eliminated.

Urinary acidifiers may be used to help prevent bacteria from adhering to the bladder wall. Blackberries and raspberries have compounds called ellagitannins that prevent bacterial adhesions to the bladder wall. Cranberries have a similar action, and all of these berries may help to lower urine pH. A second attack suggests a secondary problem, such as bladder stones, and the need for a veterinary workup. X-rays or an ultrasound may be done at this time. The second attack is treated with antibiotics selected on the basis of culture and sensitivity tests. A follow-up urine culture is obtained one to two months after discontinuing treatment. Chronic forms of cystitis may require the use of urinary antiseptics or long-term antibiotics given at bedtime.

Glucosamine and chondroitin sulfate have been shown to help some cats with recurrent urinary infections. These are safe supplements that might help dogs—although so far there is no evidence that they affect urinary tract problems in dogs.

Bladder and Urethral Stones

Kidney stones are rare in dogs. Bladder stones are common. Stones that form in the bladder may pass into the urethra. All dogs can develop bladder stones. Breeds with an increased incidence include the Miniature Schnauzer, Dalmatian, Shih Tzu, Dachshund, and Bulldog.

Bladder and urethral stones may be large or small, single or multiple, and may pass spontaneously or obstruct the lower urinary tract. Stones in the bladder eventually cause painful urination and blood in the urine.

Most bladder stones are struvites (that is, they're composed of magnesium ammonium phosphate). They form in an alkaline urine and are usually preceded by a bladder infection. The bacteria and urinary sediment form a nidus around which the ammonium phosphate is deposited.

Uric acid stones form in an acid urine, and are frequently associated with inherited alterations in urate metabolism. Dalmatians and Bulldogs are genetically predisposed.

Other stones are calcium oxalate and cystine stones. Cystine crystals have been found in Newfoundlands and many other breeds. There is a genetic test offered by VetGen, OptiGen, and PennGen to detect carriers and affected dogs with this problem. Silica stones are rare; they occur most often in male German Shepherd Dogs. These stones are not usually associated with a preexisting bladder infection.

Stones that are large or numerous can sometimes be palpated through the abdomen. In most cases the diagnosis is made by X-ray. A contrast dye study may be needed for definitive diagnosis. Stones not visible on an abdominal X-ray can often be seen by *ultrasonography* or IVP. A urinalysis is routinely obtained.

Stones that pass spontaneously and those that are removed surgically should be analyzed, if possible, since the composition of the stone influences the treatment of any remaining and future stones.

Treatment: Bladder infection, if present, is treated as described for *Cystitis* (page 414). In many cases the stones can be dissolved over weeks or months by feeding the dog a special diet. Struvite stones dissolve in an acid urine, requiring a diet low in magnesium and protein—accomplished by feeding Hill's Prescription Diet s/d, or Royal Canin Urinary SO 13. Uric acid stones respond to a low-purine diet (Hill's u/d), along with the drug allopurinol. Cystine stones also respond to Hill's u/d, along with drugs that dissolve cystine. Feeding a vegetarian diet, such as Royal Canin Vegetarian Formula, may help prevent urate stones. There are no methods currently available for dissolving calcium oxalate and silica stones. However, diets and supplements can be used to reduce the risk of recurrence.

Surgical removal is the treatment of choice for urethral stones that cause obstruction (see *Obstructed Bladder*, page 416) and for bladder stones that fail to respond to a diet change and medication. Surgery is also indicated when medical treatment is contraindicated because of congestive heart failure, or when there is a need for more rapid resolution of symptoms.

The formation of new stones occurs in up to 30 percent of cases. The dog should be seen and checked at regular intervals. Your veterinarian may recommend long-term dietary changes and/or the addition of supplements such as vitamin C, raspberry seed extracts, or cranberry extracts.

Obstructed Bladder

A stone is the most common cause of an obstructed bladder. Tumors and strictures are less common causes. Enlargement of the prostate gland is a rare cause of bladder obstruction in male dogs.

A dog with an obstructed bladder is acutely uncomfortable or in dire distress. Males and females often assume a peculiar splay-legged stance while attempting to void. A partial blockage can be suspected when the dog dribbles urine, voids frequently, and has a weak, splattery stream.

A partial obstruction, left untreated, may become a complete obstruction. With a complete obstruction no urine is passed. The lower abdomen becomes swollen and tender to pressure, and it feels as if there is a large ball in front of the pelvis. Note that the continuous straining associated with an obstructed bladder can be mistaken for constipation.

Treatment: A dog with a partial obstruction due to a urethral stone may pass the stone spontaneously. Treatment thereafter is similar to that described for *Bladder and Urethral Stones*, page 415.

A *complete obstruction is an acute emergency.* Take your dog at once to the veterinarian. If the blockage is not relieved, the dog will go into kidney failure or the bladder could rupture. Often the stone can be pushed back into the bladder using a sterile catheter, or by infusing water under pressure into the urethra. If not, surgical removal will be necessary.

Urinary Incontinence

Incontinence is loss of voluntary control over the act of voiding. This medical condition must to be differentiated from a housetraining problem and/or submissive urination, especially in young dogs. Incontinent dogs wet their bed or the floor where they are sleeping, urinate inappropriately in the house, sometimes dribble urine, and may void more frequently than normal. There may be an ammonialike odor about the dog's bedding. The skin around the penis or vulva may be scalded.

There are several types of urinary incontinence.

Hormone-Responsive Incontinence

This common incontinence is seen most often in middle-aged and older spayed females, and less commonly in young females and older neutered males. It is caused by a deficiency of estrogen in females and testosterone in males. Both these hormones are important in maintaining muscle tone of the urethral sphincter.

Hormone-responsive incontinence is much like bedwetting. The dog urinates normally, but wets when relaxed or asleep.

Treatment: Hormone-responsive incontinence in spayed females is treated by giving phenylpropanolamine, a drug that increases the tone of the urethral sphincter. Diethylstilbestrol (estrogen) can be given if phenylpropanolamine is not successful. However, diethylstilbestrol is no longer the first choice for treatment because of the risk of bone marrow suppression. Phenylpropanolamine is periodically taken off the market, because it is also used in human diet supplements and can be abused. If it unavailable, your veterinarian will work with you to use the lowest dose possible of estrogen to control your dog's incontinence.

Incontinence in neutered males responds well to giving the dog testosterone. Phenylpropanolamine has also been used successfully in males.

Submissive Urination

This is another common problem, characterized by the release of urine caused by contraction of the abdominal wall muscles along with relaxation of the muscles that support the urethra—the normal voiding process. The dog passes small amounts of urine when she is upset or in a stressful situation. It has also been called stress incontinence. This is most common in young puppies in their new homes, and many will simply outgrow it.

Treatment: Submissive urination can be treated with phenylpropanolamine and/or other drugs that increase urethral tone while behavior modification techniques are applied. Keep stress-provoking interactions low key and brief, and avoid bending over the dog or making direct eye contact with her. Do not punish the dog, as this makes the incontinence worse. Working with a dog trainer or canine behaviorist is recommended to address this behavioral issue.

Neurogenic Incontinence

Spinal cord injuries, infections, tumors, and inherited neuropathies can interfere with the nerves that control the bladder. A bladder with a compromised nerve supply lacks muscle tone and cannot contract. The bladder continues to fill until the pressure exceeds the resistance of the sphincter mechanism that closes the urethra. This results in intermittent, uncontrolled dribbling.

Neurogenic incontinence can be confirmed with a cystometrogram. This is a test that measures how forcefully the bladder contracts in response to the introduction of incremental volumes of fluid into it through a catheter. The results also suggest the site of the neurologic deficit (the spinal cord or the bladder).

Treatment: Neurogenic incontinence is treated with long-term catheterization and antibiotics to treat and suppress infection. Drugs that act on the bladder may be of help. This type of incontinence is difficult to treat. The problem may totally resolve, however, in dogs whose spinal cord injuries have been successfully treated.

Incontinence from Overdistension of the Bladder

This type of incontinence is due to a partially obstructed bladder, caused by urethral stones, tumor, or stricture. The signs and symptoms are similar to those of neurogenic incontinence, but the nerve supply to the bladder is undamaged.

Treatment: Dribbling associated with an overdistended bladder is treated by correcting the cause of the obstruction and placing an indwelling catheter until the bladder regains its muscular tone. Drug therapy is also beneficial. Since the bladder is neurologically normal, treatment may eliminate the problem entirely.

Kidney Failure

Dogs with failing kidneys are unable to concentrate their urine. They have a large urinary output and must drink more than usual to replace fluid losses. If they are not allowed to go outside to urinate as often as necessary, they may begin to urinate in the house. It is important to check kidney function in all incontinent dogs to be sure the incontinence is not due to kidney failure.

Treatment: Treatment of kidney failure is discussed on page 425.

Other Causes of Incontinence

Another cause of incontinence is ectopic ureters. Females are eight times more likely to suffer from this congenital problem than males. One or both ureters may enter the vagina instead of the bladder. There is then continuous drainage of urine into the vagina. The incontinence of ectopic ureters is present from birth, but becomes more noticeable at 3 to 6 months of age when housetraining should be complete. Breeds with a predisposition include White West Highland Terriers, Fox Terriers, and Miniature and Toy Poodles. Siberian Huskies and Labrador Retrievers may also have a familial predisposition.

Incontinence in bitches shortly after spaying is usually caused by postoperative pelvic adhesions.

Treatment: Both an ectopic ureter and pelvic adhesions may be corrected surgically.

Enlarged Prostate

The prostate is an accessory sex gland in males that completely surrounds the urethra at the neck of the bladder. The prostate produces fluid that is added to the ejaculate when a male dog mates. This fluid provides nutrients and assists in the sperm's movement. The three conditions that cause prostatic enlargement are benign prostatic hyperplasia, prostatitis, and cancer of the prostate.

The diagnosis of prostate enlargement is made by digital rectal examination, during which the size, position, and firmness of the prostate gland is assessed. *Ultrasonography* provides additional information and may be helpful in guiding a needle into the prostate to obtain a biopsy—a procedure indicated when cancer is suspected.

BENIGN PROSTATIC HYPERPLASIA

This is an increase in the size of the prostate gland. The disease is hormone-dependent and is influenced by testosterone. Benign prostatic hyperplasia begins in sexually intact males at about 5 years of age and progresses as the dog grows older. Thus, older dogs are more likely to have symptoms.

As the prostate enlarges, it gradually expands backward and may eventually obstruct the rectum, causing constipation and straining while defecating (see *Anorectal Obstructions*, page 287). The feces may appear flat or ribbon-like. Defecation is difficult. Fecal impactions are common.

Rarely, the prostate pushes forward and presses on the urethra, causing straining during urination. Blood in the urine can be a sign of benign prostatic hyperplasia.

Treatment: Treatment is not necessary unless the dog has symptoms. Neutering eliminates the stimulus for prostatic enlargement and is the treatment of choice for dogs who are not intended for breeding. A significant decrease in the size of the prostate gland occurs shortly after neutering.

An alternative to neutering is to administer megestrol acetate (Megace), a synthetic derivative of progesterone. Megace decreases the size of the prostate without impairing fertility, but long-term use may cause a dog to develop diabetes mellitus or adrenal problems. Note that estrogens, because of their potentially serious side effects, are no longer recommended for treating benign prostatic hyperplasia.

PROSTATITIS

Prostatitis is a bacterial infection of the prostate gland, usually preceded by a bout of cystitis. Signs of acute prostatitis are fever, depression, vomiting, diarrhea, and painful urination. The dog may have an arched back or a tucked-up abdomen. Blood-tinged or purulent secretions may drip from the prepuce. The prostate gland is enlarged, swollen, and tender.

The disease can become chronic, with periodic flare-ups. Chronic prostatitis is a significant cause of male infertility.

Treatment: Your veterinarian may want to collect prostatic secretions for culture and *cytology*. Once the diagnosis is made, the dog is placed on an oral antibiotic selected on the basis of culture and sensitivity tests. Antibiotics have difficulty penetrating the swollen prostate, so long-term administration is necessary.

Following treatment, the prostatic fluid should be recultured to ensure that the infection has been eliminated. Neutering helps to resolve symptoms and decreases the likelihood of recurrent prostatitis.

Prostate surgery may be necessary for dogs with serious complications, such as prostatic abscess.

PROSTATE CANCER

This type of cancer is rare in dogs. It is not influenced by testosterone, so it can occur in both neutered and intact male dogs.

Treatment: This involves surgery and/or radiation therapy. In most cases the disease is far advanced by the time it is diagnosed. Because prostate cancer in dogs is not testosterone-dependent, neutering does not slow the progress of the disease. Similarly, neutering does not protect against the development of prostate cancer.

Kidney Disease
CONGENITAL KIDNEY PROBLEMS

Congenital kidney problems are kidney problems that are present at birth. The actual signs of kidney failure may not immediately be apparent, but the process leading to the kidney problem is present—perhaps just a genetic defect or damaged tissue. Some congenital problems are hereditary, while others are a result of trauma *in utero* or at whelping, or the effects of chemicals or drugs the dam was exposed to while the pups were *in utero*.

A congenital kidney problem may involve both kidneys or just one. Dogs can do very well with just one healthy kidney.

Polycystic Kidney Disease

Dogs with this disease have multiple cysts on one or both kidneys. Depending on the degree of normal tissue versus cystic tissue, a dog may show minimal signs or be in renal failure. The disease is often diagnosed by ultrasound.

Cairn Terriers seem to have familial predisposition to this problem, along with Beagles. Bull Terriers have an autosomal dominant version of polycystic kidney disease.

Treatment: There is no medical treatment specifically for cystic kidneys — you simply manage the kidney failure as described on page 425. A kidney transplant would be an option if both kidneys are severely affected.

Renal Dysplasia

Renal dysplasia is a problem with the development of the tissues of the kidney itself. Depending on what tissues are malformed, kidney failure of various types and severity will result. Urine may not be concentrated or certain nutrients may not be retained.

Dogs start to show increased urination and drinking at 6 to 24 months of age. If the problem is unilateral, the dog may appear normal throughout her life, as long as the remaining kidney stays healthy. A kidney biopsy is the only way to definitively diagnose this problem.

Most dogs inherit this condition as an autosomal recessive gene, so both parents could be carriers and both sexes can be affected. In Samoyeds, it is an X-linked trait, which means many more males show clinical signs than females.

Renal dysplasia has been identified in more than 20 breeds, including Alaskan Malamutes, Cocker Spaniels, Lhasa Apsos, Shih Tzus, Miniature Schnauzers, Soft Coated Wheaten Terriers, Standard Poodles, Keeshonds, and Norwegian Elkhounds. VetGen offers a genetic test for Lhasa Apsos, Shih Tzus, and Soft Coated Wheaten Terriers.

Treatment: The only treatment is to follow the guidelines for kidney failure described on page 425. A kidney transplant could be considered if severe kidney failure develops.

Protein-Losing Nephropathy

In dogs with this disease, the filtering mechanism of the kidneys is defective and the body loses protein. One of the first signs is increased urination and drinking. Excess protein in the urine may be picked up by a urinalysis.

There appears to be an *immune-mediated* component to this illness. Breeds with a predisposition include Soft Coated Wheaten Terriers, Bernese Mountain Dogs, Labrador Retrievers, and Golden Retrievers.

Treatment: Treatment is aimed at controlling the kidney failure, as described on page 425.

Amyloidosis

In dogs with amyloidosis, the protein amyloid is deposited in the kidney, interfering with normal functions by blocking the normal filter mechanisms, leading to dilute urine and/or protein loss in the urine. This disease can be seen in any breed, but is a particular problem for many Chinese Shar-Peis. In this breed, the problem tends to begin before 5 years of age with swollen joints and high fevers that come and go in a cyclic pattern.

Treatment: Colchicine, a drug that reduces the inflammation caused by excess uric acid, may help as a treatment, along with supportive care for kidney failure.

Fanconi Syndrome

Fanconi syndrome is an impairment in the function of the kidney that causes certain compounds which should be absorbed into the bloodstream by the kidneys to be excreted in the urine instead. Compounds that may be lost in the urine include glucose, amino acids, uric acid, and phosphate. Loss of these compounds can cause problems such as failure to grow and bone abnormalities. When too much bicarbonate is excreted in the urine, excess acid can build up in the blood.

The disease can be seen in any breed of dog, but Basenjis have a breed predisposition. Many dogs first show signs at 4 to 8 years of age. With the dramatic nutrient loss, these dogs will rapidly lose condition and die unless they are treated.

Treatment: Regular supplements can help replace the lost nutrients. Bicarbonate is especially important due to the problems with the acid-base balance.

PYELONEPHRITIS (KIDNEY INFECTION)

Pyelonephritis is a bacterial infection of the kidney, including the renal pelvis and ureter. Most cases are caused by an ascending bladder infection. There may be a predisposing blockage or congenital malformation of the urinary tract. Occasionally, the infection is blood-borne.

Acute pyelonephritis begins with fever, loss of appetite, vomiting, and pain in the lower back. A stiff-legged gait and a hunched-up posture are characteristic. Some dogs exhibit signs of painful urination. On microscopic examination, the urine contains white blood cell casts, which are plugs of cells expelled from kidney tubules. An IVP or renal ultrasound may show an enlarged kidney or a dilated renal pelvis.

Chronic pyelonephritis is an insidious disease that may or may not be preceded by an acute pyelonephritis. Signs are loss of appetite, weight loss, and excessive urination and thirst. This disease smolders for months or years, eventually culminating in kidney failure. Early treatment of acute pyelonephritis may prevent this.

Treatment: Kidney infection is difficult to eliminate and relapse is common. Any underlying predisposing causes should be dealt with. Pyelonephritis is treated with antibiotics selected on the basis of bacterial sensitivity tests. Antibiotics should be continued for six to eight weeks. The urine should be recultured during treatment to be sure the antibiotic selected is still effective against the bacteria in question.

After treatment, it is important to reculture the urine on three separate occasions at six- to eight-week intervals before concluding that the dog is cured.

NEPHRITIS AND NEPHROSIS

Nephritis and nephrosis are diseases of the kidneys that produce scarring and kidney failure. The diagnosis of nephritis or nephrosis is established by kidney biopsy.

Nephritis is an inflammatory process associated with certain infectious diseases, including canine hepatitis, canine ehrlichiosis, Lyme disease, Rocky Mountain spotted fever, and others. Dogs with systemic lupus erythematosus and chronic pancreatitis can develop nephritis. A familial predisposition for a condition called glomerulonephritis occurs in Doberman Pinschers, Samoyeds, and Bull Terriers. In Bull Terriers this is an autosomal dominant problem.

Nephrosis is the result of degenerative changes caused by toxins and poisons that target the kidneys or by ischemia (inadequate blood flow to the kidneys). The most important nephrotoxins are aspirin, ibuprofen, and butazolidin. Certain antibiotics are nephrotoxic, particularly when given for prolonged periods or in high doses. They include polymyxin B, gentamicin, amphotericin B, and kanamycin.

The nephrotic syndrome may develop in dogs with nephritis or nephrosis. Large amounts of protein are excreted into the urine from the damaged kidneys. In consequence, serum protein levels are low. This results in loss of fluid from the blood, which pools in the legs (*edema*), the abdominal cavity (*ascites*), and the chest cavity (*pleural effusion*). The swollen limbs and potbellied appearance of the nephrotic syndrome suggest right-sided congestive heart failure, but laboratory studies will distinguish between this condition and kidney problems.

Treatment: If caught in time, nephritis and nephrosis respond to elimination of the predisposing cause. For treatment of the nephrotic syndrome, see *Uremia*, page 424. Nephritis caused by Lyme disease is usually fatal.

UREMIA (KIDNEY FAILURE)

Kidney failure is defined as the inability of the kidneys to remove waste products from the blood. The buildup of toxins produces the signs and symptoms of uremic poisoning. Kidney failure can appear suddenly (acute kidney failure) or come on gradually over months. Most cases are of the gradual onset type and are caused by nephritis and nephrosis.

Causes of acute kidney failure include:

• Complete urinary tract obstruction caused by a stone

• Rupture of the bladder or urethra

• Shock, with inadequate blood flow to the kidneys

• Congestive heart failure with low blood pressure and reduced blood flow to the kidneys

- Poisoning, especially from antifreeze
- Lyme disease
- Leptospirosis

Dogs with kidney failure do not show signs of uremia until 75 percent of functioning kidney tissue is destroyed. Thus, a considerable amount of damage occurs before the signs are noticed.

Signs of Kidney Failure

One of the first things you may notice is that your dog drinks and urinates more than usual and indicates her need to go outside to eliminate several times a day. If not allowed to do so, the dog may begin to have housetraining accidents in the house. These signs are due to the failure of the kidneys to concentrate the urine. This results in a large urine output over which the dog has no control, with subsequent dehydration and thirst.

As kidney function declines, the dog retains ammonia, nitrogen, acids, and other chemical wastes in her blood and tissues. This is called uremia. The degree of uremia is determined by measuring serum blood urea nitrogen (BUN), creatinine, and electrolytes.

Signs of uremia are apathy and depression, loss of appetite and weight, a dry haircoat, a brownish discoloration to the surface of the tongue, and an ammonialike odor to the breath. Dogs at this stage may urinate less than normal. Ulcers may arise in the mouth. With the nephrotic syndrome the dog develops ascites and edema. Vomiting, diarrhea, and gastrointestinal bleeding may occur. At the end stages of kidney failure, the dog falls into a coma.

A condition called rubber jaw may be seen with chronic kidney failure. It is characterized by loosening of the teeth and ulcerations of the mouth and gums. This can also occur with a diet low in calcium or an imbalance of calcium and phosphorus.

Your veterinarian may wish to make an exact diagnosis by performing exploratory surgery and biopsy of the kidney, or doing an ultrasound-guided biopsy. This helps to guide treatment and determine whether the disease is treatable.

Treating Kidney Failure

Dogs with kidney failure require periodic monitoring of blood chemistries to detect changes in kidney function that may require medical intervention. A most important step is to restrict salt intake. This helps prevent edema, ascites, and hypertension.

Protein is poorly metabolized by dogs with kidney failure, but what to do about protein levels in the diet is currently an area of controversy. Some veterinarians believe a diet rich in meat, or one that contains poor-quality protein, creates an increased nitrogen load that must be handled by the liver and kidneys. Dogs with weak kidneys can be thrown into uremia by feeding them more protein than they can handle. Other veterinarians believe that as long as the protein is of high biological value, it will help the kidneys retain their function. Diet may need to be customized to the individual dog.

Restricting phosphorus intake is agreed upon by all. Medications to lower phosphorus levels may be required along with dietary adjustments.

There are prescription diets available from your veterinarian that can relieve some of the symptoms of kidney failure and help control it. These include Hill's k/d, Eukanuba Early and Advanced Stage, and Purina NF.

It is extremely important to provide fresh water at all times. The dog must be able to take in enough water to compensate for her large urine output. Some dogs will need occasional boosts to their fluid intake. This can be done by giving subcutaneous (known as sub-Q or SQ) fluids. With most dogs, their owners can learn how to do this at home. In the later stages of kidney failure, dogs may need sub-Q fluids daily.

B vitamins are lost in the urine of uremic dogs. These losses should be replaced by giving vitamin B supplements. Sodium bicarbonate tablets may be prescribed by your veterinarian to correct an acid-base imbalance. A phosphorous binder, such as Amphogel, may be recommended to lower the serum phosphorus.

A dog who becomes dehydrated because of illness or failure to drink enough water may decompensate suddenly, a condition called a uremic crisis. The dog should be hospitalized and rehydrated with intravenous fluids and balanced electrolyte solutions.

Some types of kidney failure are acute, and are mild enough that if the dog is well supported medically, there will be a complete recovery. More commonly, dogs will have at least some renal function deficit and need a change in care for the rest of their lives. With chronic renal failure, there is no cure; the disease must be controlled as well as possible for the rest of the dog's life.

Two other treatment options, dialysis and kidney transplant, are described in the sections that follow.

DIALYSIS

Dialysis describes two therapies that try to duplicate the filtering tasks of the kidneys. In peritoneal dialysis, special fluid is put into the abdomen using a catheter. The fluid then washes tissues and absorbs toxins from the body across tissue barriers. After a set period of time, the fluid is removed through the same catheter, taking the toxins out with it. This technique has been used in veterinary referral centers for short-term kidney problems such as antifreeze poisonings.

Hemodialysis is the second technique. This therapy is only available at a few referral centers across the country, because the equipment is expensive and must be specially designed to work with dogs. The dog's blood is circulated through a machine with filters that tries to duplicate the filtering tasks of a healthy kidney. Special catheters are required and dogs need treatments of three to four hours, up to three times a week. This is a very expensive therapy and is ideally only needed for short-term problems such as poisoning or leptospirosis—giving the dog's own kidneys time to heal. Dogs with chronic kidney failure have been maintained on hemodialysis for up to one year, but that is unusual.

KIDNEY TRANSPLANT

Another option for dogs with terminal kidney failure is to consider a kidney transplant. Kidney transplants are only done a few veterinary referral centers, but are becoming more common. As with human transplant patients, drugs must be given post-transplant to prevent organ rejection. These drugs are quite expensive and must be carefully calibrated to minimize side effects.

The current method for finding kidney donors is to test shelter dogs for tissue compatibility. The shelter dog then donates one kidney; dogs, like people; can do fine with just one healthy kidney. The shelter dog is then adopted by the family of the recipient dog, who have to agree ahead of time to provide a home for the donor dog for the rest of her life.

SEX AND REPRODUCTION

Selective breeding for many centuries has resulted in the establishment of well-defined dog breeds that are based on features such as head type, overall size, coat, color, and body structure. The development of different breeds has been possible because of a phenomenon called genetic mutation. Mutations occur spontaneously, often for reasons unknown. A mutation changes encoded information in a gene, which results in the addition or deletion of an enzyme or protein that may perform an important cellular function. When a mutation arises in an egg or a sperm cell, it affects all the cells in the embryo and, if the animal survives, the mutation is passed on to future generations.

The majority of mutations are detrimental in that they do something that interferes with the animal's ability to adapt to his environment. In nature, such mutations usually do not become part of the gene pool, because the individuals possessing them do not survive to pass on their genes.

As wild dogs became dependent on humans for survival, matings between the most highly adapted and competitive animals gave way to a system in which breeding partners were selected by their owners for specific reasons. When mutations occurred, they often changed the appearance of the dog, but may also have given the dog a better sense of smell or the ability to burrow in pursuit of rodents. By selectively breeding such dogs to others of similar type or attribute, over a long period of time humans were able to create hundreds of breeds as diverse as St. Bernards, Chihuahuas, Pugs, and Salukis. Despite differences, these are all still dogs and are capable (at least in theory) of interbreeding.

Unfortunately, selective breeding has also resulted in the appearance of a number of genetic diseases, involving most of the organs and systems discussed throughout this book. (All of these mutations may also be seen in mixed-breed dogs, as well.) Sadly, these diseases are accepted and tolerated as part of some breed packages, even though they weaken the species and have ethical as well as financial consequences to dog breeders and owners. Inherited diseases can, however, be controlled (and in some cases even eliminated) through informed breeding practices.

The Basics of Genetics

Heredity is the result of the random combination of countless genes. In the canine *genome* there are 39 pairs of chromosomes (for a total of 78 chromosomes) and about 80,000 genes. Chromosomes are strands of DNA that contain a sequence of genes. When chromosomes pair up, their corresponding genes also pair up. The gene pair then determines the expression of a particular trait.

The sire and dam contribute equally to the genetic makeup of their offspring. Unlike other cells in the body, as the egg and sperm cells are formed, 39 chromosomes are retained and 39 are discarded. So each germ cell contains 39 single chromosomes. It is a matter of chance which chromosomes will be retained and which discarded. When the egg and sperm combine during fertilization, the 39 chromosomes in the egg and 39 in the sperm join up to form 39 pairs in the fertilized embryo.

Because the egg and the sperm each contribute one of two chromosomes to every pair, the possible number of combinations for a given chromosome pair is four. Similarly, the number of gene pair possibilities at any specific site is limited to four. However, if you consider the genetic potential of the breed as a whole, the number of different pair combinations that theoretically could occur at a specific site is twice the number of reproducing individuals in the breed. So the greater the number of reproducing individuals in the breed, the greater the genetic diversity of that breed.

A breed with a large population of unrelated dogs is genetically diverse. This is good, because reproductive efficiency and survival are high in genetically diverse populations. It also means breed clubs with only a few foundation animals, which have not been able to bring in new blood, or breeds in which a few closely related individuals are frequently bred, face problems.

INHERITING PROBLEM GENES

Overall, about one out of every 100 puppies will have a demonstrable congenital defect. Some undesirable hereditary traits commonly seen in dogs include undescended testicles, inguinal and umbilical hernias, abnormally short or absent tails, congenital heart defects, canine hip and elbow dysplasia, luxating patella, wobbler syndrome, malocclusion and incorrect bite, bleeding diseases, congenital deafness, entropion and ectropion, Collie eye anomaly, progressive retinal atrophy, glaucoma, congenital cataracts, idiopathic epilepsy, and behavioral disorders such as inherited aggression and shyness. This list is by no means complete.

A number of undesirable traits are carried by *recessive* genes. Traits controlled by recessive genes are not expressed unless both genes in the gene pair carry that trait. A recessive gene can be carried down through many generations of offspring, causing no problem until it is combined with a like recessive gene. Simple recessive disorders are relatively easy to control if there is a genetic test for the carriers. If there is no test, control is difficult.

Disorders caused by dominant genes are much easier to control, because all carriers of the genes are clinically affected. Breeders can choose not to breed such individuals and their offspring, thus eliminating the problem from their breeding stock. Sometimes these problems do not show up until later in life, however, and by then a dog may have been bred. So even problems caused by dominant genes may survive in a population.

However, simple dominant or recessive genes do not cause the majority of hereditary problems in purebred dogs. Most of the traits that breeders are interested in are *polygenic*—that is, they are controlled by multiple genes, the majority of which are unknown. Hip dysplasia, for example, is considered to be a polygenic trait because defects in muscles, ligaments, and bones must be present for dysplasia to occur.

Genetic disorders for which there is no specific genetic test can be identified and their mode of inheritance determined through test breedings and pedigree analysis. Knowing which animals in a pedigree were affected by an inherited disease makes it possible to predict whether a specific individual is at high or low risk for transmitting the disease. This helps greatly in selecting breeding stock. For example, in progressive retinal atrophy, which in some cases is controlled by a simple autosomal recessive gene, both parents must carry a defective gene for a puppy to be affected. Therefore, if a puppy does have PRA, it can be deduced that both parents were at least carriers and may even have had the disease. Other offspring of either of the two parents, and any siblings or half-siblings of the affected puppy, would be highly suspect of carrying the defective gene.

For genetic disorders caused by more than one gene, there is no way to tell whether a dog who tests normal for the disease is a carrier. The probability that the dog is a carrier increases if some of his immediate relatives have the disease. It is important to know whether his littermates, his sire and dam, and their littermates were affected. The breadth of the pedigree is more important than its depth. In other words, you want to know more about the health status of the extended family, as opposed to looking many generations into the past.

One problem is that even when the frequency of a disease is high in immediate relatives, some offspring who test normal will be carriers and some will not. If there is no genetic test for the carrier state, some genetically normal dogs who may be superior examples of the breed may not be used for breeding, because of their family history. In addition, in breeds where the gene pool is rather small, eliminating normal dogs from breeding can adversely affect genetic diversity.

Health information on the pedigrees of normal and affected animals is difficult to obtain, but may be available through open registries such as the Institute for Genetic Disease Control in Animals (GDC), registries sponsored by breed clubs, or in specific cases through the records of dedicated breeders who are willing to share that information. OFA now offers dog owners the option of making test results open.

In an open registry, the results of a dog's tests are available to anyone who makes an inquiry. This provides a real service to the public, but many breeders are understandably reluctant to come forward with information that might reflect badly on their breeding programs. Further education and acceptance of the fact that hereditary problems are a concern for all should result in more widespread sharing of this information. Enlightened breed clubs are already moving in this direction.

Certification by the Orthopedic Foundation for Animals (OFA), Canine Eye Registry Foundation (CERF), or the GDC indicates that a dog shows no clinical signs of having the diseases for which he or she has been tested (see appendix D). OFA now has checkoffs for owners to allow their dog's information to be made available to the public. AKC pedigrees now show OFA and CERF certifications. A pedigree that contains such certifications indicates a low probability of transmitting the disease. As a general rule, *the greater the number of normal relatives in a dog's pedigree, the less likely it is that the dog will carry and transmit a heritable disease*.

Carrier dogs can sometimes be identified by a blood-based DNA test, such as the test used for PRA in Irish Setters. However, these tests are available only for certain diseases in certain breeds. The canine genome has now been mapped, so that researchers will be able to isolate defective genes and sites that affect certain traits more easily. As more is known about the canine genome (and this will take several years), newer methods should become available to test for and treat genetic diseases. Already the number of genetic tests available is growing.

Breeding Purebred Dogs

It is important to begin with a mental picture of what you are trying to accomplish. A through knowledge of the breed standard is the most basic requirement. Beyond the standard, however, there is an elusive something extra, a certain almost extra-sensory perception that gives success to those who have it.

A successful breeder is one who knows the virtues and faults of all the dogs in a pedigree for four generations. He or she will have the judgment to pick the best puppies and the willingness to eliminate as breeding stock all defective or substandard animals.

Knowledge of this sort does not come quickly or easily. You need to learn everything you can about your breed, especially the bloodlines from which you plan to choose your stock. Visit as many kennels as you can, talk to the owners and see the tried-and-true producers, the winners, and the retired dogs.

Keep in mind that a pedigree ensures only that the dogs are registered with the AKC or a similar organization and are the breed they seem to be. It does not testify to the quality of the dogs in question. Pedigrees are important because they are the means to study bloodlines and learn the relationships among dogs of a particular breed. They are of greatest value when the dogs are known to you or have actually been seen. The contribution of a superior dog who appears several times in a pedigree can be determined mathematically. Now that pedigrees, such as those from AKC, include some health certifications, the pedigree will be more helpful for health studies.

Some registries are now requiring a DNA profile before a dog is bred, so that parentage can be verified. This is done with a cheek swab. This helps ensure that pedigrees are correct.

You will notice that the successful breeder is the one who sees faults in his or her own dogs as readily as those in a rival's. Perhaps the little "something extra" is the good sense to breed with the *whole* dog in mind—not to emphasize one particular attribute at the expense of the overall dog.

FOLLOWING BLOODLINES

A conscientious breeding program seeks to maintain and improve the quality of the breed. Dogs who are poor examples of breed type should be avoided in favor of those who are excellent examples. *When outstanding dogs are bred repeatedly to dogs of similar type, the type becomes fixed and the line breeds true.*

In essence, this is the strategy behind most planned breeding programs. The relationship between the various breeding individuals is kept relatively close in order to concentrate the desired genes in the offspring. This method is called inbreeding.

Inbreeding involves mating parent to offspring and full brother to full sister. A variation on inbreeding, called linebreeding, breeds individuals who are closely related through a common ancestor. Skillful linebreeding is the best method for perpetuating desired characteristics.

Inbreeding and linebreeding expose both good and bad qualities in the animals being bred. If the line carries undesirable traits, this becomes evident after a few generations. While this may seem a disaster, in the long run the exposure of such traits is in the best interests of the breed. By choosing not to breed affected animals and their relatives, the undesirable trait can be eliminated from the bloodline.

A common misconception is that inbreeding causes high-strung, nervous, or aggressive dogs. However, it is not the breeding process but the genetic potential in the bloodline that determines the animal's temperament. A kennel that uses unstable dogs in its breeding program is likely to have problems. One that uses fundamentally sound dogs produces sound dogs.

Close breeding for three or four generations generally fixes type in a line, after which further improvement becomes more difficult because of uniformity and loss of genetic diversity. In fact, the overall effect of uninterrupted linebreeding is a decline in reproductive fitness. Fewer litters are produced, the number of pups in the litter decreases, and some of the puppies fail to thrive. Most breeders have found that it is wise at this stage to bring in new breeding animals.

Using a stud dog from a totally different line may be considered. This produces an outcrossed litter and reshuffles the genes that have tended to become more or less fixed. Many times, particularly with an overly refined bitch, an outcross gives surprisingly good results. An improvement in the health and vigor of the resulting puppies may be noted from birth.

While an outcross litter sometimes lacks uniformity, some very good show dogs have been produced in this way. Puppies from such matings usually are bred back into the line of either the sire or dam, thereby recapturing the benefits of previous linebreeding.

The third and final strategy is to breed a dog and a bitch who are unrelated and of varied ancestry. In other words, neither animal has a linebred background. With this approach, it is essential that the breeder have a definite goal in mind. One dog may carry an attribute or quality that is totally lacking in the other. However, mating animals of such genetically diverse backgrounds in the hope of finding show-quality puppies is rarely rewarding. Even if outstanding puppies are produced from such matings, it is unlikely their offspring will be of similar quality.

THE BROOD BITCH

In general, it is best to begin your breeding program with a show-quality bitch rather than a male. This way, you have the flexibility to breed to stud dogs who best complement her qualities. In addition, if the litters are outstanding, you have foundation stock on which to base your bloodlines.

Before making a decision to breed your female, carefully consider the effort and expense that goes into producing a litter of healthy and active puppies. It can be both time consuming and expensive. Many pedigreed puppies cannot be sold locally because there aren't enough buyers. This means advertising and the effort and cost of finding just the right home in which to place the pups.

A reputable breeder is responsible for the puppies they breed for their entire lifetime. So if a dog you bred is in a family who is undergoing a divorce and needs to be returned to you at 8 years of age, you should be ready, willing, and able to take that dog back. Shelters and rescue groups have very few dogs show up who came from reputable breeders but many dogs from people who are not willing to put the time and effort into truly planning and taking responsibility for a litter. Also consider whether you are financially and emotionally prepared if something goes wrong, such as an emergency c-section or having to bottle-raise puppies.

Also consider your bitch's overall conformation, health, disposition, and the qualities she may pass along to her puppies. *If the bitch is not of breeding quality, she should be spayed.* Not every dog, even a champion, needs to or should be bred. Despite popular belief, a bitch does not need to have a litter in order to be psychologically fulfilled.

A bitch should not be bred until her second or third season, at which time she is physically and emotionally mature and able to adjust to motherhood. This usually does not occur before 18 to 24 months of age. Most reputable breeders wait until the bitch is at least 2 years of age so that health clearances, such as those for hip dysplasia, can be done.

Be sure to check local and state laws concerning dog breeding. In some areas there are new regulations designed to control the explosion in the dog and cat populations. They may only apply to commercial establishments, but they may apply to all breeders regardless of how many litters they have a year.

Brood bitches should be kept in excellent physical condition. Overweight bitches and those depleted by improper diet, excessive breeding, and unsanitary living conditions often do not come into season regularly, are difficult to breed, and experience problems during delivery. They should not be bred until all such problems have been corrected.

Maternal behavior is believed to be inherited. Check to see if your bitch's dam and other female relatives showed good mothering abilities. Temperament is also extremely critical in a brood bitch. Not only will she contribute her genetic behavior tendencies, but she will also directly influence her puppies for the first 7 to 10 weeks of their lives. A nervous bitch may produce nervous puppies.

The Prebreeding Examination

Schedule a veterinary examination at least one month before the date you plan to breed the bitch. Maiden bitches over 15 pounds should be examined with a gloved finger to make sure the vaginal canal is normal and that there are no constrictions or abnormalities that could interfere with breeding or conception.

A prospective brood bitch should be screened for hereditary diseases for which she may be at risk. For example, if her breed places her at increased risk for hip dysplasia, elbow dysplasia, or luxating patella, it is highly desirable to obtain certification from the OFA or GDC before breeding. Breeds at risk for inherited eye diseases should be screened by CERF. *If any of these tests are positive, do not breed the bitch.* The number of tests for individual health problems in each breed is growing all the time, so it's important to find out what screening is available before a bitch is bred.

Be sure to have her checked for dental infections. Bacteria from the mouth can be transmitted to newborn puppies when the mother bites and severs the

This bitch has a developmental anomaly of the vulva in which the rectum (above) opens into the vagina (below). This leads to reproductive failure from recurrent vaginal infections.

umbilical cord. A stool test will show whether she has intestinal parasites. If found, they should be treated with appropriate medications (see *Deworming Adult Dogs*, page 53).

Because of the seriousness of brucellosis, a sexually transmitted disease, it is extremely important to obtain a brucellosis blood test on all bitches (and stud dogs) one month before breeding. Repeat this test before each subsequent breeding. Other blood tests that may be necessary include canine herpesvirus serology, a screen for von Willebrand's disease, and a test for hypothyroidism.

Bitches who live in areas where heartworm is a problem should have a heartworm antigen test, unless they are already receiving heartworm preventives. If the test is negative, begin the preventive medication. Most heartworm preventives are safe to use during pregnancy. As an added benefit, many control intestinal parasites.

A brood bitch should be given a distemper and parvo booster (see page 91) shot two to four weeks before breeding, particularly if she is heading into year three of a three-year vaccination cycle. This boosts immunity to the common infectious diseases. In addition, high antibody levels will be transmitted to her pups in her colostrum. These maternal antibodies are the primary protection for puppies during the first three months of life.

Choosing the Right Stud Dog

Part of the preparation for breeding your bitch is to choose the stud dog well in advance. If your bitch comes from a show or breeding kennel, it is clearly a good idea to talk to her breeder before making a final decision. The breeder will be familiar with the bloodlines that lie behind your bitch. If you have an outstanding bitch, you should seriously consider using a stud from that same bloodline to reinforce her best qualities.

The show record of a prospective stud dog may include a Championship, multiple breed wins, Group placements, or even Bests in Show. Unfortunately, not all great show dogs are outstanding producers. A show record beyond a Championship is not as important as the record of the dog's offspring. If the dog has sired outstanding puppies, particularly out of several bitches, you have evidence that he is a good producer. Much of the credit, however, may belong to the breeder for using the dog wisely and with bitches who complement his attributes.

It is the responsibility of the breeder (that is, the owner of the bitch) to come to a clear understanding with the owner of the stud dog concerning the breeding terms. Usually a stud fee is paid at the time of the mating, or the stud's owner may agree to take a puppy of his or her own choosing. If the bitch does not conceive, the stud's owner may offer a return service at no extra charge. However, this is not obligatory. Terms vary with the circumstances and policies of the kennel. If the terms are in writing, there will be no misunderstandings later.

THE STUD DOG

The age at which a male dog reaches sexual maturity and begins to produce sperm varies from 6 to 12 months, the average being about 9 months. Physiologically, a male could be used at stud at about 1 year of age. Most male dogs, however, do not achieve physical maturity before 18 to 24 months of age, and should not be used before that time. This is because their full breeding potential does not become apparent until they reach physical maturity. Also, many health certifications, such as OFA clearance for hip dysplasia, require the dog to be at least 2 years of age.

A stud dog should be kept at an ideal weight with regular exercise and a sound diet. Exercise maintains physical condition, endurance, and muscle tone. Regular health checkups are important. Vaccinations must be kept current, as the stud will have close contact with a number of bitches (see *Vaccination Schedule*, page 98).

The Prebreeding Examination

Before a male is used at stud he should undergo a complete physical examination with laboratory tests similar to those described for the brood bitch. Parasites, if present, should be treated. Heartworm preventives are important in areas where the disease is known to occur. Screening tests for von Willebrand's disease and hypothyroidism may be necessary for certain breeds.

It is extremely important that all prospective stud dogs undergo screening and certification for hereditary orthopedic and eye diseases, as well as other genetic disorders for which they may be at risk. *Dogs with any of these diseases should not be used at stud.*

All prospective stud dogs should have a brucellosis test. Repeat the test every 6 to 12 months, depending on how active the dog is at stud. Once introduced into a kennel, brucellosis can cause widespread sterility and ruin a breeding program.

The reproductive tract examination includes an inspection of the penis, the prepuce, and the testicles, and digital rectal examination of the prostate. A semen analysis is not necessary unless there is some reason to suspect infertility, but should be done on a young male and on older males to be sure they are fertile. Some breed registries require this on male dogs over or under a certain age to be sure the male is fertile.

Inspection of the penis may reveal a sheath infection, phimosis, or paraphimosis. A retained fold of skin (called frenulum) may prevent protrusion of the penis. This can be treated by your veterinarian. Some males have a long, flexible forepart to the penis that can bend backward and make intromission difficult or impossible without assisted breeding.

Solitary or multiple ulcerated cauliflowerlike growths up to an inch in size that appear on the shaft of the penis may be transmissible venereal tumors (see page 541). They will not be found on virgin dogs, because they occur as a consequence of breeding. All growths on the penis should receive veterinary attention. Lacerations and erosions tend to bleed when the penis is erect. If blood gets into the ejaculate, it can reduce the motility of the sperm.

Both testicles should be present in the scrotum. They should be of similar size and have a rather firm consistency. A dog with two undescended testicles is sterile. A dog with one undescended testicle may still be fertile, but should not be used at stud because the condition is heritable.

THE ESTROUS (HEAT) CYCLE

Bitches become sexually mature when they have their first heat period, usually between 6 and 12 months of age, although there is considerable variation. Toy breeds become sexually mature several months earlier than giant breeds. Sexual maturity does not correspond to physical maturity—the attainment of adult height and weight—which generally happens at about 14 months of age in medium-size dogs.

Ovarian activity begins to decline after 6 years of age and ceases in most bitches at around 10 years of age. By 8 years of age it is marginal. Most bitches are not used for breeding after 7 to 8 years of age.

Females generally come into heat every five to nine months. (Basenjis are noted for only having a heat once a year.) The heat cycle is specific for each individual. Unlike some other animals, the heat cycle in dogs is not controlled by outside influences such as the number of hours of daylight.

The estrous, or heat, cycle is divided into four stages, each corresponding to the principal hormonal influence governing that stage. The combination of proestrus and estrus, which breeders refer to as the heat period, lasts an average of 21 days.

Proestrus

The initial stage of the heat cycle lasts an average of nine days (the range is 3 to 17 days). The first sign is a bloody discharge from the vulva. In early proestrus, the discharge may be light pink to yellow. If you are not sure about the discharge, wipe a tissue across the vulva. If you see a pinkish color, the bitch is in heat. Along with a discharge, there is firm swelling of the vulva.

During proestrus the female makes chemical substances called pheromones. These substances attract males, although many experienced stud dogs will not show strong sexual interest in a bitch until she is in estrus.

During the first four to five days of proestrus, the female shows no interest in breeding. If mating is attempted, she will sit down, jump away, growl, or snap at the male. A few days before estrus, the next phase, she may be willing to let the male mount her but she won't stand for breeding. Proestrus ends when the bitch becomes receptive to the male.

This bitch is in the proestrus stage. Note the swelling and enlargement of the vulva.

Estrus

The second phase of the heat cycle is called estrus, or standing heat. This is when the female is willing to breed. Estrus lasts seven to nine days (the range is 2 to 20 days). It ends when the bitch refuses to stand for the stud.

As estrus begins, the vulva softens and becomes pliable in preparation for intromission. The discharge becomes watermelon colored or pink. At this time the female begins to flirt with the male, raises her tail and flags it to the side, lifts her pelvis, and presents her vulva when touched in the rear.

Ovulation usually occurs on the second day of estrus, or about the 12th day of the heat cycle as measured from the first day of proestrus. *Keep in mind that ovulation may occur sooner or later than expected, owing to variations in the lengths of proestrus and estrus.*

A microscopic examination of vaginal secretions (a test called vaginal cytology) helps pinpoint the beginning of estrus. There are characteristic changes in the appearance of vaginal cells that tell your veterinarian when the bitch is in estrus, and later, when she is in diestrus.

Vaginal cytology, however, is not an accurate method of predicting when ovulation will take place. A more accurate method is to measure serum progesterone levels. The serum progesterone level remains low during early proestrus (less than 2 nanograms per milliliter). As ovulation approaches, the serum progesterone begins to rise. The reason progesterone rises is that it is stimulated to do so by the rise in luteinizing hormone (LH), as shown on the chart on this page. Note that LH peaks rapidly and drops precipitously. The LH surge triggers ovulation, which occurs two days after the peak. As LH peaks, the serum progesterone rises above 2 ng/ml. Thus, when the progesterone measures above 2 ng/ml, one can predict that ovulation will occur within the next 24 to 48 hours.

SERUM HORMONE LEVELS DURING ESTROUS

Progesterone levels can be measured by your veterinarian using a rapid in-house assay kit (*ELISA*). The test is not done for routine uncomplicated breedings. A radioimmunoassay test also is available, but blood must be sent to a reference laboratory. LH levels can also be measured, but should be studied in combination with progesterone levels to be sure you didn't miss the peak surge.

Timing the breeding with ovulation increases the probability of breeding at the most fertile time in the estrous cycle—72 hours after ovulation. This is particularly important in planning artificial insemination and in attempting to impregnate bitches with infertility related to abnormal heat cycles or failure to show heat.

Diestrus

This third stage in the estrous cycle, also called the luteal phase, begins when the female refuses to stand for breeding. The male also loses interest at this time. Diestrus can be confirmed by vaginal cytology. It lasts about 60 days, and then merges with anestrus. If the bitch becomes pregnant, diestrus lasts 56 to 58 days and is followed by whelping.

Anestrus

The fourth phase of the estrous cycle is a period of sexual quiescence during which the progesterone-stimulated endometrium undergoes repair. Progesterone levels are low, indicating little if any ovarian activity. The length of anestrus varies, lasting on average 130 to 150 days. Anestrus is followed by the beginning of a new heat cycle.

HORMONAL EFFECTS DURING ESTROUS

Heat begins when the pituitary gland releases follicle stimulating hormone (FSH), which causes the ovaries to develop egg follicles and begin to produce estrogen. Estrogen causes the vulva to swell and the lining of the uterus to shed blood. This is responsible for the bloody discharge of proestrus.

During proestrus there is a steady increase in estrogen concentration, which peaks one to two days before the beginning of estrus and then drops precipitously (see the chart on page 438). LH follows a similar course, but peaks a day or two after estrogen and then drops precipitously. The surge and drop in LH signals the onset of estrus and triggers ovulation two days later. Fertile matings can occur three days before the LH peak through six to seven days after the peak.

LH also ensures that the ovulatory follicles convert to corpora luteal cysts and begin to produce progesterone. The serum progesterone level parallels the rise in LH. It begins to rise during the last two days of proestrus, rises above 2 ng/ml as the LH peaks, continues to rise during estrus, remains elevated for 8 to 10 weeks during diestrus, and returns to baseline levels during anestrus. Progesterone is essential for keeping the uterine lining receptive to the implantation and growth of embryos. Removal of the ovaries during early pregnancy, or failure of the corpora luteal cysts to produce progesterone, results in spontaneous abortion.

The hormonal effects of the estrous cycle have implications for preventing pregnancy (see *Contraceptive Drugs*, page 457). If progesterone is given during the first three days of proestrus, it blocks the release of pituitary FSH and aborts the heat cycle. Testosterone works by blocking the release of LH from the pituitary gland. It must be given 30 days before estrous to abort the heat cycle.

When to Breed

The most common cause of an unsuccessful mating is bad timing. Many dog owners do nothing more than count the days in a cycle. They attempt to breed on the 10th through the 14th day of the heat cycle. But, as noted earlier, each female is an individual with her own breeding timetable—a timetable that can vary according to the lengths of proestrus and estrus. Ovulation cannot always be predicted just by counting the days of the heat cycle. Furthermore, counting will not be accurate if you miss the early signs of heat or if your bitch shows very little evidence of being in heat.

Fortunately, nature provides a safety factor: Fresh sperm are able to survive for up to seven days in the female oviducts. An offsetting factor is that eggs must mature in the oviducts for three days before they can be fertilized. This still leaves a window of several days before and after ovulation for successful breeding. In fact, the peak of female fertility occurs three days after ovulation.

There are reports of bitches being bred as early as the fourth day and as late as the 21st day of the heat cycle—and still conceiving a litter. When the heat cycle is this atypical, a combination of vaginal cytology and progesterone measurements can be used to determine estrus and predict the time of ovulation.

Multiple breedings are more likely than a single breeding to produce pregnancy, and may even have an influence on the size of the litter. Accordingly, most veterinarians recommend breeding a bitch every other day (or every third day) for as long as she remains in standing heat. If, for any reason, a bitch cannot be bred more than once, consider timing that breeding using progesterone assays to predict the exact time of ovulation. Using hormonal assays to determine the best time to breed is especially important if you are using fresh-shipped semen or frozen semen.

The Tie

Male dogs differ from humans in that they do not have seminal vesicles in which to store sperm. Sperm flows directly into the urethra from the spermatic ducts and does not mix with prostatic fluid first. The first part of the male's ejaculate is clear. The second part is cloudy and contains the sperm. The third part is prostate fluid that washes out the urethra and neutralizes the acidity of the vagina.

After the penis enters the bitch's vagina, a bulb of erectile tissue at the base of the penis, called the bulbus glandis, enlarges and is held inside the vagina by powerful vulvar constrictor muscles. This tight union between the two dogs is called the tie. For dogs to mate, the bulbus glandis must become enlarged *after* intromission.

The exact function of the tie is unknown. Its purpose may be to hold the penis in place while sperm flows up from the testicles. To be effective, a tie must last for at least two to three minutes. Many ties last 30 to 40 minutes. Contrary to popular belief, the length of the tie has no effect on the likelihood of pregnancy or the number of puppies conceived.

If the bulbus glandis swells up *before* intromission (an external tie), the penis cannot fully penetrate and will be withdrawn. Some inexperienced males have premature swelling of the bulbus glandis. These dogs should be led away from the female until the bulb returns to its normal size.

Mating Procedures

Breeding dogs can be surprisingly stressful, particularly when there is a great deal of emotion invested in the outcome. If you do not feel confident in handling the mating, ask your veterinarian or an experienced breeder to be present to lend support and assist, if necessary.

Be aware that more than one dog may mate with a bitch if she is not closely supervised. It is possible to get puppies with different sires in one litter. DNA testing can be done to prove parentage so the litter can be registered.

GETTING READY

When a bitch is due to come into season, she should be watched carefully for signs of proestrus. As soon as she shows color (bloody discharge), notify the owner of the stud. He or she may want the bitch to be shipped to the stud's kennel at once. This gives her time to settle into her new surroundings after a stressful trip. In addition, the stud's owner can follow her progress by exposing her to the male to see if she will stand for breeding.

If the female has a heavy or matted coat, trim away the hair under the tail to expose the vulva. On long-coated male dogs, it is a good idea to clip the hair around the penis before mating. Long hair near the head of the penis may catch on the penis during erection. As the penis returns to the sheath, the prepuce may be rolled under, causing a constriction (see *Paraphimosis*, page 464).

NORMAL MATING

Neither animal should be fed for several hours before mating. Avoid the heat of the day. In hot weather, bring both dogs into the house or kennel where it is relatively cool. Normally, the bitch should be taken to the stud's enclosure, as the male is more confident and assertive in his own surroundings. If the bitch is shy and retiring and the male is strong and assertive, it may be better to take the male to the enclosure of the bitch.

Keep the number of observers to a minimum. The fewer distractions, the better. Both dogs should be introduced to each other on leash. Once it is certain that the bitch's behavior is friendly, the dogs can be let off leash for a short period to romp and flirt. If the stud is not interested, and particularly if the female rejects the male, she is not in standing heat. Separate the dogs and try again in 48 hours. *Do not persist when it is apparent that the bitch is not receptive.* This can confuse or frighten the female and frustrate the male, making future attempts more difficult.

If the bitch is ready to mate, she will hold her tail to the side and stand quietly. As the male mounts and penetrates, he clasps her around the loins with his forelegs and thrusts forward. At full penetration he treads up and down instead of thrusting forward. The bulbus glandis swells and is clasped by the vulva. This produces the tie and stimulates the male to ejaculate.

After ejaculation, the male unclasps his forelegs and places both feet on the ground on one side of the bitch. He may lift his hind leg over the back of the bitch and swing around so that the two stand rump to rump. The dogs usually remain joined for 10 to 30 minutes.

A bitch may cry, whine, or grunt during a tie. It is a good idea to have someone posted at the bitch's head to calm her so she doesn't become frightened and try to pull free. As the dog and bitch separate, it can be momentarily painful. Be prepared for either to turn and snap.

HELPING THE MATING ALONG

Maiden bitches, nervous bitches, and bitches who do not show strong signs of estrus can be difficult to breed. With these individuals it is often necessary to hold or restrain the bitch.

The procedure for assisting large dogs requires two or three people. One person sits on a stool at the bitch's side and supports her with a knee beneath her belly. This handler also draws her tail around the outside of her hind leg, exposing the vulva. A second person holds the leash of the male. If the dog mounts at the side or front, this handler gently pulls him off and encourages him to mount from the rear. An optional third person steadies the bitch from in front. A cooperative female raises her vulva so that the male can make a straight entry into the vagina. The individual holding the bitch can make this easier for the male by raising the vulva with a hand between the bitch's legs.

Young and inexperienced males may become so excited that they ejaculate before intromission. This is more likely to happen if attempts are made to guide the male by taking hold of his penis behind the bulb.

A mating between a tall dog and a short bitch can present mechanical problems. The solution is to stand the male in a ditch or breed on a slope to equalize the difference.

Small dogs can be mated on a table with a piece of carpet or nonslip rug on it for good footing. Support the female with a hand beneath her pelvis.

A Prolonged Tie

A prolonged tie is one that lasts for an hour or longer. The problem is caused by a spasm of the constricting vulvar ring. The ring maintains the dog's erection by preventing the blood from leaving the bulbus glandis and returning to the body. Eventually the animals become frustrated and begin to tug against each other, aggravating the problem.

Do not throw water on the dogs or try to pull them apart. Instead, turn the male so that he mounts the female and then push on his rump to increase the depth of penetration. This relieves the constricting effect of the vulvar ring on the penis and allows the bulb to subside.

Shy Breeders and Dogs Who Won't Mate

The most common reason why dogs refuse to mate is that it is the wrong time in the estrous cycle. If mating is attempted too early in the cycle, the bitch may growl and snap at the dog, or she may allow the male to mount, only to sit down or jump away as he starts to thrust. This is normal proestrus behavior, but some breeders may misinterpret it as a sign that mating won't take place.

A simple test to check for estrus is to stroke the female's vulva when she is relaxed. A bitch in estrus raises her vulva and flags her tail to the side. These signs indicate that she is hormonally ready for breeding. If it is the right time and she continues to refuse the male, then quite likely the problem is psychological. Psychological factors are much more common than hormonal or physical ones.

A female raised as a house pet may be a shy breeder because of inadequate social contact with members of her own species. Mate preference, too, can be a determining factor. A bitch who runs with a certain dog may mate willingly with that dog but refuse another. Some females are willing to mate only with very aggressive males.

In males, sexual aggressiveness may be influenced by unpleasant associations with sex. Some owners scold or punish a dog for showing sexual behavior toward dogs or people. Thus the dog comes to believe he will be punished if he attempts mating. A stud may fear mating because of a traumatic experience with an aggressive bitch.

Inadequate canine socialization can be a problem in males as well as females. This is especially true for dogs who live almost exclusively with people and have little or no opportunity to form social relations with others of their own kind.

Finally, and least likely, a dog with a low libido may be suffering from a testosterone deficiency (see *Impotence*, page 447).

Treatment: Reluctance to mate is a problem that should be referred to your veterinarian for further evaluation. If an outgoing bitch consistently refuses to receive a stud, it is a good idea to have her examined for an abnormal heat cycle or a reproductive tract abnormality.

In the case of a frightened or completely uncooperative bitch, breeding by artificial insemination is preferable to a forced mating (see *Artificial Insemination*, on this page). Because the bitch won't display the usual signs of sexual receptivity, vaginal cytology and progesterone determinations should be used to time artificial insemination with ovulation (see *The Estrous Cycle*, page 436). Breeding by artificial insemination will not spoil a dog or bitch for natural breeding in the future.

A male may regain his self-confidence if he is allowed to run with an easygoing bitch who likes to be dominated. An experienced brood matron who is a willing breeder can help a bashful dog overcome his sexual inhibitions. Once he has bred successfully, usually his problems are over.

Remember that temperaments and breeding behaviors are inherited. A dog with poor temperament or inadequate breeding behavior may not be the best choice as a breeding animal.

Artificial Insemination

Artificial insemination (AI) is a procedure in which semen is collected from the male and introduced into the reproductive tract of the female. The American Kennel Club has regulations concerning the registration of dogs produced by artificial insemination. Before breeding, check with the AKC or your country's kennel club for information on how to properly register the litter. DNA profiles are required by most registries when AI is used.

Procedures for collecting and processing the semen and inseminating the bitch are well standardized, and must be followed exactly or the breeding will not be successful. Accordingly, AI should be performed by veterinarians or those who have acquired expertise under veterinary supervision. When properly performed, conception rates using fresh semen are equal to those attained by natural breeding.

AI using fresh semen is best used when natural mating is impossible or has been unsuccessful. Usually this is for psychological reasons, anatomical reasons, or problems associated with heat detection. It should be taken into account that if a dog cannot breed naturally, then perhaps he or she is not a dog who should be bred.

Cooled transported semen can be used to inseminate a bitch in another state or country who could not otherwise breed to a particular stud. Frozen semen can be stored for weeks, months, or years, possibly increasing in value as the importance of a particular stud dog is recognized through his progeny.

The success rate for AI has improved dramatically with the ability to time the insemination with ovulation using progesterone assay kits and LH testing, as well as vaginal cytology (see *The Estrous Cycle,* page 436). Predicting ovulation is particularly important when the bitch does not display the typical signs of estrus. Semen is obtained by stimulating the male and collecting the ejaculate in a rubber conical sheath connected to a receptacle such as a glass tube or the barrel of a syringe. When inseminating with fresh semen, the bitch must be present. The semen is introduced immediately into her vagina using a sterile flexible insemination pipette connected to a syringe. The semen is deposited at the entrance to the cervix.

Using an insemination pipette, the semen is deposited into the vagina at the entrance of the cervix.

The best results are obtained by collecting semen and inseminating the bitch every 48 to 72 hours, beginning at the first indication of standing heat and continuing until she refuses to breed. When insemination is timed with ovulation, insemination should be done two to three days after ovulation, as determined by progesterone assays. After AI, the bitch should be confined until she goes out of heat.

Cooled semen must be handled and shipped according to strict protocols to maintain the viability of the sperm. Properly prepared cooled semen from a fertile stud can be preserved for two to four days. Cooled semen should be inseminated twice, either on days three and five or days four and six—as measured from day zero, or the first day of estrus (standing heat). Day zero is determined by progesterone assay and the receptive behavior of the bitch.

Conception rates for frozen semen are not as high as they are for fresh or cooled semen. Frozen-thawed sperm are unable to traverse the cervix and must be inseminated directly into the uterine body. Semen can be implanted directly into the bitch's uterus using a very small surgical opening in the abdominal wall. It can also be done by passing a long stainless steel catheter through the cervix into the uterine body, but this is not as effective.

Advanced reproductive techniques using embryo transfers currently have a low rate of success.

Male Infertility

Male infertility means the inability to sire a litter. It can be congenital or acquired. A stud dog who has never sired a litter despite several matings should be considered congenitally infertile. Congenital causes of infertility include chromosomal abnormalities (intersex), underdeveloped testicles (testicular hypoplasia), undescended testicles, and abnormalities of the penis and prepuce that prevent mating.

Acquired infertility occurs in a proven stud dog who subsequently becomes infertile. This follows testicular injuries and infections, and may occur as a consequence of prostatitis and infections of the male genital tract, such as brucellosis. Drug therapy, testicular degeneration, and *immune-mediated* orchitis are other causes of acquired infertility.

Hormone diseases of the pituitary and thyroid glands can cause both congenital and acquired infertility. Hypothyroidism is the most common hormonal cause of infertility. It affects both the dog's sex drive and his sperm count.

Retrograde ejaculation is an acquired cause of infertility. It is caused by failure of the internal urethral sphincter to contract during ejaculation. As a consequence, the sperm are ejaculated into the dog's bladder.

A significant cause of reduced fertility in males is excessive use. Dogs used at stud for three consecutive days should be rested for two days. Males with high fertility can be used every other day, but should be given periods of sexual rest to prevent overuse and loss of libido.

When a stud dog is used a great deal, a single mating may not be enough to cause pregnancy. Alternatively, a dog who has not been used for some time may have a low sperm count because of reduced production. During a second mating, two days after the first, the quality of the semen may be much improved.

Prolonged elevation of body temperature damages the sperm-producing cells. Some dogs are less fertile in the summer, especially if they live outdoors where the weather is very hot. A dog with a high fever may take several weeks or months to regain a normal sperm count. An age-related decline in sperm production occurs in older dogs.

IMPOTENCE

Impotence is loss of sex drive (libido). Most cases are caused by overuse, and by physiological factors already discussed in *Shy Breeders and Dogs Who Won't Mate* (page 443).

The male sex drive is under the influence of testosterone, produced by the testicles. A dog with a normal libido is easily aroused when presented with a bitch in standing heat. A dog with a poor libido exhibits little interest in sex, despite the overtures of a willing female. Lack of libido and a low sperm count occur together in dogs with testicular diseases, hypothyroidism, and pituitary gland disorders.

In rare cases, a Sertoli cell tumor of the testicle may be responsible for impotence (see *Tumors of the Testicles*, page 540). These tumors manufacture estrogen, which neutralizes the effects of testosterone. Feminization of the male occurs, with enlargement of the mammary glands, a pendulous foreskin, and bilateral symmetrical hair loss.

EVALUATING INFERTILITY IN THE STUD DOG

A thorough exam should include a comprehensive review of past breeding performance, as well as a family history looking for predisposing hereditary causes. Other factors to consider are recent illnesses, medications, vaccinations, and diet.

Collecting and evaluating semen is a most important part of the infertility exam. The number of sperm per milliliter and the quality of the semen are the two most important considerations. When the sperm count is low (a condition called oligospermia), there may be a problem with the epididymis or testicles. The complete absence of sperm (azospermia) suggests severe testicular degeneration, a blockage in the spermatic ducts, testicular tumor, testicular hypoplasia, or retrograde ejaculation. In a dog with retrograde ejaculation, sperm will be found in urine collected from the bladder shortly after ejaculation. The semen and prostatic fluid are cultured to rule out infection.

Baseline laboratory tests screen for chronic diseases. Measuring the sex and thyroid hormones (testosterone, FSH, LH, and a complete thyroid panel) provides information on possible endocrine causes of infertility. Testicular biopsy gives information on causes of low sperm count, as well as the likelihood the dog will respond to medical treatment.

TREATING MALE INFERTILITY

Stress, sexual overuse, heat, and temporary injury to sperm-producing cells are potentially reversible and often improve with a period of prolonged sexual rest. Treating prostatitis, sheath infections, orchitis, and undescended testicles are discussed later in this chapter.

A male of marginal fertility should be bred at the peak of female fertility (72 hours after ovulation), as determined by vaginal cytology and progesterone measurements (see *The Estrous Cycle,* page 436).

Hormone therapy and drugs to correct retrograde ejaculation and immune-mediated orchitis have been of benefit in some cases. Genetic and chromosomal abnormalities associated with *intersex* may be accompanied by genitalia that appear abnormal. The diagnosis is made by *karyotyping* (analyzing the number, size, and shape of the paired chromosomes).

Dogs with congenital infertility, and those with acquired infertility who do not produce sperm after six months of treatment, usually do not become fertile.

Female Infertility

The most common cause of reproductive failure is improper breeding management—particularly in detecting the heat cycle, determining when to breed, and the number of breedings per cycle. These topics have been discussed earlier in this chapter. Other important factors that influence the outcome of a breeding are the general health and nutrition of the bitch, the effectiveness of vaccination and parasite control programs, maintaining wholesome surroundings, and avoiding overcrowding.

Diseases of the uterus (endometritis, cystic endometrial hyperplasia, and pyometra) are other important causes of female infertility.

EVALUATING INFERTILITY IN THE BITCH

This involves a comprehensive review of the bitch's past breeding performance, as well as a family history of breeding problems. Other factors to consider are recent illnesses and any medications she may be taking. The physical exam is similar to that described for the prebreeding examination. Additional studies include *ultrasonography*, vaginal cytology, and hormone assays such as FSH, LH, thyroid panel, estrogen, and progesterone.

Infertility in bitches is often associated with abnormal heat cycles, but can be caused by other factors as well. A biopsy of the uterus may be recommended.

INFERTILITY WITH A NORMAL ESTROUS CYCLE

If the bitch fails to conceive after successful matings, the most probable cause is a uterine infection—either pyometra or cystic endometrial hyperplasia. Other possible causes are brucellosis or canine herpesvirus. These two sexually transmitted diseases cause infertility by preventing conception, or by causing early loss of pregnancy or spontaneous abortion.

Infertility may result from vaginal strictures and neoplasms that prevent intromission or the ability to tie. A blockage in the oviducts can prevent the union of egg and sperm. Tumors and congenital anomalies of the uterus can interfere with conception and embryo implantation. Lethal genes and chromosomes produce defective embryos and malformed fetuses, which are reabsorbed or expelled.

ABNORMAL ESTROUS CYCLES

Abnormalities of the heat cycles can include silent heat, split heat, prolonged heat, absent heat, or irregular heat. Occasionally a bitch will skip an entire heat period. Young bitches frequently have irregular or silent heat periods. Generally, their cycles become regular by 2 to 3 years of age. Most bitches will follow the heat cycle pattern of their dams.

Silent Heat

Silent heat is a fertile heat cycle that escapes detection because of minimal vulvar swelling and vaginal bleeding. A bitch with silent heat may show no interest in the stud, except during a short period around the time of ovulation. Small breeds who achieve early sexual maturity may have one or two silent heats before exhibiting an obvious cycle. When heat goes undetected, the bitch is often given the mistaken diagnosis of absent heat.

Vaginal bleeding may go unnoticed if the female is fastidious and licks herself clean. If you are not familiar with the size of the normal vulva, you may not notice the swelling of proestrus. However, you should be able to recognize the mild vulvar enlargement and slight bloody discharge of proestrus if you carefully inspect the vulva once or twice a week. You can also expose the bitch to a stud dog twice a week and observe the behavior of both animals.

Veterinary examination using vaginal cytology and progesterone measurements is an accurate method of determining whether the bitch is cycling.

Split Heat

In bitches with this abnormality, the heat appears to be split into two separate cycles. In the first, or false, cycle the bitch attracts the male and develops the vulvar swelling and vaginal bleeding typical of proestrus. Because she does not proceed to estrus, however, she goes out of heat without becoming receptive. A second heat cycle occurs 2 to 10 weeks later. This cycle often proceeds to standing heat.

Split heat typically occurs in young females. It is caused by lack of pituitary output of LH. Because the LH does not rise, the ovaries do not produce ovulatory follicles and serum progesterone remains low (see *Hormonal Effects During Estrous*, page 439). In most cases no treatment is required. The next heat cycle is usually normal.

Prolonged Heat

This occurs when a bitch remains in heat for more than 21 days. During the prolonged heat she continues to display vaginal bleeding and remains attractive to males. Prolonged heat may occur in maiden bitches during the first heat cycle. It normalizes with maturity.

In all other cases, the hormonal basis is a persistent elevation of estrogen, caused by an estrogen-producing ovarian cyst or, occasionally, by a granulosa cell tumor of the ovary (see *Tumors of the Ovaries*, page 542). Vaginal cytology and serum estrogen measurements will confirm the diagnosis of prolonged estrus. *Ultrasonography* may show an ovarian cyst or tumor. Ovarian cysts may regress. If they do not, surgery is required. Ovarian tumors must be surgically removed.

Heat can be terminated by giving an androgen preparation for three to four months. Bitches who respond to androgens usually begin a new heat cycle four to five months later and can often be bred at that time. As an alternative, an attempt can be made to breed the bitch on the same cycle by inducing ovulation with human chorionic gonadotropin (hCG) or gonadotrophin-releasing hormone (Gn-RH). If further breeding is not desired, spaying is the treatment of choice.

Absent Heat

Absent heat is due to a failure to cycle. Bitches younger than 2 years of age may not cycle because of sexual immaturity. Some large-breed dogs do not attain sexual maturity and experience their first heat until they are 2 years old. If a bitch does not go into heat by 24 to 30 months of age, have her examined by a veterinarian.

Heat will not occur if a female has been spayed. This becomes a consideration if the medical history is unknown. Inspect the lower abdomen to find the scar that indicates she was spayed. Females who have been treated with androgens or progesterones will not cycle during treatment and for some time thereafter. The same is true for bitches receiving corticosteroids.

Bitches who are malnourished or debilitated from recent illness often do not cycle until they are in a better state of health. Hypothyroidism is a common cause of absent heat. Other signs of hypothyroidism may or may not be present. The diagnosis is made by a thyroid blood test. Cushing's syndrome is an uncommon cause. Most bitches with Cushing's are over 8 years of age and are no longer in their reproductive years.

Ovarian hypoplasia is a disease in which the ovaries do not develop to sexual maturity and are incapable of producing adequate amounts of estrogen. The mammary glands and vulva remain small and underdeveloped. Ovarian hypoplasia may be the result of sex chromosome abnormalities. An *immune-mediated* inflammation of the ovaries may be responsible for some cases of absent heat. Tumors of the ovary have also been associated with absent heat.

The diagnosis of absent heat is confirmed by weekly vaginal cytology and progesterone assays that show no hormonal effects of estrous. An elevated LH is present in bitches with ovarian hypoplasia and those with absent ovaries. Ultrasonography may reveal an immature uterus or an ovarian tumor. *Karyotyping* is recommended for bitches who show no evidence of cycling after six months of study. If the chromosomes are normal and the bitch has not cycled by 30 months of age, estrus and ovulation often can be induced by FSH and hCG in a protocol determined by your veterinarian. A bitch with major infertility problems should not be bred, as these problems may be passed on genetically.

Interestrous Interval

This is the interval between one heat cycle and the next. The average interval is five to nine months. Often a bitch's interestrous interval is either longer or shorter than normal, or occurs at irregular intervals. An abnormal interestrous interval is one in which the interval between two heat cycles is either less than four months or greater than one year.

Some bitches come into heat every four months and others every 10 to 12 months. This may be genetically influenced. Basenjis and wolf-dog crosses, for example, come into heat once a year.

Prolonged Interestrous Interval

This condition, also referred to as prolonged anestrus, occurs in previously cycling bitches who do not come into heat after 16 or more months. A common cause is cessation of ovarian activity due to an ovarian cyst that produces progesterone. The administration of progesterone and androgenic drugs produces a similar effect. Hypothyroidism and Cushing's syndrome also produce prolonged anestrus.

Hypothyroidism can be diagnosed by a thyroid blood test. Cushing's syndrome generally occurs in older females and is not a common reproductive problem.

Bitches with normal ovaries who are slow to come into heat will often do so when they are kenneled with other cycling females and regularly exposed to a male. If this is not successful, and the bitch has a low serum progesterone level and no discernible medical cause for the prolonged anestrus, consider karyotyping to rule out intersex. If the karyotype is normal, an attempt can be made to induce estrus and ovulation, as described on page 450 for *Absent Heat*.

Shortened Interestrous Interval

In bitches with this condition, the interval between one cycle and the next is four months or less. A shortened interestrous interval should be distinguished from split heat, in which the first cycle does not progress beyond proestrus, and thus is incomplete.

The problem with a shortened interval is that the lining of the uterus has not had sufficient time to repair the progesterone-induced damage caused by the previous heat cycle. Thus, the endometrium is not hormonally receptive to embryo implantation and the bitch with a shortened interestrous interval cannot become pregnant.

Treatment may not be necessary. Most young females develop normal interestrous intervals as they mature. In a mature bitch with a shortened interestrous cycle, the process of uterine repair can be expedited by using an androgen to terminate heat before ovulation, thus paving the way for a normal endometrium on the next heat cycle.

Premature Ovarian Failure

Ovarian function begins to decline at about 6 years of age and ceases, on average, when a bitch is 10 years old. This usually is not a problem, because most bitches are not bred beyond 7 to 8 years of age. The ovaries of some bitches, however, may cease to function as early as 6 years of age, resulting in permanent anestrus. This can be confirmed by FSH and LH concentrations; both will be extremely high in premature ovarian failure. There is no treatment for premature aging of the ovaries.

FETAL LOSS DURING PREGNANCY

Early embryonic loss may take place even before the embryos implant in the lining of the uterus because of unfavorable environmental conditions caused by endometritis or cystic endometrial hyperplasia. Other causes of early embryonic loss are chromosomal abnormalities and fatal genetic defects in the pups.

Pregnancy can be diagnosed at three to four weeks by palpating the bitch's abdomen. This should only be done by an experienced breeder or veterinarian. Using *ultrasonography*, it is possible to diagnose pregnancy as early as 18 days after the first breeding, although most breeders wait until 21 to 28 days. Ultrasounds are excellent for diagnosing pregnancies but tend to underestimate the number of puppies.

Checking blood levels of the hormone relaxin may also confirm a bitch's pregnancy. This is done at about 30 days into the pregnancy. X-rays are usually taken about 45 days into the pregnancy and are excellent for determining how many pups are present.

If a bitch is found to be pregnant and later does not deliver puppies, one of two things must have happened: Either her puppies were reabsorbed or she miscarried (aborted).

Fetal reabsorption can occur at any time from fertilization through about the 40th day of gestation. The products of conception are absorbed back into the mother's body. Some bitches exhibit malaise, fever, loss of appetite, and a thin, bloody, or purulent vaginal discharge. In early fetal reabsorption, symptoms usually are absent and the pregnancy and reabsorption go unnoticed. Thus the problem is often mistaken for failure to conceive.

Abortion is defined as death of the fetus followed by expulsion of the products of conception. Abortion generally occurs during the last three weeks of gestation. The signs of abortion are vaginal bleeding and the passage of tissue. These signs may not be observed if the bitch is fastidious and consumes all expelled tissue.

A well-recognized cause of third-trimester abortions and stillbirths is brucellosis. Herpesvirus is another cause of late abortions, stillbirths, a decrease in the number of pups per litter, and female infertility. Occasionally, a bacterial infection will cause an abortion. Culprit bacteria include E. coli, camphylobacter, mycoplasma, and streptococcus. Drugs that can induce abortion include corticosteroids and chloramphenicol.

Bitches who suffer repeated early pregnancy losses or abort on successive pregnancies should be suspected of having uterine infection or a progesterone deficiency. Progesterone deficiency (called hypoluteoidism) is caused by failure of the corpora lutea of the ovaries to secrete enough progesterone to support placental attachment. The condition recurs with subsequent pregnancies and becomes a likely consideration when a bitch repeatedly fails to maintain a pregnancy.

Causes of sporadic abortion include a serious illness with a high fever during pregnancy (such as distemper or leptospirosis), violent activities such as jumping from heights, a blow to the abdomen, and improper feeding and prenatal care.

Breeders may decide to invest in a monitoring system, such as Whelpwise, to keep a close check on a pregnancy if the bitch is prone to problems. The Whelpwise system measures fetal heartbeats and can also track contractions. Dog owners basically rent the equipment to monitor their bitch and are provided with some guidance from the company on results they see. However, this should not be a substitute for the direct guidance of a veterinarian.

Treatment: A bitch who has passed fetal tissue should be examined by a veterinarian. Ultrasonography may be needed to make sure the bitch has not retained fetal or placental tissue. Infectious abortions are treated with antibiotics and supportive measures, as necessary.

It is important to identify and correct the underlying cause whenever possible. Laboratory examination of the fetus and placenta, along with appropriate cultures, will reveal the cause of an abortion in about 50 percent of cases. When such studies are not done, the cause usually is never discovered. For safety, assume that all abortions are infectious. Maintain kennel hygiene and handle all discharges and tissues with disposable rubber gloves.

Bitches who abort should be screened for brucellosis and herpesvirus—if these tests were not already done in preparation for breeding. The investigation of chronic uterine infection is discussed in *Diseases of the Female Genital Tract*, page 459.

Hypoluteoidism is associated with low plasma progesterone levels in early pregnancy. Although conclusive studies are lacking, treatment with a progesterone supplement may prevent recurrent abortion in some bitches with apparent hypoluteoidism. The progesterone must be carefully monitored because of serious risks associated with its use during pregnancy. Whether these bitches should be bred is questionable.

Pseudocyesis (False Pregnancy)

Mild cases of false pregnancy are a fairly common condition in which a nonpregnant bitch acts as if she were pregnant. The condition is caused by progesterone, which is manufactured by corpora luteal cysts in the ovaries. Signs appear about six to eight weeks after estrus.

A bitch with full-blown pseudopregnancy may exhibit some or all of the physical and behavioral signs of a true pregnancy, including abdominal distension, enlargement of the mammary glands, and even lactation. Some females make a nest and become attached to small toys and other puppy substitutes, occasionally guarding them aggressively. Bitches may vomit off and on and become depressed; a few develop diarrhea. The mammary glands may become caked and can be painful.

Treatment: Most cases do not require treatment. Pseudocyesis disappears spontaneously in 12 weeks or less. Bitches with aggressive behavior or severe symptoms can be treated with hormones such as Ovaban or prolactin inhibitors. These drugs have significant side effects and are therefore not routinely used. For the treatment of caked mammary glands, see *Mastitis*, page 484.

A female with pseudocyesis is likely to have other false pregnancies. If breeding is not intended, she should be spayed. This should be done after the pseudocyesis resolves.

Unwanted Pregnancy

Accidental pregnancy is common in dogs. Male dogs are remarkably adept at getting to females in heat. The usual measures, such as confining a female in a run or pen, are not always sufficient to protect her from a determined male.

To be absolutely safe, keep your bitch indoors when she's in heat; take her out on a leash only. *When outside, do not let her out of your sight for even one minute.* She should be confined throughout the entire estrous cycle, which begins with the first show of color and continues for at least three weeks.

Chlorophyll tablets, which you can purchase from your veterinarian or at pet supply stores, may help to mask the odor of a female in heat, but are not effective in preventing mating.

If you witness a tie or suspect for any reason that your bitch may have been bred, take her at once to your veterinarian. The stage of the heat cycle can be determined by vaginal cytology and a serum progesterone assay. The bitch may not have been in her fertile period, in which case pregnancy is unlikely. Sperm in the vagina can often be identified during the first 24 hours after mating, but absence of sperm does not rule out breeding or pregnancy.

If it appears that the bitch has indeed been bred and is likely to become pregnant, there are two alternatives: One is to wait and see if she becomes pregnant, then allow her to go through with her pregnancy; the other is to treat for termination, either before or after the pregnancy is confirmed.

The first alternative, allowing the bitch to carry her litter, is the safest and best if she is valuable and you are planning to breed her in the future. However, if she is not of breeding quality and you do not have the time and facilities to raise a litter of puppies and find suitable homes for them all, your best choice is to have her spayed. This can be done during the early stages of pregnancy without added risk. During the second half of pregnancy, hysterectomy becomes more difficult.

There is no uniformly safe and effective medical alternative to spaying for preventing or terminating pregnancy in dogs. Preventing pregnancy using estradiol cyprionate (ECP), the mismate shot, is no longer recommended because of the high risks of estrogen-induced bone marrow suppression and pyometra. In addition, the shot is not reliable, even when given during the required three to five days after breeding.

Terminating pregnancy with prostaglandin PGF$_{2a}$ (Lutalyse), although associated with significant complications including rupture of the uterus and gastrointestinal and respiratory distress, may be the best medical alternative currently available for inducing abortion. There are early and late treatment protocols. The late protocol, with which there has been the most experience, uses ultrasonography or abdominal palpation to diagnose pregnancy at 30 to 35 days after breeding. If the bitch is found to be pregnant, she is hospitalized and given Lutalyse injections daily for four to seven days.

Lutalyse causes the corpora lutea in the ovaries to disappear. The corpora lutea manufacture the progesterone that maintains the pregnancy. Although treatment is successful in the majority of cases, it is important to verify that pregnancy has indeed been terminated by obtaining a follow-up ultrasound and serum progesterone level. And the possible side effects (mentioned above) can be serious.

Early pregnancy termination using Lutalyse uses a similar protocol, but the hormone is given 10 days after breeding, before pregnancy is actually confirmed. The advantage of early treatment is that no dead puppies are aborted. The disadvantage is that some nonpregnant bitches may be subjected to unnecessary treatment.

Several other drugs are available for inducing abortion in bitches. The drug RU-486 is under investigation and may prove to be an effective and relatively safe drug for inducing abortion in the first half of pregnancy. Currently, it is not approved in the United States for use in dogs. A related drug, aglepristone, is being studied in Europe for use as an abortifacient in dogs. Dexamethasone (a cortisone preparation) terminates pregnancy in midgestation, but specific protocols have not yet been established.

The inconvenience of a pregnancy must be weighed against the potential risks and complications associated with terminating the pregnancy. Discuss all these options fully with your veterinarian before making a decision.

Preventing Pregnancy
Ovariohysterectomy (Spaying)

The best way to prevent conception in a female dog is to spay her. In this operation, called an ovariohysterectomy, the entire uterus, including the body, horns, and uterine tubes, is removed, along with the ovaries. The operation is done through the abdomen. Spaying prevents the bitch from coming into season and eliminates the problems of cystic ovaries, false pregnancies, pyometra, uterine cancer, irregular heat cycles, and the need to keep her confined during estrus.

Spaying before the first heat reduces the frequency of mammary tumors by more than 90 percent. Finally, with a spayed female there is no inconvenient heat to go through twice a year.

A bitch does not need to have a litter of puppies to be fulfilled. Dogs are people-oriented. They seek human companionship and look to their owners for happiness and personal fulfillment. Spaying will not change a female's basic personality, except perhaps to make her less irritable at certain times of the year. Nor will it affect her basic breed instincts, such as hunting, pointing, retrieving, herding, coursing, or protecting livestock and property.

Spaying does not make a bitch fat and lazy. Obesity is caused by overfeeding and lack of exercise. By coincidence, a bitch is often spayed as she enters adulthood, at which time her caloric requirements diminish. If she continues to eat a high-calorie puppy food and puts on weight, the tendency is to blame the operation.

Traditionally, bitches have been spayed at about 6 months of age, before they go into heat for the first time. The American Veterinary Medical Association, the Humane Society of the United States, the American Kennel Club, and other organizations agree that it is safe to spay or neuter most puppies as early as 8 weeks of age. Research has shown that there are no adverse effects on growth (if anything, the pups will grow a bit taller) and development with early spaying. The operation is not difficult to perform at this time, provided good anesthetic equipment and expertise are available. The risk of complications is small. Early spaying before the puppies are placed in their permanent homes ensures that individuals with genetic or conformation defects will not be used for breeding. Early spaying is often practiced at animal shelters to ensure that the dog will indeed be spayed. There have been concerns about increases in urinary infections and incontinence with early spaying, but this is controversial. For dogs who participate in sporting events, many veterinarians suggest waiting until adult size is reached before spaying or neutering, as this is healthier for joints, which will be stressed over the lifetime of the dog.

When you've made arrangements to have your female spayed, be sure to withhold all food and water the evening before the surgery. For very young dogs, this protocol may be adjusted. A full stomach may result in vomiting and aspiration while the dog is under general anesthesia. Check with your veterinarian concerning other instructions or precautions to be taken before and after the surgery.

CONTRACEPTIVE DRUGS

Megestrol acetate (Ovaban) currently is the only contraceptive drug approved for use in dogs in the United States. Ovaban is a long-acting progesterone. It inhibits the estrous cycle by suppressing the pituitary output of FSH (see *Hormonal Effects During Estrous*, page 439). The drug is safe and effective when used according to the manufacturer's recommendations. A veterinary examination is advised to rule out diabetes, pyometra, pregnancy, and mammary gland tumors before starting the drug. If any of these are present, Ovaban should not be used. The first heat cycle in puppy bitches frequently is unreliable. To ensure proper drug performance, do not use Ovaban until the second heat.

To bring a bitch out of heat, start the pill at the first signs of proestrus. It must be started within the first three days of the heat cycle to prevent estrus and possible pregnancy. Ovaban is given for eight days. The next heat cycle will occur in two to nine months.

It is essential to adhere to a strict schedule with any contraceptive drug. Always confine your bitch during the first eight days of heat, since you might have missed the first signs of proestrus and started the drug too late. If an unplanned mating does take place and the bitch has not been on Ovaban for three full days, stop the pill and consult your veterinarian (see *Unwanted Pregnancy*, page 455). If mating occurs after the bitch has been on the pill for more than three days, complete the course. She will not become pregnant.

To postpone heat for a hunting trip, pleasure trip, or dog show, start the pill at least one week before leaving and continue it for 32 days. Ovaban must be started at least one week before proestrus to postpone a heat.

Bitches taking Ovaban may become hungry or lazy, gain weight, experience personality changes, or show mammary gland enlargement. These changes disappear when the drug is stopped. Because of the risk of pyometra associated with the prolonged use of progesterone, Ovaban should not be used to postpone heat or to take a bitch out of heat for more than two consecutive heat cycles.

CASTRATION (NEUTERING)

Neutering is an operation in which both testicles are removed from a male dog. It can be performed at any age. The operation is not difficult and the dog can usually go home the same day. Instructions before surgery are the same as those for spaying (see page 456).

Neutering has a number of health benefits. It eliminates the risk of testicular tumors and greatly reduces the risk of prostate enlargement and perianal adenomas. Neutered males are less territorial, more congenial with other dogs, and less likely to roam. Neutering does not, however, affect the dog's basic instincts, including his willingness to guard and protect his family.

When a dog is neutered before puberty, his sexual urges do not develop. If he is neutered after sexual maturity, his interest in estrous females may persist, although this is not common.

Neutering may be advised to eliminate unmanageable behavior, such as some forms of aggression. Unfortunately, many behavior problems arise from causes other than male hormones. Thus, neutering may not improve the dog's basic behavior.

Traditionally, dogs have been neutered after attaining most of their adult stature at about 6 to 9 months of age. It is now known that early neutering and spaying does not adversely affect growth and development, although dogs may grow a bit taller than expected. The American Veterinary Medical Association, the Humane Society of the United States, the American Kennel Club, and many veterinarians agree that neutering as early as 8 to 12 weeks is safe and may be preferable, particularly when there are genetic or conformation reasons why the individual should not be used at stud. If neutering is done before the puppies are placed in their permanent homes, there will be no concern about future breeding misuse. Early neutering is often practiced at animal shelters to ensure that the dog will indeed be neutered. There have been concerns about increases in urinary infections and incontinence with early neutering, but so far there is no definitive evidence that this is a problem. Some veterinarians recommend waiting until a dog has reached his adult size before spaying or neutering, however, because this is better for the joints, which will be stressed over the lifetime of the dog.

Diseases of the Female Genital Tract
VAGINITIS (VAGINAL INFECTION)

Vaginitis is an inflammation of the vagina. It is not necessarily accompanied by an infection. Adult vaginitis usually is caused by an anatomic abnormality of the vagina that results in urine pooling in the vaginal canal. Viral vaginitis is caused by the herpesvirus, which is transmitted during breeding. Mycoplasma vaginitis may result from an overgrowth of mycoplasma organisms, which are normally present in the vagina in small numbers.

Vaginitis can ascend into the uterus or bladder, causing endometritis or, more commonly, a urinary tract infection. Juvenile vaginitis is seen in puppies less than 1 year of age. It is often asymptomatic. In some cases there is a light purulent vaginal discharge.

Signs of vaginitis are licking at the vulva and staining of the hair around the vulva. A vaginal discharge may not be visible if the bitch keeps herself clean. Vaginal examination is painful and may require sedation. Male dogs are sometimes attracted to bitches with vaginitis. This can give the impression that the bitch is in heat.

The diagnosis is confirmed by speculum examination of the interior of the vagina. Cultures and *cytology* are obtained. There are normally bacteria present in the vagina; a culture looks for an overgrowth of a particular bacteria. A urinalysis is taken to rule out an associated urinary tract infection.

Treatment: Bacterial vaginitis is easier to clear up if an underlying cause can be identified and removed. In the absence of an underlying cause, treatment involves oral antibiotics selected based on culture and sensitivity tests,

THE FEMALE GENITOURINARY SYSTEM

along with an initial Betadine or chlorhexidine lavage to remove the accumulated discharge.

Bitches with bacterial vaginitis should not be bred until the infection has been eliminated. There is no effective treatment for herpesvirus vaginitis, but most bitches develop antibodies against the virus.

Mycoplasma cultured from vaginitis may be normal flora or the results of an infection. If other signs, such as infertility, indicate an infection, treatment usually involves antiobiotics such as the tetracyclines.

Juvenile vaginitis does not require treatment other than to keep the vulva clean to prevent skin inflammation caused by excessive licking. Most cases disappear when the female enters her first heat cycle. Spaying, if planned, should be postponed until after that time.

Vaginal Hyperplasia and Prolapse

Vaginal hyperplasia is an exaggerated swelling of the vaginal lining that occurs during proestrus and estrus in response to the influence of estrogen. When the swollen vaginal mucosa can no longer be contained within the vagina, it bulges out through the vaginal lips. The principal sign is the protrusion of a tongue-shaped mass through the vulva. Other signs include painful urination and excessive licking at the vulva.

The protruding mass prevents mating. Vaginal hyperplasia occurs most often in young bitches of the larger breeds, particularly Boxers and St. Bernards.

Severe hyperplasia may progress to prolapse. In a dog with vaginal prolapse, the apex of the vagina drops out through the vulva, resembling a donut-shaped mass. This can be mistaken for a vaginal tumor (see page 541).

Vaginal prolapse can also be caused by prolonged straining, such as that associated with anorectal obstructions and difficult labor and delivery. Another cause of vaginal prolapse is forcefully separating dogs during the tie (see A *Prolonged Tie*, page 443).

Treatment: Vaginal hyperplasia subsides during diestrus but tends to recur with each new heat cycle. For mild hyperplasia, no treatment is necessary other than to keep the vaginal membranes clean and well lubricated with antibiotic ointment to prevent drying.

If the bitch is to be bred, artificial insemination is the method of choice. If breeding is not intended, the bitch should be spayed. This cures the problem.

For severe hyperplasia or vaginal prolapse, it may be possible for your veterinarian to push the everted tissue back into the vagina and hold it in place with sutures until it regresses during diestrus. Surgical excision may be required to remove devitalized tissue and prevent hyperplasia during future cycles.

PYOMETRA AND CYSTIC ENDOMETRIAL HYPERPLASIA

Pyometra is a life-threatening infection of the uterus that occurs most often in intact females over 6 years of age. The disease often begins with a condition called cystic endometrial hyperplasia.

In a dog with cystic endometrial hyperplasia, the inner glandular layer of the uterus becomes thickened, fills with fluid, and forms open pockets like those in Swiss cheese. These endometrial changes are caused by the sustained effect of high levels of progesterone that occur during the 8 to 10 weeks of diestrus. Cystic endometrial hyperplasia provides ideal conditions for bacterial growth. The bacteria gain access to the uterus when the cervix is relaxed during estrus. The subsequent infection leads to pyometra.

A biopsy might detect cystic endometrial hyperplasia, but the condition usually goes unnoticed until it has progressed to pyometra and the bitch becomes ill.

Although estrogen does not cause cystic endometrial hyperplasia, it does increase the effects of progesterone. Estrogen given in the form of a mismate shot to prevent unwanted pregnancy has been associated with a greatly increased risk of pyometra and is no longer recommended for that purpose.

Signs of pyometra appear one to two months after the heat period. A bitch with pyometra appears depressed and lethargic, may refuse to eat, drinks a great deal of water, and urinates frequently. Vomiting and diarrhea also can occur. Her temperature may be normal or even below normal. *Suspect pyometra in any intact bitch who appears ill without obvious cause.*

There are two types of pyometra: open and closed. In open-cervix pyometra, the cervix relaxes and releases a large amount of pus that often resembles tomato soup. These bitches usually do not appear as ill as those with closed-cervix pyometra.

In closed-cervix pyometra, the undrained uterus enlarges, often producing a painful swelling in the lower abdomen. This type of pyometra is more likely to be accompanied by vomiting and diarrhea, and may produce signs of toxicity such as high fever, rapid pulse, and shock. The diagnosis of closed-cervix pyometra is made by an X-ray of the abdomen showing an enlarged uterus. *Ultrasonography* distinguishes pyometra from the enlarged uterus of pregnancy; an X-ray taken after about 45 days of pregnancy will also distinguish one from the other.

Treatment: Pyometra requires immediate veterinary attention to prevent shock and death. Ovariohysterectomy, along with antibiotics, is the treatment of choice. It is best to do this operation before the bitch becomes *septic*.

When it is important to preserve the reproductive potential of a valuable bitch, an alternative to ovariohysterectomy can be considered—provided that the cervix is open and the bitch is not septic. It involves the use of antibiotics along with prostaglandin. Prostaglandin PGF_{2a} (Lutalyse) relaxes the cervix, stimulates uterine contractions, and evacuates the pus. Lutalyse is administered by subcutaneous injection daily for three to five days. If evacuation is not complete, a second course is given. Antibiotics are selected based on sensitivity tests, and are continued for one to three weeks after evacuation of the uterus. Lutalyse is not licensed by the FDA for use in small animals, but is nevertheless widely used for this purpose.

Prostaglandin treatment is accompanied by a number of dose-related side effects, including shock. Uterine rupture may occur when the cervix is closed. Most veterinarians regard closed-cervix pyometra as a contraindication to the use of Lutalyse.

Bitches who recover from pyometra are at increased risk for developing it again on subsequent heat cycles. They should be bred on the first estrus after recovery to maximize their chances for fertility.

ENDOMETRITIS

Endometritis is a low-grade bacterial infection of the uterus that occurs as a sequel to a postpartum infection of the uterus (see *Acute Metritis,* page 483), and occasionally as a result of vaginitis that ascends to the uterus. Endometritis is a significant cause of female infertility. Unlike pyometra, the infection is limited to the lining of the uterus. Little pus is produced, but the endometrium becomes inflamed and harbors bacteria. This creates an unfavorable environment for fertilization and the implantation of embryos.

A bitch with endometritis appears to be in good health, has a normal heat period, and mates successfully, yet fails to become pregnant or is found to be pregnant but does not deliver puppies. The diagnosis should be considered whenever a bitch is bred at the right time but fails to conceive on two or more heat cycles.

Endometritis is difficult to diagnose. Abdominal palpation or ultrasonography during diestrus or anestrus may reveal a uterus that is somewhat larger or thicker than normal. Uterine biopsy confirms the diagnosis, but requires laparoscopic abdominal surgery.

Treatment: There is no effective treatment for endometritis. Hysterectomy is recommended for bitches who are not intended for breeding. This eliminates the risk of pyometra.

If future breeding is desired, consider using oral antibiotics and/or topical antibiotics infused into the uterus. Antibiotics are selected based on cultures taken from the cervix. There may be benefit in starting an antibiotic seven days before breeding and continuing it until the bitch develops the behavioral signs of heat.

Diseases of the Male Genital Tract

There are several diseases of the male genital tract. All of them discomfort the dog, and many can lead to mating problems and, in some cases, infertility. Among them are orchitis, balanoposthitis, phimosis, paraphimosis, undescended testicles, testicular degeneration, testicular tumors, and prostatitis. (Prostatitis is discussed on page 419 and testicular tumors are discussed on page 540.)

BALANOPOSTHITIS (INFECTION OF THE PREPUCE AND HEAD OF THE PENIS)

The *prepuce* is a sheath of skin that folds over the head of the penis (see *Anatomy of the Male Genitourinary System*, page 411). A small amount of yellow-green discharge from the opening of the prepuce is normal. A copious discharge indicates infection, called balanoposthitis.

Awns, dirt, or pieces of straw can get caught beneath the foreskin and cause irritation, followed by infection and abscess within the sheath. Herpesvirus produces a chronic sheath infection that can be transmitted to the female during breeding. A strictured foreskin may cause a sheath infection. Transmissible venereal tumors may produce growths on the penis, and this type of cancer is contagious.

Signs of sheath infection are excessive licking at the penis and a foul-smelling discharge from the prepuce.

Treatment: Any purulent discharge from the prepuce should be investigated and treated by a veterinarian. Antibiotics are selected based on culture and sensitivity tests. Herpesvirus is difficult to culture, but serology testing is available. A rising antibody level suggests the diagnosis. Since herpes is a virus, there is no specific treatment. Most bitches develop immunity after once losing a litter to this virus, but still should be protected from stress the last three weeks of pregnancy and the first three weeks post whelping. There is a vaccine in use in Europe, but it is not yet available in North America.

PHIMOSIS (STRICTURED FORESKIN)

In dogs with this condition, the opening of the sheath is extremely small, preventing the penis from extending and in some cases interfering with the flow of urine. Neonatal phimosis is a birth defect that occurs most often in German Shepherd Dogs and Golden Retrievers. Several pups in the litter may be affected. Adult phimosis can be caused by a sheath infection or a congenital defect.

Treatment: Some cases of phimosis resolve with treatment of the associated sheath infection. Most will require surgery to enlarge the opening. Neonatal phimosis causing urinary tract obstruction requires immediate relief.

PARAPHIMOSIS (PENIS TRAPPED OUTSIDE THE SHEATH)

In dogs with this condition, the extended penis is unable to return to its former position inside the sheath. Long hair on the skin around the sheath causes the foreskin to roll under so that the sheath cannot slide. This usually happens after the penis has been extended during mating. The sheath then serves as a constricting ring around the shaft of the penis, causing sustained engorgement. A rubber band maliciously placed around the shaft of the penis produces a similar result.

Rarely, this will occur with puppies removed from their dam too soon who will suck on each other's penises.

Treatment: The penis must be returned to its normal position inside the prepuce as quickly as possible to prevent further swelling and permanent damage. First, lubricate the shaft with K-Y Jelly, mineral oil, or olive oil. Push the prepuce back on the shaft of the penis while rolling it out to release the trapped hair. With one hand, gently draw the head of the penis toward you. With the other, slide the prepuce forward over the head of the penis. If these measures are not successful, proceed at once to the veterinary clinic. Surgery may be required to relieve the constriction.

Paraphimosis can be prevented by cutting the long hair around the foreskin before breeding. Always check the male after mating to be sure the penis has returned to its sheath.

UNDESCENDED TESTICLES

A dog in which one or both testicles have not descended and are missing from the scrotum is said to be cryptorchid. Cryptorchidism is inherited as an autosomal recessive trait. Mature dogs with two undescended testicles are sterile. A cryptorchid dog with one descended testicle may be fertile, but should not be used for breeding.

If one testicle is actually missing and the other is present, the dog is said to be monorchid.

The testicles usually descend into the scrotum by 6 to 8 weeks of age, but may not descend until 6 months of age. Occasionally a testicle can be felt in the scrotum at one time but not at another. The testicles can retract up into the inguinal canal when a puppy is cold, excited, or actively playing. These puppies are not cryptorchid.

Treatment: Hormone injections have been used to stimulate testicular descent in puppies, but the rationale is questionable. In some cases descent would have occurred spontaneously. Furthermore, cryptorchid dogs are not candidates for breeding because the condition is heritable.

Removing both testicles is the treatment of choice because of the risk of developing testicular neoplasms, which may be as high as 50 percent in dogs with undescended testicles (see *Tumors of the Testicles,* page 540). During surgery, it is important to find and remove the cryptorchid testicles. This may involve making an abdominal incision.

ORCHITIS (INFECTION OF THE TESTICLES)

Infections and injuries of the testicles are common causes of male infertility. Scrotal and testicular injuries can be caused by dog bites, puncture wounds, frostbite, and weed, chemical, and thermal burns. Infections are caused by bacteria that infect scrotal injuries or are spread through the spermatic ducts from the bladder or prostate. Distemper or brucellosis may be causative agents.

Signs of orchitis are pain and swelling of the testicles and licking at the scrotum. The testicles become enlarged and hard. The dog assumes a spread-legged stance and walks with a stilted gait. Frequently, the epididymis is also involved.

Treatment: Testicular infection is treated with antibiotics that are selected based on culture and sensitivity tests. Corticosteroids, NSAIDs, and cold packs to the scrotum reduce swelling and inflammation. Following resolution, the testicles may shrink and become small and firm. These testicles no longer produce sperm. A persistent low-grade infection may occur in some cases. Removal of the testicles is then recommended.

Dog bites and injuries to the scrotum are quite likely to become infected. To prevent orchitis, all scrotal injuries (even ones that appear minor) should be examined and treated by a veterinarian.

Testicular Hypoplasia and Degeneration

The normal testicle is smooth, oval, and has a regular outline. Both testicles should be of similar size and feel rather firm. The size of the testicle is related to its sperm-producing capacity. Accordingly, small testicles in a sexually mature dog produce a smaller number of sperm. The diagnosis of testicular disease can be confirmed by biopsy.

Testicular hypoplasia is a developmental disorder in which one or both testicles fail to reach normal size at sexual maturity. The small size and flabby consistency of these testicles is caused by poor development of sperm-producing tissue. An ejaculate will show either no sperm or a low number of sperm with numerous abnormal forms. There is no effective treatment.

Testicular degeneration is an acquired disease that can result in either permanent or temporary sterility. Unlike testicular hypoplasia, the testicles were normal before they became small. A common cause of reversible testicular degeneration is high fever. Effective sperm production requires that the scrotal temperature be at least two to three degrees below the core body temperature. Fever raises both body and scrotal temperatures. Diseases associated with fever that can cause temporary testicular degeneration include canine distemper, parvovirus, and leptospirosis. Hypothyroidism is also a major cause of infertility in mature male dogs. If any of these conditions persist, permanent infertility can occur.

Immune-mediated orchitis occurs following testicular biopsy and trauma in which sperm escape and enter the bloodstream. The escaped sperm cause the body to produce antisperm antibodies. The antibodies destroy the sperm in the dog's own testicles.

In all the conditions just described, the testicles become small and flabby like those of a dog with testicular hypoplasia.

There are also diseases that destroy the testicles: These are testicular trauma and acute bilateral orchitis. In testicles damaged in this way, the sperm-producing tissue is replaced by fibrous connective tissue. The testicles become small and hard. Sterility is irreversible in these cases.

Treatment: Testicular degeneration is treated by correcting the underlying disease and allowing time for spontaneous recovery. Sexual rest is essential. Semen examinations are used to monitor the return of spermatogenesis. It takes 50 to 60 days for regenerating sperm to reach the ejaculate, so any improvement in sperm quality will not be seen for at least two months.

PREGNANCY AND WHELPING

Pregnancy

Gestation is the period from conception to birth. It averages 63 days from the day of ovulation (the normal range is 56 to 66 days). Note that the day of ovulation is not always the same as the day of breeding.

During the first few weeks of gestation there are few signs of pregnancy, except for a slight gain in weight. Occasionally a bitch may experience morning sickness. This usually happens during the third to fourth week of pregnancy, and is caused by the effects of progesterone, combined with the stretching and distention of the uterus. You may notice that your bitch appears apathetic, lacks appetite, and may vomit from time to time. Morning sickness lasts only a few days. Unless you are particularly attentive, you may not notice it at all. If vomiting occurs, feed several small meals spaced throughout the day.

By day 40, the nipples begin to darken and enlarge, and the belly is increasing in size. As birth approaches, the breasts enlarge and a milky fluid may be expressed from the nipples. (Note that many bitches have breast enlargement after a normal heat period, so this alone should not lead you to conclude she is pregnant.)

Abdominal *ultrasonography* can detect puppies throughout pregnancy, beginning as early as 18 or 19 days after ovulation, although many veterinarians prefer to wait until 21 days for increased reliability. The technique is safe and effective, and does not use radiation.

The dog's uterus has two horns that meet in a central uterine cavity. Developing puppies, encircled by their placentas, lie within the uterine horns.

Puppies growing in the uterine horns at 35 days of gestation.

By palpating the abdomen, a veterinarian can tell by the 28th day after the last breeding whether a bitch is pregnant. The embryos can be felt as evenly spaced swellings about the size of walnuts in the average-size dog.

Abdominal palpation requires experience and a gentle hand. This should only be done by your veterinarian or an experienced breeder. There are other structures in the abdomen that may feel lumpy. Excessive poking and prodding can damage the delicate fetal-placental units and cause a miscarriage. If you would like to learn how to palpate for puppies, ask your veterinarian to demonstrate the procedure to you. After day 35, the fetuses are floating in capsules of fluid and can no longer be detected by palpation.

A blood test looking for relaxin levels can be done around 28 to 30 days of gestation. Relaxin is a hormone that increases during pregnancy. Another blood test in experimental development is for acute phase proteins. These are proteins that react to inflammation. In the case of canine pregnancies, the rise in these proteins is stimulated by the attachment of the embryos to the lining of the uterus (the endometrium).

Abdominal X-rays will show fetal bone structure at about day 45. X-rays are used as an alternative to ultrasonography, to distinguish among pregnancy, false pregnancy, and pyometra, and to estimate the size of the litter. X-rays should be avoided in early pregnancy, because the radiation could adversely affect the developing embryos before 45 days.

In late pregnancy, the abdomen becomes enlarged and pendulous. The movements of the puppies can be seen and felt during the last two weeks.

PRENATAL CHECKUPS

The first prenatal visit should be scheduled for two to three weeks after breeding. Any questions about activity and feeding during pregnancy can be answered at this time. Your veterinarian might schedule additional tests. Intestinal parasites, if present, should be treated.

Make an appointment to have the expectant mother seen again two weeks before her due date. Your veterinarian will want to discuss normal delivery procedures, alert you to potential problems, and give you instructions on how to care for the newborn puppies. Be sure to ask where you can get emergency service after hours, if it's needed. At that time, you may want to have your bitch X-rayed to determine how many puppies you can expect.

If, for any reason, you suspect there may be problems with the pregnancy, you may want to look into a pregnancy monitoring system such as Whelpwise. These systems measure fetal heart rates and uterine contractions. The data you collect should always be discussed with your veterinarian before you attempt any treatment.

CARE AND FEEDING DURING PREGNANCY

A pregnant bitch needs little in the way of special attention. During the first half of pregnancy it is not necessary to restrict her activity. Moderate exercise is beneficial, because it helps prevent undue weight gain and maintains muscle tone. Activities such as climbing fences, roughhousing with other dogs and children, and leaping up and down stairs should be avoided during the last three or four weeks of pregnancy. Long walks are an excellent way to keep the bitch fit.

Raspberry leaves are advocated by many to help a bitch when whelping. Whether or not to add a pinch of dried raspberry leaves to the bitch's food throughout pregnancy is more controversial. Consult your veterinarian before adding this or any supplement.

Deworming

It is a good practice to deworm expectant mothers during the last two weeks of gestation and during lactation. This reduces environmental exposure to roundworm eggs (a human health hazard) and helps control roundworm infection in puppies.

Panacur (febendazole) is a deworming agent that is effective against roundworms, hookworms, and whipworms. It is safe to use during pregnancy. Strongid (pyrantel pamoate) is another safe dewormer but doesn't have as broad a spectrum of efficacy as fenbendazole.

Drugs

Vaccinations, most medications, some flea and insecticide preparations, most hormones (including cortisone), and many dewormers are inadvisable during pregnancy.

Antibiotics that can effect fetal development include the tetracyclines, kanamycin, and Griseofulvin (fulvicin). Live-virus vaccines should not be given to pregnant females because of the risks of abortion and birth defects. Always check with your veterinarian before giving your bitch any drug or supplement during pregnancy.

Diet and Feeding

During the first four weeks of pregnancy, continue to feed the usual adult maintenance food. Protein and calorie requirements increase during the second half of pregnancy. More than 75 percent of puppy weight and at least 50 percent of puppy length is attained during the last three weeks of gestation. Beginning on day 35, gradually increase the amount of food so that by whelping time the dam is consuming 1.5 times her maintenance ration.

Also at this time, consider switching to a commercial food formulated for growing puppies. These products are especially suitable for pregnant and nursing females because ounce for ounce they contain more protein, calcium, and other essential nutrients. An appropriate food is one that contains at least 1,600 metabolizable kcals per pound (.45 kg) of food and at least 21 percent protein. Nutrient information is given on the package label.

Divide the day's ration into equal parts and feed two or three meals a day. Avoid supplementing the bitch's diet with treats, table scraps, or meat. To the extent that other foods supply additional calories, the dam may not eat enough of the pregnancy food to get all the nutrients she and her puppies need for a successful and healthy pregnancy.

Do not increase the caloric intake if the bitch is overweight. (How to determine the ideal weight is discussed in *Weight Reduction*, page 308.) Excessive weight gain should be strictly avoided. Overweight bitches are notorious for having whelping problems. An expectant mother should gain no more than 15 to 25 percent of her body weight by the end of gestation, and should weigh no more than 5 to 10 percent above her normal weight after whelping.

Vitamin and mineral supplements are not required unless the dam is below par from an earlier litter or recovering from an illness. In fact, excessive supplementation can cause soft tissue calcifications and physical deformities in the developing puppies.

An expectant dam may lose her appetite a week or two before whelping. Her abdomen is crowded and she may have difficulty taking in large meals. Feed her several small meals spaced throughout the day.

PREPARING FOR WHELPING

Dams should deliver at home in familiar surroundings where they are at ease. The best place to care for newborn puppies is in a whelping box. The box should be located in a warm, dry, out-of-the-way spot that is free from drafts, noise, and distractions.

An adequate wooden box for large dogs should be at least 4 to 5 feet (1.2 to 1.5 m) on each side and 12 inches (30 cm) high. A box 2 to 3 feet (61 to 91 cm) on each side and 8 inches (20 cm) high is sufficient for toy breeds. The sides should be tall enough to keep puppies from crawling out while allowing the dam to step (not jump) over. If necessary, one side can be made shorter than the others to help the dam. This side can be replaced by a taller board when the pups are older.

The floor is much easier to clean and the box easier to store if the sides are removable. Therefore, the sides of the whelping box should not be nailed to the floor. Instead, they should be held in grooves made by nailing 1-by-2-inch (2.5-by-5-cm) molding around the edges. The sides are then joined and held in place by hook-and-eye latches.

Make a shelf around the inside of the box a few inches from the floor by nailing 3-inch to 6-inch (7-cm to 15-cm) wide boards to all four sides. Puppies will instinctively crawl under these ledges and thus are less likely to be stepped or rolled on by their mother. All wood surfaces should be treated so they are safe for the pups and easy to clean and disinfect.

There are many commercial whelping boxes available that have safe, easy-to-clean surfaces. If you borrow a whelping box, be sure to thoroughly disinfect it.

Lay several sheets of newspaper in the bottom of the box to absorb moisture. If you ask at your local newspaper office, you may be able to get sheets of newsprint without any printing so you won't get ink on the pups. Because newspapers offer little traction and do not provide a good surface for crawling, cover the newspapers with heavy towels, mattress pads, or some other material that gives good traction and is either washable or disposable. Make sure there are no strings or loose strips or threads in the bedding that could entrap the puppies. Disposable baby diapers are excellent for toy breeds. Newborn puppies should never be placed in deep, loose bedding, such as blankets, in which they can smother. Also do not use straw or wood chips, because these substances can be inhaled.

Cold, damp quarters are a leading cause of newborn puppy deaths. The whelping room should be free of drafts and kept at a temperature of 85°F (29°C) for the first seven days after delivery. During the second week, reduce the temperature to 80°F (27°C). Thereafter, progressively reduce the temperature to 72°F (22°C) by the time the litter is 6 weeks old. Keep a constant check on the temperature using a thermometer placed on the floor of the whelping box (and carefully protected from the puppies).

Additional heat can be supplied by using 250-watt infrared heat bulbs, either suspended above the whelping box or mounted in a photographer's floodlight reflector stand (or by using plant lights). Be sure to leave an area of the box that is out of the direct source of heat, so the mother can rest in a cooler area and the pups can crawl out of the light if they feel overheated.

In addition to the whelping box and a good heat source, you should keep these supplies on hand in case they are needed:

- A small box with padding in which to place newborn puppies
- Sterile disposable latex gloves
- An eyedropper or small bulb syringe to aspirate mouth and nose secretions
- Dental floss or cotton thread to tie the umbilical stumps
- An antiseptic, such as iodine, to apply to the umbilical stumps
- Scissors
- Clean towels
- Plenty of fresh newspapers

Introduce the dam to her whelping box about two weeks before she is due to deliver, and encourage her to sleep in it. By the time she whelps, she will understand that she is to do so in the box and not in your bed.

One week before the dam is due to deliver, clip the long hair around her mammary glands and vulva.

Whelping

Many people use the day of first breeding as the basis for determining when the bitch will whelp. However, a bitch may not ovulate until after her second or third breeding, so a more accurate determination of the whelping date can be obtained by using serum progesterone assays during estrus to determine ovulation. Ovulation coincides with the LH surge (see *The Estrous Cycle*, page 436). The expected date of whelping is 62 to 64 days after the LH surge.

Whelping usually occurs earlier in bitches with large litters and later in those with small litters and single pups. Puppies born on the 56th day after ovulation are likely to be of low birth weight and physiologically immature. If they are born on the 55th day or before, they are premature and probably will not survive. Any gestation beyond 65 days from the day of the first breeding may be postmature and require veterinary examination.

SIGNS OF WHELPING

Two to three days before the dam is due to deliver, start taking her rectal temperature each morning. Twelve to 18 hours before labor begins, the rectal temperature drops from a normal range of 100° to 102.5°F (37.7° to 39.2°C) to 99.5°F (37.5°C) or below. This drop may not occur; if it does, it's so small that it can easily be missed. Don't assume that a normal rectal temperature means she won't deliver soon. As the day of whelping approaches, restrict her to the house.

Twelve to 24 hours before whelping the dam loses her appetite, becomes more active and restless, perhaps rummages in closets, digs in the garden, or scratches up her owners' bed. Remind her that the whelping box is nearby. An experienced dam usually takes to it without difficulty. But if she decides to have her puppies in some other spot, move the entire family to the whelping box as soon as she finishes delivering.

LABOR AND DELIVERY

The entire birthing process is seldom difficult and normally proceeds without human intervention, except in *brachycephalic* breeds such as Bulldogs. During stage one, which lasts 6 to 12 hours, involuntary uterine contractions dilate the cervix. The bitch may appear restless or uncomfortable, but exhibits no other signs.

In stage two, involuntary uterine contractions become more forceful. One uterine horn contracts and expels a puppy into the body of the uterus. The uterus contracts and pushes the presenting part of the puppy against the cervix. This stimulates active labor, with voluntary tightening of the abdominal wall muscles and purposeful straining. At this point the dam may become anxious and begin to pant and lick at her vulva. She may vomit. This is a normal reflex and should not be taken as a sign that something is wrong. Bitches usually deliver lying down, but some may stand or squat.

In this birth, the first puppy is being delivered in the common presentation with nose and feet first. The second puppy will be born backward; this usually does not cause problems.

The cervix opens into the vaginal birth canal. When the cervix is completely dilated, the puppy slides into the vagina and the water bag around the puppy can be seen bulging through the lips of the vulva. In some cases the bag ruptures before the puppy is born. If so, a yellow or straw-colored fluid is passed. After the water bag breaks, the puppy should be delivered within a few minutes. Dark green fluid—from placental wastes called biliverdin—will be passed, but normally the puppy comes first.

About 70 percent of puppies are born in the diving position, with feet and nose first. After the head is delivered, the rest of the puppy slides out easily. The mother instinctively removes the fetal membranes and vigorously licks the puppy's face to clear fluid and mucus from his nose and mouth. As the puppy gasps, the lungs inflate and breathing begins. The dam now severs the umbilical cord by shredding it with her teeth.

No attempt should be made to interfere with this normal maternal care. It is an important part of the recognition process and mother-puppy bonding. However, if the mother is occupied with another puppy and fails to remove the sac around the puppy, you should step in and strip away the fetal membranes to allow the puppy to breathe (see *Helping a Puppy to Breathe*, page 477). Similarly, if the cord is severed too cleanly or too close to the puppy's navel, it may continue to bleed. Be prepared to clamp or pinch off the cord and tie a thread around the stump.

After the mother severs the cord, the stump of each puppy should be disinfected with iodine or some other suitable antiseptic. This step helps to prevent umbilical stump infection.

During stage three labor, the placenta is expelled. A placenta is passed within a few minutes after the birth of each puppy. The dam may consume some or all of the placentas. This instinctive reaction may stem from behavior in the wild, where it is important to remove the evidence of birthing. Consuming the placentas is not essential from a health standpoint. In fact, ingesting several placentas can cause diarrhea. You may wish to remove some or all of the placentas. However, be sure to count them. If the number of placentas is less than the number of puppies, notify your veterinarian. A retained placenta can cause acute postpartum metritis.

Normally, the next puppy will be born from the opposite uterine horn. As the dam prepares for the second puppy, remove the first puppy and place him in a warm box. This way, the mother will not accidentally roll on the pup while she is distracted by the next birth. Between births put the puppies back on the dam's nipples. Their sucking action stimulates uterine contractions and helps bring on the *colostrum*, or first milk of the dam. This colostrum contains maternal antibodies that protect the pups against infectious diseases.

This puppy is being born surrounded by the water bag. Remove the membranes if the mother does not do so.

Present the puppy to the mother to lick and cuddle. This establishes the mother-puppy bond.

Encourage puppies to nurse between deliveries. This stimulates the dam's uterine contractions and helps bring down her milk.

Most puppies are born at intervals of 15 minutes to 2 hours apart, but this varies. The average time to whelp a litter of four to six puppies is six to eight hours, but large litters can take considerably longer. Dams who are whelping their first litter often take longer than experienced dams. Active straining returns 5 to 30 minutes before the delivery of the next pup. Occasionally the interval between puppies is as long as three to four hours. But if you suspect that the mother has not finished delivering all her puppies and she rests for more than four hours, or if she actively strains for 30 to 60 minutes without delivering a puppy, notify your veterinarian without delay.

Twelve to 24 hours after the dam has delivered her last puppy, have her examined by your veterinarian to be sure there are no retained puppies or placentas. An oxytocin injection (breeders call this a pit shot) may be given to clear the uterus. This also stimulates the letdown of milk.

Assisting a Normal Delivery

When labor is going well, there is no need to interfere. But on occasion a large puppy may get stuck in the vaginal birth canal. The head or presenting part appears during a forceful contraction and then slips back when the dam relaxes. In most cases this can be corrected by lubricating the birth canal liberally with K-Y Jelly. If the dam does not deliver the puppy within 15 minutes, you will have to help.

Put on a pair of sterile disposable latex gloves. As the presenting part of the puppy appears at the vaginal opening, place your thumb and index finger on either side of the mother's perineum, just below the anus, and push down gently to keep the puppy from slipping back inside. Next, grip the puppy in the birth canal and slide the lips of the vulva back over his head. Once this has been done, the lips will hold the puppy in place, giving you a chance to get another grip.

Now grip the skin of the puppy with a clean piece of cloth behind his neck or along the back. As the mother strains, apply gentle traction to the skin—not to the legs or head—and draw the puppy out. It may be helpful to rotate the puppy first one way and then the other. If these measures are not successful, see *Physical Blockage*, page 478.

HELPING A PUPPY TO BREATHE

The amniotic sac that surrounds the newborn puppy should be removed within 30 seconds so the puppy can breathe. If the mother fails to do this, tear open the sac and remove it, starting at the mouth and working it back over the body. Remove the secretions from the puppy's mouth and nose with a cotton swab, or gently suction the secretions using an eyedropper or a bulb syringe. Rub the puppy briskly with a soft towel.

Another good way to clear secretions is to hold the puppy in your hands while supporting his head. Then slowly swing him in a downward arc, stopping when his nose is pointed toward the floor. This expels water from the nostrils. Present the puppy to the mother to lick, sniff, and cuddle.

After a difficult delivery, a puppy may be too weak or too limp to breathe on his own. Squeeze the puppy's chest gently from side to side and then from front to back. If the puppy still does not draw a breath, place your mouth over his nose and blow gently until you see his chest expand. *Do not blow forcefully* because this can rupture the lungs. Remove your mouth to allow the puppy to exhale. Repeat this several times until the puppy breathes on his own.

There is an acupuncture site that can stimulate respirations. This is located on the upper lip, right under the nose. Carefully sticking a sharp, sterile needle into this spot and moving it gently in and out can help stimulate breathing.

Dystocia (Prolonged or Difficult Labor)

Prolonged labor at any stage is called dystocia. Dystocia is caused by a physical blockage or uterine inertia. The latter is a condition in which the uterus does not contract forcefully enough to expel the puppy. Dystocia usually affects the first puppy in the litter and is much more common in singleton litters.

Dystocia rarely occurs in healthy, well-conditioned dams. However, it does occur in fat, overweight brood bitches. This is one reason why it is so important to prevent excessive weight gain in pregnancy. Dystocia is common in breeds with large heads and broad shoulders, such as Bulldogs, Pugs, and Boston Terriers.

PHYSICAL BLOCKAGE

The two common causes of physical blockage are a very large puppy and a puppy who is not positioned correctly in the birth canal.

Oversized puppies may appear in litters with just a few puppies, and particularly in litters with a single puppy. Relatively large puppies may also appear when the sire was much larger than the dam. Prolonged gestation, and a puppy with a congenital defect such as hydrocephalus, are other reasons why a pup might be oversized relative to the size of the birth canal.

Physical blockage is often caused by a combination of a large puppy and a relatively narrow birth canal. Maternal causes of a narrow birth canal include a small pelvis, occasionally seen in terriers and the *brachycephalic* breeds; vaginal stenosis or a persistent hymen; a tumor of the vagina; or a previously fractured pelvis.

An incorrectly positioned puppy comes down the birth canal backward, with his hind feet or rump presenting first. Most puppies come down nose and feet first, in the diving position, with their backs along the top of the vagina. The hind foot presentation occurs about 20 percent of the time. It is probably not accurate to call this an incorrect presentation, because it seldom causes a problem.

The breech position, however, in which the rump is the presenting part, does cause problems—particularly when it occurs with the first puppy. Another presentation that can complicate delivery is when the head is bent forward or to the side.

Treatment: Physical blockage can be suspected if the mother actively strains (bears down) for more than 30 to 60 minutes without delivering a puppy, or if she exhibits weak, ineffectual labor for more than two hours instead of resting quietly between births. The obstruction must be unblocked by a veterinarian to prevent complications and allow labor to resume.

Veterinary obstetrics for an incorrect position involves manually correcting the presentation. Sterile gloves are used and the vaginal canal is lubricated with Betadine solution and K-Y Jelly. With one hand beneath the mother's abdomen in front of the pelvis, the body of the uterus is lifted to align the puppy with the birth canal. A finger is slipped into the vagina to feel for a head, tail, or leg. A tilted head can be corrected by inserting a finger into the puppy's mouth and gently guiding the head into correct alignment.

To correct a breech (rump first) presentation, first one leg and then the other is hooked with the finger, slipping the legs over the pelvic brim and into the vagina. This converts the breech to a hind foot presentation. The vaginal opening is gently stretched to stimulate a forceful push by the mother. When the puppy is part way out, delivery is assisted as described for assisting a normal delivery, page 476.

Occasionally a blockage is caused by a retained placenta. The placenta can be hooked with the fingers and then grasped with a sterile gauze pad. Steady traction is maintained until the placenta passes out of the vagina.

If the obstruction cannot be relieved by medical means, an emergency cesarean section is required.

UTERINE INERTIA

Uterine inertia is an important cause of ineffective labor. Inertia is classified as primary (insufficient stimulation to start uterine contractions) or secondary (caused by uterine muscle fatigue after prolonged straining). Giant-breed dogs seem to be predisposed to uterine inertia.

Primary Uterine Inertia

The two conditions associated with primary uterine inertia are failure to go into labor by 67 days after ovulation and failure to progress from stage one to stage two labor within 24 hours. Causes of failure to initiate labor include a small litter (particularly a single puppy), overstretching of the uterus by a large litter, the stress and anxiety of being a first-time mother (dams can voluntarily prolong, delay, and even interrupt the normal birthing process for up to 24 hours), and occasionally, a calcium deficiency called hypocalcemia.

If more than 65 days have passed from the date of first breeding and the mother shows no signs of whelping, notify your veterinarian because gestation may be prolonged. (Alternatively, the pups may not yet be mature.) An X-ray can be taken to determine the number of puppies and their sizes.

Treatment: Hypocalcemia can be diagnosed by a blood test and treated by giving oral or intravenous calcium. If postmaturity is suspected, your veterinarian may wish to confirm this with a progesterone level test and then do a cesarean section.

If the cervix is dilated, oxytocin may be effective. Oxytocin should never be used when the cervix is closed or in cases of suspected physical blockage because of the danger of uterine rupture. If primary uterine inertia does not respond to medical treatment, a cesarean section is required.

Secondary Uterine Inertia

After a mechanical blockage has been removed, the uterus may be too tired for labor to resume.

Treatment: This usually involves cesarean section.

When to Call the Veterinarian

It is better to call your veterinarian with a false alarm, if only to gain reassurance, than to hope the problem will disappear with time. Most whelping problems can be dealt with rather simply when they are attended to at once. However, the same problem, when neglected, can become complicated—often leading to emergency surgery.

Signs of birthing problems include:

- Thirty to 60 minutes of active straining without birth of a puppy
- Four hours between births when more puppies are expected
- Two hours of weak, ineffectual labor without the birth of a puppy
- A purulent or hemorrhagic vaginal discharge
- Presence of fetal membranes at the vulva for more than 15 minutes
- Apathy or weakness, with a rectal temperature above 104°F (40°C) or below 97°F (36°C)
- Passing dark green or bloody fluid *before* the birth of the first puppy

A dark green vaginal discharge indicates that the placenta is separating from the wall of the uterus. When this happens, the first puppy should be born within a few minutes. After the first puppy, the passage of dark green fluid is not a concern.

Cesarean Section

Cesarean section is the treatment of choice for all dystocias that can't be relieved by drugs or obstetrics. Common reasons for C-section include primary uterine inertia associated with postmaturity, physical blockage, and death of puppies in utero.

The decision of when to proceed with an emergency C-section rests with your veterinarian. It is based on the condition of the dam, the length of labor, results of X-rays, the size of the puppies in relation to the pelvic outlet, the dam's response to oxytocin, and whether the vaginal canal has lost its lubrication.

Because of anatomical make-up, certain breeds are prone to whelping difficulties. These include the Bulldog, Chihuahua, Pekingese, Toy Poodle, and Boston Terrier. C-section may be indicated as an elective procedure in these breeds as soon as the bitch goes into labor.

The operation is done under general anesthesia in the veterinary hospital. The risk of an elective C-section to a healthy dam is small. However, when labor has been prolonged, when the puppies are dead and beginning to decompose, or when the uterus has ruptured, the risk of surgery becomes significant.

Most dams are awake and able to nurse puppies within three hours of surgery and can be discharged from the hospital shortly thereafter.

A dam who has had a C-section may or may not require one with her next litter. This depends upon the reasons for the first C-section.

Postpartum Care of the Dam

Twelve to 24 hours after the dam delivers, ask your veterinarian to do a postpartum checkup. Many veterinarians prescribe an injection of oxytocin to help expel all the products of conception and return the uterus to its normal size. Take the mother's temperature at least once a day for the first week. A temperature of 103°F (39.4°C) or higher indicates infection. The most likely causes are acute metritis and acute septic mastitis.

Some bloody or dark green discharge (called lochia) is normal for the first few days. The lochia changes to a watery pink or a bloody discharge that may persist for four to six weeks. A dark brown or foul-smelling discharge is abnormal and suggests a retained placenta or uterine infection (see *Acute Metritis*, page 483). A pink or bloody discharge that persists for more than six weeks indicates subinvolution of placental sites. Be sure to consult your veterinarian if you see either of these discharges.

FEEDING A NURSING DAM

A nursing dam's calorie requirements increase steadily as her puppies grow. By the third or fourth week, she needs two to three times more calories than she did before pregnancy. If her diet is not adjusted to supply these calories, she may not be able to produce enough milk to nourish her puppies. Inadequate milk production is a common cause of puppy mortality.

Many commercial dog foods do not provide enough calories to support lactation. It is important to switch to a food advertised as formulated for growing puppies. You may have already done this during the second half of pregnancy. Ounce for ounce, these foods contain more calories, protein, and calcium. The food should contain at least 1,600 metabolizable kcals per pound (.45 kg) of food and at least 21 percent protein. Nutrient information is given on the package label.

Do not use table scraps or treats to supply additional calories. The calories provided will not be of the same quality and may cause the dam to eat less of the high-quality food. Kibble can be left down all the time for the dam to eat whenever she is hungry. Canned foods should be fed at least three times a day.

How much should you feed a nursing dam? During the first week, feed one and a half times the manufacturer's recommended daily maintenance ration. Increase this to twice the daily ration during the second week. By the third week, a nursing dam should be eating three times the normal maintenance ration. These amounts may need to be decreased if the litter is small. Slowly reduce the size of the portions after the fourth week in preparation for weaning. *Be sure to keep clean, fresh water available at all times.*

Vitamin and mineral supplements are not necessary, and can even be harmful. Avoid them, unless the dam refuses to eat her food or has a preexisting deficiency or a chronic illness. In these circumstances, seek veterinary consultation.

Raspberry leaves are advocated by many breeders to help a bitch when whelping. Whether or not to add a pinch of dried raspberry leaves to the bitch's food throughout pregnancy is more controversial, and some veterinarians believe it may increase the need for a C-section. Consult your veterinarian before adding any supplements to the dam's diet.

DRUGS AND LACTATION

Note that many drugs are passed on to puppies in the mother's milk. The amount depends on the blood concentration and whether the drug is soluble in fat. Fat-soluble drugs are stored in body fat and will be secreted in the milk for prolonged periods. Keep in mind that a newborn's liver and kidneys are immature and cannot detoxify and eliminate drugs as readily as those of an adult. Avoid giving the dam any drugs during lactation, unless they are prescribed by your veterinarian.

Postpartum Problems

Problems that can affect the dam after delivery include subinvolution of placental sites, acute metritis, acute mastitis, caked mammary glands, absent milk supply, and milk fever. Occasionally, a mother has problems accepting and caring for her puppies.

SUBINVOLUTION OF PLACENTA SITES

The uterus normally returns to near-normal size (a process called involution) by four to six weeks after whelping, and completes the entire process by 12 weeks postpartum. During the first four to six weeks, the dam will have a light pink to bloody vaginal discharge called the lochia.

A vaginal discharge that persists for more than six weeks is caused by subinvolution of placental sites (SIPS). These sites, where the placentas formerly attached to the wall of the uterus, are invaded by placentalike tissue called trophoblasts. The trophoblasts prevent the uterus from completing the process of involution. The associated vaginal bleeding is usually mild, but may be heavy enough to cause anemia.

SIPS tends to occur in bitches younger than 3 years old. There is no breed predisposition. The condition does not cause discomfort. SIPS can be complicated by acute metritis or perforation of the uterus, but this is not common.

The diagnosis is made by palpating the uterus and feeling lumpiness in the uterine horns. Ultrasonography shows the enlarged horns. Vaginal *cytology* may disclose trophoblastlike cells.

Treatment: The SIPS-related discharge usually resolves spontaneously. If it persists and you don't plan to breed the bitch again, have her spayed. When SIPS disappears spontaneously, future fertility is not affected. There is no predisposition for developing SIPS after subsequent litters.

ACUTE METRITIS (INFECTED UTERUS)

Acute metritis is a bacterial infection that spreads upward into the uterus during the birthing process or shortly after. Some cases are caused by a retained placenta or a mummified fetus. Others are caused by contamination of the birth canal during or after delivery. Unsanitary whelping quarters and failure to dispose of the placentas and change the bedding immediately after whelping predispose a bitch to bacterial infection.

Many cases of acute metritis can be prevented by a postpartum checkup 24 hours after delivery. The veterinarian will give the dam an injection of oxytocin to clear the uterus, if needed.

Signs of metritis appear two to seven days after whelping. A dam with acute metritis is lethargic, refuses to eat, has a fever of 103°F (39.4°C) to 105°F (40.5°C), is not attentive to her puppies, and may vomit and have diarrhea. There is a foul-smelling vaginal discharge, which should be distinguished from the normal greenish or bloody discharge common for the first few days. A normal discharge is not accompanied by high fever, excessive thirst, and other signs of toxicity, such as vomiting and diarrhea. Abdominal palpation and *ultrasonography* help determine whether there has been a retained fetus or placenta. Cultures are taken to determine the pathogens involved and their antibiotic sensitivities.

Be sure to take the dam's rectal temperature daily after whelping and notify your veterinarian if she develops fever or any of the signs just described. Acute metritis is a life-threatening illness that can rapidly progress to *toxemia* and shock.

Treatment: Treatment involves administering intravenous fluids and antibiotics to support circulation and treat toxemia. Oxytocin or prostaglandin PGF$_2$ (Lutalyse) is given to empty the uterus. Your veterinarian may insert a small catheter through the cervix and flush the uterus with sterile saline or

Betadine solution. A severely ill dam may require life-saving surgery to remove the uterus and ovaries.

Most dams with acute metritis are too ill to nurse puppies. The puppies should be taken off the mother and raised by hand, as described in chapter 17. Bitches who recover from acute metritis may develop a persistent low-grade infection of the lining of the uterus (see *Endometritis*, page 462).

Mastitis

The bitch normally has five pairs of mammary glands, or a total of 10 individual teats. There are two types of mastitis that can affect the nursing dam: caked breasts and acute septic mastitis.

Galactostasis (Caked Breasts)

Milk accumulation in late pregnancy and during lactation may increase to the point where the teats become distended, painful, and warm. They are not infected and the dam does not appear sick. Caking of the mammary glands also occurs during false pregnancy when there are no puppies to remove the milk. This may also occur when the litter is small and the dam has extra milk.

Caked breasts should be distinguished from the swollen breasts that develop when milk fails to let down after whelping (see *Agalactia*, page 486).

Treatment: Withhold water for 6 to 10 hours. Also withhold food for 24 hours and modestly restrict food intake for the next three days. Your veterinarian may prescribe a diuretic such as furosemide (Lasix).

Bitches with a false pregnancy often exhibit an excessive mothering instinct that includes licking and stimulating the teats, which makes matters worse. This can be prevented, in part, by giving a mild tranquilizer prescribed by your veterinarian. Hormonal therapy to dry up the breasts may be considered in cases of false pregnancy.

Acute Septic Mastitis

Acute mastitis is an infection or abscess of one or more of the mammary glands caused by bacteria that gain entrance from a scratch or puncture wound in the skin of the teat. Some cases are bloodborne and are associated with acute metritis. Breast infection can occur any time from day one to six weeks postpartum.

Dams with acute mastitis run a high fever, are depressed, and refuse to eat. The affected teats, usually the two largest ones close to the groin, are swollen, extremely painful, and usually reddish blue in appearance. The milk may be blood-tinged, thick, yellow, or stringlike. In some cases the milk appears normal.

Treatment: Acute mastitis should be treated under veterinary supervision. Routine measures include appropriate antibiotics and the application of warm compresses for 30 minutes three times a day, followed by gentle stripping of the infected gland to express the milk. Early treatment may prevent an abscess.

The milk of an infected breast is of poor nutritional quality, and puppies usually refuse to nurse from these teats. It is seldom necessary to tape a nipple or bind the teat to prevent nursing. However, if the puppies are trying to nurse the infected glands, you will need to do this. A mammary gland that is not suckled stops producing milk in three days.

If the dam is septic, her overall milk production may decline. She may show little interest in tending her puppies. If this happens, remove the puppies and raise them by hand. If they are 3 weeks or older, wean them and dry up the breasts as described in chapter 17.

The inflamed mammary gland of a dam with acute septic mastitis.

Prevention: Puppies should have their nails trimmed weekly beginning at 2 to 3 weeks of age to keep them from scratching the skin of the dam.

ECLAMPSIA (MILK FEVER)

Eclampsia is a seizurelike condition caused by low serum calcium (hypocalcemia). It usually appears two to four weeks postpartum. At this time there is a heavy drain on the mother's calcium stores because she is nursing.

Small dogs, particularly toys, are most likely to suffer from eclampsia. Large breeds are seldom affected. Eclampsia is also more likely to occur in dams who have not received optimum nutrition during pregnancy. It also occurs among dams with large litters and, paradoxically, in brood bitches who are given calcium supplements during pregnancy.

Signs of eclampsia are restlessness, anxiety, rapid breathing, and pale mucus membranes. The dam frequently leaves her puppies and paces up and down. Her gait may be stiff-legged, uncoordinated, and jerky. Tightening of the face muscles exposes the teeth and gives her face a pinched look. In severe cases, she falls down on her side, kicks all four legs, and salivates profusely. The rectal temperature may be elevated to 106°F (41°C).

Treatment: *Eclampsia is an emergency.* Notify your veterinarian at once. Intravenous calcium gluconate is a specific antidote. It is indicated at the first signs of muscle spasms or tremors. If the rectal temperature is over 104°F (40°C), treat as described for *Heat Stroke* (see page 22).

Puppies should be removed from the dam and fed by hand. If the puppies are 3 weeks or older, wean as described in chapter 17. After 24 hours, young puppies can be permitted to return to the mother—*if* she has completely recovered. For the first week, restrict nursing to 30 minutes two or three times a day. If the dam remains asymptomatic, these restrictions can be lifted.

Mothers who continue to nurse should be supplemented with an oral calcium preparation such as calcium carbonate. Continue the supplement for as long as the dam is nursing.

Agalactia (Absence of Milk)

Milk may be absent because it has failed to let down or because the dam is not producing milk.

Failure of Milk to Let Down

Most mothers instinctively encourage their puppies to suckle soon after delivery. Suckling stimulates the release of oxytocin from the pituitary gland. Oxytocin is responsible for milk letdown. A nervous, frightened, or stressed mother may discourage her puppies from suckling, or may release a hormone (epinephrine) that blocks the action of oxytocin.

This condition, which resembles galactostasis, should be suspected if the mammary glands are firm and swollen but no milk is found in the teat canals.

Puppies who are not receiving milk should be supplemented as described in *Raising Puppies by Hand*, page 496. Between supplements, it is important to encourage suckling to continue breast stimulation. Once the milk comes down, the dam usually accepts her puppies.

Treatment: Examine all the nipples to be sure they are open, fully formed, and erect. A deformed nipple may cause difficulty in suckling. A recessed nipple can be improved by massaging it to stimulate the flow of milk and then putting a vigorous suckler directly on that nipple.

The problem can be solved by giving oxytocin. It may be necessary to repeat the oxytocin during the first 48 hours.

Failure to Produce Enough Milk

True agalactia can be suspected if the bitch's breasts do not develop in late pregnancy. This condition may have a genetic basis. These puppies must be hand fed using artificial bitch's milk (see *Raising Puppies by Hand*, page 496).

Occasionally, a dam with a large litter is incapable of producing enough milk to satisfy all her puppies. The most common cause of insufficient milk production is failure to feed the mother an adequate number of calories, especially during the second and third weeks after whelping, when nursing demands are greatest. This problem is entirely preventable (see *Feeding a Nursing Dam*, page 481).

Treatment: There is no way to make a bitch produce more milk. If the mother is constitutionally unable to produce enough milk, her puppies should be supplemented with artificial bitch's milk.

Maternal Neglect

Mothers can neglect or injure their puppies for a number of reasons. The best way to prepare a dam for quality nurturing is to create an atmosphere conducive to a contented nest. The whelping quarters should be clean, dry, in a quiet, out-of-the-way location, and well heated to avoid chilling the puppies.

The mother-puppy bond begins during and shortly after birth. The mother recognizes each puppy by his distinctive scent. During the process of licking, cleaning, and nursing the puppy, she establishes a supportive relationship that remains until the puppy is weaned.

This bond may be less secure when puppies are born by C-section. Such mothers can have difficulty accepting their puppies for the first 24 hours. This is less likely to happen when some of the puppies are born before the surgery, or when the puppies are put to her nipples before the sedation wears off.

A bitch whelping her first litter should be watched closely. She may confuse the puppy with the placenta or injure a puppy while attempting to sever the cord and remove the membranes. Breeds with an undershot jaw or malocclusion problems are particularly prone to severing the cord too close to a pup's body or accidentally biting the puppy.

A novice mother may have difficulty coping with a litter of squirming puppies for the first few hours. With a little help, she can be shown how to nurse her puppies and keep from stepping on them. Some house pets are extremely people-oriented and show little interest in being a mother if it means loss of their human family's attention. Spend a good deal of time in the whelping area and allow the dam to have the run of the house. Lavishly praise the dam for being a good mother.

A dam may neglect her puppies if her milk does not come down during the first 24 hours. Treating of delayed milk letdown is described on page 486. Once the milk does comes down, the puppies begin to nurse and the bond is established.

It is important to keep visitors out of the whelping area for the first three to four weeks, especially when the dam is a novice or is high-strung. Letting children and unfamiliar people handle the pups is stressful for the dam.

An overprotective dam could injure her puppies by picking them up and carrying them to another spot. Return the entire family to the whelping box and stay with the mother, talking softly and stroking her often, until she settles in. Do not allow her to become frightened while carrying a puppy. Nest seeking can be prevented, in part, by introducing the dam to her whelping box two weeks before she is expected to deliver and encouraging her to sleep in it.

Other causes of puppy rejection are postpartum infections and complications such as milk fever, mastitis, and acute metritis. In these cases, puppies may have to be removed and reared by hand.

A fading puppy whose body temperature has dropped below normal due to sickness or constitutional weakness may be pushed out of the nest. This is nature's way of culling.

Maternal behavior is at least in part genetically inherited. Dams who show poor maternal behavior should not be bred and their daughters should not be bred. Before breeding your bitch, look into the maternal behavior of her dam.

Chapter 17

PEDIATRICS

Healthy newborn puppies are the picture of contentment, sleeping much of the time and awakening only to eat. For the first 48 hours, puppies sleep with their heads curled under their chests. While sleeping, they jerk, kick, and sometimes whimper. This is called activated sleep. It is the puppy's only way to exercise and helps develop muscle tone.

A good mother instinctively keeps her nest and puppies clean. By licking the belly and rectum of each puppy, she stimulates the elimination reflex.

Puppies can raise their heads at birth, but are unable to maintain an upright posture. By 5 days of age they can support their body weight with their front legs. Their eyes and ears are open at 10 to 14 days. By 2 weeks of age they should be actively crawling and may be able to stand a bit. At approximately 3 weeks of age, puppies can sit and are walking normally. They can also eat from a bowl. Puppies are fully oriented to sight and sound by 25 days.

The heart of a newborn puppy beats at 160 to 200 beats per minute. The puppy takes 15 to 35 breaths per minute and has an internal temperature ranging from 94°F (34.4°C) to 97°F (36°C). By 2 weeks of age, the normal heart rate is above 200 beats per minute and the respiratory rate 15 to 30 breaths per minute. The temperature gradually increases to 100°F (37.8°C) by 4 weeks of age.

It is best to disturb newborn puppies as little as possible—at least until they are a few weeks old. Some dams get anxious when their puppies are handled. There is a theory that too much handling interferes with the process by which puppies learn to identify and relate to their mothers and littermates. These interactions are important in establishing normal canine behavior. When these early imprints do not proceed as they should, a puppy could develop problems with shyness or aggression at a later date.

Early neurological stimulation may build up a pup's resistance to stress—the goal being a dog who handles stress well. Advocated by top breeder and author Dr. Carmen Battaglia, this program starts with five simple "stressors" from 3 to 16 days of life. The activities are tactical stimulation between the toes by gently touching between the toes with a cotton swab; holding the pup with his head supported in an erect position; holding the pup with his head pointed downward; and holding the pup on his back and gently touching his feet to a damp, chilled towel for three seconds. None of these should be done more than once a day and only for the briefest of times.

After 6 weeks of age, positive interactions with humans and exposure to new and nonthreatening situations are important for the development of a happy, well-adjusted pet.

Caring for Newborns

Newborn puppies are born with very little capacity to adapt to environmental stresses. They are extremely vulnerable. However, with proper care and attention to the special needs of these infants, many neonatal deaths can be avoided.

Two crucial factors to watch closely are the puppy's body temperature and his weight. A puppy's appearance, strength of suckle, sound of cry, and general behavior are also important indicators of his health and well-being.

GENERAL APPEARANCE AND VITALITY

Healthy puppies are round and firm. They nurse vigorously and compete for nipples. Their mouths and tongues are wet. When you insert a finger into their mouths, they have a strong, vigorous suckle.

A healthy newborn's skin is warm and pink. When pinched, it springs back resiliently. Pick up a puppy and he stretches and wiggles energetically in your hand. When removed from his mother, the puppy crawls back to her. Newborn puppies pile together for warmth.

A sick puppy presents a dramatically different picture. This puppy is limp, cold, and hangs like a dishcloth. He shows little interest in nursing and tires easily. If you insert a finger into his mouth, his suckle response is poor.

Newborn puppies seldom cry. Crying indicates that a puppy is cold, hungry, sick, or in pain. A distressed puppy crawls about looking for help and falls asleep away from the life-sustaining warmth of his mother and littermates. Later, he moves slowly and with great effort. He sleeps with his legs splayed apart and his head bent to the side. His cry is plaintive and piercing. Such a puppy is often rejected by the dam, who senses that the pup is not going to survive and pushes him out of the nest. The situation can sometimes be reversed if the puppy is treated and his body temperature is brought back to normal (see *Reviving a Weak Puppy*, page 495).

BODY TEMPERATURE

When a puppy is born, his body temperature is the same as his mother's. Immediately thereafter, his core temperature drops several degrees (how much depends upon the temperature of the room). Within 30 minutes, if the puppy is dry and snuggles close to his mother, his temperature begins to climb and reaches 94°F (34.4°C). Twenty-four hours later, his core or rectal temperature is 95° to 97°F (35°C to (36°C). It steadily increases, until at 3 weeks of age the rectal temperature is 98° to 100°F (36.6°C to (37.8°C). (How to take the newborn's rectal temperature is described in appendix A.)

During the first week of life, puppies do not have the capacity to constrict the blood vessels at the surface of their skin to retain heat. A newborn is able to maintain a body temperature 10°F to 12°F (3.8°C to 4.9°C) above his immediate surroundings for only short periods. When his mother is away for 30 minutes in a 72°F (22.2°C) room (well below the recommended level), the pup's core temperature quickly falls to 94°F (34.4°C) or below. This gravely reduces his metabolism.

Chilling is the single greatest danger to infant puppies. Low temperatures for these first few weeks are also one of the biggest reasons herpesvirus is able to successfully attack a litter. The temperature in the whelping box and surrounding area should be kept at 85° to 90°F (29.4°C to 32.2°C) for the first week. During the second week, reduce the temperature to 80°F (26.7°C). Then reduce the temperature gradually so that it is 70°F (21°C) when the litter is 6 weeks old. (Remember that the puppies still get heat from the mother dog, one another, blankets, and, often, a heat lamp over one corner of the whelping box.) Keep a constant check on the temperature using a thermometer placed on the floor of the whelping box.

THE IMPORTANCE OF NURSING

During the first 36 hours after whelping, mothers produce a special type of milk that is high in vitamins, minerals, and protein. This is the *colostrum*, or first milk of the dam. Colostrum also contains antibodies and other immune substances (primarily IgG) that provide protection against infectious diseases. Dams vaccinated one month before breeding have antibody levels high enough to protect puppies from distemper, parvovirus, and other infectious diseases for up to 16 weeks. Some veterinarians do not believe it is necessary to give the dam this booster shot; they believe she will have adequate immunity to pass on to her puppies as long as she is current on her vaccinations.

Newborn puppies nurse vigorously and compete for nipples. Puppies often nurse six to eight times a day, with suckling sessions lasting up to 30 minutes. Frequent nursing is essential to survival, because at this stage the energy for heat and metabolism is supplied principally through mother's milk.

Neonatal puppies have little subcutaneous fat, and reserve energy is supplied almost entirely by glycogen in the liver. The liver is the last organ to grow, while the brain is the organ that consumes the most energy, so a puppy with a brain too large in proportion to his liver rapidly runs out of energy. Accordingly, the weight of the liver at birth should be at least one and a half times the weight of the brain. It's even better if the liver is twice or three times the size of the brain. But even with a large liver–brain ratio, energy

Contented newborns.

reserves are limited. Therefore, the potential for low blood sugar must be offset by frequent feeding. A puppy who does not nurse frequently, for whatever reason, is headed for trouble.

The Importance of Weight Gain

After birth, puppies should gain 1 to 1.5 grams a day for each pound of anticipated adult weight, and should double their birth weights in 10 to 12 days. The anticipated adult weight is the weight of the dam. So if the dam weighs 30 pounds (13.6 kg), the puppies should gain 30 to 45 grams per day. (One ounce equals 28.35 grams.) A steady gain in weight is the best indicator that a puppy is doing well.

It is important to weigh each puppy at birth and 12 hours later on a scale that measures grams or ounces. You will need a scale that measures fine increments, because, initially, the gains are such small amounts. Then weigh each pup daily for the first two weeks and every three days thereafter until the puppies are 1 month old. Failure to gain weight is a cause for immediate concern. Notify your veterinarian.

When several puppies in the litter are not gaining at the expected rate, consider a maternal factor such as failure to produce enough milk (see *Agalactia*, page 486). A nursing dam needs two to three times more nutrition than a typical adult dog. If the mother is not getting enough calories, her milk supply will be inadequate to support a large litter. How much to feed during lactation is discussed in chapter 16.

When to Supplement

Puppies who gain weight steadily during the first seven days of life are in no danger. Puppies who lose some weight, but not more than 10 percent of their birth weight, for the first 48 hours of life and then begin to gain should be watched closely. Puppies who lose 10 percent or more of their birth weight in the first 48 hours and are not gaining by 72 hours are in trouble. Start supplemental feedings at once (see *Raising Puppies by Hand*, page 496).

If a puppy is 25 percent below the average weight of his littermates at birth, you can expect a high likelihood of mortality unless the puppy is hand fed. If possible, allow the pup to

Neonatal puppies should be weighed on a scale that measures ounces or grams.

nurse for the first 24 hours to receive colostrum. Then place him in a homemade incubator and raise him by hand. Alternatively you can supplement his nursing with hand feedings, but keep him with the litter—always checking that he is not being shoved away from the dam by larger pups. As soon as his weight approaches that of his littermates, he can be returned to the nest. Many immature puppies can be saved if supplemental feedings are started *before* they begin to fail.

DEHYDRATION

Kidney function in the newborn is 25 percent of what it will be later in life. These immature kidneys are unable to concentrate urine, and puppies therefore excrete large amounts of dilute urine regardless of whether they take in fluids. Thus, dehydration is a complicating factor whenever puppies become too weak to nurse. *This is another reason why it is important to begin supplemental feedings as soon as a puppy stops nursing or stops gaining weight.*

Signs of dehydration are lack of moisture in the mouth, a bright pink color to the tongue and mucous membranes, and loss of muscle tone and weakness. When the skin is pinched, it stays up in a fold.

Neonatal diarrhea is a serious cause of rapid dehydration and weight loss. When diarrhea occurs during hand feeding, it usually clears up when the strength of the formula is changed, as described in *Common Feeding Problems*, page 502. In all other cases of diarrhea, the puppies should be seen and treated by a veterinarian.

WHY PUPPIES DIE

The first two weeks of life is the period of greatest risk for newborn pups. Unfortunately, some early neonatal deaths are due to lack of advance preparation—especially failure to provide adequate heat in the whelping quarters, failure to vaccinate the dam (which gives neonatal infections a foothold), and failure to provide the dam with an adequate diet during pregnancy. These deaths are preventable.

Maternal factors are critical to puppy survival. Novice, obese, and elderly dams have higher puppy mortality rates than do experienced, well-conditioned, and younger dams. The quantity of the mother's milk is also of utmost importance. Genetic influences may play a role, but in most cases milk supply is insufficient because the dam has not been fed enough calories. This is especially true for dams with large litters.

Congenital and acquired birth defects are infrequent causes of newborn deaths. Cleft palate, often accompanied by harelip, prevents effective nursing. Large navel hernias allow the abdominal organs to protrude. Heart defects can be severe enough to produce circulatory failure. Other developmental disorders that may be responsible for neonatal deaths include hemophilia, esophageal atresia, pyloric stenosis, anal atresia, and malformations affecting the eyes and skeletal system.

The Physiologically Immature Puppy

An immature puppy is at a distinct disadvantage because of his low birth weight and lack of muscle mass and subcutaneous fat. This pup may be unable to breathe deeply, nurse effectively, and maintain body warmth. His liver–brain ratio may be less than 1.5:1. His birth weight will be 25 percent below that of his littermates. Such a puppy is likely to be crowded out by his brothers and sisters and forced to nurse at the least productive nipples.

A common cause of immaturity is inadequate growth while in the uterus. The fault may be placental insufficiency, perhaps due to overcrowding or a disadvantageous placement of a placenta in the wall of the uterus. These puppies are immature because of their development rather than their age, and are at risk of developing cardiopulmonary syndrome.

Cardiopulmonary Syndrome

This is a shocklike state of circulatory failure that occurs in puppies under 5 days of age. Many affected puppies are physiologically immature. Inadequate consumption of mother's milk shortly after birth may set the stage for this problem. Thereafter, weakness and hypoglycemia lead to chilling and dehydration. There is a drop in temperature and heart and breathing rates.

As the rectal temperature drops below 94°F (34.4°C), there is further depression of vital functions. Gradually, the crawling and righting reflexes are lost and the puppy lies on his side. Gagging and fluid in the nostrils may be noted. Later, poor circulation affects the brain, causing seizurelike spasms, accompanied by breathless periods lasting up to a minute. At this point, the condition is irreversible.

Early treatment is imperative to avoid death. Veterinary assistance is required.

Fading Puppies

These are puppies who are vigorous at birth but fail to gain weight and gradually lose vitality and the urge to feed. For want of a better term, the condition is called fading puppy syndrome. There is no agreement as to what causes puppies to fade. Some cases may result from immaturity, others from internal birth defects, environmental stresses, or maternal factors. The syndrome is reversible if the cause can be determined and steps taken to correct it, as discussed in the section that follows.

REVIVING A WEAK PUPPY

If a puppy is immature, weak, or fading, early treatment is imperative. New puppies are extremely fragile and can die quickly. Treatment involves slow warming to restore body temperature, oral fluids to correct dehydration, and supplemental feedings to provide calories.

A chilled puppy should be warmed *gradually.* Rapid warming using, for example, a heating pad, causes the blood vessels in the skin to dilate, increasing heat loss, expending more calories, and creating a greater need for oxygen. This harms rather than helps. However, if the puppy's rectal temperature is below 90°F (32.2°C), rapid warming under veterinary supervision may be required as a life-saving procedure.

The best way to warm a puppy gradually is to tuck him down next to your skin beneath a sweater or jacket and let your own warmth seep into the puppy. If the puppy's rectal temperature is below 94°F (34.4°C), warming will take two to three hours.

Chilled puppies are usually hypoglycemic and dehydrated. Correct mild to moderate dehydration by giving a warmed glucose-electrolyte solution such as Pedialyte, which can be purchased at drug stores and large grocery stores. Give 1 cc per ounce (28 g) of body weight every hour by eyedropper or baby nurser (see *How to Give Formula,* page 500) and warm slowly until the puppy is wiggling about. If a commercial solution is not available, as a temporary expedient you can substitute a solution of 1 teaspoon (8 g) of granulated sugar to 1 ounce (30 ml) of water. Severe dehydration, in which the puppy is too weak to nurse, should be treated by a veterinarian.

Never allow a cold puppy to nurse or receive formula. Never give chilled or cold formula to any puppy. When chilled, the stomach and small intestines will not digest or absorb milk. The puppy will bloat and perhaps vomit.

Once the puppy is warm and wiggling about, begin supplemental feedings to restore liver glycogen and supply calories, as described in *Raising Puppies by Hand*. If the puppy is immature, he will not be able to compete successfully with his littermates for milk and should be placed in a homemade incubator and raised by hand.

Raising Puppies by Hand

A dam may be incapable of raising a litter because of a uterine or mammary gland infection, eclampsia, or insufficient milk supply. In addition, an immature or sick puppy may need to be hand fed for survival. If the dam cannot raise the litter, you should inquire at your veterinarian's clinic about other recently born litters. If a litter is very close in age to yours and the healthy dam has only a few puppies, she might be convinced to foster a couple of extra pups. The dam must be of solid temperament and she must be observed closely while attempting this. The puppies to be fostered should be gently rubbed with blankets from the dam's whelping box to put the scent of that litter on them.

If no foster mother is found, you need to start supplementing. The decision to supplement a single pup (or an entire litter) is based on the puppy's general appearance and vitality, his weight at birth, and his progress in comparison to his littermates. It is far better to intervene early and start hand feeding a borderline case than to wait until a puppy is in obvious distress.

In some cases it may be possible to supplement two or three times a day and let the pup remain in the nest and continue to nurse. Other pups must be raised entirely by their breeder.

Whenever possible, puppies should nurse from the mother for the first 24 to 36 hours of life. During this period they receive antibodies in the colostrum that provide temporary immunity to the common canine infectious diseases. If the puppies do not get colostrum for whatever reason, you can use clear serum from the dam or order fresh frozen plasma to help provide immunity. Such puppies may need to be actively immunized starting at a young age.

When hand raising puppies, it is critically important to:

- Prevent chilling
- Prepare and feed the right formula
- Provide the right management

THE INCUBATOR

You can make a satisfactory incubator by dividing a cardboard box into separate compartments, one for each puppy. The compartments are important because orphaned puppies tend to suckle each other's ears, tails, and genitalia, which can cause problems. It goes on for the first three weeks. (If the puppies are nursed using a bottle and not a stomach tube, this may not happen.) After three weeks, the puppies should be put together for socialization and to establish normal behavior patterns.

The temperature in the incubator is of critical importance, since it provides the warmth that would have been provided by the mother. Place a thermometer in the incubator to monitor the surface temperature. Keep the incubator at 85° to 90°F (29.4°C to 32.2°C) for the first week. During the second week, reduce it to 85°F to 80°F (29.4°C to 26.7°C). Thereafter, gradually decrease the temperature to 75°F (23.9°C) by the end of the fourth week.

The temperature in the incubator will be the same as the room temperature if there are no drafts and you insulate the floor beneath the incubator with heavy padding. If the incubator and room temperature cannot be maintained with your existing heating system, provide additional heat using infrared heat lights or electric heaters. Avoid focusing heat directly on the puppies.

Electric heating pads can be used as a heat source, but are not as safe as heating the room. Puppies can become severely dehydrated or burned by continuous exposure to heating pads. If used, they should be heavily padded and should cover only one side of the box and one half the floor. This allows the puppies to escape from the heat if they become too hot. Cover the pad with a waterproof material such as plastic or rubber.

On the floor of the incubator place a baby diaper that can be replaced when it gets wet or soiled. This also provides a way to easily check the appearance of each puppy's stool, which is an excellent indicator of overfeeding (see *Overfeeding*, page 502).

Maintain the humidity of the room at about 55 percent to prevent dry skin and dehydration.

General Care

Everyone who handles the puppies should wash their hands before touching them—especially if they have touched other dogs. Many diseases, including distemper, can be transmitted to puppies by someone who has recently touched an infectious dog. All feeding equipment should be thoroughly cleaned and boiled. Visitors should not be allowed in the nursery for the first few weeks.

Keep the puppies clean with a damp cloth or disposable unscented baby wipes. Be sure to cleanse the anal area and the skin on the abdomen. You can rub a little baby oil on these areas and on the coat to prevent dry skin. Change the bedding often to prevent urine scalds. If they do appear, a light application of zinc oxide ointment will help. If infected, apply a topical antibiotic ointment such as neomycin or triple antibiotic.

For the first three weeks, gently swab the puppy's anal and genital areas after each feeding to stimulate elimination. (This is something the mother would do.) A wad of cotton or tissue soaked in warm water works well. Then dry the puppy.

HAND FEEDING

Commercial milk replacers that duplicate the composition of bitch's milk are the best formulas for infant puppies. These milk replacers are available through veterinarians and many pet supply stores. They have all but replaced cow's milk, goat's milk, and foster mothers.

Bitch's milk is unique in that it is high in protein and fat, low in lactose (milk sugar), and dense in calories. Cow's milk is not a suitable substitute for bitch's milk because it contains only half the number of calories per ounce and derives more calories from lactose than from protein and fat. Goat's milk, traditionally used as an animal milk substitute, does contain more calories per ounce than cow's milk, but is not ideal for puppies because it too is high in lactose and low in protein and fat. Newborn puppies do not have the intestinal enzymes to metabolize high concentrations of lactose, and feeding them cow's or goat's milk often leads to diarrhea.

Artificial bitch's milk can be purchased as a premixed liquid or a powder. Powdered products are reconstituted by adding water. Refrigerate the unused formula, but don't freeze it. Follow the directions of the manufacturer.

In the past, cataracts related to nutritional problems were reported in puppies fed home formulas and commercial milk replacers. These cataracts were found to have been caused by a deficiency of the amino acids phenylalanine and arginine. Commercial formulas have now been fortified to eliminate this problem.

While artificial bitch's milk is the best substitute for natural milk, the following home formula can be used as a *temporary* expedient until a commercial product can be purchased:

> 8 ounces (237 ml) homogenized whole milk
>
> 3 egg yolks
>
> 1 tablespoon (15 ml) corn oil
>
> 1 drop liquid pediatric vitamins
>
> Mix well and feed as you would a commercial milk replacer; refrigerate the unused portions

This formula provides 36 to 38 calories per ounce, or 1 to 1.25 calories per milliliter of formula. This is the same caloric density as commercial bitch's milk.

CALCULATING HOW MUCH FORMULA

Accurate record keeping is absolutely essential when raising puppies by hand. The best way to determine how much formula each puppy needs is to weigh the puppy and use a table of caloric requirements. Weigh them at birth on a scale that measures grams or ounces. Then weigh each puppy every eight hours for four days, daily for the next two weeks, then every three days until they reach 1 month of age.

During the first three weeks of life, puppies should receive 60 calories per pound (454 g) of body weight per day. All commercial milk replacer formulas provide 1 to 1.3 calories (kcals) per milliliter (ml). Since a liter is 1,000 ml, a milk replacer with a labeled caloric value of 1,000 kcals per liter provides 1 kcal per ml. One with a labeled caloric value of 1,300 kcals per liter provides 1.3 kcals per ml.

Daily requirements according to weight and age are given in the accompanying table. Divide the total daily requirement by the number of feedings per day to get the amount to give per feeding. This calculation must be made each day after the morning weighing.

Total Daily Calorie Requirements for New Puppies		
Age in weeks	Calories or ml per pound weight per day (using milk replacer that provides 1 kcal per ml)	Number of feedings
1	60	6
2	70	4
3	80	4
4	90	3

Here's an example of how to use the table: A 1-week-old puppy weighs half a pound (227 g) at the morning weighing. He will require 30 calories that day (that is, one half of 60 calories per pound). He requires six feedings a day, so divide that 30 calories by six and find that he needs 5 ml per feeding. If, as expected, the puppy's weight doubles in 10 days, he will weigh about 1 pound (454 g) and will require 60 ml per day, or 15 ml at each of four feedings.

Note that this chart assumes the caloric density of the milk replacer is 1 kcal per ml. If the milk replacer you use has a different density, divide the number in the middle column by that density to determine the number of ml needed per pound of body weight per day. For example, if your milk replacer is 1.3 kcals per ml, divide the number in the middle column by 1.3. Then proceed as above.

If the puppy is unable to take in the required number of milliliters per feeding, reduce the volume and increase the number of feedings to meet his daily requirements.

As long as the pup does not cry excessively, feels firm in the abdomen, gains weight, and has a light brown stool several times a day, you can be almost certain the diet is meeting his nutritional needs. Continue to increase the amount you are feeding according to the table. At 3 to 4 weeks, begin to introduce semisolid food (see *Weaning,* page 509).

HOW TO GIVE FORMULA

Puppies can be fed using a baby nursing bottle, special puppy bottles, or a stomach tube. An eyedropper can be used in an emergency. Use it as described for the baby bottle. *Always be sure to feed formula at room temperature.*

Keep in mind that all hand-fed puppies must have their anal and genital areas massaged with a wad of cotton soaked in warm water after each feeding to prevent constipation and stimulate the elimination reflexes.

Baby or Puppy Bottles

Using a bottle has the advantage of satisfying the suckling urge, but it requires a puppy who is strong enough to suck. When using a small baby bottle or a commercial puppy nurser with a soft nipple, you may need to enlarge the hole in the nipple so that the milk drips out slowly when the bottle is turned over. Otherwise, the puppy may tire after a few minutes and stop nursing. However, if the hole is too large, the milk will run out too fast and make the puppy choke.

This is the correct position for bottle feeding. Do not cradle the pup on his back as you would a human baby.

The correct position for bottle feeding is to place the puppy in an upright position as if he is standing on a flat surface, holding him under the stomach and chest. Do not cradle him like a human baby, because the formula will run into his trachea. Open the puppy's mouth with the tip of your finger, insert the nipple, and hold the bottle at a 45-degree angle to prevent the puppy from swallowing air. Keep a slight pull on the bottle to encourage vigorous sucking.

The feeding usually takes five minutes or longer. Afterward, burp the puppy by resting him on your shoulder and gently rubbing or patting the back. Then swab the anal and genital areas with a piece of cotton soaked in warm water to stimulate voiding and defecation.

Tube Feeding

The advantages of tube feeding are that it takes about two minutes to complete each feeding and little air is swallowed. Tube feeding also ensures that a proper amount of formula is administered to each puppy. And it is the only satisfactory way to feed immature or sick puppies who are too weak to nurse. Puppies fed by tube must be kept in separate incubator compartments to avoid the suckling damage caused by littermates.

Tube feeding is not difficult to do. It requires a soft rubber catheter tube, size 5 to 10 French, depending on the size of the puppy. A puppy weighing less than 10 ounces (283 g) requires a size 5. You'll also need a 10- or 20-ml plastic or glass syringe (minus the needle). These items can be bought at a drug store or from your veterinarian.

A puppy's stomach is even with his last rib. Measure the tube by holding it along the puppy's body, from the mouth to the last rib, and mark it with a piece of tape. Draw the formula into the syringe, taking care to expel all air, and warm it to body temperature by immersing the syringe in hot water.

Arouse the puppy and place him on his chest in a *horizontal* position. Moisten the tip of the tube with formula and allow the puppy to suckle it briefly.

Tube feeding is the only satisfactory way to give formula to a puppy who is too weak to nurse.

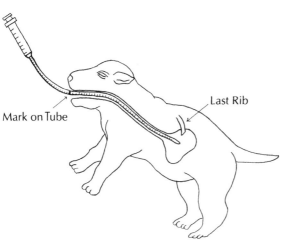

Mark on Tube

Last Rib

Then pass the tube slowly over the puppy's tongue and into the throat. With steady pressure, the puppy will swallow the tube. Pass it down the esophagus and into the stomach, to the level of the mark you made on the tube with tape.

Slowly inject a small amount of water (1 to 2 ml) into the tube. If the puppy coughs or gasps, the tube went into the trachea by mistake and the tip of the tube is in his lungs. This is not as serious a problem as if formula were injected, because water is more easily absorbed. (Putting formula into the lungs, though, can kill a puppy.) Withdraw and reposition the tube.

When the tube is in the correct position, attach the syringe to the tube and slowly inject the formula into the puppy's stomach over a two-minute period. All feedings should be injected gradually so as not to distend the stomach. If the formula is injected too rapidly, it will be regurgitated and may cause aspiration pneumonia. This is most likely to happen during the first tube feeding. The first feeding or two with a feeding tube should be at slightly less than the calculated amount, to help the puppy's stomach adjust to the volume.

When all the formula has been injected, remove the tube and raise the puppy into a vertical position to burp him. Swab the anal and genital areas with a piece of cotton soaked in warm water after each feeding to stimulate voiding and defecation.

At about 14 days of age, the trachea of many puppies becomes large enough that the feeding tube may accidentally be passed into it instead of into the esophagus. Change to a larger tube (size 8 or 10 French). Or by now, the puppy may be strong enough to suckle from a bottle.

COMMON FEEDING PROBLEMS

The two most common feeding problems are overfeeding and underfeeding. Overfeeding causes diarrhea. An underfed pup will fail to gain weight. Both of these can be avoided by monitoring the weight of the puppy and computing the correct amount of formula to give at each feeding. Steady weight gain and a normal stool (firm to semi-firm and yellow to light brown) are good indications that you are feeding the right amount.

Overfeeding

Experience has shown that breeders are more likely to overfeed than underfeed a puppy. The best way to tell whether a puppy is being overfed is to monitor his stools. If the puppy is fed four times a day, you can expect four to five stools, or about one stool after each feeding.

The first sign of overfeeding is loose stool. A loose yellow stool indicates a mild degree of overfeeding. Reduce the strength of the formula by diluting it one-third with water. As the stools become firm, gradually restore the formula to its full strength.

With moderate overfeeding, there is more rapid movement of food through the intestinal tract, indicated by a greenish stool. The green color is due to unabsorbed bile. Dilute the strength of the formula by one-half. Mix one part water or Pedialyte to one part formula. Gradually return the formula to full strength as the stools become yellow and firm.

Unchecked overfeeding leads to very rapid transit and depletion of digestive enzymes and electrolytes. This causes a grayish diarrhea. Eventually, when there is little or no digestion of formula due to rapid transit, the stool looks like curdled milk. At this point the puppy is getting no nutrition and is rapidly dehydrating. This puppy will need to be rehydrated by giving a balanced electrolyte solution subcutaneously or hourly by stomach tube; this is best done by a veterinarian.

Any diarrhea that does not respond to diluting the formula—or where the stools are gray or white—is serious and may be caused by neonatal infection. Call your veterinarian without delay. This requires professional attention.

Underfeeding

Puppies who are being underfed cry continuously, appear listless and apathetic, attempt to suckle littermates, gain little or no weight from one feeding to the next, and begin to chill. Puppies dehydrate quickly when they're not getting enough formula. Review your feeding protocol. Check the temperature of the incubator.

RAISING A SINGLETON

Raising a singleton puppy can present additional challenges. It is important to monitor his weight carefully, as the puppy will have a tendency to overeat and become overweight. You may need to bind up some of the dam's mammary glands or only allow nursing for short periods.

A single puppy will miss the litter interactions that are so important to the development of every animal. A stuffed "fake puppy" with realistic heart sounds can be purchased as a sleeping buddy for the first couple of weeks, to help mimic a littermate.

If a litter of about the same age can be found and the dam is agreeable, taking one or two puppies from that litter to foster will be good for the behavioral development of the singleton. Barring that, it will be important to arrange for puppy play dates with other litters once they are a bit older. (See *The Importance of Early Socialization*, page 512.)

Diseases of Newborn Puppies
NEONATAL ISOERYTHROLYSIS

This is a quite rare but often fatal hemolytic anemia of the newborn that sometimes occurs when a bitch with one blood type is mated to a dog with another. The puppies who inherit the blood group of the sire develop hemolytic anemia when they ingest colostrum that contains antibodies designed to attack their red blood cells. These antibodies are manufactured by the dam only if she has been previously sensitized to the sire's blood group antigens—which can occur when fetal cells of a different blood type cross the placenta.

Affected puppies are born healthy and start to nurse vigorously. But once they drink the dam's colostrum, the dam's antibodies begin to destroy their red blood cells. They start to show clinical signs within hours to days, stop nursing, and fail to thrive. They develop hemolytic anemia within one to two days after birth and some or all will die.

Early clinical signs of the disease include dark red-brown urine, weakness, failure to thrive, and jaundice. Death can occur in 24 hours. Blood tests, urinalysis, and blood typing can diagnosis the condition.

Treatment: As soon as you suspect hemolytic anemia, stop all nursing and notify your veterinarian. The puppies may require blood transfusions from a compatible donor to restore their red cells. Puppies from subsequent litters should not be allowed to receive colostrum from the dam, unless the sire and dam have compatible blood types.

UMBILICAL (NAVEL) INFECTION

A common predisposing factor in navel infection is severing the umbilical cord too close to the abdominal wall. This leaves no stump to wither up and separate cleanly. Other possible causes are a dam with dental disease who transmits bacteria when she severs the umbilical cord, and an unclean whelping box contaminated by urine and stools. An infected navel looks red and swollen and may drain pus or form an abscess.

There is a direct communication between the umbilical cord and the liver, which makes even a low-grade umbilical infection potentially dangerous. Untreated, puppy *septicemia* is likely.

Treatment: At the first indication of navel infection, seek veterinary attention for antibiotic treatment. If one puppy has an umbilical infection, it may also be present in other puppies in the litter.

Iodine applied to the navel stump at birth as a preventive measure reduces the likelihood of umbilical infection.

PUPPY SEPTICEMIA

Blood-borne infections in young puppies are caused by bacteria that gain entrance via the respiratory and gastrointestinal tracts. They occur in puppies 5 to 12 weeks of age. At this age maternal antibodies are in decline and immunity acquired through vaccinations is not as strong as it eventually will be. This creates a window of vulnerability.

Very important contributing factors include overcrowding, chilling, poor nutrition, unsanitary whelping quarters, a heavy burden of intestinal parasites, and coexistent viral infections. In a healthy environment, bacterial exposure usually produces only a mild, self-limiting illness. But when environmental stresses are added, the death rate is high.

Signs of respiratory involvement include fever, cough, nasal discharge, and rapid, noisy breathing. When the gastrointestinal tract is involved, signs include loss of appetite, vomiting, diarrhea, weakness, dehydration, and weight loss.

Treatment: Notify your veterinarian if a puppy shows any of the signs just described. Shock and dehydration are treated with antibiotics and intravenous fluids. Respiratory and GI tract infections are treated as described for *Pneumonia*, page 324, and *Acute Infectious Enteritis*, page 274.

CANINE HERPESVIRUS

Canine herpesvirus causes a fatal illness in puppies 1 to 2 weeks of age. It usually does not causes illness in puppies older than 3 weeks of age. The reason is that the body temperature of puppies younger than 3 weeks of age is below 98°F (36.6°C), and the virus replicates only at the lower temperatures.

Herpesvirus is acquired by the mother during breeding and takes up residence in her vagina. Puppies acquire the virus while in utero, during passage through the birth canal, or by direct contact with their dam and infected littermates.

This is an insidious disease. The dam is healthy and the puppies nurse in a normal manner until shortly before death. The illness begins with abrupt cessation of nursing, followed by abdominal distention, chilling, lack of coordination, and a yellow-green diarrhea. Puppies are in agony and cry out pitifully. Death usually occurs in 24 hours.

Treatment: There is no specific treatment, but survival is possible. Unaffected littermates should be placed in a homemade incubator in a room with an ambient temperature of 100°F (37.8°C). Since the virus does not multiply well at temperatures above 98°F (36.6°C), this may prevent it from reproducing and causing infection.

Puppies who recover may develop irreversible neurological symptoms, including lack of coordination, dizziness, and blindness.

Prevention: There is no available vaccine in North America at this time (there is one in Europe). Infected dams develop immunity and subsequent litters are rarely affected. Ideally, pregnant bitches should be isolated for three weeks before and after whelping—meaning no contact with dogs going to and from shows, kennels, training classes, sporting events, and so on.

FLAT (SWIMMER) PUPPIES

Puppies begin to stand at 14 days and have a semi-steady gait by 3 weeks of age. If this does not happen, the puppy may be a swimmer. This disease is caused by a weakness of the adductor muscles that pull the legs together. The hind legs usually are more severely affected.

Hobbling a swimmer puppy helps him keep his feet beneath him.

Swimmer puppies move by making swimming motions. They resemble turtles with their legs sticking out to the sides, and are flat-chested from lying on their stomachs.

The disease is more likely to occur in overweight and heavy-boned puppies. It may have a congenital basis. One theory is that puppies are infected by a viral or fungal disease in utero that results in a muscular dystrophy of the adductor muscles.

Treatment: Slippery floors aggravate the problem. Keep swimmers on indoor-outdoor carpeting or some other nonslippery surface that provides good traction.

Assist a swimmer puppy to stand and walk several times a day. Encourage him to sleep on his side, rather than splayed flat out. A hobble made from tape, placed from elbow to elbow or hock to hock, forces the pup to sleep on his side. It also keeps the legs beneath him when he stands.

In most cases the condition is self-correcting as the adductor muscles develop and strengthen.

PYLORIC STENOSIS

Congenital pyloric stenosis is caused by a thickening of the ring of muscle at the outlet of the stomach, resulting in a partial or complete obstruction of the gastric outlet. The cause is unknown. An increased incidence is seen in *brachycephalic* breeds such as Boxers and Boston Terriers.

Symptoms begin at weaning or shortly thereafter, when pups start to eat solid food. The characteristic sign of pyloric stenosis is vomiting partially digested food several hours after eating. Typically, the vomitus does not contain green bile. The vomited meal may be ingested, only to be vomited again later.

The diagnosis is made by an upper gastrointestinal X-ray examination. The presence of barium in the stomach 12 to 24 hours after ingestion indicates an obstructed stomach. *Gastroscopy* may be recommended.

Treatment: Pyloric stenosis is treated effectively with an operation that divides the enlarged muscular ring between the stomach and the duodenum. Some dogs recover without surgery, but dietary management is essential. The choice of treatment depends on a number of factors that must be determined by your veterinarian, but most cases require surgery.

An acquired form of pyloric stenosis, called hypertrophic gastropathy, occurs in middle-aged dogs (see *Chronic Gastritis*, page 268).

SKIN INFECTIONS

Scabs, blisters, and purulent crusts can develop on the skin of newborn puppies 4 to 10 days of age. These sores sometimes contain pus. They usually appear on the abdomen and are caused by poor sanitation in the whelping box.

Treatment: Keep the nest clean of food, stools, and urine. Check for any signs of external parasites, such as fleas or Cheyletiella mites, in the bedding. Cleanse scabs with a dilute solution (1:10) of hydrogen peroxide or wash with a dilute antiseptic solution such as Betadine or chlorhexidine (see *Common Drugs for Home Veterinary Use*, page 571). Then apply an antibiotic ointment such as triple antibiotic or neomycin.

CLEFT PALATE

Cleft palate is a birth defect caused by incomplete fusion of the two sides of the palate. This results in a passageway between the oral and nasal cavities that enables food and liquids to pass between them. Newborn puppies have a discharge from both nostrils and may find it impossible to create enough suction to nurse. Survival then depends on tube feeding. Many puppies do not thrive due to inhalation pneumonia and may die fairly young.

Cleft palate occurs sporadically in all breeds, but is most common in Bulldogs, Boston Terriers, Beagles, Miniature Schnauzers, Pekingese, and Cocker Spaniels. In these breeds the defect is hereditary. Affected dogs should not be bred.

Harelip is the result of incomplete development of the upper lip. It can occur independently or along with cleft palate. The problem is mainly cosmetic.

Treatment: Cleft palate and harelip can be corrected by plastic surgery. This usually is done at 3 months of age. This is a complex surgery and should only be done by a veterinarian with experience, because there is a high complication rate. For pups with severe cleft palate, euthanasia may be suggested.

HYPOGLYCEMIA (LOW BLOOD SUGAR)

Hypoglycemia is a syndrome that occurs primarily in toy breeds between 6 and 12 weeks of age. A hypoglycemic attack is often precipitated by stress. The typical signs are listlessness, depression, staggering gait, muscular weakness, and tremors—especially of the face. Puppies with a severe drop in blood sugar develop seizures or become stuporous and go into a coma. Death can follow. This particular sequence of symptoms is not always seen. though. For example, some puppies exhibit only weakness or a wobbly gait. Occasionally a puppy who seemed just fine is found in coma.

Episodes of hypoglycemia often occur without warning—for example, when a puppy is stressed by shipping. Other common causes of acute hypoglycemia are missing a meal, chilling, becoming exhausted from too much play, or having an upset stomach. These events place an added strain on the energy reserves of the liver.

Hypoglycemia can occur in adult hunting dogs as a consequence of sustained exercise and depletion of liver glycogen. It is important to feed these dogs before hunting and to increase the protein content of their diets. Hypoglycemia in diabetic dogs is caused by insulin overdose (see *Diabetes Mellitus*, page 300). Unexplained hypoglycemia that occurs in older dogs is likely to be caused by an insulin-secreting tumor of the pancreas.

Prolonged or repeated hypoglycemic attacks in toy breed puppies can cause brain damage. Puppies with frequent attacks should undergo veterinary testing to rule out an underlying problem, such as liver shunt, infection, or an enzyme or hormone deficiency.

Treatment: The treatment of an acute attack is aimed at restoring the blood sugar. Begin immediately. If the puppy is awake and able to swallow, give corn syrup or sugar water by syringe (see *How to Give Medications*, page 567), or rub corn syrup, honey, or glucose paste on the gums. You should see improvement in 30 minutes. If not, call your veterinarian.

If the pup is unconscious, do not give an oral solution because it will be inhaled. Rub corn syrup, honey, or glucose paste on the gums and proceed at once to your veterinarian. This puppy will require an intravenous dextrose solution and may need to be treated for brain swelling.

Oral glucose paste is sold at pharmacies. If you know your dog is subject to hypoglycemic attacks, keep this product on hand.

Prevention: Susceptible puppies should be fed at least four times a day. It is important to feed a high-carbohydrate, high-protein, high-fat diet. It is essential that the diet be high quality. Your veterinarian can recommend an appropriate premium food.

Food supplements and table scraps should not exceed 5 to 10 percent of the total daily ration. Owners of toy puppies should take precautions to see that they do not become excessively tired or chilled. Many (but not all) puppies outgrow this problem.

Hernia

A hernia is a protrusion of fat and/or bowel through an opening in the body wall that would normally close during development. The protrusion produces a bulge. The two common sites for hernia are the groin and navel. A hernia in the groin is called an inguinal hernia, and one in the navel area is called an umbilical hernia. Perineal hernias occur in adult dogs near the rectal area.

If the bulge can be pushed back into the abdomen, the hernia is reducible. If not, it is incarcerated. An incarcerated hernia becomes strangulated when the blood supply to the contents of the hernia sac is pinched off. An incarcerated hernia often becomes strangulated over time. Any hard or painful swelling at the navel or in the groin could be an incarcerated hernia and will require immediate veterinary attention.

Hernias have a hereditary basis, because there is a genetic predisposition for delayed closure of the abdominal ring. Dogs born with hernias that do not close spontaneously should not be bred. Rarely, a navel hernia may develop when the umbilical cord is cut too close to the abdominal wall.

Inguinal hernias are more common in female dogs. A bulge in the groin may not be seen until after the bitch has been bred or becomes very old, in which case a pregnant or diseased uterus may be incarcerated in the hernia. These hernias should be repaired. Small inguinal hernias in male puppies can be watched closely, as many will close spontaneously. If they do not, ask to have them repaired.

Umbilical hernias occur frequently in puppies at about 2 weeks of age. They usually get smaller and disappear by 6 months of age. Binding the abdominal wall with straps does not increase the chance of closure.

Treatment: If you can push a finger through the umbilical ring, the hernia should be repaired. The operation is not difficult and the pup can go home the same day. In females, repair of an umbilical hernia can often be delayed until the time of spaying.

Weaning

The right time to wean depends upon several factors, including the size of the litter, the condition of the dam, the quantity of mother's milk, and the inclinations of the breeder. If a dam with a small litter is left to her own devices, she might continue to nurse her puppies for 10 weeks or longer.

Weaning should be a *gradual* process. For larger breeds, begin at about 3 weeks of age. For toy breeds, begin at about 4 weeks. Weaning should not be completed before 6 to 8 weeks of age, unless it is necessary for medical reasons. Early weaning and separation from the mother and littermates may result in adjustment problems later in life. Some breeders, especially those with toy breeds, elect to keep the litter with the dam until 10 weeks of age.

To stimulate the pups' appetites for solid food, remove the dam from the whelping room two hours before each feeding. After the meal of solid food, let her return to nurse. She should remain with the litter at night.

Choose a commercial food formulated to meet the needs of growing puppies. A number of good products are available. Read the label to be sure the product is recommended for puppies 3 to 4 weeks of age and older. Many people prefer to use dry kibble, but canned products are equally satisfactory. Vitamin-mineral supplements are not necessary or desirable when you are feeding a nutritionally balanced puppy growth food.

How to Feed

To feed dry food, mix one part kibble to three parts water to make a gruel. Warm the food to room temperature and feed in a low-rimmed saucer or pie pan. Start by dipping your fingers into the mixture and letting the puppies lick it off. Offer this gruel three or four times a day. Do not leave a pan of gruel down for free-choice feeding. Offer the gruel for 20 minutes and remove what is not eaten. You need to supervise to be sure all the pups are getting a chance to eat.

Initially, puppies may play in the gruel more than eat it. Be prepared to clean all the puppies thoroughly after each feeding to prevent skin problems.

When the puppies are eating the gruel well, *gradually* reduce the water content over a few weeks until they are eating the mixture dry. This usually is accomplished by 5 to 7 weeks of age.

At this time there is less demand on the dam's milk supply. Decrease her food intake if you have not already begun to do so. This initiates the process of drying up her milk.

Puppies who eat too much gruel are apt to get diarrhea. Temporarily reduce the number of feedings and continue with nursing.

To feed canned food, begin by mixing two parts canned food with one part water. When the puppies are eating this mixture well, reduce the water content and follow the same general procedures described for feeding dry food.

Puppies need a lot of water and dehydrate quickly if they don't get enough fluids. Remember that before weaning, the pups' water requirements were being supplied entirely by the dam's milk. Accordingly, as milk feedings are reduced, it is vital to keep a bowl of clean fresh water available at all times. You can purchase or make waterers that won't tip or find bowls that don't flip easily. You don't want wet, chilled puppies.

To promote socialization and avoid behavior problems, feed puppies together until they are at least 6 weeks old. Allow the puppies to eat as much as they want in 20 minutes and then pick up the dish. Puppies should be fed at least three times a day from weaning to 6 months of age.

If it becomes necessary to dry up the dam's milk, withhold all food and water from her for 24 hours. The next day, feed her one-quarter of the normal amount. The third day, feed one-half the normal amount, and the fourth day feed three-quarters of the normal amount. Thereafter, feed a regular adult maintenance food.

Feeding Growing Puppies

You can determine the daily caloric requirements for growing puppies by consulting the table on this page. Compare the daily caloric needs with the number of calories per pound or kilogram of commercial food (this information is on the product label) to determine how much food to give each puppy per day. Divide by the number of feedings (three or four) to determine how much to feed at each meal.

For example, if you have a 33-pound dog who is 11 weeks old and is eating three meals a day, his daily caloric requirement is 2,179 kcals. If you're feeding a puppy food that offers 1,767 kcal per pound of food (as stated on the label), your puppy needs 1.23 pounds of food a day to meet his needs. Divide that over three meals, and he gets 6.5 ounces of food at each meal.

Daily Caloric Requirements to Maintain Average Weight Gain in Young Puppies

Body weight		Daily kcals required	
Pounds	Kilograms	Weaning to 3 months	3 to 6 months
2.2	1	268	214
6.6	3	649	520
11.0	5	915	732
15.4	7	1,107	934
19.8	9	1,394	1,115
24.3	11	1,670	1,331
28.7	13	1,929	1,543
33.1	15	2,179	1,743
37.5	17	2,415	1,932
41.9	19	2,640	2,112
46.3	21	2,856	2,285
50.7	23	3,062	2,450
55.1	25		2,618
59.5	27		2,785
63.8	29		2,945
72.8	33		3,250
81.6	37		3,551

(Modified from *Veterinary Pediatrics*, 2nd Edition, Johnny D. Hoskins, 1995)

Bear in mind, however, that these requirements are approximations based on the average dog. Your dog's needs will vary according to his activity level and temperament. The amount fed should be adjusted to maintain optimal weight and condition.

There are now many specialty foods designed for dogs of particular groups, such as sporting dogs or terriers, or for groups of dogs based on size, such as for large-breed puppies. Discuss with your veterinarian if one of those diets would be best for your puppy.

The Importance of Early Socialization

The first 12 weeks of life are extremely important and determine, to a great extent, a puppy's personality and sociability. Studies show that puppies go through a series of developmental stages. The successful negotiation of each stage is essential to avoiding future problems such as timidity, fear-biting, phobias, and dominance aggression. A pup with little or no exposure to people and dogs during the first three months of life adjusts poorly as an adult—despite attempts to compensate for this at a later date.

Separating puppies from their mothers and littermates before 6 weeks of age has been found to have adverse effects on a puppy's weight and physical condition. During the period between 3 and 8 weeks of age, puppies are receptive to and greatly influenced by interactions with their dam, littermates, and other dogs on the premises. These interactions enable the puppy to develop self-awareness and adopt appropriate dog behavior.

The ability to get along with dogs later in life is due, in part, to a smooth transition through this 3- to 8-week period. Thus, puppies should remain with their dam and littermates until they are 8 to 10 weeks of age and are fully weaned and eating puppy food.

Between 5 and 7 weeks of age, puppies become receptive to forming relationships with people. During this stage, puppies learn the leadership role of human beings and also learn that people are not threatening and provide food, pleasure, and rewards.

At 8 to 9 weeks, puppies develop strong preferences for urinating and defecating on certain types of surfaces—carpets, floors, grass, dirt, and so on. Housetraining can begin at this age. If the puppy room has been divided into two or more distinct areas, puppies will have started to housetrain themselves by using one area to eliminate. Providing such an area with a distinctive substrate, such as wood shavings, will help the pups adjust in their new homes. The new families can then put some wood shavings out in the area of their yard they wish the pup to eliminate on.

At 10 to 12 weeks, and again at 16 to 20 weeks, puppies are curious and do well exploring novel environments. This is a good time to begin car rides, obedience classes, and trips to the park.

In summary, it is critical that breeders expose puppies to other dogs starting at 3 weeks of age. Successful interactions are those that build confidence, are not stressful, and do not frighten the puppy. Handling puppies younger than 5 weeks of age is not detrimental, as long as it is not extremely stressful and does not induce fear. After 5 weeks, puppies should be picked up, petted, and handled in a pleasurable manner with increasing frequency.

Socialization should continue when a puppy goes to his new home. It is best to expose your puppy to as many positive experiences as possible. Take him with you in the car and go for walks where you will see other people and dogs. This allows the pup to get used to the noise and distractions of public life and meet and play with dogs who are gentle, friendly, and well socialized.

From about 12 to 14 or 16 weeks, your puppy's immune system will be in flux. The maternal immunity he got from nursing is wearing off and his own immune system is starting to kick in. At this time, it is best to have your pup around only those other dogs whom you know are healthy and to avoid areas where large numbers of unknown dogs may gather.

Acquiring a New Puppy
SELECTING A BREED

If you are planning to show and breed your puppy when he grows up, read *Breeding Purebred Dogs*, page 430. If you want a pet or family companion, give some thought to the type of dog that best suits your lifestyle. Dogs come in all sizes, shapes, and mixtures, and all are equally loveable. Some dogs require more exercise, more grooming, or more training. Some are too large for apartment living or too small for ranch life. Some breeds are known for their outgoing nature and love of children. Others have strong guarding and territorial instincts. These are just some of the attributes that make one breed of dog a better choice for a specific person than another. Mixed breeds generally have the characteristics of the breeds that are predominant in the mixture.

A large selection of books about specific breeds is available at most public libraries. *The Complete Dog Book* (an official publication of the American Kennel Club) is an excellent reference and contains facts and information on all breeds of dog.

A huge amount of information on dogs, breeds, and breed clubs, is available through the Internet. Many breeders and breed clubs maintain web pages and provide photographs and information on their breed and their breeding programs. Keep in mind that information on the Internet is not regulated. Use it as a good reference, but confirm what you read from other sources. If a breed sounds too good to be true—no health, behavior, or temperament problems—it undoubtedly *is* too good to be true!

Selecting a Breeder

When you know what breed you want, the next step is finding a reputable breeder. The two well-established registries in the United States, the American Kennel Club (AKC) and the United Kennel Club (UKC), both have breeder referral information on their websites (see appendix D). You can also search for local clubs devoted to the breed in which you are interested, and then call or write the secretary of the club to obtain written information and a list of breeders who are members of the club.

After you locate several breeders who have the breed of puppy you are looking for, write or call each one and explain whether you are looking for a family companion and pet, if you plan to show and/or breed, and if you prefer a male or a female. A sincere inquiry, including information about yourself, is much more likely to elicit the type of response you are looking for than a hastily scribbled note. Be prepared for the breeder to ask questions about you and your family. A responsible breeder is concerned about the future welfare of all the puppies he or she places.

It is a good policy to insist on buying the puppy pending a veterinary examination (at your expense), with a 72-hour guarantee to return the puppy if a health problem is found. Conscientious breeders who are proud of their puppies and willing to stand behind them will not object to this request. Any guarantees concerning the puppy must be discussed and agreed upon *before* the check is signed. Be sure to ask for and receive the puppy's registration paperwork, pedigree, health certificate, current diet sheet, and immunization record.

If you are interested in an older puppy or an adult dog, you may want to consider adopting a dog from the local animal shelter or a breed rescue group. Each year, animal shelters in the United States receive millions of wonderful mixed-breed and purebred dogs with one thing in common: They all need good homes. Most purebred dog clubs also maintain rescue operations for dogs of their breed who are found lost, turned in to shelters, or turned in by owners who can no longer keep the dog. These groups foster the rescued dogs, update their health care, and can offer you a very good idea of the dog's temperament and behavior.

Breeders may also have adult dogs they are looking to place. This could be a dog who didn't work out as a show or breeding prospect but has some training and is well behaved.

Choosing a Healthy Puppy

The best time to acquire a puppy is at 8 to 12 weeks of age. At this age a puppy should be well socialized, will have received the first series of immunizations, and should be weaned and eating solid food. The breeder can usually make a good guess about whether a puppy is of show or breeding quality. But keep in mind that picking a future champion at 8 weeks of age is a problem, even for breeders with considerable experience.

Most puppies 8 to 12 weeks old tolerate the stresses of being shipped by air, especially if they can travel accompanied in the cabin in a soft-sided carry bag made for pets. For toy and small breeds it is best to rely on the experience of the breeder when considering this option. Even better, try to avoid flying a puppy and plan to drive to and from the breeder if it is at all possible.

If possible, visit the kennel and make your own selection. An experienced breeder will guide you based on what you want in a puppy, the puppy aptitude test results, and the breeder's experience from living with the puppies for their first crucial weeks. Be prepared when, on the appointed day, you find yourself standing before a litter of bouncing puppies and find that all appear to be equally lovable.

Most puppies look healthy at first glance, but a closer inspection may make some puppies more desirable than others. Take your time and go over each puppy from head to tail before making the final decision.

Begin by examining the head. The nose should be cool and moist. Nasal discharge or frequent sneezing is a sign of poor health. *Brachycephalic* breeds, such as Pugs and Pekingese, often have nostrils that collapse when the dog breathes in. This is undesirable.

Check the puppy for a correct bite. The correct bite for most breeds is a scissors bite, in which the upper incisors just slightly overlap the lower ones. An even bite, in which the incisors meet edge to edge, is equally acceptable in most breeds. If the scissors bite is exaggerated so that the head of a match can be inserted between the upper and lower incisors, the bite is overshot and probably will not correct itself. In a dog with an undershot bite, the lower incisors overlap the uppers. This is characteristic and even required in some brachycephalic breeds, such as the Bulldog. If you are uncertain about the required bite, check the breed standard—the official blueprint of what an ideal dog of that breed should look like. (Breed standards can be found in *The Complete Dog Book* and on the AKC and UKC web sites.)

The gums should be pink and healthy looking. Pale gums suggest anemia, possibly caused by intestinal parasites.

Feel for a soft spot on the dome of the skull. If present, the fontanel is open. This is not desirable. In toy breeds, an open fontanel can be associated with hydrocephalus.

The eyes should be clear and bright. If you see tear stains on the muzzle, look for eyelids that roll in or out, extra eyelashes, or conjunctivitis. The pupils should be dark and have no visible lines or white spots that may indicate congenital cataracts or retained fetal membranes. The haw (third eyelid) may be visible. This should not be taken as a sign of disease unless it is swollen and inflamed.

The ears should stand correctly for the breed, although in some breeds, such as German Shepherd Dogs, the ears may not stand up fully until 4 to 6 months of age. The tips should be healthy and well furred. Crusty tips with bare spots suggest a skin disease such as sarcoptic mange. The ear canals should be clean and sweet-smelling. A buildup of wax with a rancid odor may be caused by ear mites. Head shaking and tenderness about the ears indicate an ear canal infection.

Feel the chest with the palm of your hand to see if the heart seems especially vibrant. This could be a clue to a congenital heart defect. The puppy should breathe in and out without effort. A flat chest, especially when accompanied by trouble inhaling, indicates an airway obstruction. It is seen most commonly in brachycephalic breeds such as Pugs, Boston Terriers, and Pekingese.

The skin of the abdomen should be clean and healthy looking. A bulge at the navel is caused by an umbilical hernia. This can correct itself spontaneously, but may require surgical repair.

The skin and hair around the anus should be clean and healthy looking. Skin irritation, redness, hair loss, or adherent stool suggest the possibility of worms, chronic diarrhea, or malabsorption.

A healthy coat is bright and shiny and has the correct color and markings for the breed. In long-coated breeds, the puppy coat may be fluffy and soft without a lot of shine. Excess scratching and areas of inflamed skin suggest fleas, mites, or other skin parasites. "Moth-eaten" areas of hair loss are typical of mange and ringworm.

In male puppies, push the foreskin of the penis back to confirm that it slides easily. Adhesions and strictures of the foreskin require veterinary attention. Both testicles should be present in the scrotum. If one or both are absent, they may come down before 6 months of age. However, if the puppy is intended for showing and breeding, don't take a chance, since a dog with one or two undescended testicles cannot be shown and should not be bred.

In female puppies, examine the vulva. Look for pasted-down hair around the vulva or vaginal discharge—signs of juvenile vaginitis. This is a common problem. It usually resolves spontaneously after the first heat cycle.

Next, examine the puppy for soundness and correct structure. The legs should be straight and well formed. Structural faults include legs that bow in or out, weak pasterns (the area between the wrist and the foot), flat feet with spread toes, and feet that toe in at the rear. Two inherited bone and joint diseases that may be present in puppies younger than 4 months of age (but are usually not discernable on puppy selection exams) are canine hip dysplasia and patella luxation. Certification of the puppy's sire and dam by the OFA, PennHIP, or GDC is highly desirable in breeds with a high incidence of these diseases (see *Inherited Orthopedic Diseases,* page 392).

The puppy's gait should be free and smooth. A limp or faltering gait may simply be the result of a sprain or a hurt pad, but hip dysplasia and patella luxation should be considered and ruled out. Patellas can be examined at this age, but this should only be done by an experienced breeder or veterinarian.

CONSIDERING DISPOSITION

Young puppies should be alert, playful, and full of vitality. Personalities vary with breed type, but a sweet disposition is essential to all. An unfriendly puppy certainly has no place as a family companion, especially with children. The unfriendly puppy may struggle and bite to get loose, or growl when picked up or petted. This puppy will require considerable discipline and training.

A puppy who shrinks back when spoken to or runs away and hides is shy. The puppy may possibly overcome this later, but taking a chance is hardly worthwhile. This puppy will not be easily socialized.

The ideal puppy for a family pet holds his tail high, follows you about, accepts petting, struggles when picked up, but then relaxes and licks your hand.

Most breeders use some version of the puppy aptitude test developed by well-known dog trainers Jack and Wendy Volhard. Ask if the breeder did puppy testing and if so, what the results are. Realize that a puppy may have an "off" day and the breeder can fill you in on his or her perspective of the individual personalities of each pup, as well as give you the test results.

Because good health and good disposition so often go hand in hand, it is perhaps wise, in making the final selection, to pick the individual who appears to be really bursting with vitality and self-confidence. The largest, most rambunctious puppy may be more of a handful than the average family can handle, though, especially if this is a male puppy. The pup with a middle-of-the-road temperament often makes the best family companion.

Training Advice for Your Puppy

The training advice included here is simply a start on the manners and obedience any good companion dog should know. More dogs are dropped off at shelters for training and behavior problems than for any other reason. If you start your puppy off right, you are laying the foundation for a long life and a wonderful partnership.

Start obedience training as soon as possible. The important exercises are come, sit, stay, down, and walking on the leash. It is much easier to teach a puppy how to learn and how you want him to behave in your home when he is young and hasn't developed bad habits.

The two basic principals of all training are:

1. **Once you begin an exercise, see it through to the end.** If you allow a puppy to have his own way, he is very likely to interpret your leniency as a sign that he really doesn't need to do what he's told.

2. **Always reward a puppy with praise and petting when he does the right thing.** Dogs instinctively want to please. Approval builds self-confidence and reinforces the point of the exercise. Much training

today emphasizes positive reinforcement and the liberal use of treats, toys, and praise. Remember that a reward does not always have to be food. It can be praise, or a special toy or game. Each dog is different when it comes to what motivates him.

Obedience classes will train you to train your puppy, so unless you already have dog training experience, it is important to attend classes. Classes also give the puppy an opportunity to socialize with other dogs. Puppies as young as 8 weeks can be enrolled in an obedience class, as long as they are current on their vaccinations. These early classes are called puppy kindergarten and are geared primarily toward socialization.

HOUSETRAINING

The basic procedure for housetraining a puppy is similar to potty training a child, except that puppies learn more quickly. Housetraining can be started as soon as the puppy comes home. If the breeder has divided the puppy area into different sections, the puppies have probably already started to housetrain themselves by choosing just one section to eliminate in. If you know what substrate the puppies have become accustomed to eliminating on, you can use the same substrate at home and in a small area of your yard to show the pup what you want him to do.

Puppies develop voluntary control over bladder and bowel functions beginning at 3 weeks of age. They acquire a strong preference for a surface on which to eliminate by 8 to 9 weeks of age, and they have an instinctive desire to keep their living area clean. You can take advantage of all these things. Confine an unsupervised puppy in a crate or a small area such as a utility room. Pups usually eliminate shortly after eating and when waking up from a nap, so choose these times, as well as the last thing at night and the first thing in the morning, to take the puppy outside—preferably to the same location. The surface can be gravel, dirt, grass, or concrete. It is important to allow the puppy plenty of time to eliminate. Dogs need to sniff and smell to trigger the elimination urge. If a puppy doesn't go, many times it's because he wasn't given enough time. As soon as he does go, praise him lavishly.

A good basic rule is that a puppy needs to go out as often as he is months old. So a 2-month-old pup may need to go out every two hours, and so on.

If you work during the day, you can train the puppy to use newspapers. Confine him as before and paper an area several feet square. Use several thicknesses. Remove the soiled papers on top and add new ones to the bottom. The middle layer will retain some odor and remind the pup of where to go. There are also special pads you can buy whose scent encourages puppies to eliminate on them. Later, when the puppy can control his urge to go for longer periods, you can develop a routine for going outside.

If the puppy makes mistakes in the house (and he will), you can startle him with a loud "no!" *but only if you catch him in the act.* Then pick the puppy up and take him outside. Otherwise, ignore the mistake. *Never rub a puppy's nose in the mess or punish him in any way for making a mistake.* As with toddlers, eliminating is normal. It is only a "mistake" because of the location. It takes some time for a puppy to understand this concept.

WALKING ON A LEASH

Your puppy should be taught to walk on a loose leash and have good manners. Start with a nylon or leather collar. Leave the collar on for short periods. When the puppy is no longer bothered by it, leave it on all the time. Attach a leash that he can drag behind him. (Never leave a dog unsupervised with a leash on; the leash can get caught on something and injure the dog.) Once he accepts the leash, pick up your end and follow the pup for awhile. Then switch to leading the puppy with lots of pats and praise. Treats and toys can be used to lure him at this young age.

Train the puppy to walk on your left side, to move out smartly, and to stay abreast of you—neither lunging ahead nor lagging behind. If possible, complete the leash training exercise in an obedience class.

Avoid using a choke chain (also called a training collar or slip collar), if possible, and never leave one on your dog as a permanent collar. A dog wearing a choke collar could get his paw caught between the collar and his neck and choke to death, or the collar could become snagged on something. Choke collars can also damage the throat and can aggravate some eye diseases.

If a puppy is not responsive to a leather or nylon collar, there are other options that may be even better than collars, such as halters or head collars. (Gentle Leader and Promise Collar are two examples.) Head collars, in particular, are more effective than choke collars and far more humane.

Discuss these options with an experienced obedience trainer.

COMING WHEN CALLED

Coming when called is basically an extension of leash training. Let your puppy out to the end of a 15- or 20-foot rope or check cord. Squat down, clap your hands, and call his name. If he fails to move toward you, give a tug and shorten the line. Alternatively, if you are in a safe, fenced area, turn and run away from the pup. He won't want to be left behind and will quickly run after you.

Don't fight the puppy. If he acts rebellious, stop the exercise. Eventually he will come to you all the way. Respond by giving him lavish praise and a choice tidbit. Repeat the exercise but don't overdo it. Coming should be fun—not a burden. Six times a session, three or four sessions a week, is plenty. Once the puppy has mastered the exercise, continue without the leash but practice in a safe, enclosed area.

Never call the puppy to come to you for a reprimand for anything unpleasant. Dogs are smart, and your pup will quickly learn that coming when called results in something unpleasant.

It is also good to make sure, even after the dog is trained to come, that he is not always brought inside or leashed when he is called. Then the dog learns that playtime is over when he is called to come. If he is sometimes called and simply praised, rewarded, or has a special game with you, then he is allowed to continue his free play, he never knows which time will result in the end of a fun play session and which will produce something good.

Correcting Misbehavior

Many behavior problems develop because a dog is bored or lonely. Providing adequate exercise, especially for dogs between 6 and 12 months of age, will help decrease behavior problems.

One very effective way to deal with some kinds of misbehavior is to ignore it. Dogs often engage in annoying activity just to get your attention. They find, for example, that it is easy to attract attention by jumping up on people or running away with a new shoe. Any interaction, even scolding the dog, becomes part of the game. Ignore the dog, as difficult as this may be, even if it means getting up and going outside. This removes the dog's incentive to repeat the behavior.

The best way to correct misbehavior is with the tone of your voice. Puppies are tuned in to the sounds made by their mother, and instinctively interpret a sharp sound or loud "no!" or "aht!" as a warning to stop what they are doing.

Correction is effective *only when the puppy is caught in the act.* If a pup chews up a valuable item while you are out and is reprimanded when you come home several hours later, the pup sees no connection between the destructive act and the reprimand. Obviously, there is no point in scolding the puppy after the fact.

If you do catch your pup doing something wrong, show your displeasure with a loud "no!" This gains the pup's immediate attention while you substitute a chew toy for your shoe or direct his attention to a more constructive activity.

A common mistake is to show anger (even though it may be justified). Anger equals loss of control, and usually does not teach the puppy about the cause of the anger. This creates insecurity in your pup and weakens the bond between you and your pet.

Correction should never involve physical punishment, such as hitting the puppy with an open hand or swatting him with a rolled-up newspaper. This makes a dog shy and distrustful. Fearful dogs avoid people, even their owners, and may bite when cornered.

Remember that destructive activity is age-appropriate in puppies. That means unless there is a behavior problem, such as separation anxiety, you can expect destructive behavior to diminish as the puppy matures. It also means you must provide your puppy with appropriate toys that he is allowed to destroy.

Inappropriate Chewing

Puppies chew to develop strong teeth and jaws. It is a good idea to provide high-impact rubber balls, Kongs, or nylon chew toys as a substitute for chewing on shoes and furniture. Avoid rawhide toys and bones. Rawhide may be ingested and can do damage in the gastrointestinal tract.

If you catch the puppy in the act of chewing on something inappropriate, substitute a toy or a nylon bone. Make it clear that the toy, not the other item, is for chewing. If you do not catch the puppy in the act, *do not punish him after the fact.* He will have no idea what the punishment is for.

Various commercial spray-on products are available that leave an unpleasant scent to discourage chewing on things like furniture. These products work well when applied as directed. It is also a good idea to "puppy proof" your home, making sure that potentially dangerous items your puppy could chew on are removed or blocked off, including electric cords, garbage, and small items that could cause a blockage if swallowed.

Excessive Barking

Remember that before he came home with you, your puppy spent all his time with his littermates. A puppy who is not accustomed to being left alone may demand to be let out of his enclosure and express this by barking, whining, or howling. The barking may occur when the puppy is first put into the enclosure and continue throughout the entire period of confinement. If you ignore it, the puppy usually finds little reason to continue and accepts the routine. If you let him out or pay attention to him, the barking is reinforced and the problem will take longer to correct.

Barking can also be an attention-getting device for dogs who are ignored unless they make noise. If the dog gets the attention he wants (even a reprimand, because negative attention is still attention), the behavior is reinforced. Going to the dog to quiet him down, feeding him, petting and praising him, or giving him a toy are ways of unintentionally rewarding the misbehavior. Instead, reward your dog's good behavior. Give him lots of praise, play, and attention when he is quiet and well behaved.

Barking in defense of territory is part of a dog's basic nature. Occasionally this can escalate to excessive levels. The dog barks at the slightest sound, or barks constantly for no apparent reason. Chaining up a dog outside encourages barking and is an open invitation to a bad disposition. It is far better to confine your dog in a fenced yard or a spacious enclosure that allows opportunity for exercise and play.

Barking in the house may stop if the dog is confined to a room without windows where he can't see or hear what's going on outside, and thus does not feel the need to defend the house from "outside interlopers."

Humane bark collars emit an unpleasant odor when the dog barks.

Chronic or neurotic barking may be a sign of boredom or a need for more attention. Take your dog for daily trips to the park. Regular walks on a leash provide mental and physical stimulation and allow for social interaction. Anti-bark collars are available that disrupt the barking sequence by emitting a sound or an aversive odor, usually citronella oil. These devices are humane and, in most, cases effective.

Surgery in which part or all of the vocal cord apparatus is removed is called debarking. This operation does not completely eliminate vocalization. The dog sounds hoarse, and some ability to bark often returns in time. Debarking can increase the risk of airway complications at a later date, including laryngeal stenosis.

Chronic disruptive barking should be investigated by a professional trainer to determine its cause. An effective treatment program is then based on the dog's motivation for barking, how disruptive the barking has become, and how urgently it must be stopped.

Teaching a Puppy to Be Gentle

A puppy must learn to be gentle and friendly with people, particularly children. Puppies naturally mouth and bite littermates and other puppies. As a puppy grows older, he usually learns that his bite can cause pain and usually develops a softer mouth. But playing roughly with a puppy (for example, encouraging him to growl or maul a gloved hand) can override his natural instinct to bite down softly. A young puppy playing with people may become overexcited and accidentally nip or scratch. This can be difficult to correct as the puppy grows older.

To correct a puppy who is being too rough, first yip as if you were hurt. Then leave the puppy alone and ignore him, or calmly put him in his crate. This way, he learns that playing too rough ends the game.

Children sometimes grab, pull, or otherwise frighten or hurt puppies, which can result in a child being bitten or knocked down. This type of interaction between children and puppies should be prevented. Children must be taught that a puppy is not a toy and should be treated with respect. They should also be taught not to bother a puppy when he is eating or sleeping.

A truly aggressive act by a puppy toward a person is serious. In an adult dog, it is downright dangerous. Threatening behavior includes growling, bristling, snapping, snarling, laying back the ears, standing stiff-legged, and running toward a person in a menacing manner. Actual aggression includes biting, attacking, and mauling. A threat should be taken as seriously as an actual bite, since a dog who is capable of a threat is probably capable of an attack.

Many people excuse aggressive behavior because they believe the dog was provoked or in some way justified (which may be true). Nonetheless, because of the potential consequences of dog attacks, any form of aggression should raise a red flag. More than 4 million Americans are bitten each year by dogs, nearly a quarter of these require medical attention, and about 20 Americans die each year from dog attacks. Infants and toddlers are the most frequent victims, and the attacker is most often the family pet.

Some people acquire dogs to guard their home and family. A well-trained guardian will bark at intruders without becoming a menace. However, dogs who are trained to bite usually attack the wrong person, most often a child. According to the Humane Society of the United States, of the nearly 300 people who have died in dog attacks in recent years, not one was a household intruder.

Do not attempt to discipline an aggressive dog through punishment or physical domination. You may actually provoke an attack. Isolate the dog and discuss the problem with your veterinarian or a professional dog trainer.

TUMORS AND CANCERS

A tumor is any sort of lump, bump, growth, or swelling. Tumors that are true cancers are called neoplasms. Tumors can be divided into two broad categories: benign and malignant. Benign tumors grow slowly, don't invade or destroy neighboring tissue, and don't spread to other parts of the body. These cancers aren't usually life-threatening. They are cured by surgical removal, provided that the entire tumor can be removed. Malignant tumors are potentially life-threatening cancers, and are also called carcinomas, sarcomas, or lymphomas, depending on the tissue where they originated.

Cancers invade neighboring tissue and continue to grow in an unrestricted way. At some point, malignant cells part from the primary tumor and enter the lymphatic system or the circulatory system, and establish new colonies in other areas. This process is called *metastasizing*.

Any new growth on your dog should be examined by a veterinarian. The majority of cancers in dogs are detected by physical examination. About half are visible as growths or sores on or beneath the skin. Perianal tumors, testicular tumors, mammary gland tumors, lymph gland tumors, and cancers in the mouth can be detected by inspection and palpation. Bone tumors can be recognized by a swollen limb, lameness, or the appearance of a swelling that involves the bone.

Internal cancers are most common in the spleen, liver, and gastrointestinal tract. Cancers in these areas often become advanced before they are even suspected. Usually the first signs are weight loss, a palpable mass in the abdomen, vomiting, diarrhea, constipation, or gastrointestinal bleeding. (The signs and symptoms of common tumors affecting the internal organs are discussed in the chapters dealing with these organs.)

Lung cancer is rare in dogs. However, dogs are at risk from secondhand smoke. The lungs are also a frequent site for metastases. The same is true of the liver.

The majority of cancers occur in middle-aged and older dogs. Because companion animals are living longer and enjoying a higher quality of life, it is likely that cancers will be diagnosed with increasing frequency. A routine physical exam will detect most cancers. Regular veterinary visits thus provide the opportunity to detect cancer at an early stage. This has significant implications for the life and health of your pet. As a rule, healthy dogs 7 years of age and older should have a physical examination at least once a year. If their health is questionable, they should be seen more often. If any signs develop (see *Danger Signs in the Geriatric Dog*, page 546), they should be seen at once.

What Causes Cancer?

Cancer is a condition in which rapid cell division and tissue growth occur at the expense of the host organ. Most cells in the body die and are replaced many times during the course of a dog's life. Cell reduplication follows an orderly pattern controlled by the genes. When things go smoothly, each duplicated cell is an exact clone of its ancestor and assumes the same role.

Anything that disrupts the genes that govern cell duplication results in the production of mutant cells. Mutant cells often reproduce at an extraordinary rate and form large masses that crowd out normal cells. Such a mass is called a cancer. Further, cancerous cells do not function as normal cells and thus do not provide needed services. If the cancer grows unchecked, it eventually replaces much of the organ while also metastasizing to other parts of the body. In time, it causes the death of the dog.

Some cancer-producing genes are inherent in the breed or genetic makeup of a dog. Bernese Mountain Dogs, for example, have a high incidence of cancers affecting all body systems. Approximately one in four Bernese Mountain Dogs will develop cancer; two of the cancer types seen in this breed—histiocytosis and mastocytoma—are known to be inherited as polygenic traits.

A number of genes have been identified as causing breast, colon, and other cancers in people and in some animals. The reason that all individuals with these genes do not develop cancer is that there are other specific genes that suppress the cancer genes. To complicate matters, there are still other genes that inhibit the suppressors. All these genes are turned on and off by external factors, such as diet, stress, and environment. Thus, cancer is a largely unpredictable phenomenon involving a complex interaction of genetics and the environment. A good example is bladder cancer in Scottish Terriers. Scotties have an increased risk of bladder cancer to begin with. If you add in exposure to lawn chemicals that contain 2,4 D, the risk increases four to seven times. In this case, genes and an environmental exposure work together to cause the cancer.

Carcinogens are environmental influences known to increase the likelihood of cancer in direct proportion to the length and intensity of exposure. Carcinogens gain access to tissue cells, cause alterations in genes and chromosomes, and disrupt the system of checks and balances that controls orderly growth. Examples of carcinogens known to increase the risk of cancer in humans are ultraviolet rays (which can cause skin cancers), X-rays (thyroid cancers), nuclear radiation (leukemia), various chemicals (aniline dyes cause bladder cancer), cigarettes and coal tars (lung, bladder, skin, and many other cancers), viruses (sarcoma in AIDS patients), and internal parasites (bladder cancers). Secondhand smoke exposure is associated with cancer in animals as well as in humans.

Injuries are sometimes implicated as causing cancers, but there is seldom a connection. Trauma causes hematomas, bruises, and contusions, but does not cause abnormal cell growth. However, an injured site is usually examined closely, and small preexisting tumors are sometimes discovered this way. Some veterinarians believe bone cancers may be more likely to develop at the site of previous fractures.

Some benign tumors, such as warts and papillomas, are clearly due to a virus. Other benign tumors simply grow for unknown reasons.

Treating Tumors and Cancers

A summary of the types of cancer treatment currently available can be found on page 529. The effectiveness of any type of treatment depends upon early diagnosis. In general, small cancers have a higher rate of cure than large cancers. This is true for all types of cancer.

The best possible treatment option is surgical removal of a cancer that has not spread. To prevent recurrence, a surrounding margin of normal tissue should also be removed. An initial approach that removes the tumor with an adequate margin of normal tissue may be the most important factor in controlling cancer. When a cancer recurs locally because of incomplete excision, the opportunity for cure is often lost. That's why surgeons speak of "clean margins," meaning no cancer cells are found on the outer edge of the tissue removed.

A cancer that spreads only to local lymph nodes may still be cured if all the involved nodes can be removed along with the primary tumor. Even when a cancer is widespread, removing a bleeding or infected mass, or simply a large one that is interfering with a normal physical function, can provide relief and temporarily improve the quality of life.

Electrocautery and cryosurgery are two techniques by which tumors on the surface of the body can be removed. Electrocautery means burning off the tumor using electricity; cryosurgery involves freezing the tumor to remove it. These methods provide an alternative to surgical removal and are suitable for benign tumors such as papillomas. New surgery techniques may use lasers or hyperthermy—heat treatment Radiation therapy is used primarily for local tumors that have not metastasized. Many canine tumors are sensitive to radiation. They include mast cell tumors, transmissible venereal tumors, squamous cell carcinomas, cancers of the oral and nasal cavities, and soft tissue sarcomas. A potential disadvantage of radiation therapy is that it requires special equipment and must be done at a medical center. Radiation therapy can also be done to relieve pain, especially with very painful cancers such as osteosarcoma (bone cancer).

Chemotherapy is used to prevent and control the metastatic spread of cancer cells. However, most canine cancers are only moderately sensitive to chemotherapy. It can cure only one type of cancer in dogs: transmissible venereal tumors. When used as the only form of treatment, chemotherapy usually does not extend survival. Lymphosarcoma and leukemia are exceptions. Chemotherapy drugs, even when their use is tightly controlled, can have major side effects. In humans, chemotherapy is aimed at achieving a cure. Due to their lesser efficacy in dogs, chemotherapy is aimed at controlling the disease and giving the dog a period of remission. Lower dosages are generally used and many dogs do not have the severe reactions to chemotherapy that people do.

Chemotherapy may include such new methods as injecting a photosensitive substance that is attracted to cancer cells. Light therapy then causes the destruction of those cells.

Immunotherapy using interferon, monoclonal antibodies, and other agents that stimulate the immune system is receiving renewed interest and has the potential to become an important treatment option. Immunotherapy has been used successfully to extend survival time in dogs with late-stage lymphosarcomas and mast cell tumors. (Prednisone has also been used successfully in combating these cancers.) Newer work is looking at vaccines for cancers, and this area shows quite a bit of promise.

A combination of the treatment methods (for example, surgical excision followed by radiation or chemotherapy) is often more effective than surgery alone. This is true for osteosarcoma. Only those treatments known to be effective against a particular cancer should be considered for combination therapy.

Finding Treatment

It makes sense if your dog has cancer to seek out a referral center that routinely deals with cancer cases. But that is sometimes easier said than done. Most veterinary schools and other referral centers have a veterinary oncologist on staff. These veterinarians may offer treatments at their facility or confer with your veterinarian on treatments such as chemotherapy regimens.

Most of these referral centers are also conducting research and may be looking for patients with a specific disease to be involved in clinical trials. Being included in a cancer study can help with expenses, give you access to the latest techniques, and possibly help other dogs in the future.

Cancer Treatments

Surgery	Surgery can totally remove a cancer or make it smaller so that chemotherapy and radiation are more effective. Risks include anesthesia, bleeding problems, and postoperative pain. Cures are possible with certain cancers and early intervention.
Chemotherapy	Chemotherapy uses drugs to try to kill the cancer cells with the least amount of damage to normal cells. Side effects can include nausea, lowered immunity, and bleeding problems. Dogs don't usually experience major hair loss. Not all cancers are susceptible to chemotherapy.
Radiation	Radiation uses specially calibrated X-rays to damage cancer tissues with the least amount of damage possible to normal tissues. Side effects include tissue sloughing, lowered immunity, and damage to normal tissue. Anesthesia is required. This treatment is only available at veterinary referral centers. Not all cancers are susceptible to radiation and location of the cancer may make this impossible.
Cryotherapy	Cryotherapy uses probes to freeze cancerous tissues. The goal is to destroy the cancer with the least damage to surrounding normal tissues. This is only available at veterinary referral centers. Not all cancers are susceptible to cryotherapy, and the location of the cancer may make this therapy impossible.
Hyperthermy	Hyperthermy uses heat probes or radiation to destroy cancerous tissues by overheating them. The goal is to destroy the cancer with the least damage to surrounding normal tissues. This is only available at veterinary referral centers. Not all cancers are susceptible to heat damage. The location of the cancer may make this therapy impossible.
Diet	Diet has been shown to be helpful in controlling cancer. The goal is a diet with limited simple sugars, moderate amounts of complex sugars such as carbohydrates, highly digestible protein in moderate amounts, and set amounts of certain types of fats. These dietary guidelines tend to "starve" the cancer cells and help the normal cells stay healthy. There is a commercial cancer diet called n/d from Hill's, or you can make a homemade diet that fits these criteria.
Immunotherapy	Immunotherapy use immune reactions to fight off the cancer cells. This method may use a nonspecific immune modifier such as interferon, or vaccines specifically tailored to the cancer of the individual. Much of this work is experimental but shows great promise.

Common Surface Tumors

Skin tumors are common in dogs. It is often impossible to determine whether a skin tumor is benign or malignant by appearance alone. The only conclusive way to make a diagnosis is by *biopsy*, a procedure in which tissue or cells are removed by your veterinarian and examined under a microscope by a veterinary pathologist.

For small tumors it is best for your veterinarian to remove the growth and present the entire specimen to the pathologist. For tumors larger than 1 inch (2.5 cm) across, it may be advisable for your veterinarian to obtain a tissue sample by fine needle aspiration. In this procedure, a needle connected to a syringe is inserted into the tumor and cells are obtained by pulling back on the plunger. Alternatively, the vet can use a cutting needle to obtain a core sample. An open biopsy, in which an incision is made, is preferred for suspected sarcomas and tumors that present diagnostic problems for the pathologist.

Additional information on the size of the tumor and the extent of local involvement may be important in planning treatment. *Ultrasonography,* available in many veterinary clinics, provides diagnostic information that cannot be obtained through conventional X-rays. *CT scans* and *MRI* are used to diagnose some internal cancers and determine the extent of local involvement. They are available at veterinary medical centers.

SKIN PAPILLOMAS

Skin papillomas are benign wartlike growths that occur on the skin of the body, on the foot pads, and beneath the nails. They are caused by the canine oral papilloma virus and tend to occur in older dogs, especially older Poodles.

Treatment: They do not need to be removed unless they are causing a problem because of their location on the body. Rarely, these will become injured and bleed or get infected. In these cases, removal is recommended.

HEMATOMAS

A hematoma is a blood clot beneath the skin, caused by a blow or contusion. These are not cancers. Large ones may need to be drained. Ear flap hematomas require special attention (see *Swollen Pinna*, page 210).

Calcifying hematomas are hard masses that resemble bone. They tend to occur at fracture sites, and may be found as a bump on the skull of a tall dog who strikes her head on the underside of the dining room table.

Treatment: Calcifying hematomas do not need be removed but may have to be biopsied if there is a question of bone tumor. They are difficult to treat and often recur.

Abscessed epidermal inclusion cysts such as this one are frequently mistaken for tumors.

EPIDERMAL INCLUSION CYSTS (SEBACEOUS CYSTS)

Epidermal inclusion cysts, also called sebaceous cysts, are common surface tumors found anywhere on the body. Kerry Blue Terriers, Schnauzers, Poodles, and spaniels are most often affected. Epidermal inclusion cysts begin when dry secretions block hair follicles, causing an accumulation of hair and sebum (a cheesy material), and the subsequent formation of a cyst.

These cysts produce a dome-shaped swelling up to an inch or more in size beneath the skin, though most are smaller. They can become infected and may need to be surgically drained. This sometimes leads to a cure.

Treatment: Surgical excision is the treatment of choice, although it is not always required.

LIPOMAS

A lipoma is a benign growth made up of mature fat cells interlaced with fibrous connective tissue. Lipomas are common in overweight dogs, especially females. A lipoma can be recognized by its oblong or round appearance and smooth, soft, fatlike consistency. Lipomas grow slowly and may get to be several inches in diameter. They are not painful. Rarely, what appears to be a lipoma is a malignant variant called a liposarcoma.

Treatment: Surgical removal is necessary if the lipoma is interfering with the dog's mobility, is growing rapidly, or is cosmetically bothersome. The tumor should be biopsied if there is any question about the diagnosis.

This large tumor beneath the skin of the abdomen proved to be a lipoma.

HISTIOCYTOMAS

Histiocytomas are rapidly growing tumors found in dogs 1 to 3 years of age. They occur anywhere on the body. These benign tumors are dome-shaped, raised, hairless surface growths that are not painful. Because of their appearance, they are often called button tumors. These benign growths are more common on shorthaired dogs.

Treatment: Most histiocytomas disappear spontaneously within one to two months. Those that persist should be removed for diagnosis.

Histiocytosis

This is a rare malignant cancer in which histiocytes (large cells found in normal connective tissue) are widely dispersed throughout the subcutaneous tissue and internal organs, occasionally forming nodules. The typical signs are lethargy, weight loss, and enlargement of the liver, spleen, and lymph nodes.

A raised, hairless, button-shaped growth typical of histiocytoma.

The disease tends to affect male dogs of certain breeds at 3 to 8 years of age. In Bernese Mountain Dogs, the disease is inherited as a polygenic trait, and accounts for 25 percent of all tumors in that breed. Flat-Coated Retrievers are also unusually susceptible to this type of cancer.

Treatment: Histiocytosis may respond to chemotherapy.

SEBACEOUS ADENOMAS

These are common benign tumors found more often in older dogs, particularly Boston Terriers, Poodles, and Cocker Spaniels. The average age of dogs with sebaceous adenomas is 9 to 10 years.

Sebaceous adenomas arise from the oil-producing sebaceous glands in the skin. They tend to occur on the eyelids and limbs. They may be single or multiple, usually are less than 1 inch (25 cm) across, and appear as smooth, lobulated growths on a narrow base or stem. The surface of the tumor is hairless and may be ulcerated.

A sebaceous adenoma on the body of a Cocker Spaniel.

Occasionally, a sebaceous adenoma becomes malignant (becoming a sebaceous adenocarcinoma). Suspect malignancy if the tumor is larger than 1 inch, has an ulcerated surface, and is growing rapidly.

Treatment: Small tumors do not need to be removed unless they are causing a problem. Large adenomas should be removed.

BASAL CELL TUMORS

This is a common tumor usually found on the head and neck in dogs over 7 years of age. It appears as a firm, solitary nodule with distinct borders that sets it apart from the surrounding skin. The tumor may have been present for months or years. Cocker Spaniels appear to be at increased risk.

A small percent of basal cell tumors are malignant, becoming basal cell carcinomas.

Treatment: Basal cell tumors should be removed by wide surgical excision.

MASTOCYTOMAS (MAST CELL TUMORS)

Mast cell tumors are common, accounting for 10 to 20 percent of skin tumors in dogs. About half of them are malignant. *Brachycephalic* breeds, such as

Boxers, Boston Terriers, and Bulldogs, have a higher incidence. However, mast cell tumors can occur in all dogs. In Bernese Mountain Dogs, mast cell tumors are especially common and are inherited as a polygenic trait.

The mean age for dogs to develop mast cell tumors is 9 years. Both sexes are equally affected. Multiple tumors are present in 10 percent of cases. Look for these tumors on the skin of the trunk and perineum, lower abdomen, foreskin of the penis, and hind legs.

Mast cell tumors vary greatly in appearance. The typical tumor is a multinodular growth that appears reddish, hairless, and ulcerated. It is impossible to tell by appearance whether the tumor is benign or malignant. Some growths may be present for months or years, then suddenly enlarge and metastasize to the regional lymph nodes, liver, or spleen. Others grow rapidly right from the start. Still others may be completely under the skin and look like a lipoma. For that reason, all new lumps should be checked by your veterinarian.

Mast cell tumors release histamine and other substances that cause stomach and duodenal ulcers. In fact, up to 80 percent of dogs with mast cell tumors may be suffering from ulcers. Dogs with intestinal symptoms should be evaluated for ulcer disease and treated accordingly (see *Stomach and Duodenal Ulcers*, page 261).

Treatment: The World Health Organization has established a system for staging mast cell tumors based on the size of the tumors, the number present, the degree of local involvement, and the presence or absence of metastases. Early-stage (favorable) tumors are treated by complete local excision with a margin of normal tissue. Larger tumors that cannot be removed with adequate tissue margins are treated with surgery plus prednisone and/or radiation therapy. Chemotherapy and/or immunotherapy have been of benefit in treating late-stage disease.

Squamous Cell Carcinomas

These tumors are induced by exposure to the ultraviolet radiation in sunlight, and occur on lightly pigmented areas of the body, including the underside of the belly, trunk, scrotum, nail beds, nose, and lips.

One variety of squamous carcinoma appears as a hard, flat, grayish-looking ulcer that does not heal. Another appears as a firm red patch, and still another as a cauliflowerlike growth. There may be hair loss around the tumor because of constant licking.

Squamous carcinomas invade locally and metastasize at a late stage to the regional lymph nodes and lungs.

Treatment: Complete surgical removal is the treatment of choice. When this cannot be accomplished due to widespread involvement, radiation therapy can be used. Light-skinned dogs should avoid being in the sun at peak hours of UV exposure—generally 10 a.m. to 2 p.m.

This large, pigmented growth on the leg is typical of melanoma.

MELANOMAS

Melanomas arise from melanin-producing cells in the skin. They are more common in Scottish Terriers, Boston Terriers, and Cocker Spaniels. These brown or black nodules are found on darkly pigmented areas of skin, particularly on the eyelids. Rarely, you will find an unpigmented melanoma. They also occur on the lips, in the mouth, on the trunk and limbs, and in the nail beds.

Melanomas on the skin are usually benign; those in the mouth are highly malignant. About 50 percent of nail bed melanomas are malignant and metastasize. Metastases occur in the regional lymph nodes, lungs, and liver.

Treatment: The melanoma must be removed surgically, along with a margin of normal tissue. Recurrence is common and difficult to treat. The outlook is extremely poor for melanomas in the mouth.

PERIANAL TUMORS

Perianal growths are usually benign cancers that appear around the rectum, especially in unneutered male dogs. Rarely, these will be malignant perianal adenocarcinomas. Siberian Huskies are predisposed to this type.

Anal sac gland tumors are a separate entity. These tumors are often aggressive and malignant. They arise from the anal glands on either side of the rectum and often metastasize quickly. These cancers are also associated with an increase in calcium in the blood.

Treatment: Neutering and/or surgical removal may be curative for perianal growths. Multimodal therapy is the best way to fight anal sac gland cancer: surgery, radiation, and chemotherapy.

Soft Tissue Sarcomas

Sarcomas are malignant tumors that arise from various sources, including connective tissue, fat, blood vessels, nerve sheaths, and muscle cells. Collectively they account for about 15 percent of all cancers in dogs. There is a genetic disposition among German Shepherd Dogs, Boxers, Saint Bernards, Basset Hounds, Great Danes, and Golden Retrievers.

Sarcomas occur on the surface of the body and within organs. They tend to grow slowly and metastasize only when they have been present for some time. Metastases usually involve the lungs and liver. Some sarcomas are well defined and appear to be encapsulated; others infiltrate the surrounding tissue and have no distinct margins. Sarcomas within body cavities often grow to a large size before being discovered.

Soft tissue sarcoma is diagnosed using X-rays, ultrasonography, CT scan, and tissue biopsy.

The most common sarcomas found in dogs are:

- **Hemangiopericytoma,** arising from cells surrounding small arteries
- **Fibrosarcoma,** arising from fibrous connective tissue
- **Hemangiosarcoma,** arising from cells that make up the lining of small blood vessels
- **Schwannoma,** a tumor of nerve sheaths
- **Osteosarcoma,** a tumor of bones
- **Lymphoma,** arising in lymph nodes and in organs that contain lymphoid tissue, such as the spleen, liver, and bone marrow

Treatment: The World Health Organization has established a staging system for canine soft tissue sarcomas similar to that described for mast cell tumors. Depending on the type of sarcoma and the extent of local involvement, treatment may involve surgical excision with a margin of normal tissue, radiation therapy, hyperthermia, and chemotherapy. A specific treatment plan often uses a combination of therapies. The prognosis depends on the stage of the tumor at the time of treatment.

Lymphoma (Lymphosarcoma)

Lymphoma, also called lymphosarcoma, is a type of cancer that arises (often simultaneously) in lymph nodes and in organs that contain lymphoid tissue such as the spleen, liver, and bone marrow. The disease affects middle-aged and older dogs. It should be suspected when enlarged lymph nodes are found in the groin, armpit, neck, or chest. Affected dogs appear lethargic, eat poorly, and lose weight. The liver and spleen are often enlarged.

Chest involvement results in *pleural effusion* and severe shortness of breath. Skin involvement produces itchy patches or nodules on the surface of the skin that mimic other skin diseases. Intestinal involvement causes vomiting and diarrhea.

A complete blood count may show anemia and immature white blood cells. The serum calcium is elevated in 20 percent of dogs with lymphoma. Blood and liver function tests are usually abnormal. A bone marrow biopsy is helpful in determining if the disease is widespread.

Chest and abdominal X-rays and *ultrasonography* are particularly valuable in identifying enlarged lymph nodes, organs, and masses. A diagnosis can also be made by *fine needle aspiration* of an enlarged lymph node. In questionable cases, the entire lymph node should be removed for more complete evaluation.

A company in Great Britain called Pet Screening offers a genetic screening test for canine lymphoma, based on genetic markers in a blood sample. They suggest periodic screenings to detect lymphomas early on.

Treatment: Lymphoma localized to a single lymph node may be cured by surgical removal of the involved node. However, in most dogs the disease is widespread and a cure is unlikely. Chemotherapy using several agents offers the best chance of remission, which may last a year or longer. When a dog comes out of remission, chemotherapy "rescue protocols" may be used to induce a second or even a third remission.

HEMANGIOSARCOMA

Hemangiosarcoma is a tumor of the vascular tissues. This cancer may be noticed as a lump on a rib or an abdominal swelling, but can progress unnoticed while growing on the heart, liver, or spleen. The cancerous growths are

A biopsy identified this tumor on the back as a hemangiosarcoma, which arises from cells that make up the lining of small blood vessels.

quite fragile and often break off, "seeding" cancer throughout the body. Alternatively, the first sign may be sudden death as a large area of tumor ruptures and the dog bleeds to death internally.

Treatment: Surgery and chemotherapy may help prolong survival times but cures are virtually never seen, even with surgery done before there are detectable metastases.

Transitional Cell Carcinoma of the Bladder

This is a common urinary tract cancer, especially in older female dogs. The first signs may be similar to a urinary infection: straining to urinate or passing some bloody urine. Diagnosis may require special dye studies. Scottish Terriers are predisposed to this cancer, especially if they have been exposed to lawn-care chemicals that contain 2,4D.

Treatment: Treatment may include surgery and chemotherapy, but this is a very aggressive cancer. With medication, prolonged symptom-free intervals are possible.

Bone Tumors

Bone tumors can be either malignant or benign. Osteosarcoma and chondrosarcoma are the two most common malignant bone tumors. Osteomas and osteochondromas are the most common benign types.

MALIGNANT BONE TUMORS

Osteosarcoma is by far the most common malignant bone cancer in dogs. This cancer affects dogs of all ages, with a median age of 8 years. It occurs with equal frequency in males and females. Giant breeds, such as the Saint Bernard, Newfoundland, Great Dane, and Great Pyrenees, are 60 times more likely to develop an osteosarcoma than are dogs weighing less than 25 pounds. Large breeds, such as the Irish Setter and Boxer, are eight times more likely to develop osteosarcoma. Toy breeds are rarely, if ever, affected.

Osteosarcoma occurs most often in the bones of the front legs, followed, in order of frequency, by the hind legs, the flat bones of the ribs, and the mandible. Often the first sign is a limp in a mature dog who has no history of injury. Usually this receives little attention until swelling of the leg or a bone mass is observed. Pressure over the tumor causes pain. Fractures can occur at the tumor site.

X-rays can strongly suggest the disease, but a definitive diagnosis depends on biopsy of the tumor. Osteosarcoma is an aggressive cancer that quickly spreads to the lungs.

Chondrosarcoma is the second most common malignant bone tumor in dogs. The average age of onset is 6 years. This tumor tends to involve the ribs, nasal bones, and pelvis. It presents as a large, hard, painless swelling in an area containing cartilage. This tumor also metastasizes to the lungs, but is less aggressive than osteosarcoma.

Treatment: Malignant tumors such as osteosarcomas and chondrosarcomas should be treated aggressively. Because these tumors metastasize to the lungs, it is important to obtain a chest X-ray before recommending surgery. The dog should have a complete physical examination, including a blood count and a fine needle aspiration or biopsy of any enlarged lymph nodes.

Partial or complete amputation is the only effective treatment for osteosarcomas of the limbs. Most dogs are able to get around well on three legs. Although amputation rarely cures the cancer, it does relieve pain and improves the quality of life. The amputation should be performed at least one joint above the involved bone. New surgical techniques that preserve the leg are currently being done at some veterinary referral centers.

Chemotherapy in addition to amputation increases the survival time for osteosarcoma, but not the cure rate. Radiation therapy may be considered if the cancer is metastatic or far advanced, but is also not a cure. Osteosarcoma of the mandible is treated with radiation therapy, to which it is moderately responsive. Radiation is also used for palliation of pain.

Complete surgical removal of chondrosarcomas affords relief, but should not be considered curative.

BENIGN BONE TUMORS

Osteomas are raised tumors composed of dense but otherwise normal bone. They occur about the skull and face.

Osteochondromas, also called multiple cartilaginous exostoses, are bone tumors that arise in young dogs from areas where cartilage grows prior to calcification. Osteochondromas may be single or multiple and are found on the ribs, vertebrae, pelvis, and extremities. There is a hereditary basis to osteochondromas.

A bone biopsy should be performed to determine the type of bone tumor, unless the appearance on X-ray is conclusive.

Treatment: Benign tumors can be removed by local excision. The surgery is needed when the growth impinges on structures such as nerves and tendons, producing pain or causing inactivity. Surgical removal may also be indicated for the sake of appearance.

Reproductive Tract Tumors
Tumors of the Testicles

Testicular tumors are common in male dogs. Most affected dogs are over 6 years of age, with a median age of 10. The majority of tumors occur in undescended testicles—located in the inguinal canal or abdominal cavity. In fact, tumors develop in up to 50 percent of undescended testicles. A swelling or firm mass in the inguinal canal in a dog with an undescended testicle is characteristic of a testicular tumor (although the mass may simply be the undescended testicle).

Tumors in descended testicles are less common. The affected testicle is often larger and firmer than its neighbor and has an irregular, nodular surface. At times the testicle is normal size but feels hard.

The three common testicular tumors in dogs are Sertoli cell tumors, interstitial (Leydig) cell tumor, and seminomas. A small percentage of Sertoli cell tumors and seminomas are malignant.

Some Sertoli cell tumors produce estrogen, which can result in feminization of the male with enlargement of the mammary glands, a pendulous foreskin, and bilateral symmetric hair loss. A serious complication of high estrogen levels is bone marrow suppression.

Ultrasonography is particularly useful in locating undescended testicles and determining whether a scrotal mass is a tumor, abscess, testicular torsion, or

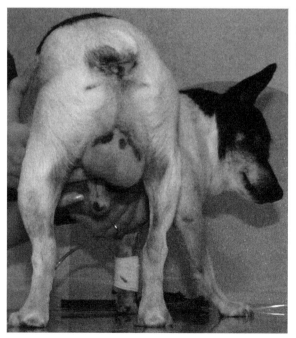

This dog has a tumor of the right testicle, causing asymmetric scrotal enlargement.

scrotal hernia. Fine needle aspiration biopsy provides information on the cell type of the tumor.

Treatment: Neutering is the treatment of choice. This is curative in nearly all cases, even when the tumor is malignant. For scrotal tumors in fully descended testicles, the normal testicle can be left if future fertility is desired. If one or both testicles are undescended, both testicles should be removed, since the condition is heritable and the dog should not be bred. Signs of feminization in Sertoli cell tumors may disappear after neutering—but this is not always the case.

Prevention: Tumors of the testicles can be prevented by neutering dogs early in life. It is particularly important to neuter all dogs with undescended testicles.

TRANSMISSIBLE VENEREAL TUMORS

An unusual neoplasm called transmissible venereal tumor occurs in both males and females. Tumor cells are transplanted from one dog to another, primarily during sexual contact, but also through licking, biting, and scratching. Transmissible venereal tumors tend to occur in free-roaming dogs, particularly those living in urban areas. They appear within seven days of contact exposure.

Transmissible venereal tumors are solitary or multiple tumors that usually appear as cauliflowerlike growths or as nodules on a stalk. The growths may be multinodular and/or ulcerated.

In females, transmissible venereal tumors develop in the vagina and on the vulva. In males, they occur on the penis. Other locations in both sexes include the skin of the perineum, face, mouth, nasal cavity, and limbs.

Transmissible venereal tumors are considered low-grade cancers. They do have the potential to metastasize, although this is rare.

Treatment: Chemotherapy is the recommended treatment. The drug of choice is vincristine, given weekly for three to six weeks. Radiation therapy is also highly effective; most dogs are cured after a single dose.

Surgery is not considered an effective treatment because it is associated with a high rate of local recurrence. Dogs and bitches not intended for breeding should be neutered or spayed.

VAGINAL TUMORS

The vaginal and vulvar areas are the most common sites for tumors of the female genital tract. These tumors tend to occur in older, sexually intact females, at an average age of 10 years. Benign tumors include leiomyomas, lipomas, and transmissible venereal tumors. They are often found on a narrow base or a long stalk.

Malignant tumors in this area are rare. They include leiomyosarcomas, squamous cell carcinomas, and mast cell tumors. Malignant tumors grow locally, infiltrate surrounding tissue, and become quite large. They rarely metastasize.

Signs include vaginal discharge or bleeding, a mass protruding through the vulvar lips, frequent urination, and excessive licking at the vulva. Large vaginal tumors can cause swelling and deformity of the perineum, block the birth canal, and cause problems in whelping. Note that a mass protruding through the vulva of a bitch in heat is most likely to be due to vaginal hyperplasia (see page 460).

Treatment: Surgical removal with a margin of normal tissue is the treatment of choice. Recurrence may follow removal.

TUMORS OF THE OVARIES

Ovarian tumors are uncommon. Most cause no symptoms and are found incidentally during a spay operation. Occasionally, a tumor becomes large enough to produce a visible or palpable swelling in the abdomen.

Papillary adenoma is a benign tumor that may arise simultaneously in both ovaries. A malignant variety, called papillary adenocarcinoma, is the most common ovarian cancer in bitches. These tumors spread throughout the abdominal cavity and are associated with *ascites*.

Granulosa cell tumors can also become quite large. Some secrete estrogen, producing signs of hyperestrogenism with abnormal heat cycles, enlargement of the vulva, and a greasy skin and coat.

Other tumors of the ovaries also occur. Ovarian cysts, which are not true tumors, are discussed in *Abnormal Estrous Cycles*, page 449.

Abdominal *ultrasonography* is particularly helpful in determining the size, structure, and location of ovarian tumors. Finding ascites and masses in the abdominal cavity suggests malignancy.

Treatment: Removal of the ovaries by ovariohysterectomy (spaying) cures benign tumors. The cure rate for malignant tumors is about 50 percent. The addition of chemotherapy for metastatic tumors may extend the time the dog is in remission.

MAMMARY GLAND (BREAST) TUMORS

The mammary glands in female dogs vary in number and can be determined by counting the nipples. The typical bitch has 10 mammary glands, five on each side of the midline, beginning on the chest and extending to the groin. The largest glands are located near the groin.

Mammary gland tumors are the most common tumors in dogs. In fact, among unspayed females the risk of a mammary tumor is 26 percent. This is three times the risk of breast tumors in women. Most mammary gland tumors occur in bitches over 6 years of age (the average age is 10). Forty-five percent are cancerous and 55 percent are benign. An increased incidence occurs in sporting breeds, Poodles, Boston Terriers, and Dachshunds. Multiple tumors are common. If a bitch has one tumor, she is three times more likely to have or develop a second tumor.

The principal sign is a painless lump or mass. Most lumps occur in the larger glands closest to the groin. A mass may be large or small, with boundaries that are distinct or indefinite. Some lumps are freely moveable, while others adhere to the overlying skin or underlying muscle. Occasionally, the mass ulcerates the skin and bleeds.

Inflammatory cancer is a rapidly progressive neoplasm that spreads throughout the chain of mammary

A bitch with mammary cancer.

glands and into surrounding skin and fat. Death usually comes in a matter of weeks. Inflammatory cancer may be difficult to distinguish from acute septic mastitis (which is discussed on page 484).

Malignant tumors spread widely, primarily to the pelvic lymph nodes and lungs. Before embarking on treatment, a chest X-ray should be taken to rule out lung metastases, present in 30 percent of these cancers. *Ultrasonography* is useful in determining whether the pelvic lymph nodes are involved. Biopsy of the tumor may not be necessary if surgical removal is contemplated. Inflammatory cancer, however, must be biopsied, because there is little to be gained in attempting aggressive treatment in these tumors.

Treatment: Removing the lump with adequate margins of normal tissue is the treatment of choice for all mammary tumors, whether benign or malignant. How much tissue will be removed depends on the size and location of the tumor. Removing a small tumor with a rim of normal tissue is called a lumpectomy. A simple mastectomy is the removal of the entire mammary gland. A complete unilateral mastectomy is the removal of all five mammary glands on one side of the body. The inguinal lymph nodes are often included in a unilateral mastectomy. A specimen is then submitted to a pathologist for a tissue diagnosis to determine the prognosis.

The success rate of surgery depends on the biological potential and the size of the tumor. Benign tumors are cured. Bitches with small malignant tumors less than 1 inch (25cm) across have favorable cure rates. Those with large, aggressive tumors are more likely to have metastatic disease and a poor prognosis.

The addition of chemotherapy, immunotherapy, and complete ovariohysterectomy does not improve cure rates, although chemotherapy may offer some relief in bitches with advanced cancers that cannot be surgically excised.

Prevention: Spaying a female before the first heat cycle reduces her risk of breast cancer to less than 1 percent. If she is spayed after one heat period, her risk is still only 8 percent. After two heat cycles, however, there is no reduction in risk.

It is important to examine the mammary glands of unspayed bitches every month, starting at 6 years of age or younger. If you feel a suspicious lump or swelling, take the dog to your veterinarian at once. Experience shows that many owners procrastinate for several months hoping that a lump will go away. Thus, the opportunity to cure many mammary cancers is lost.

Leukemia

Leukemia is a cancer involving the blood elements in the bone marrow, including the lymphocytes, monocytes, platelets, eosinophils, basophils, and erythrocytes. All of these cells can give rise to cell-specific leukemias. For example, lymphoid leukemia is a malignant transformation of the lymphocytes, or white blood cells. Leukemia is further subdivided into acute and chronic stages. Both stages are relatively rare in dogs.

Leukemia generally occurs in middle-aged dogs. Signs are nonspecific and include fever, loss of appetite, weight loss, and sometimes anemia with pale mucous membranes. Usually the disease is discovered when blood tests are drawn to diagnose these symptoms. Leukemic cells may or may not be found circulating in the blood. A bone marrow biopsy confirms the diagnosis.

Treatment: Leukemia is treated with anti-cancer drugs. Chemotherapy does not cure leukemia, but may put the disease into remission for several months or longer. Dogs with chronic leukemia have a better prognosis than those with acute leukemia.

Chapter 19

GERIATRICS

The average dog now lives about 13 years, and it is not uncommon to see dogs who are more than 20 years old. The maximum life span of dogs has been estimated to be 27 years. Large dogs have shorter lifespans than smaller dogs. St. Bernards, German Shepherd Dogs, Great Danes, and other giant breeds are considered senior at 6 to 9 years of age and old at 10 to 12. Medium dogs are seniors at 9 to 10 years of age and old at 12 to 14. Toy breeds are considered senior at 9 to 13 years of age and old at 14 to 16 years. Being a purebred or mixed-breed dog does not influence the aging process.

A table showing the comparative age of dogs and humans is found in appendix B. However, the numbers are only estimates. Dogs do not all age at the same rate. A dog's biological age depends on his genetic inheritance, nutrition, state of health, and sum of lifetime stresses

Of greatest importance is the care the dog has received throughout his life. Dogs with a poor genetic inheritance may have shorter lives due to medical problems. Well-cared-for pets suffer fewer infirmities as they grow older. When sickness, illness, or injury is neglected, the aging process is accelerated.

Adding a puppy to the household can be a rejuvenating experience for an elderly dog. When handled properly, most old dogs delight in the companionship. Through renewed interest and added exercise, they seem to recapture their youth.

Some older dogs do not enjoy the addition of a puppy. It is best to try things out first by arranging "play dates" with a friend's puppy or arranging temporary puppy visits, to be sure both dogs are compatible.

Prevent jealousy by giving attention to the old dog first. Always affirm the older dog's senior privileges. It is also important to have an area where the older dog can go to be alone when he needs a break from a rowdy puppy. Make sure the elderly dog gets special one-on-one attention every day.

The Geriatric Checkup

The care of older dogs is directed at preventing premature aging, minimizing physical and emotional stresses, and meeting the special needs of the elderly. While every dog should have an annual physical, a dog older than 7 years who is in good health should have a complete veterinary examination at least once a year—often, twice a year is preferred. For giant breeds, the age for annual exams is 5. If the health of the dog is questionable, he should be seen by a veterinarian more often. If symptoms appear, he should be seen at once.

The annual geriatric checkup should include a physical examination, complete blood count, blood chemistries, urinalysis, and parasite examination. Liver and kidney function tests, thyroid levels, chest X-ray, and electrocardiogram may be needed if specific signs and symptoms appear.

A new simple urine test called ERD, or early renal disease health screen, checks for protein leakage into the urine—specifically, albumin. This test may pick up kidney failure very early on, so you can take steps to slow its progression.

Routine dental care, including scaling the teeth, may be needed more frequently than once a year.

Danger Signs in the Geriatric Dog

If you see any of the following signs, take your dog to the veterinarian for further investigation.

- Loss of appetite or weight
- Coughing or rapid, labored breathing
- Weakness or exercise intolerance
- Increased thirst and/or frequency of urination
- Change in bowel function with constipation or diarrhea
- Bloody or purulent discharge from a body opening
- An increase in temperature, pulse, or breathing rate
- A growth or lump anywhere on the body

Behavior Changes

In general, older dogs are more sedentary, less energetic, less curious, and more restricted in their scope of activity. They adjust slowly to changes in diet, activity, and the daily routine. They are less able to tolerate extremes of heat and cold. They tend to sleep a lot and may be forgetful. When disturbed, they may be cranky and irritable.

Most of these behavior changes are the result of physical ailments (such as diminished hearing and smell, arthritic stiffness, and muscular weakness) that restrict a dog's activity and his ability to participate in family life. Arthritic changes in the dog's joints are often accompanied by pain and irritability, which can lead to aggressive encounters with family members and visitors.

Encourage your dog to participate more actively by finding a warm, comfortable resting spot near the center of family activity. Take the dog outside twice a day for a comfortable walk in the neighborhood. Extra short walks for elimination may be needed. Activities that provide human companionship will be deeply appreciated and will give the dog a sense of being valued and loved.

Old dogs don't tolerate boarding and hospitalization well. The older dog away from home often will not eat and will become overanxious or withdrawn, bark excessively, and sleep poorly. If possible, care for him at home under the guidance of your veterinarian. When leaving town, ask a friend to stay over so the dog can remain in familiar surroundings. Dog-sitting services are available in most communities. Pet Sitters International and the National Association of Professional Pet Sitters are two organizations that maintain standards through a code of ethics, certification, and attendance at national conferences. For information about these organizations and members serving your area, see appendix D.

COGNITIVE DYSFUNCTION SYNDROME

This condition, once called the senile or old dog syndrome, is a newly recognized disease, somewhat similar to Alzheimer's disease in people. In dogs with cognitive dysfunction syndrome, the brain undergoes a series of changes that result in a decline in the mental faculties associated with thinking, recognition, memory, and learned behavior. Fifty percent of dogs over age 10 will exhibit one or more symptoms of cognitive dysfunction syndrome. Cognitive dysfunction is a progressive disease with increasing signs of senile behavior.

Disorientation is one of the principal symptoms of cognitive dysfunction syndrome. The dog appears lost in the house or yard, gets stuck in corners or under or behind furniture, has difficulty finding the door (stands at the hinge side or goes to the wrong door), doesn't recognize familiar people, and fails to respond to verbal cues or his name. Hearing and vision loss must be ruled out.

Activity and sleep patterns are disturbed. The dog sleeps more in a 24-hour period, but sleeps less during the night. There is a decrease in purposeful activity and an increase in aimless wandering and pacing. Dogs with cognitive dysfunction may also exhibit compulsive behaviors with circling, tremors, stiffness, and weakness.

Housetraining is another area that suffers. The dog may urinate and/or defecate indoors, sometimes even in the view of his owners, and may signal less often to go outside.

Often, interactions with family members become much less intense. The dog seeks less attention, often walks away when being petted, shows less enthusiasm when greeted, and may no longer greet his family. Other dogs seem to need human contact 24 hours a day.

Some of these symptoms may be due to age-related physical changes and not to cognitive dysfunction. A medical condition such as cancer, infection, organ failure, or drug side effects could be the sole cause of the behavioral changes or could be aggravating the problem. Thus, medical problems must be tested for and eliminated before senile symptoms are attributed to cognitive dysfunction syndrome.

Research on the aging canine brain reveals a number of pathogenic processes that could account for many of the symptoms of cognitive dysfunction syndrome. A protein called B-amyloid is deposited in the white and gray matter of the brain and forms plaques that result in cell death and brain shrinkage. Alterations in various neurotransmitter chemicals, including serotonin, norepinephrine, and dopamine, have been described. Oxygen levels in the brains of senile dogs are decreased.

There is no specific test for cognitive dysfunction syndrome. The number of symptoms the dog exhibits and the severity of the senile behavior are important considerations in making the diagnosis. An *MRI* may show some degree of brain shrinkage, but the test is not likely to be done unless a brain tumor is suspected. Awareness of the diagnosis makes it easier to understand the dog's behavior.

Treatment: The drug Anipryl (selegiline), used by humans to treat Parkinson's disease, has been found to dramatically improve symptoms and the quality of life for many dogs with cognitive dysfunction syndrome. The drug is given once daily as a pill. Because medical treatment is now available, it is even more important to seek veterinary consultation for behavior changes in elderly dogs.

An additional benefit can come from feeding the therapeutic diet Hill's b/d. This diet is specifically formulated with extra antioxidants for older dogs. Older dogs may also benefit from treatment with acupuncture and Chinese herbs.

Physical Changes

The life cycle of the dog can be divided into three stages: puppyhood, adulthood, and old age. Puppyhood and old age are relatively short when compared to the length of adulthood. After puberty, a dog's physique changes very little until quite close to the end of his life.

Periodic physical examinations may reveal an age-related condition that can be improved by modifying the dog's care or daily routine. Although aging is inevitable and irreversible, some of the infirmities attributed to old age may,

Author Debra Eldredge's old Belgian Tervuren.

in fact, be due to disease, and therefore preventable or at least treatable. Understand that many old dog problems are not curable but can be controlled or, at the very least, the rate of progression slowed.

Care should be taken to prevent an old dog from becoming chilled. After a walk in the rain, the dog should be towel-dried and kept indoors. Many old dogs appreciate coats or sweaters when they are outside in inclement weather, and even inside on chilly days.

Musculoskeletal Problems

Signs of aging include loss of muscle tone and strength, especially in the legs. The abdomen may sag, the back may sway, and the elbows may turn out. The muscles may begin to shake when the dog physically exerts himself.

Most older dogs suffer to some extent from osteoarthritis. Stiffness in the joints is made worse by drafts and by sleeping on cold, hard, or damp floors, such as tile or cement. Make a comfortable bed for the dog indoors on a well-padded surface. Toy dogs may need to be covered at night.

There is nothing more beneficial for an older dog than regular, moderate exercise. Exercise improves muscle tone and strength, keeps the joints supple, helps prevent weight gain, and promotes a youthful attitude. However, an older dog should not be forced to exercise beyond his comfort level. If the dog has been sedentary and out of condition, gradually begin to add more exercise as his conditioning improves. A couple of short walks daily is better than one long walk that leaves the dog exhausted.

The unwillingness to exercise in a dog with arthritis is related, in part, to muscle soreness. Although there is no way to prevent arthritis, analgesics such as one of the many *NSAIDs* mentioned in chapter 13 can relieve muscle soreness and enable the dog to enjoy daily exercise. Older dogs on NSAIDs have an even greater need for regular bloodwork to be sure they aren't experiencing side effects from these medications.

Acupuncture may help with some arthritic conditions. Hydrotherapy (working in a warm tub or pool) can also be used to keep joints mobile. Physical therapy, chiropractic care, and some herbal supplements may also help. Always consult your veterinarian before adding supplements or ancillary care to be sure all treatments are compatible.

Neutraceuticals that protect joint cartilage, such as polysulfated glycosaminoglycan and chondroitin sulfate, are available through your veterinarian and from health food stores. For more information on the treatment of osteoarthritis, see page 401.

Massage and TTouch (developed by Linda Tellington-Jones) techniques can make an old, stiff dog much more comfortable.

Older dogs who have trouble getting up or handling steps will do well with special leashes that support their rear end and ramps instead of stairs, where possible. The ramps should have a nonslip covering. With loss of the use of their hind legs, many dogs, especially smaller ones, do well with specially designed carts for mobility.

While canine rehabilitation centers are primarily designed for working on injured canine athletes, many of their techniques and physical therapy programs can benefit older dogs as well. Your veterinarian can guide you to a rehab center near you.

Coat and Skin Problems

Skin tumors and coat problems are common in older dogs. The coat mats easily and the skin becomes dry and scaly because oil-producing skin glands don't work as efficiently. Symmetrical loss of coat is an indication of an endocrine disease such as Cushing's syndrome (see page 144). Stiff old dogs may have trouble keeping their anal and genital areas clean, and may need some help. The toenails may need to be trimmed more often.

Comb or brush elderly dogs three or four times a week. This may have to be done in several short sessions, for the comfort of the dog. If the dog does not handle grooming well, consider clipping or shaving the coat, especially around the rectum and underneath on the abdomen. Nails should be checked weekly, as they will not be worn down if the dog isn't exercising as much.

Regularly examining the hair and skin while grooming may reveal tumors, parasites, or other skin diseases that require prompt veterinary attention. Old dogs also enjoy the attention and companionship that accompanies these grooming sessions.

The Senses

As dogs grow older they gradually lose their hearing, but this may not become apparent until after 10 years of age. A dog with impaired hearing compensates by relying more on his other senses. (Techniques to test your dog's hearing are described in *Deafness*, page 218.) Senile deafness has no treatment.

However, hearing problems could be exacerbated by a wax blockage in the ear canal or some other problem, such as hypothyroidism or an ear tumor, all of which can be treated. A veterinary examination is the best way to determine the proper course of action. Many partially deaf dogs can still pick up a sharp whistle or clap. A blinking light can be used to help guide a deaf dog.

Loss of the senses of smell and taste may result in a decreased interest in food, with attendant problems in maintaining a healthy weight.

Loss of eyesight is difficult to assess in the dog. Senile cataracts may appear as an aging disease, usually in dogs six to eight years of age. Loss of vision may be caused by *retinal diseases, glaucoma,* and *uveitis.* These diseases are discussed in chapter 5. It is important not to move the furniture if you have an elderly blind dog. They have a "mental map" of where things are in the house and can hurt themselves not knowing when things have been moved.

Mouth, Teeth, and Gums

Periodontal disease is a gradual process that begins in early adulthood. If it goes unchecked, it culminates in advanced gum disease and tooth decay in older dogs. But this need not happen. Periodontal disease is preventable by routine dental care, as described in *Taking Care of Your Dog's Teeth*, page 249. Medicated oral gels may be gently applied to your dog's gums if he doesn't tolerate tooth brushing.

Dogs with infected gums and teeth experience mouth pain, eat poorly, and lose weight. Dental treatment relieves suffering and improves health and nutrition. Elderly dogs may need more frequent dental care, including scaling the teeth at least twice a year.

Lost and infected teeth cause old dogs to eat poorly and lose weight. Dental disease is preventable with routine dental care throughout the dog's life.

If your dog has lost teeth and is unable to chew dry kibble, switch to a homemade diet or canned food.

Functional Changes

Changes in eating and drinking patterns, voiding habits, and bowel functions are frequently seen in older dogs. Such changes are important clues to health problems.

INCREASED THIRST AND FREQUENT URINATION

These are often signs of kidney failure (see page 423) Aging alone is not a cause of kidney failure, but kidney diseases tend to be slowly progressive, so symptoms often appear later in life. The dog urinates more frequently because the kidneys have lost the ability to concentrate wastes. These dogs are thirsty and drink larger amounts of water to compensate. Note that increased thirst and urination also occur in dogs with diabetes mellitus and Cushing's syndrome—two diseases that tend to occur in middle-aged and older dogs. You may see these signs in dogs with liver problems and other health problems, as well.

A dog with failing kidneys may be unable to keep from wetting in the house, especially at night. Take the dog out several times a day and just before bedtime. Be sure to keep fresh water available at all times. *Do not* reduce water intake in an attempt to control the incontinence. This may push the dog into acute kidney failure.

The new ERD health screen is a urine test that looks for an increase in the protein albumin in the urine. This early screening test may detect kidney failure early on, so steps can be taken to control it. The screening test needs to be followed up with more specific tests to measure kidney failure.

HOUSE SOILING

Some cases of house soiling are due to musculoskeletal problems that restrict activity. Dogs with difficulty getting about may be unwilling or unable to go to the area designated for elimination. They can be helped by adding ramps and area rugs, particularly over slick surfaces.

A common cause of house soiling is hormone-responsive incontinence, seen most often in middle-aged and older spayed females, and less commonly in older neutered males. It is caused by a deficiency of estrogen in females and testosterone in males. Both these hormones are important in maintaining the muscle tone of the urethral sphincter. Hormone-responsive incontinence is much like bed wetting. The dog urinates normally but wets when relaxed or asleep. Treatment is discussed in *Urinary Incontinence*, page 416. Inappropriate defecation may be due to loss of sphincter control.

House soiling may also be due to failing memory and a decline in learned behavior associated with cognitive dysfunction syndrome. Treatment with Anipryl may help to restore a normal elimination pattern.

In all cases of house soiling, it is important to clean the soiled areas to prevent odors that might attract the dog to return to the area. *Do not punish the dog.* Most likely, the dog is unable to control himself. Scolding and punishment only produces fear and anxiety, which makes the problem worse. Special dog "diapers" can be used to help reduce soiling in the house.

Constipation

This is a common problem in geriatric dogs. Older dogs tend to drink less water and this produces hard, dry stools that are difficult to pass. Other contributing factors are lack of exercise, improper diet, reduced bowel activity, weakness of the muscles of the abdominal wall, and prostate problems. An enlarged prostate can narrow the rectal canal and cause straining to defecate.

Older dogs with reduced bowel activity can be helped by soaking their kibble with equal parts of water and letting the mixture stand for 20 minutes. Some older dogs are simply reluctant to get up and move to the water bowl. Delivering the bowl for a drink a couple of times a day can be helpful. Always use clean bowls and fresh, clean water.

Nearly all older dogs can benefit from adding fiber to their diet. The best way is to choose a high-fiber food. Dog foods advertised as "for seniors" usually contain more fiber. Compare the analysis on the labels of various products. High-fiber diets are also available through your veterinarian. Adding a small amount of plain canned pumpkin to the dog's regular food can also add fiber to the diet. For information on preventing constipation, see page 280.

Diarrhea

Older dogs with chronic diarrhea experience weakness and weight loss, and may develop kidney failure due to chronic dehydration. Like puppies, older dogs can dehydrate quickly and may need additional fluids, either subcutaneously or via an intravenous line.

Diarrhea that persists for more than two or three days is abnormal. It can be a sign of kidney or liver disease, pancreatic disease, malabsorption syndrome, parasites (especially whipworms), or cancer. The dog needs to see a veterinarian.

Abnormal Discharges

Abnormal discharges are those that contain pus or blood. They may have an offensive odor. Discharges from the eyes, ears, nose, mouth, penis, or vagina suggest infection. In older dogs, cancer must also be considered. If you see any such discharges, take your dog to the veterinarian.

Weight Changes

Weight loss is a serious problem in older dogs. Some cases are caused by kidney disease, others by heart disease, cancers, periodontal disease, loss of the senses of smell and taste, or apathy associated with inactivity and lack of attention. Weigh your dog once a month. A drop in weight is a reason for a veterinary checkup.

Excessive weight gain is a serious but largely preventable problem. Being obese is a complicating factor in heart and respiratory disease. Overweight dogs are less likely to exercise and maintain health and fitness. It is important to correct this problem, as discussed in *Diet and Nutrition*, on this page.

A pendulous, potbelly abdomen may appear to be a weight problem, but is more likely due to Cushing's syndrome or *ascites* (an accumulation of fluid in the abdomen as the result of heart or liver failure). Have it checked by your veterinarian.

Temperature, Pulse, and Respiration

Fever indicates inflammation. In the older dog, two common sites of infection are the lungs and urinary tract.

A rapid heart rate is a sign of anemia, infection, or heart disease. Anemia is suggested by paleness of the gums and tongue. Possible causes include liver disease, kidney failure, immune-mediated hemolytic anemia, and cancer.

A rapid breathing rate (more than 30 breaths per minute at rest) suggests respiratory disease or congestive heart failure. A chronic cough suggests bronchitis, airway disease, or cancer. Coughing at night in an elderly small dog suggests chronic valvular heart disease.

Diet and Nutrition

Preventing obesity is the single most important thing you can do to prolong the life of an older dog. Geriatric dogs are less active and may require up to 30 percent fewer calories than do younger dogs. Unless maintaining a good body weight is a problem, senior dogs should be on a reduced-calorie diet. In general, an elderly dog who is neither too fat nor too thin needs only 25 to 30 kcals per pound (.45 kg) of body weight per day to meet his caloric needs. If the dog's diet is not lower in calories, feeding the adult maintenance amount may result in weight gain. However, you do not need to switch your dog to a senior food if he is doing well on his current adult maintenance diet; you may simply need to feed him a little less. The actual amount to feed your senior dog will depend on the individual dog and his activity level, health, and metabolism.

Senior foods usually are more expensive per pound than maintenance foods. A senior food often contains less protein, but healthy geriatric dogs do not need to be on a protein-restricted diet. There is no evidence that limiting protein intake in dogs can prevent renal failure. In fact, studies show that older dogs actually benefit from a higher-protein diet; because the amount of food they eat is often reduced, the percentage of protein in the food may need to be higher to maintain muscle tissue. To ensure that the protein is of the highest quality, look for meat sources of protein in the first few ingredients printed on the label..

Dogs with chronic kidney or liver failure are exceptions. They lose the ability to fully metabolize protein and may need to be given a low-protein diet, as described in the treatment of *Kidney Failure*, page 423. As always, top-quality protein is important.

Older dogs are less tolerant of changes in diet, and even of changes in drinking water. When changes are necessary, make them gradually (see *Switching Diets*, page 308).

COUNTING CALORIES

Canned dog foods supply about 500 calories in a pound (.45 kg) of food; moist or "chunky" dog food, about 1,300 calories per pound; dry kibble, about 1,600 calories. (The actual calorie counts are printed in the label and vary significantly among brands.) The quantity of food you give a geriatric dog should be controlled to provide a daily intake of 25 to 30 calories a day per pound of body weight. The feeding instructions on the package should be taken only as guidelines; they often do not take into account the individual variation in dogs or the 30 percent reduction in calories required by many geriatric dogs.

The best way to determine the amount to feed is to weigh the dog and compute his caloric requirements, then determine how much to give him based on the calorie information on the package. Adjust the portions up or down, depending on the dog's activity level and whether he is looking trim. Senior foods have fewer calories per pound, so if you use one of these, the amount may not have to be reduced.

Dogs who lose weight on a calorie-adjusted feeding program may have a medical problem and should be seen by a veterinarian.

Overweight dogs should be placed on a weight-loss diet. Before doing so, consult your veterinarian to be sure there are no medical reasons for the obesity and that it is safe to cut back the number of calories. Your veterinarian will provide you with diet instructions.

Older dogs should lose weight gradually—no more than 1.5 percent of their initial body weight per week. It is important not to feed table scraps and snacks between meals, as the additional calories can unbalance the dog's diet. If you use training treats during the day, you need to adjust the daily meal amounts.

When feeding geriatric dogs, it is a good idea to divide the daily ration into two equal parts. Feed the first half in the morning and the second half in the evening. Some dogs may do even better with three meals daily, because their systems digest the smaller amounts of food more easily or they need the "pick up" of calories spread throughout the day. If your elderly dog is on a set feeding schedule due to health problems, consult your veterinarian before changing anything.

Vitamins and Minerals

Geriatric dogs may have increased mineral and vitamin requirements. B vitamins are lost in the urine of elderly dogs with reduced kidney function. The intestinal tract's ability to absorb vitamins also decreases as the dog ages. Fortunately, high-quality commercial dog foods contain enough vitamins and minerals to meet the needs of senior dogs. If you are feeding your dog a premium food, vitamin supplements should not be necessary.

Antioxidants slow down or prevent the damage done to cells by free radicals. Free radicals are the result of oxidation processes that occur in normal and damaged tissue. A free radical is a molecule that is missing an electron. This molecule basically "steals" an electron from a protein or a piece of DNA, causing damage to that cell. Antioxidants donate a molecule to the free radical, which neutralizes its effects. This also ends the usefulness of the antioxidant, so these substances need to be replaced.

There is some evidence that the accumulation of free radicals accelerates the aging process, and it may even lead to degenerative diseases such as osteoarthritis. Although specific proof is lacking, many veterinarians believe antioxidants can benefit older dogs. The antioxidants used most often are vitamin E, vitamin C, and co-enzyme Q. You can safely supplement your dog's diet using an antioxidant product prescribed by your veterinarian.

Special Diets

Prescription diets, such as those from Purina and Hill's, may be required for dogs with heart disease, kidney disease, intestinal disease, or obesity. There is also the Hill's b/d diet for older dogs with cognitive problems. They are available through your veterinarian.

Hospice Care

Hospice or home care for dogs has come to the forefront in recent years. It can be an option when your dog has a terminal illness and you don't want to pursue more aggressive medical care, but would like to provide comfort care for as long as possible. The goals of hospice are to control pain, keep the dog comfortable, and provide a decent quality of life for as long as possible.

Committing a dog to hospice care can be a very involved step. Your veterinarian will draw up a care plan for the dog, but you will be administering virtually all of the care. Some training may be required for safely giving medications and for detecting signs of problems.

Some hospice programs involve occasional home visits by a veterinarian or a veterinary technician to assist with care and evaluations. A few sites provide hospice care on site, with owners visiting or staying for the duration.

Talk to your veterinarian about possible home care that will ease this final transition for your dog.

Euthanasia

The time may come when you are faced with the prospect of having to end your pet's life. This is a difficult decision to make—both for you and for your veterinarian. Many old and infirm dogs can be made quite comfortable with just a little more thoughtfulness and tender loving care than the average healthy dog needs. Old dogs can still enjoy months or years of happiness in the company of loved ones.

But when life ceases to be a joy and a pleasure, when the dog suffers from a painful and progressive condition for which there is no hope of betterment, then perhaps at this time we owe the dog the final kindness of helping him to die easily and painlessly. Quality-of-life issues are always difficult, but questions to ask yourself include:

- Is he having more good days than bad days?
- Can he still do the things he loves to do best?
- Is he in pain or discomfort that can't be relieved?
- Is he eating and drinking?

When it is clear that comfort is no longer possible, it is time for euthanasia. This is accomplished by an intravenous injection of an anesthetic agent in a sufficient amount to cause immediate loss of consciousness and cardiac arrest. Some dogs will vocalize at the last instant or appear to take a deep breath after death; this is normal, as is the loss of urine and/or stool. While adults must make the final decisions, children often handle all of this better than adults suspect, and should be involved in the decisions following the death of the dog.

How involved children will be in this process will depend on their age and emotional maturity. Euthanasia should not be referred to as "putting to sleep," as this may frighten children at bedtime and/or lead to expectations that the dog will "wake up" and return.

Grieving for a dog may involve different stages. These include denial, bargaining, anger, sadness, and acceptance. Not everyone will go through all these stages, and the length of time and order for each stage is individual. There are pet loss hotlines available and grief counselors are now better equipped to deal with pet loss.

Pet loss hotlines include:

- University of California–Davis Veterinary Students; (530) 752-3602 or (800) 565-1526; www.vetmed.ucdavis.edu/petloss/index.htm
- Colorado State University–Argus Institute; (970) 491-4143; www.argusinstitute.colostate.edu/grief.htm
- Cornell University Veterinary Students; (607) 253-3932; web.vet.cornell.edu/public/petloss/
- University of Illinois, College of Veterinary Medicine; (217) 244-2273 or (877) 394-2273; www.cvm.uiuc.edu/CARE/
- Washington State University, College of Veterinary Medicine; (509) 335-5704; www.vetmed.wsu.edu/plhl/index.htm

Almost all veterinary colleges offer some grief counseling. Your veterinarian can guide you to local groups and resources such as helpful books.

A Final Memorial

Ideally, you need to think about how to handle the body before your dog has died. Burial is the choice of many families. Local laws may prohibit burying pets in your yard, but most communities have a pet cemetery close by. There will be a fee for this—particularly if perpetual care is included.

Cremation is ideal for many people who don't have a burial site. Costs vary dramatically, especially if you want a private cremation so that you can receive all of your own dog's ashes back. The ashes can then be spread in your dog's favorite places, buried in a small area, or kept by you in an urn.

There are many ways to memorialize your dog. A lock of hair enclosed in a locket can be comforting. Having ashes sealed in a locket is another possibility. Many families decide to make a donation in their dog's memory to a local humane society, a rescue group, or a canine health research fund. All of these are worthy causes and keep your dog's memory alive in a very positive way.

MEDICATIONS

Before discussing the specifics of the most common medications used in veterinary medicine, it's important to review some basic rules that apply to all medications you give your dog.

- The label should list the name of the drug, its strength, how much there is in the container, the expiration date, and how to give it.
- Be sure you understand the dose. For example, is it two pills once a day or one pill twice a day?
- Make sure you know how the medication is to be given. For example, are the drops to go in the mouth or in the ears?
- Make sure you know whether the medication can be given with food.
- Ask your veterinarian about side effects to be aware of.
- Make sure you know how the medication is to be stored and if it needs to be refrigerated or shaken.
- Always be sure your veterinarian is aware of all supplements and other medications your dog is taking.

Anesthetics and Anesthesia

Anesthetics are drugs used to block the sensation of pain. They are divided into two categories: local and general.

Local anesthetics are used to numb the surface of the body. They are injected into tissue and around regional nerves. They may also be applied topically to mucous membranes. Local anesthetics, such as xylocaine, have fewer risks and side effects than general anesthetics, but they are not suitable for major surgery.

General anesthetics render the dog unconscious. They can be given by injection or inhalation. Light anesthesia sedates or relaxes the dog and may be suitable for short procedures, such as removing porcupine quills. For prolonged surgeries or extremely painful procedures such as surgery on the eye or orthopedic procedures, the dog may need to be kept at a deeper level of anesthesia. This is normally done using inhaled anesthetics. Inhaled gases, such as isoflurane, are administered through a tube placed in the dog's trachea. By adjusting the flow of the gas, the dog can be kept at a lighter or deeper level of anesthesia.

The guideline dose of an injectable anesthetic is computed according to the weight of the dog. For gas anesthesia, the mixture of oxygen and anesthetic is balanced and the dose adjusted according to the breathing of the dog. Many factors require that the exact dosage be customized to the individual dog.

Certain breeds have an increased sensitivity to barbiturates and other anesthetics, and that must also be taken into account. Toy breeds and breeds with a low percentage of body fat, particularly Greyhounds and Border Collies, require less anesthetic per pound of body weight. This is one reason why anesthetics should be given by someone who is trained to determine the degree of sedation each drug produces.

Combinations of anesthetics are often given to lessen the potential toxicity of each.

Anesthetics are removed from the bloodstream by the lungs, liver, and kidneys. Impaired function of these organs can cause dose-related complications. If your dog has a history of lung, liver, kidney, or heart disease, the risk from anesthesia and surgery is increased. Presurgery bloodwork will help your veterinarian to determine the safest drug and dose for your dog.

A major risk of general anesthesia is the dog vomiting when going to sleep or waking up. The vomitus refluxes into the trachea and produces asphyxiation. This can be avoided by keeping the stomach empty for 12 hours before scheduled surgery. If you know your dog is going to have an operation the next day, *do not give him anything to eat or drink after 6 p.m. the night before*. This means picking up the water dish and keeping the dog away from the toilet bowl and other sources of water. The endotracheal tube used to administer anesthesia has a small inflatable balloon that helps block off the trachea and inhaling vomitus.

Analgesics

Analgesics are drugs used to relieve pain. There are many classes of painkillers. Demerol, morphine, codeine, and other narcotics are subject to federal regulation and cannot be purchased without a prescription.

Buffered or enteric-coated aspirin (acetylsalicylic acid) is an over-the-counter analgesic that is reasonably safe for a short time for home veterinary care in the recommended dosage for dogs. (Aspirin has a very low margin of safety for cats and should not be used.) Buffered or enteric-coated aspirin is much safer than regular aspirin because it is less likely to cause stomach and duodenal ulcers.

Aspirin remains effective as a short-term analgesic to control the pain associated with musculoskeletal injuries. It is no longer recommended for long-term control of osteoarthritis, because of its destructive effects on joint cartilage. There are better analgesics available that do not have this disadvantage. Aspirin should not be given to dogs with any bleeding or clotting disorders. Aspirin should be stopped at least one week before any surgery and should not be used during pregnancy, due to its effects on clotting mechanisms.

Note that individual dogs metabolize aspirin at very different rates. This inconsistency can lead to an unexpected accumulation of dangerous breakdown products in the animal's body. As few as two regular-strength aspirin tablets can produce severe organ damage in some medium-size (30 pounds, 13.6kg) dogs. Follow the exact dosage given in the table on page 571 to avoid this complication.

Aspirin belongs to the general class of drugs collectively known as nonsteroidal anti-inflammatory drugs (NSAIDs). To treat arthritis and other inflammations, newer NSAIDs have been tested extensively in dogs. (See the chart *Osteoarthritis Medications*, page 404, for more about NSAIDs.) These are generally less upsetting to the stomach than buffered aspirin and appear to be more effective for long-term treatment.

However, all NSAIDs irritate the stomach and are capable of causing stomach and duodenal ulcers. Your veterinarian may prescribe a gastric mucosal protectant, such as misoprostol (Cytotec) or sucralfate (Carafate), to prevent this complication. Remember, never use more than one NSAID (including aspirin) at the same time. Also, do not combine NSAIDs with any corticoteroids, such as prednisone.

Any dog who is going on one of the NSAIDs should have bloodwork done before the drug is administered. The bloodwork should be repeated every three to six months if the dog will be on one of these medications long term. Liver problems have been seen in some dogs, and Labrador Retrievers may have an idiosyncratic reaction to carprofen. If liver or kidney problems develop, even if they are not due to the drug itself, the dosage may need to be adjusted or the dog may be switched to another pain medication.

Many NSAIDs that can be purchased over the counter have unpredictable absorption rates and low margins of safety. *None of these should be used without specific instructions from your veterinarian.*

Naproxen and ibuprofen (Motrin) are powerful analgesics, but both have a high incidence of gastrointestinal side effects. This makes them unsuitable for long-term administration. Ibuprofen, in particular, is not recommended for dogs.

Phenylbutazone (Butazolidin) is an analgesic that is widely used in horses. In dogs it appears to have harmful effects on joint cartilage. Its other main drawback is that it can cause bone marrow suppression, especially when given in high doses for long periods. It is no longer recommended now that safer analgesics are available.

Flunixin meglumine (Banamine) is a potent analgesic and anti-inflammatory that is also useful in fighting the toxins produced by bacteria. This makes it useful in treating *septic* shock. Gastrointestinal toxicity limits its use in dogs for routine care. There are also other options available, and new pain medications are being developed all the time.

When pain relievers are used for treating sprains and acute injuries of muscles, tendons, and joints, the dog should be confined or restricted from exercising. Pain relief may cause the dog to overuse the limb, which can delay recovery.

Antibiotics

Antibiotics are used to fight bacteria and fungus in and on the body. Bacteria are classified according to their ability to cause disease. Pathogenic bacteria are capable of producing a particular illness or infection. Nonpathogenic bacteria live on or within the host but do not cause illness under normal conditions. These bacteria are called normal flora. Some actually produce substances necessary to the well-being of the host. For example, bacteria in the bowel synthesize vitamin K, which is necessary for blood clotting. Rarely, nonpathogenic bacteria will overgrow and cause symptoms due to their sheer numbers.

Antibiotics fall into two categories: Bacteriostatic and fungistatic drugs inhibit the growth of microorganisms but don't kill them; bactericidal and fungicidal drugs destroy the microorganisms outright.

WHY ANTIBIOTICS FAIL

Antibiotics may not always be effective, for a number of reasons.

Inadequate Wound Care

Antibiotics enter the bloodstream and are carried to the source of the infection. Abscesses, wounds that contain devitalized tissue, and wounds with foreign bodies (dirt or splinters, for example) are resistant areas. Under such circumstances, antibiotics can't penetrate the wound completely. Accordingly, it is essential to drain abscesses, clean dirty wounds, and remove foreign bodies.

Inappropriate Selection

An antibiotic chosen to treat an infection must be effective against the specific type of bacteria that is infecting the body. The best way to determine susceptibility is to sample the organism, grow it on a culture plate, and identify it by the way

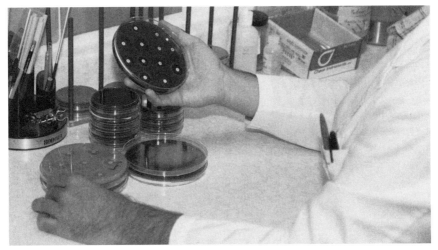

This is an antibiotic sensitivity test. Discs containing antibiotics on an agar plate show which antibiotics inhibit the growth of the cultured bacteria.

its colony appears and by microscopic characteristics. Antibiotic discs are then applied to the culture plate to see which discs inhibit the growth of bacteria colonies. The results are graded according to whether the bacteria are sensitive, indifferent, or insensitive to the effects of the antibiotic. Laboratory findings, however, do not always coincide with results in the patient. Nonetheless, sensitivity testing is the best way to select the most effective antibiotic.

Route of Administration

An important medical decision is choosing the best route for administration. In a dog with severe infections, antibiotics may be given intravenously or by intramuscular or subcutaneous injection. Some oral antibiotics should be given on an empty stomach; others with a meal. Incomplete absorption is one cause of inadequate levels of antibiotics in the blood. If the dog is vomiting, oral medications may not be absorbed.

Dose and Frequency of Administration

The dose is computed by weighing the dog, then dividing the total daily dose into equal parts and giving them at prescribed intervals. Other factors that must be accounted for when computing the daily dose are the severity of the infection, the age of the dog, her overall health and stamina, and whether the dog is taking another antibiotic. When the total dose is too low or the antibiotic is not given often enough, the drug may not be effective.

Resistant Strains

Antibiotics can destroy the normal flora in the body, which crowds out pathogens. This allows harmful bacteria to multiply and cause disease. Furthermore, strains of bacteria may develop that are resistant to antibiotics and thus cannot be effectively controlled. This is particularly likely to occur when antibiotics are used:

- For too short a time
- In too low a dosage
- When the antibiotic is not bactericidal

Microorganisms that are resistant to one antibiotic are usually resistant to other antibiotics of the same class. The development of antibiotic-resistant bacteria is one of the main reasons why antibiotics should be used exactly as prescribed and only in situations in which they will clearly benefit the dog. If antibiotics are given at a lower than effective dose or for a shorter time period than prescribed, this may select for bacteria that have resistance to that drug. For example, if five days of treatment would kill all the bacteria and you administer antibiotics for only four days, the only bacteria left are those that managed to survive through four days of treatment. The most resistant bacteria are then left to reproduce.

ANTIBIOTICS AND STEROIDS

Steroids are often combined with antibiotics, particularly in topical preparations for the eyes and ears, and on the skin. Corticosteroids have anti-inflammatory effects. By reducing swelling, redness, and tenderness, they often give the impression that the dog is getting better when actually, she is not.

Steroids have one other side effect that is undesirable: They depress the normal immune response. This can impair the dog's ability to fight the infection. Antibiotic medications that contain steroids should be used only under the guidance of a veterinarian.

Drug Complications

Virtually all drugs have side effects. Side effects are changes caused by the drug that are not related to the intended use of the drug. For example, prednisone often causes a dog to drink more and consequently urinate more. This is a side effect to its primary purpose of influencing immune reactions. Side effects can range form very mild, such as mild sedation, to serious, such as gastric ulcers. Most side effects lie somewhere between those extremes.

TOXICITY

All drugs are poisons and are capable of causing greater harm than good. This includes herbal and "natural" remedies. There is a margin of safety between a therapeutic dose and a toxic dose. A safe drug has a wide margin of safety. Toxicity is caused by overdose, impaired elimination of the drug, giving the drug for too long a time, or using a drug with a narrow margin of safety.

If a dog has advanced liver or kidney disease, drugs are not detoxified and excreted. The dosage of any drug must therefore be reduced accordingly. Young pups require a lower dose per pound of body weight than do adult dogs, because puppies' kidneys are immature.

Drug toxicity can affect one or more systems. Signs are difficult to recognize in dogs, and can be far advanced before they come to your attention. The symptoms of drug toxicity include:

- **Ears.** Damage to the otic nerves leads to ringing in the ears, hearing loss, and deafness; the hearing loss can be permanent
- **Liver.** Jaundice and liver failure
- **Kidneys.** Nitrogen retention, uremia, and kidney failure
- **Bone marrow.** Depresses the production of red blood cells, white blood cells, and platelets, resulting in anemia, impaired immunity, and spontaneous bleeding
- **Gastrointestinal.** Vomiting and/or diarrhea, nausea, loss of appetite
- **Neurological signs.** Disorientation, *ataxia*, coma

ALLERGIC REACTIONS

Antibiotics cause more allergic reactions in dogs than any other group of drugs. Signs of a mild allergic reaction are hives, rash, itching, scratching, and watering eyes. Hives are characterized by the sudden appearance of raised, circular areas in which the hair sticks out in patches. Hives generally appear within 30 minutes of exposure and disappear within 24 hours. (Other types of allergic reactions are discussed in *Allergies*, page 135.) Eruptions on the skin, hemolytic anemia, or thrombocytopenia from a drug reaction may all be classified as allergic reactions to a drug.

Anaphylactic shock is an uncommon, severe allergic reaction usually caused by exposure to foreign proteins, such as penicillin or a vaccine. The signs are vomiting, diarrhea, weakness, *stridor*, difficulty breathing, collapse, and sometimes death. Anaphylactic shock is a medical emergency and is discussed on page 13.

A dog who has had any type of allergic drug reaction should not be given that drug again.

How to Give Medications

Don't give your dog any medication until you have spoken to your veterinarian to make sure it is the right medicine for the dog and the circumstances. You should also ask for instructions on how to give the drug and the correct dosage for your dog.

Pills, Capsules, and Tablets

To give a dog a pill, slip your thumb into the space behind one of the canine teeth and press upward on the roof of the mouth. As the mouth begins to open, press down on the lower jaw with the opposite thumb. Alternatively, press in on both lips from above the muzzle. As the skin pushes in behind the canines, the dog will open her mouth.

Insert the pill well to the back of the tongue in the middle of the mouth. If you place the pill too far forward or to the side of the tongue, the dog will spit it out. Close the dog's mouth and massage or rub her throat until she swallows. If the dog licks her nose, the pill has been swallowed. Blowing briefly into the dog's nose may also cause her to quickly swallow the pill. You can also give her a syringe full of water to make sure she swallows, or give the dog a small treat after the pill goes down.

Do not break the pill up into a powder. Powders have an unpleasant taste that dogs don't accept well. Some pills also have a protective coating that is important for the delayed release of the medication, and crushing the pill will destroy the coating.

Some pills can be given in food. This can be done by making up small "meatballs" of dog food. Give the dog one or two undoctored meatballs, then

The correct way to give a pill—in the middle and well at the back of the tongue.

Liquids are administered
into the cheek pouch
using a plastic syringe or a
medicine squeeze bottle.

one with the pill pushed deep into the center. Follow up with an undoctored one so the dog will continue to take the treats even if she gets a small taste of the medicine.

There are also commercial treats available made specfically for administering medication that are sticky enough to make it difficult for the dog to extract a pill while eating the treat. They are soft so they mold easily around the pill. Pill Pockets and Flavor Doh are two examples.

Always check with your veterinarian before giving any pills with food.

LIQUIDS

Liquid medicines, including electrolytes and water solutions, are administered into the cheek pouch between the molars and the cheek. A medicine bottle, eyedropper, or plastic syringe without the needle can be used to dispense the liquid.

Pinch the dog's lips together as shown in the photo on this page. Insert the end of the dispenser into the cheek pouch and seal the lips with your fingers. Tilt the dog's chin upward and slowly dispense the liquid. The dog will swallow automatically. If you must give the dog a large quantity of liquid, you will need to pause periodically and give her time to swallow. Do not try to push a full syringe of liquid quickly down the dog's throat!

INJECTIONS

Injecting any foreign substance into the body always carries with it the danger of causing an acute allergic or anaphylactic reaction, as described on page 13. Treating anaphylactic shock requires immediate intravenous adrenaline and oxygen. This is one reason why it is best to have your veterinarian give injections. As a precaution, do not administer a drug by injection to a dog who has had any sort of past history of an allergic reaction (such as hives) to that drug.

If it becomes necessary to give injections at home (for example, if the dog is diabetic), have your veterinarian demonstrate the procedure. Some injections are given under the skin (subcutaneous) and others into the muscle (intramuscular). Directions that come with the product will indicate the correct route of injection.

The injection itself usually is not painful, although intramuscular injections may hurt somewhat as the medicine is injected. Dogs should be restrained as described in *Handling and Restraint*, page 2. Having an assistant is helpful.

Begin by drawing the medicine up into the syringe. If there is an air bubble inside, flick the syringe to get the bubble to the top. Then point the needle toward the ceiling or into a sink and press the plunger to expel all air from the syringe and needle. Make sure the correct amount is still in the syringe after the air bubble is expelled. Select the injection site, part the hair, and cleanse the dog's skin with cotton soaked in alcohol.

Subcutaneous Injections

These are given under the skin on the back of the neck or the shoulder. Here the skin is loose and easily forms a fold when pinched. Grasp a fold of skin to form a ridge. Firmly push the point of the needle through the skin into the subcutaneous fat at an angle somewhat parallel to the surface of the body.

Subcutaneous injections are given beneath the skin on the back of the neck or shoulder.

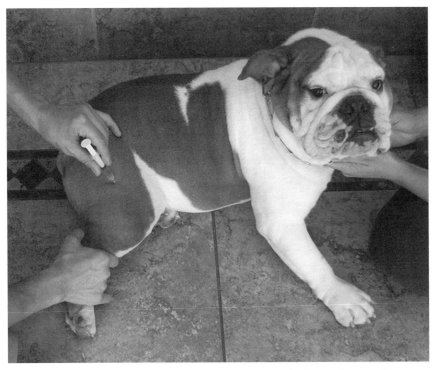

Intramuscular injections are given into the back of the thigh muscle away from the bone.

Before giving the injection, pull back a bit on the plunger and look for blood. If blood appears, the medicine might be injected into a vein or artery. Withdraw the syringe and start again. When you see no blood, push in the plunger. Withdraw the needle and rub the skin for a few seconds to disperse the medicine.

Intramuscular Injections

Most intramuscular injections will be given by your veterinarian or a veterinary technician at the clinic. They are given into the muscle at the back of the thighs, halfway between the hip and the knee. Use a ¾-inch-long (1.8cm) needle. Note the location of the bone and plan to place the injection into muscle well away from the bone. Injections into bones, nerves, and joints can be avoided by giving the shots in the location described.

Insert the needle rapidly through the skin to minimize pain. Withdraw the plunger and check for blood before giving the injection. Inject the medication slowly over five to seven seconds.

SUPPOSITORIES

When a dog cannot take a drug orally (for example, when she is vomiting), medications can sometimes be given by suppository. Your veterinarian may also prescribe a suppository to treat a bout of severe constipation.

Lubricate the suppository with petroleum jelly, then slip it all the way into the rectum, where will dissolve.

Suppositories for constipation contain a mild irritant, which draws water into the rectum and stimulates a bowel movement. Check with your veterinarian for pediatric suppositories that might be suitable for your dog. Do not give suppositories to dogs who are dehydrated or may have an intestinal obstruction. A dog with *Acute Painful Abdomen*, as described on page 14, also should not be given a suppository.

COMPOUNDED MEDICINES

Compounding uses new ways of combining or formulating medications to make them easier to give to your dog. This could mean mixing the medication into a flavored treat or liquid. Some medications can also be transferred to gels that can then be rubbed onto an ear. Fentanyl patches are an example of a medication that is absorbed through the skin.

Occasionally, compounding is used to combine medications that can be mixed together safely so fewer pills need to be given. Compounding may be used for medications that are not commercially available or are not available in dosages for dogs, such as potassium bromide for seizures. More research is needed to determine if the dosage in compounded drugs is appropriate and consistent for most medications.

OTHER MEDICATIONS

The proper way to medicate the eyes is discussed in *How to Apply Eye Medicines*, page 174. Medicating the ears is discussed in *How to Apply Ear Medicines*, page 208. Enemas are discussed in *Fecal Impactions*, page 282.

Over-the-Counter Drugs for Home Veterinary Use

Note that these medications are not approved for use in dogs and should only be used under the guidance of your veterinarian. Do not give your dog any drug without first consulting your veterinarian. The doses given here will need to be adjusted if your dog has other health problems, such as liver or kidney disease. 1 teaspoon = 5 ml; 1 pound = .45 kg

Drug	Action	Dosage	Method of administration	Frequency of administration
Aspirin (buffered; enteric coated)	Analgesic, anti-inflammatory	4 to 10 mg per pound of body weight (dose varies with the purpose of the medication)	With food	Once daily
Benadryl (diphenhydramine)	Antihistamine	2 mg per pound of body weight	Orally	Every eight hours
Betadine solution (povidone-iodine)	Antiseptic	Dilute to 0.2 percent (2 ml to 2 quarts tap water)	Topically	As prescribed for cleaning the wound
Charcoal (compressed activated charcoal)	Binds stomach poisons	5 g per 10 pounds of body weight	Orally	Keep at least 30 tablets available; give once, and only under the direction of a veterinarian
Chlorhexidine solution (Nolvasan and others)	Antiseptic	Dilute to 0.05 percent (25 ml to 2 quarts, 1.9 l, tap water)	Topically	As prescribed for cleaning the wound
Dramamine (dimenhydrinate)	For motion sickness	2 to 4mg per pound of body weight	Orally	Every eight hours
Hydrogen peroxide (3%)	Induce vomiting	1 teaspoon per 10 pounds of body weight	Orally	May repeat every 15 to 30 minutes (3 times only)
Kaolin and pectin (beware: some formulations contain salicylates)	For persistent diarrhea	½ to 1 ml per pound of body weight (or 1 to 2 teaspoons per 10 pounds)	Orally	Every 6 hours

continued

Over-the-Counter Drugs for Home Veterinary Use (*continued*)

Drug	Action	Dosage	Method of administration	Frequency of administration
Metamucil (psyllium)	For constipation or to add fiber to the diet	1 teaspoon per 11 to 22 pounds of body weight	Add to meals	Once daily; for short-term use, unless otherwise directed
Milk of Magnesia, Mylanta, Maalox (magnesium hydroxide)	Antacid, laxative	2 to 4 ml per pound of body weight	Orally	Every 12 to 24 hours
Mineral oil	Lubricant, laxative	5 ml per 20 pounds of body weight	Add to food; do not give separately due to aspiration risk	Twice daily; only for 2 to 3 days
Pepcid (famitodine)	Histamine blocker for antacid effect	1 mg per pound of body weight	Injection or orally	Once or twice daily
Pepto-Bismol, Kaopectate (bismuth subsalicylate)	For diarrhea	0.5 to 1.5 ml per pound of body weight	Orally	Every 12 hours
Prilosec (omeprazole)	Antacid, ulcer medication	.25 to .5 mg per pound of body weight	Orally	Once daily
Zantac (ranitidine)	Histamine blocker for antacid effect	150 to 300 mg per pound of body weight	Add to meals	Daily; divide total dose over several meals throughout the day
Robitussin DM, Benylin Expectorant (dextromethorphan)	Cough suppressant	0.5 to 1 mg per pound of body weight (or 1 teaspoon per 20 pounds)	Orally	Every 6 hours
Tagamet (cimetidine)	Histamine blocker for antacid effect	10 mg per pound of body weight	Orally	2 or 3 times a day

NORMAL PHYSIOLOGICAL DATA

Normal Body Temperature

Adult dog: 100° to 102.5°F (37.7° to 39.2°C)

Average: 101.3°F (38.5°C)

Newborn puppy: 94° to 97°F at birth (34.4° to 36.1°C); 100°F (37.3°C) at 4 weeks old

HOW TO TAKE YOUR DOG'S TEMPERATURE

The only effective way to take your dog's temperature is to use a rectal thermometer. Bulb and digital rectal thermometers are equally acceptable, but the digital thermometer is more convenient and records the temperature faster.

If you're using a bulb thermometer, shake it down until the bulb registers 96°F (35.5°C). Lubricate the bulb with petroleum or K-Y jelly. Have someone gently restrain the dog, holding his head and making sure the dog can't move around. Raise the dog's tail holding, it firmly to keep him from sitting down. Using a twisting motion, gently insert the bulb into the anal canal one to three inches (2.5 to 7.6cm), depending on the size of the dog.

For newborn puppies, use a pediatric thermometer and insert the tip of the thermometer only as far as necessary to completely cover the bulb or tip.

Hold the thermometer in place for three minutes. Then remove it, wipe it clean, and read the temperature by the height of the silver column of mercury on the thermometer scale. Clean the thermometer with alcohol to prevent the transfer of diseases.

If you're using a digital thermometer, insert it the same way and follow the manufacturer's directions.

If the thermometer breaks off—this usually happens because the dog sits down—do not attempt to find and extract the broken end. Instead, notify your veterinarian immediately.

Normal Heart Rate

Adult dog: 60 to 160 beats per minute

Toy breeds: Up to 180 beats per minute

Newborn puppy: 160 to 200 beats per minute at birth; 220 beats per minute at 2 weeks of age

To learn how to take your dog's pulse, see *Pulse*, page 8.

Normal Respiratory Rate

Adult dog: 10 to 30 breaths per minute

Average: 24 breaths per minute at rest

Newborn puppy: 15 to 35 breaths per minute, up to 2 weeks of age

Gestation

Averages 63 days from the day of ovulation. The normal range is 56 to 66 days.

COMPARATIVE AGE OF DOGS AND HUMANS

An old general rule is that one dog year is equivalent to seven human years, but this is not always accurate. Dogs age at different rates than humans do. Some dog years are equivalent to more than seven years, and some are equivalent to fewer years. For example, it takes puppies about a year to grow into their adult bodies, while it takes children a lot longer. Thus, the first year of a dog's life is perhaps equivalent to about 15 years of a child's.

Dogs also vary in how quickly they age. In general, small breeds live longer than large ones—occasionally, twice as long.

The chart below indicates average figures for all breeds of dogs, based on their size. The numbers in bold indicate that the dog is considered senior; the numbers in italics indicate that the dog is considered geriatric.

A Dog's Age in Human Years

	Human Years			
Canine Age	Up to 20 pounds (9.07 kg)	21–50 pounds (9.52–22.7 kg)	51–90 pounds (23.1–40.8 kg)	Over 90 pounds
5	36	37	40	**42**
6	40	42	**45**	**49**
7	**44**	**47**	50	**56**
8	**48**	**51**	55	**64**
9	**52**	**56**	**61**	**71**
10	**56**	**60**	66	78
11	**60**	**65**	72	86
12	**64**	69	77	93
13	**68**	74	82	101
14	72	78	88	108
15	76	83	93	115
16	80	87	99	123
17	84	92	104	
18	88	96	109	
19	92	101	115	
20	96	105	120	

Chart developed by Dr. Fred L. Metzger, DVM, State College, Pennsylvania. Courtesy of Pfizer Animal Health.

C

LABORATORY TESTS

At some time in your dog's life, it is highly likely that laboratory tests will be performed. These can range from very simple tests, such as fecal checks for parasites or heartworm tests looking for *antigens*, to sophisticated bloodwork checking out various organs and their functioning. The most common tests done to the blood and urine are discussed here. Blood samples are normally taken from your dog's vein—either a leg or the jugular vein in the neck. Fasting is recommended before blood tests.

Complete Blood Count (CBC) or Hemogram

A CBC is done on blood taken directly from your dog's vein. The goal is to count the different types of cells present in your dog's blood. At the same time, an evaluation is made about the types of cells and their health and life stages. Blood counts may be lowered overall in dogs with bone marrow disorders and those undergoing certain types of chemotherapy.

PCV OR HEMATOCRIT

This test checks to see approximately how many red blood cells your dog has. Blood in a tiny tube is spun in a centrifuge and the number of red blood cells is given as a percent of the total blood volume. Normal dogs run about 35 to 50 percent. A low PCV indicates anemia, which could have a number of causes from hemorrhage to liver or kidney disease. A high PCV is often present in dogs who are dehydrated.

RBC Data

With the red blood cells (RBC), an actual count is made by estimating from the number of cells spread on a slide and examined under a microscope. The amount of hemoglobin present and the age and size of the red blood cells are also measured. MCV is mean corpuscular volume, which is the average size of the red blood cells. MCH is mean corpuscular hemoglobin (the substance in the red blood cells that transports oxygen), which is the average amount of hemoglobin inside a red blood cell. MCHC is the mean corpuscular hemoglobin concentration, which is the average concentration of hemoglobin in the red blood cells, expressed as a percentage. Your veterinarian or the laboratory technician will also examine cells for maturity and for any blood-borne parasites.

WBC Data

An estimate will also be made of the total number of white blood cells (WBC) in the sample. White blood cells include eosinophils (cells that fight parasite infestations and are involved in allergies), and cells that fight infections or cellular invaders, including neutrophils, lymphocytes, basophils, and monocytes. The number of white blood cells such as lymphocytes may be increased in dogs with certain cancers, as well. Normally, white blood cell counts rise with bacterial infections, but if the infection is winning the battle, counts may be lower than expected. Viruses may also lower the white blood cell count.

Platelets

Platelets are cells that assist in clotting and coagulation. An estimate of their numbers is also made from a blood sample on a slide examined under a microscope. Platelets can be low in number in dogs with certain immune disorders, some cancers, and bleeding disorders. Some breeds, such as Cavalier King Charles Spaniels, can have platelet anomalies that cause their numbers to be low.

Blood Chemistry Panel

A blood chemistry panel evaluates the enzymes that are important to many organ functions, and also looks at certain proteins and minerals that are important for normal body functions. Important tests include:

> **Albumin.** This is an important protein made by the liver. It decreases in dogs with certain types of liver and kidney damage or intestinal problems, and can increase in dehydrated dogs.

ALT. Alanine aminotransferase is a liver enzyme that can increase in dogs with virtually any liver damage.

ALP. Alkaline phosphatase is an enzyme that may increase in dogs with liver or bone disease, or along with steroid use or Cushing's disease. It could also indicate bile problems. Phenobarbital, used to control seizures, may also increase the levels of this enzyme.

Amylase. This is an enzyme manufactured primarily by the pancreas and released into the digestive tract to help digest starch and glycogen. It may be elevated in dogs with pancreatitis, kidney disease, or steroid use.

AST. Aspartate aminotransferase is an enzyme normally found in red blood cells, the liver, the heart, muscle tissue, the pancreas, and the kidneys. The test is used primarily as a measure of liver function. AST levels may also increase in dogs with heart damage.

Bile acids. These tests are important for evaluating liver function. In this case, two blood samples are needed: one taken before eating and one two hours after eating.

Bilirubin. This is made in the liver from old red blood cells. This value may increase in dogs with liver or gallbladder disease, or with diseases that destroy red blood cells. Accumulation of this pigment in the body may cause a yellow coloring or jaundice.

BUN. Blood urea nitrogen is protein waste material made by the liver and eliminated via the kidneys. A low BUN may indicate liver disease and a high BUN indicate kidney disease or dehydration.

Calcium. This mineral is very important for muscle and nerve action as well as bone development. High calcium can be seen in dogs with certain cancers, kidney failure, certain rodenticide poisonings, and parathyroid problems. Low calcium can be seen in bitches after whelping and nursing large litters and with some parathyroid problems.

Cholesterol. This level isn't nearly as important in dogs as it is in humans, and is not a factor in canine heart disease. Still, it is a fat and increases can be seen in dogs with hypothyroidism, Cushing's disease, and diabetes, among other problems.

Creatinine. This is a waste product of muscles and is normally removed by the kidneys. An increase can indicate kidney disease.

CPK or CK. Creatinine phosphokinase or creatinine kinase are different names for a muscle enzyme that increases with muscle damage, including damage to the heart muscle.

Glucose. This is blood sugar. Levels are increased in dogs with diabetes mellitus or Cushing's disease, and with steroid use. Low blood sugar may be due to certain cancers, insulin overdose, liver problems or infection.

Phosphorus. Abnormal levels of this mineral indicate parathyroid problems, kidney problems, and possible dietary inadequacies.

Potassium. This mineral is very important for muscle and nerve functions and for proper regulation of the heart. Kidney failure, an obstructed bladder, Addison's disease, and antifreeze poisoning can all increase potassium levels.

Sodium. This mineral is important for normal muscle and nerve function. Levels can be affected by vomiting and diarrhea, and by Addison's disease.

Total protein. This is a measure of the proteins in the blood, including albumin and globulins (which are associated with infections and inflammations). High levels can occur in dogs with dehydration or immune stimulation. Low levels may indicate liver problems.

Urinalysis

Urinalysis involves looking at a urine specimen. Urine samples may be collected as a "free catch" when the dog is voiding or by using a catheter or a needle inserted directly into the bladder. The last two methods are much better if an infection is suspected, because the sample collected is sterile and any bacteria cultured from it is likely to be the culprit.

The urine is checked for certain components, such as glucose and pH. Concentration and the presence of any cells are also evaluated. Some of this is done with a specially coated test strip that gives a range for results and some is done with special instruments.

Dilute urine may mean kidney problems or increased drinking. Concentrated urine could mean dehydration or liver or kidney problems.

The urine is checked for glucose, indicating diabetes mellitus, and for protein, indicating kidney damage. The pH will tell if the urine is acidic or alkaline, which can be influenced by diet and may cause bladder crystals or stones to form.

The urine is also spun in a centrifuge and the cells collected and examined. The presence of red blood cells or white blood cells may indicate infections or damage to the urinary tract. Crystals suggest stone formation. Bacteria can indicate infection, in which case the sample may also be cultured to look for bacterial infections.

USEFUL RESOURCES

AKC Canine Health Foundation
P.O. Box 37941
Raleigh, NC 27627-7941
www.akcchf.org

American Animal Hospital Association
12515 W. Bayaud Ave.
Lakewood, CO 80228
(303) 986-2800
www.aahanet.org
www.healthypet.com

American Holistic Veterinary Medical Association
2218 Old Emmorton Rd.
Bel Air, MD 21015
(410) 569-0795
www.ahvma.org

American Kennel Club
260 Madison Ave.
New York, NY 10016
(212) 696-8300
www.akc.org

American Veterinary Medical Association
1931 North Meacham Rd., Suite 100
Schaumburg, IL 60173
(847) 925-8070
www.avma.org

ASPCA Animal Poison Control Center
424 East 92 St.
New York, NY 10128
(888) 426-4435
www.aspca.org/apcc

Canadian Kennel Club
89 Skyway Ave.
Etobicoke, Ontario
Canada M9W 6R4
(800) 250-8040 or (416) 675-5511
www.ckc.ca

Canine Eye Registration Foundation (CERF)
1717 Philo Rd.
P.O. Box 3007
Urbana, IL 61803-3007
(217) 693-4800
www.vmdb.org/cerf.html

Center for Veterinary Medicine
Food and Drug Administration
Communications Staff
7519 Standish Pl., HFV-12
Rockville, MD 20855
(240) 276-9300
www.fda.gov/cvm

Delta Society
875 124th Ave. NE
Suite 101
Bellevue, WA 98005
(425) 226-7357
www.deltasociety.org

Institute for Genetic Disease Control in Animals (GDC)
P.O. Box 222
Davis, CA 95617
(530) 756-6773
www.gdcinstitute.org

International Association of Animal Behavior Consultants
505 Timber Lane
Jefferson Hills, PA 15025
www.iaabc.org

International Veterinary Acupuncture Society
P.O. Box 271395
Ft. Collins, CO 80527-1395
(970) 266-0666
www.ivas.org

Morris Animal Foundation
45 Inverness Dr. East
Englewood, CO 80112
(800) 243-2345
www.morrisanimalfoundation.org

National Association of Professional Pet Sitters
15000 Commerce Pkwy.
Suite C
Mt. Laurel, NJ 08054
(856) 439-0324
www.petsitters.org

OptiGen
Cornell Business & Technology Park
767 Warren Rd.
Suite 300
Ithaca, NY 14850
(607) 257 0301
www.optigen.com

Orthopedic Foundation for Animals (OFA)
2301 East Nifong Blvd.
Columbia, MO 65201
(573) 442-0418
www.offa.org

PennHIP
University of Pennsylvania School of Veterinary Medicine
3800 Spruce St.
Philadelphia, PA 19104
(215) 573-3176
www.pennhip.org

Pet Sitters International
201 East King St.
King, NC 27021-9161
(336) 983-9222
www.petsit.com

United Kennel Club
100 E. Kilgore Rd.
Kalamazoo, MI 49001-5598
(616) 343-9020
www.ukcdogs.com

VetGen
3728 Plaza Dr.
Suite 1
Ann Arbor, MI 48108
(800) 483-8436
www.vetgen.com

Web Sites for General Health Information

Dog Hobbyist
www.doghobbyist.com

Dog Owner's Guide
www.canismajor.com/dog

The Senior Dogs Project
www.srdogs.com

Veterinary Partner
www.veterinarypartner.com

Web Sites for Dog Food and Nutrition Information

Eukanuba
www.eukanuba.com

Hill's Science Diet
www.hillspet.com

The Honest Kitchen
www.thehonestkitchen.com

Iams
www.iams.com

Pet Diets
www.petdiets.com

Purina
www.purina.com

Royal Canin
www.royalcanin.us

Therapeutic Diets
www.prescriptiondiets.com

GLOSSARY

Words in italics are defined elsewhere in the Glossary.

Abortion   Death of a fetus after organ development (28 days), followed by expulsion of the products of conception.

Abscess   A collection of pus in a cavity. It may be beneath the skin, in an organ, or in a body space.

Accommodate   The process by which the lens of the eye changes shape to focus light on the retina.

Acidosis   A buildup of acids in the blood, resulting in a lower pH than normal.

ACTH   Adrenocorticotropic hormone, the pituitary hormone that stimulates the adrenal cortex to produce corticosteroids.

Acute   Occurring suddenly. Often indicates the early stage of a disease, when symptoms are most pronounced. Acute symptoms are usually short term.

Afebrile   Without fever.

AKC   American Kennel Club

Allergen   Any substance that is capable of causing an allergic reaction. Drugs, insect toxins, pollens, molds, dust mites, foods, and vaccinations are common allergens for dogs.

Alopecia   Loss of hair or failure to regrow hair, resulting in an area of thinning or baldness.

Analgesia   Pain relief.

Anomaly   Out of the ordinary; a condition that departs from the normal.

Anestrus   The fourth phase of the estrous cycle in which there is little, if any, ovarian activity. The length of this phase varies, lasting on average 130 to 150 days.

Anorectal   Anatomically, the area encompassed by the anus, anal canal, and rectum.

Anorexia   Loss of appetite and failure to eat.

Anthelmintic   A medication that acts to dispel or destroy parasitic intestinal worms.

Antibody A protein substance produced by the immune system to neutralize the effects of an *antigen*.

Antigen A substance recognized by the immune system as foreign to the body. The immune system develops antibodies that bind the antigen and prevent it from harming the animal or causing disease.

Arrhythmia An abnormal heart rhythm. It may be inconsequential, or serious enough to cause cardiac arrest.

Ascarids Roundworms.

Ascites An abnormal accumulation of fluid in the *peritoneal cavity*. Congestive heart failure and liver failure are the most common causes.

Assay Testing the *serum* to determine the relative proportion of a substance, such as the concentration of an *antigen* or *antibody*.

Ataxia Incoordination; an inability to coordinate voluntary muscle movements that is symptomatic of some central nervous system disorders and injuries and is not due to muscle weakness. The adjective is ataxic.

Atresia Failure of a channel or passage to open in the course of fetal development.

Atrophy Shrinkage in the size of an organ or tissue due to disuse or death of cells.

Auto-antibodies Antibodies that a host makes against its own tissues. Auto-antibodies cause destruction of the targeted cells.

Autoimmune disease A disease resulting from *auto-antibodies* targeting host tissue.

Autosomal All chromosomes that are not the X and Y sex chromosomes.

Bactericidal Capable of killing bacteria, as opposed to just inhibiting their growth.

Benign An abnormal growth that is not a malignant cancer. Benign growths are usually not life threatening and do not spread to other areas of the body.

Bezoars Foreign bodies in the stomach composed of hair and other ingested materials that form hard concretions too large to pass out of the stomach.

Bilateral On both sides.

Biopsy The removal of tissue for microscopic examination and diagnosis.

Bitch A female dog.

Bleb A skin blister filled with *serum* or blood.

Boil A small skin *abscess*, usually at the site of a hair follicle.

BPH Benign prostatic hyperplasia, a noncancerous form of prostate enlargement.

Brachycephalic   A dog with a broad skull and a short muzzle, resulting in a flat face, as in the Pug and Pekingese.

Breeder   The owner of the bitch when the dog was bred.

Brisket   The lower chest, particularly the sternum.

Bronchoscopy   A procedure in which an *endoscope* is passed into the trachea and bronchi to directly visualize the interior of the respiratory tract.

Brood bitch   A female dog used for breeding.

Bulla   A large skin blister filled with clear fluid. Or, in the case of the lungs, air sacs filled with air. May also refer to the tympanic bulla, a part of the inner ear.

Calculus   Dental calculus (also called tartar) is a plaquelike material composed of calcium salts, food particles, and bacteria.

Cancer   A tumor on the surface of the body or within an organ that has the potential to destroy tissue and kill the animal through local growth and/or spread to distant parts.

Canids   Foxes, wolves, coyotes, jackals, and other cousins of dogs.

Capillary refill time   The time it takes for the gums to pink up after being firmly pressed with a finger—normally one to two seconds or less. A measure of the quality of the circulation.

Cardiac massage   Compression of the heart, resulting in temporary support of the circulation.

Castrate   To remove the testicles of a male dog.

Cellulitis   Infection of all layers of the skin along with inflammation of the connective tissue, characterized by redness, swelling, tenderness, and increased warmth. Usually very painful.

Cerebral edema   Swelling of the brain following injury or a period of oxygen deprivation.

Chemotherapy   The use of drugs that are cellular poisons to attack and kill cancer cells, or to suppress the immune system in the treatment of *autoimmune disease*.

Chondroprotective   Compounds that protect joint cartilage from the destructive effects of degenerative joint disease.

Chromosomes   The collection of DNA proteins that are organized into genes and aligned to provide genetic information to the body. Dogs have 78 chromosomes (arranged in 39 pairs).

Chronic   Present for a long period. Often indicates that stage of a disease in which symptoms persist in a milder form.

Cilia   Hairlike projections on cells in the respiratory tract.

Colonoscopy A procedure that uses an *endoscope* to view the interior of the colon and rectum.

Colostrum The first milk of the dam, containing the all-important maternal antibodies that protect puppies from common diseases for the first three months of life.

Conceptus The products resulting from the union between egg and sperm.

Condition (of the body) A subjective term that refers to overall health as shown by the coat, general appearance, body weight, and musculature.

Conformation How the various angles, shapes, and parts of the dog's body conform to the breed standard. At dog shows, dogs are judged by how well they conform to the standard for their breed.

Congenital A condition that exists at birth, although it is not always clinically evident until later in life. Congenital conditions can be either genetically determined or acquired before or during delivery.

Corpus luteum A growth that forms in the ovary at the site of ovulation. The corpus luteum manufactures progesterone, essential to the support of pregnancy. The plural is corpora lutea.

CPK Creatine phosphokinase, an enzyme found in muscle tissue that is released when there is muscle injury or disease.

CPR Cardiopulmonary resuscitation; the combination of mouth-to-mouth resuscitation and cardiac massage.

Crossbred A dog whose sire and dam are of different breeds.

Cryopreservation Freezing and storing tissue for later use.

Cryotherapy A procedure in which tissue is destroyed by freezing it with liquid nitrogen.

Cryptorchid A male dog with one or both testicles retained in the abdomen or the inguinal area instead of in the scrotum.

CT scan Computerized tomography, a diagnostic X-ray procedure that produces cross-sectional views of a body structure. CT scans may be available only at veterinary referral centers. Sometimes called CAT scan, an acronym for computer-assisted tomography.

Cyanosis A bluish discoloration of the gums and tongue due to inadequate oxygen in the blood.

Cytology The microscopic examination of cells to determine the cause of a disease.

Dam The mother of a puppy.

Dementia Loss of memory and reasoning power characterized by varying degrees of confusion, disorientation, apathy, and stupor.

Depigmentation Loss of dark color in the skin caused by destruction of *melanin*-producing cells. Depigmented areas are shades of white.

Depression A marked decrease in activity in which the dog withdraws, spends most of her time lying down, is disinterested in her surroundings, and exhibits little or no interest in eating.

Dermis The sensitive connective tissue layer of the skin located below the epidermis.

Dewclaws Vestigial toes; the equivalent of a fifth digit high on the inside of each foot. Normally present on the front feet, unless they are removed. Double dewclaws are required by the breed standard on the back feet of Briards, Great Pyrenees, and Icelandic Sheepdogs.

Diestrus The third stage in the *estrous cycle,* also called the *luteal phase,* which begins when the female refuses to stand for mating. It lasts, on average, about 60 days, then merges with *anestrus.*

Dominant A gene is dominant if it alone is capable of determining the expression of a particular trait.

Duodenum The first part of the small intestines, after the stomach.

Dysfunction Abnormal performance of an organ or system.

Dysphagia Painful and/or difficult swallowing.

Dysplastic Developmentally malformed.

Dysuria Painful and/or difficult urination.

Early embryonic loss Loss of the productions of conception before 28 days gestation, often by internal resorption so that no external evidence of the loss is found.

ECG Electrocardiogram; the readings from an electrocardiograph, which measures the changes in electrical currents associated with heart activity. An ECG is used to measure heart function and detect abnormalities. Sometimes called EKG.

Echocardiogram A test that uses plain and doppler ultrasound (high-frequency sound waves) to create a computerized image of structures within the heart and a detail of blood flow. The procedure that uses an echocardiogram to diagnose heart disease is called echocardiography.

Edema The accumulation of fluid beneath the skin or within an organ.

EEG Electroencephalography; a procedure that records the electrical activity of the cerebral cortex. It is used to diagnose epilepsy, *tumors,* and brain diseases. It is only available at some veterinary referral centers.

Ejaculate The total volume of semen emitted by the stud dog during breeding.

Electrocautery The use of an electric probe to destroy tissue using heat.

Electrolytes   Sodium, chloride, potassium, bicarbonate, calcium, phosphorus, and other minerals required for organ functioning.

ELISA   Enzyme-Linked Immunosorbent Assay, a *serologic* test used to detect antibodies to a protein, such as those associated with a bacteria or virus.

Embolus   A blood clot that develops at another site and travels through the circulatory system to a smaller vessel, where it becomes lodged and interrupts blood flow.

Embryo   A *conceptus* younger than 28 days gestation, before the stage of organ development.

Encapsulated   Surrounded by a capsule that creates a distinct boundary between two tissue planes.

Encephalitis   Inflammation and/or infection of the brain.

Endemic   Occurring in or native to a particular population or region.

Endometrium   A layer of glandular tissue lining the cavity of the uterus.

Endoscope   An instrument that uses lights and fiber optics or a miniaturized video camera to view the interior of a body cavity. The procedure of using an endoscope to visualize the interior of a body cavity is called endoscopy.

Enteritis   Inflammation of the lining of the intestines, caused by bacterial, parasitic, or viral infection as well as *immune-mediated* diseases.

Eosinophil   A type of white blood cell that is often associated with diseases that have an allergic component.

Epididymis   The coiled tube on top of the testicle that stores the sperm.

Epithelium   A layer of nonliving cells that forms the surface of the skin, mucous membranes, and cornea.

Erosion   An area where a body surface has been destroyed by trauma or inflammation.

Erythrocytes   Red blood cells; the cells that carry oxygen and carbon dioxide.

Estrous cycle   The entire reproductive cycle, as determined from one ovulation to the next, normally occurring about every five to nine months in the sexually mature *bitch.*

Estrus   Same as *heat.* The first phase of the *estrous cycle,* during which the bitch is receptive to the male; lasts on average seven to nine days.

Etiology   Cause of the disease.

Euthanasia   The humane process of giving an animal a fatal, painless injection to end suffering.

Excision   The surgical removal of a *tumor* or *lesion.*

Excoriation   A deep scratch or abrasion of the skin.

Exudate   A liquid discharge that contains pus and bacteria.

FDA   Food and Drug Administration; licenses the use of human and veterinary drugs.

Fertility   In stud dogs, the ability to impregnate the bitch. In brood bitches, the ability to conceive and carry a litter.

Fetus   A *conceptus* older than 28 days' gestation, generally after the stage of organ development.

Fibrosis   The replacement of normal tissue by scar tissue.

Flatus   Breaking wind; passing gas from the rectum.

Follicle   A growth within the ovary that contains an egg. Also, the cells in the skin from which hairs grow.

Fontanel   The soft spot on the top of the skull where the bones of the skull come together. It normally closes before or shortly after birth.

Fresh semen   *Semen* that is artificially inseminated into the bitch within a few hours of collection.

FSH   Follicle-stimulating hormone; produced by the pituitary gland. It causes the ovaries to produce egg *follicles*.

Furuncle   A small skin *boil*, about 2 to 3 millimeters in size.

Gastroesophageal junction   The anatomical area formed by the junction of the esophagus and the stomach.

Gastroscopy   A procedure that uses an *endoscope* to view the interior of the esophagus, stomach, and duodenum.

GDC   Institute for Genetic Disease Control in Animals.

Gene   The basic unit of heredity. Each gene contains the code that produces a specific protein or molecule.

Genome   The map that gives the locus (chromosome and site) of all the genes that control the makeup of an animal (80,000 in dogs); the complete set of hereditary factors.

Genotype   The combination of genes that determine a physical characteristic.

Gestation   Length of pregnancy; the period from conception to birth. It averages 63 days from the day of ovulation, with a normal range of 56 to 66 days.

GI   An abbreviation for gastrointestinal. GIT is sometimes used to denote the gastrointestinal tract.

Gn-RH   Gonadotrophin-releasing hormone; triggers the release of *FSH* and *LH* from the pituitary gland.

Gonadotropins   Hormones released from the pituitary gland or placenta, acting on the ovaries or testicles to cause them to manufacture and release the sex hormones.

Grand mal   A type of seizure that is typical of epilepsy. It usually involves loss of consciousness and falling down.

Hackles   Hairs on the neck and back; they are raised when the dog is experiencing fright or anger.

Haw   A visible third eyelid at the inner corner of the eye.

hCG   Human chorionic gonadotropin, used to induce ovulation.

Head-pressing   Pressing the head against the wall or furniture without apparent purpose.

Heat   See *estrus*.

Hematocrit   The percentage of red blood cells in whole blood.

Hematoma   A collection of clotted blood beneath the skin at the site of an injury.

Hematuria   The passage of blood in the urine, recognized by red-colored urine or blood clots in the urine. Microscopic hematuria is the presence of red cells on microscopic exam.

Hemolytic anemia   The disease that results when red blood cells are destroyed in the dog's circulation.

Hepatic   Referring to the liver.

Histiocyte   A cell that is part of the immune system that wanders in the connective tissue and kills foreign cells, such as bacteria.

Histology   The microscopic study of the structure of tissue to determine the cause of disease.

Hives   Small, raised, red, pruritic areas, generally caused by an allergic reaction.

Hydrotherapy   Cold water delivered to the site of injury using a showerhead or nozzle. May also involve warm water pools or underwater treadmills.

Hyperpigmentation   A darkening of the skin due to the deposition of *melanin* in the *dermis*. Associated with chronic inflammation of the skin.

Hypertrophy   Enlargement of an organ or tissue; an increase in size and volume.

Hypoxia   Lack of oxygen in the blood and tissues. If untreated, it results in coma and death.

Iatrogenic   An unintended disease that results from a medical treatment or procedure.

Idiopathic   A disease or condition for which no cause is known.

IFA   Immunofluorescent antibody test; a *serologic* test used to detect antibodies to bacteria and viruses.

Ileocecal valve   A flap of *mucosa* at the junction of the small bowel and the colon that acts like a valve.

IM   Abbreviation for intramuscular; an injection given into the muscle.

Immune-mediated   A process in the body in which proteins in the immune system lead the body to destroy its own cells. This can happen for unknown reasons (*idiopathic*) or due to a secondary cause such as infection, parasites, cancer, or a drug reaction.

Immunosuppressants   Medications that suppress the immune response—a desirable effect in *autoimmune* diseases.

Intubation   Placing a breathing tube into the trachea to establish an airway for assisted breathing.

In utero   Occurring in the uterus.

Incarceration   Trapping an organ or part of an organ within a closed space. Most commonly refers to intestine trapped in a hernia.

Infarction   Death of tissue as a consequence of an interruption in the blood supply.

Infection   Disease caused by a bacteria or a virus.

Infertility   Absence of *fertility*. A bitch who can't conceive or a dog who can't sire a litter.

Infestation   The presence of parasites in numbers that may be sufficient to cause an infection.

Intact   An animal who has not been *spayed* or *neutered*.

Intersex   The condition in which an animal has sex organs that have characteristics of both sexes and/or has chromosomes containing both male and female genetic material. Such animals are usually relatively or absolutely infertile.

Intromission   The introduction of the penis into the vagina during breeding.

Involution   The process by which the uterus empties and returns to normal size after *whelping*.

IV   Abbreviation for intravenous; an injection given into a vein.

IVP   Intravenous pyelogram; an X-ray of the kidneys taken after injecting a dye into a vein. This test provides an assessment of the renal circulation, ureters, bladder, and urethra.

Jaundice   A yellow discoloration in the whites of the eyes and mucous membranes of the mouth, caused by an accumulation of bile in the *serum* and tissues. Usually associated with liver disease or the destruction of red blood cells.

Karotype   A "picture" of all the chromosomes in a cell.

Karyotyping Analysis of the number, size, and shape of the paired chromosomes of a specific dog to determine the dog's sex.

Killed vaccine A vaccine made from killed virus particles. Killed vaccines are generally safe, but may not be as effective as *modified live vaccines* (MLV).

Laparoscopy A surgical procedure in which an *endoscope* and surgical instruments are inserted into the abdomen through several small incisions.

Lavage Flushing out a wound or cavity with large amounts of irrigating solution.

Lesion Damage to tissue caused by an injury or a specific disease.

LH Luteinizing hormone, produced by the pituitary gland. It causes ovarian *follicles* to mature and ovulate.

Ligation Tying off a vessel.

Lobulated Having the appearance of several lobes or swellings.

Luteal activity The influence of the *corpora lutea*, particularly the effects of *progesterone*.

Luteal phase See *diestrus*.

Luteolysis The process that results in the regression and disappearance of the *corpora lutea*. Accompanied by a fall in *serum progesterone*.

Luxation The displacement of a bone from its normal position within a joint.

Lymphadenopathy The enlargement of one or more lymph nodes as the result of inflammation or cancer.

Macule A spot on the skin that is a different color (such as red or whitish) but is not elevated.

Malignant A growth that is a cancer that is likely to spread throughout the body and may be life threatening.

Megaesophagus An enlarged esophagus that does not contract well and interferes with normal swallowing.

Melanin Naturally occurring dark pigment.

Melena The dark or tarry black stools associated with upper gastrointestinal bleeding (bleeding in the stomach, duodenum, or small intestines).

Meniscus A cushioning pad of cartilage interposed between two bones.

Merle A color pattern involving a dominant gene and characterized by dark splotches against a lighter background of the same pigment (seen in Collies, Shetland Sheepdogs, Australian Cattle Dogs, and some other breeds).

Metastasize The spread of a cancer from its site of origin to another part of the body.

MLV   Modified live virus vaccine; a vaccine made from live bacteria or viruses that have been treated so that they cannot cause disease.

Monorchid   A dog who truly has only one testicle. True monorchids are unusual. See also *cryptorchid*.

MRI   Magnetic resonance imaging, a diagnostic procedure that uses a nuclear magnetic spectrometer to produce computerized images of body structures. Usually available only at veterinary referral centers.

Mucociliary blanket   The mucosal lining of the upper respiratory tract that contains cells with *cilia* that are capable of propelling inhaled irritants into the back of the throat.

Mucopurulent   A discharge containing mucus and pus.

Mucosa   The inner layer of mucus-producing cells that lines the respiratory, gastrointestinal, and genitourinary tracts.

Mucus   The slippery substance that is secreted as a protective coating by cells and glands of the mucosa. The adjective is mucoid.

Multinodular   A growth composed of *nodules*, giving it an irregular, bumpy surface.

Mutation   An alteration in a gene causing a change in some bodily function that is perpetuated in all the cells that descend from the original mutant cell.

Myelitis   An infection or inflammation of the spinal cord.

Myelogram   An X-ray study in which a contrast material is injected into the fluid around the spinal cord to show whether a disc or tumor is impinging on the spinal cord.

Myopathy   A disease of muscle or muscle tissue.

Necrosis   The death of a cell or group of cells that are in contact with living tissue.

Nephron   The basic working unit of the kidney, composed of a glomerulus that filters urine and a system of tubules that concentrates the urine and reabsorbs water and *electrolytes*.

Neutering   Removing both testicles in the male. Also known as castration or orchiectomy.

Nictitating membrane   The third eyelid; a membrane at the inner corner of the eye that comes out across the eye in response to eye pain and other conditions.

NSAID   Nonsteroidal anti-inflammatory drug.

Nutraceutical   A nutritional supplement that can have disease-modifying effects.

Nystagmus A rhythmic movement of the eyeballs in which the eyes slowly wander a few degrees in one direction and then jerk back. Seen in dogs with diseases of the inner ear and brain.

Occlusion An obstruction or closure of a passageway or vessel.

Occult Not evident by clinical signs.

OFA Orthopedic Foundation for Animals, a group that certifies dogs are screened for certain inheritable health problems, such as hip dysplasia.

Off-label Using a medication in a dog that is not approved by the FDA for use in dogs. This may be a drug that is in common use for another species and it simply is not financially viable for a company to go through FDA testing.

Opacity Loss of transparency of the cornea or lens of the eye.

Organisms Living members of the animal or plant kingdom; usually refers to bacteria, viruses, and other small one-celled beings.

OTC Over-the-counter; refers to drugs.

Ovariohysterectomy Removal of the uterus and ovaries of a female dog. Also called spaying or OVH.

Oviduct The tube that carries the egg from the ovary to the uterus.

Ovulation The process during which the egg *follicle* releases the egg into the *oviduct*.

Palliation Treatment that affords relief but not a cure. The adjective is palliative.

Palpation Feeling, pressing on, and examining the body with the hands.

Papule A small bump on the surface of the skin, varying in size from a pinpoint to a split pea.

Parturition Giving birth; the period covered by labor and delivery.

Pathogenic Having the potential to cause disease.

Pathogens Agents such as bacteria, viruses, and fungi that are capable of causing disease.

Pedigree The written record of a dog's genealogy, covering three generations or more.

Perianal The glands and skin structures surrounding the anal opening.

Perineum The area extending from the anus to the bottom of the vulva in the female, and to the scrotum in the male.

Peristalsis Rhythmic contractions that propel ingested foods and liquids from the mouth to the anus.

Peritonitis Inflammation or infection of the peritoneal or abdominal cavity.

Peritoneal cavity   The abdominal cavity, containing organs of the intestinal, urinary, and reproductive tracts.

Placentitis   Infection of the placenta, usually caused by bacteria that ascend into the uterus through the cervix.

Plaque   A soft, yellow-brown material deposited on teeth that hardens into *calculus*.

Pleural effusion   An accumulation of fluid in the chest cavity caused by right-side heart failure, infection, or *tumor*.

PMN   Polymorphonuclear leukocyte; inflammatory cells that make up *pus*.

Pneumothorax   Air in the chest caused by a tear in the lung or a wound in the chest wall. The lung collapses, resulting in respiratory distress.

Polygenic traits   Heritable traits that are controlled by the effects of multiple *genes*.

Polyuria   The passage of large amounts of urine, usually recognized by more frequent voiding.

Postmaturity   The condition in which the puppies are mature and ready to be born but the *dam* does not go into labor, especially after 67 days' *gestation*.

Postpartum   After giving birth; the period after *whelping* that lasts four to six weeks.

Premature puppy   A pup born alive before 56 days' gestation.

Prepuce   The foreskin; the sheath that surrounds the *glans*, or head of the penis.

Productive cough   One that brings up a quantity of phlegm. Also known as a moist cough.

Prodromal   The period in a disease just before the onset of symptoms.

Proestrus   The initial stage of the *estrous* cycle, lasting, on average, nine days. The first sign is a bloody discharge from the vulva.

Progeny   Descendents or offspring.

Progesterone   The pregnancy hormone, produced by the ovaries (*corpora lutea*).

Prognosis   A forecast based on the probable outcome of the disease.

Prolapse   The *protrusion* or falling out of a body part; generally referring to the gland of the third eyelid, the intestines, or the uterus.

Prophylactic   A medication or a procedure used as a preventive.

Protrusion   Extending beyond the normal location, such as a protruding eyeball.

Psychogenic   Caused by emotional or psychological factors, as opposed to a specific disease.

Pulmonary edema   The accumulation of fluid in the lungs, usually caused by congestive heart failure.

Pruritic   Itchy.

Purulent   Puslike; a discharge containing *pus*.

Pus   A discharge that contains *serum*, inflammatory cells, and sometimes bacteria and dead tissue.

Pustule   A small bump on the surface of the skin that contains *pus*.

Pylorus   The part of the stomach that forms a channel between the stomach and the *duodenum*.

Pyoderma   A *purulent* skin infection including *pustules*, boils, *abscesses, cellulitis*, and infected scabs.

Radiograph   The use of X-rays to take an image of the inside of the body; commonly referred to as X-ray.

Recessive   A *gene* that expresses a trait only when it is combined with another recessive gene.

Recombinant vaccine   A vaccine made by splicing gene-sized fragments of DNA from one organism (a virus or bacteria) and transferring them to another organism (the dog), where they stimulate the production of antibodies.

Reflux   A reversal in the normal direction of flow.

Regurgitation   The passive expulsion of esophageal contents without conscious effort.

Reinfestation   An *infestation* of parasites that occurs after the original group was eliminated.

Remission   The period during which the dog remains free of symptoms.

Renal   Referring to the kidneys.

Renal pelvis   The funnel that collects the urine excreted by the kidney. It tapers and becomes the ureter.

Resection   Removing *malignant*, dead, or unwanted tissue by surgically cutting it out.

Retrobulbar space   A space between the back of the eyeball and the bony socket, occupied by fat and blood vessels.

Sarcoma   A cancer that arises from muscle, bone, or other connective tissue.

Scaly   Shedding flakes of skin.

Sclera   The white membrane surrounding the cornea of the eye.

Scrotum   The bag of skin and connective tissue that surrounds and supports the testicles.

Semen   The contents of the *ejaculate*, containing sperm cells, gel, and the secretions of the accessory sex glands.

Senile   An age-related decline in physical and mental faculties.

Sepsis   The presence of infection, often accompanied by fever and other signs of illness, such as vomiting and diarrhea. The adjective is septic.

Septicemia   The stage of *sepsis* in which microorganisms and/or their toxins are found in the blood.

Serosanguinous   A discharge, generally pink or red, that contains *serum* and blood.

Serum   The clear fluid component of the blood. The adjective is *serous*. *Serologic* refers to blood tests that evaluate or measure antibody responses.

Sire   The father of a puppy.

Soundness   Mental and physical health when all the organs and systems are functioning as intended.

Spay   Neutering a *bitch* by removing the ovaries and uterus.

Spermatogenesis   The production of sperm by the testicles.

Spinal tap   A procedure in which a needle is inserted into the spinal canal to remove cerebrospinal fluid for laboratory analysis.

Sporadic   Isolated, occasional, or infrequent.

SQ   Abbreviation for subcutaneous; an injection given beneath the skin. Also sometimes called sub-Q or SC.

Staging   A system developed to determine the extent and *prognosis* of a cancer, as well as its treatment.

Stenosis   Constriction or narrowing, especially of a channel or passage. The adjective is stenotic.

Stillbirth   A full-term puppy who is born dead.

Strangulated   The compression or pinching off of the blood supply to an abdominal organ, such as a segment of bowel. Leads to death of tissue.

Stridor   A high-pitched, raspy sound caused by air passing through a narrowed larynx.

Stud dog   A male dog used for breeding.

Subclinical   A stage of illness in which infection occurs without apparent signs.

Subfertility   Less than normal *fertility*.

Subluxation A partial dislocation, in which the bone is partly out of the joint.

Superinfection The development of a second infection on top of (or following) the first infection.

Synovial fluid analysis A procedure in which a needle is inserted into a joint to remove fluid for chemical and microscopic examination.

Systemic Into the system; used in reference to widespread dissemination of infection or cancer, or a drug given orally, intramuscularly, intravenously, or subcutaneously.

Tartar See *calculus*.

Teratogenic That which causes developmental malformations in the fetus.

Testosterone The male hormone, produced by the testicles.

Thromboembolism The process by which a blood clot forms in a vein or artery and then moves up or down in the circulatory system, where it causes further clotting.

Titer The concentration of a measured substance in the *serum*.

Torsion The twisting of an organ and its blood supply, resulting in insufficient blood flow and death of that organ.

Toxemia A state of shock induced by the absorption of bacterial toxins from an infected area in the body.

Tracheobronchitis A viral or bacterial infection of the cells lining the trachea and bronchi.

Tracheostomy Surgery in which an opening is made through the skin into the windpipe to establish a new airway.

Transtracheal washings Cells obtained by flushing the trachea with saline; used to diagnose the causes of upper respiratory infections.

Tucked up A tightening of the muscles of the abdominal wall, creating a narrow waist and a hunched-up back.

Tumor Any growth or swelling (such as an *abscess*). A cancerous growth is called a *neoplasm*.

Ulcer A defect on the surface of an organ or tissue. A skin ulcer is an open sore with an inflamed base, involving the outer layer of the skin and often the *dermis*. A gastrointestinal ulcer is an open sore in the lining of the stomach or intestines. A corneal ulcer is on the clear surface of the eye.

Ultrasonography A diagnostic procedure that uses high-frequency sound waves to map a picture of an organ or structure inside the body.

Unilateral On one side only (as opposed to bilateral—on both sides).

Urethra The tube that conveys urine from the bladder to outside the body.

Uterine inertia   Failure of the uterus to contract to start labor or to continue to contract during labor.

Vaginal cytology   A procedure in which cells are obtained from the vaginal lining and examined microscopically to determine the stage of the *estrous cycle*.

Ventricle   A cavity or chamber. Ventricles within the brain contain cerebrospinal fluid. Within the heart, the ventricles are the larger chambers on both sides.

Vesicle   A small skin blister filled with clear fluid.

Vulva   The labia (lips) of the vagina.

Wheal   An intensely itchy, raised patch of skin with a white center and a red rim. Varies in size from a pinhead to several inches. Often transient.

Whelp   To give birth.

Zoonosis   A disease that is communicable from humans to animals and vice versa under natural conditions. The adjective is zoonotic.

ABOUT THE
AUTHORS

Debra M. Eldredge, DVM

Debra Eldredge graduated from the New York State College of Veterinary Medicine at Cornell and was the first recipient of Cornell's Gentle Doctor Award, given for patient care. She has been in private practice, primarily small animal, since 1980, with two years as the staff veterinarian for the Humane Society of Huron Valley in Michigan Dr. Eldredge is a member of the American Veterinary Medical Association and the New York State Veterinary Medical Association, and received the public service award from the Central New York Veterinary Medical Association.

Dr. Eldredge is a professional member of the Dog Writers Association of America and the Cat Writers' Association. She has been a finalist in their writing contests many times and is the recipient of Muse Medallions and Maxwell Awards. Her previous books include the award-winning *Pills for Pets*; *Everything Guide to Dog Health* with Kim Thornton; the award-winning *Cancer and Your Pet* with Margaret Bonham; and *Head of the Class*, a dog training book with her daughter, Kate Eldredge. She is also the co-author of *Cat Owner's Home Veterinary Handbook*.

Dr. Eldredge is very active in organized dog activities and has competed successfully in most dog sports, from herding to conformation, agility, obedience, rally, tracking, and freestyle. Her true canine love is the Belgian Tervuren, but she has also shared her life with a Kuvasz, a Labrador Retriever, German Shepherd Dogs, Australian Shepherds, and Pembroke Welsh Corgis.

She currently lives in upstate New York with seven dogs, one cat, two donkeys, twelve sheep, one goat, five horses, one miniature horse, twelve ducks, and three primates: her husband, Chuck, her daughter, Kate, and her son, Tom.

Delbert G. Carlson, DVM

Del Carlson received his veterinary medical degree from the University of Minnesota Veterinary School in 1954 and interned at the Rawley Memorial Hospital in Springfield, Massachusetts.

He was a member of the Missouri Veterinary Medical Association and a past president of the Greene County Human Society.

Dr. Carlson is also the co-author of *Cat Owner's Home Veterinary Handbook*.

Until his death, "Doc" could be found on his farm, caring for his horses, cats, and dogs. He consulted at the Carlson Pet Hospital, often volunteering to spend the night with a sick dog or cat.

Liisa D. Carlson, DVM

Liisa Carlson received her veterinary medical degree from the University of Missouri College of Veterinary Medicine and was a member of the Veterinary Honor Society, Phi Zeta. In 1988, Dr. Carlson returned to Springfield, Missouri, to join her father, Dr. Delbert Carlson, at the Carlson Pet Hospital.

She is a member of the American Veterinary Medical Society, the Southwestern Veterinary Medical Association, and a founding member of the Emergency Clinics of Southwest Missouri. Dr. Carlson is also the co-author of *Cat Owner's Home Veterinary Handbook*.

In 1994, Dr. Carlson was honored as Humanitarian of the Year by the Southwest Humane Society of Springfield.

James M. Giffin, MD

Jim Giffin graduated from Amherst College and received his medical degree from Yale University School of Medicine. After years of private surgery practice in Missouri and Colorado, Dr. Giffin was activated during Operation Desert Storm, serving as Chief of Surgery at military hospitals in Alabama, Korea, and Texas.

Dr. Giffin had lifelong experience with cats, dogs, and horses. In 1969 he established a Great Pyrenees kennel and became active in breeding, showing, and judging. He finished several champions, campaigned a Best-in-Show winner, and served on the board of directors of the Great Pyrenees Club of America. He is co-author of the award winning books *The Complete Great Pyrenees, Cat Owner's Home Veterinary Handbook, Horse Owner's Veterinary Handbook*, and *Veterinary Guide to Horse Breeding*, and was a professional member of the Dog Writers' Association of America.

Until his death in 2000, he made his home in Colorado.

TECHNICAL REVIEWER

Sandra Young, DVM, graduated with distinction from the New York State College of Veterinary Medicine at Cornell University. Since then, she has worked primarily with dogs and cats in small animal practice, but also with zoo, wildlife, and exotic species, and in shelter medicine. She has been in practice 14 years. She is certified in veterinary acupuncture and has additional training in Western and Chinese herbal medicine. She is co-author of *The Eden Alternative: Animal Welfare Guidelines*, an animal care manual for long-term care facilities for humans that incorporate live-in animals. Dr. Young shares her life with her husband, Rodger, their two sons, Evan and Alex, and a Greyhound.

ART CREDITS

Unless otherwise noted here, photographs have been provided by Krist Carlson and James A. Giffin and drawings have been provided by Rose Floyd and Karen Wyatt.

James Clawson: 50, 70, 173, 174, 209, 331 (bottom), 567

Dr. T. J. Dunn, DVM: 16, 125, 232, 241, 243, 390, 543, 566, 569

Tom Eldredge: 9 (bottom), 549, 603

Jean Fogle: 105

Bridget Olerenshaw: 384

Dusty Rainbolt: 10 (middle), 291, 331 (top)

Susan Stamilio (SKS Designs): 41, 52, 102, 108 (bottom), 128, 170, 189, 206, 253, 256, 264, 290, 312, 314, 330, 333, 342, 377, 391–393, 411, 438, 460, 468, 473

JoAnn Thompson: 476

Valerie Toukuly. 120, 174

Emergency Pet Hospital of Collier County: 12

Sydney Giffin Wiley: 181, 492

Courtesy of American Veterinary Publications: 76

Courtesy of BiteNot Products: 5 (bottom)

Courtesy of Bristol-Meyers Squibb: 148, 165, 167

Courtesy of Liisa Carlson, DVM: 604

Courtesy of James M. Giffin, MD: 605

Reprinted with permission of the copyright owner, Hill's Pet Nutrition, Inc.: 292

LIST OF TABLES

GENERAL INDEX

NOTE: Page numbers shown in boldface contain detailed coverage of the subject.